PRINCIPLES OF PROGRAMMING LANGUAGES

Principles of Programming Languages

Editor:

Ivan Stanimirović, Ph.D.

ArclerPress

www.arclerpress.com

Principles of Programming Languages

Editor: Ivan Stanimirović, Ph.D.

© 2017 Arcler Press LLC
708 3rd Avenue, 6th Floor
New York
NY 10017
United States of America
www.arclerpress.com

ISBN: 978-1-68094-452-5

Library of Congress Control Number: 2016913464

Arcler Press LLC publishes wide variety of books and eBooks. For more information about Arcler Press and its products, visit our website at www.arclerpress.com

About the Editor

Ivan Stanimirović, Ph.D.

Ivan Stanimirović gained his PhD from University of Niš, Serbia in 2013. His work spans from multi-objective optimization methods to applications of generalized matrix inverses in areas such as image processing and computer graphics and visualisations. He is currently working as an Assistant professor at Faculty of Sciences and Mathematics at University of Niš on computing generalized matrix inverses and its applications.

Contents

List of Contributors

Nabil el Boustani Jurriaan Hage
Center for Software Technology, Department of Information and Computing Sciences,
Universiteit Utrecht, 3508 TB Utrecht, The Netherlands

Wouter Swierstra
Vector Fabrics, Paradijslaan 28, Eindhoven, The Netherlands

Stefan Holdermans
Vector Fabrics, Paradijslaan 28, 5611 KN Eindhoven, The Netherlands

Jurriaan Hage
Department of Information and Computing Sciences, Utrecht University, TB Utrecht, The Netherlands

Arie Middelkoop Atze Dijkstra S. Doaitse Swierstra
Department of Information and Computing Sciences, Universiteit Utrecht, Utrecht, Netherlands

MAURO JASKELIOFF
CIFASIS, CONICET, Argentina FCEIA, Universidad Nacional de Rosario, Argentina

RUSSELL O'CONNOR
Google Canada Kitchener, Ontario, Canada

Lee Naish
University of Melbourne Melbourne 3010, Australia

Alberto Rodrigues da Silva
INESC-ID & Instituto Superior Técnico - Universidade de Lisboa, Lisbon, Portugal

Christian Häubl
Institute for System Software, Christian Doppler Laboratory for Automated Software Engineering, Johannes Kepler University Linz, Altenbergerstrasse 69, 4040 Linz, Austria

Hanspeter Mössenböck
Institute for System Software, Christian Doppler Laboratory for Automated Software Engineering, Johannes Kepler University Linz, Altenbergerstrasse 69, 4040 Linz, Austria

Christian Wimmer
Oracle Labs, 500 Oracle Parkway, Redwood Shores, CA 94065, USA

Khalid Aljasser
Information and Computer Science Department, King Fahd University of Petroleum and Minerals, Dhahran, Saudi Arabia

Jim Davies
Department of Computer Science, University of Oxford, Oxford OX1 3QD, UK

Jeremy Gibbons
Department of Computer Science, University of Oxford, Oxford OX1 3QD, UK

James Welch
Department of Computer Science, University of Oxford, Oxford OX1 3QD, UK

Edward Crichton
Department of Computer Science, University of Oxford, Oxford OX1 3QD, UK

Zahir AlHashami
Research Center, 420-Oman-Muscat

Francesco Tiezzi
University of Camerino, Italy

Nobuko Yoshida
Imperial College London, UK

Jeremy Gibbons
Department of Computer Science, University of Oxford, United Kingdom

Cliff B. Jones
School of Computing Science, Newcastle University, UK

Ian J. Hayes
School of Information Technology and Electrical Engineering, The University of Queensland, Australia

Matthew Edmunds
Department of Computer Science, Swansea University, Swansea, SA2 8PP, Wales, UK

Chao Tong
Department of Computer Science, Swansea University, Swansea, SA2 8PP, Wales, UK

Robert S. Laramee
Department of Computer Science, Swansea University, Swansea, SA2 8PP, Wales, UK

Preface

Recent years, a large focus on fundamental principles in the design, analysis, implementation of programming languages and programming interfaces has been conducted. A novel research of the basic structure of programming languages, including data types, control structures, naming conventions is presented. To give insight into different programming language paradigms, such as functional, imperative, object-oriented and logic paradigms, several reports are given. Procedural programming is represented as a flow chart where a linear sequence of statements is defined for the program to complete. When this sequence is followed, data is manipulated by the program to create the desired execution.

The combination of parametric polymorphism and inclusion polymorphism in programming language Java is complicated, particularly so for Generic Java. It is described how to adapt the type inference process of Java to obtain better error diagnostics for generic method invocations. This subject is discussed in detail in the first section of this book.

The following five chapters of the book present new approaches in well-known concepts in programming languages, such as functional and logic programming, distributed arrays and 'stricterness'. The remaining content of this book focuses on the advances of object-oriented programming paradigm and specific logical and algebraic methods used in programming and the principles of programming languages. The specific advances discussed in this book include the use of concurrency and kernels in programming languages. The particular design of a flow visualisation framework is discussed in the final section of this book.

Locality-aware algorithms over distributed arrays can be very difficult to write. It is shown how a dependently-typed programming language can aid in the development of these algorithms and statically ensure that every well-typed program will only ever access local data. Such static guarantees can help catch programming errors early on in the development cycle and maximise the potential speedup that multicore machines offer.

Adapting a strictness analyser to have it take into account explicit strictness annotations can be difficult. Straightforward extensions of analyses based on relevance typing are likely to either be unsafe or fail to pick the fruits of increases in strictness that are introduced through annotations. A more involved adaptation of relevance typing is proposed, that can be used to derive strictness analyses that are both safe and effective in the presence of explicit strictness annotations. The resulting type system provides a firm foundation for implementations of type-based strictness analysers in compilers for lazy programming languages such as Haskell and Clean.

Generalized Algebraic Data Types are a generalization of Algebraic Data Types with additional type equality constraints. These found their use in many functional programs, including the development of embedded domain specific programming languages and generic programming. To make the integration of GADTs in languages easier, an orthogonal specification for GADTs is presented. This specification exploits the Church encoding of data types to describe GADT matches in terms of conventional lambda abstractions.

Representation theorems relate seemingly complex objects to concrete, more tractable ones. The advantages of the abstraction power of category theory is taken and a datatype-generic representation theorem is provided. More precisely, a representation theorem for a wide class of second-order functionals which are polymorphic over a class of functors is derived. Types polymorphic over a class of functors are easily representable in languages such as Haskell, but are difficult to analyse and reason about.

A probabilistic approach to the search strategy for declarative debugging is presented, which focuses on diagnosing wrong answers in pure Prolog programs but the approach can be adapted to other languages (for example, functional languages) and bug symptoms. Drawing information from source code and the execution of passed and failed test cases, different search heuristics are combined using probability theory.

Method inlining is one of the most important optimizations in method-based just-in-time (JIT) compilers. It widens the compilation scope and therefore allows optimizing multiple methods as a whole, which increases the performance. However, if method inlining is used too frequently, the compilation time increases and too much machine code is generated. This has negative effects on the performance. The effect of trace inlining on the performance and the amount of generated machine code is evaluated.

Reports upon ten years of experience in the development and application of model-driven technology are provided. The technology in question was inspired by work on formal methods: in particular, by the B toolkit. It was used in the development of a number of information systems, all of which were successfully deployed in real world situations. Section 10 reports upon three systems: one that informed the design of the technology, one that was used by an internal customer, and one that is currently in use outside the development organization.

Reversibility is incorporated into structured communication-based programming, to allow parties of a session to automatically undo, in a rollback fashion, the effect of previously executed interactions. This permits to take different computation paths along the same session, as well as to revert the whole session and start a new one.

An important issue in concurrency is interference. Rely/guarantee approaches have been shown to be useful in specifying and reasoning compositionally about concurrent programs. The use of a "possible values" notation is explored for reasoning about variables whose values can be changed multiple times by interference.

Research software often consists of individual, isolated prototype applications. Utilizing previously implemented techniques, researchers are able to combine visualization options in new ways that typical research prototypes cannot. The software application can be made available to the domain expert for evaluation and future use. These goals are in part realized by utilizing recent advancements in game design technology and by leveraging features available with recent graphics hardware. In contrast to most research prototypes, the system presented in the last section handles real-world simulation datasets by interfacing directly with the commercial package called tecplot, whereat the effectiveness and scalability of the approach is also discussed.

Editor
Ivan Stanimirović, Ph.D.

CHAPTER 1

IMPROVING TYPE ERROR MESSAGES FOR GENERIC JAVA

Nabil el Boustani Jurriaan Hage

Center for Software Technology, Department of Information and Computing Sciences, Universiteit Utrecht, 3508 TB Utrecht, The Netherlands

ABSTRACT

Since version 1.5, generics (parametric polymorphism) are part of the Java language. However, the combination of parametric polymorphism and inclusion polymorphism is complicated, particularly so for Generic Java. Indeed, the main Java compilers, Eclipse's EJC and Sun's JAVAC, do not even accept the same set of programs. Moreover, experience with these compilers shows that the error messages provided by them leave more than a little to be desired.

To alleviate the latter problem, we describe how to adapt the type inference process of Java to obtain better error diagnostics for generic method invocations. Although the extension by itself already helps to improve type error messages to some extent, another major advantage of the new type inference process is that it also paves the way for further heuristics can provide additional diagnostic information. The extension has been implemented into the JastAdd Extensible Java Compiler.

INTRODUCTION

Since the introduction of generics in Java, the programmers who seek to actually use this powerful feature may have discovered that production strength compilers such as Eclipse's EJC and Sun's JAVAC, do not always carefully explain why a given generic method invocation fails to type check.

Consider the code and the corresponding error messages[1] in Fig. 1. Both EJC and JAVAC merely claim that there is no method declared with the signature foo(Map). However, they do not explain why the foo method that is declared does not match the invocation. Our message, on the other hand, does make such an attempt.

[1]All examples in the paper first give the code to be compiled, followed by a number of error messages, accompanied by an indication of which compiler generated the message. The indication ejc refers to the Eclipse Java Compiler (0.883_R34x, 3.4.1 release, in mode 1.5, MacOSX), javac to Sun's Javac (version 1.5.0_22, MacOSX), and ours refers to our own implementation based on the JastAdd Extensible Java Compiler (see Sect. 8 for information on how to obtain this implementation). In our examples we sometimes write (. . .) to indicate that part of the error message has been deleted. These omitted parts are hints that serve to suggest how to fix the type error and are considered outside the scope of the current paper [2].

Citation: Nabil el Boustani Jurriaan Hage, Improving type error messages for generic Java, DOI 10.1007/s10990-011-9070-3.

```
import java.util.*;

class Listing1{
    <T> void foo(Map<T,T> a){
        Map<Number, Integer> m1 = null;
        foo(m1);
    }
}
```

```
listings/Listing1.java:6: <T>foo(java.util.Map<T,T>) in Listing1 cannot be
applied to (java.util.Map<java.lang.Number,java.lang.Integer>)
        foo(m1);
        ^
```
JAVAC

```
1. ERROR in listings/Listing1.java (at line 6)
    foo(m1);
    ^^^
The method foo(Map<T,T>) in the type Listing1 is not applicable for the
arguments (Map<Number,Integer>)
```
EJC

```
listings/Listing1.java:6
Method <T>foo(Map<T, T>) of type Listing1 is not applicable for the argument of
type (Map<Number, Integer>), because:
  [*] The type variable T is invariant, but the types:
  - Integer in Map<Number, Integer> on 5:9(5:21)
  - Number in Map<Number, Integer> on 5:9(5:13)
  are not the same type.
```
ours

Figure. 1 A Java code fragment harbouring a type equality conflict, and the type error messages for JAVAC, EJC and our implementation respectively.

In this paper, we describe how to rearchictect the Java type checking process in order to obtain more informative error messages. We have implemented our solution into the JastAdd Extensible Java Compiler and provide many examples of programs that benefit from our approach. Our modifications also pave the way for the implementation of special heuristics that can go beyond explaining what the problem is, by showing how the problem can be fixed. These heuristics are, however, considered in another paper [2].

Having some experience in improving type error messages for functional languages [9, 13], it turns out that in the current study we faced a number of additional problems. The first problem is that the Java Language Specification (JLS) [7] is large, complicated and full of all kinds of restrictions and limitations that the programmer needs to know about. The fact that not even EJC and JAVAC always agree on the type correctness of a program suggests that also the implementers of Java have problems coming to grips with it. Furthermore, Smith and Cartwright have shown that type inference in Generic Java is neither sound nor complete [27]. It is worthwhile to note here that type inference is not the same as type checking: type inference, in the case of Java, refers to the process that tries to come up with suitable instantiations for type variables that occur in the program. In the case of Java this process can come up with instantiations that will later be found to be inconsistent. In that sense, type inference can be considered to be unsound, but it does not mean that the speci- fication allows type incorrect programs. A further illustration of the complexity of Generic Java is the sizable FAQ maintained by Angelika Langer [16].

The second problem is that the combination of generics with subtyping, i.e., the fact that you can bind an object of type T to an identifier of type S if T is a subtype of S, yields a type system that is inherently complex. This is further complicated by other demands on the language, such as backwards compatibility and the recent addition of various other features such as variable arity methods and autoboxing and unboxing.

Given the size of the language, we restrict ourselves to type error diagnosis for generic method invocations. In our solution we adhere to three general principles: we do not change, but only add to the original type checking process, in that our extension only comes into play after an inconsistency has been detected. Second, in order to provide more elaborate error messages, we retain the constraints generated for an inconsistent invocation in order to better explain what went wrong, and to be able to execute heuristics that work directly on the constraints. The final principle is to avoid acting on those parts of the program that are more likely to contain mistakes. Since we believe that the generic arguments of the generic types are likely to be the source of a mistake when an inconsistency arises, this implies we should ignore these arguments as long as we can.

To better substantiate and position our contribution, we consider the properties proposed by Yang and others [34] that a good type error message should have: correctness, accuracy, intuitiveness, succinctness and source-basedness. Although these properties tend to be hard to establish formally, we believe the examples in this paper show that compared to the error messages provided by EJC and JAVAC our messages are more intuitive and source-based. We also believe that we strike a better balance in being more informative, although at the price of being less concise. Finally, we believe our implementation is not less correct than that of the compiler into which our research has been implemented (but proving that would be very hard). In general, we think that we have improved the situation with respect to JAVAC and EJC in particular by striking a better balance between verbosity and terseness, and that our messages are less tied the internal type inference process.

The paper is structured as follows. In Sect. 2 we reiterate some of the essential elements of the Generics extension in Java, and introduce some basic notations. Section 3 then provides quite a number of examples of type error messages constructed by our implementation, together with the messages provided by EJC and JAVAC. In Sect. 4 we explain in some detail the type checking process as specified by the JLS, and discuss our extension to that process in Sect. 5. In Sect. 6 we briefly describe our implementation, Sect. 7 describes related work, and Sect. 8 reflects, concludes and gives directions for future work.

AN OVERVIEW OF JAVA GENERICS

For completeness we run through the essentials of the generics of Java. We assume the reader is familiar with the non-generic part of Java. For more details, the reader can consult the Java standard [7] and the Java Generics FAQ [16].

Arguably, the main reason for introducing generics into Java was to counter the large number of casts needed to deal with collection classes, e.g., sets and vectors. Before generics, all collection classes were defined so that any Object could be stored in them. However, this makes all collections potentially heterogeneous and makes it necessary to explicitly downcast objects obtained from such a collection. This is both cumbersome and potentially unsafe.

With generics, the programmer can specify upper bounds, besides Object, for the objects that can be stored in a collection. For example, a List can store Numbers and objects of any type that is a subclass of Number, such as Integer. If an object is retrieved from such a list, then it can be stored as a Number without any type cast, and if the need arises it can be further downcast to, say, Integer.

An important and maybe subtle point is that although Integer is a subclass of Number, List is not a subclass of List. Indeed, this holds for all collection classes: they are all invariant type constructors. All things considered, this is not so strange: a List is not supposed to store Numbers, but if we assign it to a variable of type List we cannot safely guarantee this. However, a value of type HashMap may be passed safely to a parameter of type Map, because HashMap extends Map.

A consequence of the invariance restriction is that there is no type that denotes a list of any kind of element. We still need such a type, for example to write a length method for lists. This is why the wildcard was introduced: List denotes a list for which nothing is known of the element type. We can store a List for any type T in a variable of such a type. The price to be paid is that we cannot store anything into the list, and we can only read Objects from it.

The wildcard introduces a problem by itself. If we would like to write a method that computes the reverse of a list, we can easily do so for non-wild card types, and only for wild-card types if we do not mind losing the knowledge that the input list and the output list have the same element type. In Java this can, in some cases, be solved by wildcard capture conversion [30], in which case the compiler can determine that although it may not know the concrete type at compile-time, it is still known to be safe at run-time.

In many cases, we can be more precise in our estimation of the possible types that a certain type variable or a wildcard may have. For that reasons bounds were introduced. For example T extends Number expresses that the type inferred for T should be a subtype of Number. Similarly, T super Number expresses the inverse relation. The same applies to wildcards. For example, the declaration void foo (Map<? extends Number, ? super Integer> mp)expresses that the key type of an actual parameter should be a subtype of Number and that the value type should be a supertype of Integer. Note however, that the fact that a wildcard ? refers to both key and value type does not imply that the types are the same, or even related. For example, we can pass a value of type Map, Map or even Map to foo.

In Generic Java, the raw type, e.g., a type constructor such as List without its type arguments, is assignment compatible with all instantiations of the generic type. So, if you write List as a type somewhere, the inferencer can decide to interpret it as List for whatever T it finds suitable at that point. This mixing of type constructor and type is used in dealing with legacy code.

The JLS imposes a number of seemingly arbitrary restrictions. To give a few examples: Wildcard capture conversion only works when wildcards are at top-level, and not for a type like List<List>. Wildcards may only occur as arguments to a generic type constructor, i.e, you cannot write ? x = ... to describe an identifier of unknown type. Primitive types may not occur as parameters of a generic type constructor, e.g., Vector is not allowed, but Vector is. There are also some restrictions on how type variables may be bounded: we may write T extends Number, but not T super Number [7, §4.4]. This restriction does not apply to wildcards: both ? extends Number and ? super Number are allowed [7, §4.5.1].

Notation and Terminology

We shortly introduce some notation used throughout the paper, linking these to the pertinent paragraphs of the JLS [7], to which we refer for more details.

Since we deal exclusively with method invocations in this paper, and focus on generic classes and interfaces, the basic operation is that of method invocation conversion (§5.3). It specifies when actual arguments are compatible with formal parameters. In our case, the main conversion operation is widening reference conversion (§5.1.5), which basically specifies that compatibility is governed by the subtype relation (§4.10): T T for T is defined as the reflexive and transitive closure of the direct supertype relation >1, which contains the extends relationship between classes and interfaces: if A extends B then B >1 A. As §4.10.2 of the JLS makes clear, the subtyping relation among (generic) classes and interfaces is quite complicated. For the purposes of the examples in this paper, we need not to consider these definitions in full detail. Instead, we prefer to give a restricted version of the definition[2]:

[2]For example, we restrict C and D to have the same number of arguments, there are no intersections, and no capture conversion is performed.

```
C<S1,...,Sn> <:D<T1,...,Tn>
```

if and only if C <: D and for all $1 \leq i \leq n$: Si $\leq$: Ti (pronounced Si contains Ti) where

- T $\leq$: T,
- T $\leq$: ? extends T,
- T $\leq$: ? super T,
- ? extends T $\leq$: ? extends S, if T <: S,
- ? super T $\leq$: ? super S, if S <: T.

Intersection types are written T_1 & ... & T_n, $n > 0$, where the T_i are type expressions (Sect. 4.9). At most one of these types may specify a class type, since Java does not support multiple inheritance.

The least upper bound (lub) of a collection of classes and interfaces S is the most specific type that is a supertype of each S ∈ S. For example, lub({Integer,Double}) = Number. Often, the lub is not simply a class name, but also specifies a number of interfaces. For example, lub({Integer,String}) equals

```
Object & Serializable &
      Comparable<? extends Object & Serializable &
      Comparable<?>>.
```

Dually, the greatest lower bound (glb) of S is the most general type in the hierarchy that extends each S ∈ S. Note that the glb is sometimes undefined, e.g., glb({String,Number}).

EXAMPLES

To illustrate what can be gained from the developments in this paper, we compare the messages generated by our implementation with those generated by the standard compilers for Java, EJC (0.883_R34x, 3.4.1 release, in mode 1.5, MacOSX) and JAVAC (version 1.5.0_22, MacOSX). We have taken the liberty to insert some newlines in order to make the output fit the width of a page. The examples we show tend to be contrived in the sense that they show a particular phenomenon with as little code as possible. We shall however start with a somewhat more realistic and intuitive longer example. The number of examples is relatively small, but Appendix describes where to obtain programs to generate many more examples of the messages we can provide, as part of the test set for our implementation.

Consider the code in Fig. 2 which describes a class for doing static operations on HashMaps. Four methods are provided: copy adds the pairs in from to those in to, and project restricts the domain of the map to the list of elements in the second argument. The method printRange can be used to show that the operations work as expected. The final operation is selfcompose which composes a map with itself: the result contains a pair (x,y) if there is some u such that (x,u) and (u,y) are pairs in the argument HashMap. A critical requirement is that in the argument to selfcompose, the map may not have an arbitrary range and domain, but that these should coincide. We believe the code to be sufficiently standard to need no further explanation. If the type-incorrect invocation hm1 = MapOps. selfcompose(hm1); is deleted, then the output of the program is [twenty].

If the classes in Fig. 2 are compiled, then we obtain the type error messages given in Fig. 3. We note that JAVAC and EJC are not very informative, and only say that no matching method could be found. Our message explains the inconsistency between the defined selfcompose and the invocation: the method expects a map from a type to the same type, but this is not the case for hm1 which maps numbers to strings.

It is quite easy to change MapOps.java to show the behaviour of our system for other kinds of errors. Consider that the line marked as incorrectly typed is omitted. We shall now describe three modifications of the signature of project. In each case, EJC and JAVAC continue to generate messages similar to those in Fig. 3, which we omit. The first modification is to change extends into super in the signature of project. If we compile the MapOps.java after this first modification, then the error message reads:

```
listings/MapOps.java:49
Method <T, S>project(HashMap<T, S>, ArrayList<? super T>)
of type MapOps is not applicable for the arguments
of type (HashMap<Number, String>, ArrayList<Integer>), because:
  [*] The type Integer in ArrayList<Integer> on 46:8(46:18)
      is not a supertype of the inferred type for T: Number.
```

If we write ? extends S instead of ? extends T, then we obtain the message

```
listings/MapOps.java:49
Method <T, S>project(HashMap<T, S>, ArrayList<? extends S>)
of type MapOps is not applicable for the arguments
of type (HashMap<Number, String>, ArrayList<Integer>), because:
  [*] The type Integer in ArrayList<Integer> on 46:8(46:18)
      is not a subtype of the inferred type for S: String.
```

Finally, if we replace ? extends T with T, then the message becomes:

```
import java.util.*;

class MapOps {
    MapOps() {
    }

    static <T,S> void copy(HashMap<T,S> from, HashMap<T,S> to) {
      for (T key : from.keySet()) {
         to.put(key, from.get(key));
      }
    }

    static <T,S> HashMap<T,S> project(HashMap<T,S> cmap,
                                  ArrayList<? extends T> dom) {
        HashMap<T,S> retmap = new HashMap<T,S>();
        copy(cmap,retmap);
        Set<T> keyset = retmap.keySet();
        keyset.retainAll(dom);
        return retmap;
    }

    static <T,S> void printRange(HashMap<T,S> cmap) {
        System.out.println(cmap.values().toString());
    }

    static <T> HashMap<T,T> selfcompose(HashMap<T,T> map) {
        HashMap<T,T> twm = new HashMap<T,T>();
        Set<T> domain = map.keySet();

        for (T key : domain) {
          T img = map.get(key);
          if (domain.contains(img)) {
            twm.put(key, map.get(img));
          }
        }
        return twm;
    }
}

class Main {
    public static void main(String[] parameters)
    {
       HashMap<Number, String> hm1 = new HashMap<Number,String>();
       hm1.put(10,"ten");
       hm1.put(20,"twenty");
       hm1.put(21.5,"twenty-one-and-a-half");
       ArrayList<Integer> l1 = new ArrayList<Integer>();
       l1.add(20);
       l1.add(30);
       hm1 = MapOps.project(hm1,l1);
       hm1 = MapOps.selfcompose(hm1); // Type-incorrect
       MapOps.printRange(hm1);
    }

}
```

Figure. 2 A class defining operations on HashMaps that is used type incorrectly.

```
listings/MapOps.java:50: <T>selfcompose(java.util.HashMap<T,T>) in MapOps cannot
be applied to (java.util.HashMap<java.lang.Number,java.lang.String>)
       hm1 = MapOps.selfcompose(hm1);
                   ^
```
JAVAC

```
1. ERROR in listings/MapOps.java (at line 50)
    hm1 = MapOps.selfcompose(hm1);
                 ^^^^^^^^^^^

The method selfcompose(HashMap<T,T>) in the type MapOps is not applicable for
the arguments (HashMap<Number,String>)
```
EJC

```
listings/MapOps.java:50
Method <T>selfcompose(HashMap<T, T>) of type MapOps is not applicable for the
argument of type (HashMap<Number, String>), because:
  [*] The type variable T is invariant, but the types:
  - String in HashMap<Number, String> on 42:8(42:24)
  - Number in HashMap<Number, String> on 42:8(42:16)
  are not the same type.
```
ours

Figure. 3 The three error messages for the inconsistency caused by the wrong invocation to selfCompose.

```
listings/MapOps.java:49
Method <T, S>project(HashMap<T, S>, ArrayList<T>)
of type MapOps is not applicable for the arguments
of type (HashMap<Number, String>, ArrayList<Integer>), because:
  [*] The type variable T is invariant, but the types:
  - Integer in ArrayList<Integer> on 46:8(46:18)
  - Number in HashMap<Number, String> on 42:8(42:16)
  are not the same type.
```

We now continue with the smaller, more contrived examples in order to show the kind of situations we can handle. We already saw an example of a type equality conflict, but we shall list a few more to illustrate some further differences between our compiler and EJC and JAVAC. The first example can be found in Fig. 4. Note that our message explains that there are in fact two independent errors (indicated by [*]), and that it also explains why the invocation does not match the given definition. Again, neither EJC nor JAVAC explains what the problem is, only that the invocation does not match.

In Fig. 5, the conflicts are not independent, because all inconsistencies involve the same type variable, and our message reflects this. We have omitted the messages of EJC and JAVAC since they follow the same pattern as in Fig. 4.

As a final type equality conflict consider the fragment in Fig. 6. In this case, both calls are inconsistent, and although the return type of the inner foo does not depend on the types of its inputs, all three compilers only mention the inconsistency arising from the inner invocation: the inconsistency will only show up after fixing the innermost one.

We now continue with an example of a subtyping conflict. Consider the code fragment and associated messages in Fig. 7. Such a conflict arises when an equality constraint determines the type of a particular type variable; in this case T becomes equal to Integer, which then leads to an inconsistency in the second parameter, because Number is not a subtype of Integer. Neither EJC nor JAVAC explain why the invocation does not match the declared type of bar; our message does provide such an explanation.

It is quite easy, but not very interesting, to come up with a similar mistake to that in Fig. 7, but which involves super rather than extends. A more interesting source of mistakes, that is typical for supertype constraints, is due to the inability to find a single type that extends two different types. In the case of the code fragment in Fig. 8, the return type of foo is void so the assignment context cannot be used to find a proper instance for T. Following the JLS, the type T is then computed by taking the largest type that extends both Number and String. However, such a type does not exist, as our error message explains. As usual, both EJC and JAVAC simply complain that the invocation does not match the method. In Sect. 3.1 we show that these compilers sometimes exhibit strange behaviour for this kind of example.

```
class Listingindep{
    <T,S> void foo(Map<T,T> a, Map<S,S> b){
        Map<Number,String> m1 = null;
        Map<Integer,String> m2 = null;
        foo(m1,m2);
    }
}
```

```
listings/Listingindep.java:7: <T,S>foo(java.util.Map<T,T>,java.util.Map<S,S>)
in Listingindep cannot be applied to (java.util.Map<java.lang.Number,
java.lang.String>,java.util.Map<java.lang.Integer,java.lang.String>)
        foo(m1,m2);
        ^
```

JAVAC

```
1. ERROR in listings/Listingindep.java (at line 7)
    foo(m1,m2);
    ^^^
The method foo(Map<T,T>, Map<S,S>) in the type Listingindep is not applicable
for the arguments (Map<Number,String>, Map<Integer,String>)
```

EJC

```
listings/Listingindep.java:7
Method <T, S>foo(Map<T, T>, Map<S, S>) of type Listingindep is not applicable
for the arguments of type (Map<Number, String>, Map<Integer, String>), because:
  [*] The type variable T is invariant, but the types:
  - String in Map<Number, String> on 5:9(5:20)
  - Number in Map<Number, String> on 5:9(5:13)
  are not the same type.
  [*] The type variable S is invariant, but the types:
  - String in Map<Integer, String> on 6:9(6:21)
  - Integer in Map<Integer, String> on 6:9(6:13)
  are not the same type.
```

ours

Figure. 4 A code fragment with two independent equality type conflicts (one in each argument), and the type error messages for JAVAC, EJC and our implementation respectively.

```
import java.util.*;

class Listingref{
    <T> void foo(Map<T,Map<T,T>> a){
        Map<Number, Map<Integer,String>> m1 = null;
        foo(m1);
    }
}
```

```
listings/Listingref.java:6
Method <T>foo(Map<T, Map<T, T>>) of type Listingref is not applicable for the
argument of type (Map<Number, Map<Integer, String>>), because:
  [*] The type variable T is invariant, but the types:
  - Integer in Map<Number, Map<Integer, String>> on 5:9(5:25)
  - String in Map<Number, Map<Integer, String>> on 5:9(5:33)
  - Number in Map<Number, Map<Integer, String>> on 5:9(5:13)
  are not the same type.
                                   ours
```

Figure. 5 A code fragment with multiple conflicts arising from the variable m1, and the error message we provide.

```
import java.util.*;

class Listingnested{
    <T> Map<Number,Integer> foo(Map<T,T> a){
        Map<Number,String> m1 = null;
        foo(foo(m1));
    }
}
```

```
listings/Listingnested.java:6: <T>foo(java.util.Map<T,T>) in Listingnested
cannot be applied to (java.util.Map<java.lang.Number,java.lang.String>)
        foo(foo(m1));
            ^
                                   JAVAC
```

```
1. ERROR in listings/Listingnested.java (at line 6)
    foo(foo(m1));
        ^^^
The method foo(Map<T,T>) in the type Listingnested is not applicable for
the arguments (Map<Number,String>)
                                   EJC
```

```
listings/Listingnested.java:6
Method <T>foo(Map<T, T>) of type Listingnested is not applicable for the
argument of type (Map<Number, String>), because:
  [*] The type variable T is invariant, but the types:
  - String in Map<Number, String> on 5:9(5:20)
  - Number in Map<Number, String> on 5:9(5:13)
  are not the same type.
                                   ours
```

Figure. 6 Although our error message provides more explanation, for all three compilers the type inconsistency in the inner invocation of foo eclipses the inconsistency in the outer invocation.

```
import java.util.*;

class Listing2{
    static <T> void bar(Map<T, ? extends T> a){
        Map<Integer, Number> m2 = null;
        bar(m2);
    }
}
```

```
listings/Listing2.java:6: <T>bar(java.util.Map<T,? extends T>) in Listing2
cannot be applied to (java.util.Map<java.lang.Integer,java.lang.Number>)
        bar(m2);
        ^
                                   JAVAC
```

```
1. ERROR in listings/Listing2.java (at line 6)
    bar(m2);
    ^^^
The method bar(Map<T,? extends T>) in the type Listing2 is not applicable for
the arguments (Map<Integer,Number>)
                                   EJC
```

```
listings/Listing2.java:6
Method <T>bar(Map<T, ? extends T>) of type Listing2 is not applicable for the
argument of type (Map<Integer, Number>), because:
  [*] The type Number in Map<Integer, Number> on 5:9(5:22) is not a subtype of
      the inferred type for T: Integer.
                                   ours
```

Figure. 7 A code fragment with a subtyping conflict and the three corresponding type error messages.

```
import java.util.*;

class Listing6{
    <T extends Number> void foo(Map<? super T, ? super T> a){
        Map<Number, String> m = null;
        foo(m);
    }
}
```

```
listings/Listing6.java:7: <T>foo(java.util.Map<? super T,? super T>) in Listing6
cannot be applied to (java.util.Map<java.lang.Number,java.lang.String>)
        foo(m);
        ^
```
JAVAC

```
1. ERROR in listings/Listing6.java (at line 6)
    foo(m);
    ^^^
The method foo(Map<? super T,? super T>) in the type Listing6 is not applicable
for the arguments (Map<Number,String>)
```
EJC

```
listings/Listing6.java:7
Method <T extends Number>foo(Map<? super T, ? super T>) of type Listing6 is not
applicable for the argument of type (Map<Number, String>), because:
  [*] The types Number in Map<Number, String> on 5:9(5:13) and String in
      Map<Number, String> on 5:9(5:21) do not share a common subtype.
```
ours

Figure. 8 A code fragment without assignment context, so that in absence of equality and subtype constraints the supertype constraints determine the type.

A similar kind of situation occurs in Fig. 9, but here the cause of the problem is a subtype conflict: because of the second argument type for Map and the invariance of collection class type constructors, T will be instantiated to Number. However, this choice clashes with the fact that Number is not a subtype of Integer.

We continue with some examples that involve a bound conflict, starting with Fig. 10. Surprisingly, JAVAC gives exactly the same error messages as in Fig. 1, although the reason why this particular invocation fails is completely different: it is illegal, because the type that the type variable T should be instantiated with must be a subtype of Number. Since the type Comparable of the actual parameter is not a subtype of Number, the invocation is incorrect.

A second example of a bound error can be found in Fig. 11. In this case the error message of EJC is quite reasonable, although our message does not resort to mentioning an intersection type, which is an artifact constructed by the type inference phase. Surprisingly, some versions of JAVAC crash for this particular program due to an infinite number of calls to the least upper bound function, while some other version of JAVAC generate an internal error.

```
import java.util.*;

class Listing8{
   <T> void foo(Map<? super T, T> a) {
      Map<Integer, Number> m = null;
      foo(m);
   }
}
```

```
listings/Listing8.java:6: <T>foo(java.util.Map<? super T,T>) in Listing8 cannot
be applied to (java.util.Map<java.lang.Integer,java.lang.Number>)
      foo(m);
      ^
```
JAVAC

```
1. ERROR in listings/Listing8.java (at line 6)
    foo(m);
    ^^^
The method foo(Map<? super T,T>) in the type Listing8 is not applicable for the
arguments (Map<Integer,Number>)
```
EJC

```
listings/Listing8.java:6
Method <T>foo(Map<? super T, T>) of type Listing8 is not applicable for the
argument of type (Map<Integer, Number>), because:
  [*] The type Integer in Map<Integer, Number> on 5:7(5:11) is not a supertype
      of the inferred type for T: Number.
```
ours

Figure. 9 A conflict due to the fact that Integer is not a supertype of Number, a constraint that follows from the second argument to Map.

```
import java.util.*;

class Listing3{
    <T extends Number> void baz(List<T> a){
        List<Comparable<Integer>> x = null;
        baz(x);
    }
}
```

```
listings/Listing3.java:6: <T>baz(java.util.List<T>) in Listing3 cannot be
applied to (java.util.List<java.lang.Comparable<java.lang.Integer>>)
        baz(x);
        ^
```

JAVAC

```
1. ERROR in listings/Listing3.java (at line 6)
    baz(x);
    ^^^
Bound mismatch: The generic method baz(List<T>) of type Listing3 is not
applicable for the arguments (List<Comparable<Integer>>). The inferred type
Comparable<Integer> is not a valid substitute for the bounded parameter
<T extends Number>
```

EJC

```
listings/Listing3.java:6
Method <T extends Number>baz(List<T>) of type Listing3 is not applicable for the
argument of type (List<Comparable<Integer>>), because:
  [*] The type Comparable<Integer> in List<Comparable<Integer>> on 5:9(5:9) is
      not a subtype of T's upper bound Number in 'T extends Number'.
```

ours

Figure. 10 A code fragment with a bound conflict followed by the three corresponding type error messages.

```
class JavacError1 {
  <T extends Number> void foo(T a, T b){
    foo(1, false);
  }
}
```

```
listings/JavacError1.java:3: internal error; cannot instantiate <T>foo(T,T) at
JavacError1 to (int,boolean)
    foo(1, false);
       ^
```

JAVAC

```
1. ERROR in listings/JavacError1.java (at line 3)
    foo(1, false);
    ^^^
Bound mismatch: The generic method foo(T, T) of type JavacError1 is not
applicable for the arguments (Integer, Boolean). The inferred type
Object&Comparable<?>&Serializable is not a valid substitute for the bounded
parameter <T extends Number>
```

EJC

```
listings/JavacError1.java:3
Method <T extends Number>foo(T, T) of type JavacError1 is not applicable for the
arguments of type (int, boolean), because:
  [*] The type boolean of the expression 'false' on 3:12 is not a subtype of T's
      upper bound Number in 'T extends Number'.
```

ours

Figure. 11 The value false cannot be considered an element of any type that extends Number; everything is okay for the first argument 1.

An example of a type error involving wildcards can be found in Fig. 12. The code fragment shows what might be a typical mistake on the part of a novice programmer: assuming that the type ? extends Number equals ? extends Number which, if provable, would make the invocation correct. However, these types are not equivalent. Our message follows the tenets of the manifesto of Yang [33] in that an error message should never reveal anything internal to compiler. However, the error messages provided by EJC and JAVAC explicitly refer to a captured wildcard.

Strange Behaviour

In some cases we have observed that the compilers may behave strangely, or simply not according to the JLS.

Sometimes the type inferencer computes the largest subtype of a pair of types, and recall from the preliminaries that such a type may not always exist. This is the case for the program given in Fig. 13, in which T should be instantiated to the largest subtype of Number and String, which is not a valid type. Surprisingly, JAVAC accepts the program, due to the fact that it ignores the bound constraint when inferring a type for T.

A second example of a program that is erroneously accepted by JAVAC can be found in Fig. 14. In fact, none of the method invocations in this program should be allowed according to the JLS. Both EJC and our own compiler generate the type error messages as provided.

So why are these invocations type incorrect? The type of a generic type variable T for which no constraints of the form $T = \ldots$ or $\ldots <: T$ are generated, is determined by the type to which the result of the call to bar is assigned (if present). This, in the case of bar(m1) results in T being instantiated to Integer due to the type given for l. For the second call, T is instantiated to Integer. However, in both cases, and the third one as well, the constraint derived from the invocation itself T then cannot be satisfied.

```
import java.util.*;

class Listing4{
    <T> void bar(Map<T, T> a){
        Map<? extends Number, ? extends Number> m = null;
        bar(m);
    }
}
```

```
listings/Listing4.java:6: <T>bar(java.util.Map<T,T>) in Listing4 cannot be
applied to (java.util.Map<capture of ? extends java.lang.Number,
capture of ? extends java.lang.Number>)
        bar(m);
        ^
```
JAVAC

```
1. ERROR in listings/Listing4.java (at line 6)
    bar(m);
    ^^^
The method bar(Map<T,T>) in the type Listing4 is not applicable for the arguments
(Map<capture#1-of ? extends Number,capture#2-of ? extends Number>)
```
EJC

```
listings/Listing4.java:6
Method <T>bar(Map<T, T>) of type Listing4 is not applicable for the argument of
type (Map<? extends Number, ? extends Number>), because:
  [*] The type variable T is invariant, but the type '? extends Number' is not.
```
ours

Figure. 12 Two wildcards (even with the same bounds) are never provably the same, which is a likely reason for the inconsistency. Both JAVAC and EJC make explicit reference to captured variables, while our message does not.

```
import java.util.*;

class JavacError2 {
  <T extends Number> void foo(List<? super T> a){
    List<String> x = null;
    foo(x);
  }
}
```

```
1. ERROR in listings/JavacError2.java (at line 6)
    foo(x);
    ^^^
Bound mismatch: The generic method foo(List<? super T>) of type JavacError2 is
not applicable for the arguments (List<String>). The inferred type String is not
a valid substitute for the bounded parameter <T extends Number>
```
EJC

```
listings/JavacError2.java:6
Method <T extends Number>foo(List<? super T>) of type JavacError2 is not
applicable for the argument of type (List<String>), because:
  [*] The types String in List<String> on 5:5(5:10) and Number do not share a
      common subtype. (...)
```
ours

Figure. 13 The argument type implies that T is String, which is clearly not a subtype of Number. Still, the program is accepted by JAVAC.

```
import java.util.*;

class JavacError3{
    <T extends Number> List<T> bar(Map<? super T, ? super T> a){
        Map<List<String>, List<String>> m1 = null;
        Map<Double, Number> m2 = null;
        List<Integer> l = bar(m1);
        List<Integer> s = bar(m2);
        s = bar(m1);
        return null;
    }
}
```

```
1. ERROR in listings/JavacError3.java (at line 7)
    List<Integer> l = bar(m1);
                      ^^^
The method bar(Map<? super T,? super T>) in the type JavacError3 is not
applicable for the arguments (Map<List<String>,List<String>>)
----------
2. ERROR in listings/JavacError3.java (at line 8)
    List<Integer> s = bar(m2);
                      ^^^
The method bar(Map<? super T,? super T>) in the type JavacError3 is not
applicable for the arguments (Map<Double,Number>)
----------
3. ERROR in listings/JavacError3.java (at line 9)
    s = bar(m1);
        ^^^
The method bar(Map<? super T,? super T>) in the type JavacError3 is not
applicable for the arguments (Map<List<String>,List<String>>)
```

EJC

```
listings/JavacError3.java:7
Method <T extends Number>bar(Map<? super T, ? super T>) of type JavacError3
is not applicable for the argument of type (Map<List<String>, List<String>>),
because:
   [*] The type List<String> in Map<List<String>, List<String>> on 5:9(5:9) is
       not a supertype of the inferred type for T: Integer.

listings/JavacError3.java:8
Method <T extends Number>bar(Map<? super T, ? super T>) of type JavacError3
is not applicable for the argument of type (Map<Double, Number>), because:
   [*] The type Double in Map<Double, Number> on 6:9(6:13) is not a supertype of
       the inferred type for T: Integer.

listings/JavacError3.java:9
Method <T extends Number>bar(Map<? super T, ? super T>) of type JavacError3
is not applicable for the argument of type (Map<List<String>, List<String>>),
because:
   [*] The type List<String> in Map<List<String>, List<String>> on 5:9(5:9) is
       not a supertype of the inferred type for T: Integer.
```

ours

Figure. 14 Another code fragment erroneously accepted by JAVAC.

The EJC compiler also sometimes exhibits strange behaviour. Consider the code fragments in Figs. 15 and 16. The only difference between the two is in the order of the type arguments of the value passed to the method. The constraints generated for both method calls are the same according to the JLS:

$$\{\mathtt{T} <: \mathtt{Number}, \mathtt{T} <: \mathtt{String}\}$$

```
import java.util.Map;

class Listing51{
    <T extends Number> void foo(Map<? super T, ? super T> a){
        Map<String, Number> m = null;
        foo(m);
    }
}
```

```
listings/Listing5-1.java:6: <T>foo(java.util.Map<? super T,? super T>) in
Listing51 cannot be applied to
(java.util.Map<java.lang.String,java.lang.Number>)
        foo(m);
        ^
```
JAVAC

```
1. ERROR in listings/Listing5-1.java (at line 6)
    foo(m);
    ^^^
Bound mismatch: The generic method foo(Map<? super T,? super T>) of type
Listing51 is not applicable for the arguments (Map<String,Number>). The inferred
type String is not a valid substitute for the bounded parameter
<T extends Number>
```
EJC

```
listings/Listing5-1.java:6
Method <T extends Number>foo(Map<? super T, ? super T>) of type Listing51 is not
applicable for the argument of type (Map<String, Number>), because:
  [*] The types String in Map<String, Number> on 5:9(5:13) and Number in
      Map<String, Number> on 5:9(5:21) do not share a common subtype. (...)
```
ours

Figure. 15 An inconsistency that for EJC reveals some of the underlying type checking machinery: the diagnosis given by EJC for the erroneous invocation should be the same as that for Fig. 16, but this is not the case.

One would expect, therefore, the error messages for the two programs to be identical, as they are for our implementation. However, the type error diagnosis for these programs by EJC is quite different. This is due to how EJC resolves subtype constraints. Note that although the error messages generated by JAVAC are the same, neither is very informative.

Obtaining different type error messages for very similar, in some sense isomorphic, programs is an often observed but not so pleasant phenomenon. It is typically due to the fact that the implementation of the type checking process leaks through to the type error messages. Since programmers typically do not have any knowledge of the implementation, they are at a disadvantage when trying to interpret the messages. We saw two examples of this earlier: the captured wildcards (Fig. 12) and the intersection types (Fig. 11) computed by the inference process.

THE TYPE CHECKING PROCESS

To be able to describe our modifications to the Java type checking process, we first discuss the original process. The modifications are then described in the next section.

```
import java.util.Map;

class Listing52{
    <T extends Number> void foo(Map<? super T, ? super T> a){
        Map<Number, String> m = null;
        foo(m);
    }
}
```

```
listings/Listing5-2.java:6: <T>foo(java.util.Map<? super T,? super T>) in
Listing52 cannot be applied to (java.util.Map<java.lang.Number,
java.lang.String>)
        foo(m);
        ^
```
JAVAC

```
1. ERROR in listings/Listing5-2.java (at line 6)
    foo(m);
    ^^^
The method foo(Map<? super T,? super T>) in the type Listing52 is not applicable
for the arguments (Map<Number,String>)
```
EJC

```
listings/Listing5-2.java:6
Method <T extends Number>foo(Map<? super T, ? super T>) of type Listing52 is not
applicable for the argument of type (Map<Number, String>), because:
  [*] The types Number in Map<Number, String> on 5:9(5:13) and String in
      Map<Number, String> on 5:9(5:21) do not share a common subtype. (...)
```
ours

Figure. 16 The inconsistency is very similar to that in Fig. 15, but nonetheless diagnosed differently by EJC.

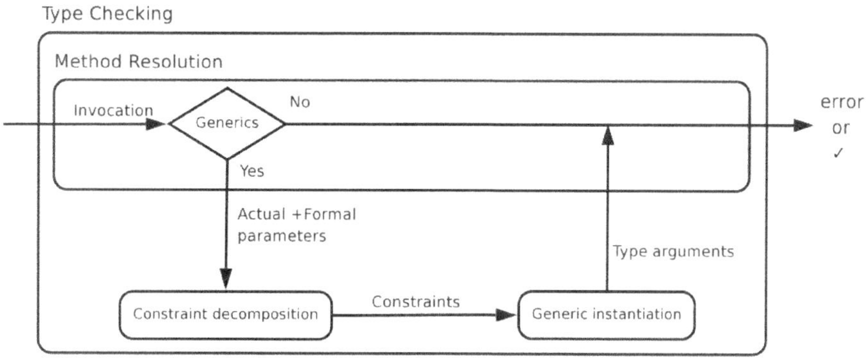

Figure. 17 The type checking process.

To avoid any misunderstanding, we first explain our terminology. In this paper, type checking process refers to the complete process of determining the type correctness of a particular program fragment. In our particular case these program fragments are always method invocations.

The type checking process is depicted in Fig. 17. It starts off by performing method resolution, which determines, for a given invocation, a set of methods that the programmer may be invoking. We describe the complex process of method resolution in some detail below.

The set of methods obtained by method resolution may contain a number of generic methods. Pairing the concrete parameter types to the formal parameter types of a generic method:

```
<T, S> List<S> foo (Map<T, T> a,
                   List <? super S> b);
...
Map<Integer, Number> m = ...;
List<String> l = ...;
List<Integer> ret = foo(m, l);
```

results in a set of constraints

{Map<Integer, Number> <: Map<T, T>,
List<String> <: List<? super S>}.

that should hold if this invocation is to typecheck.

The set of constraints is subsequently decomposed into atomic constraints between type variables on the one hand and types on the other. Although there are quite a few cases to be covered, this part of the process is conceptually quite easy and is described in detail in §15.12.2.7 of [7]. Here, we give only the result of decomposition for our example:

{T = Integer, T = Number, String :> S}.

The type checking process then proceeds with generic instantiation to infer the types of the generic variables, essentially a process of finding a concrete type for each type variable. Although its name might imply otherwise, the inference process has a surprising property: if multiple, conflicting instantiations for a type variable are possible, then the inference process simply selects one, leaving it up to the later type checking phase to find that the instantiation is incorrect. The JLS states that if a conflict exists, then it will indeed not show up until in the type checking phase at the end of the type checking process. In the above example, a possible outcome of the inference phase is:

T = Integer.

In the presence of multiple supertype constraints, say

{Integer <: T, Double <: T},

this results in the instantiation of T to the least upper bound (lub) of the two, Number. However, things are not always so simple: for {Integer <: T, String <: T}, the lub is

Object & Serializable & Comparable<? extends Object & Serializable & Comparable<?>>,

because both Integer and String implement these interfaces. Note that in many compilers, not only are these types computed by the inference process, they are sometimes also used in the type error message displayed to the programmer. This contradicts one of the crucial properties that we, and others [33], believe a type checking process should have: it should only refer to types or expressions that are part of the original source program. Without any information on how the lub was computed, it can be very difficult for programmers to reconstruct what has happened and why.

The dual of the least upper bound is the greatest lower bound (glb), which is used to capture the most general type that extends both argument types (which may include classes and interfaces). However, if all constraints in which a type variable is involved are of this kind and the invocation occurs in an assignment context, then the JLS specifies that the type of the variable to which the result is assigned should, if possible, be used to determine to what type a type variable should be instantiated. This happens to be the case in our example for S. Therefore, the constraint List<S> <: List<Integer> is added to the constraint set. It decomposes into S = Integer. Together, the decomposed constraints are

{T = Integer, T = Number, S = Integer, String :> S}.

The inference process then instantiates S to Integer on the basis of the third constraint above; note that T was already instantiated to Integer.

One may wonder what happens if a declared type variable is not constrained in any way. The JLS specifies that the variable should then be instantiated to Object; this helps the JLS deal with legacy code.

In the final step, it is determined whether the remaining constraints, which are by now all equivalence and subtype relations between concrete types, are consistent. This part of the type checking process we call the type checking phase.

It is important to realize that in the type checking phase

each invocation is considered in isolation. This even holds for nested invocations foo(bar(x),y), where first the bar invocation will be considered in isolation from its context. It can therefore well be that the bar invocation type checks, but that types chosen by the inference phase turn out to be inconsistent with the enclosing call to foo. Or, it may be that the call to bar is not valid due to a case of ambiguous method invocation, but that on the basis of the type of foo, this ambiguity could have been resolved. By contrast, in the polymorphic lambda-calculus type information from the encapsulating call would be used to determine the proper instantiations for bar. This lack of propagation in Java has its advantages, as types are instantiated based on local information only and not through a long and complicated sequence of unifications. But this may also surprise the programmer, particularly in the case of an ambiguous method invocation.

Method Resolution

The goal of method resolution, for a given invocation, is to come up with a single method in the program that the programmer intends to call. This decision has to be made statically, and cannot depend on run-time type information.

The process of method resolution is rather complex, due to such features as overloading (multiple methods having the same name), overriding (methods can be overridden by subclasses), variable arity methods, and visibility. Visibility depends not only on lexical scope, but also on, e.g., the access modifiers of the method. This includes the fact that you may not call a private method from certain contexts, but also that you cannot access (non-static) instance fields from a static method.

Method resolution consists of three main steps. For a given method invocation,

1. Determine the name of the method to be invoked, say mthd, and the class or interface that receives the invocation. Java has five different forms of method invocation. Examples respectively are a.byteValue(), this.Foo(), super.intVal(), Baz.super.intVal() and Collections.emptySet(). In the case of the invocation a.byteValue(), byteValue() is the name of the method, and the receiver is the innermost class or interface that encloses the method declaration (if indeed, byteValue is visible from the invocation site). Note that for this case alone there are two additional variants: a. may be omitted, and a type name may be used instead of a. For more details see the JLS.
2. Consider every method of the receiver in turn to find all possible accessible and applicable method members. A method potential in the receiver is a candidate if and only if
   - the names potential and mthd are the same,
   - potential is accessible from the invocation site,
   - if potential is a variable arity method of arity, say n, then the number of arguments passed to mthd must be greater than or equal to n − 1,
   - if potential is a fixed arity method of arity n, then the number of arguments passed to mthd must be equal to n,
   - if the method invocation includes explicit type parameters, and potential is a generic method, then the number of actual type parameters must equal the number of formal type parameters.

   Then the compiler tries to weed out potential methods by comparing actual to formal parameters. Due to the presence of subtyping, auto-boxing, and variable arity methods, this is quite a complicated process, consisting of three alternative decision procedures. A decision procedure is only applied if all the preceding decision procedures eliminated all candidates. Below, we assume the method invocation is mthd(A_1,...,A_n).

   a. Identify methods mthd(F_1,...,F_n), and in which only "weakening by subtyping" is allowed to match actual argument types to formal argument types. In other words, for all $1 \leq i \leq n$:
      - $A_i <: F_i$, or
      - A_i is a raw type that can be parametrized into a type C_i so that $C_i <: F_i$.

      If the method is generic, then all type variables in the Fi are bound to a concrete type provided by the method invocation. If such type information is unavailable then type inference, as described earlier, is used to find concrete types. The potential method is then only applicable if all instantiated type variables are within their stated bounds.

   b. Similar to the previous case, but now in combination with (un)boxing.

   c. Similar to the previous case, but now allowing also variable arity methods. Details can be found in the JLS.

   If all the sets of candidates delivered by the three previous cases are empty, then no matching method exists, and an error message is produced. Otherwise, we take the first non-empty one, say S, and proceed to try to eliminate candidates until only one is left. For example, we remove from S those methods for which a more specific signature in S exists, e.g., if both `mthd(List<T>)` and `mthd (List<Integer>` are in S, then the former is deleted. A similar but more complicated rule can be formulated for variable arity methods.

   If for any pair of methods it cannot be decided which is the most specific, the compiler has a few rules to deal with this, largely by preferring non-abstract over abstract methods. In the absence of the former, an arbitrary abstract method with the most specific return type is chosen.

   If that still does not work, then an ambiguous method invocation error message is generated.

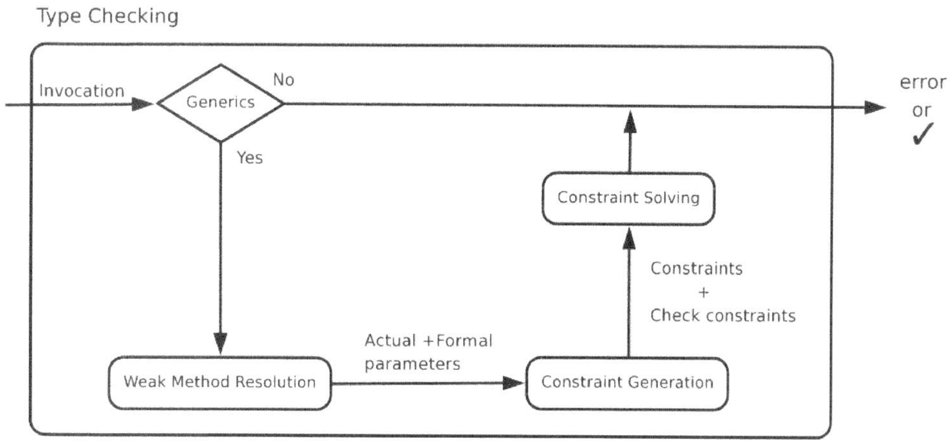

Figure. 18 The modified type checking process.

3. In the third and final step, the method chosen in the previous step is screened for appropriateness. For example, an instance method cannot be invoked from a static context.

   As the reader can see, method resolution is indeed a complicated, stepwise process. In our extension of the type checking process, which we describe in the following section, we relax the constraints somewhat to try and figure out which method the programmer might have been trying to call, and to use that information in our type error message.

THE MODIFIED TYPE CHECKING PROCESS

Figure 18 shows the overall architecture of our modified type checking process. The structure of the process is not much different, only the contents of the phases themselves change. It is important to realize that this modified process is only invoked after the original process has found a particular invocation to be type incorrect.

Weakened Method Resolution

First, we define a weaker form of method resolution that allows more candidate methods to be targeted by the method invocation. We are not interested in identifying a single method that is being called, but want to consider multiple candidate methods and provide a diagnosis for each method that is reasonably close to what the programmer intended to call.

A major decision we have to make is how exactly we weaken method resolution. Our choice here is to erase generic information from the invocation and the candidate method. In other words, when we are looking for a suitable method in the second step (ii) of method resolution we base our comparison between the signatures on the raw types, instead of the generic types. Conversion to raw types involves replacing type variables (and possible bounds) with Object and changing generic types like List to the raw type List.

The original process of method resolution aims to come up with a single method to be called (or it may fail to find one at all). Because we drop information that might be used during the original method resolution phase, the set of candidates might now be larger. This is not a problem. Remember that we already know that in the end none of these methods will be acceptable. But since we have more candidates to pass on to the part of the process that is still to come, that part of the process may then be able to tell us more precisely why each of the candidates fails to qualify. In our particular case, for example, we have defined and implemented a number of heuristics [2] that work directly on the constraints derived from a particular method invocation and method definition, but these heuristics will only be applied to method definitions that pass (weakened) method resolution.

The (heuristic) assumption we make is that when it comes to the types of arguments, the generic parts of Java are more likely to contain mistakes than the raw types. This assumption derives from the fact that the generic part of Java is pretty complicated and therefore more easily misunderstood. Moreover, it is a fairly recent addition to the language, and a refinement of the raw types.

Another way to view our assumption, is that we prefer not to commit too early to certain choices because that immediately biases the type checking process, in that it becomes less likely that we shall ever blame that which we commit upon first. This indicates that, as a rule, it pays to commit first to facts in which your confidence is the highest. Since our assumption is that we should have less confidence in the generic parts of the types, it makes sense to ignore them in the early phases of the process.

Another instance of this idea can be found in work on removing the bias from Algorithm W [3]: in a standard implementation, constraints are solved (i.e., unifications are performed) while traversing the abstract syntax tree of the program (from left to right), thereby building a type substitution on the fly. So if we have multiple, inconsistent constraints for a particular type variable, the leftmost constraint is seen first and will determine the type we find for the type variable, even in cases where we find that all other constraints for that type variable say differently. In [9] it was shown how the bias can be removed by a constraint solving approach in which sets of constraints are considered simultaneously, and heuristics that work on these sets of constraints, either select the constraint(s) that are most likely to be the cause of the inconsistency, or eliminate constraints for which the opposite is the case.

The specification of weakened method resolution in the form of pseudocode can be found in Figs. 19, 20 and 21. The function methodResolution takes a method invocation as an argument and returns a set of most specific method declarations. The procedure starts by searching for potentially applicable methods, by considering all methods that are members of the receiver of the invocation. These are methods with the same name as the method that is invoked, and have an arity equal the number of arguments in the invocation (if the method is of fixed arity), or an arity less than the number of arguments in the invocation (if the method is of variable arity). This part is performed by the procedure potentiallyApplicable in Fig. 19. As explained before, three attempts will be made to come to a non-empty set of methods: first we are only allowed to match up to subtyping, then we allow method conversion (methodConvertible, that considers candidate methods modulo boxing, unboxing and various forms of widening, §5.3 of [7]), and finally we also allow methods of variable arity to be considered.[3]

[3]The construct foreach (x, y) in (xs,ys) iterates through the lists xs and ys in a way that if x is the ith element of xs, then y is the ith element of ys.

In each case, methods will be eliminated if they are less specific than at least one other in the list. This check is implemented for the fixed arity and variable arity case in mostSpecificMethodFixed and mostSpecificMethodVariable, as given in Fig. 20. The methods behave exactly as in the original type checking process, except that they ignore any kind of generic information. The specification of the auxiliary function moreSpecificVariable in Fig. 21 is rather lengthy, because we have to deal with the fact that the number of parameters can be unequal in two ways, but that the subtype relation is independent of the respective lengths. Note that we could have abstracted away from the particular type comparison operator in order to save code, but for reasons of clarity and correspondence with the JLS (§15.12.2.5) we preferred to write it out.

```
[Method] methodResolution(invocation)
  potentialMethods = [m in invocation.receiver
                      | potentiallyApplicable(m,invocation)]
  specificMethods = [m in potentialMethods
                     | m of fixed arity and
                       applicableBySubtyping(m,invocation)]
  mostSpecificMethods = mostSpecificMethodFixed(specificMethods)
  if empty mostSpecificMethods then
    methodConvertedMethods = [m in potentialMethods
                              | m of fixed arity and
                                applicableByMethodConversion(m,invocation)]
    mostSpecificMethods = mostSpecificMethodFixed(methodConvertedMethods)
    if empty mostSpecificMethods then
      methodVarArity = [m in potentialMethods
                        | m of variable arity and
                          applicableByMethodConversion(m,invocation)]
      mostSpecificMethods = mostSpecificMethodVariable(methodConvertedMethods)
  return [m in mostSpecificMethods | m appropriate]

boolean potentiallyApplicable(method, invocation)
  return
     method.name == invocation.name and
     method accessible from invocation.location and
     (method.arity == length(invocation.arguments) or
      (method of variable arity and
       length(invocation.arguments) >= method.arity-1))

boolean applicableBySubtyping(method, invocation)
  foreach (parameter,argument) in (method.arguments,invocation.arguments) do
    erasedParameter = wideErasure(parameter)
    if (argument <: erasedParameter) then
      continue
    else
      return false
  return true

boolean applicableByMethodConversion(method, invocation)
  (* Works both for variable and fixed arity methods *)
  k = method.arity-1
  for i = 1 to k
    erasedParameter = wideErasure(method.arguments[i])
    argument   = invocation.arguments[i]
    if methodConvertible(argument, erasedParameter) then
      continue
    else
      return false
  (* The "variable" part *)
  erasedParameter = wideErasure(method.arguments[k+1]
  for i = k+1 to n
    argument   = invocation.arguments[i]
    if methodConvertible(argument, erasedParameter) then
      continue
    else
      return false
  return true
```

Figure. 19 Pseudocode for weakened method resolution (part 1).

```
Type wideErasure(tp)
  if tp is a type variable then
    return Object
  else
    if tp is generic then
      return raw form of tp
    else
      return tp

[Method] mostSpecificMethodFixed(methods)
  foreach m1 in methods
    foreach m2 in methods
      if moreSpecificFixed(m1,m2) then
        methods.delete(m2)

[Method] mostSpecificMethodVariable(methods)
  foreach m1 in methods
    foreach m2 in methods
      if moreSpecificVariable(m1,m2) then
        methods.delete(m2)
```

Figure. 20 Pseudocode for weakened method resolution (part 2).

After having constructed a set of most specific methods, methodResolution will remove any method declaration that is not appropriate from the set (e.g. not accessible from the call site), and returns the set of remaining methods.

We illustrate the process by means of an example. Consider the code in Fig. 22 where we define a many-times overloaded method foo (we designate foo on line x by foo_x). Consider first the invocation on line 20. The method foo_2 does not qualify as a candidate because it has the wrong number of parameters. All the other declarations have the right number of parameters, so they are marked as candidates in step (i). Their signatures are converted into their raw form, and we obtain

foo_4(Map, Collection), foo_7(Map, List), foo_{10}(HashMap, List), foo_{13}(HashMap, LinkedList), foo_{16}(HashMap, Set).

In the absence of primitive types and variable arity methods, the applicable methods can be determined using subtyping only, i.e., we only need to look at case (a) of step (ii) in the method resolution phase. The second parameter LinkedList in the invocation is not a subtype of the generic interface type Set. Therefore, foo_{16} is disqualified as a candidate. Next, our weak method resolution reduces the set of applicable methods

$\{foo_4, foo_7, foo_{10}, foo_{13}\}$

to a set of most specific methods. Comparing foo_4 with foo_7 results in the removal of foo_4, because `List <: Collection` Similarly, foo_7 and foo_{10} are removed in favour of foo_{13}. For the second and third invocation in Fig. 22 the same set of candidates is obtained.

```
boolean moreSpecificFixed(m1,m2)
  (* In case both methods are of fixed arity *)
  foreach (paramm1,paramm2) in (m1.arguments, m2.arguments) do
    paramm1 = wideErasure(paramm1)
    paramm2 = wideErasure(paramm2)
    if (paramm1 <: paramm2) then
      continue
    else
      return false
  return true

boolean moreSpecificVariable(m1,m2)
  (* In case both methods are of variable arity *)
  if m1.arity >= m2.arity then
    k = m2.arity - 1
    m = m1.arity
    for i = 1 to k
      paramm1 = wideErasure(m1.arguments[i])
      paramm2 = wideErasure(m2.arguments[i])
      if (paramm1 <: paramm2) then
        continue
      else
        return false
    paramm2 = wideErasure(m2.arguments[k+1])

    for i = k+1 to n
      paramm1 = wideErasure(m1.arguments[i])
      if (paramm1 <: paramm2) then
        continue
      else
        return false
    return true

  else
    k = m1.arity - 1
    m = m2.arity
    for i = 1 to k
      paramm1 = wideErasure(m1.arguments[i])
      paramm2 = wideErasure(m2.arguments[i])
      if (paramm1 <: paramm2) then
        continue
      else
        return false
    paramm1 = wideErasure(m1.arguments[k+1])

    for i = k+1 to n
      paramm2 = wideErasure(m2.arguments[i])
      if (paramm1 <: paramm2) then
        continue
      else
        return false
    return true
```

Figure. 21 Pseudocode for weakened method resolution (part 3).

In all cases, we ended up with a singleton set, but our resolution method does not demand this, contrary to the original resolution method. For example, for the code fragment of Fig. 28, which we shall discuss in more detail later, both declarations of bar pass method resolution.

```
class FooLib{
   <T> void foo(Map<T, ? extends T> a){}

   <T> void foo(Map<T, ? extends T> a,
                Collection<? super T> b){}

   <T> void foo(Map<T, ? extends T> a,
                List<? super T> b){}

   <T> void foo(HashMap<T, ? extends T> a,
                List<? super T> b){}

   <T> void foo(HashMap<T, ? extends T> a,
                LinkedList<? super T> b){}

   <T> void foo(HashMap<T, ? extends T> a,
                Set<? super T> b){}
}
...
UtilLib.foo(new HashMap<Integer, Integer>(),
            new LinkedList<Number>());
UtilLib.foo(new HashMap<Double, Number>(),
            new LinkedList<Integer>());
LinkedList<? extends Number> wl = ...;
UtilLib.foo(new HashMap<Number, Double>(), wl);
```

Figure. 22 A utility class for illustrating weakened method resolution.

```
<T> void foo(List<T> a, List<? super T> b){
...
List<Number> l1 = ...;
List<? extends Number> l2 = ...;
foo(l1, l2);
```

Figure. 23 Inference succeeds to find instantiations for all variables, but then checking fails.

Constraint Generation

Constraint generation is our version of the phase of constraint decomposition. Recall that the original type inference phase does not check for inconsistencies. Inconsistencies are discovered later during the type checking phase. This choice leads to type error messages that cannot explain very well what the problem is, because information has been lost between the type inferencing and type checking phase.

Consider the code fragment in Fig. 23. Here, the type parameter T is instantiated to Number, because l1 is passed as the first argument. But unfortunately, List is not a subtype of List. In this situation, an implementation based on the JLS will typically say that foo cannot be applied to the variables l1 and l2, but it cannot for example explain to the programmer why the error occurred or how to fix it: it does not have enough knowledge to do so.

In our extension, we provide the constraint solver, introduced in detail below, with more constraints that will ensure that a type is inferred only if all type constraints are satisfied and no type-checking error will occur. To that purpose, the original constraint decomposition algorithm is extended to keep track of constraints that were left alone during decomposition, because they did not match any of the cases of the constraint decomposition procedures. In fact, the new procedures can be obtained from the old ones (based on §15.12.2.7 of [7]), simply by adding cases that store the non-atomic constraints for which no case is defined, into a special set of constraints. In the following we therefore keep track of two sets of constraints X and Y by writing X $\Cup$ Y. Here, the left operand X contains the decomposed constraints, and Y contains those constraints that could not be decomposed.

For the example in Fig. 23, the new constraint generation algorithm will collect the following constraints:

$$\{T = \texttt{Number}\} \Cup$$

$$\{\texttt{List<? extends Number>} <: \texttt{List<? super T>}\}$$

Coming back to the example of Fig. 22, we generate constraints for the invocation of foo at line 20 to type check. The only remaining candidate method is foo$_{13}$, in which case we obtain

$$\{T = \texttt{Integer}, \texttt{Integer} <: T, T <: \texttt{Number}\} \Cup \emptyset$$

For the second invocation we obtain

$$\{T = \texttt{Double}, \texttt{Number} <: T, T <: \texttt{Integer}\} \Cup \emptyset$$

and for the third

$$\{T = \texttt{Number}, \texttt{Double} <: T\} \Cup$$

$$\{\texttt{LinkedList<? extends Number>} <: \texttt{LinkedList<? super T>}\}$$

The Constraint Solving Phase

In Fig. 24 we summarize the constraint solving phase. In the pre-check for bounds, we check that all types in the atomic constraints of a type parameter T satisfy the bounds of T. If not, a type error message is generated for each failed check. Then it infers the instantiations for every type variable, based on the decomposed constraints (the left operand of $\Cup$). This either results in a substitution or, in case of failure, a list of type error messages. If there are still bounds for T left unchecked, e.g., they involve also other type variables, then these bounds checks are performed next. Finally, we verify that the non-atomic constraints (the right operand of $\Cup$) are satisfied.

```
<T, S extends T> void foo(Map<S, S> a, T a){
...
Map<Integer, String> m = ...;
foo(m, 1);
```

Figure. 25 The order of inference for type variable matters.

The reason for doing the pre-check is best illustrated by an example. Consider the following set of constraints

$$\{\texttt{String} <: T, \texttt{Integer} <: T, T <: \texttt{Number}\}.$$

The original algorithm instantiates T to Object, the lub of String and Integer. [4] Later, during type checking it finds that Object is not a subtype of Number. Since the type checker does not have information available about how T got its type, it cannot really say what went wrong. If on the other hand, the bound had been checked immediately (or alternatively, information about the inference of T had been retained), we would have found that $\texttt{String} <: T$ is not consistent with $T <: \texttt{Number}$; and choosing any type that is a supertype of String is not going to help. In other words, for constraints of the given form, it can be determined at an early stage that an inconsistency will result, and a type error message can be generated immediately.

[4]Actually, the type is somewhat more complicated, but never mind that now.

The second modification we made is to tune the order in which type inference instantiates the type variables. It is well known that for the polymorphic lambda-calculus the different implementations of the type system solve constraints in different orders and that the order influences the error message the implementations provide [12, 18]. In our inference algorithm, type variables are considered separately, but because we involve the bounds constraints at an early stage, the inferred type for a particular type variable may impact that of another.

To illustrate, consider the code fragment in Fig. 25. If we first infer the type of S, then we cannot exploit the information that the bound S extends T might give us. On the other hand, if we first infer T (to be Integer, obviously), then we obtain an additional pre-check bound for S: $\texttt{S <: Integer}$.

During the pre-check we can then establish that the constraint S = Integer is consistent with the bound and S = String is not.

It should not be a surprise, therefore, that we have chosen the degree heuristic for determining the order of inference [26]. This heuristic selects first the type variables that determines the largest number of other variables. Consider the following generic parameter:

```
<T, S extends T, R, U extends Map<R, S> &
  T, V extends Map<U, T>>
```

From this generic parameter we can construct the graph in Fig. 26 as follows: the type variables form the vertices of the graph, and we have a solid edge from S to T if T occurs in a bound for S. The dashed edges in the graph are edges that additionally result from taking the transitive closure of the direct dependencies. The degree heuristic now specifies that we should first instantiate the type variable that has the highest number of incoming edges, whether solid or dashed. The reasoning is that an instance for such a type variable provides the most information, i.e., the largest number of type variables can potentially profit from the additional information. Hence, in the example type inference should start by inferring T.

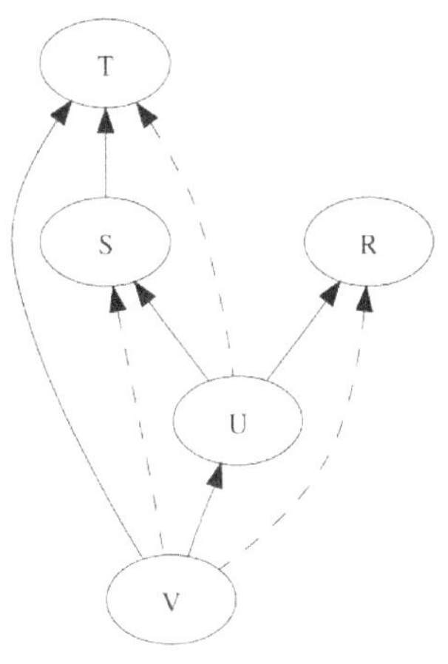

Figure. 26 A type variable dependency graph, with solid edges denoting a direct dependency, and dashed edges for indirect ones.

```
if empty E then
  if empty P then
    if empty B then
      set T = Object
    else
      set C = constraints from the context
      if T inferred on the basis of union(B,C)
        set T = inferred type
      else
        generate error message
  else
    set A = { alpha | alpha <: T in P }
    set T = lub(A)
    if B are satisfied then
      okay
    else
      generate error message
else
  if all constraints in E of the form T = X then
    set T = X
    if union(P, B) are satisfied then
      okay
    else
      generate error message
  else
    generate error message
```

Figure. 27 A pseudocode algorithm for type inference.

The Inferencer

The large rounded rectangle in Fig. 24 is the core of the constraint solving phase, where inference takes place. The algorithm processes the type variables one at the time, in the order obtained using the dependency graph, as described in Sect. 5.3.

Suppose we now deal with type variable T, and E, P and B contain the type equality, supertype and subtype constraints involving T, respectively. Then Fig. 27 gives the pseudocode to describe the inference process.

We conclude this section by revisiting the running example of Fig. 22.

For the first invocation we find

$$\{\texttt{T} = \texttt{Integer}, \texttt{Integer} <: \texttt{T}, \texttt{T} <: \texttt{Number}\} \uplus \emptyset.$$

In this case, there is a single equality constraint for T, so we infer T to be Integer and proceed to verify the remaining constraints: the supertype and subtype constraints turn out to be satisfied as well. Because the set of non-atomic constraints is empty, and therefore trivially satisfied, the invocation on line 20 invokes the method on line 13 correctly and unambiguously.

For the second invocation we obtained

$$\{\texttt{T} = \texttt{Double}, \texttt{Number} <: \texttt{T}, \texttt{T} <: \texttt{Integer}\} \uplus \emptyset.$$

The type variable T is inferred to be Double, but in this case both subtype and supertype constraints fail to be satisfied. Hence an error message is generated.

Finally, for the third

$$\{\texttt{T} = \texttt{Number}, \texttt{Double} <: \texttt{T}\} \uplus$$

$$\{\texttt{LinkedList<? extends Number>} <: \texttt{LinkedList<? super T>}\}$$

we infer T to be Number, and since $\texttt{Double} <: \texttt{Number}$, the constraints are satisfied. However, the non-atomic constraint is not satisfied, so the method invocation fails to type check.

For a somewhat different example, consider the code fragment in Fig. 28. Because in both cases the names match, and the number of formal parameters matches the number of actual arguments in the call, both methods are considered candidates and will be considered further. Since weak method resolution ignores all generic information, both method signatures are implicitly converted to void bar(Object a, Object b). Because the arguments to the call happen to be of primitive type, weak method resolution will attempt to match the call to a method by means of method invocation conversion (§5.3 of [7]). This results in both methods to be considered applicable. Then the type checking process will consider each method in turn to determine which of these, if any, matches the call.

Let us consider the first definition of bar. Matching the types of the invocation with that of the first definition of bar results in the following constraints, in which the primitive types are automatically promoted to their corresponding reference type:

$$\{\texttt{Character} <: \texttt{T}, \texttt{Double} <: \texttt{T}\} \uplus \emptyset.$$

Because only one type variable is involved, the ordering phase for type variables can be ignored, and we proceed to perform bounds checking. Bounds checking ensures that for all types S with $S <: T$, that S is a subtype of all the types U that bound T from above. Choices for S in this particular case are Double and Character, the only possibility for U is Number. The combination Double and Number is fine, but since Character $\not<:$ Number, the method does not match. Notwithstanding, the process does set T equal to the lub of Double and Character. This type is not returned as the type for T, but, instead, used to further uncover potential type conflicts. For example, if there would be another constraint on T, say $T <: \texttt{Integer}$, then this may help establish more firmly that the types used in computing the lub to obtain T are not the right ones. When we provide an error message to fix the problem, we can then avoid to suggest fixing it in a way that in the next compile a clash with the constraint $T <: \texttt{Integer}$ can occur.

```
class BarUtil{
   static <T extends Number>void bar(T a, T b){}
   static <T extends Integer>void bar(T a, T b){}
   void dummy() {
     BarUtil.bar('0', 3.14);
   }
}
```

```
listings/Listing7.java:5: internal error; cannot instantiate <T>bar(T,T) at
BarUtil to (char,double)
      BarUtil.bar('0', 3.14);
                 ^
```

JAVAC

```
1. WARNING in listings/Listing7.java (at line 3)
     static <T extends Integer>void bar(T a, T b){}
                       ^^^^^^^
The type parameter T should not be bounded by the final type Integer. Final
types cannot be further extended
----------
2. ERROR in listings/Listing7.java (at line 5)
     BarUtil.bar('0', 3.14);
             ^^^
Bound mismatch: The generic method bar(T, T) of type BarUtil is not applicable
for the arguments (Character, Double).
The inferred type Object&Serializable& Comparable<?> is not a valid substitute
for the bounded parameter <T extends Number>
```

EJC

```
listings/Listing7.java:5
Method <T extends Number>bar(T, T) of type BarUtil is not applicable for the
arguments of type (char, double), because:
   [*] The type char of the expression ''0'' on 5:18 is not a subtype of T's
       upper bound Number in 'T extends Number'.

listings/Listing7.java:5
Method <T extends Integer>bar(T, T) of type BarUtil is not applicable for the
arguments of type (char, double), because:
   [*] The type char of the expression ''0'' on 5:18 is not a subtype of T's
       upper bound Integer in 'T extends Integer'.
   [*] The type double of the expression '3.14' on 5:23 is not a subtype of T's
       upper bound Integer in 'T extends Integer'.
```

ours

Figure. 28 A code fragment with two candidate methods, both of which fail to qualify. JAVAC and EJC provide only one message, but our system provides a diagnosis for both failures.

For the second definition of bar, we similarly obtain an inconsistent set of constraints. In this case U ranges over the set {Integer}, and neither the constraint `Double <: T` nor the constraint `Character <: T` can be satisfied. For both method definitions an error message will be provided by our implementation, as seen in Fig. 28. Both EJC and JAVAC give only a single type error message for the invocation. It is not made clear why the method call matches neither, and, in the case of JAVAC it is even not clear to which of the two method definitions the method invocation has been compared.

As an aside, EJC also warns that it makes little sense to have T extend a final class. This is quite similar to one of the heuristics we describe in [2]. However, before we would give such a hint, we make sure that replacing T by its upper bound actually solves the problem. Since that is not the case here, our implementation does not provide such a hint.

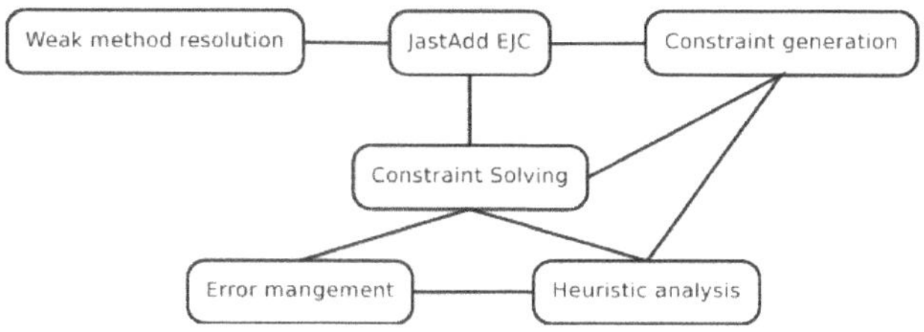

Figure. 29 Architecture of our extension to the JastAdd EJC.

IMPLEMENTATION

We have implemented our work as an extension to the JastAdd Extensible Java Compiler (JastAdd EJC) [6], which in turn was built on top of JastAdd [11]. The latter is an attribute grammar compiler that allows specifying compiler semantics in an aspect-oriented way by means of declarative attributes and semantic rules using ordinary Java code. Some more information on this implementation can be found in Appendix.

For the convenience of the weak method resolution, the ordering of type variables and the computation of greatest lower bound have been implemented using JastAdd. We have contributed the module that we have developed for computing the greatest lower bound to the maintainers of JastAdd EJC; it has been added to the repository.

The architecture of the resulting compiler is shown in Fig. 29: the type checker sends a method invocation which fails to typecheck to the weak method resolution which returns a set of methods. The type checker then generates type constraints for the method invocation and each method declaration using the constraint generation algorithm described in Sect. 5. The type checker passes these constraints along to our constraint solver together with the return type of the method declaration under consideration and the type of the value if the invocation appears in an assignment context. The constraint solver will then solve the constraints and return an error message to the type checker if the constraints are unsatisfiable. The error messages returned by the constraint solver are maintained and collected by a separate error manager. This is mainly to facilitate the implementation of a number of heuristics that we use to suggest fixes for the type error [2].

Although we have only discussed method invocations, our extension already gives some limited support for constructor invocations.

Related Work

Thus far, work on improving type error diagnosis has concentrated on strongly typed, higherorder, polymorphic functional languages, such as ML and Haskell. Indeed, one of the reasons we set out to do the current study was to see how far our experience in improving type error diagnosis for Haskell would help us in a different setting.

The PhD thesis of Bastiaan Heeren [12] compiles a number of papers with the second author and includes an extensive bibliography on improving type error messages for functional languages. We mention a few of the more important papers. We omit [34], which was already discussed in the introduction.

Heeren categorises papers based on their approach. The simplest approach to improve type error messages is to change the order in which unifications take place, i.e., constraints are solved, because that will change the unification that will be held responsible for the inconsistency [10, 17, 18, 20].

The second category consists of explanation systems, which in one way or another keep track of how a conclusion about a particular type was derived in order to provide that explanation to the programmer [5, 9, 32, 33, 35]. We make in particular note of Yang et al. [35], because at its basis lies algorithm H, which was inspired by how human subjects (in an experimental setting) perform type checking. In particular, they discovered that human subjects focus on the concrete types derived from the use of literals, and make heavy use of the two-dimensional inspection of code. Contrary to how most algorithms work, humans avoid type variables when explaining the type of an expression.

A potential problem of explanation systems is that explanations can quickly become very verbose, because type information can potentially propagate to all corners of the program. This is less of a problem in the context of Generic Java, because each method invocation is considered in isolation; reasoning is thereby much more localised.

Repair systems try to isolate a particular cause of a problem, suggesting that this part of the program should be changed to remedy the mistake. Particular examples are [2, 9, 21, 31]. The danger of these systems is that they are heuristic: there are always situations where they will suggest the wrong fix. Thus, some researchers prefer to report a set of program locations, usually with some guarantee that no location outside this set can be responsible for the problem. Such a set forms a program slice, and such approaches are said to perform type error slicing [4, 8, 25]. It is still unknown, however, whether such a system can be useful in practice as there is not enough information yet on how large slices can become, and how well the system works in the presence of multiple independent and/or somewhat related mistakes. We believe that the combination of type error slicing with type error repair to be very promising, but we have not yet seen any substantial work in this direction.

A final category consists of systems that allow the programmer to interactively investigate the types of expressions in the program. Such a system can usually give more precise feedback, because from the interaction it may obtain more information from the programmer about his/her intentions. The most well-known attempts in this direction are Typeview [14] and Chameleon [28, 29].

Characteristic of all these attempts is that the authors redesign the type inference process to come up with better error messages. A totally different approach can be found in [19], which uses a Caml compiler as a black box, and presents programmers with complete program fixes for parts of their program. This is done by enumerating variations on the faulty program and submitting these to the compiler to decide on type correctness.

We consider the current paper to belong to the category of explanation systems, although our explanations typically will not be long. Our work also has some elements from [19]: although our work is implemented directly in a Java compiler, we do leave the original type inference process intact.

What sets our work somewhat apart from the literature above is that we need to deal with subtyping and overloading. Because a programmer may be attempting to call any number of methods, our method compares the invocation to multiple method definitions, and for each describes why the call is inconsistent with that method. For the languages that are the subject of the papers above, such a situation never occurs. Moreover, our work is complicated by the fact that instead of the elegant Hindley-Milner type system for the polymorphic lambdacalculus [22], we have to cope with the large, operational specification of Java's type system, which actually coincides with its type checking process.

We are not aware of any other work on improving type error messages for languages besides functional ones, except for el Boustani and Hage [1], which is a shorter version of the current paper, and a follow-up paper that deals with heuristics that can offer suggestions on how to fix the type error [2]. Changes with respect to the former can be summarized as follows: since we have fewer restrictions on length we have recompiled all the programs with the three tools and have included all the outcomes without changing the content of the messages. We made one exception: our implementation also sometimes suggests how to change the program to get rid of a type error. Since these suggestions are the subject of [2], we have omitted these from our messages, and replaced them with (...). We have also added quite a few examples including a realistic one, and a related work section. Finally, we describe more details of the processes involved.

Somewhat related to our work is that of Jadud who performed an extensive study of parse errors and compiler usage for Java [15].

CONCLUSIONS, REFLECTIONS AND FUTURE WORK

We have described how the type checking process of Generic Java can be extended to provide more informative type error messages, particularly for method invocations that involve generics. We have illustrated our work by a sizable number of examples and have made a download available in which our work is implemented as an extension to the JastAdd Extensible Java Compiler.

Our work follows three design principles: Principle number one is to leave the (very complicated) type checking process intact, because any modification of the process risks changing the set of typable programs. The second principle is to avoid acting on what you trust the least, e.g., a major hurdle to obtain good type error messages when following the JLS, is that candidate methods may be disqualified at an early stage of the type checking process. In this paper, we chose to ignore the generic parts of types, based on the assumption that this is where programmers make the most mistakes. The third and final principle is to hold on to type information longer than is necessary for following the JLS. In our particular case, we kept some of the original constraints around to make a more informed decision on the causes of the inconsistencies.

There are plenty of directions for future work. The first is to perform a more global analysis to come up with an even better estimate of what might be the mistake. For example, type inference is highly compartmentalized in the JLS: each method invocation is considered more or less in isolation and independent of others. However, if a lack of understanding of this particular fact is the reason for a mistake, we can only find that out by going beyond these compartments. This is an often observed pattern, and one that makes type error diagnosis significantly more complicated than type checking by itself: to find out what kind of faulty reasoning on the part of the programmer is responsible for a type error, the improved type inference process must be able to distinguish between these forms of reasoning, and therefore be able to maintain and manipulate what, according to the original type system, is inconsistent information.

Beyond method invocations, a particularly interesting and complicated language construct is that of inner classes. In that case, we have the additional problem of dealing with the scope/shadowing of type variables, and all the mistakes programmers can make in these situations.

Furthermore, although we have weakened method resolution somewhat so that we may determine the method the programmer might have wanted to invoke, there are plenty of variations left unconsidered: why not also consider methods that are not visible or accessible and suggest to modify the program so that they become visible and accessible? There is, in fact, a huge number of possibilities here, and thus far we have barely scratched the surface.

To have some idea in which direction to look it would be really helpful to know what kind of mistakes programmers make. Program logging systems like BlueJ might be able to help us there [15]. Having consulted Jadud on the subject, however, we have learned that the programs he has collected do not contain generics. One promising idea, suggested by Pierre-Evariste Dagand in private communication, is to offer our system as a web-based service for Java programmers, and, as part of the service, ask them to rate the output of our system and that of the standard compilers. As a bonus, we obtain a collection of programs that we can use to validate and improve on our work. Recently, we found another valuable source of information which is Angelika Langer's FAQ on Java Generics [16]. Based on this FAQ, we plan to perform a systematic study of the kind of mistakes programmers make, and misunderstandings they might have about Java Generics. As a more labour-intense alternative to the two previous two, the empirically based route followed in [35] could be explored to find out, e.g., what kind of mistakes programmers make, and how they themselves derive the types of expressions in their program. The work presented here can serve to prepare the way for such further studies.

We note that our work takes the JLS as a starting point, and we have yet to consider alternative approaches to combining generics with subtyping, as part of, e.g., Scala [24] and Timber [23]. However, the second author, together with the developers of the Timber language, has recently started to look at the latter language, as an example of a language that adds subtyping to a language based on the polymorphic lambda-calculus.

Finally then, in [27] it is shown how the generics of Java might be “fixed” to obtain a process that is sound and complete. Although soundness and completeness are clearly important issues, we believe that intuitiveness and elegance of the type system is important too, particularly for a language that may well be the first programming language novice programmers encounter. We therefore hope that any fix will take those properties into consideration as well.

ACKNOWLEDGEMENTS

We acknowledge the involvement of Martin Bravenboer during the early stages of this project, and thank the anonymous referees for their suggestions and corrections.

APPENDIX: USING THE SYSTEM

To compile the system you need subversion (http://subversion.tigris.org/) and Ant obtainable from http://ant.apache.org. Once you have these installed on your system, checkout the repository

```
staff.jur.javagenerics/project
```

on the subversion server located at

```
https://subversion.cs.uu.nl/
```

(click on info to get the exact location for the checkout). The README file that you obtain in the process explains how to proceed: run ant in the Java1.5Backend directory, and afterwards proceed to the bin directory where the invocation java JavaCompiler - help tells you how the compiler should be invoked. The subdirectory testing contains a large number of example programs on which to try out the compiler. Most of these programs also explain in comments which constraints are generated and how these are used to determine type (in) correctness. Note that many error messages also suggest a problem fix using heuristics; that part of our work is discussed in another paper [2]. The examples in the current paper have all been included in the special subdirectory testing/listings. To compile, e.g., Listing1.java simply write the following at the command prompt while inside the testing subdirectory:

```
java -cp ../bin JavaCompiler -d /tmp listings/Listing1.java
```

REFERENCES

1. el Boustani, N., Hage, J.: Improving type error messages for Generic Java. In: Puebla, G., Vidal, G. (eds.) Proceedings of the ACM SIGPLAN 2009 Symposium on Partial Evaluation and Semantics-Based Program Manipulation (PEPM’09), pp. 131–140. ACM Press, New York (2009)
2. el Boustani, N., Hage, J.: Corrective hints for type incorrect Generic Java programs. In: Gallagher, J., Voigtländer, J. (eds.) Proceedings of the ACM SIGPLAN 2010 Workshop on Partial Evaluation and Program Manipulation (PEPM’10), pp. 5–14. ACM Press, New York (2010)
3. Damas, L., Milner, R.: Principal type-schemes for functional programs. In: Conference Record of the Ninth Annual ACM Symposium on Principles of Programming Languages, Albuquerque, New Mexico, January 1982, pp. 207–212. ACM Press, New York (1982)
4. Dinesh, T.B., Tip, F.: A slicing-based approach for locating type errors. In: 264, Centrum voor Wiskunde en Informatica (CWI), p. 24 (1998). ISSN 1386-369X
5. Duggan, D., Bent, F.: Explaining type inference. Sci. Comput. Program. 27, 37–83 (1996)MATH
6. Ekman, T., Hedin, G.: The JastAdd extensible Java compiler. In: OOPSLA’07: Proceedings of the 22nd Annual ACM SIGPLAN Conference on Object-Oriented Programming Systems and Applications, pp. 1–18. ACM, New York (2007)
7. Gosling, J., Joy, B., Steele, G., Bracha, G.: Java(TM) Language Specification, 3rd edn. Addison-Wesley Professional, Reading (2005)
8. Haack, C., Wells, J.B.: Type error slicing in implicitly typed higher-order languages. In: Proceedings of the 12th European Symposium on Programming (ESOP). Lecture Notes in Computer Science, vol. 2618, pp. 284–301. Springer, Berlin (2003)
9. Hage, J., Heeren, B.: Heuristics for type error discovery and recovery. In: Horváth, Z., Zsók, V., Butterfield, A. (eds.) Implementation of Functional Languages—IFL 2006, vol. 4449, pp. 199–216. Springer, Heidelberg (2007)
10. Hage, J., Heeren, B.: Strategies for solving constraints in type and effect systems. Electron. Notes Theor. Comput. Sci. 236, 163–183 (2009). Proceedings of the 3rd International Workshop on Views On Designing Complex Architectures (VODCA 2008)
11. Hedin, G., Magnusson, E.: The JastAdd system—an aspect-oriented compiler construction system. Sci. Comput. Program. 47(1), 37–58 (2003).http://www.cs.lth.se/~gorel/publications/2003-JastAdd-SCP-Preprint.pdfMathSciNetMATH
12. Heeren, B.: Top quality type error messages. PhD thesis, Universiteit Utrecht, The Netherlands (2005). http://www.cs.uu.nl/people/bastiaan/phdthesis
13. Heeren, B., Hage, J., Swierstra, S.D.: Scripting the type inference process. In: Eighth International Conference on Functional Programming, pp. 3–13. ACM Press, New York (2003)
14. Huch, F., Chitil, O., Simon, A.: Typeview: a tool for understanding type errors. In: Mohnen, M., Koopman, P. (eds.) Proceedings of 12th International Workshop on Implementation of Functional Languages (IFL 00). Aachner Informatik-Berichte, pp. 63–69 (2000)
15. Jadud, M.C.: A first look at novice compilation behaviour using BlueJ. Comput. Sci. Educ.15(1), 25–40 (2005)

16. Langer, A.: Java generics FAQs—frequently asked questions (2008).http://www.angelikalanger.com/GenericsFAQ/JavaGenericsFAQ.html
17. Lee, O., Yi, K.: Proofs about a folklore let-polymorphic type inference algorithm. ACM Trans. Program. Lang. Syst. 20(4), 707–723 (1998)
18. Lee, O., Yi, K.: A generalization of hybrid let-polymorphic type inference algorithms. In: Proceedings of the First Asian Workshop on Programming Languages and Systems, pp. 79–88. National University of Singapore, Singapore (2000)
19. Lerner, B., Grossman, D., Chambers, C.: Seminal: searching for ml type-error messages. In: ML'06: Proceedings of the 2006 Workshop on ML, pp. 63–73. ACM, New York (2006)
20. McAdam, B.J.: On the Unification of Substitutions in Type Inference. In: Hammond, K., Davie, A.J.T., Clack, C. (eds.) Implementation of Functional Languages (IFL'98), London, UK. LNCS, vol. 1595, pp. 139–154. Springer, Berlin (1998)
21. McAdam, B.J.: How to repair type errors automatically. In: Hammond, K., Curtis, S. (eds.) Trends in Functional Programming, Intellect, Bristol, UK, vol. 3, pp. 87–98 (2002)
22. Milner, R.: A theory of type polymorphism in programming. J. Comput. Syst. Sci. 17, 348–375 (1978) MathSciNetMATH
23. Nordlander, J., Carlsson, M., Gill, A., Lindgren, P., von Sydow, B.: The Timber homepage (2008). http://www.timber-lang.org
24. Odersky, M.: The Scala homepage (2008). http://www.scala-lang.org/
25. Rahli, V., Wells, J.B., Kamareddine, F.: A constraint system for a SML type error slicer. Tech. Rep. HW-MACS-TR-0079, Herriot Watt University, Edinburgh, Scotland (2010)
26. Russell, S., Norvig, P.: Artificial Intelligence: A Modern Approach, 2nd edn., pp. 137–151. Pearson Education, Upper Saddle River (2003). Chap. 5
27. Smith, D., Cartwright, R.: Java type inference is broken: can we fix it. In: Proceedings of the 23rd Conference on Object-Oriented Programming, Systems, Languages, and Applications (OOPSLA'08), pp. 505–524. ACM, New York (2008)
28. Stuckey, P.J., Sulzmann, M., Wazny, J.: Interactive type debugging in Haskell. In: Haskell'03: Proceedings of the ACM SIGPLAN Workshop on Haskell, pp. 72–83. ACM Press, New York (2003)
29. Stuckey, P.J., Sulzmann, M., Wazny, J.: Improving type error diagnosis. In: Haskell'04: Proceedings of the ACM SIGPLAN Workshop on Haskell, pp. 80–91. ACM Press, New York (2004)
30. Torgersen, M., Hansen, C.P., Ernst, E., von der Ahé, P., Bracha, G., Gafter, N.: Adding wildcards to the Java programming language. In: Proceedings of the 2004 ACM Symposium on Applied Computing (SAC'04), pp. 1289–1296. ACM Press, New York (2004)
31. Walz, J.A., Johnson, G.F.: A maximum flow approach to anomaly isolation in unification-based incremental type inference. In: Conference Record of the 13th Annual ACM Symposium on Principles of Programming Languages, St. Petersburg, FL, pp. 44–57 (1986)
32. Wand, M.: Finding the source of type errors. In: 13th Annual ACM Symp. on Principles of Prog. Languages, pp. 38–43 (1986)
33. Yang, J.: Explaining type errors by finding the sources of type conflicts. In: Michaelson, G., Trinder, P., Loidl, H.W. (eds.) Trends in Functional Programming. Intellect Books, pp. 58–66 (2000)
34. Yang, J., Michaelson, G., Trinder, P., Wells, J.B.: Improved type error reporting. In: Proceedings of 12th International Workshop on Implementation of Functional Languages. LNCS, vol. 2011, pp. 71–86. Springer, Berlin (2000)
35. Yang, J., Michaelson, G., Trinder, P.: Explaining polymorphic types. Comput. J. 45(4), 436–452 (2002)

CHAPTER 2

MORE DEPENDENT TYPES FOR DISTRIBUTED ARRAYS

Wouter Swierstra

Vector Fabrics, Paradijslaan 28, Eindhoven, The Netherlands

ABSTRACT

Locality-aware algorithms over distributed arrays can be very difficult to write. Yet such algorithms are becoming more and more important as desktop machines boast more and more processors. This paper shows how a dependently-typed programming language can aid in the development of these algorithms and statically ensure that every well-typed program will only ever access local data. Such static guarantees can help catch programming errors early on in the development cycle and maximise the potential speedup that multicore machines offer. At the same time, the functional specification of effects presented here facilitates the testing of and reasoning about algorithms that manipulate distributed arrays.

INTRODUCTION

Computer processors are not becoming significantly faster. To satisfy the demand for more and more computational power, manufacturers are now assembling computers with multiple microprocessors. It is hard to exaggerate the impact this will have on software development: tomorrow's programming languages must embrace parallel programming on multicore machines.

Researchers have proposed several new languages to maximise the potential performance gain that multicore processors offer [1, 6–8, 12, 21]. Although all these languages are different, they share the central notion of a distributed array, where the elements of an array may be distributed over separate processors or even over separate machines. To write effi- cient code, programmers must ensure that processors only access local parts of a distributed array—it is much faster to access data stored locally than remote data on another core.

When writing such locality-aware algorithms it is all too easy to make subtle mistakes. Programming languages designed specifically for distributed computing, such as X10 [8], require all arrays operations to be local. Any attempt to access non-local data results in an exception. To preclude such errors, X10's type system guarantees that programs only access local parts of a distributed array [9, 17]. The proposed type system is fairly intricate and consists of a substantial number of type rules that keep track of locality information. Proving meta-theoretical results about such a system, such as the decidability of type checking, is no trivial result.

This paper explores an alternative avenue of research. Designing and implementing a type system from scratch is a lot of work. New type systems typically require extensive proofs of various meta-theoretical results. Instead, this paper shows how to tailor a powerful type system to enforce certain properties—resulting in a domain-specific embedded type

Citation: Wouter Swierstra, More dependent types for distributed arrays, DOI 10.1007/s10990-011-9075-y.

system. This type system immediately inherits all the desirable properties of our dependentlytyped host type system, such as subject reduction, decidable type checking, and principle typing. Functional programmers have studied domain-specific embedded languages for years [11]; the time is ripe to take these ideas one step further.

Previous work described a pure specification of several parts of the IO monad [23], the interface between pure functional languages such as Haskell [19] and the 'real world.' By providing functional, executable specifications you can test, debug, and reason about impure programs as if they were pure. When you release the final version of your code, you can replace these pure specifications with their impure, more efficient, counterparts. In the presence of dependent types, these specifications can provide even stronger static guarantees about our programs. To this end, this paper makes several contributions:

- We will begin by giving a pure specification of arrays (Sect. 3). This specification is total: there is no way to access unallocated memory; there are no 'array index out of bounds' exceptions. As a result, these specifications can not only be used to program with, but also facilitate formal proofs about array algorithms. To make this specification usable, we must overcome a problem related to the weakening of address locations.
- Distributed arrays pose more of a challenge. Section 4 shows how to enforce locality constraints, while still providing programmers with place-shifting operators. The pure speci- fication is, once again, executable and total: it can be interpreted both as a domain-specific embedded language for writing algorithms on distributed arrays and as an executable denotational model for specifying and proving properties of such algorithms.
- Finally, we will see how programmers may write their own locality-aware control structures (Sect. 4.3), how to implement simple distributed algorithms using these control structures (Sect. 4.4), and how to define combinators that describe data distributions (Sect. 4.5). We will conclude by discussing further work and the limitations of this approach (Sect. 5).

Throughout this paper, I will use the dependently-typed programming language Agda [16] as a vehicle of explanation. In fact, using lhs2TeX [13], the sources of this paper generate an Agda program that can be compiled and executed. In the coming section, I will briefly introduce the syntax of Agda by means of several examples, as it may be unfamiliar to many readers.

AN OVERVIEW OF AGDA

Data types in Agda can be defined using a similar syntax to that for Generalized Algebraic Data Types, or GADTs, in Haskell [20]. For example, consider the following definition of the natural numbers.

```
data Nat : ⋆ where
  Zero : Nat
  Succ : Nat → Nat
```

There is one important difference with Haskell. We must explicitly state the kind of the data type that we are introducing; in particular, the declaration Nat : states that Nat is a base type.

We can define functions by pattern matching and recursion, just as in any other functional language. To define addition of natural numbers, for instance, we could write:

```
_+_ : Nat → Nat → Nat
Zero + m = m
Succ n + m = Succ (n + m)
```

Note that Agda uses underscores to denote the positions of arguments when defining new operators.

Polymorphic lists are slightly more interesting than natural numbers:

```
data List (a : ⋆) : ⋆ where
  Nil : List a
  Cons : a → List a → List a
```

To uniformly parameterise a data type, we can write additional arguments to the left of the colon. In this case, we add $(a : \star)$ to our data type declaration to state that lists are type constructors, parameterised over a type variable a of kind ⋆.

Just as we defined addition for natural numbers, we can define an operator that appends one list to another:

```
append : (a : ⋆) → List a → List a → List a
append a Nil           ys = ys
append a (Cons x xs) ys = Cons x (append a xs ys)
```

The append function is polymorphic. In Agda, such polymorphism can be introduced via the dependent function space, written (x : a) → y, where the variable x may occur in the type y. This particular example of the dependent function space is not terribly interesting: it corresponds to parametric polymorphism. Later we will encounter more interesting examples, where types depend on values.

One drawback of using the dependent function space for such parametric polymorphism, is that we must explicitly instantiate polymorphic functions. For example, the recursive call to append in the Cons case takes a type as its first argument. Fortunately, Agda allows us to mark certain arguments as implicit. Using implicit arguments, we could also define append as in any other functional language:

```
append : {a : ⋆} → List a → List a → List a
append Nil           ys = ys
append (Cons x xs) ys = Cons x (append xs ys)
```

Arguments enclosed in curly brackets, such as $\{a : \star\}$, are implicit: we do not write a to the left of the equals sign and do not pass a type argument when we make a recursive call. The Agda type checker will automatically instantiate this function whenever we call it, much in the same way as type variables are automatically instantiated in Haskell. By enclosing a function's argument in curly brackets, we can explicitly instantiate or pattern match on an implicit argument.

Besides polymorphic data types, Agda also supports indexed families, a dependently typed analogue of Haskell's GADTs. Indexed families, however, are more general as they also capture data types that are indexed by values instead of types. For example, we can define the family of finite types:

```
data Fin : Nat → ⋆ where
  Fz : {n : Nat} → Fin (Succ n)
  Fs : {n : Nat} → Fin n → Fin (Succ n)
```

The type Fin n corresponds to a finite type with n distinct values. For example, Fin 1 is isomorphic to the unit type; Fin 2 is isomorphic to Bool. Note that the argument n is left implicit in both the constructors of Fin. From the types of these constructors, it is easy to see that Fin 0 is uninhabited. For every n, the Fs constructor embeds Fin n into Fin (Succ n); the Fz constructor, on the other hand, adds a single new element to Fin (Succ n) that was not in Fin n. This inductive argument shows that Fin n does indeed have n elements.

Agda has many other features, such as records and a module system, that we will hardly use in this paper. Although there are a few more concepts we will need, we will discuss them as they pop up in later sections.

MUTABLE ARRAYS

With this brief Agda tutorial under our belt, we can start our specification of mutable arrays. We will specify three different operations on arrays: the creation of new arrays; reading from an array; and updating a value stored in an array. Before we can define the behaviour of these operations, we need to introduce several data types to describe the layout and contents of memory. Using these data types, we can proceed by defining an IO type that captures the syntax of array operations. To program with these operators, we need to resolve a few technical problems. Finally, we will define a run function that describes how the array operations affect the heap, assigning semantics to our syntax. This semantics can be used to simulate and reason about computations on mutable arrays in a pure functional language. When compiled, however, these operations should be replaced by their more efficient, low-level counterparts.

To keep things simple, we will only work with flat arrays storing natural numbers. This is, of course, a drastic oversimplification. The techniques we present here, however, can be adapted to cover multidimensional arrays that may store different types of data using a universe construction, as is done in my PhD thesis [22].

To avoid confusion between numbers denoting the size of an array and the data stored in an array, we introduce the Data type synonym. Throughout the rest of this paper, we will use Data to refer to the data stored in arrays; the Nat type will always refer to the size of an array.

```
Data : ⋆
Data = Nat
```

Using the Fin type, we can give a functional specification of arrays of a fixed size by mapping every index to the corresponding value.

```
Array : Nat → ⋆
Array n = Fin n → Data
```

How should we represent the heap? We need to be a bit careful—as the heap will store arrays of different sizes its type should explicitly state how many arrays it stores and how large each array is. To accomplish this, we begin by introducing a data type representing the shape of the heap:

```
Shape : ⋆
Shape = List Nat
```

The Shape of the heap is a list of natural numbers, representing the size of the arrays stored in memory.

We can now define a Heap data type that is indexed by a Shape. The Empty constructor corresponds to an empty heap; the Alloc constructor adds an array of size n to any heap of shape ns to build a larger heap with the layout Cons n ns.

```
data Heap : Shape → ⋆ where
  Empty : Heap Nil
  Alloc : {n : Nat} → {ns : Shape} → Array n → Heap ns → Heap (Cons n ns)
```

Finally, we will want to model references, denoting locations in the heap. A value of type Loc n ns corresponds to a reference to an array of size n in a heap with shape ns. The Loc data type shares a great deal of structure with the Fin type. Every non-empty heap has a Top reference; any existing reference can be modified to denote the same location in a larger heap using the Pop constructor.

```
data Loc : Nat → Shape → ⋆ where
  Top : {n : Nat} → {ns : Shape} → Loc n (Cons n ns)
  Pop : forall {n k ns} → Loc n ns → Loc n (Cons k ns)
```

Note that in the type signature of the Pop constructor, we omit the types of three implicit arguments and quantify over them using the forall keyword. When we use the forall-notation, the types of n, k, and ns are inferred from the rest of the signature by the Agda type checker. Alternatively, we could also have written the more verbose:

```
Pop : {n : Nat} → {k : Nat} → {ns : Shape}
  → Loc n ns → Loc n (Cons k ns)
```

We will occasionally use the forall-notation to make large type signatures somewhat more legible.

With these data types in place, we can define a data type capturing the syntax of the permissible operations on arrays. Crucially, the IO type is indexed by two shapes: a value of type IO a ns ms denotes a computation that takes a heap of shape ns to a heap of shape ms and returns a result of type a. This pattern of indexing operations by an initial and final 'state' is a common pattern in dependently-typed programming [14].

```
data IO (a : ⋆) : Shape → Shape → ⋆ where
  Return : {ns : Shape} → a → IO a ns ns
  Write : forall {n ns ms}
    → Loc n ns → Fin n → Data → IO a ns ms → IO a ns ms
  Read : forall {n ns ms}
    → Loc n ns → Fin n → (Data → IO a ns ms) → IO a ns ms
  New : forall {ns ms}
    → (n : Nat) → (Loc n (Cons n ns) → IO a (Cons n ns) ms) → IO a ns ms
```

The IO type has four constructors. The Return constructor returns a pure value of type a without modifying the heap. The Write constructor takes four arguments: the location of an array of size n; an index in that array; the value to write at that index; and the rest of the computation. Similarly, reading from an array requires a reference to an array and an index. Instead of requiring the data to be written, however, the last argument of the Read constructor may refer to data that has been read. Finally, the New constructor actually changes the size of the heap. Given a number n, it allocates an array of size n on the heap; the second argument of New may then use this fresh reference to continue the computation in a larger heap.

The IO data type is a parameterised monad [3]—that is, a monad with return and bind operators that satisfy certain coherence conditions with respect to the Shape indices.

$$
\begin{aligned}
&\mathit{return} : \textbf{forall}\ \{a\ ns\} \to a \to \mathit{IO}\ a\ ns\ ns \\
&\mathit{return}\ x = \mathit{Return}\ x
\end{aligned}
$$

$$
\begin{aligned}
&\_ \gg\!= \_ : \textbf{forall}\ \{a\ b\ ns\ ms\ ks\} \\
&\quad \to \mathit{IO}\ a\ ns\ ms \to (a \to \mathit{IO}\ b\ ms\ ks) \to \mathit{IO}\ b\ ns\ ks \\
&\mathit{Return}\ x \gg\!= f \quad = f\ x \\
&\mathit{Write}\ a\ i\ x\ wr \gg\!= f = \mathit{Write}\ a\ i\ x\ (wr \gg\!= f) \\
&\mathit{Read}\ a\ i\ rd \gg\!= f \quad = \mathit{Read}\ a\ i\ (\lambda x \to rd\ x \gg\!= f) \\
&\mathit{New}\ n\ io \gg\!= f \quad = \mathit{New}\ n\ (\lambda a \to io\ a \gg\!= f)
\end{aligned}
$$

The return of the IO data type lifts a pure value into a computation that can run on a heap of any size. Furthermore, return does not modify the shape of the heap. The bind operator, >>=, can be used to compose monadic computations. To sequence two computations, the heap resulting from the first computation must be a suitable starting point for the second computation. This condition is enforced by the type of the bind operator.

To facilitate programming using these array operations, we could define the functions readArray and newArray as follows:

$$
\begin{aligned}
&\mathit{readArray} : \textbf{forall}\ \{n\ ns\} \to \mathit{Loc}\ n\ ns \to \mathit{Fin}\ n \to \mathit{IO}\ \mathit{Data}\ ns\ ns \\
&\mathit{readArray}\ a\ i = \mathit{Read}\ a\ i\ \mathit{Return}
\end{aligned}
$$

$$
\begin{aligned}
&\mathit{newArray} : \textbf{forall}\ \{ns\} \to (n : \mathit{Nat}) \to \mathit{IO}\ (\mathit{Loc}\ n\ (\mathit{Cons}\ n\ ns))\ ns\ (\mathit{Cons}\ n\ ns) \\
&\mathit{newArray}\ n = \mathit{New}\ n\ \mathit{Return}
\end{aligned}
$$

There is a slight problem with these definitions. As we allocate new memory, the size of the heap changes; correspondingly, we must explicitly modify any existing pointers to denote locations in a larger heap. This problem is best illustrated with an example. Consider the following sequence of array manipulations:

$$
\begin{aligned}
&\mathit{newArray}\ 4 \gg\!= \lambda \mathit{array1} \\
&\quad \to \mathit{newArray}\ 8 \gg\!= \lambda \mathit{array2} \\
&\quad \to \mathit{readArray}\ \mathit{array1}\ \mathit{Fz}
\end{aligned}
$$

This allocates two arrays, before performing reading an index from the first array. The first array, stored at array1, has type Loc 4 (Cons 4 Nil); the second array has type Loc 8 (Cons 8 (Cons 4 Nil)). When we want to read from the first array after the second allocation, the type checker expects an array location in a heap of shape (Cons 8 (Cons 4 Nil)), and not Cons 4 Nil. Fortunately, adding a Pop constructor around array1 yields a type correct program:

$$
\begin{aligned}
&\mathit{newArray}\ 4 \gg\!= \lambda \mathit{array}_1 \\
&\quad \to \mathit{newArray}\ 8 \gg\!= \lambda \mathit{array}_2 \\
&\quad \to \mathit{readArray}\ (\mathit{Pop}\ \mathit{array}_1)\ \mathit{Fz}
\end{aligned}
$$

We will refer to this as weakening the reference array1, in line with the usual terminology used for the weakening rules present in many logics.

Adding these extra Pop constructors by hand is tiresome and error-prone. In the coming sections, we will see how this process can be automated to some degree.

Manual Weakening

Before we revisit our smart constructors, we need to develop a bit of machinery. We need to decide how many Pop constructors are necessary to weaken a location to denote a position in a larger heap. Put differently, we need to prove that one shape is a suffix of a larger shape. One way to represent such a proof is using an inductive data type:

$$
\begin{aligned}
&\textbf{data}\ \mathit{IsSuffix} : \mathit{Shape} \to \mathit{Shape} \to \star\ \textbf{where} \\
&\quad \mathit{Base} : \textbf{forall}\ \{ns\} \to \mathit{IsSuffix}\ ns\ ns \\
&\quad \mathit{Step} : \textbf{forall}\ \{m\ ns\ ms\} \to \mathit{IsSuffix}\ ns\ ms \to \mathit{IsSuffix}\ ns\ (\mathit{Cons}\ m\ ms)
\end{aligned}
$$

Every proof that ns is a suffix of ms is built from two constructors Base and Step. The base case corresponds to stating that every list is a suffix of itself; the step case states that if ns is a suffix of ms then ns is also a suffix of Cons m ms for any natural number m.

If we have such a proof that ns is a suffix of ms, we can weaken any location of type Loc n ns to make a new location of type Loc n ms. The weaken function does exactly this:

$$
\begin{aligned}
&\mathit{weaken} : \textbf{forall}\ \{n\ ns\ ms\} \to \mathit{IsSuffix}\ ns\ ms \to \mathit{Loc}\ n\ ns \to \mathit{Loc}\ n\ ms \\
&\mathit{weaken}\ \mathit{Base}\ \mathit{loc} \quad = \mathit{loc} \\
&\mathit{weaken}\ (\mathit{Step}\ i)\ \mathit{loc} = \mathit{Pop}\ (\mathit{weaken}\ i\ \mathit{loc})
\end{aligned}
$$

It proceeds by induction over the proof argument, adding a Pop constructor for every step. While the weaken function adds the necessary Pop constructors, there is still no way to compute its proof argument automatically. There is an alternative representation of such proofs that does facilitate such automation.

An Alternative Proof

In type theory, one way to formulate the proposition that two values are equal is by constructing an inhabitant of the following type:

$$
\begin{aligned}
&\textbf{data}\ \_ \equiv \_\ \{a : \star\}\ (x : a) : a \to \star\ \textbf{where} \\
&\quad \mathit{Refl} : x \equiv x
\end{aligned}
$$

That is, the only canonical proof that two objects are equal is by reflexivity. This type plays a fundamental role in intensional type theory [15].

Whenever we pattern match on an equality proof, we learn how two values are related. For example, suppose we want to write the following function:

$$\mathit{subst} : \{a : \star\} \to (P : a \to \star) \to (x : a) \to (y : a) \to x \equiv y \to P\ x \to P\ y$$

What patterns should we write on the left-hand side of the definition? Clearly, any argument of type $x \equiv y$ must be Refl. As soon as we match on that argument, however, we learn something about x and y, i.e., they must be the same. We will write this as follows:

$$\mathit{subst}\ P\ x\ .x\ \mathit{Refl}\ px = \cdots$$

The pattern .x means 'the value of this argument can only be equal to x.' Such 'dot-patterns' appear naturally once you start programming with data types indexed by values.

We can decide whenever two shapes are equal, that is, we can define a function with the following type:

$$\mathit{decEqShape} : (s : \mathit{Shape}) \to (t : \mathit{Shape}) \to \mathit{Either}\ (s \equiv t)\ ((s \equiv t) \to \bot)$$

Here Either denotes the disjoint sum of two types and $\bot$ is the empty type. The definition of decEqShape is fairly unremarkable. We traverse the lists s and t, comparing every element. If the elements of both lists are equal at every position, the entire lists are equal; if the lists have different lengths or store different elements, the two shapes are distinct.

Using this function, we can define the following function that checks whether or not one list is a suffix of another:

```
_ ≤ _ : Shape → Shape → Bool
Nil ≤ s          = True
Cons u s ≤ Nil = False
Cons u s ≤ Cons v t with decEqShape (Cons u s) (Cons v t)
Cons u s ≤ Cons .u .s | Inl Refl = True
Cons u s ≤ Cons v t | Inr q = (Cons u s) ≤ t
```

Here we use a with clause, a local pattern match similar to Haskell's case expressions. In the inductive step, we make a call to the auxiliary function decEqShape. On the next lines we repeat the left-hand side of the function definition, followed by the new patterns Inl Refl and Inr q. We separate the new patterns introduced by the with clause from the original function arguments by a vertical bar. If we learn that the two lists are equal, it follows that the first list is a suffix of the second. Otherwise, we continue with a recursive call.

Now we can reflect any Bool into ⋆ as follows:

```
So : Bool → ⋆
So True = ()
So False = ⊥
```

Using this definition, we give an alternative definition of the IsSuffix predicate: a shape s is a suffix of a shape t if and only if So (s ≤ t) is inhabited. This alternative definition is equivalent to the definition using IsSuffix. Proving the equivalence in one direction corresponds to defining a function with the following type:

```
equiv : (s : Shape) → (t : Shape) → So (s ≤ t) → IsSuffix s t
```

The definition is reasonably straightforward: we pattern match on s and t, using the proof argument to kill off any impossible branches.

So why go through all this effort to write an equivalent representation of the inductive IsSuffix data type? The two forms of proof are useful for different reasons:

IsSuffix s t By defining the proof as an inductive data type, we can pattern match on proofs.

We use this to define the weaken function. Unfortunately, we need to write an inhabitant of IsSuffix by hand to pass to the weaken function.

So (s ≤ t) By defining the ≤-operator we have written a function that decides when one list is a suffix of another. In particular, for any pair of closed shapes s ≤ t reduces to either True or False. Correspondingly, the type So (s ≤ t) is either trivial or uninhabited.

The central idea behind our smart constructors is to weaken using the inductive representation, but to require a trivial implicit witness.

Smart Constructors

With this in mind, we revise our smart constructors for reading from and writing to references. These smart constructors now require an implicit proof that s is a suffix of t. Using our equiv function, we can compute the inductive representation of such a proof. Using this inductive representation, we can weaken locations as necessary

```
readArray : forall {n ns ms} → {p : So (ns ≤ ms)}
  → Loc n ns → Fin n → IO Data ms ms
readArray {n} {ns} {ms} {p} a i = Read (weaken (equiv ns ms p) a) i Return
```

The beauty of this solution is that Agda will automatically instantiate implicit arguments of type (). In other words, for any closed IO term a programmer need not worry about passing proof arguments. For example, we can now write:

```
f : IO Nat Nil (Cons 8 (Cons 4 Nil))
f = newArray 4 >>= λarray₁
  → newArray 8 >>= λarray₂
  → readArray array₁ Fz
```

The smart constructors will now automatically weaken array$_1$ after array$_2$ has been allocated.

Unfortunately, not all in the garden is rosy. If we have an open term, Agda will warn you that it cannot find a suitable proof argument. For example, consider the following function that reads the first and only location of any array storing a single element:

```
readOne : {ns : Shape} → Loc 1 ns → IO Nat ns ns
readOne a = readArray a Fz
```

While any particular call to readOne is safe, Agda fails to automatically deduce that So (ns ≤ ns) reduces to the unit type. Even though it is clearly true for any particular choice of ns and we can fill in the proof argument manually, the techniques we have outlined here fail to provide the required proof automatically.

Without more language support it is unlikely that we can avoid this restriction.

Denotational Model

We have described the syntax of array computations using the IO data type, but we have not specified how these computations behave. Recall that we can model arrays as functions from indices to natural numbers:

```
Array : Nat → ⋆
Array n = Fin n → Data
```

Before specifying the behaviour of IO computations, we define several auxiliary functions to update an array and lookup a value stored in an array

```
lookup : forall {n ns} → Loc n ns → Fin n → Heap ns → Data
lookup Top      i (Alloc a _) = a i
lookup (Pop k) i (Alloc _ h) = lookup k i h
```

The lookup function takes a reference to an array l, an index i in the array at location l, and a heap, and returns the value stored in the array at index i. It dereferences l, resulting in a function of type Fin n → Data; the value stored at index i is the result of applying this function to i.

Next, we define a pair of functions to update the contents of an array.

```
updateArray : {n : Nat} → Fin n → Data → Array n → Array n
updateArray i d a = λj → if i ≡ j then d else a j

updateHeap : forall {n ns}
  → Loc n ns → Fin n → Data → Heap ns → Heap ns
updateHeap Top      i x (Alloc a h) = Alloc (updateArray i x a) h
updateHeap (Pop k) i x (Alloc a h) = Alloc a (updateHeap k i x h)
```

The updateArray function overwrites the data stored at a single index. The function updateHeap updates a single index of an array stored in the heap. It proceeds by dereferencing the location on the heap where the desired array is stored and updates it accordingly, leaving the rest of the heap unchanged.

We now have all the pieces in place to assign semantics to IO computations. The run function below takes a computation of type IO a ns ms and an initial heap of shape ns as arguments, and returns a pair consisting of the result of the computation and the final heap of shape ms.

```
data Pair (a : ★) (b : ★) : ★ where
  pair : a → b → Pair a b

run : forall {a ns ms} → IO a ns ms → Heap ns → Pair a (Heap ms)
run (Return x) h       = pair x h
run (Read a i rd) h    = run (rd (lookup a i h)) h
run (Write a i x wr) h = run wr (updateHeap a i x h)
run (New n io) h       = run (io Top) (Alloc (λi → Zero) h)
```

The Return constructor simply pairs the result and heap; in the Read case, we lookup the data from the heap and recurse with the same heap; for the Write constructor, we recurse with an appropriately modified heap; finally, when a new array is created, we extend the heap with a new array that stores Zero at every index, and continue recursively. Note that, by convention, the Top constructor always refers to the most recently created reference. Our smart constructors will add additional Pop constructors when new memory is allocated.

We refer to this specification as a denotational model. Agda is a programming language based on a consistent type theory. In a sense, the run function constitutes a denotational semantics of mutable arrays. By implementing these semantics in Agda, we build an executable denotational model in Agda's type theory.

Example

Using our smart constructors and the monad operators, we can now define functions that manipulate arrays. For example, the swap function exchanges the value stored at two indices:

```
swap : forall {n ns} → Loc n ns → Fin n → Fin n → IO () ns ns
swap a i j = readArray a i >>= λval_i
           → readArray a j >>= λval_j
           → writeArray a i val_j
           >> writeArray a j val_i
```

In a dependently-typed programming language such as Agda, we can prove properties of our code. For example, we may want to show that swapping the contents of any two array indices twice, leaves the heap intact :

```
swapProp : forall {n ns}
  → (l : Loc n ns) → (i : Fin n) → (j : Fin n) → (h : Heap ns)
  → (h ≡ snd (run (swap l i j >> swap l i j) h))
```

The proof requires a lemma about how updateHeap and lookupHeap interact and is not terribly interesting in itself. The fact that we can formalise such properties and have our proof verified by a computer is much more exciting.

DISTRIBUTED ARRAYS

Arrays are usually represented by a continuous block of memory. Distributed arrays, however, can be distributed over different places—where every place may correspond to a different core on a multiprocessor machine, a different machine on the same network, or any other configuration of interconnected computers.

We begin by determining the type of places, where data is stored and code is executed. Obviously, we do not want to fix the type of all possible places prematurely: you may want to execute the same program in different environments. Yet regardless of the exact number of places, there are certain operations you will always want to perform, such as iterating over all places, or checking when two places are equal.

We therefore choose to abstract over the number of places in the module we will define in the coming section. Agda allows modules to be parameterised:

```
module DistrArray (placeCount : Nat) where
```

When we import the DistrArray module, we are obliged to choose the number of places. Typically, there will be one place for every available processor. From this number, we can define a data type corresponding to the available places:

```
Place : ★
Place = Fin placeCount
```

The key idea underlying our model of locality-aware algorithms is to index computations by the place where they are executed. The new type declaration for the IO monad corresponding to operations on distributed arrays will become:

```
data DIO (a : ★) : Shape → Place → Shape → ★ where
```

You may want to think of a value of type DIO a ns p ms as a computation that can be executed at place p and will take a heap of shape ns to a heap of shape ms, yielding a final value of type a.

We strive to ensure that any well-typed program written in the DIO monad will never access data that is not local. The specification of distributed arrays now poses a twofold problem: we want to ensure that the array manipulations from the previous section are 'localityaware,' that is, we must somehow restrict the array indices that can be accessed from a certain place; furthermore, X10 facilitates several place-shifting operations that change the place where certain chunks of code are executed. As we shall see in the rest of this section, both these issues can be resolved quite naturally.

Regions, Points, and Distributed Arrays

Before we define the DIO monad, we need to introduce several new concepts. In what follows, we will try to stick closely to X10's terminology for distributed arrays. Every array is said to have a region associated with it. A region is a set of valid index points. A distribution specifies a place for every index point in a region.

Once again, we will only treat flat arrays storing natural numbers and defer any discussion about how to deal with more complicated data structures for the moment. In this simple case, a region merely determines the size of the array.

```
Region : ★
Region = Nat
```

As we have seen in the previous section, we can model array indices using the Fin data type:

```
Point : Region → ⋆
Point n = Fin n
```

To model distributed arrays, we now need to consider the distribution that specifies where this data is stored. In line with existing work [9], we assume the existence of a fixed distribution. Agda's postulate expression allows us to assume the existence of a distribution, without providing its definition.

```
postulate
  distr : forall {n ns} → Loc n ns → Point n → Place
```

We have implemented several of X10's combinators for defining distributions, which we will present shortly

Now that we have all the required auxiliary data types, we proceed by defining the DIO monad. As it is a bit more complex than the data types we have seen so far, we will discuss every constructor individually.

The Return constructor is analogous to one we have seen previously for the IO monad: it lifts any pure value into the DIO monad.

```
Return : {p : Place} → {ns : Shape} → a → DIO a ns p ns
```

The Read and Write operations are more interesting. Although they correspond closely to the operations we have seen in the previous section, their type now keeps track of the place where they are executed. Any read or write operation to point pt of an array l can only be executed at the place specified by the distribution. This invariant is enforced by the types of our constructors:

```
Read : forall {n ns ms}
  → (l : Loc n ns) → (pt : Point n)
  → (Data → DIO a ns (distr l pt) ms)
  → DIO a ns (distr l pt) ms
Write : forall {n ns ms}
  → (l : Loc n ns) → (pt : Point n) → Data
  → DIO a ns (distr l pt) ms
  → DIO a ns (distr l pt) ms
```

In contrast to Read and Write, new arrays can be allocated at any place.

```
New : forall {p ns ms}
  → (n : Nat)
  → (Loc n (Cons n ns) → DIO a (Cons n ns) p ms)
  → DIO a ns p ms
```

Finally, we add a constructor for a place-shifting operator. Using this At operator lets us execute a computation at another place.

```
At : forall {p ns ms ps}
  → (q : Place) → DIO () ns q ms → DIO a ms p ps → DIO a ns p ps
```

Note that we will discard the result of the computation that is executed at another place. We therefore require this computation to return an element of the unit type. We can add our smart constructors for each these operations, as we have done in the previous section.

We can also show that DIO is indeed a parameterised monad. We have omitted the definitions of the return and bind operators for the sake of brevity:

```
return : forall {ns a p} → a → DIO a ns p ns
_ ≫= _ : forall {ns ms ks a b p}
  → DIO A ns p ms → (A → DIO B ms p ks) → DIO B ns p ks
```

It is worth noting that the bind operator >>= can only be used to sequence operations at the same place.

Denotational Model

To run a computation in the DIO monad, we follow the run function defined in the previous section closely. Our new run function, however, must be locality-aware. Therefore, we parameterise the run function explicitly by the place where the computation is executed.

```
run : forall {a ns ms}
  → (p : Place) → DIO a ns p ms → Heap ns → Pair a (Heap ms)
run p (Return x) h             = pair x h
run .(distr l i) (Read l i rd) h   = run (distr l i) (rd (lookup l i h)) h
run .(distr l i) (Write l i x wr) h = let h′ = updateHeap l i x h
                                      in run (distr l i) wr h′
run p (New n io) h             = run p (io Top) (Alloc (λi → Zero) h)
run p (At q io1 io2) h         = run p io2 (snd (run q io1 h))
```

Now we can see that the Read and Write operations may not be executed at any place. Recall that the Read and Write constructors both return computations at the place distr l i. When we pattern match on a Read or Write, we know exactly what the place argument of the run function must be. Correspondingly, we do not pattern match on the place argument—we know that the place can only be distr l i, as is indicated by the dot-pattern.

The other difference with respect to the previous run function, is the new case for the At constructor. In that case, we sequence the two computations io1 and io2. To do so, we first execute the io1 at q, but discard its result; we continue executing the second computation io2 with the heap resulting from the execution of io1 at the location p. Conform to previous proposals [10], we have assumed that io1 and io2 are performed synchronously—executing io1 before continuing with the rest of the computation. Using techniques to model concurrency that we have presented previously [23], we believe we could give a more refined treatment of the X10's globally asynchronous/locally synchronous semantics and provide specifications for X10's clocks, finish, and force constructs.

Locality-aware Combinators

Using the place-shifting operator at, we can define several locality-aware control structures. With our first-class distribution and definition of Place, we believe there is no need to define more primitive operations.

The distributed map, for example, applies a function to all the elements of a distributed array at the place where they are stored. We define it in terms of an auxiliary function, for, that iterates over all the indices of an array:

```
for : forall {n ns p} → (Point n → DIO () ns p ns) → DIO () ns p ns
for {Succ k} dio = dio Fz ≫ (for {k} (dio . Fs))
for {Zero}   dio = return ()

dmap : forall {n ns p} → (Data → Data) → Loc n ns → DIO () ns p ns
dmap f l = for (λi → at (distr l i) (readArray l i ≫= λx
                                     → writeArray l i (f x)))
```

Besides dmap, we implement two other combinators: forallplaces and ateach. The forallplaces operation executes its argument computation at all available places. We define it using the for function to iterate over all places. The ateach function, on the other hand, is a generalisation of the distributed map operation. It iterates over an array, executing its argument operation once for every index of the array, at the place where that index is stored.

$$
\begin{aligned}
&\mathit{forallplaces} : \textbf{forall}\ \{p\ ns\} \\
&\quad \rightarrow ((q : \mathit{Place}) \rightarrow \mathit{DIO}\ ()\ ns\ q\ ns) \rightarrow \mathit{DIO}\ ()\ ns\ p\ ns \\
&\mathit{forallplaces}\ io = \mathit{for}\ (\lambda i \rightarrow \mathit{at}\ i\ (io\ i))
\end{aligned}
$$

$$
\begin{aligned}
&\mathit{ateach} : \textbf{forall}\ \{n\ ns\ p\} \\
&\quad \rightarrow (l : \mathit{Loc}\ n\ ns) \rightarrow ((pt : \mathit{Point}\ n) \rightarrow \mathit{DIO}\ ()\ ns\ (\mathit{distr}\ l\ pt)\ ns) \\
&\quad \rightarrow \mathit{DIO}\ ()\ ns\ p\ ns \\
&\mathit{ateach}\ l\ io = \mathit{for}\ (\lambda i \rightarrow \mathit{at}\ (\mathit{distr}\ l\ i)\ (io\ i))
\end{aligned}
$$

Example

We will now show how to write a simple algorithm that sums all the elements of a distributed array. To do so efficiently, we first locally sum all the values at every place. To compute the total sum of all the elements of the array, we add together all these local sums. In what follows, we will need the following auxiliary function, increment:

$$
\begin{aligned}
&\mathit{increment} : \textbf{forall}\ \{n\ ns\ p\} \\
&\quad \rightarrow (l : \mathit{Loc}\ n\ ns) \rightarrow (i : \mathit{Fin}\ n) \rightarrow \mathit{Nat} \rightarrow (\mathit{distr}\ l\ i \equiv p) \rightarrow \mathit{DIO}\ ()\ ns\ p\ ns \\
&\mathit{increment}\ l\ i\ x\ \mathit{Refl} = \mathit{readArray}\ l\ i \gg\!= \lambda y \rightarrow \mathit{writeArray}\ l\ i\ (x + y)
\end{aligned}
$$

Note that increment is a bit more general than strictly necessary. We could return a computation at distr l i, but instead we choose to be a little more general: increment can be executed at any place, as long as we have a proof that this place is equal to distr l i. The ≡ –type is inhabited by single constructor Refl.

We can use the increment function to define a simple sequential sum function:

$$
\begin{aligned}
&\mathit{sum} : \textbf{forall}\ \{n\ ns\ p\} \rightarrow \mathit{Loc}\ n\ ns \rightarrow \mathit{Loc}\ 1\ ns \rightarrow \mathit{DIO}\ ()\ ns\ p\ ns \\
&\mathit{sum}\ l\ \mathit{out} = \mathit{ateach}\ l\ (\lambda i \rightarrow \mathit{readArray}\ l\ i \gg\!= \lambda n \\
&\qquad\qquad \rightarrow \mathit{at}\ (\mathit{distr}\ \mathit{out}\ \mathit{Fz})\ (\mathit{increment}\ \mathit{out}\ \mathit{Fz}\ n\ \mathit{Refl}))
\end{aligned}
$$

The sum function takes an array as its argument, together with a reference to a single-celled array, out. It reads every element of the array, and increments out accordingly.

Finally, we can use both these functions to define a parallel sum:

$$
\begin{aligned}
&\mathit{psum} : \textbf{forall}\ \{n\ ns\} \\
&\quad \rightarrow (l : \mathit{Loc}\ n\ ns) \rightarrow (\mathit{localSums} : \mathit{Loc}\ \mathit{placeCount}\ ns) \\
&\quad \rightarrow ((i : \mathit{Place}) \rightarrow \mathit{distr}\ \mathit{localSums}\ i \equiv i) \\
&\quad \rightarrow (\mathit{out} : \mathit{Loc}\ 1\ ns) \rightarrow \mathit{DIO}\ \mathit{Nat}\ ns\ (\mathit{distr}\ \mathit{out}\ \mathit{Fz})\ ns \\
&\mathit{psum}\ l\ \mathit{localSums}\ \mathit{locDistr}\ \mathit{out} \\
&\quad = \mathit{ateach}\ l\ (\lambda i \rightarrow (\mathit{readArray}\ l\ i \gg\!= \lambda n \\
&\qquad\qquad \rightarrow \mathit{increment}\ \mathit{localSums}\ (\mathit{distr}\ l\ i)\ n\ (\mathit{locDistr}\ (\mathit{distr}\ l\ i)))) \\
&\quad \gg \mathit{sum}\ \mathit{localSums}\ \mathit{out} \\
&\quad \gg \mathit{readArray}\ \mathit{out}\ \mathit{Fz}
\end{aligned}
$$

The psum function takes four arguments: the array l whose elements you would like to sum; an array localSums that will store the intermediate sums; an assumption regarding the distribution of this array; and finally, the single-celled array to which we write the result.

For every index i of the array l, we read the value stored at index i, and increment the corresponding local sum. We then add together the local sums using our previous sequential sum function, and return the final result. We use our assumption about the distribution of the localSums array when calling the increment function. Without this assumption, we would have to use the place-shifting operation at to update a (potentially) non-local array index.

There are several interesting issues that these examples highlight. First of all, as our at function only works on computations returning a unit type, the results of intermediate computations must be collected in intermediate arrays.

More importantly, however, whenever we want to rely on properties of the global distribution, we need to make explicit assumptions in the form of proof arguments. This is rather unfortunate: it would be interesting to research how a specific distribution can be associated with an array when it is created. This would hopefully allow for a more fine-grained treatment of distributions and eliminate the need for explicit proof arguments.

Defining Distributions

Throughout this section we have assumed the existence of a distribution, specifying how an array is distributed over the available places. Several built-in distributions are provided by X10, some of which we will now define. For the moment, we focus on defining a distribution of a single array, that is, functions of type Fin n → Place.

There are two atomic distributions: the constant distribution maps all the points of an array to a single place; the unique distribution maps the i-th index of an array to the i-th place.

$$
\begin{aligned}
&\mathit{constDistr} : \{n : \mathit{Nat}\} \rightarrow \mathit{Place} \rightarrow \mathit{Point}\ n \rightarrow \mathit{Place} \\
&\mathit{constDistr}\ p = \lambda i \rightarrow p
\end{aligned}
$$

$$
\begin{aligned}
&\mathit{unique} : \mathit{Point}\ \mathit{placeCount} \rightarrow \mathit{Place} \\
&\mathit{unique}\ i = i
\end{aligned}
$$

We can compose any two such distributions, to form a larger distribution:

$$
\begin{aligned}
&\mathit{compose} : \textbf{forall}\ \{n\ m\} \\
&\quad \rightarrow (\mathit{Point}\ n \rightarrow \mathit{Place}) \rightarrow (\mathit{Point}\ m \rightarrow \mathit{Place}) \rightarrow (\mathit{Point}\ (n + m) \rightarrow \mathit{Place})
\end{aligned}
$$

Although the definition of compose is a bit tricky, there is a particularly elegant definition in the literature using views [2]. Of course, we can iterate the compose operator:

$$
\begin{aligned}
&\mathit{cycle} : \{n : \mathit{Nat}\} \\
&\quad \rightarrow (k : \mathit{Nat}) \rightarrow (\mathit{Point}\ n \rightarrow \mathit{Place}) \rightarrow (\mathit{Point}\ (k * n) \rightarrow \mathit{Place}) \\
&\mathit{cycle}\ Z\ f\ () \\
&\mathit{cycle}\ (\mathit{Succ}\ k)\ f\ i = \mathit{compose}\ f\ (\mathit{cycle}\ k\ f)\ i
\end{aligned}
$$

In the case where k is equal to Zero, we need to define a function of type Fin Zero → Place. As Fin Zero has no inhabitants, this function will never be applied and we may omit the definition accordingly.

Using similar combinators, we can define distributions over all arrays, exploiting the obvious similarity between Loc and Fin. There are several other distributions supported by X10, that can be implemented along the same lines.

DISCUSSION

Using a dependently-typed host language, we have seen how to implement a domain-specific library for distributed arrays, together with an embedded type system that guarantees all array access operations are both safe and local. In contrast to existing work [10], there is no specific set of type rules; instead, equivalent properties are enforced by a general-purpose language with dependent types. We have defined semantics for our library in the form of a total, functional specification. Although this semantics may not take the form of deduction rules, they are no less precise or concise. Besides these functional specifications are both executable and amenable to computer-aided formal verification. More generally, this approach can be extended to other domains: a dependently-typed language accommodates domain specific libraries with their own embedded type systems [18].

Having said this, there are clearly several serious limitations of this work as it stands. First and foremost, I have assumed that every array only stores natural numbers, disallowing more complex structures such as multi-dimensional arrays. This can be easily fixed by defining a more elaborate Shape data type. In its most general form, the Shape data type could be defined as a list of types; a heap then corresponds to a list of values of the right type. I have decided to impose this restriction for the purpose of presentation. I believe that there is no fundamental obstacle preventing us from incorporating the rich region calculus offered by X10 in the same fashion.

Furthermore, the pure model is rather naive. It would be interesting to explore a more refined model, where every place maintains its own heap. As our example in the previous section illustrated, assuming the presence of a global distribution does not scale well. Decorating every array with a distribution upon its creation should help provide localityinformation when it is needed.

We have not discussed how code in the IO or DIO monad is actually compiled. At the moment, Agda can only be compiled to Haskell. Agda does provide several pragmas to customise how Agda functions are translated to their Haskell counterparts. The ongoing effort to support data parallelism in Haskell [4, 5] may therefore provide us with a most welcome foothold.

The domain-specific language for manipulating arrays presented in this paper contains an operation for the allocation of memory, but no operation for memory deallocation. The system presented here assumes garbage collection is handled automatically. This is not a fundamental limitation of this approach: in principle, dependently typed programming languages can enforce any invariant that can be described in constructive predicate logic. In particular, we could extend the shape data type not only capture the amount of data that has been allocated, but also record the locations that are still valid. Any memory access operation then needs to provide a proof that the location being accessed has not been deallocated. Where this is certainly feasible, there is still a substantial challenge in engineering a solution that does not put a strain on the programmer to provide explicit proofs or clutter type signatures with too much information.

There are many features of X10 that have not been discussed here at all. Most notably, I have refrained from modelling many of X10's constructs that enable asynchronous communication between locations, even though I would like to do so in the future.

Finally, it is necessary to explore larger examples to acquire a better understanding of how this approach scales. At the moment, I cannot predict how efficient the resulting code will be; nor do I know how difficult it will be to reason about large, realistic distributed algorithms.

ACKNOWLEDGEMENTS

A previous version of this article was published at the Symposium on Trends in Functional Programming in 2008. Thorsten Altenkirch, my PhD supervisor, suggested this line of research and helped prepare our original submission, for which I am grateful. I would also like to thank the anonymous reviewers for their valuable comments on both versions of this paper.

REFERENCES

1. Allen, E., Chase, D., Luchangco, V., Maessen, J.-W., Ryu, S., Steele, G.L. Jr., Tobin-Hochstadt, S.: The Fortress language specification. Technical report, Sun Microsystems, Inc. (2005)
2. Altenkirch, T., McBride, C., Morris, P.: Generic programming with dependent types. In: Backhouse, R., Gibbons, J., Hinze, R., Jeuring, J. (eds.) Spring School on Datatype-Generic Programming. LNCS, vol. 4719. Springer, Berlin (2007)
3. Atkey, R.: Parameterised notions of computation. In: Proceedings of the Workshop on Mathematically Structured Functional Programming (2006)
4. Chakravarty, M.M.T., Keller, G., Lechtchinsky, R., Pfannenstiel, W.: Nepal—nested data-parallelism in Haskell. In: Euro-Par 2001: Parallel Processing, 7th International Euro-Par Conference. LNCS, vol. 2150 (2001)
5. Chakravarty, M.M.T., Leshchinskiy, R., Jones, S.P., Keller, G., Marlow, S.: Data parallel Haskell: a status report. In: Proceedings of the 2007 Workshop on Declarative Aspects of Multicore Programming (2007)
6. Chamberlain, B.L., Choi, S.-E., Lewis, E.C., Lin, C., Snyder, L., Weathersby, D.: ZPL: a machine independent programming language for parallel computers. Softw. Eng. 26(3) (2000)
7. Chamberlain, B., Deitz, S., Hribar, M.B., Wong, W.: Chapel. Technical report, Cray Inc. (2005)
8. Charles, P., Grothoff, C., Saraswat, V., Donawa, C., Kielstra, A., Ebcioglu, K., von Praun, C., Sarkar, V.: X10: an object-oriented approach to non-uniform cluster computing. In: OOPSLA '05 (2005)
9. Grothoff, C., Palsberg, J., Saraswat, V.: Safe arrays via regions and dependent types. doi:10.1.1.98.8038
10. Grothoff, C., Palsberg, J., Saraswat, V.: A type system for distributed arrays. Unpublished draft
11. Hudak, P.: Building domain-specific embedded languages. ACM Comput. Surv. 28 (1996)
12. Liblit, B., Aiken, A.: Type systems for distributed data structures. In: POPL '00: Proceedings of the 27th ACM SIGPLAN-SIGACT Symposium on Principles of Programming Languages, pp. 199–213 (2000)

13. Löh, A.: lhs2TeX. http://people.cs.uu.nl/andres/lhs2tex/

14. McKinna, J., Wright, J.: A type-correct, stack-safe, provably correct, expression compiler in Epigram. J. Funct. Program. doi:10.1.1.105.4086

15. Nordström, B., Petersson, K., Smith, J.M.: Programming in Martin-Löf's Type Theory: An Introduction. Oxford University Press, London (1990)

16. Norell, U.: Towards a practical programming language based on dependent type theory. PhD thesis, Chalmers University of Technology (2007)

17. Nystrom, N., Saraswat, V., Palsberg, J., Grothoff, C.: Constrained types for object-oriented languages. In: OOPSLA '08: Proceedings of the 23rd ACM SIGPLAN Conference on Object-Oriented Programming Systems Languages and Applications, pp. 457–474 (2008)

18. Oury, N., Swierstra, W.: The power of Pi. In: ICFP '08: Proceedings of the 13th ACM SIGPLAN International Conference on Functional Programming (2008)

19. Jones, S.P. (ed.): Haskell 98 Language and Libraries—The Revised Report. Cambridge University Press, Cambridge (2003)

20. Jones, S.P., Vytiniotis, D., Weirich, S., Washburn, G.: Simple unification-based type inference for GADTs. In: ICFP '06: Proceedings of the 11th ACM SIGPLAN International Conference on Functional Programming (2006)

21. Scholz, S.-B.: Single assignment C—efficient support for high-level array operations in a functional setting. J. Funct. Program. 13(6), 1005–1059 (2003)

22. Swierstra, W.: A functional specification of effects. PhD thesis, University of Nottingham (2009)

23. Swierstra, W., Altenkirch, T.: Beauty in the beast: a functional semantics of the awkward squad. In: Proceedings of the ACM SIGPLAN Haskell Workshop (2007)

CHAPTER 3 MAKING "STRICTERNESS" MORE RELEVANT

Stefan Holdermans[1], Jurriaan Hage[2]

[1]Vector Fabrics, Paradijslaan 28, 5611 KN Eindhoven, The Netherlands

[2]Department of Information and Computing Sciences, Utrecht University, TB Utrecht, The Netherlands

ABSTRACT

Adapting a strictness analyser to have it take into account explicit strictness annotations can be a tricky business. Straightforward extensions of analyses based on relevance typing are likely to either be unsafe or fail to pick the fruits of increases in strictness that are introduced through annotations. We propose a more involved adaptation of relevance typing, that can be used to derive strictness analyses that are both safe and effective in the presence of explicit strictness annotations. The resulting type system provides a firm foundation for implementations of type-based strictness analysers in compilers for lazy programming languages such as Haskell and Clean.

INTRODUCTION

In the design of strictness analyses, lazy functional languages are typically modelled in terms of nonstrict lambda-calculi. However, such calculi fail to account for the semantic properties of constructs such as Haskell's primitive function seq [31] and Clean's strictness annotations [32], that allow programmers to selectively make their functions stricter. As a result, it is not always clear how strictness analyses and the optimisations they enable scale to real-world programming languages. In this context, this article makes the following contributions:

- We present an optimising transformation for a call-by-name lambda-calculus. The transformation is driven by a strictness analysis based on relevance typing (Sect. 4). We show how two straightforward extensions for dealing with a construct for selective strictness (Sect. 3) yield transformations that are either unsafe or otherwise ineffective in the sense that they fail to pick up on any increases in strictness that are incurred from the use of this construct (Sect. 5).
- Moreover, we present a more involved adaptation of the transformation that makes use of a relevance typing discipline that, in addition to demand propagation, also keeps track of applicativeness: i.e., which expressions in a program are guaranteed to give rise to functions that, during the evaluation of the program, receive arguments (Sect. 6). The transformations obtained by this approach are both safe and effective, and so our approach can serve as a basis for optimisations in compilers for real-world languages.

BACKGROUND

The praises of lazy evaluation [20] have been sung in many voices and its benefits (the ability to construct infinite data structures, the ability to define custom control structures, the

Citation: Stefan Holdermans, Jurriaan Hage, Making "stricterness" more relevant, DOI 10.1007/s10990-011-9079-7

inherent avoidance of unnecessary computations, the facilitation of increased modularisation—to name a few) are well-known. Equally well-known are its drawbacks, most notably the excessive use of memory that is frequently associated with the deferral of computations. Accurate strictness analysers have therefore proven themselves indispensable tools in the optimisation of lazy programs.

The goal of strictness analysis is to identify which functions within a nonstrict program are in fact strict, i.e., always diverge on diverging input. Changing the evaluation strategy for applications of such functions from a nonstrict strategy (call-by-name or call-by-need) into a strict strategy (call-by-value) does not change the semantics of the program and avoids the cost that is otherwise incurred by deferring the evaluation of argument expressions. Because strictness is generally an undecidable property, strictness analysers need to be conservative and cannot be expected to successfully identify all strict functions in a program. Moreover, in practice, many functions written in lazily evaluated languages turn out to be almost strict. For example, a function that consumes a given argument in all but one of the arms of a case analysis on another argument. Obviously, in these situations, no help can be expected from strictness analysis. As a countermeasure, modern lazy languages like Haskell and Clean offer the programmer a means to make such programs stricter: Clean offers explicit strictness annotations in type signatures and strict local definitions, while Haskell provides a primitive binary function seq, that evaluates its first argument (that is, forces it to weak head normal form) and returns its second. Furthermore, both languages allow for strictness annotations to occur in datatype declarations.

As an example of the use of such constructs, consider the definition of a function that returns its first argument, while ignoring its second argument, in some lazily evaluated functional language,

$$\lambda x.\lambda y.x,$$

and the following—stricter—version, that is defined in terms of a function seq with semantics as described above:

$$\lambda x.\lambda y.seq\ y\ x.$$

Whereas the former is strict only in its first argument (and lazy in its second), the latter is strict in both its arguments.

Of particular interest is that the increase in strictness induced by primitive operations like seq also propagates through function application. For instance, because of its use of the stricter version of the function that ignores its second argument, the otherwise lazy function

$$\lambda z.(\lambda x.\lambda y.seq\ y\ x)\ \text{true}\ z,$$

that always produces the Boolean constant true, is now strict itself as well. Of course, one would hope that such "stricterness" would be picked up by automatic strictness analysers, so that calls to functions like λz.(λx.λy.seq y x) true z could be evaluated eagerly rather than lazily. However, faithfully accounting for the effects of this so-called selective strictness is a tricky business as it comes with some peculiar semantic properties.

For one thing, selective strictness can be used to tell the programs ⊥ and λx. ⊥ apart. As a simple example, the term seq ⊥ true diverges whereas seq (λx.⊥) true produces the constant true. Note that this distinction cannot be made in either the "pure" call-by-name or call-byneed lambda-calculus;[1] yet studies into programming languages typically assume one or the other of these calculi as a model for nonstrict functional languages. Then, having seq (or a similar construct) in a language has profound repercussions. For example, in the presence of strictness annotations, polymorphic functions generally do not possess the parametricity property [40] and, so, optimisations such as short-cut deforestation [12] that are justified by parametricity are no longer sound.

[1]From within these calculi, that is: one cannot write a function that behaves differently for ⊥ and λx.⊥.

Unsurprisingly, similar issues arise when adapting a strictness analysis for a mere nonstrict lambda-calculus for use in a lazy language with constructs for selective strictness.

PRELIMINARIES

To be able to consider the problem from a formal angle, we introduce a small, implicitly typed, nonstrict expression language. Assuming a countable infinite set of variable symbols ranged over by x,

x ∈ Var variables,

its terms,

t ∈ Term terms,

are given by

$$t ::= \text{false} \mid \text{true} \mid 0 \mid x \mid \lambda x.t_1 \mid t_1\ t_2 \mid t_1 \bullet t_2 \mid \text{if } t_1 \text{ then } t_2 \text{ else } t_3$$
$$\mid \text{succ } t_1 \mid \text{pred } t_1 \mid \text{iszero } t_1 \mid \text{error}.$$

That is, terms include the Boolean constants false and true, the numeral 0, variables x, and lambda-abstractions $\lambda x.t_1$. Furthermore, we distinguish between nonstrict function applications $t_1\ t_2$ and strict function applications $t_1 \bullet t_2$. Conditionals are written as if t_1 then t_2 else t_3; succ t_1 and pred t_1 denote, respectively, the successor and predecessor operations on natural numbers, while iszero t_1 tests whether or not a given natural-number computation results in a zero result. Finally, error denotes a failing computation.

Evaluation $\boxed{t \longrightarrow w}$

$$\frac{}{\mathsf{false} \longrightarrow \mathsf{false}}\ [\textit{e-false}] \qquad \frac{}{\mathsf{true} \longrightarrow \mathsf{true}}\ [\textit{e-true}] \qquad \frac{}{0 \longrightarrow 0}\ [\textit{e-zero}]$$

$$\frac{}{\lambda x.\,t_1 \longrightarrow \lambda x.\,t_1}\ [\textit{e-abs}]$$

$$\frac{t_1 \longrightarrow \lambda x.\,t_0 \quad [x \mapsto t_2]t_0 \longrightarrow w}{t_1\ t_2 \longrightarrow w}\ [\textit{e-app}] \qquad \frac{t_1 \longrightarrow \lambda x.\,t_0 \quad t_2 \longrightarrow w_2 \quad [x \mapsto w_2]t_0 \longrightarrow w}{t_1 \bullet t_2 \longrightarrow w}\ [\textit{e-sapp}]$$

$$\frac{t_1 \longrightarrow \mathsf{true} \quad t_2 \longrightarrow w}{\mathsf{if}\ t_1\ \mathsf{then}\ t_2\ \mathsf{else}\ t_3 \longrightarrow w}\ [\textit{e-if-true}] \qquad \frac{t_1 \longrightarrow \mathsf{false} \quad t_3 \longrightarrow w}{\mathsf{if}\ t_1\ \mathsf{then}\ t_2\ \mathsf{else}\ t_3 \longrightarrow w}\ [\textit{e-if-false}]$$

$$\frac{}{\mathsf{succ}\ t_1 \longrightarrow \mathsf{succ}\ t_1}\ [\textit{e-succ}] \qquad \frac{t_1 \longrightarrow 0}{\mathsf{pred}\ t_1 \longrightarrow 0}\ [\textit{e-pred-zero}]$$

$$\frac{t_1 \longrightarrow \mathsf{succ}\ t_0 \quad t_0 \longrightarrow w}{\mathsf{pred}\ t_1 \longrightarrow w}\ [\textit{e-pred-succ}]$$

$$\frac{t_1 \longrightarrow 0}{\mathsf{iszero}\ t_1 \longrightarrow \mathsf{true}}\ [\textit{e-iszero-zero}] \qquad \frac{t_1 \longrightarrow \mathsf{succ}\ t_0}{\mathsf{iszero}\ t_1 \longrightarrow \mathsf{false}}\ [\textit{e-iszero-succ}]$$

Figure. 1 Natural semantics.

We adopt the Barendregt convention and assume that all bound variables are named distinctly from any free variables. As always, lambda-abstractions extend as far to the right as possible, while function application is left-associative.

To ease the presentation in the sequel, strict function application is included instead of a primitive operation seq t_1 t_2. Note that this choice is by no means essential as—under a call-by-need semantics at least—strict function application and seq can always be defined in terms of each other. That is, given seq t_1 t_2 as part of the language, strict function application is given by

$$\lambda f.\,\lambda x.\,\mathsf{seq}\ x\ (f\ x),$$

whereas in the term language defined above, seq can be defined as

$$\lambda x.\,\lambda y.\,((\lambda z.\,y) \bullet x).$$

A natural semantics [24] for the term language is given in Fig. 1 by means of rules for deriving judgements of the form t $\longrightarrow$ w. That is, successful evaluation of a term t yields a weak head normal form w,

$w \in$ Whnf weak head normal forms,

given by

$w ::= \mathsf{false} \mid \mathsf{true} \mid 0 \mid \lambda x.t_1$.

As reflected by the rules [e-false], [e-true], [e-zero], [e-abs], and [e-succ], Boolean constants, the numeral 0, abstractions, applications of the successor operator are already in weak head normal form. Nonstrict and strict function applications are evaluated under a call-by-name and a call-by-value strategy, respectively; in the rules [e-app] and [e-sapp] beta-substitution is denoted by $[\cdot \mapsto \cdot]$. For conditionals if t_1 then t_2 else t_3, rules [e-if-true] and [e-if-false] evaluate the condition t_1 and proceed by evaluating one of the branches t_2 and t_3. Taking the predecessor of a computation that results in 0, yields 0 (rule schema [e-pred-zero]), while taking the predecessor of a computation that produces a result of the form succ t_0 for some t_0 amounts to evaluating t_0 (rule schema [e-pred-succ]). Rules [eiszero-zero] and [e-iszero-succ] denote that a zero-equality test iszero t_1 for a term t_1 results in true if t_1 evaluates to 0 and false if t_1 evaluates to succ t_0 for some t_0.

Typing $\boxed{\Gamma \vdash t : \tau}$

$$\frac{}{\Gamma \vdash \mathsf{false} : \mathsf{bool}}\ [\textit{t-false}] \qquad \frac{}{\Gamma \vdash \mathsf{true} : \mathsf{bool}}\ [\textit{t-true}] \qquad \frac{}{\Gamma \vdash 0 : \mathsf{nat}}\ [\textit{t-zero}]$$

$$\frac{}{\Gamma_1[x \mapsto \tau] \vdash x : \tau}\ [\textit{t-var}] \qquad \frac{\Gamma[x \mapsto \tau_1] \vdash t_1 : \tau_2}{\Gamma \vdash \lambda x.\,t_1 : \tau_1 \to \tau_2}\ [\textit{t-abs}]$$

$$\frac{\Gamma \vdash t_1 : \tau_2 \to \tau \quad \Gamma \vdash t_2 : \tau_2}{\Gamma \vdash t_1\ t_2 : \tau}\ [\textit{t-app}] \qquad \frac{\Gamma \vdash t_1 : \tau_2 \to \tau \quad \Gamma \vdash t_2 : \tau_2}{\Gamma \vdash t_1 \bullet t_2 : \tau}\ [\textit{t-app}]$$

$$\frac{\Gamma \vdash t_1 : \mathsf{bool} \quad \Gamma \vdash t_2 : \tau \quad \Gamma \vdash t_3 : \tau}{\Gamma \vdash \mathsf{if}\ t_1\ \mathsf{then}\ t_2\ \mathsf{else}\ t_3 : \tau}\ [\textit{t-if}]$$

$$\frac{\Gamma \vdash t_1 : \mathsf{nat}}{\Gamma \vdash \mathsf{succ}\ t_1 : \mathsf{nat}}\ [\textit{t-succ}] \qquad \frac{\Gamma \vdash t_1 : \mathsf{nat}}{\Gamma \vdash \mathsf{pred}\ t_1 : \mathsf{nat}}\ [\textit{t-pred}] \qquad \frac{\Gamma \vdash t_1 : \mathsf{nat}}{\Gamma \vdash \mathsf{iszero}\ t_1 : \mathsf{bool}}\ [\textit{t-iszero}]$$

$$\frac{}{\Gamma \vdash \mathsf{error} : \tau}\ [\textit{t-error}]$$

Figure. 2 The underlying type system.

We say that evaluation of a term t fails if there is no weak head normal form w such that t → w. Note that we do not have rules for evaluating error; hence, evaluation of error always fails.

A type system for our language is presented in Fig. 2 as a set of type-assignment rules for deriving judgements $\Gamma \vdash t : \tau$, , expressing that, in the type environment Γ , the term t can be assigned the type τ . Here, types,

$\tau \in$ Type types,

are given by

$\tau ::= \text{bool} \mid \text{nat} \mid \tau_1 \rightarrow \tau_2$,

with bool the type of Booleans, nat the type of natural numbers, and $\tau_1 \rightarrow \tau_2$ the type of functions that take arguments of type τ_1 to results of type τ_2. Type environments are finite maps from variables to types:

$\Gamma \in \mathbf{TEnv} = \mathbf{Var} \rightarrow_{\text{fin}} \mathbf{Type}$ type environments.

We write [ ] for the empty map, $[x \mapsto \tau]$ for the singleton map that binds x to τ, and $\Gamma_1[x \mapsto \tau]$ for the map that is obtained by extending Γ_1 with a binding from x to τ.

The assignment rules in Fig. 2 are completely standard. Note in particular that nonstrict applications $t_1\ t_2$ and strict applications $t_1 \bullet t_2$ have the same static semantics, and that error can be assigned any type. In the sequel, we are only concerned with well-typed terms, i.e., terms for which, in a given environment Γ, there is at least one type τ with $\Gamma \vdash e : \tau$. The type system of Fig. 2 is referred to as the underlying type system.

ELEMENTARY RELEVANCE TYPING

Let us now consider a simple approach to strictness analysis that makes use of a nonstandard type system for keeping track of relevance. Similar systems have been considered by Wright [42] and Amtoft [1]; the presentation below is largely inspired by Walker [41].

We will use the analysis to drive program transformations that safely replace nonstrict function applications by strict applications. Here, "safely" means "without changing the meaning of the program". For now, we will only deal with transformations of programs that themselves do not already contain strict function applications. In Sect. 5 and Sect. 6, we will then admit strict applications in source programs as well and show that dealing with these in an adequate manner is actually quite involved.

Annotated Types

A variable x is relevant to a term t if any term bound to x is guaranteed to be evaluated whenever t is evaluated. We say that an abstraction $\lambda x.t_1$ is a relevant abstraction if its formal parameter x is relevant to its body t_1.

To distinguish between expressions that evaluate to relevant abstractions and expressions that evaluate to abstractions that may not be relevant, we introduce annotated types,

$\widehat{\tau} \in \widehat{\mathbf{Type}}$ annotated types,

given by

$\widehat{\tau} ::= \text{bool} \mid \text{nat} \mid \widehat{\tau}_1 \xrightarrow{\varphi} \widehat{\tau}_2$.

That is, an annotated type $\widehat{\tau}$ is either one of the base types bool and nat or else a function type $\widehat{\tau}_1 \xrightarrow{\varphi} \widehat{\tau}_2$ where φ ranges over annotations,

$\varphi \in \mathbf{Ann}$ annotations,

for which we have

$\varphi ::= \mathsf{S} \mid \mathsf{L}$.

In our analysis, the annotation S is used to designate the types of terms that, when successfully evaluated to weak head normal form, produce relevant abstractions, while L is used to annotate the types of terms that may or may not produce relevant abstractions.

As an illustration of how to assign annotated types, consider the terms λx.x and λx. true. The former term denotes a relevant abstraction, whereas the latter does not. Hence, for any annotated type $\widehat{\tau}$, the type $\widehat{\tau} \xrightarrow{\mathsf{S}} \widehat{\tau}$ would be a valid type for λx.x, while λx. true should always receive a type of the form $\widehat{\tau} \xrightarrow{\mathsf{L}}$ bool.

Note that relevance implies strictness: if a variable x is relevant to a term t, then t is strict in x and, so, relevant abstractions denote strict functions.[2] Now, while S and L can thus be thought of as mnemonics for "strict" and "lazy", they can also be taken to stand for "small" and "large" as we will impose a partial order $(\mathbf{Ann}, \sqsubseteq)$ on annotations that is characterised by $\mathsf{S} \sqsubseteq \mathsf{L}$. Hence, $(\mathbf{Ann}, \sqsubseteq)$ is a complete lattice with least element S and greatest element L, and joins and meets given by

[2]However, relevance and strictness are not equivalent: for instance, λx.error is strict but not relevant.

$\mathsf{S} \sqcup \varphi = \varphi$,

$\mathsf{L} \sqcup \varphi = \mathsf{L}$

and

$\mathsf{S} \sqcap \varphi = \mathsf{S}$,

$\mathsf{L} \sqcap \varphi = \varphi$.

Type-Driven Call-By-Value Transformation

Our goal will now be to transform programs by turning as many nonstrict applications of strict functions into strict applications as possible. That is, if for a given nonstrict application $t_1\ t_2$ it can be shown that successfully evaluating t_1 will always result in a relevant abstraction, then we optimise away the assumed overhead of nonstrict evaluation by replacing the application by its strict counterpart $t_1 \bullet t_2$. This optimisation is justified by the observation that from the implied relevance of the function t_1 it follows that, for the application to produce a result, evaluation of the argument t_2 is required anyway.

We define the transformation through rules for deriving judgements of the form $\widehat{\Gamma} \vdash t \rhd t' : \widehat{\tau}^{\varphi}$, expressing that, in the annotated type environment $\widehat{\Gamma}$, the source term t, of type $\widehat{\tau}$ and annotated with φ, can be safely transformed into the target term t'. Here, the annotation φ is used to indicate whether or not the context in which t appears guarantees its evaluation: t is said to be demanded if φ = S. When analysing the body of an abstraction, we will set its annotation to S and observe whether the modelled demand propagates to its parameter: if it does, the abstraction is relevant; if it does not, the abstraction may be irrelevant. Annotated type environments,

$$\widehat{\Gamma} \in \mathbf{TEnv} = \mathbf{Var} \rightarrow_{\text{fin}} \widehat{\mathbf{Type}} \times \mathbf{Ann} \quad \text{annotated type environments},$$

map variables x to pairs $(\widehat{\tau}, \varphi)$ consisting of an annotated type $\widehat{\tau}$ and an annotation φ. Analogously to the unannotated environments from Sect. 3, we write [ ] for the empty environment, $[x \mapsto (\widehat{\tau}, \varphi)]$ for the singleton environment that maps x to $(\widehat{\tau}, \varphi)$, and $\widehat{\Gamma}_1[x \mapsto (\widehat{\tau}, \varphi)]$ for the environment that is obtained by extending $\widehat{\Gamma}_1$ with a binding from x to $(\widehat{\tau}, \varphi)$.

The rules of the transformation relation are given in Fig. 3.

Relevance typing constitutes a so-called substructural typing discipline [41], which is reflected by a careful treatment of type environments throughout the rules. The all-important invariant that we maintain is that any S-annotated variable in an annotated type environment $\widehat{\Gamma}$ is to appear in an S-context at least once. The rules [r-false], [r-true], [r-zero], and [r-error], for instance, require that any constant terms are transformed in an empty type environment. All constants can be typed and transformed in any context; false and true always have the type bool, 0 always has the type nat, and error can be assigned any type. Variables, as per rule schema [r-var], are typed and transformed in singleton environments that agree with the types and annotations assigned.

Interesting is the rule schema for lambda-abstractions, [r-abs]. It states that typing and transforming an abstraction $\lambda x.\ t_1$ depends on the typing and transformation of its body t_1 in a type environment that is extended with a binding for the formal parameter x. As far as deriving the argument and result types τ_1 and τ_2 is concerned, the rule is completely standard; what remains is to consider how annotations are dealt with. To determine whether the parameter x is relevant to the body t_1— and thus whether the abstraction itself is relevant— we “reset” the demand context for t_1 to S. If x can then be annotated with S as well, we conclude that $\lambda x.t_1$ is relevant; otherwise, we classify the abstraction as possibly irrelevant. To ensure that resetting the demand for the body does not propagate to any variables other than the formal parameter, we require that none of the bindings in the original type environment $\widehat{\Gamma}$ carries an annotation that is smaller than the demand φ of the abstraction. Hence, the rule for abstractions includes a so-called containment restriction $\varphi \blacktriangleright \widehat{\Gamma}$, the rules for

Transformation $\qquad \boxed{\widehat{\Gamma} \vdash t \rhd t' : \widehat{\tau}^{\varphi}}$

$$\frac{}{[\,] \vdash \mathsf{false} \rhd \mathsf{false} : \mathsf{bool}^{\varphi}}\ [\textit{r-false}] \qquad \frac{}{[\,] \vdash \mathsf{true} \rhd \mathsf{true} : \mathsf{bool}^{\varphi}}\ [\textit{r-true}]$$

$$\frac{}{[\,] \vdash 0 \rhd 0 : \mathsf{nat}^{\varphi}}\ [\textit{r-zero}] \qquad \frac{}{[x \mapsto (\widehat{\tau}, \varphi)] \vdash x \rhd x : \widehat{\tau}^{\varphi}}\ [\textit{r-var}]$$

$$\frac{\varphi \blacktriangleright \widehat{\Gamma} \quad \widehat{\Gamma}[x \mapsto (\widehat{\tau}_1, \varphi_1)] \vdash t_1 \rhd t_1' : \widehat{\tau}_2^{\mathsf{S}}}{\widehat{\Gamma} \vdash \lambda x.\,t_1 \rhd \lambda x.\,t_1' : (\widehat{\tau}_1 \xrightarrow{\varphi_1} \widehat{\tau}_2)^{\varphi}}\ [\textit{r-abs}]$$

$$\frac{\widehat{\Gamma}_1 \vdash t_1 \rhd t_1' : (\widehat{\tau}_2 \xrightarrow{\mathsf{S}} \widehat{\tau})^{\varphi} \quad \widehat{\Gamma}_2 \vdash t_2 \rhd t_2' : \widehat{\tau}_2^{\varphi}}{\widehat{\Gamma}_1 \diamond \widehat{\Gamma}_2 \vdash t_1\ t_2 \rhd t_1' \bullet t_2' : \widehat{\tau}^{\varphi}}\ [\textit{r-app}_1]$$

$$\frac{\widehat{\Gamma}_1 \vdash t_1 \rhd t_1' : (\widehat{\tau}_2 \xrightarrow{\mathsf{L}} \widehat{\tau})^{\varphi} \quad \widehat{\Gamma}_2 \vdash t_2 \rhd t_2' : \widehat{\tau}_2^{\mathsf{L}}}{\widehat{\Gamma}_1 \diamond \widehat{\Gamma}_2 \vdash t_1\ t_2 \rhd t_1'\ t_2' : \widehat{\tau}^{\varphi}}\ [\textit{r-app}_2]$$

$$\frac{\widehat{\Gamma}_1 \vdash t_1 \rhd t_1' : \mathsf{bool}^{\varphi} \quad \widehat{\Gamma}_2 \vdash t_2 \rhd t_2' : \widehat{\tau}^{\mathsf{L}} \quad \widehat{\Gamma}_2 \vdash t_3 \rhd t_3' : \widehat{\tau}^{\mathsf{L}}}{\widehat{\Gamma}_1 \diamond \widehat{\Gamma}_2 \vdash \mathsf{if}\ t_1\ \mathsf{then}\ t_2\ \mathsf{else}\ t_3 \rhd \mathsf{if}\ t_1'\ \mathsf{then}\ t_2'\ \mathsf{else}\ t_3' : \widehat{\tau}^{\varphi}}\ [\textit{r-if}]$$

$$\frac{\widehat{\Gamma} \vdash t_1 \rhd t_1' : \mathsf{nat}^{\mathsf{L}}}{\widehat{\Gamma} \vdash \mathsf{succ}\ t_1 \rhd \mathsf{succ}\ t_1' : \mathsf{nat}^{\varphi}}\ [\textit{r-succ}] \qquad \frac{\widehat{\Gamma} \vdash t_1 \rhd t_1' : \mathsf{nat}^{\varphi}}{\widehat{\Gamma} \vdash \mathsf{pred}\ t_1 \rhd \mathsf{pred}\ t_1' : \mathsf{nat}^{\varphi}}\ [\textit{r-pred}]$$

$$\frac{\widehat{\Gamma} \vdash t_1 \rhd t_1' : \mathsf{nat}^{\varphi}}{\widehat{\Gamma} \vdash \mathsf{iszero}\ t_1 \rhd \mathsf{iszero}\ t_1' : \mathsf{bool}^{\varphi}}\ [\textit{r-iszero}]$$

$$\frac{}{[\,] \vdash \mathsf{error} \rhd \mathsf{error} : \widehat{\tau}^{\varphi}}\ [\textit{r-error}] \qquad \frac{\widehat{\Gamma} \vdash t \rhd t' : \widehat{\tau}^{\mathsf{L}}}{\widehat{\Gamma} \vdash t \rhd t' : \widehat{\tau}^{\mathsf{S}}}\ [\textit{r-sub}] \qquad \frac{\widehat{\Gamma}_1 \vdash t \rhd t' : \widehat{\tau}^{\varphi}}{\widehat{\Gamma}_1[x \mapsto (\widehat{\tau}_0, \mathsf{L})] \vdash t \rhd t' : \widehat{\tau}^{\varphi}}\ [\textit{r-weak}]$$

Figure. 3 Relevance typing and call-by-value transformation.

Containment $\qquad \boxed{\varphi \blacktriangleright \widehat{\Gamma}}$

$$\frac{}{\varphi \blacktriangleright [\,]}\ [\textit{c-nil}] \qquad \frac{\mathsf{S} \blacktriangleright \widehat{\Gamma}_1}{\mathsf{S} \blacktriangleright \widehat{\Gamma}_1[x \mapsto (\widehat{\tau}, \varphi_0)]}\ [\textit{c-cons-s}] \qquad \frac{\mathsf{L} \blacktriangleright \widehat{\Gamma}_1}{\mathsf{L} \blacktriangleright \widehat{\Gamma}_1[x \mapsto (\widehat{\tau}, \mathsf{L})]}\ [\textit{c-cons-l}]$$

Figure. 4 Containment.

which are given in Fig. 4. Note in particular that $L \blacktriangleright \widehat{\Gamma}$ if and only if all bindings in $\widehat{\Gamma}$ carry the annotation L.

There are two rule schemata that deal with nonstrict function applications t_1 t_2. Recall that we are not dealing with strict function applications yet. The first, [r-app$_1$], is applicable whenever the function term t_1 can be assigned an S-annotated function type and thus constitutes a strict function. Then, the argument t_2 is demanded whenever the result of the application is and, hence, the demand φ of the application propagates to t_2. Importantly, here we seize on the opportunity and transform the nonstrict application t_1 t_2 into the strict application $t_1' \bullet t_2'$. The second schema, [r-app$_2$], deals with the application t_1 t_2 of a possibly nonstrict function t_1. In that case, there are no guarantees about the demand for the argument and so t_2 receives the demand L. Both rules, of course, require that the type τ_2 of the argument matches the argument type of the function and that the type τ of the application equals the result type of the function. Moreover, both rules insist that the environment in which the application is analysed corresponds to the pointwise meet $\widehat{\Gamma}_1 \diamond \widehat{\Gamma}_2$ of the environments $\widehat{\Gamma}_1$ and $\widehat{\Gamma}_2$ in which, respectively, the subterms t_1 and t_2 are analysed. That is, $\cdot \diamond \cdot$ is a partial operation on annotated type environments with:

$$[\,] \diamond [\,] = [\,],$$
$$\widehat{\Gamma}_{11}[x \mapsto (\widehat{\tau}, \varphi_1)] \diamond \widehat{\Gamma}_{21}[x \mapsto (\widehat{\tau}, \varphi_2)] = (\widehat{\Gamma}_{11} \diamond \widehat{\Gamma}_{21})[x \mapsto (\widehat{\tau}, \varphi_1 \sqcap \varphi_2)].$$

This "context split" [8] reflects that a variable is relevant to t_1 t_2 if its relevance can be established in at least one of the subanalyses for t_1 and t_2. The same operation is used in the rule schema for conditionals, [r-if], in which the type environment is split in two parts: one for the guard and one for the conditional branches. As only one of them will be evaluated, both branches are analysed in an L-context.

The rules [r-succ], [r-pred], and [r-iszero] are straightforward. Operands t_1 in succ t_1 receive L-contexts to reflect that weak head normal form has been reached when a successor operation is produced.

The rule [r-sub] implements subeffecting [36] and, by enabling derivations to selectively "forget" about the demand of an expression, allows for more programs to be considered well-typed and hence transformable. Intuitively, it states that any conclusions that may be drawn from the assumption that a term is not demanded are still valid if the term is in fact demanded.

Finally, the weakening rule [r-weak], expresses that any transformation that is derivable in a given annotated type environment $\widehat{\Gamma}_1$ that does not contain a binding for a variable x can also be derived in an annotated type environment that is obtained by adding an L-annotated binding for x to $\widehat{\Gamma}_1$.

Examples

Let us now consider two examples of transformations in our system. First, consider the term

$$(\lambda x.\lambda y.x)\ \mathsf{true}\ \mathsf{false}$$

and its transformation into

$$((\lambda x.\lambda y.x) \bullet \mathsf{true})\ \mathsf{false},$$

justified by the following derivation of

$$[\,] \vdash \lambda x.\lambda y.x \rhd \lambda x.\lambda y.x : (\mathsf{bool} \xrightarrow{S} \mathsf{bool} \xrightarrow{L} \mathsf{bool})^S$$

in our system (the target terms are omitted for clarity):

$$\frac{\dfrac{}{S \blacktriangleright [\,]} \qquad \dfrac{\dfrac{}{S \blacktriangleright [x \mapsto (\mathsf{bool}, S)]} \qquad \dfrac{\dfrac{}{[x \mapsto (\mathsf{bool}, S)] \vdash x : \mathsf{bool}^S}}{[x \mapsto (\mathsf{bool}, S)][y \mapsto (\mathsf{bool}, L)] \vdash x : \mathsf{bool}^S}}{[x \mapsto (\mathsf{bool}, S)] \vdash \lambda y.x : (\mathsf{bool} \xrightarrow{L} \mathsf{bool})^S}}{[\,] \vdash \lambda x.\lambda y.x : (\mathsf{bool} \xrightarrow{S} \mathsf{bool} \xrightarrow{L} \mathsf{bool})^S}$$

Here, the assigned typed $(\mathsf{bool} \xrightarrow{S} \mathsf{bool} \xrightarrow{L} \mathsf{bool})$ reflects that the function that is produced by λx. λy.x is strict in its first argument. Hence, the innermost application in

$(\lambda x.\lambda y.x)\ \mathsf{true}\ \mathsf{false}$ can be transformed into a strict application.

As an example of a case in which the use of subeffecting is crucial, consider the analysis of the term

$$\lambda x.\,(\lambda y.\,\mathsf{true})\ (\lambda z.\,x).$$

As the abstraction λy. true results in a lazy function, the function argument λz. x must be analysed in an L-context. The containment restriction for λz. x then prescribes that x, in the type environment for the abstraction, has to be L-annotated. However, because the body of the abstraction must be analysed in an S-context, we have to somehow be able to derive the judgement

$[x \mapsto (\widehat{\tau}, L)] \vdash x \rhd x : \widehat{\tau}^S$ for some annotated type $\widehat{\tau}$. Here, subeffecting allows us to obtain the desired judgement from the trivially fulfilled premise

$$[x \mapsto (\widehat{\tau}, L)] \vdash x \rhd x : \widehat{\tau}^L.$$

DEALING WITH STRICT APPLICATIONS

The call-by-value transformation in the previous section has a somewhat limited scope in that it does not support the transformation of expressions that include strict applications: in our relevance type system of Sect. 4.2 such expressions are simply considered ill-typed. As a result, the source language for the transformation does not quite model real-world languages such as Haskell and Clean. In this section, we will try to overcome this limitation by admitting strict applications in source terms. Naturally, when doing so, we want to make sure that transformation remains safe. Moreover, we want the transformation to be effective, in the sense that it is able to pick up on the increase in strictness that is induced by strict applications and have the resulting stricterness propagate.

At first glance, the task at hand seems as simple as adding one or two appropriate rules for strict applications to the type system: below, we will describe two of the most straightforward approaches. However, as it turns out, these are either safe but ineffective (Sect. 5.1) or effective but unsafe (Sect. 5.2).

A Conservative Approach

Arguably the simplest way to extend the transformation with support for strict applications is to treat strict applications as if they were nonstrict applications. That is, we add two rules,

$$\frac{\widehat{\Gamma}_1 \vdash t_1 \rhd t_1' : (\widehat{\tau}_2 \xrightarrow{S} \widehat{\tau})^{\varphi} \qquad \widehat{\Gamma}_2 \vdash t_2 \rhd t_2' : \widehat{\tau}_2^{\varphi}}{\widehat{\Gamma}_1 \diamond \widehat{\Gamma}_2 \vdash t_1 \bullet t_2 \rhd t_1' \bullet t_2' : \widehat{\tau}^{\varphi}}$$

and

$$\frac{\widehat{\Gamma}_1 \vdash t_1 \rhd t_1' : (\widehat{\tau}_2 \xrightarrow{\mathsf{L}} \widehat{\tau})^{\varphi} \quad \widehat{\Gamma}_2 \vdash t_2 \rhd t_2' : \widehat{\tau}_2^{\mathsf{L}}}{\widehat{\Gamma}_1 \diamond \widehat{\Gamma}_2 \vdash t_1 \bullet t_2 \rhd t_1' \bullet t_2' : \widehat{\tau}^{\varphi}},$$

that are identical to the rules [r-app$_1$] and [r-app$_2$] except that they deal with strict applications rather than nonstrict applications.

However, while these additions do bring strict applications in scope of the transformation and perserve its safety, they do not enable us to profit from any increase in strictness caused by the use of strict application. For example, the rules cannot derive the relevance of the following abstraction (cf. Sect. 2),

$$\lambda z.\,(((\lambda x.\,\lambda y.\,x)\ \mathsf{true}) \bullet z), \qquad (1)$$

and, hence, nonstrict applications of this abstraction are unaffected by associated call-byvalue transformations—even though it would be completely safe to replace them by strict applications.

A More Ambitious Attempt

To be able to have •-induced increases in strictness propagate, we must record that a strict application always evaluates its argument in order to produce a result. In other words, that the argument of a strict application is demanded whenever the result of the application is. This can be easily expressed by means of a single transformation rule for strict application:

$$\frac{\widehat{\Gamma}_1 \vdash t_1 \rhd t_1' : (\widehat{\tau}_2 \xrightarrow{\varphi_0} \widehat{\tau})^{\varphi} \quad \widehat{\Gamma}_2 \vdash t_2 \rhd t_2' : \widehat{\tau}_2^{\varphi}}{\widehat{\Gamma}_1 \diamond \widehat{\Gamma}_2 \vdash t_1 \bullet t_2 \rhd t_1' \bullet t_2' : \widehat{\tau}^{\varphi}}.$$

Note how this rule resembles the rule for nonstrict applications of strict functions, [r-app$_1$], with the notable exception that the actual relevance φ_0 of the function expression t_1 is completely ignored here.

This new rule seems to capture the semantics of strict application much better than the rules that we considered in the previous subsection and, indeed, we are now able to derive that abstractions like expression (1) above are relevant, effectively enabling local increases in strictness to propagate. Unfortunately, and perhaps surprisingly, addition of the rule completely breaks the transformation system! To see this, consider the abstraction

$$\lambda x.\,((\lambda y.\,0) \bullet (\lambda z.\,x)) \qquad (2)$$

and note that it is lazy in its argument x; in particular, that the application

$$(\lambda x.\,((\lambda y.\,0) \bullet (\lambda z.\,x)))\ \mathsf{error} \qquad (3)$$

evaluates to the numeral 0, while evaluation of the stricter

$$(\lambda x.\,((\lambda y.\,0) \bullet (\lambda z.\,x))) \bullet \mathsf{error} \qquad (4)$$

obviously fails. Still, with the suggested rule for strict applications we can derive that $\lambda x.\,((\lambda y.\,0) \bullet (\lambda z.\,x))$ has type $\widehat{\tau} \xrightarrow{\mathsf{S}}$ nat for any annotated type $\widehat{\tau}$:

$$\frac{\dfrac{}{\mathsf{S} \blacktriangleright [\,]} \quad \dfrac{\dfrac{\vdots}{[x \mapsto (\widehat{\tau}, \mathsf{L})] \vdash \lambda y.\,0 : ((\widehat{\tau}_0 \xrightarrow{\mathsf{L}} \widehat{\tau}) \xrightarrow{\mathsf{L}} \mathsf{nat})^{\mathsf{S}}} \quad \dfrac{\dfrac{\mathsf{S} \blacktriangleright [\,]}{\mathsf{S} \blacktriangleright [x \mapsto (\widehat{\tau}, \mathsf{S})]} \quad \dfrac{\overline{[x \mapsto (\widehat{\tau}, \mathsf{S})] \vdash x : \widehat{\tau}^{\mathsf{S}}}}{[x \mapsto (\widehat{\tau}, \mathsf{S})][z \mapsto (\widehat{\tau}_0, \mathsf{L})] \vdash x : \widehat{\tau}^{\mathsf{S}}}}{[x \mapsto (\widehat{\tau}, \mathsf{S})] \vdash \lambda z.\,x : (\widehat{\tau}_0 \xrightarrow{\mathsf{L}} \widehat{\tau})^{\mathsf{S}}}}{[x \mapsto (\widehat{\tau}, \mathsf{S})] \vdash (\lambda y.\,0) \bullet (\lambda z.\,x) : \mathsf{nat}^{\mathsf{S}}}}{[\,] \vdash \lambda x.\,((\lambda y.\,0) \bullet (\lambda z.\,x)) : (\widehat{\tau} \xrightarrow{\mathsf{S}} \mathsf{nat})^{\mathsf{S}}}$$

That is, we can—wrongfully—derive that term (2) is a relevant abstraction. As a result, it allows term (3) to be transformed into term (4)—which is clearly unsafe.

Now, with such transformations admitted, the proposed rule for strict applications is of course not fit for inclusion in our system. However, rather than completely abandoning the proposed approach to dealing with strict applications, in the next section we will analyse exactly what prohibits the resulting transformation from being safe and show what can be done to compensate. This will lead us to an extension of the original system that is more involved than the extensions considered in the present section—but that is both safe and effective.

A REFINED APPROACH TO RELEVANCE TYPING

In the previous section, we have seen that safely extending the transformation system of Sect. 4 with support for eager function applications in the source language does not require much effort in itself (Sect. 5.1); but also that our desire to have the system reflect the semantics of these eager applications apparently complicates matters considerably (Sect. 5.2). And, indeed, there is no such thing as a free lunch: in this section, we show how transformations that are both safe and faithful to the nature of eager applications can be realised at the cost of extending the system in more essential ways than those that we have considered before. As it turns out, the key to success lies in establishing where the approach of Sect. 5.2 went wrong.

Stocktaking

Let us have a closer look at how the derivation tree for term (2) in Sect. 5.2,

$$\frac{\dfrac{}{\mathsf{S} \blacktriangleright [\,]} \quad \dfrac{\dfrac{\vdots}{[x \mapsto (\widehat{\tau}, \mathsf{L})] \vdash \lambda y.\,0 : ((\widehat{\tau}_0 \xrightarrow{\mathsf{L}} \widehat{\tau}) \xrightarrow{\mathsf{L}} \mathsf{nat})^{\mathsf{S}}} \quad \dfrac{\dfrac{\mathsf{S} \blacktriangleright [\,]}{\mathsf{S} \blacktriangleright [x \mapsto (\widehat{\tau}, \mathsf{S})]} \quad \dfrac{\overline{[x \mapsto (\widehat{\tau}, \mathsf{S})] \vdash x : \widehat{\tau}^{\mathsf{S}}}}{[x \mapsto (\widehat{\tau}, \mathsf{S})][z \mapsto (\widehat{\tau}_0, \mathsf{L})] \vdash x : \widehat{\tau}^{\mathsf{S}}}}{[x \mapsto (\widehat{\tau}, \mathsf{S})] \vdash \lambda z.\,x : (\widehat{\tau}_0 \xrightarrow{\mathsf{L}} \widehat{\tau})^{\mathsf{S}}}}{[x \mapsto (\widehat{\tau}, \mathsf{S})] \vdash (\lambda y.\,0) \bullet (\lambda z.\,x) : \mathsf{nat}^{\mathsf{S}}}}{[\,] \vdash \lambda x.\,((\lambda y.\,0) \bullet (\lambda z.\,x)) : (\widehat{\tau} \xrightarrow{\mathsf{S}} \mathsf{nat})^{\mathsf{S}}},$$

enabled us to inappropriately conclude that the given abstraction was relevant. To do so, it had to derive that the formal parameter x of the abstraction was relevant to its body. Since the body is an application, this is achieved by deriving that x is relevant to at least one of the two subterms of the application. Clearly, x cannot be relevant to the function term λy. 0 as it does not even occur in it. The only possibility left is then to establish that x is relevant to the argument abstraction λz. x. Recall that we always analyse the body of an abstraction as if it were demanded. Then, as x occurs in the body, we can conclude that x is at least locally relevant. As x is a free variable of λz. x, the containment restriction prescribes that this conclusion can only be propagated globally if the abstraction λz. x is itself demanded. However, as the demand for λz. x is implied by its use as an argument in a demanded strict application, the containment restriction is met trivially and so we indeed derive that x is relevant to (λy. 0) • (λz. x).

Now—where did we go wrong? A moment's reflection reveals that, with a progressive rule for strict applications in place, the containment restriction does not serve its purpose anymore. It was there to ensure that we could not conclude that a term bound to a free variable of an abstraction was demanded while, in fact, it was not. Still, that is exactly what happened for the free variable x of λz. x in the derivation in Sect. 5.2. So, why is the containment restriction adequate in the language of Sect. 4, but not in the language of Sect. 5.2?

The answer lies in the observation that, if we leave strict applications out of the source language, an abstraction can only ever be considered demanded if it can be guaranteed to appear in the function position of an application at least once during evaluation. In simpler terms: the only way to force the evaluation of a function is to apply it to an argument. Thus, if the evaluation of a function is forced, then it is applied to an argument and if it is applied to an argument, then its body is evaluated. Hence, the demands for an abstraction and its body coincide, and this invariant is exploited by the containment restriction: if an abstraction is demanded, then so are all variables that are relevant to its body.

Note that the coinciding of demands for an abstraction and its body is reflected by the inability of nonstrict lambda-calculi to distinguish between ⊥ and λx.⊥. However, as we demonstrated in Sect. 2, with constructs like seq this is no longer the case. Indeed, with strict applications in the source language, we can force the evaluation of an abstraction without ever evaluating its body and this is what happens to λz. x in the expression (λy. 0) • (λz. x). In our relevance type system this is reflected as follows: for the original language, parameter types are permitted to be annotated with S only if the corresponding parameters are relevant to the bodies of their functions. However, with the suggested rule for strict applications, Sannotations can cross over to the environments of abstractions even if they are irrelevant to these abstractions.

These considerations suggest replacing the containment restriction by either a stronger constraint that does not allow free variables to be relevant to an abstraction, or a more refined constraint that takes into account why abstractions are demanded. The first of these options is easy to realise but gives rise to transformations that are even less effective than the conservative transformations of Sect. 5.1, as it would prevent us from detecting the strictness of curried functions in any but the last of their arguments. For example, to type λx. λy. x, we first have to analyse the inner abstraction λy. x in which x occurs free. If we can no longer assign x an S-annotation there, then we cannot derive that it is relevant to the outer abstraction. Below, we shall therefore proceed along the path of the second option and extend our relevance typing discipline with a facility for recording which functions are guaranteed to be applied to arguments.

Type-driven call-by-value Transformation (Revised)

In the transformation system of Sect. 4, we used annotations S and L to keep track of whether or not terms were demanded by their contexts. We will now refine the transformation system and have these annotations also indicate the applicativeness of terms. We say that a term is applicative if it is guaranteed to be applied to an argument at least once. We will repeat the essential parts of the development of Sect. 4 for our refined system and call attention to any differences with respect to the original system.

Let us start with the annotations. Since we are using the same set of annotations {S, L} to express both demand and applicativeness, we commit to the convention that annotations are ranged over by the metavariable φ if they are used to indicate demand and by the metavariable ψ if they are used to indicate applicativeness:

$\varphi, \psi \in \mathbf{Ann}$ annotations,

$\varphi, \psi ::= \mathsf{S} \mid \mathsf{L}.$

When expressing applicativeness, the smaller annotation S is to be read as "guaranteed to be applied to an argument" and the larger annotation L as "may not be applied to an argument".

As before, we let $\widehat{\tau}$ range over annotated types,

$\widehat{\tau} \in \widehat{\mathbf{Type}}$ annotated types.

Function types are now decorated with information about the applicativeness of the arguments and results of functions:

$\widehat{\tau} ::= \mathsf{bool} \mid \mathsf{nat} \mid \widehat{\tau}_1^{\psi_1} \xrightarrow{\varphi} \widehat{\tau}_2^{\psi_2}.$

Furthermore, annotated type environments now map from variables x to triples $(\widehat{\tau}, \varphi, \psi)$, consisting of an annotated type $\widehat{\tau}$, a demand annotation φ, and an annotation ψ that reflects the applicativeness of any expressions bound to x:

$\widehat{\Gamma} \in \widehat{\mathbf{TEnv}} = \mathbf{Var} \to_{\text{fin}} \widehat{\mathbf{Type}} \times \mathbf{Ann} \times \mathbf{Ann}$ annotated type environments.

The judgements of the refined transformation relation read

$$\widehat{\Gamma} \vdash t \rhd t' : \widehat{\tau}^{(\varphi,\psi)},$$

where the annotation ψ indicates the applicativeness of the term t. Note that applicativeness implies relevance: if an expression can be guaranteed to be applied to an argument, it can also be guaranteed to be evaluated. Therefore, in our refined transformation system, we maintain the invariant that whenever we have that $\widehat{\Gamma} \vdash t \rhd t' : \widehat{\tau}^{(\varphi,\psi)}$, it holds that $\varphi \sqsubseteq \psi$.

The rules for deriving judgements of the given form are listed in Fig. 5. The rules for constants—[r-false], [r-true], and [r-zero]—express that constants can never appear in contexts in which they are applied to arguments. In rule [r-var] the applicativeness of variables is obtained from the environment.

Crucially, in the rule for abstractions, [r-abs], the containment restriction is dominated by applicativeness rather than demand: terms bound to the free variables that are relevant to the body of an abstraction are only guaranteed to be demanded if the abstraction itself is guaranteed to be applied. The rules for deriving containment need to be updated as well to reflect that type environments now also contain annotations for applicativeness: see Fig. 6. The refined transformation system has three rules for applications, which all make use of a revised context-split operation:

$$
\begin{aligned}
[\,] \diamond [\,] &= [\,].\\
\widehat{\Gamma}_{11}[x \mapsto (\widehat{\tau}, \varphi_1, \psi_1)] \diamond \widehat{\Gamma}_{21}[x \mapsto (\widehat{\tau}, \varphi_2, \psi_2)] &= (\widehat{\Gamma}_{11} \diamond \widehat{\Gamma}_{21})[x \mapsto (\widehat{\tau}, \varphi_1 \sqcap \varphi_2, \psi_1 \sqcap \psi_2)].
\end{aligned}
$$

In each of the rules [r-app$_1$], [r-app$_2$], and [r-sapp], the applicativeness of the function term t_1 follows from the demand for the application. In the two rules for nonstrict applications, the applicativeness of the argument term t_2 is obtained by taking the join of the demand for the application and the applicativeness of arguments of t_1. That is, arguments are guaranteed to be used applicatively if the application is guaranteed to be performed and the function is guaranteed to use its argument applicatively. In the case for strict applications, we ignore, as we did in Sect. 5.2, the strictness of the function expression t_1 and propagate the demand for the application directly to the argument term t_2; furthermore, the applicativeness of t_2 is obtained by combining the demand φ for the application and the applicativeness ψ_2 of the parameter of t_1.

Transformation $\qquad \boxed{\widehat{\Gamma} \vdash t \triangleright t' : \widehat{\tau}^{(\varphi,\psi)}}$

$$
\frac{}{[\,] \vdash \mathsf{false} \triangleright \mathsf{false} : \mathsf{bool}^{(\varphi,\mathsf{L})}}\ [\textit{r-false}]
\qquad
\frac{}{[\,] \vdash \mathsf{true} \triangleright \mathsf{true} : \mathsf{bool}^{(\varphi,\mathsf{L})}}\ [\textit{r-true}]
$$

$$
\frac{}{[\,] \vdash 0 \triangleright 0 : \mathsf{nat}^{(\varphi,\mathsf{L})}}\ [\textit{r-zero}]
\qquad
\frac{}{[x \mapsto (\widehat{\tau}, \varphi, \psi)] \vdash x \triangleright x : \widehat{\tau}^{(\varphi,\psi)}}\ [\textit{r-var}]
$$

$$
\frac{\psi \blacktriangleright \widehat{\Gamma} \quad \widehat{\Gamma}[x \mapsto (\widehat{\tau}_1, \varphi_1, \psi_1)] \vdash t_1 \triangleright t_1' : \widehat{\tau}_2^{(\mathsf{S},\psi_2)}}{\widehat{\Gamma} \vdash \lambda x.\, t_1 \triangleright \lambda x.\, t_1' : (\widehat{\tau}_1^{\psi_1} \xrightarrow{\varphi_1} \widehat{\tau}_2^{\psi_2})^{(\varphi,\psi)}}\ [\textit{r-abs}]
$$

$$
\frac{\widehat{\Gamma}_1 \vdash t_1 \triangleright t_1' : (\widehat{\tau}_2^{\psi_2} \xrightarrow{\mathsf{S}} \widehat{\tau}^{\psi})^{(\varphi,\varphi)} \quad \widehat{\Gamma}_2 \vdash t_2 \triangleright t_2' : \widehat{\tau}_2^{(\varphi,\varphi \sqcup \psi_2)}}{\widehat{\Gamma}_1 \diamond \widehat{\Gamma}_2 \vdash t_1\ t_2 \triangleright t_1' \bullet t_2' : \widehat{\tau}^{(\varphi,\psi)}}\ [\textit{r-app}_1]
$$

$$
\frac{\widehat{\Gamma}_1 \vdash t_1 \triangleright t_1' : (\widehat{\tau}_2^{\psi_2} \xrightarrow{\mathsf{L}} \widehat{\tau}^{\psi})^{(\varphi,\varphi)} \quad \widehat{\Gamma}_2 \vdash t_2 \triangleright t_2' : \widehat{\tau}_2^{(\mathsf{L},\varphi \sqcup \psi_2)}}{\widehat{\Gamma}_1 \diamond \widehat{\Gamma}_2 \vdash t_1\ t_2 \triangleright t_1'\ t_2' : \widehat{\tau}^{(\varphi,\psi)}}\ [\textit{r-app}_2]
$$

$$
\frac{\widehat{\Gamma}_1 \vdash t_1 \triangleright t_1' : (\widehat{\tau}_2^{\psi_2} \xrightarrow{\varphi_0} \widehat{\tau}^{\psi})^{(\varphi,\varphi)} \quad \widehat{\Gamma}_2 \vdash t_2 \triangleright t_2' : \widehat{\tau}_2^{(\varphi,\varphi \sqcup \psi_2)}}{\widehat{\Gamma}_1 \diamond \widehat{\Gamma}_2 \vdash t_1 \bullet t_2 \triangleright t_1' \bullet t_2' : \widehat{\tau}^{(\varphi,\psi)}}\ [\textit{r-sapp}]
$$

$$
\frac{\widehat{\Gamma}_1 \vdash t_1 \triangleright t_1' : \mathsf{bool}^{(\varphi,\mathsf{L})} \quad \widehat{\Gamma}_2 \vdash t_2 \triangleright t_2' : \widehat{\tau}^{(\mathsf{L},\psi)} \quad \widehat{\Gamma}_2 \vdash t_3 \triangleright t_3' : \widehat{\tau}^{(\mathsf{L},\psi)}}{\widehat{\Gamma}_1 \diamond \widehat{\Gamma}_2 \vdash \mathsf{if}\ t_1\ \mathsf{then}\ t_2\ \mathsf{else}\ t_3 \triangleright \mathsf{if}\ t_1'\ \mathsf{then}\ t_2'\ \mathsf{else}\ t_3' : \widehat{\tau}^{(\varphi,\psi)}}\ [\textit{r-if}]
$$

$$
\frac{\widehat{\Gamma} \vdash t_1 \triangleright t_1' : \mathsf{nat}^{(\mathsf{L},\mathsf{L})}}{\widehat{\Gamma} \vdash \mathsf{succ}\ t_1 \triangleright \mathsf{succ}\ t_1' : \mathsf{nat}^{(\varphi,\mathsf{L})}}\ [\textit{r-succ}]
\qquad
\frac{\widehat{\Gamma} \vdash t_1 \triangleright t_1' : \mathsf{nat}^{(\varphi,\mathsf{L})}}{\widehat{\Gamma} \vdash \mathsf{pred}\ t_1 \triangleright \mathsf{pred}\ t_1' : \mathsf{nat}^{(\varphi,\mathsf{L})}}\ [\textit{r-pred}]
$$

$$
\frac{\widehat{\Gamma} \vdash t_1 \triangleright t_1' : \mathsf{nat}^{(\varphi,\mathsf{L})}}{\widehat{\Gamma} \vdash \mathsf{iszero}\ t_1 \triangleright \mathsf{iszero}\ t_1' : \mathsf{bool}^{(\varphi,\mathsf{L})}}\ [\textit{r-iszero}]
$$

$$
\frac{}{[\,] \vdash \mathsf{error} \triangleright \mathsf{error} : \widehat{\tau}^{(\varphi,\psi)}}\ [\textit{r-error}]
\qquad
\frac{\widehat{\Gamma} \vdash t \triangleright t' : \widehat{\tau}^{(\mathsf{L},\mathsf{L})}}{\widehat{\Gamma} \vdash t \triangleright t' : \widehat{\tau}^{(\mathsf{S},\psi)}}\ [\textit{r-sub}]
$$

$$
\frac{\widehat{\Gamma}_1 \vdash t \triangleright t' : \widehat{\tau}^{(\varphi,\psi)}}{\widehat{\Gamma}_1[x \mapsto (\widehat{\tau}_0, \mathsf{L}, \mathsf{L})] \vdash t \triangleright t' : \widehat{\tau}^{(\varphi,\psi)}}\ [\textit{r-weak}]
$$

Figure. 5 Relevance typing and call-by-value transformation. (Cf. Fig. 3).

Containment $\qquad \boxed{\psi \blacktriangleright \widehat{\Gamma}}$

$$
\frac{}{\psi \blacktriangleright [\,]}\ [\textit{c-nil}]
\qquad
\frac{\mathsf{S} \blacktriangleright \widehat{\Gamma}_1}{\mathsf{S} \blacktriangleright \widehat{\Gamma}_1[x \mapsto (\widehat{\tau}, \varphi_0, \psi_0)]}\ [\textit{c-cons-s}]
\qquad
\frac{\mathsf{L} \blacktriangleright \widehat{\Gamma}_1}{\mathsf{L} \blacktriangleright \widehat{\Gamma}_1[x \mapsto (\widehat{\tau}, \mathsf{L}, \mathsf{L})]}\ [\textit{c-cons-l}]
$$

Figure. 6 Containment. (Cf. Fig. 4).

Adapting the rules for terms of the forms if t_1 then t_2 else t_3, succ t_1, pred t_1, and iszero t_1 is straightforward. Note that Booleans and natural numbers are never to occur in function position and hence can never be used applicatively. Rule [r-error] expresses that whether an occurrence of error is applicative depends on its context.

As expressed by rule [r-sub], subeffecting applies to applicativeness as well as to demand. Similarly, as far as weakening is concerned, by rule [r-weak], no differences arise between the annotations for applicativeness and those for demand.

As an example of how our revised transformation system is indeed faithful to the semantics of strict applications, consider the analysis of term (1),

$\lambda z.\,((\lambda x.\,\lambda y.\,x)\ \mathsf{true} \bullet z),$

from Sect. 5.1:

$$\dfrac{\dfrac{}{\mathsf{L} \blacktriangleright [\,]} \qquad \dfrac{\dfrac{\vdots}{[z \mapsto (\hat{\tau}, \mathsf{L}, \mathsf{L})] \vdash (\lambda x.\,\lambda y.\,x)\ \mathsf{true} : (\hat{\tau}^{\mathsf{L}} \xrightarrow{\mathsf{L}} \mathsf{bool}^{\mathsf{L}})^{(\mathsf{S},\mathsf{S})}} \qquad \dfrac{}{[z \mapsto (\hat{\tau}, \mathsf{S}, \mathsf{L})] \vdash z : \hat{\tau}^{(\mathsf{S},\mathsf{L})}}}{[z \mapsto (\hat{\tau}, \mathsf{S}, \mathsf{L})] \vdash ((\lambda x.\,\lambda y.\,x)\ \mathsf{true}) \bullet z : \mathsf{bool}^{(\mathsf{S},\mathsf{L})}}}{[\,] \vdash \lambda z.\,((\lambda x.\,\lambda y.\,x)\ \mathsf{true} \bullet z) : (\hat{\tau}^{\mathsf{L}} \xrightarrow{\mathsf{S}} \mathsf{bool}^{\mathsf{L}})^{(\mathsf{S},\mathsf{L})}}$$

Even though the subterm (λx. λy. x) true produces a lazy function, reflected by its relevance type $\hat{\tau}^{\mathsf{L}} \xrightarrow{\mathsf{L}} \mathsf{bool}^{\mathsf{L}}$, the argument z of the strict application ((λx. λy. x) true) • z is still assigned the relevance annotation S and so the term as a whole can be recognised as producing a strict function, i.e., a function of relevance type $\hat{\tau}^{\mathsf{L}} \xrightarrow{\mathsf{S}} \mathsf{bool}^{\mathsf{L}}$.

To illustrate that our refined system handles strict applications correctly, reconsider term (2),

$\lambda x.\,((\lambda y.\,0) \bullet (\lambda z.\,x)),$

for which an unsafe derivation was given in Sect. 5.2. As the following derivation shows, the inner abstraction λz. x does not appear in an applicative position and hence the revised containment restriction for this abstraction now forces all bindings in its type environment to be annotated with L exclusively. That is, writing $\hat{\tau}_{\lambda y.0}$ as an abbreviation for the annotated type

$(\hat{\tau}_0^{\mathsf{L}} \xrightarrow{\mathsf{L}} \hat{\tau}^{\mathsf{L}})^{\mathsf{L}} \xrightarrow{\mathsf{L}} \mathsf{nat}^{\mathsf{L}},$

we have

$$\dfrac{\dfrac{}{\mathsf{L} \blacktriangleright [\,]} \qquad \dfrac{\dfrac{\vdots}{[x \mapsto (\hat{\tau}, \mathsf{L}, \mathsf{L})] \vdash \lambda y.\,0 : \hat{\tau}_{\lambda y.0}^{(\mathsf{S},\mathsf{S})}} \qquad \dfrac{\dfrac{\mathsf{L} \blacktriangleright [\,]}{\mathsf{L} \blacktriangleright [x \mapsto (\hat{\tau}, \mathsf{L}, \mathsf{L})]} \qquad \dfrac{\dfrac{\dfrac{}{[x \mapsto (\hat{\tau}, \mathsf{L}, \mathsf{L})] \vdash x : \hat{\tau}^{(\mathsf{L},\mathsf{L})}}}{[x \mapsto (\hat{\tau}, \mathsf{L}, \mathsf{L})] \vdash x : \hat{\tau}^{(\mathsf{S},\mathsf{L})}}}{[x \mapsto (\hat{\tau}, \mathsf{L}, \mathsf{L})][z \mapsto (\hat{\tau}_0, \mathsf{L}, \mathsf{L})] \vdash x : \hat{\tau}^{(\mathsf{S},\mathsf{L})}}}{[x \mapsto (\hat{\tau}, \mathsf{L}, \mathsf{L})] \vdash \lambda z.\,x : (\hat{\tau}_0^{\mathsf{L}} \xrightarrow{\mathsf{L}} \hat{\tau}^{\mathsf{L}})^{(\mathsf{S},\mathsf{L})}}}{[x \mapsto (\hat{\tau}, \mathsf{L}, \mathsf{L})] \vdash (\lambda y.\,0) \bullet (\lambda z.\,x) : \mathsf{nat}^{(\mathsf{S},\mathsf{L})}}}{[\,] \vdash \lambda x.\,((\lambda y.\,0) \bullet (\lambda z.\,x)) : (\hat{\tau}^{\mathsf{L}} \xrightarrow{\mathsf{L}} \mathsf{nat}^{\mathsf{L}})^{(\mathsf{S},\mathsf{L})}}$$

In particular, the variable x can now no longer be considered relevant to the body of the outer abstraction λx.((λy. 0) • (λz. x)) and so we can no longer derive that the function produced by this abstraction is strict.

Properties

The transformations that arise from the revised system can be shown to preserve the behaviour of programs. To this end, let us write t for the term that is obtained by turning all strict applications in t into nonstrict applications.

Theorem 1 (Correctness) If $\hat{\Gamma} \vdash t \rhd t' : \hat{\tau}^{(\mathsf{S},\mathsf{L})}$, then (1) $\lfloor t \rfloor = \lfloor t' \rfloor$, and (2) if t → w for some weak head normal form w, then there exists a weak head normal form w', such that $t' \longrightarrow w'$.

Proof (Sketch.) The first part follows from a trivial structural induction on a derivation of $\hat{\Gamma} \vdash t \rhd t' : \hat{\tau}^{(\varphi,\psi)}$.

For the second part, we first show that in our system well-typed terms can only go wrong if during evaluation the constant error shows up in head position. The property is then demonstrated by induction on a derivation of $\hat{\Gamma} \vdash t \rhd t' : \hat{\tau}^{(\varphi,\psi)}$. The only interesting case is the one for [r-app1] for which we need as an auxiliary result that $\hat{\Gamma} \vdash \lambda x.\,t_0 \rhd t' : (\hat{\tau}_1^{\psi_1} \xrightarrow{\mathsf{S}} \hat{\tau}_2^{\psi_2})^{(\varphi,\psi)}$ implies that during the evaluation of $[x \mapsto t_2]t_0$ the term t_2 is guaranteed to show up in head position.

The required result follows from a lemma for $\hat{\Gamma} \vdash t \rhd t' : \hat{\tau}^{(\mathsf{S},\mathsf{L})}$ that states that, for every $x, \hat{\tau}_0, \varphi_0$, and ψ_0 with $\hat{\Gamma}(x) = (\hat{\tau}_0, \varphi_0, \psi_0)$, $\varphi_0 = \mathsf{S}$ implies that terms substituted for x in t show up in head position during evaluation, while ψ_0 = S implies that such terms show up in function position.

To show that our transformation is indeed applicable to all terms that are well-typed in the underlying type system, including those that contain strict applications, let us write $\lfloor \hat{\tau} \rfloor$ for the underlying type that is obtained by removing all annotations from the annotated type $\hat{\tau}$ and $\lfloor \hat{\Gamma} \rfloor$ for the underlying type environment that is obtained by removing all annotations from the annotated type environment $\hat{\Gamma}$.

Theorem 2 (Conservative Extension)

1. If $\Gamma \vdash t : \tau$, then there exist $\hat{\Gamma}, t', \hat{\tau}, \varphi$, and ψ with = $\lfloor \hat{\Gamma} \rfloor = \Gamma$ and $\lfloor \hat{\tau} \rfloor = \tau$ such that $\hat{\Gamma} \vdash t \rhd t' : \hat{\tau}^{(\varphi,\psi)}$.
2. If $\hat{\Gamma} \vdash t \rhd t' : \hat{\tau}^{(\varphi,\psi)}$, then $\lfloor \hat{\Gamma} \rfloor \vdash t : \lfloor \hat{\tau} \rfloor$ and $\lfloor \hat{\Gamma} \rfloor \vdash t' : \lfloor \hat{\tau} \rfloor$

Proof Trivial structural inductions on derivations of $\Gamma \vdash t : \tau$ and $\hat{\Gamma} \vdash t \rhd t' : \hat{\tau}^{(\varphi,\psi)}$, respectively. For the first part, we simply annotate all terms and bindings with L.

RELATED WORK

While strictness analysis has been around for over two decades, the problem of adapting strictness analysers to deal with seq and the like is ignored by most authors. A notable exception is the article by Schmidt-Schauß et al. [33], who consider the semantics of seq in a safety proof for the strictness analysis of Nöcker [29], which is based on abstract reduction and implemented in the Clean compiler. As far as we are aware, we are the first to consider the problem of extending a relevance-based strictness analysis to deal with both lazy and eager application.

An excellent introduction to substructural type systems is given by Walker [41]. Examples of the application of substructural typing to program analyses other than strictness analysis include work on uniqueness analysis [37] and sharing analysis [15]. The contextsplit operation has been attributed to Cervesato and Pfenning [8] and shows up in recent formulations of uniqueness analysis [14, 38].

Looking through a Curry-Howard lens, relevance type systems are connected to relevance logics [2, 3, 30]. Relevance has been put to use as an approximation of strictness by several authors, most prominently Wright [42], Baker-Finch [4], and Amtoft [1]. While strictness is an extensional property of the functions defined by a program, relevance is an intensional property. Operationally, the focus of relevance type systems is on identifying the needed redexes [5] in a program. Now, whereas conventional relevance typing disciplines are foremost concerned with terms that appear in the argument position of needed betaredexes, our refined system also aims at predicting which terms are guaranteed to appear in function position.

Type-based approaches to strictness analysis that keep track of totality rather than relevance are given by Kuo and Mishra [25], Jensen [21, 22], Benton [6], Solberg Gasser [35], Glynn et al. [13], and Coppo et al. [9]. Of these, only the formulations of Glynn et al. and Coppo et al. can distinguish between diverging functions and functions that produce diverging results. Hence, for the others, when applied to languages with explicit strictness annotations, the drawbacks reported in this paper arise. A general discomfort of totality-based approaches is that, in comparison to relevance-based approaches, it is harder to read off the strictness of functions from their assigned types; on the other hand, totality-based formulations are arguably easier to grasp. However, as this paper specifically deals with type-based strictness analysis based on relevance typing, our refined approach does not directly apply to totality-based systems. Similar observations can be made for more traditional strictness analyses that are expressed as either abstract interpretations [7, 27, 39] or projection analyses [10, 16, 19].

An elaborate exposition of the rôle played by seq in the design of Haskell is given by Hudak et al. [18]. In the process, they point out an interesting point in the design space: having the (indirect) use of seq be reflected in the types assignable to polymorphic functions in order to recover the parametricity property. Seidel and Voigtländer [34], however, demonstrate that the concrete method described by Hudak et al. is flawed and not adequate for regaining parametricity. They then propose an alternative type-based approach that does actually allow for parametricity to be recovered. This approach, which thus serves a somewhat different purpose than ours, is dual to the one taken in the present paper, in the sense that, rather than in establishing that a term is never used as an argument to seq, we are interested in demonstrating that a particular function is used at least once in a context in which it is not an argument to seq.

A precise account of the impact of seq on the so-called free theorems derivable from polymorphic types and some program transformations that are based on these theorems is given by Johann and Voigtländer [23]. Van Eekelen and De Mol [11] discuss how properties derived for lazy programs can be adapted when these programs are decorated with explicit strictness annotations and show how the techniques involved can be incorporated in a proof assistant.

CONCLUSIONS AND FURTHER WORK

We have demonstrated how a relevance type system for a completely lazy language can be adapted to a language with a construct for selectively making programs stricter. We have argued that it is not trivial to keep such an adaptation sound and, at the same time, have it satisfactorily account for the propagation of programmer-induced increases in strictness. In our approach, safe and effective analyses are derived in the context of an extended relevance type system that not only keeps track of demand propagation, but also of the so-called applicativeness of expressions.

While our system can be used as a basis for the design and implementation of typebased strictness analyses for modern lazy functional languages such as Haskell and Clean, it is not yet applicable to such languages as it fails to account for some essential features, such as type polymorphism and algebraic data types. Extending our type system to deal with such features remains future work, as is subjecting the analysis to techniques—such as subtyping and annotation polymorphism [28]—that make it truly applicable to programming in the large. We stress, however, that these extensions are completely orthogonal to the issues focussed on in the present paper and fairly straightforward to implement. The authors are currently planning to have the described approach implemented in a full-scale Haskell compiler; the resulting implementation may then serve as a basis for benchmarks and quantitative comparisons with other realisations of strictness analysis.

While the correctness property that was stated in Sect. 6 captures the main property of a strictness analyser, i.e., that changing nonstrict applications into strict applications does not worsen the termination behaviour of the program under analysis, a stronger property is desirable. We would like to make explicit that our transformation preserves the semantics of terms. That is, if $\widehat{\Gamma} \vdash t \triangleright t' : \widehat{\tau}^{(S,L)}$, then t and t' are contextually equivalent [26].

Another direction for future work follows from the observation that applicativeness implies relevance: if an expression of function type is guaranteed to be applied to an argument, it is also guaranteed to be evaluated. This suggests that all properties of interest can be captured in terms of elements of a single ternary lattice rather than in terms of the squared binary lattice that we implicitly used in the present paper. It would be interesting to see whether a seq-aware strictness analysis can then be elegantly formulated as an abstract interpretation in such a ternary abstract domain.

ACKNOWLEDGEMENTS

This work was generously supported by the Netherlands Organisation for Scientific Research through its project on "Scriptable Compilers" (612.063.406) and initiated while the first author was employed at Utrecht University.

Some early results were presented under the title "Spreading the Joy" on June 3rd, 2009 at the 2009 Symposium on Trends in Functional Programming in Komárno, Slovakia. The present article is a revised version of a paper [17] that was presented on January 19th, 2010 at the 2010 ACM SIGPLAN Workshop on Partial Evaluation and Program Manipulation in Madrid, Spain. The authors wish to express their gratitude to the anonymous reviewers of TFP 2009 and PEPM 2010, and the reviewers and editors of the current volume for their insightful comments and helpful suggestions.

That S and L may serve as mnemonics not only for "strict" and "lazy", but also for "small" and "large" was pointed out to us by Jeroen Fokker.

REFERENCES

1. Amtoft, T.: Minimal thunkification. In: Cousot, P., Falaschi, M., Filé, G., Rauzy, A. (eds.) Static Analysis, Third International Workshop, WSA'93, Proceedings, Padova, Italy, 22–24 September 1993. Lecture Notes

of Computer Science, vol. 724, pp. 218–229. Springer, Berlin (1993)

2. Anderson, A.R., Belnap, N.D. Jr.: Entailment: The Logic of Relevance and Necessity, vol. 1. Princeton University Press, Princeton (1975)

3. Anderson, A.R., Belnap, N.D. Jr., Dunn, J.M.: Entailment: The Logic of Relevance and Necessity, vol. 2. Princeton University Press, Princeton (1992)

4. Baker-Finch, C.A.: Relevant logic and strictness analysis. In: Billaud, M., Castéran, P., Corsini, M.-M., Musumbu, K., Rauzy, A. (eds.) Actes WSA'92 Workshop on Static Analysis (Bordeaux), Laboratoire Bordelais de Recherche en Informatique (LaBRI), Proceedings, 23–25 September 1992. Series Bigre, vols. 81–82, pp. 221–228. Atelier Irisa, Rennes (1992)

5. Barendregt, H.P., Kennaway, R., Klop, J.W., Sleep, M.R.: Needed reduction and spine strategies for the lambda calculus. Inf. Comput. 75(3), 191–231 (1987)

6. Benton, N.: Strictness analysis of lazy functional programs. Ph.D. thesis, University of Cambridge (1992)

7. Burn, G.L., Hankin, C., Abramsky, S.: The theory of strictness analysis for higher order functions. In: Ganzinger, H., Jones, N.D. (eds.) Programs as Data Objects, Proceedings of a Workshop, Copenhagen, Denmark, 17–19 October 1985. Lecture Notes in Computer Science, vol. 217, pp. 42–62. Springer, Berlin (1986)

8. Cervesato, I., Pfenning, F.: A linear logical framework. Inf. Comput. 179(1), 19–75 (2002)

9. Coppo, M., Damiani, F., Giannini, P.: Strictness analysis, totality, and non-standard-type inference. Theor. Comput. Sci. 272(1–2), 69–112 (2002)

10. Davis, K., Wadler, P.: Backwards strictness analysis: Proved and improved. In: Davis, K., Hughes, J. (eds.) Functional Programming, Proceedings of the 1989 Glasgow Workshop, Workshops in Computing, 21–23 August 1989, Fraserburgh, Scotland, UK, pp. 12–30. Springer, Berlin (1990)

11. van Eekelen, M., de Mol, M.: Proof tool support for explicit strictness. In: Butterfield, A., Grelck, C., Huch, F. (eds.) Implementation and Application of Functional Languages, 17th International Workshop, Revised Selected Papers, IFL 2005, Dublin, Ireland, September 19–21. Lecture Notes in Computer Science, vol. 4015, pp. 37–54. Springer, Berlin (2006)

12. Gill, A., Launchbury, J., Jones, S.P.: A short cut to deforestation. In: FPCA'93 Conference on Functional Programming and Computer Architecture, Copenhagen, Denmark, 9–11 June 1993, pp. 223–232. ACM Press, New York (1993)

13. Glynn, K., Stuckey, P.J., Sulzmann, M.: Effective strictness analysis with HORN constraints. In: Cousot, P. (ed.) Static Analysis, 8th International Symposium, SAS 2001, Proceedings, Paris, France, 16–18 July 2001. Lecture Notes in Computer Science, vol. 2126, pp. 73–92. Springer, Berlin (2001)

14. Hage, J., Holdermans, S.: Heap recycling for lazy languages. In: Hatcliff, J., Glück, R., de Moor, O. (eds.) Proceedings of the 2008 ACM SIGPLAN Symposium on Partial Evaluation and Semantics-Based Program Manipulation, PEPM'08, San Francisco, California, USA, 7–8 January 2008, pp. 189–197. ACM Press, New York (2008)

15. Hage, J., Holdermans, S., Middelkoop, A.: A generic usage analysis with subeffect qualifiers. In: Hinze, R., Ramsey, N. (eds.) Proceedings of the 12th ACM SIGPLAN International Conference on Functional Programming, ICFP 2007, Freiburg, Germany, 1–3 October 2007, pp. 235–246. ACM Press, New York (2007)

16. Hinze, R.: Projection-based strictness analysis: theoretical and practical aspects. Ph.D. thesis, Bonn University (1995)

17. Holdermans, S., Hage, J.: Making "stricterness" more relevant. In: Gallagher, J.P., Voigtländer, J. (eds.) Proceedings of the 2010 ACM SIGPLAN Workshop on Partial Evaluation and Program Manipulation, PEPM 2010, Madrid, Spain, 18–19 January 2010, pp. 121–130. ACM Press, New York (2010)

18. Hudak, P., Hughes, J., Jones, S.P., Wadler, P.: A history of Haskell: Being lazy with class. In: Ryder, B.G., Hailpern, B. (eds.) Proceedings of the Third ACM SIGPLAN History of Programming Languages Conference, HOPL-III, San Diego, California, USA, 9–10 June 2007, pp. 1–55. ACM Press, New York (2007)

19. Hughes, J.: Backwards analysis of functional programs. In: Björner, A., Jones, N.D., Ershov, A.P. (eds.) Partial Evaluation and Mixed Computation: Proceedings of the IFIP TC2 Workshop, Gammel Avernaes, Denmark, 18–24 Oct. 1987, pp. 187–208. North-Holland, Amsterdam (1988)

20. Hughes, J.: Why functional programming matters. Comput. J. 32(2), 98–107 (1989)

21. Jensen, T.P.: Strictness analysis in logical form. In: Hughes, J. (ed.) Functional Programming Languages and Computer Architecture, 5th ACM Conference, Proceedings, Cambridge, MA, USA, 26–30 August 1991, pp. 352–366. Springer, Berlin (1991)

22. Jensen, T.P.: Inference of polymorphic and conditional strictness properties. In: POPL'98, Proceedings of the 25th ACM SIGPLAN-SIGACT Symposium on Principles of Programming Languages, 19–21 January 1998, San Diego, CA, USA, pp. 209–221. ACM Press, New York (1998)

23. Johann, P., Voigtländer, J.: The impact of seq on free theorems-based program transformations. Fundam. Inform. 69(1–2), 63–102 (2006)

24. Kahn, G.: Natural semantics. In: Brandenburg, F.-J., Vidal-Naquet, G., Wirsing, M. (eds.) STACS 87, 4th Annual Symposium on Theoretical Aspects of Computer Science, Proceedings, Passau, Germany, 19–21 February 1987. Lecture Notes in Computer Science, vol. 247, pp. 22–39 (1987)

25. Kuo, T.-M., Mishra, P.: Strictness analysis: A new perspective based on type inference. In: FPCA'89, Conference on Functional Programming Languages and Computer Architecture, Imperial College, London,

England, 11–13 September 1989, pp. 260–272. ACM Press, New York (1989)

26. Morris, J.: Lambda-calculus models of programming languages. Ph.D. thesis, Massachusetts Institute of Technology (1968)
27. Mycroft, A.: The theory and practice of transforming call-by-need into call-by-value. In: Robinet, B. (ed.) International Symposium on Programming, Proceedings of the Fourth 'Colloque International sur laProgrammation', Paris, France, 22–24 April 1980. Lecture Notes in Computer Science, vol. 83, pp. 269–281. Springer, Berlin (1980)
28. Nielson, F., Nielson, H.R.: Type and effect systems. In: Olderog, E.-R., Steffen, B. (eds.) Correct System Design, Recent Insight and Advances (to Hans Langmaack on the occasion of his retirement from his professorship at the University of Kiel). Lecture Notes in Computer Science, vol. 1710, pp. 114–136. Springer, Berlin (1999)
29. Nöcker, E.: Strictness analysis using abstract reduction. In: FPCA'93 Conference on Functional Programming Languages and Computer Architecture, Copenhagen, Denmark, 9–11 June 1993, pp. 255– 265. ACM Press, New York (1993)
30. Orlov, I.E.: Ischislenie sovmestimosti predlozhenii. Mat. Sb. 35(3–4), 263–286 (1928)
31. Jones, S.P. (ed.): Haskell 98 Language and Libraries: The Revised Report. Cambridge University Press, Cambridge (2003)
32. Plasmeijer, R., van Eekelen, M.: Concurrent Clean language report—version 1.3. Technical Report CSIR9816, University of Nijmegen (1998)
33. Schmidt-Schauß, M., Sabel, D., Schütz, M.: Safety of Nöcker's strictness analysis. J. Funct. Program. 18(4), 503–551 (2008)
34. Seidel, D., Voigtländer, J.: Refined typing to localize the impact of forced strictness on free theorems. Acta Inform. 48(3), 191–211 (2011)
35. Gasser, K.L.S., Nielson, H.R., Nielson, F.: Strictness and totality analysis. Sci. Comput. Program. 31(1), 113–145 (1998)
36. Talpin, J.-P., Jouvelot, P.: Polymorphic type, region and effect inference. J. Funct. Program. 2(3), 245– 271 (1992)
37. de Vries, E.: Making uniqueness typing less unique. Ph.D. thesis, Trinity College Dublin (2008)
38. de Vries, E., Plasmeijer, R., Abrahamson, D.: Uniqueness typing simplified. In: Chitil, O., Horváth, Z., Zsók, V. (eds.) Implementation and Application of Functional Languages, 19th International Symposium, Revised Selected Papers, IFL 2007, Freiburg, Germany, September 2007. Lecture Notes in Computer Science, vol. 5083, pp. 201–218. Springer, Berlin (2008)
39. Wadler, P.: Strictness analysis on non-flat domains (by abstract interpretation over finite domains). In: Abramsky, S., Hankin, C. (eds.) Abstract Interpretation of Declarative Languages, pp. 266–275. Ellis Horwood, Chichester (1987)
40. Wadler, P.: Theorems for free! In: FPCA'89 Conference on Functional Programming and Computer Architecture, Imperial College, London, England, 11–13 September 1989, pp. 347–359. ACM Press, New York (1989)
41. Walker, D.: Substructural type systems. In: Pierce, B.C. (ed.) Advanced Topics in Types and Programming Languages. The MIT Press, Cambridge (2005)
42. Wright, D.A.: A new technique for strictness analysis. In: Abramsky, S., Maibaum, T. (eds.) TAPSOFT'91: Proceedings of the International Joint Conference on Theory and Practice of Software Development. Vol. 2: Advances in Distributed Computing (ADC) and Colloquium on Combining Paradigms for Software Development (CCPSD), Brighton, UK, 8–12 April 1991. Lecture Notes in Computer Science, vol. 494, pp. 235–258. Springer, Berlin (1991)

CHAPTER 4

A LEAN SPECIFICATION FOR GADTS: SYSTEM F WITH FIRST-CLASS EQUALITY PROOFS

Arie Middelkoop Atze Dijkstra S. Doaitse Swierstra

Department of Information and Computing Sciences, Universiteit Utrecht, Utrecht, Netherlands

ABSTRACT

Generalized Algebraic Data Types are a generalization of Algebraic Data Types with additional type equality constraints. These found their use in many functional programs, including the development of embedded domain specific programming languages and generic programming.

Recently, several authors published novel inference algorithms and corresponding type system specifications. These approaches tend to be more algorithmic than declarative in nature, and tied to a given compiler infrastructure. This results in complex specifications. For a language implementor, adopting such a complex approach is hard, due to conflicting infrastructure and language features. Similarly, type inference is difficult to comprehend for a programmer when the specification is complex.

To make the integration of GADTs in languages easier, we thus need a more orthogonal specification. We present an orthogonal specification for GADTs: the language System $F_{\sim}$, consisting of System F augmented with first-class equality proofs. This specification exploits the Church encoding of data types to describe GADT matches in terms of conventional lambda abstractions.

INTRODUCTION

Generalized Algebraic Data Types (GADTs) allow for additional equalities to hold between types of a data constructor. These equalities must hold when constructing a value with this data constructor. When a match against this constructor succeeds in a pattern match, these equalities hold between the types of the constructor, and may be used to coerce the type of an expression to an equivalent type.

This particular feature found many application areas. Many Haskell-related projects make use of GADTs, such as a diversity of generic programming approaches [6], and transformations on typed abstract syntax for the implementation of domain-specific languages [2]. Therefore, we added support for GADTs in UHC [5], the Haskell compiler that we develop at Universiteit Utrecht.

Dijkstra [4] describes the implementation of UHC as a combination of many specifications. Similarly, we wanted to add GADTs to UHC by taking a specification as guidance. However, it was not straightforward to match existing specifications to UHC's infrastructure, for the following reasons:

Citation: Arie Middelkoop Atze Dijkstra S. Doaitse Swierstra, A lean specification for GADTs: system F with first-class equality proofs, DOI: 10.1007/s10990-011-9065-0

- GADT pattern matching is defined in terms of case-expressions. In a programming language such as Haskell, there are several other ways to pattern match, such as in letbindings and list-comprehensions. Furthermore, Haskell has a concept of lazy pattern matching (irrefutable patterns). It is not directly clear if GADT matching is allowed in these situations, and what the side conditions are.
- For many approaches, it turns out that the effectiveness of inference for GADTs depends on what type information can be derived a priori from type annotations given by the programmer (Sect. 6). Specifications for inference of GADTs use a variety of techniques such as shape inference to describe that process. The implementation of such techniques crosscut the type inference implementation of the compiler, thus we are reluctant to incorporate them, unless absolutely necessary. Additionally, UHC already analyzes a program to derive type information from type signatures. Since the above techniques are intertwined with the specifications, it is not directly clear how to compare our infrastructure with the infrastructure used in the aforementioned specifications.

In this paper, we present a specification for GADT inference that addresses the above points, and has the following distinguishing features:

- We introduce a variation of System F, named System F~, extended with equality assumptions. In contrast to other GADT specifications, System F~ does not have syntax for data types or case expressions. These are redundant in our specification, because we exploit the folklore Church encoding of data types as conventional lambda expressions. The result is an abstract and concise description without the redundant syntax, while it is on the other hand more general, because it (necessarily) answers how to treat arbitrary pattern matching, including let-bindings and irrefutable patterns.
- Our specification is orthogonal to type inference infrastructure. Like System F, System F~ is explicitly typed. These explicit types represent the type information that can be derived using analysis on type signatures and conventional type inference. Our specification thus focusses in isolation on how to infer type coercions.

We thus claim that our specification is lean: it is concise because it does not require the notion of data types and case expressions, and abstract because it is orthogonal to infrastructure (in particular regarding type annotation analysis). However, our specification only specifies when explicit type information is needed, not when type annotations may be omitted, which depends largely on the effectiveness of the algorithms we abstracted from.

In an earlier version of this paper [9], we presented this work in terms of an extension of System FA [18], using explicit syntax for data types and case expressions. The encoding in System F~ is significantly less complex.

Roadmap We introduce GADTs in Sect. 2, and motivate the design choices for our speci- fication in Sect. 3. We formally define System F~ and its type system in Sect. 4. In Sect. 5, we define the semantics of System F~ via a translation to a subset of System FC, which is a System F -like language with explicit type coercions, defined by Sulzmann et al. [18]. The relation to various other approaches, we discuss in Sect. 6. Finally, in Sect. 7, we briefly mention our experiences with the integration of GADTs in the UHC.

INTRODUCTION TO GADTS

We start this section with an introduction to GADTs. GADTs, combined with the Haskell class system, form an essential ingredient for many Haskell libraries. In this section, we picked two simplified examples as illustration.

Typed Abstract Syntax

One popular use of GADTs is related to the embedding of domain-specific languages in such a way that Haskell's type system can be used to type check the domain-specific language.

A typical implementation of an embedded domain specific language consists of some combinators to construct an abstract syntax tree, and some functionality in the host language to manipulate this abstract syntax tree. After analysis and transformation, the abstract syntax tree is translated to some denotation in the host language in order to use it.

For example, assume that we use Haskell as a host language and embed an expression language containing only tuples and numbers, using the following abstract syntax:

```
data Expr
  = Num Int
  | Tup  Expr Expr
```

The following straightforward translation of the expression to a tuple in the host language does not type check, because the inferred types for the case alternatives are not the same:

```
eval e = case e of
           Num i   → i                       -- expected: Int
           Tup p q → (eval p, eval q)        -- expected: (a,b)
```

We bypass this restriction imposed by the Haskell type system with typed abstract syntax and encode a proof that the generated tuples are type correct. For that, we add a type parameter t to the abstract syntax, which represents the type of the expression, and embed in the constructors a proof (with type Equal $t\,t'$) that states that this t is equal to the real type t' of this specific expression (an Int for a Num and some tuple type for a Tup):

```
data Expr t
  =          Num (Equal t Int)     Int
  | ∀a b . Tup  (Equal t (a, b)) (Expr a) (Expr b)
```

Baars and Swierstra [1] give a definition of this Equal data type and some operations, including a function coerce that converts the type to a proved equivalent type, and some combinators to construct equality proofs:

```
coerce :: Equal a b → a → b
sym :: Equal a b → Equal b a
refl :: Equal a a
trans :: Equal a b → Equal b c → Equal a c
congr :: Equal a b → Equal (f a) (f b) -- has a more general signature
subsum :: Equal (f a) (f b) → Equal a b -- than written here
```

A non-bottom value with the type Equal τ_1 τ_2 is a proof that the types τ_1 and τ_2 are equal. The coerce function applied to such a proof is technically the identity function.

As a hypothetical example, consider the proof p_1 out of assumptions a_1 and a_2:

```
a1 :: Equal v1 (Int, v2)
a2 :: Equal v1 (v3, v4)

p1 :: Equal (Int, v2) (v3, v4)
p1 = trans (sym a1) a2

p2 :: Equal (Int, v4) (v3, v2)
p2 = ... congr ... subsum ...
```

We continue with the running example in this section and modify the eval function such that the case alternatives have the same type, namely the t in Expr t:

```
eval :: Expr t → t
eval e = case e of
    Num ass i     → coerce (sym ass) i
    Tup  ass p q  → coerce (sym ass) (eval p, eval q)
```

The assumptions used by eval need to be proved when constructing values of type Expr t, which we achieve by using refl:

```
Tup refl (Num refl 4) (Num refl 2)      :: Expr (Int, Int)
```

The important observation to make at this point is that the proofs are a static property of the program. Hence, the goal is to construct these proofs automatically.

GHC, the mainstream compiler for Haskell, has built-in support for GADTs. It offers two ways of writing GADTs. One can use qualified type notation, which resembles the example above. Instead of an additional field of the type Equal, we write an equality constraint:

```
data Expr t
  =        (t~Int)      ⇒ Num Int
  | ∀a b.(t~(a, b)) ⇒ Tup (Expr a) (Expr b)
```

Alternatively, one can use special notation for GADTs:

```
data Expr t where
  Num :: Int → Expr Int
  Tup :: Expr a → Expr b → Expr (a, b)
```

These two forms of notation are interchangeable. To convert from the above qualified-type notation to GADT notation, turn each equality constraint into a substitution and apply it exhaustively to the type signature of the constructor. The other way around, given a type signature of the constructor, take the result type as written (e.g. Expr (a, b)), and match it against the actual result type (Expr t).

Proofs do not have to be written manually. These are automatically constructed by GHC. The eval function can simply be written using either function alternatives or a case expression:

```
eval :: Expr t → t
eval (Num i)     = i
eval (Tup p q) = (eval p, eval q)
```

GHC (version 6.12.1) requires the type signature to be given. We discuss in Sect. 3.2 if this type signature could be inferred and if it is desirable to do so.

Generic Programming

Cheney and Hinze [3] show how GADTs, called Phantom Types in their work, can be used to implement generic functions that work for many data types. The idea is to have a representation of types as a first class value, then use this representation to navigate generically over a particular value:

```
data Rep t where
  RInt   :: Rep Int
  RChar :: Rep Char
  RList  :: Rep a → Rep [a]
  RTup   :: Rep a → Rep b → Rep (a, b)

x :: [(Int, Char)]       r :: Rep [(Int, Char)]
x = [(3, '4')]           r = RList (RTup RInt RChar)
```

In this example, x is a value of some type, and r is a value of a representation of that type. The following function, for example, traverses a value of any type for which we have a representation, and increments all integers with one:

```
replace :: Rep t → t → t
replace RInt        x      = x + 1
replace RChar       c      = c
replace (RList r)   xs     = map (replace r) xs
replace (RTup a b) (p, q)  = (replace a p, replace b q)
```

Values of Rep t can typically be obtained automatically at replace's call site using Haskell's class system.

Cheney and Hinze [3] continue from here, and define a data type for the sum of products representation of data types, and use this representation to define combinators to express generic traversals over arbitrary data types for which there is a representation.

DESIGN RATIONALE

In this section, we discuss the design decisions of System F~. We are liberal concerning syntax in this section, without loss of generality. In Sect. 4.1, we treat System F~ formally.

Church Encoding of Data Types

In other GADT specifications and algorithms, GADT matches are described in combination with case-expressions. In many type system descriptions, however, data types and case expressions are not part of the language, because these are implied by using a Church encoding or Mogensen-Scott encoding [10] of the data types. In our specification, we take a similar approach and consider a Church encoding of GADTs.

Church encoding of ADTs As a prelude, we informally sketch the Church encoding of algebraic data types.

The easiest example to start with are Church booleans. The constructors True and False can be represented as functions that take two continuation-expressions as parameters and return the appropriate one:

```
type Bool′ = ∀α.α → α → α
mkTrue, mkFalse :: Bool′
mkTrue  t f = t
mkFalse t f = f
```

The functions mkTrue and mkFalse can be used instead of the original constructors. To pattern match against such a constructor, we give it the continuations. For example, the following function:

```
ifThenElse :: Bool → a → a → a
ifThenElse b f g
  = case b of
     True  → f
     False → g
```

can be encoded as:

```
ifThenElse :: Bool′ → a → a → a
ifThenElse b f g = b f g
```

In general, the Church encoding of a data constructor is a function that takes (Church encoded) values for each of its fields, and several continuation functions, one for each constructor. The values are passed on to the appropriate continuation function. For example, given the following data type:

```
data D
  = C1 Int
  | C2 D
```

We introduce a (recursive) type D' for Church-encoded Ds, and constructor functions mkC1 and mkC2:

```
type D′ = ∀r.(Int → r) → (D′ → r) → r
mkC1 :: Int → D′
mkC1 x f1 _ = f1 x

mkC2 :: D′ → D′
mlC2 r _f2  = f2 r
```

In this example, we assume that built-in types are not encoded. As a technical detail, we require a number of built-in types in order to map recursive types to System F [19].

When we pattern match in a case-expression, we get a value of type D', and parameterize it with functions that deal with each of the cases. For example, given the following case expression:

```
case x of
  C1 y → y + 1
  C2 _ → ⊥
```

In the Church encoding, this corresponds to:

$x\ (\lambda y.y+1)\ (\backslash\_.\bot)$

Likewise, we can look at encodings of other forms of pattern matching. A let-binding can be encoded by means of a lambda and application:

let $(C1\ y) = x$ **in** $y + 1$

The pattern match takes place when y is evaluated. We can encode such a let-expression as a lambda, if we assume that patterns in a lambda match lazily:

$(\lambda y.y+1)\ ((\lambda (C1\ y).y)\ x)$

As continuation functions we take ⊥, except for the continuation corresponding to the data constructor matched on.

$$(\lambda y.y+1)\ ((\lambda d.d\ (\lambda y.y)\ \bot)\ x)$$

If a let-binding involves multiple variables, we use the Church encoding of tuples. Haskell has irrefutable (or, lazy) patterns. A match against such pattern always succeeds, and is actually only performed when values of variables that are bound by the pattern are needed. In the following example, the pattern match against C1 is only performed when the value of y is needed:

```
case x of
  ~(C1 y) → y + 1
```

We can write the irrefutable pattern with a let-binding.

```
case x of
  z → let (C1 y) = z
      in y + 1
```

This expression can be encoded again in a similar way as above.

Church encoding of GADTs The above approach has as advantage that we only need to consider lambda applications in our specification, and from it, the behavior for caseexpressions, let-bindings, etc. can be derived.

In the previous section, we showed that the mechanism underlying GADTs is the construction and application of equality proofs. These proofs are constructed and stored as fields in the constructor, such that they can be taken out when the match succeeds. In the Church encoding, a field has become a lambda. We thus introduce two new forms of expressions. An expression $\tau \sim \sigma$ that builds a proof of the equality between τ and σ , and an expression $\lambda(\tau \sim \sigma).e$ that matches against such a proof and allows it to be used for coercions in e.

For example, for a GADT (written using qualified-type notation):

data *Rep a*
  $= (a \sim Int) \Rightarrow RInt$

The encoding for RInt takes an equality proof, and passes it on to the continuation:

type $Rep'\ a = \forall r.((a \sim Int) \rightarrow r) \rightarrow r$
$mkRInt :: (a \sim Int) \rightarrow Rep'\ a$
$mkRInt = \lambda(a \sim Int).\lambda f.f\ (a \sim Int)$

In order to construct a value of Rep' a using mkRInt, we first need to pass a proof that a ~ Int. Lazy equalities We choose the equality-lambda to bind lazily. The following example gives an explanation. The pattern occurs in a let-expression and does not define any variables, which essentially means that it will never be evaluated.

$f :: Rep\ a \rightarrow a \rightarrow Int$
$f\ x\ y =$ **let** $RInt = x$
  in 3

In the encoding, x is only evaluated if its equality proof is needed when equalities bind lazily:

$$\lambda(x :: Rep\ a).\lambda(y :: a).(\lambda(a \sim Int).3 :: Int)\ (x\ (\lambda(a \sim Int).(a \sim Int)))$$

However, if we replace the 3 by y, the equality proof is needed to coerce the type a to Int. This subsequently leads to evaluation of x.

It is, however, undesirable that the construction of an equality proof influences the evaluation of the program. With our encoding, we have a model to reason about these effects. For example, it is straightforward to verify that the encoding of GADT matches in a case expression, and the encoding of GADT matches in a lambda, do not influence the evaluation of the program.

Type Inference

Above, we gave type signatures to all expressions involving GADTs. Several authors showed that there are situations where coercions can be inferred without an accompanying type annotation. So far, such approaches are not predictable: it is not intuitive when an annotation may be omitted or when it is obligatory. Several examples in this section illustrate the difficulties regarding inference. We therefore decided to allow coercions only when directed to via a type annotation, and describe how this shows up in the specification.

The main problem regarding GADT inference is that without a type annotation, it is not clear whether or not to coerce a type. In the following example, the pattern match on Num brings an equality on Int in scope, which may be applied to coerce the type of 3:

data *Expr t* **where**
  $Num\ :: Int \rightarrow Expr\ Int$
  $Tuple :: Expr\ a \rightarrow Expr\ b \rightarrow Expr\ (a, b)$
$eval\ (Num\ x) = x$

There are several types possible for eval:

(1) $eval :: \forall t\ .\ Expr\ t \rightarrow t$
(2) $eval :: Expr\ Int \rightarrow Int$
(3) $eval :: \forall t\ .\ Expr\ t \rightarrow Int$

The second type seems appropriate in this case. However, the first type is more general than the second, and the first and third are incomparable. We cannot choose between the first and third type, unless we know precisely how eval is to be used. Many inference approaches analyze the usages of such a function to make a choice. When usage of such a function changes due to modifications of the programmer, this may affect the choice, and cause type errors in other parts of the program. This leads to an unpredictable type inference. We choose only to apply equalities when directed to via a type annotation. In the above case, no type annotation is present, we do not apply the equality, which results in type (3).

In the above example, the usage of x in the body seems to suggest a relation to type t in Expr t. However, the following example demonstrates that this is not a good criterium, because there are also expressions that have a coercible type, aside from variables occurring in the pattern:

flex True (Num x) = x

flex False (Num x) = 3

Multiple pattern matches pose additional challenges. In the following example, there are two possible equalities on Int to choose from:

choose (Num x) (Num y) = 3

There are now many alternative types possible, including:

choose :: ∀t s . Expr t → Expr s → t

choose :: ∀t s . Expr t → Expr s → s

choose :: ∀t s . Expr t → Expr s → Int

During inference of the body of choose, the problem boils down to making a choice between either coercion to a Skolem constant such as s or t, or not coerce types at all. Again, we refrain from applying an equality unless directed to by a type annotation, and thus end up with the last type.

When there are multiple function or case alternatives, there is often no choice. The equalities have to be applied to have branches with equal types.

eval (Num x) = x

eval (Tup a b) = (a, b)

$e, f, g, a \in Expr$		$\tau, \rho, \varrho, \sigma \in Type$	
$::= x$	(E.VAR)	$::= \alpha$	(T.VAR)
$\mid \tau \sim \sigma$	(E.EQ)	$\mid \sigma \to \tau$	(T.ARR)
$\mid \lambda x.e$	(E.LAM.ABS)	$\mid \forall \alpha.\tau$	(T.FORALL)
$\mid \lambda \alpha.e$	(E.UNIV.ABS)	$\mid \tau \sim \sigma$	(T.EQS)
$\mid \lambda(\tau \sim \sigma).e$	(E.EQ.ABS)		
$\mid f\ e$	(E.APP.EXPR)	$\Gamma \in Env$	
$\mid f\ \tau$	(E.APP.UNIV)	$::= \Gamma, x :: \tau,$	(E.TY)
		$\mid \Gamma, \alpha$	(E.VAR)
$x, y \in Ident$			
$\alpha, \beta \in TyIdent$			

Figure. 1 Syntax of System F~.

We still require a type annotation. The design rationale is here that adding additional cases to a function without changing the existing cases, should only make a type less specific. In the above case, adding the Tup alternative causes the type of eval to change to an incomparable type, which again makes type inference hard to predict from the perspective of the programmer. Also, we point out that in the situation that multiple function or case alternatives are written, the overhead of the annotation (expressed for example in terms of lines of code) decreases.

In our specification, we abstract from the type inference algorithm. Moreover, we require type inference to be completed before the inference of coercions. The language System F~, based on System F, is explicitly typed. These explicit types represent the types derived from type annotations and those inferred. This makes it unambiguous where to find the locations where a coercion is needed: at those locations where the actual type does not match the expected type (Sect. 4.4). What remains is to specify how coercions are inferred, and that we make explicit in the specification.

SPECIFICATION

In this section, we present our specification for GADT inference. We start with the language System F~ in Sect. 4.1, present System F~'s typing rules in Sect. 4.2, and show how to deal with equality proofs in Sect. 4.3.

SYSTEM F~

Figure 1 lists the syntax of System F~, which consists of System F with the addition of equality proofs. These additions consist of:

- The abstraction λ(τ ~ σ).e matches against an equality proof for τ ~ σ, and brings it in scope by adding it to the environment. The equalities in scope are called equality assumptions, and can be used in equality proofs. The process of constructing a proof is fully automatic.
- The proof expression (τ ~ σ) constructs an equality τ ~ σ.
- The type language contains a type for equality proofs. Furthermore, we assume a number of primitive types to be present in the type language, such as Int.

Environments record Skolem constants introduced by type abstraction, and types for identifiers. Since we present equality proofs as conventional types, these can be stored in the environment as well, when we give them a name.

As illustration, we encode the following fragment of a program that generically increments integers in data types:

$$
\begin{array}{l}
\textbf{data}\ Rep\ \alpha\ \textbf{where} \\
\quad RInt :: Rep\ Int \\
inc :: Rep\ \alpha \to \alpha \to Int \\
inc = \lambda r.\lambda x.\textbf{case}\ r\ \textbf{of} \\
\qquad\qquad RInt \to x + 1 \\
z :: Int \\
z = inc\ RInt\ 3
\end{array}
$$

As an intermediate step, we write:

$$
\begin{array}{l}
\textbf{type}\ Rep'\ \alpha = \forall \beta.((\alpha \sim Int) \rightarrow \beta) \rightarrow \beta \\
mkRInt :: \alpha \sim Int \rightarrow Rep'\ \alpha \\
mkRInt = \lambda eq.\lambda f.f\ eq \\
inc :: Rep'\ \alpha \rightarrow \alpha \rightarrow Int \\
inc = \lambda r.\lambda x.r\ (\lambda(\alpha \sim Int).x + 1)) \\
z :: Int \\
z = inc\ (mkRInt\ (Int \sim Int))\ 3
\end{array}
$$

Finally, expressed in System F~:

$$
\begin{array}{l}
\text{-- } mkRInt \\
\Lambda\alpha.\lambda(eq :: \alpha \sim Int) \\
\quad .\lambda(f :: \forall\beta.((\alpha \sim Int) \rightarrow \beta) \rightarrow \beta) \\
\quad .f\ \alpha\ eq \\
\text{-- } inc \\
\Lambda\alpha.\lambda(r :: \forall\beta.((\alpha \sim Int) \rightarrow \beta) \rightarrow \beta) \\
\quad .\lambda(x :: \alpha) \\
\quad .r\ Int\ (\lambda(\alpha \sim Int).(+)\ x\ 1) \\
\text{-- } z \\
inc\ Int\ (mkRInt\ Int\ (Int \sim Int))\ 3
\end{array}
$$

Note that the type of x in inc is α, and is required to have type Int. In System F, this expression is not correctly typed. It has a valid type in System F~'s type system, which we discuss below.

TYPE RULES

The typing relation (rules in Fig. 2) states that in environment Γ, the expression e has type τ . These rules are syntax directed, except for rule COERCE. The idea is that the shape of the expression determines which rules to apply, and we resort to rule COERCE when there is a mismatch between the types. We illustrate this process briefly with inference for the inc example of the previous section, then explain the rules in more detail.

$$\boxed{\Gamma \vdash e : \tau}$$

$$
\frac{x :: \tau \in \Gamma}{\Gamma \vdash x : \tau}\ \text{VAR}
\qquad
\frac{\Gamma \vdash e : \sigma \quad \Gamma \Vdash \sigma \sim \tau \quad \mathtt{ftv}\,\tau \subseteq \mathtt{ftv}\,\Gamma}{\Gamma \vdash e : \tau}\ \text{COERCE}
\qquad
\frac{\Gamma \Vdash \tau \sim \sigma \quad \mathtt{ftv}\,\tau \subseteq \mathtt{ftv}\,\Gamma \quad \mathtt{ftv}\,\sigma \subseteq \mathtt{ftv}\,\Gamma}{\Gamma \vdash \tau \sim \sigma : \tau \sim \sigma}\ \text{EQ}
$$

$$
\frac{\Gamma \vdash f : \sigma \rightarrow \tau \quad \Gamma \vdash e : \sigma}{\Gamma \vdash f\ e : \tau}\ \text{APP.EXPR}
\qquad
\frac{\Gamma \vdash f : \sigma \rightarrow \tau \quad \mathtt{ftv}\,\sigma \subseteq \mathtt{ftv}\,\Gamma}{\Gamma \vdash f\ \sigma : \tau}\ \text{APP.TY}
$$

$$
\frac{\Gamma, x :: \sigma \vdash e : \tau}{\Gamma \vdash \lambda(x :: \sigma).e : \sigma \rightarrow \tau}\ \text{LAM.EXPR}
\qquad
\frac{\Gamma, \alpha \vdash e : \tau \quad \alpha \notin \mathtt{ftv}\,\Gamma}{\Gamma \vdash \Lambda\alpha.e : \forall\alpha.\tau}\ \text{LAM.TY}
$$

$$
\frac{\Gamma, x :: \rho \sim \sigma \vdash e : \tau \quad x \notin \Gamma}{\Gamma \vdash \lambda(\rho \sim \sigma).e : (\rho \sim \sigma) \rightarrow \tau}\ \text{LAM.EQ}
$$

Figure. 2 Expression type rules.

Example To type the inc expression (see Fig. 3), we apply first rule LAM.TY, then rule LAM.EXPR twice. The former administers the Skolem constant α in the environment, the second two the types of r and x. The type of r, we extract again using the rule VAR, then use rule APP.TY to instantiate the universally quantified β of the type of r to the result type Int.

To type the subexpression (λ(α ~ Int).(+) x 1), we use rule LAM.EQ to introduce the equality into the environment, bound to a fresh name (not important for now). The subexpression (+) x 1 must have type Int. Assuming that (+):: Int → Int → Int is in the environment, this means that x must have type Int. However, the type we get for x by applying the VAR-rule is α. So, we apply the COERCE-rule to convert the type α to Int. This requires us to prove that $\Gamma \Vdash \alpha \sim Int$, for which we give the rules later. This is in this case not difficult, because exactly this equality we added just before into the environment.

Type rules overview Most of the rules are vanilla System F rules. Via the ftv relation, we state that the types chosen in rules COERCE, EQ, and APP.TY are closed (and well-formed). The ftv relation is defined as:

$$
\begin{array}{ll}
\mathtt{ftv}\,\alpha & = \{\alpha\} \\
\mathtt{ftv}\,(\tau \rightarrow \sigma) & = \mathtt{ftv}\,\tau \cup \mathtt{ftv}\,\sigma \\
\mathtt{ftv}\,(\forall\alpha.\tau) & = \mathtt{ftv}\,\tau - \{\alpha\} \\
\mathtt{ftv}\,(\tau \sim \sigma) & = \mathtt{ftv}\,\tau \cup \mathtt{ftv}\,\sigma
\end{array}
$$

We overload ftv to work on environments as well:

$$
\begin{array}{ll}
\mathtt{ftv}\,\emptyset & = \emptyset \\
\mathtt{ftv}\,(\Gamma, \alpha) & = \mathtt{ftv}\,\Gamma \cup \{\alpha\} \\
\mathtt{ftv}\,(\Gamma, x :: \tau) & = \mathtt{ftv}\,\Gamma \cup \mathtt{ftv}\,\tau
\end{array}
$$

$$
\frac{\dfrac{\dfrac{\dfrac{\dfrac{\Gamma_1 \vdash r : \forall\beta.(((\alpha \sim \beta) \rightarrow \beta) \rightarrow \beta)}{\Gamma_1 \vdash r\ Int : ((\alpha \sim Int) \rightarrow Int) \rightarrow Int} \qquad \Gamma_1 \vdash \lambda(\alpha \sim Int).(+)\ x\ 1 : \ldots}{\Gamma_1 \vdash r\ Int\ (\lambda(\alpha \sim Int).(+)\ x\ 1) : Int}}{\ldots \vdash \lambda x.r\ Int\ (\lambda(\alpha \sim Int).(+)\ x\ 1) : \ldots \rightarrow Int}}{\ldots \vdash \lambda r.\lambda x.r\ Int\ (\lambda(\alpha \sim Int).(+)\ x\ 1) : \ldots \rightarrow \ldots \rightarrow Int}}{\emptyset \vdash \Lambda\alpha.\lambda r.\lambda x.r\ Int\ (\lambda(\alpha \sim Int).(+)\ x\ 1) : \forall\alpha.\ldots \rightarrow \ldots \rightarrow Int}
$$

$$
\frac{\dfrac{\dfrac{\Gamma_2 \vdash (+) : \ldots \qquad \dfrac{\Gamma_2 \vdash x : \alpha \qquad \Gamma_2 \Vdash \alpha \sim Int}{\Gamma_2 \vdash x : Int}}{\Gamma_2 \vdash (+)\ x : Int \rightarrow Int} \qquad \Gamma_2 \vdash 1 : Int}{\Gamma_2 \vdash (+)\ x\ 1 : Int}}{\Gamma_1 \vdash \lambda(\alpha \sim Int).(+)\ x\ 1 : (\alpha \sim Int) \rightarrow Int}
$$

$$
\begin{array}{l}
\Gamma_0 = \emptyset, 1 :: Int, (+) :: Int \rightarrow Int \rightarrow Int \\
\Gamma_1 = \Gamma_0, \alpha, r :: \forall\beta.(((\alpha \sim \beta) \rightarrow \beta) \rightarrow \beta, x :: \alpha \\
\Gamma_2 = \Gamma_1, e :: \alpha \sim \beta
\end{array}
$$

Figure. 3 Typing Derivation of inc.

Rules COERCE and EQ specify the construction of equality proofs. In the former, the equality proof is used to coerce a type, in the latter to pass it on as a first-class value. In rules LAM.EXPR, LAM.TY, and LAM.EQ, we extend the environment. Extension of an environment with a binding shadows a possible previous binding with the same name. In rule LAM.EQ, we introduce an equality in the environment, using a fresh name x. This name is of consequence for the next section, but has no meaning in this section.

Type Conversions

Figure 4 lists the inference rules for equality proofs. The rules REFL, SYM and TRANS correspond to the conventional rules of an equality theory. An equality assumption can be applied through rule ASSUM.

In the example of the beginning of this section, we need to prove $\Gamma \Vdash Int \sim Int$ (by means of the REFL-rule), and $\Gamma \Vdash a \sim Int$ (with the ASSUM-rule). In Sect. 2.1 we showed some examples using more involved equality proofs. Simply put, proving an equality is a matter of exhaustively applying all the rules.

To be able to apply coercions deeper into types, we have congruence and subsumption rules for each member of the type language that has a substructure. In our case, for arrows and universal quantification. We do not need nor allow coercions on equality proofs.

With congruence rules, if two types share a common structure, we only need to prove the equality between the components that differ. The other way around, with subsumption rules, we lift a proof on smaller type into a proof on bigger types.

$$\boxed{\Gamma \Vdash \tau_1 \sim \tau_2}$$

$$\Gamma \Vdash \tau \sim \tau \ \text{REFL} \qquad \frac{\Gamma \Vdash \sigma \sim \tau}{\Gamma \Vdash \tau \sim \sigma}\ \text{SYM} \qquad \frac{\Gamma \Vdash \tau \sim \rho \quad \Gamma \Vdash \rho \sim \sigma}{\Gamma \Vdash \tau \sim \sigma}\ \text{TRANS} \qquad \frac{x :: \tau \sim \sigma \in \Gamma}{\Gamma \Vdash \tau \sim \sigma}\ \text{ASSUM}$$

$$\frac{\Gamma \Vdash \sigma \sim \tau \quad \Gamma \Vdash \rho \sim \varrho}{\Gamma \Vdash \tau \to \rho \sim \sigma \to \varrho}\ \text{CON.ARR} \qquad \frac{\Gamma, \beta \Vdash \tau\,[\alpha := \beta] \sim \sigma \quad \beta \notin \mathtt{ftv}\,\tau \cup \mathtt{ftv}\,\Gamma}{\Gamma \Vdash \forall \alpha.\tau \sim \sigma}\ \text{CON.UNIV.LEFT}$$

$$\frac{\Gamma \Vdash \tau \sim \sigma\,[\beta := \alpha] \quad \beta \in \mathtt{ftv}\,\Gamma \quad \alpha \notin \mathtt{ftv}\,\sigma}{\Gamma \Vdash \tau \sim \forall \alpha.\sigma}\ \text{CON.UNIV.RIGHT}$$

$$\frac{x :: (\tau_3 \sim (\forall \alpha.\tau_4)) \in \Gamma \quad y :: (\tau_5 \sim (\forall \alpha.\tau_6)) \in \Gamma \quad \Gamma \Vdash \tau_3 \sim \tau_5 \quad x' :: \tau_4 \sim \tau_6 \Vdash \tau_1 \sim \tau_2 \quad x' \notin \Gamma}{\Gamma \Vdash \tau_1 \sim \tau_2}\ \text{SUB.UNIV}$$

$$\frac{x :: (\tau_3 \sim (\tau_4 \to \tau_5)) \in \Gamma \quad y :: (\tau_6 \sim (\tau_7 \to \tau_8)) \in \Gamma \quad \Gamma \Vdash \tau_3 \sim \tau_6 \quad x' :: \tau_4 \sim \tau_7, y' :: \tau_5 \sim \tau_8 \Vdash \tau_1 \sim \tau_2 \quad x', y' \notin \Gamma}{\Gamma \Vdash \tau_1 \sim \tau_2}\ \text{SUB.ARR}$$

Figure. 4 Equality proof inference rules.

In other specifications Schrijvers et al. [14], Sulzmann et al. [18], the subsumption rules e.g. on arrows are typically specified as:

$$\frac{\Gamma \Vdash \tau \to \rho \sim \sigma \to \varrho}{\Gamma \Vdash \tau \sim \sigma}\ \text{SUB.L} \qquad \frac{\Gamma \Vdash \tau \to \rho \sim \sigma \to \varrho}{\Gamma \Vdash \tau \sim \sigma}\ \text{SUB.R}$$

These rules appear simpler than the rule in our specification. However, we have objections against these rules:

- For any environment Γ, the other rules have a finite number of unique instantiations. However, when we include the above subsumption rule, arbitrary big types can be constructed. Thus the search space can be infinite. In practice, we only need to consider a finite portion of the search space to prove or disprove the equality of two types, but this rule does not force us to.
- The subsumption rule does not give us an intuition when to actually apply this rule. To construct an equality proof, one first decomposes the equality to prove using the congruence rules, then apply subsumption rules to work up to assumptions in the environment. We thus restrict the subsumption rule to assumptions in the environment.

$$\begin{array}{lll}
\gamma \in \mathit{Coercion} & & \\
\quad ::= x & & \text{(C.VAR)} \\
\quad \mid \gamma_1\ \gamma_2 & & \text{(C.APP)} \\
\quad \mid \tau & & \text{(C.REFL)} \\
\quad \mid \mathtt{sym}\ \gamma & & \text{(C.SYM)} \\
\quad \mid \gamma_1 \circ \gamma_2 & & \text{(C.TRANS)} \\
\quad \mid \mathtt{right}\ \gamma & & \text{(C.RIGHT)} \\
\quad \mid \mathtt{left}\ \gamma & & \text{(C.LEFT)} \\
\quad \mid \forall \alpha\,.\,\gamma & & \text{(C.UNIV)} \\
\quad \mid \gamma @ \rho & & \text{(C.INST)}
\end{array}
\qquad
\begin{array}{lll}
\hat{e} \in \mathit{Expr} & & \\
\quad \mid e \rhd \gamma & & \text{(E.APP.COE)} \\
\quad \mid \mathbf{case}\ \hat{e}\ \mathbf{of}\ \overline{p \to \hat{e}} & & \text{(E.CASE)} \\
 & & \\
p \in \mathit{Pat} & & \\
\quad \mid C\ \overline{\gamma : \tau \sim \sigma}\ \overline{\alpha : \star}\ \overline{x : \rho} & & \text{(P.CON)} \\
 & & \\
d \in \mathit{Decl} & & \\
\quad \mid \mathbf{data}\ D\ \overline{a} \mid \overline{C\ \overline{\tau \sim \sigma}\ \overline{\alpha : \star}\ \overline{\rho}} & &
\end{array}$$

Figure. 5 Subset of syntax of System FC.

Our rule simply expresses that if there are two equalities in the environment, and these equalities can be shown equal on one side, then we may assume that each pairwise subtype on the other side is equal as well.

Algorithm

The specification of this section has a straightforward implementation, even combined with type inference. We first infer types of a program in the conventional way, but for each type conflict, we generate a coercion constraint. At the end of type inference for e.g. a binding group, we try to solve these coercion constraints, using an exhaustive application of the above equality rules. For those constraints that cannot be solved we generate a type error. For those we can, we generate a coercion. In the next section, we show how to generate these coercions.

SEMANTICS

We define the semantics of System F∼ in terms of System FC [18]. We introduction to System FC, then show the important parts of the translation.

System F_C

System FC extends System F with equality coercions. It has a built-in syntax to represent values of the Equal data type mentioned in the Sect. 2.1.

We limit our explanation to a simplified fragment of System FC, which contains what we need: System F (lambda abstraction, etc.), data types, case expressions, and coercions. Figure 5 lists the extensions to System F. A data constructor C consists of three components: equality coercions, existentials, and fields, respectively, hence it is a representation of the qualified-type style of GADT constructors.

A coercion γ can be applied to an (System FC) expression $\hat{e}$, denoted as $\hat{e} \rhd \gamma$, which changes the type of e^ according to coercion. A coercion γ of type $\tau_1 \sim \tau_2$ represents a proof of the equality of τ_1 and τ_2. Figure 6 lists the typing rules of coercion terms. See [18] for the full listing.

$$\boxed{\Gamma \vdash \gamma : \tau_1 {\sim} \tau_2}$$

$$\frac{x :: \tau_1 {\sim} \tau_2 \in \Gamma}{\Gamma \vdash x : \tau_1 {\sim} \tau_2}\ \text{VAR} \qquad \frac{\Gamma \vdash \gamma_1 : \tau_1 {\sim} \tau_3 \qquad \Gamma \vdash \gamma_2 : \tau_2 {\sim} \tau_4}{\Gamma \vdash \gamma_1\ \gamma_2 : \tau_1\ \tau_2 {\sim} \tau_3\ \tau_4}\ \text{APP} \qquad \Gamma \vdash \tau : \tau {\sim} \tau\ \text{REFL}$$

$$\frac{\Gamma \vdash \gamma : \tau_2 {\sim} \tau_1}{\Gamma \vdash \mathtt{sym}\,\gamma : \tau_1 {\sim} \tau_2}\ \text{SYM} \qquad \frac{\Gamma \vdash \gamma_1 : \tau_1 {\sim} \tau_2 \qquad \Gamma \vdash \gamma_2 : \tau_2 {\sim} \tau_3}{\Gamma \vdash \gamma_1 \circ \gamma_2 : \tau_1 {\sim} \tau_3}\ \text{TRANS}$$

$$\frac{\Gamma \vdash \gamma : \tau_1\ \tau_2 {\sim} \tau_3\ \tau_4}{\Gamma \vdash \mathtt{left}\,\gamma : \tau_1 {\sim} \tau_3}\ \text{LEFT} \qquad \frac{\Gamma \vdash \gamma : \tau_1\ \tau_2 {\sim} \tau_3\ \tau_4}{\Gamma \vdash \mathtt{right}\,\gamma : \tau_2 {\sim} \tau_4}\ \text{RIGHT}$$

$$\frac{\Gamma \vdash \gamma : \tau_1 {\sim} \tau_2 \qquad \alpha \notin \mathtt{ftv}\,\Gamma}{\Gamma \vdash \forall \alpha . \gamma : \forall \alpha . \tau_1 {\sim} \forall \alpha . \tau_2}\ \text{FORALL} \qquad \frac{\Gamma \vdash \gamma : \forall \alpha . \tau_1 {\sim} \forall \beta . \tau_2}{\Gamma \vdash \gamma @ \rho : \tau_1\,[\alpha := \rho] {\sim} \tau_2\,[\beta := \rho]}\ \text{INST}$$

Figure. 6 Coercion type rules.

Coercion application $\gamma_1\ \gamma_2$ builds a coercion that applies γ_1 to the function part f and γ_2 to the argument part a of a type application f a. With transitivity $\gamma_2 \circ \gamma_1$, the second coercion is applied to the result of applying the first coercion. The right-coercion extracts the coercion of the arguments from a coercion on a type application f a. 5.2 Translation overview We use a type-directed translation. The typing relations have the form:

Translation Overview

We use a type-directed translation. The typing relations have the form:

$\Gamma \vdash e : \tau \rightsquigarrow \hat{e}$ -- System F_C-expr $\hat{e}$ is the translation of System F

$\Gamma \Vdash \tau_1 \sim \tau_2 \rightsquigarrow \gamma$ -- γ is a System F_C-coercion term of type $\tau_1 {\sim} \tau_2$.

The translation consists of two challenges: we need to represent System F~'s equality proofs in System F_C, and need to associate with each equality-proof rule of the previous section a well-typed System F_C-coercion term.

System F~ expressions

The first-class equality proofs in System F~ have no direct counterpart in System F_C. However, in System F_C, equality proofs may be stored in a data constructor. For example, for an equality proof of type $\alpha \sim \beta \rightarrow$ Int, we can associate a data type:

data D α β = C (α ~ β → Int)

In general, we associate a data type $D_{key\,(\tau,\sigma)}\overline{\alpha}$ with a System F~ proof of type $\tau \sim \sigma\ (\overline{\alpha} = \mathtt{ftv}\ \tau \cup \mathtt{ftv}\ \sigma).$, as well as a constructor $C_{key\,(\tau,\sigma)}$ storing the System F_C-coercion. We denote with $[\![\tau \sim \sigma]\!]$the conversion from a System F~-proof type to a System F_C data type, or data constructor according to the above procedure. Similarly, $[\![\sigma]\!]$ denotes the translation of a System F~ type to a System F_C type, by recursively mapping each coercion type τ ~ σ to $D_{key\,(\tau,\sigma)}\overline{\alpha}$.

Figure 7 shows the translation rules, which are the type rules of the previous section extended with the resulting eˆ expression.

$$\boxed{\Gamma \vdash e : \tau \rightsquigarrow \hat{e}}$$

$$\frac{x :: \tau \in \Gamma}{\Gamma \vdash x : \tau \rightsquigarrow x}\ \text{VAR} \qquad \frac{\begin{array}{c}\Gamma \vdash e : \sigma \rightsquigarrow \hat{e}\\ \Gamma \Vdash \sigma \sim \tau \rightsquigarrow \gamma\\ \mathtt{ftv}\,\tau \subseteq \mathtt{ftv}\,\Gamma\end{array}}{\Gamma \vdash e : \tau \rightsquigarrow \hat{e} \triangleright \gamma}\ \text{COERCE}$$

$$\frac{\begin{array}{c}\Gamma \Vdash \tau \sim \sigma \rightsquigarrow \gamma\\ \mathtt{ftv}\,\tau \subseteq \mathtt{ftv}\,\Gamma\\ \mathtt{ftv}\,\sigma \subseteq \mathtt{ftv}\,\Gamma\end{array}}{\Gamma \vdash \tau \sim \sigma : \tau \sim \sigma \rightsquigarrow [\![\tau \sim \sigma]\!]\ \gamma}\ \text{EQ} \qquad \frac{\begin{array}{c}\Gamma \vdash f : \sigma \rightarrow \tau \rightsquigarrow \hat{f}\\ \Gamma \vdash e : \sigma \rightsquigarrow \hat{e}\end{array}}{\Gamma \vdash f\ e : \tau \rightsquigarrow \hat{f}\ \hat{e}}\ \text{APP.EXPR}$$

$$\frac{\begin{array}{c}\Gamma \vdash f : \sigma \rightarrow \tau \rightsquigarrow \hat{f}\\ \mathtt{ftv}\,\sigma \subseteq \mathtt{ftv}\,\Gamma\end{array}}{\Gamma \vdash f\ \sigma : \tau \rightsquigarrow \hat{f}\ [\![\sigma]\!]}\ \text{APP.TY} \qquad \frac{\Gamma, x :: \sigma \vdash e : \tau \rightsquigarrow \hat{e}}{\Gamma \vdash \lambda(x :: \sigma).e : \sigma \rightarrow \tau \rightsquigarrow \lambda(x :: [\![\sigma]\!]).\hat{e}}\ \text{LAM.EXPR}$$

$$\frac{\begin{array}{c}\Gamma, \alpha \vdash e : \tau \rightsquigarrow \hat{e}\\ \alpha \notin \mathtt{ftv}\,\Gamma\end{array}}{\Gamma \vdash \Lambda\alpha.e : \forall\alpha.\tau \rightsquigarrow \Lambda\alpha.\hat{e}}\ \text{LAM.TY}$$

$$\frac{\Gamma, x :: \rho \sim \sigma \vdash e : \tau \rightsquigarrow \hat{e} \qquad x, y \notin \Gamma}{\Gamma \vdash \lambda(\rho \sim \sigma).e : (\rho \sim \sigma) \rightarrow \tau \rightsquigarrow \lambda y.\mathbf{case}\ y\ \mathbf{of}\,[\![\rho \sim \sigma]\!]\ (x : [\![\rho]\!] \sim [\![\sigma]\!]) \rightarrow \hat{e}}\ \text{LAM.EQ}$$

Figure. 7 System F~-expr translation rules.

Translation of Proofs

Figure 8 shows how to produce coercion terms from the equality proof. We omitted the rules for universal quantification: these are analogous. The rules REFL, SYM, TRANS, and ASSUM have a direct mapping to a coercion-term.

Each individual rule is a solution to a small puzzle. For a proof of τ ~ σ, we combine coercions γ until they have exactly the same type according to coercion type rules in Figure 6. For example, we can verify that rule SUB.ARR constructs a coercion with the right type as follows:

$$\begin{array}{ll}
\gamma_1 & :: \tau_3 \sim (\tau_4 \rightarrow \tau_5)\\
\gamma_2 & :: \tau_6 \sim (\tau_7 \rightarrow \tau_8)\\
\gamma_3 & :: \tau_3 \sim \tau_6\\
\mathtt{sym}\,\gamma_1 \circ \gamma_3 \circ \gamma_2 & :: (\tau_4 \rightarrow \tau_5) \sim (\tau_7 \rightarrow \tau_8)\\
\mathtt{right}\,(\mathtt{sym}\,\gamma_1 \circ \gamma_3 \circ \gamma_2) & :: \tau_4 \sim \tau_7\\
\mathtt{right}\,(\mathtt{right}\,(\mathtt{sym}\,\gamma_1 \circ \gamma_3 \circ \gamma_2)) & :: \tau_5 \sim \tau_8
\end{array}$$

$$\boxed{\Gamma \Vdash \tau_1 \sim \tau_2 \rightsquigarrow \gamma}$$

$$\Gamma \Vdash \tau \sim \tau \rightsquigarrow [\![\tau]\!]\ \text{REFL} \qquad \frac{\Gamma \Vdash \tau' \sim \tau'' \rightsquigarrow \gamma}{\Gamma \Vdash \tau'' \sim \tau' \rightsquigarrow \mathtt{sym}\,\gamma}\ \text{SYM} \qquad \frac{\Gamma \Vdash \tau_1 \sim \tau_2 \rightsquigarrow \gamma_1 \quad \Gamma \Vdash \tau_2 \sim \tau_3 \rightsquigarrow \gamma_2}{\Gamma \Vdash \tau_1 \sim \tau_3 \rightsquigarrow \gamma_2 \circ \gamma_1}\ \text{TRANS}$$

$$\frac{x : \tau_1 \sim \tau_2 \in \Gamma}{\Gamma \Vdash \tau_1 \sim \tau \rightsquigarrow x}\ \text{ASSUM} \qquad \frac{\Gamma \Vdash \sigma \sim \tau \rightsquigarrow \gamma_1 \quad \Gamma \Vdash \rho \sim \varrho \rightsquigarrow \gamma_2}{\Gamma \Vdash \tau \to \rho \sim \sigma \to \varrho \rightsquigarrow \gamma_1 \to \gamma_2}\ \text{CON.ARR}$$

$$\frac{\begin{array}{c} \gamma_1 :: (\tau_3 \sim (\tau_4 \to \tau_5)) \in \Gamma \qquad \gamma_2 :: (\tau_6 \sim (\tau_7 \to \tau_8)) \in \Gamma \\ \Gamma \Vdash \tau_3 \sim (\tau_6 \rightsquigarrow \gamma_3) \\ \gamma_5 = \mathtt{right}\,(\mathtt{sym}\,\gamma_1 \circ \gamma_3 \circ \gamma_2) \\ \gamma_6 = \mathtt{right}\,(\mathtt{right}\,(\mathtt{sym}\,\gamma_1 \circ \gamma_3 \circ \gamma_2)) \\ \gamma_5 :: \tau_4 \sim \tau_7, \gamma_6 :: \tau_5 \sim \tau_8 \Vdash \tau_1 \sim \tau_2 \rightsquigarrow \gamma_4 \\ \gamma_1, \gamma_2 \notin \Gamma \end{array}}{\Gamma \Vdash \tau_1 \sim \tau_2 \rightsquigarrow \gamma_4}\ \text{SUB.ARR}$$

Figure. 8 Equality proof translation rules.

Correctness

It is easy to show that a well-typed equality-proof is translated to a well-typed coercion term (see above). It is also easy to show that a System F$\sim$ expression is translated to a well-typed System F_C expression. Because System F_C has type soundness, we thus obtain that System F$\sim$ also has type soundness.

RELATED WORK

Several approaches propose limitations to make inference for GADTs tractable. Many specifications and algorithms for GADTs consist of two components: a type information propagation component and a type conversion component. A type information propagation strategy determines what is known type information based on user-supplied type signatures, and what is inferred type information. A type conversion strategy deals with the construction of coercion terms.

Restricting Expressiveness for Tractable Inference

Sulzmann et al. [16] show that inference for GADTs is undecidable without a helping hand from the programmer in the form of type annotations, and show that principal typing is lost. They present an inference algorithm that generates implication constraints, and apply a technique called Herbrand abduction [8] to solve these constraints. A solution to these constraints is a normalized constraint that implies the generated constraints. The authors define a notion of a sensible solution; under these conditions the resulting type is principal. These conditions are specified in terms of the algorithm.

We are reluctant to adopt such an approach, because it requires programmers to think in terms of an algorithm. To discover why their program is (not) accepted by the type inferencer, the steps of the algorithm have to be performed by hand.

Schrijvers et al. [14] recently presented two type systems for GADTs, and the inference algorithm OutsideIn. The first type system is relatively simple, but inference for it is undecidable. The latter is more restricted, but has OutsideIn as a sound and complete inference algorithm. Both specification and inference algorithm are given in terms of implication constraints.

When type inference is combined with coercion inference, additionally a coercion $\tau_1 \sim \tau_2$ may be constructed when τ_1 unifies with τ_2 (the result then corresponds to the REFL rule). The main idea of OutsideIn is that binding of variables during such a unification is not allowed on variables that are free in the environment (of the enclosing let-expression or casebranch). These are called the "untouchable" unification variables. Type checking proceeds as normal, except that a unification of a Skolem constant or with an untouchable requires a coercion to be constructed. The actual construction of these coercions is done after type checking is complete.

The approach is presented as a general solution to inference for GADTs. Although this approach is sound and complete with respect to their specification, their specification still requires type annotations for most functions with GADT patterns. For example, with OutsideIn, a type signature is needed for the following code that uses GADTs in the typical way:

```
data D a where
  C1 :: Int → D Int
  C2 :: Bool → D Bool
  -- needs: f :: D α → α
f x = case x of
  C1 y → y
  C2 z → z
```

The reason is that α is free in the environment, and thus not unified.

This approach still lacks a good specification: it introduces "suspended judgments" to encode a two-phase typing of an expression, which is actually harder to comprehend than the algorithm itself. A problem here is that the untouchable variables do not appear explicitly in conventional type system specifications. They might be eliminated by unification during conventional type inference, and are notationally equal to the type the variable is unified with. Thus, such a specification requires a programmer to know how the algorithm is distributing its type variables over the program.

Lin and Sheard [7] propose the Pointwise GADT type system. The notion pointwise comes from the correspondence between the range-type of a constructor and the type of the scrutinee in a GADT case expression. During inference in case branches, type information flows from and to such types. The authors identify two typical usage-patterns for GADTs, and make a case to restrict the use of GADTs to these patterns. Parametric instantiation entails that each case branch assumes the same specific instance of a polymorphic data type. Type indexing entails that each case branch assumes a different instance of a polymorphic data type. The authors propose a unification technique to restrict this bidirectional information flow. From an implementation point-of-view, this approach is promising: the authors performed several case studies of typical uses of GADTs and presented a mechanism that types many typical usages of GADT programs without explicit type annotations. However it is not clear how this approach relates to the challenges we pointed out in Sect. 3.2. Furthermore, the approach lacks a specification to serve as an explanation to the programmer.

Type Annotation Propagation Strategies

Pottier and Régis-Gianas [13] use shape inference. A shape represents known type information based on user-supplied signatures. These shapes are spread throughout the syntax tree in order to locate possible coercions. Their approach uses complex algorithms to spread the shapes as far as possible, iteratively. More iterations give rise to a better spread of annotations, at a cost of performance. The essential part concerning GADTs is that incompatible shapes are normalized with respect to some equation system, which is not made explicit in their work. From an implementer's point of view, this description is a concrete description of the equation system, and it requires infrastructure for spreading shapes.

Similarly, Peyton Jones et al. [11, 12] define a notion of wobbly types to combine type checking and type inference, which is based on earlier work on boxy types [20]. A rigid type represents known type information based on user-supplied type information, whereas a wobbly type is based on inferred information. The idea is then that type conversions are only applied on rigid types, for reasons of predictability and most-general typing. Aside from wobbly types, the authors use concepts such as "fresh most general unifiers" and lexically scoped type variables in their presentation. It is hard to distinguish which of these concepts are really required, and which of these concepts are actually related to other language features that are covered by their approach (such as type families). We incorporated a notion of wobbly and rigid types in our specification: in an explicitly typed System F - variant, the skolemnized type constants are rigid types, and we only allow type conversions on those.

The exact choice of propagation strategy is an orthogonal issue. By allowing type conversions only on known type information, a better propagation strategy just means that less explicit types have to be given by the programmer. This is the reason why we have chosen an explicitly typed source language in the first place. In fact, for our own implementation of this specification, we piggybacked on the infrastructure of the implementation of a higherranked impredicate type system. It has two propagation strategies, of which the advanced one has a concept of hard and soft type context, which can be compared to rigid and boxy types [4].

Type Conversion Strategies

Peyton Jones et al. [11, 12] use a unification-based strategy, where type conversion is called type refinement. A fixpoint substitution is constructed that, for each type equation introduced by pattern matching, contains a mapping for each (non-wobbly) type component of the left hand side of an equation, to the corresponding type component on the right hand side of an equation. The substitution is then used to normalize the types under consideration. The presentation is intertwined with the type propagation strategy, which makes it hard to separate these concepts.

Wazny [21] uses a constraint-based strategy. The GADT aspect of this strategy is covered separately by Sulzmann et al. [17], Stuckey and Sulzmann [15]. They also formulate the typing problems in terms of solving constraints with CHRs. The difference is that we restrict ourselves to equality constraints, and do not need the machinery required to solve implication constraints. Their typing/translation rules do not mention how to deal with existential data types, which may be transparent to the given approach, but is of interest to a reader because GADT examples often use them. In contrast to Peyton Jones et al. [12], restrictions on type conversions are not mentioned.

CONCLUSION

We presented a specification for GADT inference in terms of the language System F~. This language deviates from System F in three ways: it has syntax to request an equality proof, a lambda to take an equality proof as argument and bring it in scope, and automatic coercions based on equality proofs in scope. In this language, we can express GADTs using the folklore Church encoding for data types.

Compared to other approaches, our specification is a small extension of a bare System F, which allows us to treat data types and case expressions as syntactic sugar. Furthermore, our specification describes what to do with other forms of pattern matching and binding, exploiting encodings as conventional System F terms.

As future work, it may be worthwhile to investigate if algorithms such as OutsideIn [14] can be specified in a simpler way by taking an implicitly typed variation on System F~ as a basis.

ACKNOWLEDGEMENTS

This work was supported by Microsoft Research through its European PhD Scholarship Programme. We thank the anonymous reviewers of TFP 08 and TFP-HOSC for extensive comments on earlier versions of this paper.

REFERENCES

1. Baars, A.I., Swierstra, S.D.: Typing dynamic typing. In: ICFP, pp. 157–166 (2002)
2. Baars, A.I., Swierstra, S.D., Viera, M.: Typed transformations of typed abstract syntax. In: Kennedy, A., Ahmed, A. (eds.) TLDI, pp. 15–26. ACM, New York (2009)
3. Cheney, J., Hinze, R.: First-class phantom types. Tech. rep., Cornell University (2003)
4. Dijkstra, A.: Stepping through Haskell. PhD thesis, Utrecht University, Department of Information and Computing Sciences (2005). http://www.cs.uu.nl/wiki/Ehc/WebHome, papers/dijkstra05phd.pdf
5. Dijkstra, A., Fokker, J., Swierstra, S.D.: The architecture of the Utrecht Haskell compiler. In: Weirich, S. (ed.) Haskell, pp. 93–104. ACM, New York (2009)
6. Jeuring, J., Leather, S., Magalhães, J.P., Yakushev, AR: Libraries for generic programming in Haskell. In: AFP, pp. 165–229 (2008)
7. Lin, C., Sheard, T.: Pointwise generalized algebraic data types. In: Kennedy, A., Benton, N. (eds.) TLDI, pp. 51–62. ACM, New York (2010)
8. Maher, M.J.: Herbrand constraint abduction. In: LICS, pp. 397–406. IEEE Computer Society, Washington (2005)
9. Middelkoop, A., Dijkstra, A., Swierstra, S.D.: A leaner specification for generalized algebraic data types. In: TFP, vol. 9, pp. 65–80 (2008)
10. Mogensen, T.Æ.: Efficient self-interpretations in lambda calculus. J. Funct. Program. 2(3), 345–363 (1992)
11. Peyton Jones, S.L., Washburn, G., Weirich, S.: Wobbly types: type inference for generalised algebraic data types.

Tech. Rep. MS-CIS-05-26, University of Pennsylvania, Computer and Information Science Department, Levine Hall, 3330 Walnut Street, Philadelphia, Pennsylvania, 19104-6389 (2004)

12. Peyton Jones, S.L., Vytiniotis, D., Weirich, S., Washburn, G.: Simple unification-based type inference for GADTs. In: ICFP, pp. 50–61 (2006)
13. Pottier, F., Régis-Gianas, Y.: Stratified type inference for generalized algebraic data types. In: POPL, pp. 232–244 (2006)
14. Schrijvers, T., Jones, S.L.P., Sulzmann, M., Vytiniotis, D.: Complete and decidable type inference for GADTs. In: ICFP, pp. 341–352 (2009)
15. Stuckey, P.J., Sulzmann, M.: Type inference for guarded recursive data types. CoRR abs/cs/0507037 (2005)
16. Sulzmann, M., Schrijvers, T., Stuckey, P.J.: Type inference for GADTs via Herbrand constraint abduction. Manuscript (2006)
17. Sulzmann, M., Wazny, J., Stuckey, P.J.: A framework for extended algebraic data types. In: FLOPS, pp. 47–64 (2006)
18. Sulzmann, M., Chakravarty, M.M.T., Peyton Jones, S.L., Donnelly, K.: System F with Type Equality Coercions. In: TLDI, pp. 53–66 (2007)
19. Urzyczyn, P.: Positive recursive type assignment. Fundam. Inform. 28(1–2), 197–209 (1996)
20. Vytiniotis, D., Weirich, S., Peyton Jones, S.L.: Boxy types: inference for higher-rank types and impredicativity. In: Reppy, J.H., Lawall, J.L. (eds.) ICFP, pp. 251–262. ACM, New York (2006)
21. Wazny, J.R.: Type inference and type error diagnosis for Hindley/Milner with extensions. PhD thesis, The university of Melbourne (2006)

CHAPTER 5

A REPRESENTATION THEOREM FOR SECOND-ORDER FUNCTIONALS

MAURO JASKELIOFF[1], RUSSELL O'CONNOR[2]

[1]CIFASIS, CONICET, Argentina FCEIA, Universidad Nacional de Rosario, Argentina

[2]Google Canada Kitchener, Ontario, Canada

ABSTRACT

Representation theorems relate seemingly complex objects to concrete, more tractable ones. In this paper, we take advantage of the abstraction power of category theory and provide a datatypegeneric representation theorem. More precisely, we prove a representation theorem for a wide class of second-order functionals which are polymorphic over a class of functors. Types polymorphic over a class of functors are easily representable in languages such as Haskell, but are difficult to analyse and reason about. The concrete representation provided by the theorem is easier to analyse, but it might not be as convenient to implement. Therefore, depending on the task at hand, the change of representation may prove valuable in one direction or the other.

We showcase the usefulness of the representation theorem with a range of examples. Concretely, we show how the representation theorem can be used to prove that traversable functors are finitary containers, how coalgebras of a parameterised store comonad relate to very well-behaved lenses, and how algebraic effects might be implemented in a functional language.

INTRODUCTION

When dealing with a type which uses advanced features of modern type systems such as polymorphism and higher-order types and functions, it is convenient to analyse whether there is another datatype that can represent it, as the alternative representation might be easier to program or to reason about. A simple example of a datatype that might be better understood through a different representation is the type of polymorphic functions $\forall A . A \to A$ which, although it involves a function space and a universal quantifier, has only one nonbottom inhabitant: the identity function.

Hence, a representation theorem opens the design space for programmers and computer scientists, providing and connecting different views on some construction. When a representation is an isomorphism, we say that it is exact, and the change of representation can be done in both directions.

In this article we will consider second-order functionals that are polymorphic over a class of functors, such as monads or applicative functors. In particular we will give a concrete representation for inhabitants of types of the form

$$\forall F. (A_1 \to F\, B_1) \to (A_2 \to F\, B_2) \to \ldots \to F\, C$$

Here A_i, B_i, and C are fixed types, and F ranges over an appropriate class of functors. There is a condition on the class of functors which will be made precise during the presentation

Citation: MAURO JASKELIOFF, RUSSELL O'CONNOR, A Representation Theorem for Second-Order Functionals

of the theorem, but basically it amounts to the existence of free constructions. The representation is exact, as it is an isomorphism.

We will express the representation theorem using category theory. Although the knowledge of category theory that is required should be covered by an introductory textbook such as (Awodey, 2006), we introduce the more important concepts in Section 2. The usefulness of the representation theorem (Section 3) is illustrated with a range of examples. Concretely, we show how coalgebras of a specific parameterised comonad are related to very well-behaved lenses (Section 4), and how traversable functors, subjected to certain coherence laws, are exactly the finitary containers (Section 5). Finally we show how the representation theorem can help when implementing free theories of algebraic effects (Section 6) and discuss related work (Section 7).

There is a long tradition of categorically inspired functional programming (Bird & de Moor, 1997) even though functional programming languages like Haskell usually lack some basic structure such as products or coproducts. The implementation of our results in Haskell, as shown in Section 4.1 and Section 6, should be taken simply as categorically-inspired code. Nevertheless, the code could be interpreted to be "morally correct" in a precise technical sense (Danielsson et al., 2006).

A Taste of the Representation Theorem

In order to get a taste of the representation theorem, we reason informally on a total polymorphic functional language. Consider the type

$$T = \forall F : \mathsf{Functor}.\ (A \to F\,B) \to F\,C.$$

What do the inhabitants of this type look like? The inhabitants of T are functions h = λg.r. Given that the functor F is universally quantified, the only way of obtaining a result in F C is that in the expression r there is an application of the argument g to some a : A. This yields something in F B rather than the sought F C, so a function k : B → C is needed in order to construct a map F(k): F B → F C. This informal argument suggests that all inhabitants of T can be built from a pair of an element of A and a function B → C. Hence, it is natural to propose the type A×(B → C) as a simpler representation of the inhabitants of type T. More formally, in order to check that the inhabitants of T are in a one-to-one correspondence with the inhabitants of A×(B → C), we want to find an isomorphism

$$\forall F : \mathsf{Functor}.\ (A \to F\,B) \to F\,C \underset{\varphi^{-1}}{\overset{\varphi}{\cong}} A \times (B \to C).$$

We define φ^{-1} using the procedure described above.

$$\varphi^{-1} : A \times (B \to C) \to \forall F : \mathsf{Functor}.\ (A \to F\,B) \to F\,C$$
$$\varphi^{-1}\,(a, k) = \lambda g.\ F\,(k)\,(g\,a)$$

In order to define φ, notice that R C = A × (B → C) is functorial on C, with action on morphisms given by R (f) (a,g) = (a,f ∘ g). Hence, we can instantiate a polymorphic function h: T to the functor R and obtain hR : (A → R B) → R C, which amounts to the type hR : (A → (A×(B → B))) → A×(B → C).

$$\varphi : (\forall F : \mathsf{Functor}.\ (A \to F\,B) \to F\,C) \to A \times (B \to C)$$
$$\varphi\,h = h_R\,(\lambda a.\ (a, id_B))$$

The proof that φ and φ^{-1} are indeed inverses will be given for a Set model in Section 3. The simple representation A×(B → C) is possible due to the restrictive nature of the type T: all we know about F is that it is a functor. What happens when F has more structure?

Consider now the type

$$T' = \forall F : \mathsf{Pointed}.\ (A \to F\,B) \to F\,C.$$

In this case F ranges over pointed functors. That is, F is a functor equipped with a natural transformation ηX : X → F X. An inhabitant of T ′ is a function h = λg.r, where r can be obtained in the same manner as before, or else by applying the point ηC to a given c ∈ C. Hence, a simpler type representing T ′ seems to be (A×(B → C)) +C.

More formally, we want an isomorphism

$$\forall F : \mathsf{Pointed}.\ (A \to F\,B) \to F\,C \underset{\varphi'^{-1}}{\overset{\varphi'}{\cong}} (A \times (B \to C)) + C.$$

The definition of φ'^{-1} is the following.

$$\varphi'^{-1} : (A \times (B \to C)) + C \to \forall F : \mathsf{Pointed}.\ (A \to F\,B) \to F\,C$$
$$\varphi'^{-1}\,(\mathsf{inl}\,(a, k)) = \lambda g.\ F\,(k)\,(g\,a)$$
$$\varphi'^{-1}\,(\mathsf{inr}\,c) \quad = \lambda\_.\ \eta_C\,c$$

In order to define φ', notice that $R'\,C = (A \times (B \to C)) + C$ is a pointed functor on C, with η = inr. Hence, we can instantiate a polymorphic function h: T′ to the pointed functor R ′ to obtain $h_{R'}$: (A → R′ B) → R′ C, or equivalently $h_{R'}$: (A → ((A×(B → B)) +B)) → (A×(B → C)) +C.

$$\varphi' : (\forall F : \mathsf{Pointed}.\ (A \to F\,B) \to F\,C) \to (A \times (B \to C)) + C$$
$$\varphi'\,h = h_{R'}\,(\lambda a.\ \mathsf{inl}\,(a, id_B))$$

We can play the same game in the case where the universally quantified functor is an applicative functor.

$$T'' = \forall F : \mathsf{Applicative}.\ (A \to F\,B) \to F\,C.$$

An applicative functor is a pointed functor F equipped with a multiplication operation ⋆X,Y : (FX × FY) → F(X ×Y) natural in X and Y, which is coherent with the point (a precise definition is given in Section 5.1). An inhabitant of T″ is a function h = λg.r, where r can be obtained by applying the argument g to n elements of A to obtain an $(F\,B)^n$, then joining the results with the multiplication of the applicative functor to obtain an $F\,(B^n)$, and finally applying a function B^n → C which takes n elements of B and yields a C.

$$\forall F : \mathsf{Applicative}.\ (A \to F\,B) \to F\,C \underset{\varphi''^{-1}}{\overset{\varphi''}{\cong}} \sum_{n \in \mathbb{N}} (A^n \times (B^n \to C)).$$

The definition of φ''^{-1} is the following.

$$\varphi''^{-1} : (\Sigma_{n \in \mathbb{N}}\,(A^n \times (B^n \to C))) \to \forall F : \mathsf{Applicative}.\ (A \to F\,B) \to F\,C$$
$$\varphi''^{-1}\,(n, as, k) = \lambda g.\ F\,(k)\,(\mathsf{collect}_n\,g\,as)$$

Here, $\mathsf{collect}_n$: ∀F: Applicative. $(A \to F\,B) \to A^n \to F\,(B^n)$ is the function that uses the applicative multiplication to collect all the applicative effects, i.e

$$\mathsf{collect}_n\ h\ (x_1, \ldots, x_n) = h\, x_1 \star \ldots \star h\, x_n.$$

In order to define φ'', notice that $R''\ C = \Sigma_{n \in \mathbb{N}} (A^n \times (B^n \to C))$)) is an applicative functor on C, with $\eta c = (0, *, \lambda x : 1.\ c)$, where $*$ is the sole inhabitant of 1, and the multiplication is given by

$$(n, as, k) \star (n', as', k') = (n + n', as +\!\!+ as', \lambda bs.\ (k\ (\mathsf{take}\ n\ bs), k'\ (\mathsf{drop}\ n\ bs)))$$

Hence, we can instantiate a polymorphic function h : T″ to the applicative functor R″ to obtain $h_{R''} : (A \to R''\ B) \to R''\ C$, or equivalently $h_{R''} : (A \to \Sigma_{n \in N} (A^n \times (B^n \to B))) \to \Sigma_{n \in N} (A^n \times (B^n \to C))$.

$$\varphi'' : (\forall F : \mathsf{Applicative}.\ (A \to F\ B) \to F\ C) \to \Sigma_{n \in \mathbb{N}} (A^n \times (B^n \to C))$$
$$\varphi''\ h = h_{R''}\ (\lambda a.\ (1, a, id_B))$$

We have seen three different isomorphisms which yield concrete representations for second-order functionals which quantify over a certain class of functors (plain functors, pointed functors, and applicative functors, respectively.) The construction of each of the three isomorphisms has a similar structure, so it is natural to ask what the common pattern is. In order to answer this question and provide a general representation theorem we will make good use of the power of abstraction of category theory.

CATEGORICAL PRELIMINARIES

A category $\mathscr{C}$ is said to be locally small when the collection of morphisms between any two objects X and Y is a proper set. A locally small category is said to be small if its collection of objects is a proper set. We denote by $X \xrightarrow{\mathscr{C}} Y$ the (not necessarily small) set of morphisms between X and Y and extend it to a functor $X \xrightarrow{\mathscr{C}} -$ (the covariant Hom functor). When the category is Set (the category of sets and total functions) we will omit the category from the notation and write X → Y. Given two categories $\mathscr{C}$ and $\mathscr{D}$ we will denote by $\mathscr{D}^{\mathscr{C}}$ the category which has as objects functors $F : \mathscr{C} \to \mathscr{D}$ and natural transformations as morphisms. A subcategory $\mathscr{D}$ of a category $\mathscr{C}$ consists of a collection of objects and morphisms of $\mathscr{C}$ which is closed under the operations domain, codomain, composition, and identity. When, for every object X and Y of $\mathscr{D}$ subcategory of $\mathscr{C}$, we have $X \xrightarrow{\mathscr{D}} Y = X \xrightarrow{\mathscr{C}} Y$, we say that $\mathscr{D}$ is a full subcategory of $\mathscr{C}$.

The Yoneda lemma

The main result of this article hinges on the following famous result:

Theorem 2.1 (Yoneda lemma)

Given a locally small category $\mathscr{C}$, the Yoneda Lemma establishes the following isomorphism:

$$(B \xrightarrow{\mathscr{C}} -) \xrightarrow{\mathsf{Set}^{\mathscr{C}}} F \quad \cong \quad F\,B$$

natural in object B : $\mathscr{C}$ and functor F : $\mathscr{C}$ → Set.

That is, the set F B is naturally isomorphic to the set of natural transformations between the functor $(B \xrightarrow{\mathscr{C}} -)$ and the functor F.

Naturality in B means that given any morphism h : B → C, the following diagram commutes:

$$\begin{array}{ccc} ((B \xrightarrow{\mathscr{C}} -) \xrightarrow{\mathsf{Set}^{\mathscr{C}}} F) & \xrightarrow{\cong} & FB \\ \Big\downarrow{\scriptstyle (h \xrightarrow{\mathscr{C}} -) \xrightarrow{\mathsf{Set}^{\mathscr{C}}} F} & & \Big\downarrow{\scriptstyle Fh} \\ ((C \xrightarrow{\mathscr{C}} -) \xrightarrow{\mathsf{Set}^{\mathscr{C}}} F) & \xrightarrow[\cong]{} & FC \end{array}$$

Naturality in F means that given any natural transformation α : F → G, the following diagram commutes:

$$\begin{array}{ccc} ((B \xrightarrow{\mathscr{C}} -) \xrightarrow{\mathsf{Set}^{\mathscr{C}}} F) & \xrightarrow{\cong} & FB \\ \Big\downarrow{\scriptstyle (B \xrightarrow{\mathscr{C}} -) \xrightarrow{\mathsf{Set}^{\mathscr{C}}} \alpha} & & \Big\downarrow{\scriptstyle \alpha_B} \\ ((B \xrightarrow{\mathscr{C}} -) \xrightarrow{\mathsf{Set}^{\mathscr{C}}} G) & \xrightarrow[\cong]{} & GB \end{array}$$

The construction of the isomorphism is as follows:

- Given a natural transformation α : $\alpha : (B \xrightarrow{\mathscr{C}} -) \to F$, its component at B is a function $\alpha_B : (B \xrightarrow{\mathscr{C}} B) \to FB$. Then, the corresponding element of F B is $\alpha_B(id_B)$.
- For the other direction, given x: F B, we construct a natural transformation $\alpha : (B \xrightarrow{\mathscr{C}} -) \to F$ in the following manner: the component at each object C, namely $\alpha_C : (B \xrightarrow{\mathscr{C}} C) \to FC$ is given by λ f : B → C.F(f)(x).

We leave as an exercise for the reader to check that this construction indeed yields a natural isomorphism.

In order to make the relation between the programs and the category theory more evident, it is convenient to express the Yoneda lemma in end form:

$$\int_{X \in \mathscr{C}} (B \xrightarrow{\mathscr{C}} X) \to FX \quad \cong \quad FB \tag{2.1}$$

The intuition is that an end corresponds to a universal quantification in a programming language (Bainbridge et al., 1990), and therefore the above isomorphism could be understood as stating an isomorphism of types:

$$\forall X.\ (B \to X) \to F\,X \quad \cong \quad F\,B$$

Hence, functional programmers not used to categorical ends can get the intuitive meaning just by replacing in their minds ends by universal quantifiers. More details can be found in the standard reference (Mac Lane, 1971).

A simple application of the Yoneda lemma which will be used in the next section is the following proposition.

Proposition 2.2

Consider an endofunctor F : Set → Set, and the functor R : Set×Set^{op}×Set → Set defined as R(A,B,X) = A × (B → X), R(f,g,h)(a,x) = (f a,g ∘ x ∘ h), where we write $R_{A,B}X$ for R(A,B,X). Then

$$A \to F\,B \cong R_{A,B} \xrightarrow{\mathsf{Set}^{\mathsf{Set}}} F \tag{2.2}$$

Proof

$$
\begin{array}{ll}
& A \to F\,B \\
\cong & \quad \{ \text{ Yoneda } \} \\
& A \to \int_X ((B \to X) \to F\,X) \\
\cong & \quad \{ \text{ Hom functors preserve ends (Remark A.4) } \} \\
& \int_X A \to ((B \to X) \to F\,X) \\
\cong & \quad \{ \text{ Adjoints (currying) } \} \\
& \int_X A \times (B \to X) \to F\,X \\
\cong & \quad \{ \text{ Definition of } R_{A,B} \text{ } \} \\
& \int_X R_{A,B}X \to F\,X \\
\cong & \quad \{ \text{ Natural transformations as ends } \} \\
& R_{A,B} \xrightarrow{\mathsf{Set}^{\mathsf{Set}}} F
\end{array}
$$

More concretely, the isomorphism is witnessed by the following functions:

$$
\begin{array}{lll}
\alpha_F & : (A \to F\,B) \to R_{A,B} \xrightarrow{\mathsf{Set}^{\mathsf{Set}}} F & \\
\alpha_F(f) & = \tau \quad \text{where} \quad \tau_X & : A \times (B \to X) \to F\,X \\
& & \tau_X(a,g) = F(g)(f(a)) \\
\alpha_F^{-1} & : (R_{A,B} \xrightarrow{\mathsf{Set}^{\mathsf{Set}}} F) \to A \to F\,B & \\
\alpha_F^{-1}(h) & = \lambda a.\ h_B(a, id_B) &
\end{array}
$$

This isomorphism is natural in A and B.

Adjunctions

An adjunction is a relation between two categories which is weaker than isomorphism of categories.

Definition 2.3 (Adjunction)

Given categories $\mathscr{C}$ and $\mathscr{D}$, functors $L : \mathscr{C} \to \mathscr{D}$ and $R : \mathscr{D} \to \mathscr{C}$, an adjunction is given by a tuple (L, R, $\lfloor - \rfloor$, $\lceil - \rceil$), where $\lfloor - \rfloor$ and $\lceil - \rceil$ are the components of the following isomorphism:

$$\lfloor - \rfloor : LC \xrightarrow{\mathscr{D}} D \quad \cong \quad C \xrightarrow{\mathscr{C}} RD : \lceil - \rceil \tag{2.3}$$

which is natural in $C \in \mathscr{C}$ and $D \in \mathscr{D}$. That is, for f : LC → D and g : C → RD we have

$$\lfloor f \rfloor = g \quad \Leftrightarrow \quad f = \lceil g \rceil \tag{2.4}$$

The components of the isomorphism $\lfloor - \rfloor$ and $\lceil - \rceil$ are called adjuncts. That the isomorphism is natural means that for any $C, C' \in \mathscr{C}; D, D' \in \mathscr{D}; h : C' \to C; k : D \to D'; f : LC \to$ D; and g: C → RD, the following equations hold:

$$Rk \circ \lfloor f \rfloor \circ h \quad = \quad \lfloor k \circ f \circ Lh \rfloor \tag{2.5}$$

$$k \circ \lceil g \rceil \circ Lh \quad = \quad \lceil Rk \circ g \circ h \rceil \tag{2.6}$$

We indicate the categories involved in an adjunction by writing $\mathscr{C} \rightharpoonup \mathscr{D}$ (note the asymmetry in the notation), and often leave the components of the isomorphism implicit and simply write L ⊣ R.

The unit η and counit ε of the adjunction are defined as:

$$\eta = \lfloor id \rfloor \qquad \varepsilon = \lceil id \rceil; \tag{2.7}$$

The adjuncts can be characterised in terms of the unit and counit:

$$\lfloor f \rfloor = Rf \circ \eta \qquad \lceil g \rceil = \varepsilon \circ Lg. \tag{2.8}$$

For more details, see (Mac Lane, 1971; Awodey, 2006).

A REPRESENTATION THEOREM FOR SECOND-ORDER FUNCTIONALS

Consider a small subcategory $\mathscr{F}$ of $\mathsf{Set}^{\mathsf{Set}}$, the category of endofunctors on Set. [1] By Yoneda,

[1] We are interested in functors representable in a programming language, such as realisable functors (Bainbridge et al., 1990; Reynolds & Plotkin, 1993). Therefore, it is reasonable to assume smallness.

$$\int_{F \in \mathscr{F}} (G \xrightarrow{\mathscr{F}} F) \to HF \quad \cong \quad HG \tag{3.1}$$

Note that G is any functor in $\mathscr{F}$ and H is any functor $\mathscr{F} \to \mathsf{Set}$. In particular, given a set X, we obtain the functor $(-X) : \mathscr{F} \to \mathsf{Set}$ that applies a functor in $\mathscr{F}$ to X. That is, the action on objects is $F \mapsto F\,X$. The above equation, specialised to (−X) is

$$\forall G \in \mathscr{F}. \qquad \int_F (G \xrightarrow{\mathscr{F}} F) \to F\,X \quad \cong \quad G\,X \tag{3.2}$$

For example, let $R_{A,B}\,X = A \times (B \to X)$ as in Proposition 2.2, and let $\mathscr{E}$ be a small full sub-category of $\mathsf{Set}^{\mathsf{Set}}$ such that $R_{A,B} \in \mathscr{E}$.

Then, we calculate

$$
\begin{array}{ll}
& \int_{F \in \mathscr{E}} (A \to F\,B) \to F\,X \\
\cong & \quad \{ \text{ Equation (2.2) } \} \\
& \int_{F \in \mathscr{E}} (R_{A,B} \xrightarrow{\mathscr{E}} F) \to F\,X \\
\cong & \quad \{ \text{ Equation (3.2) } \} \\
& R_{A,B}X
\end{array}
$$

That is, we have proven that

$$\int_F (A \to F\,B) \to F\,X \cong R_{A,B}X \tag{3.3}$$

This isomorphism provides a justification for the first isomorphism of the introduction, namely:

$$\forall F : \mathsf{Functor}.\ (A \to F\,B) \to F\,C \quad \cong \quad A \times (B \to C)$$

Unary Representation Theorem

Let us now consider categories of endofunctors that carry some structure. For example, a category $\mathscr{F}$ may be the category of monads and monad morphisms, or the category of applicative functors and applicative morphisms. Then we have a functor that forgets the extra structure and yields a plain functor. For example, the forgetful functor $U : \mathscr{Mon} \to \mathscr{E}$ maps a monad (T,μ,η) ∈ Mon to the endofunctor T, forgetting that the functor has a monad structure given by μ and η. It often happens that this forgetful functor has a left adjoint $(-)^* : \mathscr{E} \to \mathscr{F}$. Such an adjoint takes an arbitrary endofunctor F and constructs the free structure on F. For example, in the monad case, F* would be the free monad on F. The adjunction establishes the following natural isomorphism between morphisms in $\mathscr{F}$ and $\mathscr{E}$:

$$E^* \xrightarrow{\mathscr{F}} F \quad \cong \quad E \xrightarrow{\mathscr{E}} UF \tag{3.4}$$

In this situation we have the following representation theorem.

Theorem 3.1 (Unary Representation)

Consider an adjunction $((-)^*, U, \lfloor - \rfloor, \lceil - \rceil) : \mathscr{E} \rightharpoonup \mathscr{F}$, where $\mathscr{F}$ is small and $\mathscr{E}$ is a full subcategory of $\mathrm{Set}^{\mathrm{Set}}$ such that the family of functors $R_{A,B}\, X = A \times (B \to X)$ is in $\mathscr{E}$. Then, we have the following isomorphism natural in A, B, and X

$$\int_F (A \to UF\,B) \to UF\,X \quad \cong \quad UR^*_{A,B}X \tag{3.5}$$

Proof

$$\begin{array}{ll} & \int_F (A \to UF\,B) \to UF\,X \\ \cong & \quad \{ \text{ Equation (2.2) } \} \\ & \int_F (R_{A,B} \xrightarrow{\mathscr{E}} UF) \to UF\,X \\ \cong & \quad \{ \ (-)^* \text{ is left adjoint to } U \text{ (see Eq. 3.4) } \} \\ & \int_F (R^*_{A,B} \xrightarrow{\mathscr{F}} F) \to UF\,X \\ \cong & \quad \{ \text{ Yoneda } \} \\ & UR^*_{A,B}X \end{array}$$

Every isomorphism in the proof is natural in *X*, the first one is natural in *A* and *B*, and the last two are natural in $R_{A,B}$. Therefore, the resulting isomorphism is also natural in *A* and *B*.

Since the free pointed functor on *F* is simply $F^* = F + Id$, and the free applicative functor on small functors such as $R_{A,B}$ exists (Capriotti & Kaposi, 2014), this theorem explains all the isomorphisms in the introduction. Furthermore, it explains the structure of the representation functor (it is the free construction on $R_{A,B}$) and what's more, it tells us that the isomorphism is natural.

For the sake of concreteness, we present the functions witnessing the isomorphism in the theorem:

$$\begin{array}{ll} \varphi & : (\int_F (A \to UF\,B) \to UF\,X) \to UR^*_{A,B}X \\ \varphi(h) & = h_{R^*_{A,B}}(\alpha^{-1}_{UR^*_{A,B}}(\eta_{R_{A,B}})) \end{array}$$

$$\begin{array}{llll} \varphi^{-1} & : UR^*_{A,B}X \to \int_F (A \to UF\,B) \to UF\,X & & \\ \varphi^{-1}(r) = \tau & \text{where} & \tau_F & : (A \to UF\,B) \to UF\,X \\ & & \tau_F(g) & = (U\lceil \alpha_{UF}(g) \rceil_X)(r) \end{array}$$

Here, h is the unit of the adjunction, and α is the isomorphism in Proposition 2.2.

Generalisation to Many Functional Arguments

Let us consider functionals of the form

$$\forall F.\,(A_1 \to F\,B_1) \to \ldots \to (A_n \to F\,B_n) \to F\,X$$

The representation theorem, Theorem 3.1, can be easily generalised to include the above functional.

Theorem 3.2 (N-ary representation)

Consider an adjunction $((-)^*, U, \lfloor - \rfloor, \lceil - \rceil) : \mathscr{E} \rightharpoonup \mathscr{F}$, where $\mathscr{F}$ is small and $\mathscr{E}$ is a full subcategory of $\mathrm{Set}^{\mathrm{Set}}$ closed under coproducts such that the family of functors $R_{A,B}\, X = A \times (B \to X)$ is in $\mathscr{E}$. Let A_i, B_i be sets for $i \in \{1, \ldots, n\}, n \in \mathbb{N}$. Then, we have the following isomorphism

$$\int_F (\prod_i (A_i \to UF\,B_i)) \to UF\,X \quad \cong \quad U(\sum_i R_{A_i,B_i})^* X \tag{3.6}$$

natural in A_i, B_i, and *X*.

Proof

The proof follows the same path as the one in Theorem 3.1, except that now we use the isomorphism $(A \to C) \times (B \to C) \cong (A + B) \to C$ that results from the universal property of coproducts. More precisely, the proof is as follows:

$$\begin{array}{ll} & \int_F (\prod_i (A_i \to UF\,B_i)) \to UF\,X \\ \cong & \quad \{ \text{ Equation (2.2) } \} \\ & \int_F (\prod_i (R_{A_i,B_i} \xrightarrow{\mathscr{E}} UF)) \to UF\,X \\ \cong & \quad \{ \text{ Coproducts } \} \\ & \int_F (\sum_i R_{A_i,B_i} \xrightarrow{\mathscr{E}} UF) \to UF\,X \\ \cong & \quad \{ \ (-)^* \text{ is left adjoint to } U \text{ (see Eq. 3.4) } \} \\ & \int_F ((\sum_i R_{A_i,B_i})^* \xrightarrow{\mathscr{F}} F) \to UF\,X \\ \cong & \quad \{ \text{ Yoneda } \} \\ & U(\sum_i R_{A_i,B_i})^* X \end{array}$$

Naturality follows from naturality of its component isomorphisms.

PARAMETERISED COMONADS AND VERY WELL-BEHAVED LENSES

The functor $R_{A,B}\, X = A \times (B \to X)$ plays a fundamental role in Theorems 3.1 and 3.2. Such a functor *R* has the structure of a parameterised comonad (Atkey, 2009b; Atkey, 2009a) and is sometimes called a parameterised store comonad. As a first application of the representation theorem we analyse the relation between coalgebras for this parameterized comonad and very well-behaved lenses (Foster *et al.*, 2007).

Definition 4.1 (Parameterised Comonad)

Fix a category $\mathscr{P}$ of parameters. A $\mathscr{P}$-parameterised comonad on a category $\mathscr{C}$ is a triple (C, ε, δ), where:

- *C* is a functor $\mathscr{P} \times \mathscr{P}^{\mathrm{op}} \times \mathscr{C} \to \mathscr{C}$. We write the parameters as (usually lowercase) subindexes. That is, $C_{a,b}X = C(a, b, X)$.
- the *counit* ε is a family of morphisms $\varepsilon_{a,X} : C_{a,a}X \to X$ which is natural in *X* and dinatural in *a* (dinaturality is defined in Definition A.1),
- the *comultiplication* d is a family of morphisms $\delta_{a,b,c,X} : C_{a,c}X \to C_{a,b}(C_{b,c}X)$ natural in *a*,*c* and *X* and dinatural in *b*.

These must make the following diagrams commute:

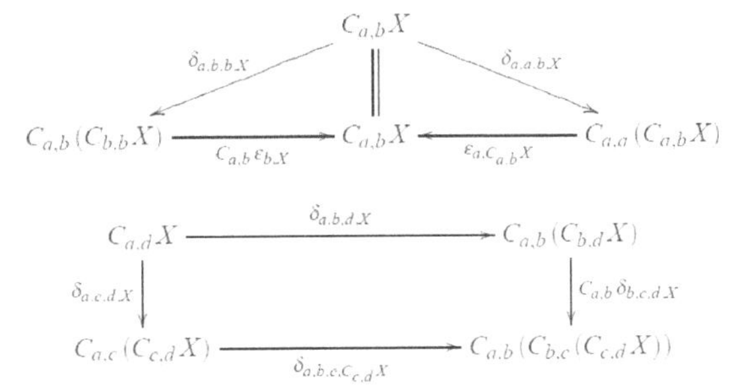

Definition 4.2 (Coalgebra for a parameterised comonad)

Let C be a $\mathscr{P}$-parameterised comonad on $\mathscr{C}$. Then a C-coalgebra is a pair (J,k) of a functor $J:\mathscr{P}\rightarrow\mathscr{C}$, and a family $k_{a,b}:Ja\rightarrow C_{a,b}(Jb)$ natural in a and dinatural in b, such that the following diagrams commute:

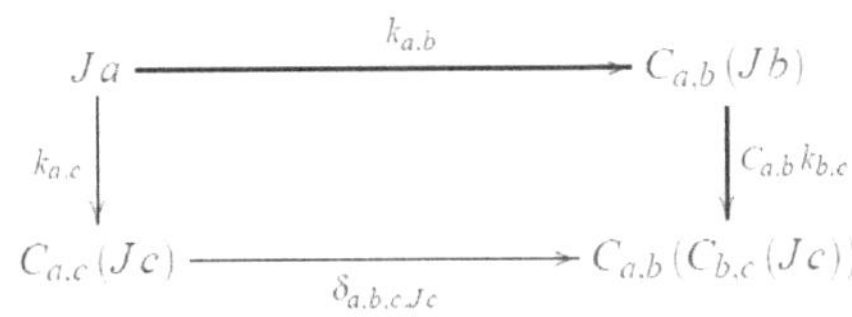

comultiplication-coalgebra law

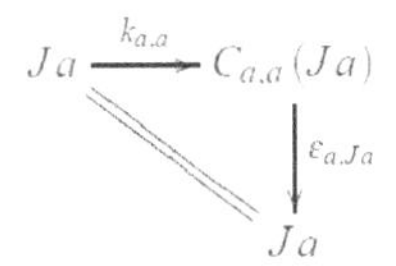

counit-coalgebra law

The definitions of parameterised comonad and of coalgebra for a parameterised comonad are dualisations of the ones for monads found in (Atkey, 2009a).

Example 4.3

The functor $R_{a,b}X=a\times(b\rightarrow X)$ is a parameterised comonad, with the following counit and comultiplication:

$$
\begin{array}{lcl}
\varepsilon_{a,X} & : & R_{a,a}X\rightarrow X \\
\varepsilon_{a,X}\,(x,f) & = & fx
\end{array}
$$

$$
\begin{array}{lcl}
\delta_{a,b,c,X} & : & R_{a,c}X\rightarrow R_{a,b}\,(R_{b,c}X) \\
\delta_{a,b,c,X}\,(x,f) & = & (x,\lambda y.\,(y,f))
\end{array}
$$

Example 4.4

Given a functor $K:\mathscr{P}\rightarrow Set$, define the functor $R^{(K)}_{a,b}X=Ka\times(Kb\rightarrow X):\mathscr{P}\times\mathscr{P}^{op}\times Set\rightarrow Set$

For every functor K, $R^{(K)}$ is a parameterised comonad, with the following counit and comultiplication:

$$
\begin{array}{lcl}
\varepsilon_{a,X} & : & R^{(K)}_{a,a}X\rightarrow X \\
\varepsilon_{a,X}\,(x,f) & = & fx
\end{array}
$$

$$
\begin{array}{lcl}
\delta_{a,b,c,X} & : & R^{(K)}_{a,c}X\rightarrow R^{(K)}_{a,b}\,(R^{(K)}_{b,c}X) \\
\delta_{a,b,c,X}\,(x,f) & = & (x,\lambda y.\,(y,f))
\end{array}
$$

The parameterised comonad R from Example 4.3 is the same as $R^{(I)}$ where I is the identity functor.

The proposition below shows how the comonadic structure of $R^{(K)}$ interacts nicely with the isomorphism of Proposition 2.2.

Proposition 4.5

Let $F, G: Set\rightarrow Set$, $f: a\rightarrow Fb$, and $g: b\rightarrow Gc$, then the following equations hold.

a) $\varepsilon_{a,X}=\alpha_I(id_{Ka})_X \quad : R^{(K)}_{a,a,X}\rightarrow X$

b) $(\alpha_F(f)\cdot\alpha_G(g))_X\circ\delta_{a,b,c,X}=\alpha_{F\cdot G}(Fg\circ f)_X \quad : R^{(K)}_{a,c}X\rightarrow F(GX)$

where $F\cdot G$ is functor composition and where $\alpha\cdot\beta$ is the horizontal composition of natural transformations. That is, given natural transformations $\alpha:F\rightarrow G$, and $\beta:F'\rightarrow G'$, , horizontal composition $\alpha\cdot\beta:F\cdot F'\rightarrow G\cdot G'$ is given by $\alpha\cdot\beta=G(\beta)\circ\alpha_{F'}$.

Example 4.6

The pair ((×C),k) is an R-coalgebra with

$$
\begin{array}{lcl}
k_{a,b} & : & a\times C\rightarrow R_{a,b}(b\times C) \\
k_{a,b}\,(a,c) & = & (a,\lambda b.\,(b,c))
\end{array}
$$

Coalgebras of $R^{(K)}$ play an important role in functional programming as they are precisely the type of very well-behaved lenses, hereafter called lenses (Foster et al., 2007). A lens provides access to a component B inside another type A. More formally a lens from A to B is an isomorphism $A\cong B\times C$ for some residual type C. A lens from A to B is most easily implemented by a pair of appropriately typed getter and setter functions

$$
\begin{array}{lcl}
get & : & A\rightarrow B \\
set & : & A\times B\rightarrow A
\end{array}
$$

satisfying three laws[2]

[2] In Foster et al. (2007), the less well-behaved lenses do not satisfy all three laws.

$$
\begin{array}{rcl}
set(x,get(x)) & = & x \\
get(set(x,y)) & = & y \\
set(set(x,y_1),y_2) & = & set(x,y_2)
\end{array}
$$

More generally, given two functors $J:\mathscr{P}\rightarrow Set$ and $K:\mathscr{P}\rightarrow Set$, we can form a parameterised lens from J to K with a family of getters and setters

$$
\begin{array}{lcl}
get_a & : & Ja\rightarrow Ka \\
set_{a,b} & : & Ja\times Kb\rightarrow Jb
\end{array}
$$

satisfying the same three laws, and with get being natural in a and set being natural in b. By some simple algebra we see that the type of lenses is isomorphic to the type of coalgebras of the parameterised comonad $R^{(K)}$

$$
(Ja\rightarrow Ka)\times(Ja\times Kb\rightarrow Jb)\quad\cong\quad Ja\rightarrow R^{(K)}_{a,b}(Jb)
$$

Furthermore the coalgebra laws are satisfied if and only if the corresponding lens laws are satisfied (O'Connor, 2010; Gibbons & Johnson, 2012). For instance, the coalgebra given in Example 4.6 is a parameterised lens into the first component of a pair.

Using the representation theorem and some simple manipulations we can define a third way to represent a parameterised lens from J to K. The so-called Van Laarhoven representation (Van Laarhoven, 2009a; O'Connor, 2011) is defined by a family of ends

$$\int_{F:\mathscr{E}} (Ka \to F(Kb)) \to Ja \to F(Jb)$$

that is natural in the sense that given two arrows from $\mathscr{P}$, $p : a \to a'$ and $q : b \to b'$, and given $f : Ka' \to F(Kb)$ for some $F : \mathscr{E}$ then

$$F(Jq) \circ v_{a',b,F}(f) \circ Jp = v_{a,b',F}(F(Kq) \circ f \circ Kp).$$

The corresponding laws for the Van Laarhoven representation of lenses are

- the linearity law

  For all $f : Ka \to F(Kb)$ and $g : Kb \to G(Kc)$,

$$v_{a,c,F \cdot G}(Fg \circ f) = Fv_{b,c,G}(g) \circ v_{a,b,F}(f)$$

- and the unity law

$$v_{a,a,I}(id_{Ka}) = id_{Ja}.$$

The following theorem proves that the coalgebra representation and Van Laarhoven representation of parameterised lenses are equivalent.

Theorem 4.7 (Lens Representation)

Given $\mathscr{E}$, a small full subcategory of Set^{Set} and given functors $J, K : \mathscr{P} \to Set$, then the families $k_{a,b} : Ja \to R^{(K)}_{a,b}(Jb)$ which form $R^{(K)}$-coalgebras (J, k) are isomorphic to the families of ends

$$\int_{F:\mathscr{E}} (Ka \to F(Kb)) \to Ja \to F(Jb)$$

which satisfy the linearity and unity laws.

Proof

First, we prove the isomorphism of families without regard to the laws

$$\begin{array}{ll} & Ja \to R^{(K)}_{a,b}(Jb) \\ \cong & \quad \{ \text{definition of } R^{(K)} \} \\ & Ja \to R_{Ka,Kb}(Jb) \\ \cong & \quad \{ \text{Equation 3.3} \} \\ & Ja \to \int_F (Ka \to F(Kb)) \to F(Jb) \\ \cong & \quad \{ \text{Hom functors preserve ends (Remark A.4)} \} \\ & \int_F Ja \to (Ka \to F(Kb)) \to F(Jb) \\ \cong & \quad \{ \text{Swap argument} \} \\ & \int_F (Ka \to F(Kb)) \to Ja \to F(Jb) \end{array}$$

This isomorphism is witnessed by the following functions:

$$\begin{array}{ll} \gamma & : (\int_F (Ka \to F(Kb)) \to Ja \to F(Jb)) \to (Ja \to R^{(K)}_{a,b}(Jb)) \\ \gamma(h) & = h_{R^{(K)}_{a,b}}(\alpha^{-1}_{R^{(K)}_{a,b}}(id)) \end{array}$$

$$\begin{array}{lll} \gamma^{-1} & : (Ja \to R^{(K)}_{a,b}(Jb)) \to \int_F (Ka \to F(Kb)) \to (Ja \to F(Jb)) & \\ \gamma^{-1}(k) = \tau & \text{where } \tau_F & : (Ka \to F(Kb)) \to Ja \to F(Jb) \\ & & \tau_F(g) = \alpha_F(g)_{Jb} \circ k \end{array}$$

In order to prove that the laws of coalgebras for parameterised comonads correspond to unity and linearity, we first prove two technical lemmas.

Lemma 4.8

$$\gamma^{-1}(k_{a,c})_{F \cdot G}(Fg \circ f) = (\alpha_F(f) \cdot \alpha_G(g))_{Jc} \circ \delta_{a,b,c,Jc} \circ k_{a,c}$$

Proof

This follows from Proposition 4.5(b).

Lemma 4.9

$$F(\gamma^{-1}(k_{b,c})_G(g)) \circ \gamma^{-1}(k_{a,b})_F(f) = (\alpha_F(f) \cdot \alpha_G(g))_{Jc} \circ R^{(K)}_{a,b}(k_{b,c}) \circ k_{a,b}$$

Proof

This follows from the definition of γ^{-1} and properties of functors and natural transformations.

Generalised versions of Lemma 4.8 and Lemma 4.9 appear with detailed proofs in Lemma B.4 and Lemma B.5.

By the previous two lemmas, to prove that the comultiplication-coalgebra law is equivalent to the linearity law it suffices to prove the following:

$$\begin{array}{rcl} R^{(K)}_{a,b}(k_{b,c}) \circ k_{a,b} & = & \delta_{a,b,c,Jc} \circ k_{a,c} \\ & \Longleftrightarrow & \\ \forall F, G, f, g. (\alpha_F(f) \cdot \alpha_G(g)) \circ R^{(K)}_{a,b}(k_{b,c}) \circ k_{a,b} & = & (\alpha_F(f) \cdot \alpha_G(g)) \circ \delta_{a,b,c,Jc} \circ k_{a,c} \end{array}$$

The forward implication is clear. To prove the reverse implication take $F = R^{(K)}_{a,b}$ and f = $\alpha^{-1}_{R^{(K)}_{a,b}}(id)_{Jb}$. Also take $G = R^{(K)}_{b,c}$ and $g = \alpha^{-1}_{R^{(K)}_{b,c}}(id)_{Jc}$. Then $\alpha_F(f) = id$ and $\alpha_G(g) = id$. Therefore, $\alpha_F(f) \cdot \alpha_G(g) = id$ and the result follows.

To prove that the counit-coalgebra law is equivalent to the unity law it suffices to prove that $\varepsilon_{a,Ja} \circ k_{a,a} = \gamma^{-1}(k_{a,a})_I(id)$.

$$\begin{array}{ll} & \gamma^{-1}(k_{a,a})_I(id) \\ = & \quad \{ \text{definition of } \gamma^{-1} \} \\ & \alpha_I(id)_{Ja} \circ k_{a,a} \\ = & \quad \{ \text{Proposition 4.5(a)} \} \\ & \varepsilon_{a,Ja} \circ k_{a,a} \end{array}$$

The previous theorem can be generalised to the case where we have an adjunction.

Theorem 4.10 (Generalised Lens Representation)

Let $\mathscr{E}$ and $\mathscr{F}$ be two small categories of Set-endofunctors, such that $\mathscr{E}$ and $\mathscr{F}$ are (strict) monoidal with respect to the identity functor I and functor composition $- \cdot -$, and $\mathscr{E}$ is a full sub-category. Let $(-)^* \dashv U : \mathscr{E} \to \mathscr{F}$, be an adjunction between them, such that U is strict monoidal. Then

1. $UR^{(K)*}$ is a parameterised comonad.
2. Given functors $J, K : \mathscr{P} \to Set$, then the family $k_{a,b} : Ja \to UR^{(K)*}_{a,b}(Jb)$ which form the $UR^{(K)*}$-coalgebras (J,k) are isomorphic to the family of ends

   $$\int_{F:\mathscr{F}} (Ka \to UF(Kb)) \to Ja \to UF(Jb)$$

   which satisfy the linearity and unity laws.

Proof

Proposition B.3.

By considering the identity adjunction between $\mathscr{E}$ and itself, Theorem 4.7 can be recovered from this generalised version.

Implementing Lenses in Haskell

The Lens representation theorem demonstrates that the coalgebra representation of lenses and the Van Laarhoven representation are isomorphic. Both representations can be implemented in Haskell.

```
-- Parameterised store comonad
data PStore a b x = PStore (b → x) a
-- Coalgebra representation of lenses
newtype KLens ja jb ka kb = KLens (ja → PStore ka kb jb)
-- Van Laarhoven representation of lenses
type VLens ja jb ka kb = ∀f . Functor f ⇒ (ka → f kb) → ja
→ f jb
```

There are a few observations to make about this Haskell code. Firstly, neither the coalgebra laws nor the linearity and unity laws of the Van Laarhoven representation can be enforced by Haskell's type system, as it often happens when implementing algebraic structures such as monoids or monads. We have accordingly omitted writing out the parameterised comonad operations of PStore. Secondly, rather than taking J and K as parameters, we take source and target types for each functor. By not explicitly using functors as parameters, we avoid newtype wrapping and unwrapping functions that would otherwise be needed. Consider the example of building a lens to access the first component of a pair.

```
fstLens         :: VLens a b (a,y) (b,y)
fstLens f (a,y) = (λb → (b,y)) `fmap` (f a)
```

Above we are constructing a VLens value but the argument applies equally well to a KLens value. The pair type is functorial in two arguments. For fstLens, we care about pairs being functorial with respect to the first position. If we were required to pass a J functor explicitly to VLens, we would need to add a wrapper around (a,b) to make it explicitly a functor of the first position. Furthermore, we are implicitly using the identity functor for the K functor. If we were required to pass a K functor explicitly to VLens we would have to wrap and unwrap the Identity functor in Haskell in order to use the lens. Fortunately, all lens functionality can be implemented without explicitly mentioning the functor parameters.

The third thing to note about the VLens formulation is that we use a type alias rather than a newtype. This allows us to compose a lens of type VLens ja jb ka kb and another lens of type VLens ka kb la lb by simply using the standard function composition operator. There is another advantage that the type alias gives us, which we will see later.

The isomorphism between the two representations can be written out explicitly in Haskell.

```
instance Functor (PStore i j) where
  fmap f (PStore h x) = PStore (f ∘ h) x

kLens2VLens    :: KLens ja jb ka kb → VLens ja jb ka kb
kLens2VLens k f = (λ(PStore h x) → h `fmap` f x) ∘ k
vLens2KLens    :: VLens ja jb ka kb → KLens ja jb ka kb
vLens2KLens v   = v (PStore id)
```

The generalised lens representation theorem gives us pairs of representations of various lens derivatives. Using pointed functors, i.e. using the free pointed functor generated by PStore in the case of the coalgebra representation, or quantifying over pointed functors in the case of the Van Laarhoven representation, gives us the notion of a partial lens (O'Connor et al., 2013), also known as an affine traversal (Kmett, 2013).[3]

[3] An affine traversal from A to B is so called because it specifies an isomorphism between A and F B for some affine container F, i.e. for some functor F where $F X \cong C_1 \times \dot{X} + C_2$.

```
data FreePointedPStore a b x = Unit x
                             | FreePointedPStore (b → x) a
  -- coalgebra representation of partial lenses
newtype KPartialLens ja jb ka kb = KPartialLens (ja → FreePointedPStore ka kb jb)
class Functor f ⇒ Pointed f where
  point :: a → f a
  -- Van Laarhoven representation of partial lenses
type VPartialLens ja jb ka kb = ∀f. Pointed f ⇒ (ka → f kb) → ja → f jb
```

A partial lens provides a reference to 0 or 1 occurrences of K within J. If we instead use applicative functors (Section 5.1), we get a reference to a sequence of 0 or more occurrences of K within J. This lens derivative is called a traversal.

```
data FreeApplicativePStore a b x =
    Unit x
  | FreeApplicativePStore (FreeApplicativePStore a b (b → x)) a
  -- coalgebra representation of traversals
newtype KTraversal ja jb ka kb = KTraversal (ja → FreeApplicativePStore ka kb jb)
  -- Van Laarhoven representation of traversals
type VTraversal ja jb ka kb = ∀f. Applicative f ⇒ (ka → f kb) → ja → f jb
```

The Haskell implementation of the isomorphism between KPartialLens and VPartialLens and the isomorphism between KTraversal and VTraversal is left as an exercise to the interested reader.

The second advantage of using a type synonym for the Van Laarhoven representation is that values of type VLens are values of type VPartialLens and VTraversal, while the values of type KLens need to be explicitly converted to KPartialLens and KTraversal. If Haskell's standard library were modified such that Pointed was a super-class of Applicative, then values of type VPartialLens would be of type VTraversal as well.

THE FINITENESS OF TRAVERSALS

In this section we show another application of the representation theorem. We show that traversable functors are exactly the finitary containers. We first introduce the relevant definitions and then provide the proof.

Applicative Functors

The cartesian product gives the category Set a monoidal structure (Set,×,1,α,λ,ρ), where $\alpha_{X,Y,Z} : X \times (Y \times Z) \to (X \times Y) \times Z$, $\lambda_X : 1 \times X \to X$, and $\rho_X : X \times 1 \to X$ are natural isomorphisms expressing associativity of the product, left unit and right unit, respectively.

Definition 5.1 (Applicative Functor)

An applicative functor is a functor F: Set → Set which is strong lax monoidal with respect to this monoidal structure. That is, it is equipped with a map and a natural transformation:

$u : 1 \to F\,1$ (monoidal unit)

$\star_{X,Y} : F\,X \times F\,Y \to F\,(X \times Y)$ (monoidal action)

such that

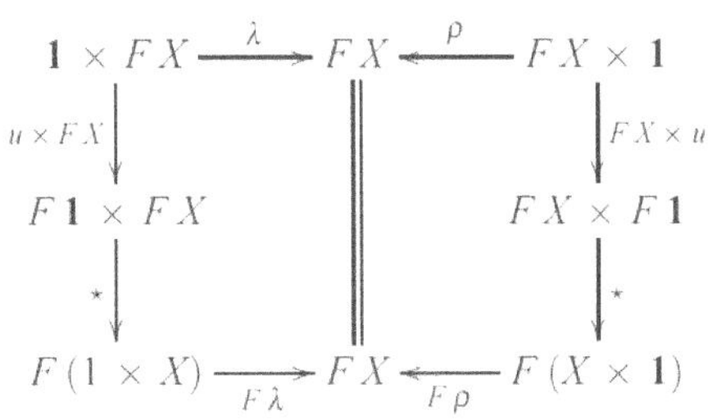

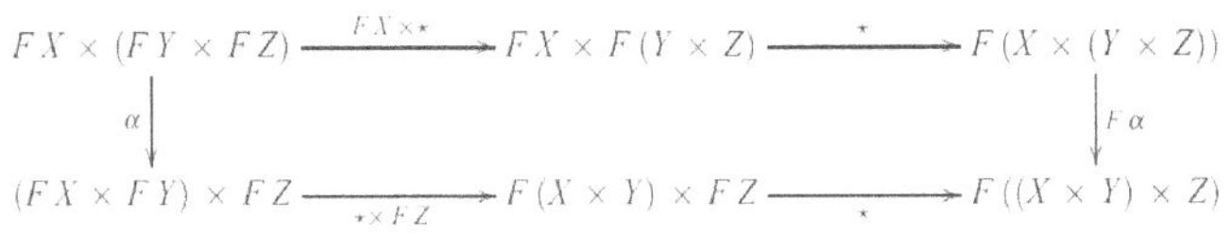

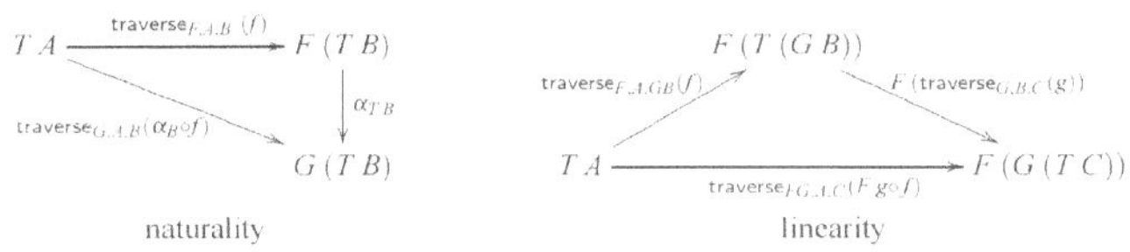

All Set functors are strong, but the strength $\tau : F\,X \times Y \rightarrow F\,(X \times Y)$ of an applicative functor F is required to be coherent with the monoidal action, i.e. the following diagram commutes.

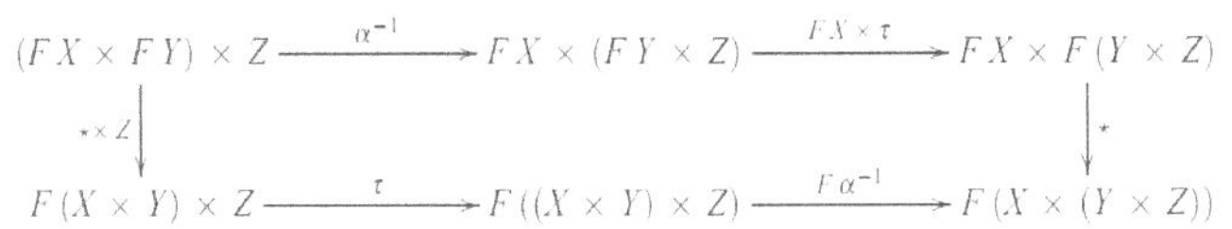

Applicative functors may alternatively be given as a mapping of objects F: |Set| → |Set| equipped with two natural transformations $pure_X : X \rightarrow F\,X$ and $\circledast_{X,Y} : F\,(X \rightarrow Y) \times F\,X \rightarrow F\,Y$, together with some equations (see (McBride & Paterson, 2008) for details). This presentation is more useful for programming and therefore is the one chosen in Haskell. However, for our purposes, the presentation of applicative functors as monoidal functors is more convenient. This situation where one presentation is more apt for programming, and another presentation is better for formal reasoning also occurs with monads, where bind (>>=) is preferred for programming and the multiplication (join) is preferred for formal reasoning.

Definition 5.2 (Applicative Morphism)

Let F and G be applicative functors. An applicative morphism is a natural transformation $\tau : F \rightarrow G$ that respects the unit and multiplication. That is, a natural transformation τ such that the following diagrams commute.

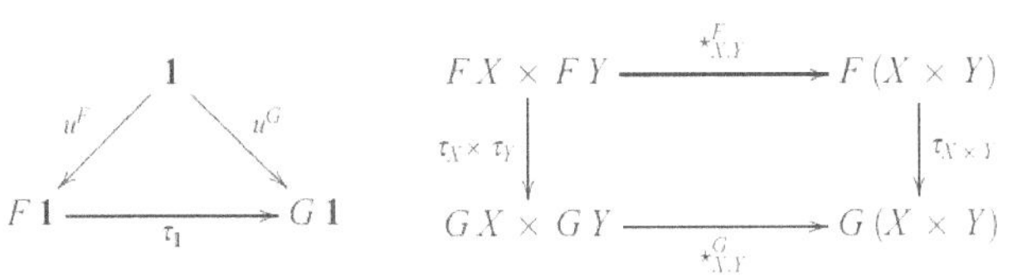

Applicative functors and applicative morphisms form a strict monoidal category $\mathscr{A}$. The identity functor is an applicative functor, and the composition of applicative functors is an applicative functor. Hence, $\mathscr{A}$ has the structure of a strict monoidal category.

Traversable Functors

McBride and Paterson (2008) characterise traversable functors as those equipped with a family of morphisms $traverse_{F,A,B} : (A \rightarrow FB) \times TA \rightarrow F(T\,B)$, natural in an applicative functor F, and sets A and B (cf. the type synonym VTraversable from Section 4.1.) However, without further constraints this characterisation is too coarse. Hence, Jaskelioff and Ryp´a˘cek (2012) proposed the following notion:

Definition 5.3 (Traversable Functor)

A functor T : Set → Set is said to be traversable if there is a family of functions

$$\mathsf{traverse}_{F,A,B} : (A \rightarrow FB) \times TA \rightarrow F(TB)$$

natural in F, A, and B that respects the monoidal structure of applicative functor composition. More concretely, for all applicative functors F,G : Set → Set and applicative morphisms α : F → G, the following diagrams should commute:

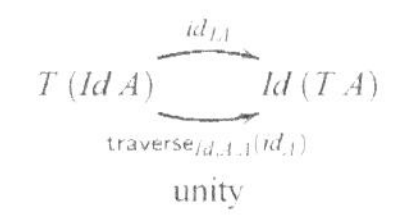

Characterising Traversable Functors

Let $\mathscr{A}$ be the category of applicative functors and applicative morphisms. In order to prove that traversable functors are finitary containers, we first note that the forgetful functor U from the category of applicative functors $\mathscr{A}$ into the category of endofunctors has a left adjoint $(-)^*$ (Capriotti & Kaposi, 2014) and therefore we can apply Theorem 4.10 to any traversal which satisfies the linearity and unity laws. Hence for every traversal on T

$$\mathsf{traverse}_{A,B} : \int_{F:\mathscr{A}} (A \rightarrow UFB) \rightarrow TA \rightarrow UF(TB)$$

there is a corresponding coalgebra

$$t_{A,B} : TA \rightarrow UR^*_{A,B}(TB)$$

where $R^*_{A,B}$ is the free applicative functor for $R_{A,B}$. The following proposition tells us what this free applicative functor looks like.

Proposition 5.4

The free applicative functor on $R_{A,B}$ is

$$R^*_{A,B}X = \Sigma n : \mathbb{N}.\ A^n \times (B^n \rightarrow X)$$

with action on morphisms $R^*_{A,B}(h)\,(n,as,f) = (n,as,h \circ f)$, and applicative structure:

$$\begin{aligned} u &: R^*_{A,B}1 \\ u &= (0,*,\lambda bs.*) \\ \star_{X,Y} &: R^*_{A,B}X \times R^*_{A,B}Y \rightarrow R^*_{A,B}(X \times Y) \\ (n,as,f) \star (m,as',g) &= (n+m,\ as +\!\!+ as',\ \lambda bs.(f\,(\mathsf{take}\ n\ bs), g\,(\mathsf{drop}\ n\ bs))) \end{aligned}$$

where we write X^n for vectors of length n, i.e. the n-fold product n times $\overbrace{X \times \cdots \times X}^{n\ \text{times}}$, ++ for vector append, and take n and drop n for the functions that given a vector of size n+m return the first n elements and the last m elements respectively.

The datatype FreeApplicativePStore given in Section 4.1 is a Haskell implementation of the free applicative functor on $R_{A,B}$, namely $R^*_{A,B}$.

Hence $R^*_{A,B}X$ consists of a natural number, which we call the dimension, a finite vector, which we call the position,

- a function from a finite vector, which allows us to peek into new positions.

In order to make it easier to talk about the different components we define projections: let $r = (n, i, g) : R^*_{A.B} X$, then dim r = n, pos r = i, and peek r = g.

Theorem 4.10 tells us that UR* is a parameterised comonad with the following counit and comultiplication operations.

$$\begin{array}{lcl} \varepsilon_{A.X} & : & UR^*_{A.A} X \to X \\ \varepsilon_{A.X}(n, as, f) & = & f\ as \\ \\ \delta_{A.B.C.X} & : & UR^*_{A.C} X \to UR^*_{A.B}(UR^*_{B.C} X) \\ \delta_{A.B.C.X}(n, as, f) & = & (n, as, \lambda bs.(n, bs, f)) \end{array}$$

Furthermore, given a traversal of T, a coalgebra for UR* ,(T,t)is given by $t_{A,B}$ = traverse$_{A,B}$ wrap$_{A,B}$, where

$$\begin{array}{lcl} \mathsf{wrap}_{A.B} & : & A \to UR^*_{A.B} B \\ \mathsf{wrap}_{A.B}\ a & = & (1, a, id_b) \end{array}$$

In the other direction, given a coalgebra for UR* , (T,t), we obtain a traversal for T:

$$\mathsf{traverse}_{A.B} f\ x = \mathbf{let}\ (n, as, g) = t\ x\ \mathbf{in}\ F(g)\ (\mathsf{collect}_n f\ as)$$

where $\mathsf{collect}_n f\ (x_1, \ldots, x_n) = f(x_1) \star \cdots \star f(x_n)$.

Finitary Containers

A finitary container (Abbott et al., 2003) is given by a set of shapes S, and an arity function $ar : S \to \mathbb{N}$. The extension of a finitary container (S,ar) is a functor $[\![S, ar]\!] : \mathsf{Set} \to \mathsf{Set}$ defined as follows.

$$[\![S, ar]\!]\ X = \Sigma\, s : S.\ X^{(ar\ s)}$$

Given an element of an extension of a finitary container $c = (s, xs) : \Sigma\, s : S.\ X^{(ar\ s)}$, we define projections shape c = s, and contents c = xs.

As an example, lists are given by the finitary container $(\mathbb{N}, id_{\mathbb{N}})$, where the set of shapes indicates the length of the list. Therefore its extension is

$$[\![\mathbb{N}, id]\!]\ X = \Sigma\, n : \mathbb{N}.\ X^n.$$

Vectors of length n are given by the finitary container (1,λx.n). They have only one shape and have a fixed arity. Streams are containers (Abbott et al., 2003) with exactly one shape, but are not finitary.

Lemma 5.5 (Finitary containers are traversable)

The extension of any finitary container (S,ar) is traversable with a canonical traversal given by:

$$\begin{array}{lcl} \mathsf{traverse}_{F.X.Y} & : & (X \to F\,Y) \times [\![S, ar]\!] X \to F\,[\![S, ar]\!]\,Y \\ \mathsf{traverse}_{F.X.Y}(f, (s, xs)) & = & F(\lambda c.(s, c))(\mathsf{collect}_{ar(s)}\ f\ xs) \end{array}$$

Finitary Containers from Coalgebras

For the first part of our proof we already showed that every traversal is isomorphic to an UR* -coalgebra. For the second part, we show that if (T, t) is a UR* -coalgebra then T is a finitary container.

Theorem 5.6

Let X: Set and let (T,t) be a coalgebra for UR*. That is, T: Set → Set is a functor and $t_{A.B} : T\,A \to UR^*_{a.b}(T\,B)$ is a family natural in A and dinatural in B such that certain laws hold (see Definition 4.2). Then T X is isomorphic to the extension of the finitary container $[\![T1, \lambda s.\ \mathsf{dim}\ (t\,s)]\!]\ X$.

Proof

We define an isomorphism between T X and $\Sigma\, s : T1.\ X^{(\mathsf{dim}\ (t\,s))}$.

Given a value x: T X, the contents of the resulting container are simply the position of (t x). The shape of the resulting container is obtained by peeking into (t x) at the trivial vector $*^n : 1^n$ where n is the dimension of (t x). More formally we define one direction of the isomorphism as

$$\begin{array}{l} \Phi\ :\ T\,X \to \Sigma\, s : T1.\ X^{(\mathsf{dim}\ (t\,s))} \\ \Phi\,x = \mathbf{let}\ (n, i, g) = t\,x\ \mathbf{in}\ (g\ (*^n), i) \end{array}$$

Given a value $(s, v) : \Sigma\, s : T1.\ X^{(\mathsf{dim}\ (t\,s))}$ we can create a T X by peaking into (t s) at v. More formally, the other direction of the isomorphism is defined as

$$\begin{array}{l} \Psi\ :\ \Sigma\, s : T1.\ X^{(\mathsf{dim}\ (t\,s))} \to T\,X \\ \Psi\ (s, v) = \mathsf{peek}\ (t\,s)\ v \end{array}$$

First we prove that $\Psi\ (\Phi\,x) = x$.

$$\begin{array}{ll} & \Psi\ (\Phi\,x) \\ = & \quad \{\ \text{definition of } \Psi, \Phi\ \} \\ & \mathbf{let}\ (n, i, g) = t\,x\ \mathbf{in}\ \mathsf{peek}\ (t\ (g\ (*^n)))\ i \\ = & \quad \{\ \text{map on morphisms of } UR^*_{a.b}\ \} \\ & \mathbf{let}\ (n, i, h) = UR^*_{a.b}\ (t)\ (t\,x)\ \mathbf{in}\ \mathsf{peek}\ (h\ (*^n))\ i \\ = & \quad \{\ \text{comultiplication-coalgebra law}\ \} \\ & \mathbf{let}\ (n, i, h) = \delta\ (t\,x)\ \mathbf{in}\ \mathsf{peek}\ (h\ (*^n))\ i \\ = & \quad \{\ \text{definition of } \delta \text{ and peek}\ \} \\ & \mathbf{let}\ (n, i, g) = (t\,x)\ \mathbf{in}\ g\ i \\ = & \quad \{\ \text{definition of } \varepsilon\ \} \\ & \varepsilon\ (t\,x) \\ = & \quad \{\ \text{counit-coalgebra law}\ \} \\ & x \end{array}$$

Last we prove that $\Phi\ (\Psi\ (s, v)) = (s, v)$.

$$\begin{array}{ll} & \Phi\ (\Psi\ (s, v)) \\ = & \quad \{\ \text{definition of } \Psi, \Phi, \text{ and map on morphisms of } UR^*_{a.b}\ \} \\ & \mathbf{let}\ \{(\_, \_, h) = UR^*_{a.b}\ t\ (t\,s); (n, i, g) = h\ v\}\ \mathbf{in}\ (g\ (*^n), i) \\ = & \quad \{\ \text{comultiplication-coalgebra law}\ \} \\ & \mathbf{let}\ \{(\_, \_, h) = \delta\ (t\,s); (n, i, g) = h\ v\}\ \mathbf{in}\ (g\ (*^n), i) \\ = & \quad \{\ \text{definition of } \delta\ \} \\ & \mathbf{let}\ (n, j, g) = t\,s\ \mathbf{in}\ (g\ (*^n), v) \\ = & \quad \{\ j = (*^n) \text{ because } 1^n \text{ has a unique element}\ \} \\ & \mathbf{let}\ (n, j, g) = t\,s\ \mathbf{in}\ (g\,j, v) \\ = & \quad \{\ \text{definition of } \varepsilon\ \} \\ & (\varepsilon\ (t\,s), v) \\ & \quad \{\ \text{counit-coalgebra law}\ \} \\ & (s, v) \end{array}$$

Corollary 5.7

Let X : Set and T : Set → Set be a traversable functor. Then T X is isomorphic to the finitary container $[\![T1, \lambda s.\ \mathsf{dim}\ (\mathsf{traverse\ wrap}\ s)]\!]\ X$

.

Proof

Apply Theorem 5.6 with the UR* -coalgebra t = traversewrap.

All that remains to show is that this isomorphism maps the traversal of T to the canonical traversal of the finitary container.

Theorem 5.8

Let T: Set → Set be a traversable functor and let $\Phi : T\,X \to [\![T1, \lambda s.\ \mathrm{dim}\ (\mathrm{traverse\ wrap}\ s)]\!]\,X$ be the isomorphism defined above. Let F be an arbitrary applicative functor and let f: A → F B and x: T A. Then, F (Φ) (traverse f x) = traverse f (Φ x).

Proof

Before beginning we prove two small lemmas. First that pos(traverse wrap x) = contents(Φ x)

$\mathrm{pos}\ (\mathrm{traverse\ wrap}\ x)$
$=\quad \{ \text{definition of pos} \}$
$\mathbf{let}\ (\_, i, \_) = \mathrm{traverse\ wrap}\ x\ \mathbf{in}\ i$
$=\quad \{ \text{definition of } \Phi \}$
$\mathrm{contents}\ (\Phi\, x)$

Second, we prove that Φ (peek (traverse wrap x) w) = (shape (Φ x),w)

$\Phi\ (\mathrm{peek}\ (\mathrm{traverse\ wrap}\ x)\ w)$
$=\quad \{ \text{definition of peek} \}$
$\mathbf{let}\ (\_, \_, g) = \mathrm{traverse\ wrap}\ x\ \mathbf{in}\ \Phi\ (g\ w)$
$=\quad \{ \text{definition of } \Phi \}$
$\mathbf{let}\ \{ (\_, \_, g) = \mathrm{traverse\ wrap}\ x; (n, i, h) = \mathrm{traverse\ wrap}\ (g\ w) \}\ \mathbf{in}\ (h\ (*^n), i)$
$=\quad \{ \text{definition of } UR^*_{a,b} \}$
$\mathbf{let}\ \{ (\_, \_, g) = UR^*_{a,b}\ (\mathrm{traverse\ wrap})\ (\mathrm{traverse\ wrap}\ x); (n, i, h) = g\ w \}\ \mathbf{in}\ (h\ (*^n), i)$
$=\quad \{ \text{coalgebra law for } \delta \}$
$\mathbf{let}\ \{ (\_, \_, g) = \delta\ (\mathrm{traverse\ wrap}\ x); (n, i, h) = g\ w \}\ \mathbf{in}\ (h\ (*^n), i)$
$=\quad \{ \text{definition of } \delta \}$
$\mathbf{let}\ (\_, \_, g) = \mathrm{traverse\ wrap}\ x\ \mathbf{in}\ (g\ (*^n), w)$
$=\quad \{ \text{definition of } \Phi \}$
$(\mathrm{shape}\ (\Phi\, x), w)$

Lastly, we prove our main result.

$F\ (\Phi)\ (\mathrm{traverse}\ f\ x)$
$=\quad \{ \text{isomorphism in Theorem 4.10} \}$
$\mathbf{let}\ (n, i, g) = \mathrm{traverse\ wrap}\ x\ \mathbf{in}\ F\ (\Phi)\ (F\ (g)\ (\mathrm{collect}_n\ f\ i))$
$=\quad \{ \text{functors respect composition} \}$
$\mathbf{let}\ (n, i, g) = \mathrm{traverse\ wrap}\ x\ \mathbf{in}\ F\ (\Phi \circ g)\ (\mathrm{collect}_n\ f\ i)$
$=\quad \{ \text{application of above two lemmas} \}$
$\mathbf{let}\ (s, v) = \Phi\, x\ \mathbf{in}\ F\ (\lambda c.\ (s, c))\ (\mathrm{collect}_n\ f\ v)$
$=\quad \{ \text{definition of canonical traverse for finitary containers} \}$
$\mathrm{traverse}\ f\ (\Phi\, x)$

The isomorphism between T and $[\![T1, \lambda s.\ \mathrm{dim}\ (\mathrm{traverse\ wrap}\ s)]\!]$ must be natural by construction. However, naturality is also an immediate consequence of the preceding theorem because traversing with the identity functor I is equivalent to the mapping on morphisms of a traversable functor.

IMPLEMENTING ALGEBRAIC THEORIES

As a last application of the representation theorem, we take a look at the case where we consider $\mathcal{M}$, the category of monads with monad homomorphisms. In this situation, the functor $(-)^* : \mathcal{E} \to \mathcal{M}$, maps any functor $F : \mathcal{E}$ to F^*, the free monad on F, while the functor $U : \mathcal{M} \to \mathcal{E}$ forgets the monad structure. The representation theorem then states that

$$\int_{M \in \mathcal{M}} (A \to UMB) \to UMX \quad \cong \quad UR^*_{A,B}X \tag{6.1}$$

where, $R_{A,B}X = A \times (B \to X)$ is the parameterised store comonad.

In Haskell, we can write the isomorphism (6.1) as

$\forall m.\ \mathrm{Monad}\ m \Rightarrow (a \to m\ b) \to m\ x \quad \cong \quad \mathit{Free}\ (\mathit{PStore}\ a\ b)\ x$

where PStore (as given in Section 4.1) and the free monad construction are as follows:

$\mathbf{newtype}\ \mathit{PStore}\ a\ b\ x = \mathit{PStore}\ (b \to x)\ a$

$\mathbf{data}\ \mathit{Free}\ f\ x = \mathit{Unit}\ x \mid \mathit{Branch}\ (f\ (\mathit{Free}\ f\ x))$

$\mathbf{instance}\ \mathrm{Functor}\ f \Rightarrow \mathrm{Monad}\ (\mathit{Free}\ f)\ \mathbf{where}$
$\quad \mathit{return} \qquad = \mathit{Unit}$
$\quad \mathit{Pure}\ x \gg\!= f \quad = f\ x$
$\quad \mathit{Branch}\ xs \gg\!= f = \mathit{Branch}\ (\mathrm{fmap}\ (\gg\!= f)\ xs)$

This way of constructing a free monad from an arbitrary functor requires a recursive datatype. The isomorphism (6.1), on the other hand, shows a non-recursive way of describing the free monad on functors of the form PStore a b.

While this result seems to be of limited applicability, we note that every signature of an algebraic operation with parameter a and arity b determines a functor of this form. Hence, the theorem tells us how to construct the free monad on a given signature of a single algebraic operation. Intuitively the type

∀m. Monad m ⇒ (a → m b) → m x

describes a monadic computation m x in which the only source of impurity is the operation of type a → m b in the argument. This type can be implemented in Haskell in the following manner, where we have abstracted over the types of the argument operation.

newtype FreeOp primOp x = FreeOp {runOp :: ∀m. Monad m ⇒ primOp m → m x}

instance Monad (FreeOp primOp) where

return x = FreeOp (const (return x))

x>>=f = FreeOp (λop → runOp x op>>=λa → runOp (f a) op)

Notice that the bind operation for FreeOp is not recursive, but is implemented in terms of the bind operation for an arbitrary abstract monad.

For example, exceptions in a type e can be given by a nullary operation throw with parameter e. [4]

[4] In order to avoid clutter, we sometimes use a type synonym where a real implementation would require a newtype, with its associated constructor and destructor.

$\mathbf{type}\ \mathit{Exc}\ e\ m = e \to m\ \emptyset$

where $\emptyset$ is the empty type, and hence FreeOp (Exc e) is the type of monadic computations which can throw an exception using the following operation:

$\mathit{throw} \quad :: e \to \mathit{FreeOp}\ (\mathit{Exc}\ e)\ \emptyset$
$\mathit{throw}\ e = \mathit{FreeOp}\ (\lambda\_\mathit{throw} \to \_\mathit{throw}\ e)$

We may model environments in r by an operation ask with parameter () and arity r.

$\mathbf{type}\ \mathit{Env}\ r\ m = () \to m\ r$

Hence, FreeOp (Env r) is the type of monadic computation which can read an environment using the following operation:

```
ask :: FreeOp (Env r) r
ask = FreeOp (λ_ask → _ask ())
```

More generally, we may want to consider algebraic theories with more than one operation. Following the same argument as before, but considering the N-ary representation theorem, we can construct the free monad on any signature of algebraic operations and express it by its generic effects (Plotkin & Power, 2003) by means of a polymorphic type. For example, a simple teletype interface can be represented by the following functor (Swierstra, 2008):

```
data Teletype x = GetChar (Char → x)
               | PutChar Char x
```

The free monad generated by this Teletype functor produces a tree representing all the interactions with a teletype machine a user can have. The Teletype functor is isomorphic to a sum of instances of R

$$Teletype\ x \cong ((), Char \to x) + (Char, () \to x) \cong (R\ ()\ Char + R\ Char\ ())\ x$$

By the N-ary representation theorem, the free monad generated by Teletype is isomorphic to

$\forall m.\ Monad\ m \Rightarrow (() \to m\ Char) \to (Char \to m\ ()) \to m\ x$

We define a type for representing teletype operations. In order to reuse our previous definition of FreeOp and to get names for each argument, we define the type as a record in which each field corresponds to an operation.

```
data TTOp m = TTOp { _ttGetChar :: m Char
                   , _ttPutChar :: Char → m ()
                   }
```

We obtain the free monad for TTOp and define operations on it that basically choose the corresponding field from the record.

```
type FreeTT = FreeOp TTOp
ttGetChar :: FreeTT Char
ttGetChar = FreeOp _ttGetChar
ttPutChar   :: Char → FreeTT ()
ttPutChar c = FreeOp (λpo → _ttPutChar po c)
```

Values of type FreeTT can easily be interpreted in IO, by providing operations of the appropriate type.

```
runTTIO :: FreeTT a → IO a
runTTIO = runOp ttOpIO
  where ttOpIO :: TTOp IO
        ttOpIO = TTOp { _ttGetChar = getChar
                      , _ttPutChar = putChar
                      }
```

Of course, the larger purpose is that FreeTT values can be interpreted in other ways, for example, by logging input, or for use in automated tests by replaying previously logged input. Furthermore, a FreeOp monad can easily be embedded into another FreeOp monad with a larger set of primitive commands, or interpreted into another FreeOp monad with a smaller, more primitive set of commands, providing a simple way of implementing handlers of algebraic effects (Plotkin & Pretnar, 2009). Hence, Theorem 3.2 might provide the basis for a simple implementation of an algebraic-effects library.

RELATED WORK

Traversable functors were introduced by McBride and Paterson (2008), generalising a notion of traversal by Moggi et al. (1999). The notion proposed was too coarse and Gibbons and Oliveira (2009) analysed several properties that should hold for all traversals. Based on some of these properties, Jaskelioff and Ryp´aˇcek (2012) proposed a characterisation of traversable functors, and conjectured that they were isomorphic to finitary containers (Abbott et al., 2003). The conjecture was proven correct by Bird et al. (2013) by a means of a change of representation. The proof of this same fact presented in Section 5 uses a similar change of representation and was found independently.

The representation of the free applicative functor on the parameterised store comonad, R, is a dependently typed version of Van Laarhoven'sFunList data type (Van Laarhoven, 2009b). Van Laarhoven's applicative and parameterised comonad instances for this type have been translated to work on the dependently typed implementation. A particular case of the representation theorem has been conjectured by Van Laarhoven (2009c), and proved by O'Connor (2011). The proof of representation theorem for functors via the Yoneda lemma was discovered independently by Bartosz Milewski (2013).

The representation theorems applied to the case where the structured functors are monads (as in Section 6) yields isomorphisms analogous to the ones presented by Bauer et al. (2013). However, our proof is based on a categorical model, while theirs is based on a parametric model. Also, as opposed to us, they do not explore the connection with algebraic effects.

Bernardy et al. (Bernardy et al., 2010) use a representation theorem to transform polymorphic properties of a certain shape into monomorphic properties, which are easier and more efficient to test. This suggests that another application for the representation theorems in this article is to facilitate the testing of polymorphic properties.

ACKNOWLEDGEMENTS

Jaskelioff is funded by ANPCyT PICT 2009-15. Many thanks go to Edward Kmett who assisted the authors with the isomorphism between KLens and VLens, and to Exequiel Rivas, Jeremy Gibbons, and the anonymous referees for helping us improve the presentation of the paper. We also thank Shachaf Ben-Kiki for explaining why affine traversals are called so, and Gabor Greif for finding some typos.

REFERENCES

1. Abbott, Michael, Altenkirch, Thorsten, & Ghani, Neil. (2003). Categories of containers. Pages 23–38 of: Proceedings of Foundations of Software Science and Computation Structures.
2. Atkey, Robert. (2009a). Algebras for parameterised monads. Pages 3–17 of: Kurz, Alexander, Lenisa, Marina, & Tarlecki, Andrzej (eds), Algebra and Coalgebra in Computer Science, Third International Conference, CALCO 2009, Udine, Italy, September 7-10, 2009.

Proceedings. Lecture Notes in Computer Science, vol. 5728. Springer.

3. Atkey, Robert. (2009b). Parameterised notions of computation. Journal of functional programming, 19(3 & 4), 335–376.
4. Awodey, Steve. (2006). Category theory. Oxford University Press, USA.
5. Bainbridge, Edwin S., Freyd, Peter J., Scedrov, Andre, & Scott, Philip J. (1990). Functorial polymorphism. Theoretical computer science, 70(1), 35–64.
6. Bauer, Andrej, Hofmann, Martin, & Karbyshev, Aleksandr. (2013). On monadic parametricity of second-order functionals. Pages 225–240 of: Pfenning, Frank (ed), Foundations of Software Science and Computation Structures. Lecture Notes in Computer Science, vol. 7794. Springer Berlin Heidelberg.
7. Bernardy, Jean-Philippe, Jansson, Patrik, & Claessen, Koen. (2010). Testing polymorphic properties. Pages 125–144 of: Gordon, Andrew D. (ed), Programming languages and systems. Lecture Notes in Computer Science, vol. 6012. Springer Berlin Heidelberg.
8. Bird, Richard, & de Moor, Oege. (1997). Algebra of programming. Upper Saddle River, NJ, USA: Prentice-Hall, Inc.
9. Bird, Richard, Gibbons, Jeremy, Mehner, Stefan, Voigtl¨ander, Janis, & Schrijvers, Tom. (2013). Understanding idiomatic traversals backwards and forwards. Pages 25–36 of: Proceedings of the 2013 ACM SIGPLAN Symposium on Haskell. Haskell '13. New York, NY, USA: ACM.
10. Capriotti, Paolo, & Kaposi, Ambros. 2014 (April). Free applicative functors. Proceedings of the fifth Workshop on Mathematically Structured Functional Programming. MSFP '14.
11. Danielsson, Nils Anders, Hughes, John, Jansson, Patrik, & Gibbons, Jeremy. (2006). Fast and loose reasoning is morally correct. Sigplan not., 41(1), 206–217.
12. Foster, J. Nathan, Greenwald, Michael B., Moore, Jonathan T., Pierce, Benjamin C., & Schmitt, Alan. (2007). Combinators for bidirectional tree transformations: A linguistic approach to the view-update problem. Acm trans. program. lang. syst., 29(3).
13. Gibbons, Jeremy, & Johnson, Mike. (2012). Relating algebraic and coalgebraic descriptions of lenses. vol. 49 (Bidirectional Transformations 2012).
14. Gibbons, Jeremy, & Oliveira, Bruno c. d. s. (2009). The essence of the iterator pattern. Journal of Functional Programming, 19(July), 377–402.
15. Jaskelioff, Mauro, & Rypacek, Ondrej. (2012). An investigation of the laws of traversals. Pages 40–49 of: Chapman, James, & Levy, Paul Blain (eds), Proceedings of the Fourth Workshop on Mathematically Structured Functional Programming. EPTCS, vol. 76.
16. Kmett, Edward. 2013 (Oct.). lens-4.0: Lenses, folds and traversals. http://ekmett.github.io/lens/Control-Lens-Traversal.html.
17. Van Laarhoven, Twan. 2009a (Aug.). CPS based functional references. http://twanvl.nl/blog/haskell/cps-functional-references.
18. Van Laarhoven, Twan. 2009b (Apr.). A non-regular data type challenge. http://twanvl.nl/blog/haskell/non-regular1.
19. Van Laarhoven, Twan. 2009c (Apr.). Where do I get my non-regular types? http://twanvl.nl/blog/haskell/non-regular2.
20. Mac Lane, Saunders. (1971). Categories for the working mathematician. Graduate Texts in Mathematics, no. 5. Springer-Verlag. Second edition, 1998.
21. McBride, Conor, & Paterson, Ross. (2008). Applicative programming with effects. Journal of functional programming, 18(01), 1–13.
22. Milewski, Bartosz. 2013 (Oct.). Lenses, stores, and yoneda. http://bartoszmilewski.com/2013/10/08/lenses-stores-and-yoneda.
23. Moggi, Eugenio, Bell`e, Giana, & Jay, C. Barry. (1999). Monads, shapely functors and traversals. Electronic notes in theoretical computer science, 29, 187 – 208. CTCS '99, Conference on Category Theory and Computer Science.
24. O'Connor, Russell. 2010 (Nov.). Lenses are exactly the coalgebras for the store comonad. http://r6research.livejournal.com/23705.html.
25. O'Connor, Russell. (2011). Functor is to lens as applicative is to biplate: Introducing multiplate. Corr, abs/1103.2841v1.
26. O'Connor, Russell, Kmett, Edward A., & Morris, Tony. 2013 (Oct.). data-lens-2.10.4: Haskell 98 lenses. http://hackage.haskell.org/package/data-lens-2.10.4/docs/Data-Lens-Partial-Common.html.
27. Plotkin, Gordon, & Power, John. (2003). Algebraic operations and generic effects. Applied categorical structures, 11(1), 69–94.
28. Plotkin, Gordon, & Pretnar, Matija. (2009). Handlers of algebraic effects. Pages 80–94 of: Castagna, Giuseppe (ed), Programming languages and systems. Lecture Notes in Computer Science, vol. 5502. Springer Berlin Heidelberg.
29. Reynolds, John C., & Plotkin, Gordon D. (1993). On functors expressible in the polymorphic typed lambda calculus. Information and computation, 105(1), 1–29.
30. Swierstra, Wouter. (2008). Data types `a la carte. Journal of functional programming, 18(4), 423–436.

CHAPTER 6 PROBABILISTIC DECLARATIVE DEBUGGING

Lee Naish

University of Melbourne Melbourne 3010, Australia

ABSTRACT

We present a probabilistic approach to the search strategy for declarative debugging. We focus on diagnosing wrong answers in pure Prolog programs but the approach can be adapted to other languages (for example, functional languages) and bug symptoms. Drawing information from source code and the execution of passed and failed test cases, different search heuristics are combined using probability theory. This reduces the expected number and complexity of questions. We appeal to rationality to compare several search algorithms. Algorithms such as ours, which use more information and make weaker assumptions, generally have better performance. Examples are also given to illustrate how the algorithm can perform extremely well when certain heuristics are effective, and reasonably well even when the heuristics are ineffective.

INTRODUCTION

Declarative debugging [20] has long been recognized as an attractive way to diagnose errors in logic, constraint and functional programs. The advantages are two-fold. First, the user is only required to understand the relatively simple declarative semantics, instead of the procedural semantics. Complex details of the execution such as backtracking, constraint propagation and lazy evaluation are not exposed to the user. It is only necessary for the user to be clear about what is true in their intended interpretation — what should be computed, rather than how it is computed. Second, the high level reasoning and decision making programmers traditionally perform is done by the debugging system — this is why it was originally named algorithmic debugging in [20]. The debugger ultimately draws the conclusion that a particular part of the source code is buggy by reasoning about bug symptoms (and lack of symptoms) in various parts of the execution. In order to do so, it must make a series of decisions about which parts of the execution should be examined for bug symptoms. The debugger (hopefully) only examines parts of the execution which may help find the bug — it searches for the bug in a rational way. The term rational debugging is used in [18] [19] to emphasize this point.

In declarative debugging a computation can be seen as a tree and a diagnosis is a single "buggy" node in the tree corresponding to a step in the execution which is at odds with the programmer's intentions. Even in the earliest work on declarative debugging (for Prolog) [20], several search strategies were proposed. The central idea we propose in this paper is a probabilistic approach to the search problem. We use various heuristics to estimate the probability of a buggy node appearing in a subtree and search the tree in a way which attempts to minimizes the expected cost. Our use of the term "probability" may be questioned by some — bugs and their

Citation: Lee Naish, Probabilistic Declarative Debugging

symptoms are arguably not the result of a randomness during programming or execution. However, probability theory is a useful tool for reasoning with uncertainty. It gives us systematic methods for combining information from different sources, something we don't have if we use numerical estimates of likelihood in a more ad hoc way. We give some examples to argue the superiority of our algorithm compared with others proposed. Although we focus on the problem of diagnosing wrong answers in pure Prolog programs without negation, diagnosing wrong answers in functional programs is very similar (see Section 2) and our algorithms can be applied directly. Diagnosing some other bug symptoms, such as inadmissible calls [18] [15] require only minor adaptation. For missing answers (incompleteness) [20] our probabilistic search algorithm could still be used, though the way probabilities are estimated would have to change more substantially. Similarly, application of the technique to other languages may require substantial changes in probability calculations.

Although we do report some experimental results, the contribution of this paper is not a practical implementation. The algorithms presented are based on an appeal to rationality and our implemetation and experiments have primarily been used to validate the approach. Rationality is also used to explain the relative performance of various search strategies. We also present a game of dice which is analogous to part of the problem of debugging and reveals the importance of explicitly estimating how "consistent" bugs are (how often the execution of buggy code returns incorrect versus correct results).

This paper is structured as follows. We first give a more detailed background summary of declarative debugging and search strategies. Next we describe a search algorithm which is similar to a previously proposed algorithm but takes advantage of probability and cost estimates to reduce the total expected cost. Next we describe various sources of estimated probabilities and how they can be combined so as to be used by the search algorithm. We provide some experimental results to compare our algorithm with previously proposed algorithms. Finally, we discuss related work and possible further work including a more practical implementation which take resource limits into consideration, then conclude.

BACKGROUND

Declarative debugging of wrong answers in Prolog uses the proof tree (see [9]) associated with the program execution. The nodes of a proof tree are Prolog atomic goals which have succeeded. The children of a node are the successful subgoals in the body of the matching clause used to prove the goal. Nodes may be correct (the goal is valid, all instances are true, in the user's intended interpretation of the program) or erroneous (not valid) — we use the terminology of [14]. An erroneous node with no erroneous children is buggy. Buggy nodes correspond to clause instances which are not true in the intended interpretation — the body is valid but the head is not.

To diagnose wrong answers in functional programs an evaluation dependence tree (EDT) [17] is used. The relationship with diagnosis of logic programs is given in [13]: if the "flattening" transformation (converting functions of N arguments to predicates of N + 1 arguments and nested expressions into conjunctions) is applied to a functional program and a corresponding EDT the result is a logic program and a corresponding proof tree. For strict functional programs and deterministic logic programs the correspondence is exact. For non-strict evaluation of functional programs some subtrees are eliminated — unevaluated applications are leaves of the EDT. For nondeterministic evaluation of logic programs a single top level goal can have multiple answers and multiple proof trees. However, neither of these variations affect our debugging algorithm. Where we refer to (instances of) clauses, (instances of) equations can be used.

A declarative debugger searches the proof tree (or EDT) for a buggy node. It uses information from an oracle to determine if nodes are correct or erroneous. The oracle relies on asking the user to determine correctness of nodes, but generally stores the information so a question is not repeated. It may also allow more general assertions (see [4], for example) about correctness to be made. During the search the debugger finds out (via the oracle) that certain nodes are erroneous and certain others are correct. Every erroneous node is on a path of erroneous nodes going down the tree which terminates at a buggy node. It is normal to search for one bug at a time, so if an erroneous node is found everything except the subtree rooted at that node is eliminated from the search space. Similarly, nodes which are correct, and their descendants, are normally eliminated from the search space. We call these correct subtrees. Erroneous nodes in correct subtrees are rare and typical search algorithms cannot find them. We call the remaining search space the suspect part of the tree. It is a tree with an erroneous root with any correct subtrees removed.

Many search algorithms have been proposed. One of the simplest is a topdown left to right search of the tree. Given an erroneous node, we check the correctness of its children left to right. If an erroneous one is found we recursively search that subtree, otherwise the root of the tree is a buggy node and is returned. For a tree with N nodes, up to N questions may be asked. The divide and query algorithm [20] was designed to improve the worst case complexity. Instead of checking a child of the root, we find a subtree whose "weight" (normally the number of nodes) is as close as possible to half the weight of the tree, and check the root of the subtree. If it is erroneous the rest of the tree can be eliminated and if it is correct the subtree can be eliminated; either way the size of the search is reduced by (approximately) half, resulting in O(log N) complexity. Constant factors depend on the branching factor — with a branching factor of M the subtree may be of size 1/M rather than the ideal case of 1/2 the tree. In practice, a top-down search is often comparable with divide and query, particularly if the children are ordered in a sensible way (not necessarily left to right), and is much easier to implement. Bottom-up search was also proposed, but this typically performs poorly.

In [18] [19] several other search heuristics were presented. As well as allowing the user to say a node is erroneous, it was suggested that they be able to say a particular sub-term is wrong. Detailed dependency information can then be used to determine where that sub-term was "produced", and the search directed accordingly. Nodes which do not help produce the sub-term cannot be eliminated from the search space (since if they had failed the incorrect result would have been avoided) but can be given a lower priority in the search. It was also noted that buggy nodes are derived from buggy procedures or clauses. Potentially we can find a subtree which uses half the clauses. If it is erroneous the search space in terms of clauses has been halved. If it is correct the clauses used cannot be eliminated from the search space (since a buggy clause may have both buggy and correct instances) but, again, can be given a lower priority in the search. We call this idea static divide and query as it is based on the (static) source code, which is typically much smaller than the proof tree.

There are many other ideas for improving the search strategy (and we provide several more in this paper), so a question arises as to how we can best combine them. One possibility is to have several different search strategies implemented and have the user pick one. Although this may be suitable for expert users, non-experts are unlikely to know which strategy is best in a given situation. It is also somewhat counter to the philosophy of declarative debugging, where the responsibility for the search strategy is given to the debugger rather than the user. One of the advantages of our proposed approach is that it is relatively simple to combine many search ideas into the same framework. Our key idea is to estimate the probability of each subtree containing a buggy node and use a search algorithm which attempts to minimize the expected cost of diagnosis.

We first describe our search algorithm, which can be applied to any tree with probability estimates for each subtree. Different sets of bug symptoms, such as wrong answers, missing answers or both, and different languages can be diagnosed using different kinds of trees [14], so the search algorithm can potentially be applied to all of these. In Section 5 we suggest an algorithm for computing probability estimates for wrong answer diagnosis, where the tree is a proof tree.

PROBABILISTIC SEARCH

Our probabilistic search algorithm can be seen as a variation of binary search. The basic operation of the search algorithm is to probe some element of the search space to determine in which of two parts of the search space the target appears. In the case of classical binary search the probe will be a comparison and a sorted array segment is used so the two parts of the search space are the array segments to the left and right of the probed element. In the case of declarative debugging the probe involves determining the correctness of a node in the tree and the two parts of the search tree are the subtree and the rest of the tree. Determining which node to probe at each stage can require significant computation (possibly evaluating some objective function for each node in order to find the optimal one), but the probes themselves are the most important cost and this is what we attempt to minimize. We know the target exists, so if there is only one element we need no probes. The maximum number of probes to search a space of size N by splitting into two parts of size XN and (1 − X)N, where $0 \leq X \leq 1$, is thus:

$$m(1) = 0$$
$$m(N) = 1 + max(m(XN), m((1-X)N))$$

It is clear that m(N) is monotonically increasing, which is sufficient to conclude that X = 1/2 is optimal, giving standard binary search where m(N) is (around) $\log_2 N$.

Reducing the Expected Number of Probes

We believe debugging is one of the many search applications where the average case behavior is more important than the worst case. Given a probability distribution for the target being in the different parts of the space, the expected number of probes (which should be close to the average number over many cases) is:

$$e(1) = 0$$
$$e(N) = 1 + Pr(< XN)e(XN) + Pr(> XN)e((1-X)N) \quad (1)$$

To simplify presentation we have written the probability terms as if we were searching a sorted array (in general there is no simple < relationship to specify a part of the search space) and assume X is fixed for all probes (in reality, it may vary). If the probabilities are proportional to the search space size the optimal solution is again binary search. We give a more precise version of equation 1 later, but for now we make the (conservative) assumption that e(N) is O(log N), in which case the optimal choice for X minimizes

$$Pr(< XN)\log X + Pr(> XN)\log(1-X)$$

The base for the logarithms doesn't affect the optimal choice used but using base 2 allows simple comparison with binary search or divide and query in the ideal case. These algorithms are optimal if we assume probabilities are proportional to subtree (or sub-array) sizes. In the ideal case, where the probed subtree is exactly half the tree size (X = 1/2) this objective function has value −1. If the root node has four subtrees of equal size, three probes may be required to reduce the search space by a factor of four, which is 2/3 of the ideal effectiveness. The expected effectiveness is somewhat better than the worst case, due to the possibility the buggy subtree will be probed earlier: the objective function value for each root child is −0.81 rather than −2/3 (with probabilities of 1/4 for each subtree). Given additional clues as to the bug location we can calculate probabilities which are not just proportional to the subtree sizes and the performance may be better than the ideal case for divide and query. For example, if one of the subtrees has a bug probability of 3/4 and the rest, collectively, have a probability of 1/4 then probing the root of that subtree will give an objective function value of −1.6 and nodes within the subtree may given even better performance.

So far we have been assuming the probabilities sum to one. For debugging, the analogy with binary search breaks down somewhat when we consider there may be several buggy nodes and the sum of the probabilities will generally be greater than one. When we probe a node during debugging, the probability of that subtree will be eliminated from the search depends on the probability of that subtree having a bug. It does not depend on the probability of the rest of the tree having a bug. Thus we want to pick a subtree S which minimizes the following objective function, where X_S is the size of S divided by the size of the whole suspect tree:

$$o(S) = Pr(S \texttt{ has bug})\log X_S + (1 - Pr(S \texttt{ has bug}))\log(1 - X_S) \quad (2)$$

Refining the Objective Function

Equations 1 and 2 attempt only to estimate the number of probes (the traditional measure of the cost when comparing different search strategies) and are somewhat oversimplified, as discussed earlier. In reality, different probes have greatly differing costs. The correctness of some nodes can be determined quickly and easily, but others may require examining extremely large data structures, for example, and be very difficult and time consuming. Complexity of questions is one of the main problems of declarative debugging, and if this could be significantly reduced it would be of great benefit, even if there was a moderate increase in the number of questions. In our refined formulas we therefore use an estimate of the cost c(N) of probing a node N. For the experiments reported in this paper we use a cost estimate based on the size A of the atom in the node: log8 (A + 7). This is conservative since it grows very slowly (multiplying the size by 8 just increases the cost by around 1) but can still have a significant effect on the complexity of questions asked. A faster growing function is probably more realistic and would tend to ask even simpler questions, though more of them.

Divide and query can also use the size of atoms as well as the number of nodes to compute the weight of a subtree. However, this can often increase the average cost of diagnosis rather than reduce it. Probes generally split the tree less evenly, the part with fewer nodes having larger atoms. Unless there is a correlation between larger atoms and buggy (not just erroneous) nodes, the number of probes tends to increase. Furthermore, because there is a strong correlation between the size of adjacent nodes whenever large data structures are present, the probed node tends to be larger than average, leading to more costly probes. The examples we use in the rest of this paper illustrate this point.

The choice of probes, and hence the total cost, also depend on information we have gathered to estimate probabilities, and this information can grow as we perform the search. If we probe a node and it is correct, the extra information that some subtree S is correct can change the probability calculations when the rest of the tree is searched. Section 5 describes how we compute the probability that a subtree S of tree T has a bug, using information I, written P r(S, T, I). The expected cost estimate and objective function can thus be defined as follows (|T| is the size of tree T, T \ S is tree T with subtree S deleted and correct(S) is the information that subtree S is correct):

$$
\begin{aligned}
e'(T,I) &= \begin{cases} 0 & \text{if } |T| = 1 \\ \min_{S\in T} o'(S,T,I) & \text{otherwise} \end{cases} \\
o'(S,T,I) &= c(root(S)) + Pr(S,T,I)e'(S,I) + \\
&\quad (1 - Pr(S,T,I))e'(T \setminus S, I \cup \text{correct}(S))
\end{aligned}
\tag{3}
$$

Ideally we would like to minimize this objective function, but applying these definitions naively takes time exponential in the size of the tree. Using dynamic programming methods to improve the complexity appears difficult due to the way the information I is gathered. Equations 1 and 2 can be seen as a first order approximation to equation 3, where the recursive calls to e' are replaced by logarithms, leading to complexity linear in the tree size, and the cost of each probe is one. Clearly, it would be possible to use a kth order approximation, using equation 3 for k levels of recursion with complexity $O(N^k)$, and perhaps vary k depending on the tree size.

Using even a second order approximation is likely to be prohibitive most of the time. Experimentation has revealed that a first order approximation can work very effectively when there is a small subtree with a high probability of containing a bug. Although the estimated number of probes for the rest of the tree may be significantly over-estimated, this is multiplied by the (small) probability that the subtree is correct. For example, if there is a buggy fact (or equation with no function applications on the right side) in a program the search typically "zooms in" on a leaf of the tree quickly. However, if the buggy node is the root of the tree and the root has several large subtrees a first order approximation works poorly, even if the probability of the root being buggy is computed to be quite high. In order to find the bug we must ultimately probe all of the children. In all probes but the last, both the subtree and the rest of the tree can be large. We need a kth order approximation, where k is the number of children, in order to avoid the objective function significantly over-estimating the number of probes required. We need to "look ahead" k probes to see the eventually reduction of the search space size to one.

To overcome this problem, we propose a refinement to equation 2 where the cost of each probe is considered and children of the root node are treated specially. This could be refined further and extended to more levels of the tree; even if applied to all nodes the complexity would be O(N). We compute the probability R of the root being a buggy node, which is just the product of the probabilities of each of its subtrees being correct (since the root is known to be erroneous). For each child, if it is correct we say there is probability 1 − R of the normal logarithmic cost and a probability R of finding the bug by probing S_1, S_2, . . . , S_M, the siblings of S. The minimum of this value and the normal objective function value is used. Note that the logarithmic cost estimates for the number of probes for a subtree S is multiplied by $c_a(S)$, the average cost of probes in S.

$$
\begin{aligned}
o''(S,T,I) &= c(root(S)) + Pr(S,T,I)c_a(S)\log|S| + \\
&\quad (1 - Pr(S,T,I))o^s(S,T) \\
o^s(S,T) &= \begin{cases} C_{TS} & \text{if } S \text{ is not a root child} \\ \min(C_{TS}, o^c(S,T)) & \text{otherwise} \end{cases} \\
o^c(S,T) &= (1-R)C_{TS} + R\sum_{i=1}^{M} c(S_i) \\
\text{where } C_{TS} &= c_a(T \setminus S)\log(|T \setminus S|)
\end{aligned}
\tag{4}
$$

SOURCES OF PROBABILITY AND COST ESTIMATES

The probabilities used in the search algorithm encapsulate domain knowledge. Our knowledge that the tree has a specific relationship with a program which is an artifact of human ingenuity (and fallibility) allows us to locate bugs more efficiently. In this section we discuss some of the multitude of sources of information we could use. The algorithm we present later uses some of this information explicitly some implicitly and some it ignores, but could potentially be incorporated in the future. There are two distinct kinds of probabilities we can estimate. The first is the correctness of sub-computations (nodes in the tree, which are Prolog atoms in our prototype). Note that if a node is erroneous a buggy node exists somewhere in the subtree but not necessarily at the root. The second is the correctness of sections of source code and their instances (some code may work correctly for some instantiation of variables but not others). We use (instances of) Prolog clauses. This is a more important source of information but is more complex to incorporate because multiple tree nodes are involved. There are also two ways we can obtain estimates. The first is what we call "static" — unrelated to the program execution. The other is from the "dynamic" execution of the program using the test case(s) supplied to the debugger.

Static Sources

The more important sources of information concerning the likelihood of an atom being erroneous are dynamic, and our current algorithm does not use static information for atoms. However, information about atoms can be incorporated in an ad hoc way by adjusting the cost function. Lowering the cost estimate for atoms considered more likely to be erroneous directs the search to those parts of the tree. Cost estimation can also be refined with information from the programmer and heuristics such as whether the procedure is part of an interface or just local (declarations or the static call graph could be used), whether the procedure has any comments, et cetera.

There are many heuristics for determining if a clause is incorrect. Users often have a reasonable feel for which procedures are suspect and this could be communicated to the debugger. Many static checks for suspicious code have been developed, for example, those incorporated into the NU-Prolog Debugging Environment [16], and could be used for estimating bug likelihood. More complex clauses (by measures such as total size, number of variables and number of conjuncts) are more likely to be buggy. If modification time of clauses or procedures is maintained by a programming environment this could also be used. Simple analysis of comments in code may also be very useful — many embarrassingly long bug searches end close to a comment containing the string "BUG" or similar. Our current algorithm uses information such as this implicitly — it assumes some method is used to compute relatively likelyhoods of different clauses being buggy.

Dynamic Sources

The debugger oracle is a very useful source of information about the truth value of atoms, especially if assertions have been provided. With a suitable oracle interface the whole tree can be traversed in search of nodes which can be determined to be erroneous or correct without asking the user any questions. Correct computations are also an excellent source of correct atoms; the root of the proof tree is known to be correct and is typically stored by the oracle, but every other atom in the tree is very likely to be correct also. Polymorphism in declared or inferred types can be used to generalize information about (probably) correct atoms. For example, if we know that append([1],[2],[1,2]) is probably correct (Figure 3 contains the definition) and append/3 is polymorphic in the type of the list elements, we can conclude append([X],[Y],[X,Y]) is probably correct for all X and Y. If users can specify incorrect terms as well as incorrect atoms, dependency information can be used to determine the producers of the term (in Mercury [22] and functional languages this can generally be computed statically). Even without dependency information we can still say a node in the tree containing this term is likely to be erroneous. The producers of the term must be connected to the root of the tree via a path in which each node contains the term. Occurrences of the term not on such a path could be ignored or given less elevated probability of being erroneous.

Program slicing is based on the idea that bugs are likely to be in parts of the program which are executed in test cases which exhibit buggy behavior but are not executed in test cases which exhibit correct behavior. Originally introduced for imperative programs [23], it has also been applied to logic programs (see [5], for example). Given a proof tree, we can identify clauses used in the suspect part of the tree but not in correct parts of the tree and adjust probabilities accordingly. This is one of the key parts of our algorithm. Measures of how well a set of test cases "covers" a program can be used to refine this idea. Clauses can contain disjunctions and conditionals and a clause body succeeds using a particular execution path [21]. We could consider execution paths used in suspect but not correct parts of the tree, and preferably also note that different execution paths can share some parts, so they are not completely independent. We can also consider different variable instantiations within a single execution path. For example, if all instances of some clause in correct parts of the tree have a certain variable instantiated to the empty list, it does not give us such a strong indication of the correctness of an instance where that variable is a non-empty list.

Work on "most specific" logic programs [11] can be used to combine information on execution paths and clause instances. Clause instances are obtained from correct parts of the tree and disjuncts not on the execution path are replaced by a special value, "bottom". All instances of each clause can be "anti-unified" to obtain a "more specific" version of the program (the least general instance of the program capable of reproducing all the correct parts of the tree). If a variant of a clause in the original program is obtained, that clause is covered; all paths have been used and every variable has been instantiated to distinct terms with different top level function symbols. Clause instances in the suspect part of the tree which are subsumed by the more specific clauses generated are very likely to be correct; others are less likely to be correct. More specific programs and path and clause usage are ways of summarizing the information in an execution tree using space related to the size of the program[1]. More detailed analysis which considers every clause instance in the tree could also be used if resources permit.

[1]Technically, the number of execution paths can be exponential in the program size and a more specific program can be arbitrarily larger, but these do not seem to occur in practice.

Note that any method which uses correct parts of the tree can benefit from correct test cases as well as correct subcomputations within buggy test cases. Ideally, a programming environment should retain information about correct cases so it can be used to help diagnose incorrect cases. If this is not implemented, a similar result can be achieved by the user explicitly running a more complex goal which contains subgoals which are known to behave correctly, as well as the buggy subgoal. Estimates of the cost of probes could be refined by noting the time it takes to answer questions, whether users answer "don't know" (which the better debuggers support) and gathering explicit cost information from users.

Learning

The most appropriate way of interpreting the "probabilities" is as a guide to predictive power in the longer term, similar to weather forecasts which give a numerical chance of rain (a style of forecasting which is gaining popularity internationally). If the system computes the chance of a bug (or rain) is 10% in particular circumstances then (over time and/or places within a program) then there should be a bug (rain) in around 10% of the cases where those circumstances arise. If it turns out to be significantly more or less than this, the mechanism for estimating the "probability" (code within the debugging environment or weather model) should be adjusted accordingly. A debugging environment could maintain statistics so probability estimates could be refined over time, either manually or perhaps using machine learning algorithms. The suggestions we make here are a starting point for such refinements.

COMPUTING PROBABILITIES

We first discuss some naive approaches, which ignore certain information. Interestingly, this forms a rational basis for explaining the relative performance of various proposed search algorithms. Next we introduce a game of dice which is analogous to the debugging problem. Being a simpler domain where we have fewer preconceptions, this can clarify some issues of rationality and what information is used. Finally we present our algorithm and discuss some possible refinements.

Naive Approaches

Our search algorithm relies on an estimate of the probability of each subtree in the suspect part of the search space having a buggy node. A naive approach is to assume each node in the tree has a small probability ϵ of being buggy. The probability of a subtree of N nodes having at least one buggy node can be calculated as $1-(1-\epsilon)^N$. Using the first order approximation of $N\epsilon$ and assuming all probes have the same cost, our search algorithm is equivalent to the divide and query algorithm, as explained in Section 3.1. Unfortunately, at the heart of many probability calculations there is a dubious assumption of independence. Here $(1-\epsilon)^N$ assumes the probability of the N different nodes being buggy is independent. If we know nothing about the tree nodes or the program it was derived from this is the simplest assumption we can make and thus is rational according to Occam's Razor. Thus divide and query has a rational basis if we assume there are few (or just one) buggy nodes and certain information is unavailable.

An example where divide and query is clearly not rational is a tree where we know more than half the nodes are in a subtree which computes an append/3 call. It is not rational to abandon our (presumably high) expectation that append/3 is correct, conclude an append/3 node is most likely buggy and probe a node within that subtree. If we know a collection of nodes use the same procedure (or clause) we should generally not assume independent probabilities and the probability that one of the nodes is buggy should be bounded by the probability that the code is buggy. We discuss this further in Section 5.2.

If we have no information about the program, tree nodes or sizes of subtrees then it is reasonable to assume that the subtrees of the root node all have the same size, and top-down search is then the rational choice. The assumption that ϵ is small is based on our knowledge of how debuggers are typically used. With no knowledge of debugging the rational choice would be much larger, around 0.5, which would make bottom-up search the best choice. Thus the relative performance of bottom-up, top-down and divide and query search algorithms can be explained by an appeal to rationality which is consistent with our approach. All are rational given certain limited knowledge, with more knowledge corresponding to better performance.

Of course there is potentially far more information available about the tree, the program and debugging in general, though some effort may be needed to gather it. Our algorithm uses (some of) this additional information to further improve performance. If some information is inconvenient to obtain or hard to condense into a probability we can consider algorithmic factors when probabilities are estimated. For example, our algorithm inputs estimates of the (prior) probability of each clause being buggy. If the probabilities are high the resulting search is similar to bottom-up whereas if they are very low the search is more like divide and query. It is therefore safer to (if anything) under -estimate such probabilities. Our algorithm also scales up these probabilities (using the knowledge that at least one clause is buggy), so they can be grossly under-estimated without significant performance decrease.

An Analogy with Dice

An analogy in a more familiar domain is a collection of ten dice, nine of which are normal but one is blank on five sides. Dice are analogous to clauses, the defective one being buggy. Die throws are analogous to tree nodes (or clause instances); blanks are considered buggy and other results correct. If we repeatedly select a die randomly and throw it, the probabilities are independent and the chance of at least one blank in S throws is $1-(1-5/60)^S$, which approaches 1. If we select a die randomly then repeatedly throw the same die the probabilities are not independent and the chance of at least one blank in S throws approaches 1/10.

More generally, the debugging problem is analogous to having N dice (which may have blanks on any number of sides and may be loaded), corresponding to the N clauses (or equations et cetera) in the program. Each die i, $1 \leq i \leq N$ is thrown S_i times, $S_i > 0$ and we are told at least one throw of some die is blank; this corresponds to a suspect tree in which each clause i is used S_i times. Each die i may also be thrown K_i more times, $K_i \geq 0$, with no blanks occurring, corresponding to trees which are known to be correct. Given this information, the challenge is to estimate the following probabilities:

- the probability that each die i is defective and
- the probability a given throw of die i comes up blank, given that it is defective.

Determining the most rational estimates is complex. We may also have some additional information available. For example, we may be told that defective dice are very rare and this may lead us to introduce simplifying assumptions, such as only one of the dice is defective (there is only one bug).

The first probability is clearly related to which parts of the program are most likely to be buggy. The second is more subtle but important because during debugging we observe instances of code which is executed and the ultimate diagnosis in declarative debugging is an incorrect clause (or equation) instance: the debugger works with throws of dice rather than the dice per s´e. Essentially, it is a measure of how "consistent" a bug is. A high value means most executions of the buggy code produce incorrect results, whereas a low value means the bug is spasmodic, being evident in relatively few executions. The consistency of bugs greatly influences the performance of some search strategies, for example, the effectiveness of program slicing.

Note that this measure of bug consistency is a conditional probability. Bayes theorem states the probability of A given B, written P r(A|B) is

$$\frac{Pr(A)Pr(B|A)}{Pr(B)}$$

where P r(A) and P r(B) are the prior probabilities of A and B, respectively (making no assumptions about the truth of the other proposition). The probability that a clause (die) is buggy given that a corresponding node (throw) is buggy is simply 1. For the dice example above, P r(Blank throw|Buggy Die) = (5/60) × 1/(1/10) = 5/6. Using Bayes theorem we can devise a method where, as the append/3 subtree size increases, the probability estimate approaches the estimate for the definition being buggy. In our technique several such refinements are used, incorporating the various sources of probability estimates given earlier. From one perspective we are incorporating more knowledge into the search algorithm. From another perspective we are weakening the assumptions of independence. Although some assumptions of independence remain, they are certainly much weaker and more reasonable than those used to justify algorithms such as divide and query from a probabilistic perspective. Similarly, although explicitly estimating prior probabilities may be difficult to do accurately, the alternative is to assume all prior probabilities are equal, which is generally even less accurate.

Algorithm *subtree_probs*:
Inputs: A suspect tree $\mathcal{T}$, a set of clauses $\mathcal{C}$ with instances in $\mathcal{T}$,
    counts of instances of each of these clauses in correct trees
Outputs: For each subtree S of suspect tree $\mathcal{T}$, an estimated
    probability $P(S)$ that S contains a buggy node

% $P_0(C)$ is the initial estimate of relative likelihood of clause C
% being buggy (compared to other clauses); can be much less than
% the actual probability
For each clause $C \in \mathcal{C}$
    Let $P_0(C)$ be the prior likelihood of C being buggy

% $P_1(C)$ is the probability that an instance of clause C with
% a correct body is buggy, given that C is buggy
For each clause $C \in \mathcal{C}$
    If C is ground $P_1(C) = 1$, otherwise
    let $0 \leq P_1(C) \leq 1$ maximize $(1 - P_1(C))^{K_C}(1 - (1 - P_1(C))^{S_C})$, where
        K_C is the number of instances of C in correct trees and
        S_C is the number of instances of C in $\mathcal{T}$

% Scale down relative likelihoods of clauses being buggy
% using number of instances in correct subtrees and P_1 values
For each clause $C \in \mathcal{C}$
    $P_2(C) = P_0(C)(1 - P_1(C))^{K_C}$, where K_C is as above

% $P_3(C)$ is the probability that clause C is buggy
% given that at least one clause is buggy
For each clause $C \in \mathcal{C}$
    $P_3(C) = P_2(C)/(1 - \prod_{C' \in \mathcal{C}}(1 - P_2(C')))$

% $P_4(S,C)$ is the probability that an instance of C in S is buggy
For each clause $C \in \mathcal{C}$ and subtree S of $\mathcal{T}$
    $P_4(S,C) = P_3(C)(1 - (1 - P_1(C))^{M_C})$, where
        M_C is the number of occurrences of C in S

% $P_5(S)$ is the probability that a clause instance in S is buggy
For each subtree S of $\mathcal{T}$
    $P_5(S) = 1 - \prod_{C \text{ in } S}(1 - P_4(S,C))$

% $P(S)$ is the probability that a clause instance in S is buggy
% given that a clause instance in $\mathcal{T}$ is buggy
For each subtree S of $\mathcal{T}$
    $P(S) = P_5(S)/P_5(\mathcal{T})$

Figure 1: Algorithm for computing probabilities of subtrees being buggy.

Our Algorithm

The algorithm is given in figure 1; here we discuss various details. As well as the inputs described in figure 1, we assume a method for computing prior relative likelihoods of clauses being buggy based on (possibly) the code and additional clues as to likely bug locations from the user or other sources. Ideally, we would like to to start with accurate prior probabilities $P_0(C)$ of each clause C being buggy. Unfortunately, this is rather difficult, though the machine learning suggestion in Section 4.3 may help. However, our approach still works well if these prior probabilities are underestimated by a constant factor. Instead of attempting to estimate accurate probabilities it is sufficient to choose relative likelihoods of clause being buggy which are much smaller than actual probabilities (around one millionth, say). Static information and possibly information from the programmer can be used to increase or decrease $P_0(C)$ compared to this base value. We don't propose any systematic method for this, but suggest a factor of more than ten with just static sources is placing too much reliance on them. If the static analysis is accurate it should be reinforced by the dynamic information anyway.

As mentioned, to weaken assumptions of independence and obtain a measure of bug consistency we can estimate the probability of a clause instance being buggy given that the clause is buggy (essentially the proportion of instances of the clause in the suspect tree which are buggy). Furthermore, we can ignore clause instances for which the body is false. An instance where both the head and body are false is indicative of a bug somewhere lower in the tree but is not buggy in itself. Thus, for each suspect clause C, we estimate the probability $P_1(C)$ of any instance of C in the tree being buggy given that C is buggy and the body instance is true. With very low P_1 values, the probability of a subtree containing a bug is more related to the number of clause instances used (the size of the subtree) than the number of clauses, and our search algorithm behaves like divide and query. With high values, our search algorithm gives more weight to the program slicing heuristic and behaves more like static divide and query. We treat ground clauses as a special case since the probability is clearly 1. For non-ground clauses we pick a value which gives the "best" explanation the observations: the choice of $P_1(C)$ maximizes the probability that all occurrences of C in correct trees are correct and least one occurrence in the suspect subtree is buggy. We discuss alternative ways of computing $P_1(C)$ in section 5.4.

The probability of a clause C being buggy given static information and information that certain nodes contain true atoms (correct computations) is the prior probability of C being buggy times the probability of the nodes being true given that C is buggy. These $P_2(C)$ values are based on the $P_0(C)$ values and are thus are relative likelihoods rather than realistic probabilities. They are further reduced by a factor dependent of the number of times C is used in correct trees ($P_2(C) = P_0(C)$ if C is not used in any correct tree). The algorithm assumes the correctness of instances of a buggy clause at different tree nodes are independent. It could be refined by considering only the number of distinct instances of a clause or using more sophisticated measures of similarity. For example, if a subset of the instances are considered to cover the clause then subsequent instances could affect the overall probability less. It is possible that correct trees contain buggy clause instances and our algorithm could be refined to take account of this. For example, slightly smaller P1 values could be used (currently it is assumed all K_C instances of clause C are correct).

Knowing at least one clause is buggy allows us to scale up each (possibly tiny) value by the same factor so they become realistic probability estimates. The sum of the $P_3(C)$ values will always be greater than 1 but if the P_0 (and P_2) values approach zero the sum approaches 1. Thus choosing very small $P_0(C)$ values corresponds to assuming there is a single buggy clause and simply scaling the P_2 values so the sum is 1 is a reasonable alternative to our more complex formula for P_3 (and is what our current implementation uses). From the perspective of the debugger we are always searching for a single bug and it does not hurt to assume every other clause is correct. Also, it is helpful to optimize the search for the "last" bug (the hardest one to find) and divide and query essentially assumes an extremely low probability. When there are many bugs a higher probability would be appropriate, but in this case we can often find one easily, with a simple test case, a small proof tree and few questions even with a far from optimal search strategy.

The way we compute the probability of a subtree S of the suspect part of the tree containing a buggy instance of clause C (given static information and information from correct computations), $P_4(S, C)$ assumes independence (as with the correct trees, we could just consider distinct clause instances, et cetera). Similarly, computing $P_5(S)$, the probability that at least one clause instance in S is buggy, we assume that the probabilities of different clauses being buggy is independent. The P_5 values are scaled up to give the final probabilities using the information that at least one clause instance in the suspect subtree is buggy.

As mentioned previously, we currently only support atom-based heuristics by ad hoc adjustment of the function which estimates the cost of a single probe. We simply make a few brief comments here. First, care must be taken with assumptions of independence. Clearly, atoms are more likely to be erroneous if they are derived from procedures which are likely to be buggy. However, the search algorithm already takes this into account; only information which is independent of clause probabilities should generally be used. Second, applying atom-based heuristics just locally within the tree is unlikely to be as effective as a more global analysis. For example, assume the user says atoms containing 42 are considered likely to be erroneous. If there are only a few such atoms in the tree it may be reasonable to change the search significantly, whereas if there are many such atoms (especially if some are found in correct sub-computations) less attention should be paid to the information. Third, procedural information may be used to affect probabilities. For example, a procedure which outputs 42 is more likely to be buggy than one which inputs 42 given the information above. Although declarative debugging can be done with only declarative information, procedural information can provide heuristics to help the search.

S_C	K_C	P_1 maximum	P_1 median	P_1 Bayesian U=0.2, R=3	P_1 Bayesian U=0.5, R=50
2	0	1.000	0.653	0.781	0.888
1	1	0.500	0.500	0.561	0.610
10	0	1.000	0.545	0.722	0.866
9	1	0.226	0.359	0.430	0.508
5	5	0.129	0.191	0.212	0.271
1	9	0.100	0.148	0.165	0.209
100	0	1.000	0.505	0.706	0.863
99	1	0.045	0.300	0.386	0.491
50	50	0.014	0.024	0.025	0.032
1	99	0.010	0.017	0.017	0.021

Figure 2: P1 values computed using maximum, median and Bayesian methods.

Alternative Methods of Computing P_1

In our first experiments we used a fixed P_1 value for all clauses. Many buggy clauses have all their instances buggy, so a relatively high P_1 value is appropriate. However, for spasmodic bugs there can be many correct instances of the clause used in the test cases and few (perhaps just one) buggy instances. Having a constant P_1 value which is too high directs the search away from such bugs, leading to poor performance — the estimated probability that a clause C is buggy, $P_3(C)$, becomes very small when many correct instances are found. With $P_1 = 0.8$, just ten correct occurrences of a clause reduces its P_3 value by a factor of around ten million. It is a mistake to explain correct instances of a clause C only by a (very) small $P_3(C)$ value. Instead, they should be explained by a combination of small $P_3(C)$ and $P_1(C)$ values.

With our proposed method of maximizing the probability of the observations, $P_1(C) = 1$ if there are no known instances of C in correct computations. As the search progresses, $P_1(C)$ drops (sometimes quite substantially) when instances of C are found in a correct computation and increases (if it is not 1) when suspect instances of C are eliminated from the search space. Instead of using the value corresponding to the maximum probability (for discreet values it would be called the mode), we could use some other measure of central tendency. For example, we could use the median, the 50th percentile of the integral of $(1 - P_1(C))^{KC} (1 - (1 - P_1(C))^{SC})$ between 0 and 1. Figure 2 gives some sample P_1 values computed using both maximum and median methods.

Alternatively, the Bayesian philosophy (which we have used elsewhere) could be embraced fully. In the Bayesian view we have prior expectations of P_1 values and these expectations, not just the observations, should be taken into account. With one correct occurrence and 99 suspect occurrences, the "best" explanation (using the maximum method and ignoring any prior expectations about P_1; see Figure 2) is only 4.5% of the instances are buggy. This intuitively may seem rather low, because most bugs we encounter are exhibited in more than 4.5% of the instances of the clause. Our expectations can be modelled by a probability distribution. For example, very simple code which manipulates data structures commonly has consistent bugs (though spasmodic bugs are still possible) whereas complex numerical code has spasmodic bugs relatively often. Our implementation supports distributions which are linear in the interval [0, 1), with a special case for 1. The function in the interval is specified by a the ratio R of the prior probabilities of very consistent bugs to very inconsistent bugs. Additionally, a value U gives the prior probability of a totally consistent bug (this becomes irrelevant as soon as an incorrect instance is found). The median method corresponds to having a uniform probability distribution for P_1 (U = 0, R = 1). A low R value such as this may be appropriate for some complex clauses. For simpler clauses, higher values for both U and R are reasonable — Figure 2 includes two examples. For ground clauses U = 1 is the rational choice.

Although the maximum method seems less rational, it often performs better than the other methods. For simple bugs where the program slicing heuristic is effective and there are no correct instances of the buggy clause, the very high P_1 value leads to outstanding performance. For spasmodic bugs where every clause has multiple correct instances and the search space is large, the P_1 values quickly become small. They typically underestimate the true values, but this simply makes the search algorithm more like divide and query, which is a good default when heuristics are not effective. We conjecture that our algorithm with the maximum method asymptotically has the same number of probes as divide and query if the size of the program is fixed. Going back to the dice game analogy, the maximum method is better than we might expect because the payoff is not symmetric. Consistently overestimating P_1 can be much worse than underestimating it and a rational choice should take this into consideration. The dice game we described relates to a single probe; a more complex version is required to model strategies over several probes. For simply ranking clauses according to the probability of them being buggy (see Section 7) we would expect the method using prior probability distributions to be most effective.

EXPERIMENTS

A simple thought experiment illustrates how our algorithm performs far more rationally than top-down search or divide and query when the tree is much larger than the program. Consider the case where the suspect subtree is a naive reverse computation with a list length L (see Figure 3.) Note that although we normally consider this code to be correct, someone may have written this code (or equivalent) with different intentions in mind. The tree has height L+ 1 and number of instances of the different clauses is 1, L, L and L.(L−1)/2, respectively; the number of nodes N = (L + 1).(L + 2)/2. With top-down search which selects the recursive child first, the next probe would be naive reverse computation with a list length L − 1. Divide and query attempts to halve the tree size, the list length being reduced by a factor of (around) √ 2, to 0.71L. With L = 256 (N = 33153), the first probe for divide and query will be the subtree which computes the reverse of a list of length 181 (16653 nodes). Although the tree has just half as many nodes, common sense suggests it is still almost certain to be buggy. It is hard to think of a realistic intended interpretation of such a simple four clause program for which the larger tree exhibits a bug but the smaller tree does not. Divide and query with weights computed using atom size will probe an even larger subtree, with a larger atom at its root.

```
% reverse of a list
reverse([], []).
reverse([A|As], Bs) :- reverse(As, Cs), append(Cs, [A], Bs).

% concatenation of two lists
append([], As, As).
append([A|As], Bs, [A|Cs]) :- append(As, Bs, Cs).
```

Figure 3: Definition of naive reverse.

Algorithm	L=4 N=15	L=16 N=153	L=64 N=2145	L=256 N=33153
Divide and query	6	78	1081	16653
$P_1(C) = \{1.0, 1.0, 1.0, 1.0\}$	3	6	6	6
$P_1(C) = \{1.0, 0.8, 0.8, 0.8\}$	3	6	6	10
$P_1(C) = \{1.0, 0.5, 0.5, 0.5\}$	3	6	10	15
$P_1(C) = \{1.0, 0.1, 0.1, 0.1\}$	1	1	36	55
median, $K_C = \{1, 1, 1, 1\}$	6	10	21	28
median, $K_C = \{1, 1, 5, 50\}$	6	10	45	136
maximum, $K_C = \{1, 1, 1, 1\}$	6	21	171	1653
maximum, $K_C = \{1, 1, 5, 50\}$	3	21	171	1830

Figure 4: Size of first subtree probed for naive reverse.

The behavior of our algorithm depends in part on the $P_0(C)$ estimates for each of the four clauses. If we have no clues as to the bug location and use the same very low $P_0(C)$ for each clause and have no known correct subtrees, the $P_3(C)$ values will be around 0.25. Assuming a constant $P_1(C)$ value of 0.8 for all (non-ground) clauses, the probability of the reverse subtree for list length 2 (6 nodes) being buggy is close to 0.95. With such a high probability of this subtree being buggy, probing a node higher in the tree is only worthwhile if there are several thousand nodes. Figure 4 shows how the tree size relates to the size of the first subtree probed for divide and query and variations of our algorithm with different ways of computing the P_1 values. Lower P_1 values generally lead to somewhat larger subtrees being probed (there are some exceptions because the reverse/2 fact is ground and hence always has a P_1 value of 1). Using the maximum method, with 50 correct and 32640 suspect instances, P_1 for the append/3 rule is 0.0002. Even with such tiny values, that rational choice for the next probe is around one tenth the size of that used by divide and query.

```
merge_sort(Us, Ss) :-
        length(Us, N),
        msort_n(N, Us, Ss, _). % last arg should be []

% Ss is first N element of Us sorted, RestUs is the rest.
% First clause only used for merge_sort of empty list.
msort_n(0, Us, [], Us).
msort_n(1, [U|Us], [U], Us).
msort_n(N, Us, Ss, RestUs) :-
        N > 1,
        N1 is N // 2,
        msort_n(N1, Us, Ss1, Us2),
        msort_n(N1, Us2, Ss2, RestUs),                  % BUG
        % N2 is N - N1, msort_n(N2, Us2, Ss2, RestUs), % correct
        merge(Ss1, Ss2, Ss).

% merge of two sorted lists
merge([], Ss, Ss).
merge([S|Ss], [], [S|Ss]).
merge([A|As], [B|Bs], [A|Ss]) :-
        A =< B,
        merge(As, [B|Bs], Ss).
merge([A|As], [B|Bs], [B|Ss]) :-
        A > B,
        merge(As, [B|Bs], Ss).                          % BUG
        % merge([A|As], Bs, Ss).                        % correct
```

Figure 5: Buggy merge sort/1 definition.

Figure 5 shows a (slightly) larger example, a buggy definition of merge sort. The code initially computes the length of the list then uses msort_n/4 to sort the first N elements and return the rest of the list (which should be empty at the top level); this method avoids multiple list scans to split lists in half. There is a "cut and paste" error in the definition of merge/3 which results in larger elements being replaced by smaller ones; all instances of this clause are buggy and buggy nodes have just one child (we assume calls to built-in procedures are ignored for debugging purposes). The recursive case for msort_n/4 is also buggy, losing an element from the sorted list if N is odd. This bug will show up if the list length at the top level is not a power of two but not all instances of the clause are buggy, it appears higher in the tree and buggy nodes have three children.

```
 ?- wrong(merge_sort([⟨(up to) 56 elements⟩,3,5,8,1,2,4,6,7],
           [⟨(up to) 56 elements⟩,1,1,1,1,2,4,6,7])).
msort_n(2,[6,7],[6,7],[]) valid?  y
merge([8],[1],[1,1]) valid?  n
merge([],[1],[1]) valid?  y
Bug:  merge([8],[1],[1,1]) :- merge([],[1],[1]).
-------------------------------------------------------------
 ?- wrong(merge_sort([⟨120 elements⟩,3,5,8,1,2,4,6,7],
           [⟨120 elements⟩,1,1,1,1,2,4,6,7])).
msort_n(4,[3,5,8,1,2,4,6,7],[1,1,1,1],[2,4,6,7]) valid?  n
merge([3],[5],[3,5]) valid?  y
merge([8],[1],[1,1]) valid?  n
merge([],[1],[1]) valid?  y
Bug:  merge([8],[1],[1,1]) :- merge([],[1],[1]).
```

Figure 6: Finding the consistent merge sort/1 bug: two "worst case" sessions.

Suppose we initially have a single test case for merge_sort/2 with a list of length some power of two, use very small P_0 values with facts all having values 1/4 of those used for all the rules and the maximum method for computing P_1. For lengths of 4 to 64 (tree size 15 and 378, respectively), the first probe will be a msort_n/4 node where the first argument is 2 (subtree size 5, P value of 0.68). There are typically several such nodes with the same probabilities and the search algorithm ensures the one with the least cost (smallest atom) is probed. It is the rightmost such atom in the tree and the list in the second argument has two elements; the leftmost such atom has an additional 62 elements in the second and fourth arguments. The msort_n/4 node may be correct or erroneous, depending on whether the last two elements of the input list are sorted or not. If the node is erroneous there is a subtree which uses the buggy merge/3 clause and this is probed next, followed by its child, and the bug is found.

If the msort_n/4 node is correct the remaining suspect tree is much larger (373 nodes) but the probabilities are recomputed so there is a better idea of the likely bug location. The buggy clause and the merge_sort/2 clause have higher P_3 values and much higher P_1 values than the other clauses (the two recursive merge/3 clauses have P_3 values of 0.22 and 0.23 and P_1 values of 0.03 and 1). The second subtree probed again has just a single occurrence of the buggy clause (see Figure 6). Although the computed probability is not particularly high ($P = 0.35$), the fact that only two probes would be required to find the bug and the cost of both are relatively small make it the optimal choice. Thus only three simple questions are asked in all cases compared with 7 significantly more complex questions for divide and query. Using our conservative logarithmic cost function our algorithm out-performs divide and query by a factor of about 3. If a linear cost measure is used the factor is between 12 and 27, depending on where in the tree the buggy node is found.

For a 128 element list (around 830 tree nodes) divide and query asks 8 questions, with the extra question almost as large as all the other questions combined. With our algorithm the first probe is typically the smallest msort_n/4 node with first argument 4 which uses both merge/3 recursive clauses (if this node has a high cost or no such node exists the questions are the same as for shorter lists). This node must be erroneous. The next probe is a merge/3 subtree of size two; if it doesn't use the buggy clause the next probe is to similar subtree which does. The second example in Figure 6 illustrates this worst case for a 128 element list: a more complex first question and an extra question about merge/3. These examples demonstrate the algorithm has outstanding performance when the program slicing heuristic is effective.

```
 ?- wrong(merge_sort([9,0,3,5,8,1,2,4,6,7],[0,1,2,3,4,5,8,9])).
merge([5,9],[8],[5,8,9]) valid?  y
msort_n(2,[2,4,6,7],[2,4],[6,7]) valid?  y
msort_n(10,[9,0,3,5,8,1,2,4,6,7],[0,1,2,3,4,5,8,9],[6,7]) valid?n
msort_n(5,[8,1,2,4,6,7],[1,2,4,8],[6,7]) valid?  n
merge([1,8],[2,4],[1,2,4,8]) valid?  y
merge([8],[1],[1,8]) valid?  y
msort_n(2,[8,1,2,4,6,7],[1,8],[2,4,6,7]) valid?  y
Bug:  msort_n(5,[8,1,2,4,6,7],[1,2,4,8],[6,7]) :-
           5 > 1,
           2 is 5 // 2,
           msort_n(2,[8,1,2,4,6,7],[1,8],[2,4,6,7]),
           msort_n(2,[2,4,6,7],[2,4],[6,7]),
           merge([1,8],[2,4],[1,2,4,8]).
```

Figure 7: Finding the more spasmodic bug without prior test cases.

Having found and corrected the bug in merge/3, the programmer may make the mistake of deleting all the information gained from the debugging session then later discover merge_sort/2 is still buggy. Figure 7 shows a sample debugging session chosen to illustrate how our algorithm can perform less well. Despite the relatively large number of probes, we believe each choice of probe is reasonable under the circumstances; in some sense the choices are unlucky rather than foolish. There are 15 instances of the buggy clause used but only 2 are incorrect (those used for sorting five elements). They are at level 3 (of 7) in the tree and are neither top-most nor bottom-most occurrences of this clause.

The first probe is a merge/3 subtree of size 3 (the merge/3 bug in the previous example distorted subsequent clause usage in merge/3, resulting in a different first probe). The second probe is the smallest msort_n/4 node with 2 in the first argument and which uses a different merge/3 fact to that in the first probe. Although this node is correct, the probe is not wasted because it is a child of the buggy node which is eventually found. At this point, all clauses but that of merge_sort/2 are known to have correct instances, leading to the child of the root being probed. The rest of the search proceeds as divide and query would, except for the fact that the first question about msort_n/4 has already been asked. Thus our algorithm results in two more questions than divide and query. If the list is duplicated (the length is doubled) our algorithm asks the same questions, only one more than divide and query, and if the length is quadrupled the same number of questions asked for both algorithms. For examples such as these there are several buggy msort_n/4 nodes at the same level of the tree, with subtrees of similar sizes. Our algorithm generally finds the right-most one, since the right-most msort_n/4 nodes have the smallest atoms and least costly probes. Because msort_n/4 nodes have three subtrees, each with strictly less than half the nodes, divide and query generally finds the one with the greatest weight, usually requiring much more complex probes, especially if weights are computed using atom sizes.

```
 ?- wrong(merge_sort([9,0,3,5,8,1,2,4,6,7],[0,1,2,3,4,5,8,9])).
msort_n(10,[9,0,3,5,8,1,2,4,6,7],[0,1,2,3,4,5,8,9],[6,7]) valid?n
msort_n(5,[8,1,2,4,6,7],[1,2,4,8],[6,7]) valid?  n
merge([1,8],[2,4],[1,2,4,8]) valid?  y
msort_n(2,[2,4,6,7],[2,4],[6,7]) valid?  y
merge([8],[1],[1,8]) valid?  y
msort_n(2,[8,1,2,4,6,7],[1,8],[2,4,6,7]) valid?  y
Bug:  ⟨as before⟩
```

Figure 8: Finding the more spasmodic bug with prior test cases.

Our final example debugging session, Figure 8, locates the same bug, but assumes the debugger has information from two prior (correct) test cases for merge_sort/2 with 16-element lists. There are only two instances of the top level merge_sort/2 clause, thirty instances of the buggy clause and between 15 and 43 instances of the other clauses. The merge_sort/2 clause therefore has the highest P_3 value and by far the lowest P_1 value, and its child is the first probed. The rest of the probes are same as those used by divide and query due to the relatively low P_1 values. The first probe can be eliminated by having more small test cases, increasing the number of correct occurrences of the merge_sort/2 clause without greatly increasing the count for the other clauses. Even with somewhat misleading prior test cases and bugs for which our heuristics are ineffective, the performance of our algorithm is typically not much worse than divide and query and in cases where the heuristics are effective its performance can be dramatically better, especially if the tree is very large.

RELATED WORK

We have already compared our work with related declarative debugging work such as divide and query. One of the contributions of declarative debugging is to view the computation as a tree rather than a sequence of states. The tree nodes can be queried for correctness in a natural way due to the semantics of the programming languages it has been applied to. Complex execution strategies such as coroutining, backtracking and lazy evaluation can be hidden and strategies for searching the tree can be automated.

There is also some related work on bug localization which has been applied to imperative programs. The Tarantula system [6] takes information about which statements are used in successful and failed test cases and displays the program statements with varied color and brightness to be used as a heuristic for (manual) debugging. Color is used to indicate how likely a statement is buggy, varying from red through yellow to green. Brightness is used to indicate confidence — if a statement is used in all successful or all failed test cases it will maximally bright; if it is never used it is black. By comparing Tarantula with our work it can be seen that both can be improved by using more information, and Tarantula could use a more rational approach to computing colors.

In comparing Tarantula and a similar visual debugging system $_\chi$Slice [3] it was noted that Tarantula used multiple failed test cases to identify likely bugs whereas $_\chi$Slice uses just one [6]. Similarly, declarative debugging systems use a single suspect subtree. There is a general assumption that probes are costly and hence there is no advantage in searching for more than one suspect subtree. However, some probes cost little (if the oracle is partially automated), and multiple suspect subtrees can give us additional information which can be used to improve the search strategy. For example, the probabilistic approach could potentially be modified to use this information, or the suspect subtree with the lowest estimated cost could be searched with our proposed algorithm. Although Tarantula may use more test cases, each test case provides less information — it is known whether a particular statement is used in each test case, but not how often (this is known as "binarization"). It would be reasonable to say that a statement being used 100 times in a single passed test case provides more evidence of its correctness than it being used once in each of two passed test cases. Clearly this information could be gathered and Tarantula modified to make use of it.

The color of a statement in Tarantula is determined by the percentage of passed test cases which use the statement divided by the sum of the percentages of passed cases using the statement and failed cases using the statement. Color discrimination between different suspect statements is reduced by increasing the number of passed test cases which don't use the code. An extreme case is a system with two entry points, one of which calls only correct code and the other calls buggy code. By executing enough test cases for the correct entry point, all the code using in incorrect test cases can be made uniformly red. Code which is not used in any failed test cases (and test cases which only use such code) may be useful for validation but are best ignored for debugging purposes.

A more subtle criticism is the relative color of two statements used in the same number of failed test cases depends only on the ratio of the number of passed test cases they have been used in. Suppose there is a single failed test case which uses two statements, S_1 and S_2. The same colors (and brightness) are used whether S_1 and S_2 are used in one and four passed test cases, respectively, or in 25 and 100 passed test cases. However, it would be rational to have more distinction between the two statements in the latter case, where there is more information. In our probabilistic approach (using equal tiny P_0 values and the maximum method for P_1) the ratio of P_3 values is 1:0.328 and 1:0.254, respectively. As the number of passed test case grows the P_3 ratio approaches the ratio of the number of passed test cases, but for small numbers of tests this approximation is inaccurate.

The metric used for ranking in Tarantula is just one of many which have been proposed for debugging and also other domains [12] and some of them have been compared impirically for debugging [1][2]. Effectiveness of declarative debugging overall cannot easily be compared with such systems because declarative debugging uses a tree to structure the computation and support an iterative search for the bug instance. However, our method of computing P_3 values could be used just for ranking, allowing (simplistic) comparison. We would expect the more sophisticated ways of computing P_1, using prior probability distributions, would perform better than the other methods we have suggested.

The SOBER system [8] is also a ranking method which uses probability theory, philosophically similar to ours, but uses different information. Instead of using statement counts it uses counts of the truth and falsity of certain predicates, such as conditions in if-then-else statements, and these predicates are ranked. The "probability" that each predicate is true is determined in successful and failed test cases; differences are used for ranking (more complex ranking metrics have also been proposed [7]). For example, if our buggy merge/3 was coded using a conditional, the predicate A>B would be always false in passed test cases (probability zero) but would have a significantly higher probability for failed test cases. Although such information may not point directly to the bug, it can be very helpful for a programmer. One advantage of the approach is that it allows additional domain knowledge to be incorporated. For example, predicates can be automatically added to compare the result of a C function with zero —

something which often has semantic significance. It may be that diagnosis methods using predicates and statement execution counts of could be combined to good effect. For example, by adding dummy conditionals which do nothing but test a predicate, the same domain knowledge can be reflected in the statement execution counts of "then" and "else" branches. However, for the most spasmodic bugs, it is doubtful that any ranking method can perform well overall as the signal to noise ratio in the data gathered will be extremely small. Impirical studies [2] comparing accuracy of ranking with "error detection accuracy", qe (essentially, a binarized approximation to P1) suggest some ranking methods still perform reasonably well with qe as little as 1%, which is encouraging.

Delta debugging [24] is very effective at diagnosing certain classes of bugs. This method runs the program multiple times with different subsets of the bug-inducing input in order to find two very similar inputs, only one of which exhibits the bug symptom. An oracle is needed to determine if the bug symptom appears in a run — if the symptom is a program crash this is simple (note that declarative languages attempt to automate such things as memory management which are the main cause of crashes). Failure cause-effect chains are then used to provide a relatively concise explanation of the bug symtom. These are stateoriented and it is not clear how usefully they could be adapted to the declarative paradigm. However, any method which can simplify the test data which causes a bug symptom is useful in any diagnosis system.

FURTHER WORK

There are clearly many areas in which our work can be extended. One important area we have discussed is estimating the consistency of bugs (P_1 values). The way we have approximated Equation 3 to obtain our objective function could also be revisited. Currently we use the logarithms of subtree sizes, which is reasonable if the bug is expected to be spasmodic. However, for consistent bugs the number of probes is more like the logarithm of the number of clauses used in the subtrees; some interpolation between these two based on probability estimates could be used. Heuristics for estimating prior probabilities and probe costs also need development. Another possible source of probabilities is to allow users to give probabilistic answers to questions rather than "don't know" (or definite answers which may be incorrect).

Any real application of this work will also have to address resource considerations, particularly memory. Its is not feasible to store the whole tree explicitly, yet our current algorithm relies on it. Divide and query suffers from the same potential problem, but the Mercury[2] debugger has an implementation of (an approximation to) divide and query which uses a modest amount of memory: the tree is incrementally constructed top-down by re-executing parts of the program [10]. Where a subtree is not explicitly constructed, some information is retained, so its (approximate) size can be computed, for example. Clause usage information can be maintained in a similar way.

[2]http://www.cs.mu.oz.au/mercury

Search for the optimal node according to our objective function is more difficult than for divide and query, but a top-down search using heuristics may often find a node with a near-optimal value (or at least significantly better than divide and query). The Mercury system currently has a "deep profiler" which accumulates information such as procedure and clause usage using a data structure which may be very useful for computing approximate probabilities and navigating down the tree. Instead of a tree, a graph is used; cycles are introduced by recursive calls. For example, a single merge/3 sub-computation would introduce a cycle and use constant space though the two textual calls to merge/3 from msort_n/4 would accumulate information separately. Alternatively, a non-top-down search could be used, constructing some nodes without constructing their ancestors. For example, constructing a node corresponding to a bottom-most occurrence of each clause would be very helpful for diagnosing consistent bugs.

There may also be other applications of our approach. One possibility[3] is to use the algorithm for generating or simplifying test cases to help validate programs. Given a complex test case where the correctness of the result is very hard to determine, our algorithm can be run to produce a sequence of probes.

[3]Suggested by Ralph Beckett

If any are incorrect a bug can be diagnosed, otherwise each one helps validate the program. The probes have (relatively) low cost and automatically produce good coverage of the program (relative to the complex test case). The algorithm estimates probabilities of nodes being erroneous given that the top level test case is erroneous, and since the probed nodes never have small probabilities, each correct probe contributes to our confidence that the top level test is correct. Depending on the relative importance of validation and diagnosis when a bug symptom is found, the objective function could be adjusted.

CONCLUSION

People draw on many sources of information when debugging: prior suspicions of where the bug may be, correct computations, incorrect sub-terms and dependencies, et cetera. Ideally, automated systems should do the same — debugging is a difficult task and to make it easier, all potentially useful information should be considered. However, there must be some way of combining information from disparate sources and making it available in a form which can be used directly in a debugging algorithm, something which (to our knowledge) has not previously been done. In this paper we have suggested using probability theory to ultimately compute estimates of the likelihood of subcomputations being buggy. This, combined with knowledge of the sizes of the subcomputations and estimates of the cost of probing different nodes is used to determine the next question to ask in the search algorithm. The effect of the information is to reduce the expected number and complexity of questions asked in order to find a bug.

Our approach has been guided by rationality and results of experimentation. Experimentation has revealed that explicit estimation of how consistent bugs are is important, something which (to our knowledge) has not been done previously. Interestingly, other search algorithms can also be considered rational if we assume limited information is available; the algorithms which perform better use more information. Unfortunately, there is actually too much potentially useful information in the execution in most practical cases. Some compromises must be introduced in order to limit memory use especially. Precisely which compromises are made is best determined by detailed implementation considerations which we have not addressed. We have built very simple prototypes of some of the ideas presented here, but are keen to see a more substantial implementation.

REFERENCES

1. R. Abreu, P. Zoetewij, and A.J.C. van Gemund. An evaluation of similarity coefficients for software fault localization. In Proceedings of PRDC'05, pages 39–46, Riverside, CA, USA, Dec 2006. IEEE Computer Society.
2. R. Abreu, P. Zoetewij, and A.J.C. van Gemund. On the accuracy of spectrum-based fault localization. In Proceedings of Testing: Academic and Industrial conference — Practice and Research Techniques, pages 89– 98. IEEE Computer Society, 2007.
3. H. Agrawal, J. Horgan, S. London, and W. Wong. Fault localization using execution slices and dataflow tests. In Proceedings of the Sixth IEEE International Symposium on Software Reliability Engineering, pages 143–151, Toulouse, France, October 1995.
4. Wlodek Drabent, Simin Nadjm-Tehrani, and Jan Maluszynski. The use of assertions in algorithmic debugging. In Proceedings of the 1988 International Conference on Fifth Generation Computer Systems, pages 573–581, Tokyo, Japan, December 1988.
5. Mireille Ducass´e and S. Schoenig. A backward slicing algorithm for Prolog. In R. Cousot and D. Schmidt, editors, Third International Static Analysis Symposium (SAS'96), pages 317–331, Aachen, Germany, 1996.
6. J. Jones, M. Harrold, and J. Stasko. Visualization of test information to assist fault localization. In Proceedings of the International Conference on Software Engineering, pages 467–477, Orlando, Florida, May 2002.
7. B. Liblit, M. Nauk, A.X. Zheng, A. Aiken, and M.I Jordan. Scalable statistical bug isolation. In Proceedings of PLDI'05, Chicago, IL, USA, June 2005. ACM.
8. C. Liu, X. Yan, L. Fei, J. Han, and S.P. Midkiff. SOBER: Statistical modelbased bug localization. In Proceedings of ESEC-FSE'05, pages 286–295, Lisbon, Portugal, September 2005.
9. John W. Lloyd. Foundations of logic programming. Springer series in symbolic computation. Springer-Verlag, New York, 1984.
10. Ian MacLarty, Zoltan Somogyi, and Mark Brown. Divide-and-query and subterm dependency tracking in the Mercury declarative debugger. In C. Jeffery, J.-D. Choi, and R. Lencevicius, editors, Proceedings of the Sixth International Workshop on Automated and Analysis-Driven Debugging, pages 59–68, Monterey, California, September 2005. ACM.
11. K. Marriott, Lee Naish, and J.L. Lassez. Most specific logic programs. Annals of mathematics and artificial intelligence, 1(2), 1990.
12. A. Meyer, A. Garcia, A. de Souza, and C. de Souza. Comparison of similarity coefficients used for cluster analysis with dominant markers in maize (Zea mays L). Genetics and Molecular Biology, 27(1):83–91, 2004.
13. Lee Naish. Declarative debugging of lazy functional programs. Australian Computer Science Communications, 15(1):287–294, 1993.
14. Lee Naish. A declarative debugging scheme. Journal of Functional and Logic Programming, 1997(3), April 1997.
15. Lee Naish. A three-valued declarative debugging scheme. Australian Computer Science Communications, 22(1):166–173, January 2000.
16. Lee Naish, P. W. Dart, and J. Zobel. The NU-Prolog debugging environment. In Antonio Porto, editor, Proceedings of the Sixth International Conference on Logic Programming, pages 521–536, Lisboa, Portugal, June 1989.
17. Henrik Nilsson and Peter Fritzson. Algorithmic debugging of lazy functional languages. Proceedings of The Fourth International Symposium on Programming Language Implementation and Logic Programming, to appear, August, 1992.
18. Luis Moniz Pereira. Rational debugging in logic programming. In Ehud Shapiro, editor, Proceedings of the Third International Conference on Logic Programming, pages 203–210, London, England, July 1986. published as Lecture Notes in Computer Science 225 by Springer-Verlag.
19. Luis Moniz Pereira and Miguel Calejo. A framework for Prolog debugging. In Kenneth A. Bowen and Robert A. Kowalski, editors, Proceedings of the Fifth International Conference/Symposium on Logic Programming, pages 481–495, Seattle, Washington, August 1988.
20. Ehud Y. Shapiro. Algorithmic program debugging. MIT Press, Cambridge, Massachusetts, 1983.
21. Zoltan Somogyi and Fergus J. Henderson. The implementation technology of the Mercury debugger. In Proceedings of the Tenth Workshop on Logic Programming Environments, pages 35–49, Las Cruces, New Mexico, November 1999.
22. Zoltan Somogyi, Fergus J. Henderson, and Thomas Conway. Mercury: an efficient purely declarative logic programming language. In Proceedings of the Australian Computer Science Conference, pages 499–512, Glenelg, Australia, February 1995.
23. M. Weiser. Programmers use slices when debugging. Communications of the ACM, 25(7):446–452, 1982.
24. A. Zeller. Isolating cause-effect chains from computer programs. In Proceedings of SIGSOFT/FSE-10, Charston, SC, USA, Nov 2002. IEEE Computer Society.

CHAPTER 7 MODEL-DRIVEN ENGINEERING: A SURVEY SUPPORTED BY THE UNIFIED CONCEPTUAL MODEL

Alberto Rodrigues da Silva

INESC-ID & Instituto Superior Técnico - Universidade de Lisboa, Lisbon, Portugal

ABSTRACT

During the last decade a new trend of approaches has emerged, which considers models not just documentation artefacts, but also central artefacts in the software engineering field, allowing the creation or automatic execution of software systems starting from those models. These proposals have been classified generically as Model-Driven Engineering (MDE) and share common concepts and terms that need to be abstracted, discussed and understood. This paper presents a survey on MDE based on a unified conceptual model that clearly identifies and relates these essential concepts, namely the concepts of system, model, metamodel, modeling language, transformations, software platform, and software product. In addition, this paper discusses the terminologies relating MDE, MDD, MDA and others. This survey is based on earlier work, however, contrary to those, it intends to give a simple, broader and integrated view of the essential concepts and respective terminology commonly involved in the MDE, answering to key questions such as: What is a model? What is the relation between a model and a metamodel? What are the key facets of a modeling language? How can I use models in the context of a software development process? What are the relations between models and source code artefacts and software platforms? and What are the relations between MDE, MDD, MDA and other MD approaches?

INTRODUCTION

A model is an abstraction of a system often used to replace the system under study [40], [20] and [37]. In general a model represents a partial and simplified view of a system, so, the creation of multiple models is usually necessary to better represent and understand the system under study. Modeling is a well-known technique adopted by Engineering fields as well as other areas such as Physics, Mathematics, Biology, Economy, Politics and Philosophy [20]. However, in this research we focus on models in the context of Software Engineering and Information Systems fields. That means that our models are thus language-based in nature and tend to describe or prescribe some system as opposed, for example, to models in Mathematics which are understood as interpretation of a theory [11].

Models allow sharing a common vision and knowledge among technical and non-technical stakeholders, facilitating and promoting the communication among them. Furthermore, models make the project planning more effective and efficient while providing a more appropriate view of the system to be developed and allowing the project control to be achieved according to objective criteria [8] and [85].

In the last decades numerous techniques and modeling languages have been proposed to support the design and the

Citation: Alberto Rodrigues da Silva, Model-driven engineering: A survey supported by the unified conceptual model, doi:10.1016/j.cl.2015.06.001

development of complex software systems. Many of these languages were defined in the context of methodological approaches – such as structured, object oriented or unified methodologies/processes, fundamentally with the purpose of facilitating and sharing a common and coherent vision of the system under study and, consequently, of easing the communication among stakeholders [8], [84],[85] and [34]. However, during this last decade a new trend of approaches has emerged considering models not just as documentation artefacts, but as central artefacts in the software engineering process. In addition to the benefits referred above, it also allows – through complex techniques such as meta-modeling, model transformation, code generation or model interpretation – the creation or automatic execution of software systems based on those models. These proposals – such as MDA [51] and [21], Software Factories [24], or recently DSL Engineering [83] – have been classified generically as Model-Driven Engineering (MDE) but also by related names such as model-based engineering (MBE), model-driven development (MDD), model-driven software development (MDSD) [45], [3], [74] and [67], or model-based testing (MBT) [80]. Regardless of the adopted term and the particular application, all of them share common concepts and terms that need to be abstracted, discussed and understood.

The objective of this paper is to survey and discuss the essential concepts of MDE and, in particular, to propose a unified conceptual model that clearly identifies and relates those concepts, namely the concepts of system, model, metamodel, modeling language, transformation, software platform and software product. For the sake of simplicity and readability this unified conceptual model is described through a coherent set of UML class diagrams complemented by descriptions and discussions in natural language. The proposed conceptual model is based on earlier work, in particular, on work that relates the conceptualization of models and metamodels [64], [20], [19] and [37], modeling languages [46] and [66], and relations between models, transformations, platforms and software products [74]. However, as further discussed in the Related Work section, unlike these former works, this paper intends to give a simple, broad and integrated view of the key concepts and respective terminology commonly involved in the MDE, answering to common questions like: What is a model? What is the relation between a model and a metamodel? What are the key facets of a modeling language? How can I use models in the context of a software development process? What are the relations between models and source code artefacts and software platforms? and What are the relations between MDE, MDD, MDA and other MD approaches?

This paper is organized in 7 sections. Section 2 introduces the concepts and definitions of system, model and metamodel that are central in MDE. Section 3 defines the concept of a modeling language with its different facets (i.e., abstract syntax, concrete syntax, semantics and pragmatics) and also asserts that a modeling language provides one or more viewpoints and can be classified according the abstraction and perspective dimensions. Section 4 extends the proposed conceptual model by introducing and relating the concepts of software product, software platform, artefacts and model transformations. Section 5 relates and analyses the terms used around the MD approaches. Section 6 compares and discusses our research with the related work. Finally, Section 7 presents the conclusion and identifies issues for future work.

MODELS AND METAMODELS

This section introduces the essential concepts underlying MDE, namely the concepts of system, model, metamodel and their relations.

In the context of MDE, we define "***system** as a generic concept for designating a software application, software platform or any other software artefact*". Additionally, as suggested in Fig. 1, a system might be composed of other subsystems and a system may have relations with other systems (e.g., a system may communicate with others).

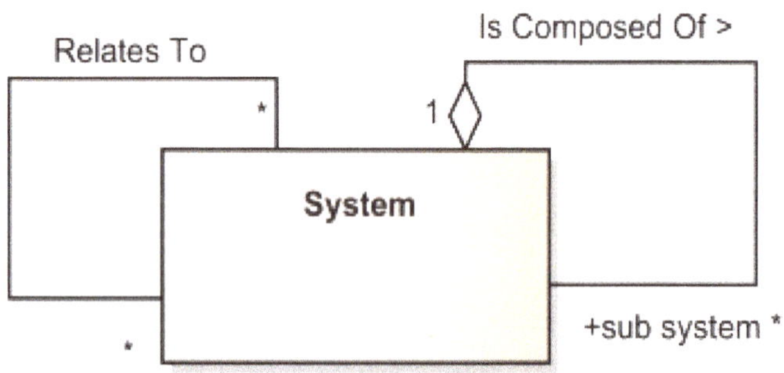

Figure. 1. The System definition.

Model

A model is an abstraction of a *system under study* (*SUS*, also known as the "Universe of Discourse" or just "system"), which may already exist or is intended to exist in the future.

Model Definition

In the absence of a common definition for "model", it is relevant to refer some of its popular attempts, namely the following: (1) model is a set of statements about the system under study [64]; (2) model is an abstraction of a (real or language-based) system allowing predictions or inferences to be made [37]; (3) model is a reduced representation of some system that highlights the properties of interest from a given viewpoint [65]; and (4) model is a simplification of a system built with an intended goal in mind so a model should be able to answer questions in place of the original system [6].

From these definitions there is a consensus that a *model defines a system under study (SUS) and* vice-versa. However, a *model is itself a system*, with its own identity, complexity, elements, relations, etc. In particular, when we think about a model of a model we have to consider that one of them plays the role of the system under study and, consequently, it is itself a system. To sum up, and as suggested in Fig. 2 we define "***model** as a system that helps to define and to give answers of the system under study without the need to consider it directly*".

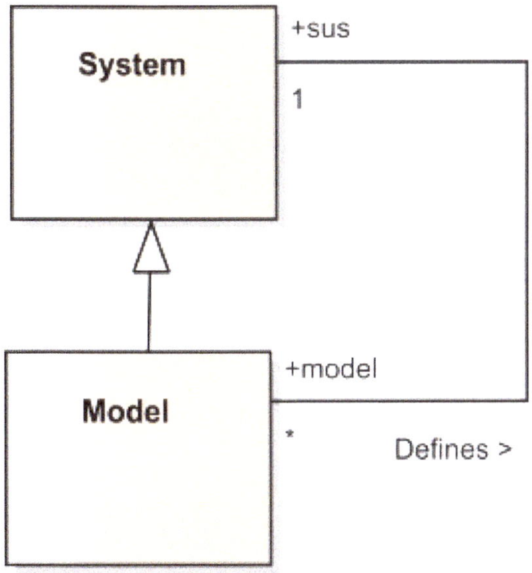

Figure. 2. The Model definition: relationships between model and system.

Criteria and Principles

To distinguish a model from any other type of artefact, Stachowiak proposes three criteria for their unique identification [40]: (1) *Mapping criteria*: It must be possible to identify the object or original phenomenon (of the system) that is represented or mapped in the model; (2) *Reduction criteria*: The model must be a simplified version of the original, so not all aspects of the original must be depicted in the model; and (3) *Pragmatism criteria*: The model has to be useful; namely it should be able to replace the original for certain purposes.

The mapping criteria do not require the existence of the original. As in most engineering areas, usually temporally models precede the original and are used extensively to check the completion of the original. The reduction criteria suggests that the model is a simplification of the original, which for instance ignores original features not relevant in the model, or adds features that can enrich the model. Finally, the pragmatism criteria refer to the useful character of models in the sense that they must serve some purpose.

On the other hand, Booch identifies a *set of purposes and benefits* deriving from the existence of models, namely that [7]: models help to visualize a system, as it is or as we want it to be; models allow to specify the structure and the behavior of a system; models give a template that help guide the development process; and models help to document the decisions taken along the project lifecycle.

Metamodel

Like for the model definition, there is a variety of definitions for metamodel, some of them are unclear or too weak, such as the OMG's definition that simply states that "a metamodel is a model of models" [51]. However, some authors have reflected extensively on these concepts, and give the following definitions: (1) a metamodel is a model that defines the language for expressing a model [51]; (2) a metamodel is a model of a language of models [19]; (3) a metamodel is a specification model for which the systems under study being specified are models in a certain modeling language [64]. However, the deepest analysis of this subject is maybe authored by Kühne that introduced important concerns for this discussion, such as the classification of models as token (or instance) versus type models, ontological versus linguistic instantiations, and the language definition stack [37].

Metamodel Definition

Based on the previous referred works we define "*metamodel as a model that defines the structure of a modeling language*". However, from Fig. 3 we still have to understand the following facts: First, through the relationship *Element Of*, between *Model* and *Modeling Language*, a modeling language is a set of models (or a model is an element of a modeling language). Second, through the relationship *Defines*, between *Metamodel* and *Modeling Language*, a metamodel is a model of a modeling language structure (or a modeling language is defined by a metamodel). Third, a metamodel is a model of a set of models or is a model of models. Finally, a model conforms with a metamodel (via the *Conforms With* relation), meaning that the model should satisfy the rules defined at the level of its metamodel as extensively discussed by Kühne and others [37], [73] and [57].

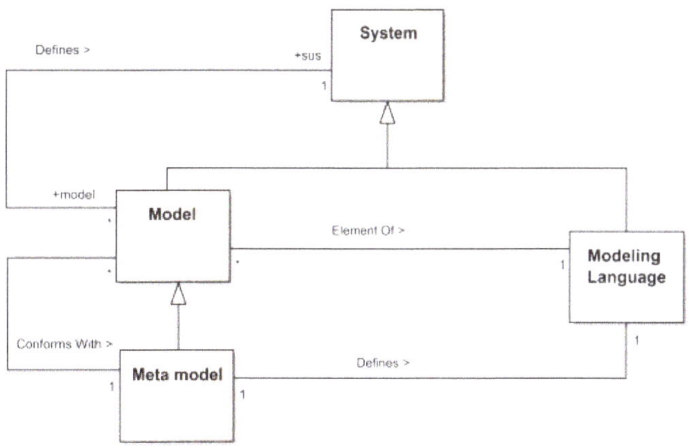

Figure. 3. The metamodel definition: relationships between metamodel and model.

Meta-metamodel, Metamodel and Model

A well-known and recurring problem of metamodeling is how to set the initial metamodel. If a metamodel is a model of a modeling language, there must be a *meta-metamodel*describing its modeling language, and so on, in higher levels and more abstract meta-metamodels. The common solution to overcome this problem is to use a language that, at a particular level of this hierarchy, describes itself in its own language. There are numerous examples of this solution. In the field of natural languages, the English Language describes itself in English at the level of grammar definition, dictionaries, etc. In the field of programming languages, Lisp is a well-known example of a language that describes itself, providing in particular a Lisp compiler written in Lisp [44].

In the field of modeling languages the solution proposed by OMG, based on a four-layer architecture and directly supported through the *Meta Object Facility* (MOF) [55] is a popular example. At the top of that hierarchy there is the meta-metamodeling layer (designated as M3) that is mainly responsible for providing a language to specify metamodels.

MOF is a unique meta-metamodel layer because it is instantiated from its own model, i.e., the MOF is defined in MOF (technically using a restricted set of meta-classes designated by *InfrastructureLibrary*). In the layer below (designated as M2), metamodels are defined by instantiation of the meta-metamodel (i.e., each element of the metamodel is an instance of an element defined in the meta-metamodel). UML [53] or Common Warehouse Metamodel (CWM) [52] are some examples of those metamodels, i.e. examples of MOF instances. In the layer below M2 (designated as M1), the models are defined according to the interest and needs of its users: typically for different application domains and different levels of abstraction, e.g. at the level of business definition, technical requirements, or software design. Note that a user model can contain either model elements (i.e., classes and concrete types e.g., *Video*) or instances of these types (e.g., the instance*:Video*). Finally, the lowest level of the hierarchy (the M0 layer) contains real instances of elements defined in the model that actually exist in the context of a computational environment or even in the real world (e.g., a specific Video in your own laptop).

MODELING LANGUAGE

As mentioned in the previous section, a modeling language is defined by a metamodel and is a set of all possible models that are conformant with its respective metamodel. However, to provide a complete definition we should consider other aspects or facets (as suggested in Fig. 4), and consequently we define "*modeling language as a set of all possible models that are conformant with the modeling language s abstract syntax, represented by one or more concrete syntaxes and that satisfy a given semantics. Additionally, the pragmatics (of a modeling language) helps and guides how to use it in the most appropriate way*". Metamodel and notation are common synonyms to, respectively, abstract syntax and concrete syntax [25].

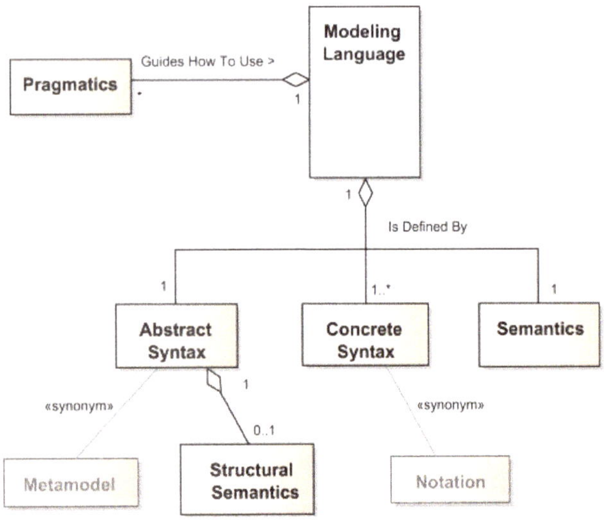

Figure. 4. The Modeling Language definition.

Abstract Syntax

The definition of a modeling language usually starts with the capture and identification of the concepts, abstractions and relations underlying the application domain, which represents domain analysis phase of DS(M)L development [46] and [32]. This is primarily an exercise of abstraction and conceptualization, and then synthesis ofthe domain knowledge, that the architect of the modeling language has to know or has to obtain from the direct interaction with the domain experts. The result of this activity produces the*modeling language s abstract syntax*, which corresponds to a metamodel with all the concepts identified at the meta domain level.

The usual techniques to the definition of abstract syntaxes are, in general, *grammars* for natural languages, or *context free grammars* (e.g., specified in compact formalism based on Backus-Naur Form (BNF) notation) for programming languages [57]. However, in the scope of modeling languages the common practice is the use of *metamodeling techniques* [79], [46] and [66]. For example in the context of OMG, the common practice for defining modeling languages is through the use of the UML profile mechanism or directly by using the MOF language (or some of its variations) [66] and [55].

The abstract syntax defines all the names of the identified concepts, and their respective relations, so it is important that those names would be close to the application domain to be easily understood by its users. On the other hand, its simplicity should be promoted, for example to avoid introducing additional concepts with misunderstood terms that could make it more expressive, but also more difficult to use and to maintain.

As illustrated in Fig. 4, the abstract syntax still includes the *"structural semantics"* (*or static semantics*) that is mainly focused on setting binding rules among its elements. For example, and in a simplified way, structural semantics allows to define that an element of type A can be related to other elements of type B according to this or that constraint; or you can determine that elements of type A can never be related to elements of type C. In general, structural semantics of a modeling language can be described in the different ways: either through a declarative constraints language (e.g., Object Constraint Language (OCL) [56] in the case of UML); through informal natural language specification; or through a blending approach. For example, the structural semantics of UML itself is described extensively in natural language, class diagrams, and some few aspects defined in OCL [7].

The structural semantics is needed because the structure of a language (abstract syntax) is many times context dependent and this cannot be capture by context free metamodels (i.e. grammars) [57]. Additionally, the structural semantics prevents its users from creating models that violate the rules of liaison and the orchestration of its elements, but this can only be achieved if there is proper tool support where such structural semantics are duly captured and validated.

Concrete Syntax

The *concrete syntax of a modeling language refers to its notation*, i.e. the way users will learn and will use it, either by reading or by writing and designing the models. The*notation* is an important aspect of a modeling language because it corresponds to the perspective and user experience that users would have. So, the success of a modeling language will depend on the right balance between simplicity and expressiveness, and in particular the following concerns should be addressed when designing a concrete syntax: writability, readability, learnability and effectiveness [83].

Different notations can be provided, namely graphical, textual, tabular and forms-based, or combinations of them. In general, graphical notations tend to be more suitable to illustrate relations between concepts, changing values in a spatial or temporal distribution, causal and temporal sequences between events, or data and control flows in process modeling scenarios. However, graphical models are not so scalable as textual or tabular-based models, that means they are not the most appropriate to support large models; also they are poorly applicable to write or visualize logical expressions or complex actions – for such, textual notations tend to be more appropriate [74] and [83]. Finally, because a modeling language might have multiple concrete syntaxes, it would be possible to combine both for the sake of their users: for example to adopt a textual notation for writing/authoring and a graphical notation for just reading/visualization.

Semantics

In general the semantics reveals the meaning of syntactically valid expressions (or models) specified in a given language. For natural languages, this means correlating sentences and phrases with the concepts, thoughts and feelings based on our experiences and background. For programming languages, semantics describes the behavior that a computer should follow when executing a program in that language. This specification can describe the relationship between the input and output of a program or can provide a step-by-step explanation on how a program will execute on a real or virtual machine.

For modeling languages, and depending on the concepts and models involved, there are two types of *semantics* [26]: executable and non-executable semantics. *Executable semantics* concerns concepts directly related to programming languages, i.e. related to the order of execution of programs, such as those found in state machines, sequence and activity diagrams. On the other hand, *non-executable semantics* concerns concepts not directly related to software execution (or any other kind of execution), such as those concepts involved on the deployment of software components on hardware nodes (e.g., UML component and deployment diagrams), or specification of user requirements (e.g., through UML use case diagrams).

Most of the existing semantics frameworks, developed originally for programming languages [71], are also used to define the semantics of executable models (such as UML state machines or BPMN business process diagrams). Some of these frameworks are "structural operational semantics" and "translational semantics" [71] and [29]. The *structural operational semantics (SOS)* describes formally a language's semantics by means of a set of inference rules: the individual computation steps are the interpretation of a given concept of the language that will produce an equivalent symbolic representation in a real or virtual machine. The *translational semantics* is a formal way to describe the language's semantics, where the abstract syntax of a source language is mapped into the abstract syntax of a target language which is supposed to be formally defined (e.g., as finite state machine or abstract state machine). Furthermore, the mappings between the source and the target languages might be supported by model language transformations such as QVT, ATL or DSLTrans (see a further discussion below, in Section 4). Regarding non-executable models their semantics can also be defined according a translational framework.

However, and in many cases the semantics of a modeling language is defined in an informal way (by using natural language specifications) instead of following the referred formal frameworks. In the end, and in those situations, the semantics is just taken into consideration during the software system development, preferably through code generation mechanisms, but also by implementing them through source code directly written in a specific programming language.

Finally and based on this discussion, we may classify the semantics of a modeling language according two-orthogonal dimensions: *executable* vs. *non-executable semantics* and *formal* vs. *informal semantics*. A further analysis and discussion of the challenges and directions in formalizing the semantics of modeling languages is proposed by Byrant and others [10].

Pragmatics

The *pragmatics of a natural language* has been treated as an area of linguistics and is concerned with the study of its use in communication acts in which the factors regarding the context are decisive, such as social, cultural, psychological, historical or geographical factors. While the semantics is concerned with the meaning of language's constructs, pragmatics is concerned with the meaning and interpretation of the language in a context dependent way, i.e. it depends on its users' knowledge and on the various factors on which the communication occurs.

On the other hand, the *pragmatics of a modeling language* has not drawn particular interest from the community, with a few exceptions such as [43] and [65]. The pragmatics of modeling languages has been focused on the definition and discussion of aspects related to their use in practical contexts, namely in the definition of its types of users or roles (e.g., domain experts, requirements engineers, software architects and end-users), the activities to be conducted (e.g., drawing/writing, refinement, reading, analysis and validation of models), and various factors (e.g., social, environmental or psychological) that may constraint themselves.

Most of the work on pragmatics is concerning how modeling languages can be used in a more efficient and appropriate way, generally involving a set of principles, recommendations and guidelines for their use. There are languages (such as UML) that do not define explicitly any pragmatics, i.e., they deliberately do not define or give any guidance or practices for how they should be used, while others (e.g., SSADM [84], Booch [8] or Yourdon [85]) include the pragmatics in their own definition, in some cases including a well-defined process (or methodology) with practical recommendations and guidelines. Furthermore, the pragmatics might also refers practical aspects of using modeling languages and MDE on real-world projects, such as scalability of the technologies, information overload of large models, efficiency of automatically generated code, and integration with other development tools.

Classification of a Modeling Language

In addition to the aspects of a modeling language (introduced above) there is some controversy and debate in the community in what concerns their classification. For example a modeling language might be classified as *general-purpose* (GPML) or *domain-specific modeling language* (DS(M)L) [16], [31], [41], [46] and [33]. A GPML is characterized by having a greater number of generic constructs, which encourages a wider and widespread use in different fields of application. UML or SysML are popular examples of GPMLs by providing large sets of constructs and notations used for specifying and documenting, respectively, software systems according to the object-oriented paradigm, or any kind of systems as understood by the system engineering discipline. On the other hand, DSLs tend to use few constructs or concepts which are closer to its application domain. Since a DSL is expressed using domain concepts, it is normally easier to read, understand, validate and communicate with, facilitating cooperation between developers and domain experts. Moreover, some argue that DSLs can improve productivity, reliability, maintainability and portability [16] and [27]. On the other hand, the use of a DSL can raise some problems, such as the cost of learning, implementing and maintaining a new language, as well as the support tools to develop with it [46].

However, others argue that, due to the high-quality and sophistication level of current language workbenches, the tool support is not anymore a main constraint (see further discussion below in Section 5.2). Furthermore, some recent studies have shown that software language engineers do not even have the common practice of evaluating their own languages [22], and conclude that more research is mandatory in the area of software language processes, particularly in what concerns the design, development and evaluation of these languages [22], [4] and [47].

Fig. 5 shows that a modeling language can be classified according its application domain attribute (e.g., based on the values defined in the *Application Domain Kind* enumeration) and can be structured by one or more viewpoints.

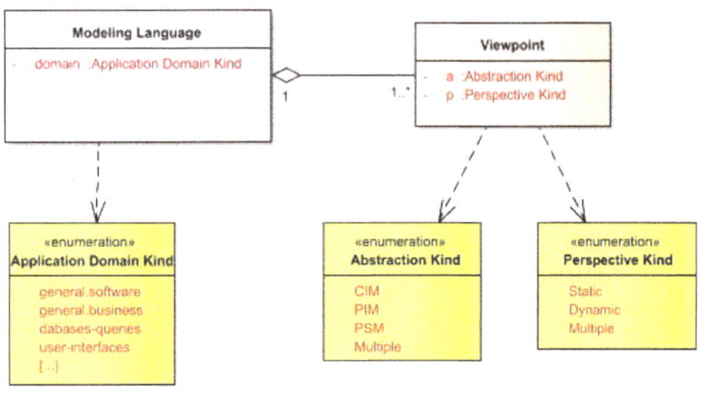

Figure. 5. The classification of a modeling language and its companion viewpoints.

A viewpoint defines a reusable set of criteria for the construction, selection, and presentation of a portion of a model, addressing particular stakeholder concerns. A *viewpoint* is a general concept that allows applying the *multi-viewpoint modeling principle* or the *separation of concerns principle* that states that a complex system is better defined by multiple views, considering both static and dynamic aspects [7] and [9]. Therefore, a modeling language provides one or more viewpoints that can be classified according the abstraction and perspective properties. On the *abstraction dimension*, a viewpoint can be classified, for example using the MDA terminology [51], as computational independent model (CIM), platform independent model (PIM), platform specific model (PSM) or multiple (meaning that viewpoint may involve elements defined at multiple abstraction levels). On the *perspective dimension*, a viewpoint can be classified as static, dynamic or multiple (meaning that a viewpoint may involve both static and dynamic elements). A static viewpoint describes a system mainly from its structural perspective with concepts such as classes, objects, nodes, blocks and respective relations. For example, UML class diagrams or component diagrams are static viewpoints. On the other hand, a dynamic viewpoint describes the behavior of a system from a certain perspective with concepts such as tasks, operations, states, events, messages and respective relations. Activity diagrams or state machines in UML or business process diagrams in BPMN are examples of dynamic viewpoints.

Discussion

Based on the proposed conceptual model, we can better analyse, understand and compare modeling languages. We can also use this conceptual model to help defining our own modeling languages, with their specific facets, principles and guidelines.

For example Table 1 shows the application of this conceptual model to classify two well-known general purpose languages, UML [53] and BPMN [54], and two domain-specific languages, XIS-Mobile ([58]) and DSL3S [72] languages. UML is a GPML for modeling software systems at multiple abstraction levels, and to that purpose UML provides many viewpoints, such as class, object, sequence, use cases, state machine, component diagrams, etc. BPMN may be classified as a GPML for modeling business systems from a dynamic perspective and mainly at a computational independent abstraction level; BPMN provides four viewpoints: process, collaboration choreography and conversation diagrams. XIS-Mobile is a DSML for modeling mobile applications in a cross-platform (or platform independent) way; XIS-Mobile is defined as a UML profile and provides the following viewpoints: domain, business entities, architectural, use cases, navigation space, and interaction space views (or diagrams). Finally, DSL3S is a DSML for spatial simulation in the field of Geographic Information Systems; DSL3S provides the following viewpoints to organized static and platform-independent models: simulation, scenario, animat and animat interactions views.

Table 1. Classification of modeling languages: UML2, BPMN, XIS-Mobile and DSL3S

Modeling Language				
Name	**Application Domain**	**Viewpoint**	**Abstraction**	**Perspective**
UML (Unified Modeling Language)	General/Software	Class Diagram	Multiple	Static
		Object Diagram	Multiple	Static
		Sequence Diagram	Multiple	Dynamic
		Use Case Diagram	PIM	Dynamic
		State Machine Diagram	Multiple	Dynamic
		Component Diagram	PSM	Static
		–	–	–
BPMN (Business Process Modeling Notation)	General/Business Processes	Process Diagram	CIM	Dynamic
		Collaboration Diagram	CIM	Dynamic
		Choreography Diagram	CIM	Dynamic
		Conversation Diagram	CIM	Dynamic
XIS-Mobile (DSL for Mobile Apps)	Specific/Mobile Apps	Domain View	PIM	Static
		BusinessEntities View	PIM	Static
		Architectural View	PIM	Static
		UseCases View	PIM	Dynamic
		NavigationSpace View	PIM	Static
		InteractionSpace View	PIM	Static
DSL3S (DSL for Spatial Simulation Scenarios)	Specific/Spatial Apps	Simulation View	PIM	Static
		Scenario View	PIM	Static
		Animat View	PIM	Static
		Animat Interactions View	PIM	Static

Furthermore, there are other discussion topics that are worthwhile to mention, namely in what concern the quality of modeling languages. An open topic is the discussion of *what should be these key qualities for analyzing and comparing modeling languages* and their corresponding trade-offs, as for example simplicity, expressiveness, focus, multiple views, or usability.

The *simplicity* of a modeling language can be analyzed at various levels, such as at the level of its abstract syntax (through the definition of its concepts and relations) and its concrete syntax (through the definition of textual or graphical representation). A simple language should have few concepts and its notation should be simple and consistent. Notwithstanding, an expressive modeling language may require the introduction of additional concepts and notations, which would facilitate the work of its users, but, on the other hand, make it less simple. For example, in the context of business process modeling, UML activity diagrams are simpler (but also less expressive and more informal) than Business Process Model and Notation (BPMN) diagrams [54].

Krogstie proposed and discussed extensively this topic of quality of modeling languages and quality of models, in particular with the SEQUAL framework [34]. On the other hand, Barišić proposed a process for evaluating the usability of DSLs [4]. Recently, Morais and Silva also proposed the ARENA framework and used it to compare and evaluate user-interface modeling languages [47].

SOFTWARE PRODUCTS, PLATFORMS AND TRANSFORMATIONS

MDE approach claims that the use of modeling languages help to specify models in a certain level of abstraction, and also that those models are used to support the development of software applications [3], [74] and [67]. As suggested in Fig. 6, we define "*software application (or software product) as a system composed of a nontrivial integration of software platforms, artefacts generated through model-to-text transformations, artefacts directly written by developers, and eventually models directly executable in the context of a particular software platform*". (For the sake of simplicity it is not illustrated in Fig. 6, but software applications, platforms, artefacts and models should all be considered "systems" according to the discussion above in Section 2.1.1., see Fig. 1).

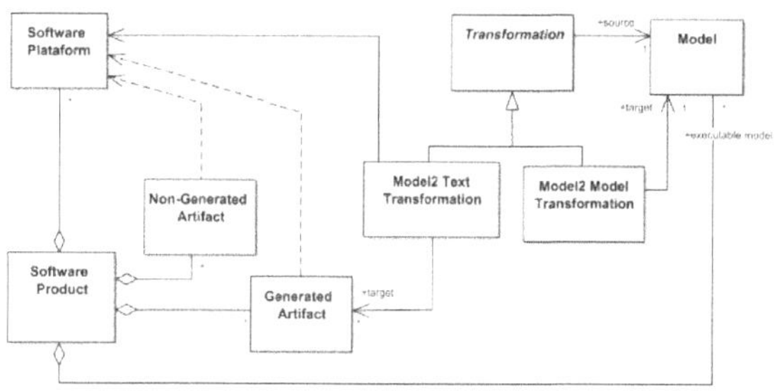

Figure. 6. Software product, platforms, transformations, and models.

First, *software platforms* mean an integrated set of computational elements that enable the development and execution of a class of software products [9], [83] and [24]. Usually these elements provide different functionalities through reuse and extensibility mechanisms and are referred to technologies such as middleware, software libraries, application frameworks, and software components, but also database management systems, web servers, content management and document management systems, workflow management systems, etc. Thus, it is common for a certain class of software product the use and integration of several software platforms, which might have constraints and dependencies among them. For example a mobile application developed for Android depends on the Android platform and on the SQLite database, which depend on the Java Virtual Machine and so on.

Second, *generated and non-generated artefacts* are also elements of the software application. These artefacts might be only relevant during the development time while other artefacts might be relevant at application runtime. Nevertheless, both types of artefacts are tightly dependent on the involved platforms. Many examples of these artefacts might be considered such as: source and binary code files, configuration and deployment scripts, database scripts, and even documentation files, including the models themselves.

Third, two main types of *transformations* tend to be considered in MDE approach. On the one hand, *model-to-text transformations* (M2T) that generate or produce software artefacts – typically source code, XML and other text files –, from models. The most common technique for this class of transformations is known as code generation, and there are multiple solutions and techniques as discussed by Czarnecki and others[14] and [74]. On the other hand, *model-to-model transformations* (M2M) allow translating models into another set of models, typically closer to the solution domain or that satisfy specific needs for different stakeholders. These transformations are specified through distinct languages, such as the mainstream programming languages, but also by specialized model transformation languages, for different purposes and with different modeling paradigms such as QVT, [1] Acceleo,[2] ATL,[3] VIATRA,[4] DSLTrans[5] as extensively discussed by Syriani and others [76], [36], [15], [23] and [2].

Fourth, as suggested in Fig. 6, *models* are a central concept of the MDE approach. On one hand, a model can be created directly by users (i.e. model designers) or can be produced automatically from model-to-model transformations and, then, still edited and refined. On the other hand, models can be used to produce generated or non-generated software artefacts, respectively by means of M2T transformations or direct authoring by their users (i.e. software developers). Furthermore, in some particular situations, models can be directly interpreted and executed by specific platforms integrated with the software application [42] and [13]. Of course, it is important to emphasize that *to be effectively used in the context of the MDE models must be defined in a consistent and rigorous way*. In general, it is required a certain level of quality in order that those models might be properly used in M2M or M2T scenarios. For this purpose there are features that the tools should provide, such as model analysis, validation and simulation as discussed in [81].

FROM ABSTRACT TO CONCRETE MODEL-DRIVEN APPROACHES

This section discusses the final research question of this paper: What are the relations between MDE, MDD, MDA and other MD approaches? This question is still important because these terms are used in the community many times without a clear understanding of their meanings and respective relations.

Fig. 7 shows the proposed conceptual model that introduces these terms and their relations. This model defines a hierarchical structure of MD approaches, each one at a level of abstraction, with the respective generalization and specialization relationships. On the top of this hierarchy it is the most abstract term (MDE) while in the bottom there are some concrete MD approaches that are briefly introduced below. It is not the purpose of this paper to give a complete or exhaustive identification of all middle-level and concrete-level approaches.

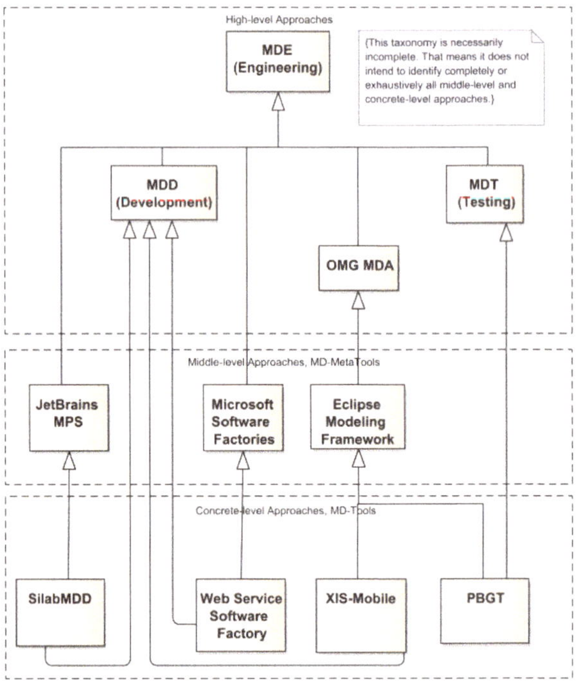

Figure. 7. MDE, related terminology and concrete approaches.

Table 2 complements Fig. 7 to help understand and discuss the proposed model. There are a certain number of aspects that were considered to support the analysis and comparison of those MD approaches, namely: abstraction level, software engineering disciplines, models, transformations, meta-modeling languages, application domain, and tool support. The aspect "abstraction level" defines how abstract or concrete is an approach. For simplicity reasons we define just 3 levels: high, medium and low. The aspect "software engineering disciplines" defines the engineering tasks addressed by each approach. For this classification we considered the following disciplines, as defined in Rational Unified Process (RUP) [35]: business modeling, requirements, analysis and design, implementation, testing, deployment; of course this list can be extended with other disciplines such as maintenance and simulation. The aspect "models" defines the abstraction levels (e.g., CIM, PIM, PSM) and the modeling languages supported by each approach, as discussed in Section 3. The aspect "transformations" defines the types (e.g., M2M and M2T) and the languages used by each approach to support the model transformations. The aspect "meta-modeling languages" defines the technologies used to define modeling languages. The aspect "domain" defines the application domains of each approach; usually only concrete approaches are domain-specific. Finally, the aspect "tool support" defines the type of tool supported by each approach.

Table 2.Classification of model-driven approaches: from abstract to concrete approaches

Model-Driven Approaches	Abstraction Level	Software Eng. Disciplines	Models		Transformations		Meta modeling languages	Domain	Tool Support
			Levels	Language	Types	Languages			
MDE	High	Any	ND	ND	ND	ND	ND	Any	ND
MDD		Requirements, Analysis and design, Implementation	ND	ND	ND	ND	ND	Any	ND
MBT		Testing	ND	ND	ND	ND	ND	Any	ND
OMG MDA		Analysis and design, Implementation	CIM, PIM, PSM	UML, UML Profiles	M2M, M2T	QVT	MOF, EMOF, Ecore, UML	Any	Several, e.g., Eclipse Modeling Framework, Enterprise Architect MDG
EMF (Eclipse Modeling Framework)	Medium	Any	Any	UML, UML Profiles	M2M, M2T	Several	Ecore, EMOF	Any	Eclipse and Eclipse Modeling Framework
Microsoft Software Factories		Any	Any	DSLs	ND	.NET languages	UML	Any	Microsoft Visual Studio - Visualization & Modeling SDK
JetBrains MPS		Any	Any	Textual DSLs	M2M, M2T	Java	MPS's Base Language	Any	JetBrains IntelliJ IDEA and MPS
Web Service Software Factory	Concrete	Design, Implementarion	PSM	DSL	M2T	.NET languages	UML	Web Services	Microsoft Visual Studio
XIS-Mobile		Analysis and design, Implementation	PIM	XIS-Mobile (UML Profile)	M2M, M2T	C#, Acceleo	UML	Mobile Apps	Sparx EA, Eclipse Modeling Framework, Accelo
SillaMDD		Requirements, Analysis and design, Implementation	CIM	SilabReq (Textual DSL)	M2T	Java	MPS's Base Language	Requirements of Business Apps	JetBrains IntelliJ IDEA and MPS
PBGT (Pattern Based GUI Testing)		Testing	PIM	PARADIGM	M2T	Java	Ecore	Software Testing	Eclipse Modeling Framework, Selenium

Legend: ND (Not defined or not relevant); Models Levels: CIM (Computing independent Model); PIM (Platform Independent Model); PSM (Platform Specific Model); Transformations Types: M2M (Model to Model), M2T (Model to Text).

High-level Approaches

MDE is on the top of abstraction of MD approaches. MDE is a software engineering approach that considers models not just as documentation artefacts but also as first-class citizens, where models might be used throughout all engineering disciplines and in any application domain. In this context, MDE is better classified as a software engineering paradigm and so, it does not have any concrete tool support. At this same level of abstraction are MDD and MBT (as well as other concerns could be considered such as enterprise engineering [17] or ontologies and knowledge representation [68]).

Model-Driven Development (MDD) approach is mainly focused on the requirements, analysis and design, and implementation disciplines [45], [3], [74] and [67]. Concrete MDD approaches tend to define modeling languages to specify the System Under Study (SUS) at different levels of abstraction, to provide M2M and M2T transformations in order to improve the productivity and quality of the process and the final software system.

On the other hand, *Model-Based Testing (MBT)* [80] is mainly focused on the automation of the testing discipline. Testing models are used to represent the desired behavior of the "System Under Test" (SUT), to represent testing strategies and the testing environment. A testing model describing the SUT is usually an abstract, partial representation of the SUT's desired behavior. Test cases derived from such a model are functional tests on the same level of abstraction as the model, and might then be mapped into executable tests that can communicate directly with the SUT under specific testing tools and frameworks.

Model Driven Architecture (MDA) is the MD approach proposed by OMG, available since early 2000, and focused primarily on the definition of models and their transformations [51] and [21]. MDA supports the definition of models at different levels of abstraction, namely Computational Independent Models (CIM), Platform Independent Models and Platform Specific Models PSM (PIM). Computational platforms correspond to concrete implementations of application servers, database servers, content management systems, frameworks and software architectures; these platforms can be described themselves through Platform Description Models (PDM). MDA also considers different types of model-to-model transformations, namely: CIM-CIM, CIM-PIM, PIM-PIM, PIM-PSM and PSM-PSM. Additionally, it considers the transformation of PSM models into source code and other types of textual artefacts (PSM-Text). In theory, an application developed under the MDA approach is platform-independent, which allows it to be installed on different computing platforms and properly supports different technologies thanks to these transformations, particularly to PIM-PSM PSM-PSM and PSM-Text transformations.

In spite not being a concrete MD approach, because it did not specify concrete modeling languages and associated tools, MDA still defends the use of several concrete OMG specifications (that is the reason that we put it in Fig. 7 a little below MDD and MBT), namely: (1) MOF as a core component of its meta-modeling architecture; (2) QVT[6] as a set of languages for model query and transformations; and (3) UML Profiles[7] as a simple but practical way to define graphical DSMLs. However, the creation of DSMLs based on UML profile mechanism – i.e., based on the definition of stereotypes, tags and constraints –, is not free of criticism. For example, the definition of a UML stereotype allows adding new properties to the original element, but not to eliminate or inhibit the properties of the original element. In addition, modeling tools that support the UML Profile mechanism usually do not check properly the quality of these models. On the other hand, this mechanism is broadly supported by UML CASE tools and development environments and, consequently, it is used easily to define DSMLs.

Middle-level Approaches (MD MetaTools)

In the middle-level of Fig. 7 we identify MD approaches as proposed by their respective companies or communities. These approaches are conducted by technologies and usually supported by complex tools that we refer as "MD MetaTools" and are commonly known as "language workbenches" [18]. Most of these tools provide a collection of features to help users to define DS(M)Ls, with specific editors, model validation, model transformation, etc. Below we briefly introduce Eclipse EMF, Microsoft Software Factories, and JetBrains MPS, but many others could be considered as well, namely: MetaEdit+ [79], SDF/Stratego/Spoofax [30], xText [5], Obeo Designer/ Sirius [82] or some academic proposals such as MIC (Model Integrated Computing) [78] with the tool GME (Generic Modeling Environment) [1], VMTS [38], MetaSketch [50], or AtomPM ([77]).

A detailed analysis of Microsoft DSL Tools, alongside with equivalent tools (e.g., Enterprise Architect, MetaSketch or MetaEdit+) is discussed in [60] and other comparison of MDE approaches for Web-application development in [61]. Savić et al. report their experience using MPS to implement the SilabReq language, a text language for requirements specification [62]. Additionally, they compare MPS with other alternative tools – namely Spoofax, Obeo Designer, MetaEdit+, XText, Papyrus and EMFText – in what respect the following criteria: support for the abstract and concrete syntax definition, and supported IDEs. Furthermore the annual Language Workbench Challenge (LWC) is another initiative that promotes the comparison and discussion of DSL workbenches. Erdweg et al. present and discuss 10 language workbenches that participated in LWC'2013 [18]. The set of tools analyzed was defined according to the tools that applied to solve an assignment and were subsequently accepted. The assignment was to implement a DSL for questionnaires, which should be rendered as an interactive GUI reactive to user input to present additional questions. Additionally, the DSLs produced did not have the restriction of being graphical.

Eclipse Modeling Project [8] focuses on the evolution and promotion of model-based development technologies within the Eclipse community by providing a unified set of modeling frameworks, tooling, and standards implementations. Eclipse Modeling Project involves an integrated set of extensible tools and frameworks, including EMF (at the core), graphical modeling, textual modeling, and concrete modeling tools particularly supporting OMG specifications, such as UML, OCL, SysML, and BPMN. *EMF (Eclipse Modeling Framework)* [75] is the core modeling framework and code generation facility for building tools and applications based on models defined in the Ecore meta metamodel. There are several tools and frameworks developed on top of EMF such as GMF, Sirius, GMF-Tooling, MoDisco, Papyrus, Acceleo, ATL, Epsilon, MMT, Xtext, etc. In general, most of these tools are popular, relatively easy to use and maintain, and they have an open and strong community support.

Microsoft Software Factories [24] is the approach proposed by Microsoft strongly inspired by the "assembly line" metaphor, found in industrial automation areas, which has also been adopted by software engineering through initiatives such as Software Product Lines [12]. A software factory is a structured collection of related software assets used for creating specific types of software, and may include processes, DSLs, templates, integrated development environment, configurations and views. Microsoft Visual Studio offers an integrated suite of tools, called Visualization and Modeling SDK[9] (previously named DSL Tools), which supports the realization of software factories, in particular by providing support to the definition of DSLs, with their respective source code or documentation generators.

Finally, *JetBrains Meta Programing System (MPS)* [10] is open source and is developed by JetBrains. MPS is is a projectional language workbench, which means that no grammar and parser is involved. Instead, an editor allows changing directly the underlying abstract syntax tree, which is projected in a way that looks like text. MPS supports mixed notations (such as textual, symbolic, tabular, graphical) and a wide range of language composition features based on the BaseLanguage, which is the MPS's meta metamodel. MPS users extend this BaseLanguage to define their own languages: during the process of creating a new language the users directly derive concepts from the BaseLanguage or combine concepts from other existent languages [83].

Concrete-level Approaches (MD tools)

Finally, the bottom of Fig. 7 shows some example of concrete MD approaches, namely XIS-Mobile, WebService Software Factory, SilabMDD, and PBGT. These examples show the applicability of the proposed model in a way that it allows clearly classifying and describing these (and other) MD approaches.

XIS-Mobile [11] is a MDD approach to increase the productivity of developing cross-plaform mobile applications. The XIS-Mobile DSL was defined as a UML profile, with a multi-view organization that supports two design approaches: the dummy and the smart design approach. XIS-Mobile has a supporting framework based on Sparx Systems Enterprise Architect MDG Technology and EMF, which intends to generate source code for multiple platforms from a single PIM model specification, through M2M and M2T transformations. Composed of four major components, this framework suggests developing a mobile application in four steps whenever possible: defining of the required views using the Visual Editor, validating them using the Model Validator, generating the User-Interfaces View models with the Model Generator, and finally generating the application's source code through the Code Generator. This way the developer takes advantage of the MDD benefits, namely increasing his productivity by using a single specification of the system, by avoiding the implementation of boilerplate code and reducing errors ([58] and [59]).

Web Service Software Factory [12] (also known as the Service Factory) is an example of the Microsoft Software Factories and is a concrete MDD approach that provides an integrated collection of resources designed to help to quickly and consistently build Web services that adhere to well-known architecture and design patterns. These resources consist of patterns and architecture topics in the form of written guidance and models with code generation in the form of tools integrated with Visual Studio.

SilabMDD is a MDD approach particularly focused on the Requirements discipline and, consequently, also known as a MDRE (Model-driven Requirement Engineering) approach [39]. SilabMDD includes the SilabReq language which is implemented with JetBrains MPS. SilabReq is a textual DSL that allow users to define and manage requirements based on use-cases specification. Consequently, SilabReq imposes a rigorous definition of use case specification, particularly based on the description of sequences of actions, pre- and post-conditions, and the relations between use cases and elements defined at domain models (still specified textually). The goal of SilabMDD is to provide a complete software development workbench (by extending JetBrains MPS) to be used by requirements engineers, developers, as well as non-technical stakeholders[62] and [63].

PBGT is a MBT approach that provides generic test strategies (based on user interface (UI) Test Patterns), with multiple configurations for testing different implementations of UI Patterns. PBGT approach is supported by the PBGT tool, in which the UI Test Patterns are defined within a domain specific language, PARADIGM, developed on top of the Eclipse Modeling Framework using the Ecore meta metamodel. PBGT tool is freely available as an Eclipse plugin. [13] It is a fully integrated testing environment that provides functionalities for modeling (either manually or automatically), configuration, automated test case generation, automated test case execution and test coverage analysis. Currently the PBGT tool is able to test both web and mobile (Android based) applications on top of the Selenium framework[14] ([48], 2014).

RELATED WORK

As mentioned in Section 1, the objective of this paper is to survey and discuss the essential concepts of MDE and supporting this survey by a unified conceptual model that would help to clearly identify and relate those concepts. This research started from earlier work, in particular on the conceptualization of models and metamodels [64], [20], [19] and [37], modeling languages [46] and [66], and relations between models, transformations, platforms and software products [74]. However and differently from those works, this paper intends *to give a simple but broad and integrated view of the key concepts and respective terminology, and answering to common questions* as defined in Table 3. Table 3 and Table 4 summarize the comparative analysis of the related work, those that are more related with this paper, namely focused on the following references [64], [19], [74] and [37].

Table 3.Related work analysis – Part 1

Related Work		Seidewitz, 2003 (2003)[64] What models mean	Stahl et al., (2005) [74], Model-Driven Software Development	Favre et al., (2005)[19], Towards a megamodel to model software evolution through transformations	Kühne, 2006 (2006) [37], Matters of (meta-) modeling
Research Questions	What is a model?	Y	Y	Y	Y
	What is the relation between a model and a metamodel?	Y	Y	Y	Y
	What are the key facets of a modeling language?	N (not explicit)	Y	N (not explicit)	N (not explicit)
	How can I use models in the context of a software development process?	N (not explicit)	Y	N (not explicit)	N (not explicit)
	What are the relations between models and source code artefacts and software platforms?	N (not explicit)	Y	N (not explicit)	N (not explicit)
	What are the relations between MDE, MDD, MDA and other MD approaches?	N	N	N	N

Table 4.Related work analysis – Part 2

Related Work		Seidewitz, 2003 (2003) [64] What models mean	Stahl et al., (2005) [74], Model-Driven Software Development	Favre et al., (2005)[19], Towards a megamodel to model software evolution through transformations	Kühne, 2006 (2006) [37], Matters of (meta-) modeling
Definition of	System	Y	N (not explicit)	Y	Y
	Model	Y	Y (Formal Model)	Y	Y
	System to Model relation	N (not explicit)	N (not explicit)	Y (RepresentationOf)	Y (model-of)
	Metamodel	Y	Y	Y	Y
	Model to Metamodel relationships	N (not explicit)	Y (instanceof)	Y (ConformsTo)	Y (instance-of)
	Modeling Language	Y	Y	Y (with the ElementOf association)	Y
	Modeling Language Facets	N	Y	N	N
	Transformation	N	Y	Y (with the IsTransformedIn association)	N
	Software Platform	N	Y	N (not explicit)	N (not explicit)
	Software Product	N	Y	N (not explicit)	N (not explicit)

Approach	Discussed	Textually, with a generic and informal discussion of concepts	Textually and UML class diagrams, deep discussion of concepts	Textually and UML class diagrams, deep discussion of concepts	Textually and mathematically, deep discussion of concepts
	Key concepts discussed	models, metamodels, modeling languages, in general terms	models, metamodels, modeling languages, transformations, platforms, products	models, metamodels, modeling languages, transformations	models, metamodels, modeling languages
	Complementary issues discussed	four-layer metamodeling architecture; meaning of models	domains, domain-specific languages, model2model and model2platform transformation, software system families	transformation models; software evolution	descriptive vs prescriptive models; token models vs type models; classification vs generalization; ontological vs linguistic instatiation

The paper "What models mean" [64] introduced the concepts of system, model, metamodel and modeling language and proposed respective definitions. However, this paper did not present any type of conceptual model, and so it is not clear the relations between those concepts. Also this paper did not discuss any other of the MDE concepts like we did in this paper.

The book "Model-Driven Software Development" [74] gives a good and broad overview of the main concepts of MDE, and also tries to explain them through a UML-based model. However, it is not completely clear the definitions of system and model, as well as its relations. However, in spite not being a research paper this is a relevant reference.

The paper "Towards a megamodel to model software evolution through transformations"[19] gave a good inspiration and starting point to propose this survey, in particular with the idea of a "megamodel for MDE". The focus of that paper was just on modeling large-scale software evolution processes. Nevertheless, it also provided some discussion and definitions on concepts such as system, model, metamodel and model transformations. However, contrary to this paper, only system and transformation were defined as first citizen concepts in that megamodel. Additionally, that paper did not define concepts, such as of modeling language, software product, software artefact and software platform.

The paper "Matters of (Meta-) Modeling" [37] provides a formal and extensive definition on the concepts of system, model, metamodel and modeling language. Additionally, it gives a deep discussion on related subjects such as: token models, type models, classification versus generalization, ontological versus linguistic instantiation. That is a significant paper that adopted a formal approach (based on Mathematics expressions) to clearly and unambiguously defined the referred concepts. However, this paper did not refer the other concepts discussed throughout this paper, such as modeling language facets, model transformations, software platform and software products.

Finally, none of these papers try to answer and discuss our last research question concerning the relations between MDE and other MD approaches.

CONCLUSION

MDE is a relatively new engineering approach with some expectations and challenges to be addressed in the next years [49]. As discussed throughout this paper there are some concrete proposals and many more tools and platforms that, in some way would achieve that general vision and relevance.

For an effective implementation of MDE several features should be supported and integrated into appropriate tools, typically classified as IDEs, CASEs and MetaCASEs. Among those we refer the following that can exist in most of these tools, namely to support: (1) the creation of modeling languages, in particular the creation of their abstract and concrete syntaxes and the corresponding structural semantics; (2) multi-user and collaborative environment for models design and management; (3) model validation, with eventual support for model analysis and simulation; (4) model-to-model transformations; (5) model-to-text transformations; and even in some cases (6) models interpretation and execution.

A variety of tools that embody the main ideas of MDE have been developed and improved over this last decade. Some of them correspond to tools developed in an academic environment, as is the case of experiments carried out under GME [1], ProjectIT ([69]), VMTS [38], MetaSketch [50], or AtomPM ([77]). Other tools are commercial, such as the case of Microsoft Visual Studio Visualization and Modeling SDK, Sparx Enterprise Architect,[15] Metacase MetaEdit+,[16] or Obeo Designer.[17] Beyond these, it is worth to highlight some tools and technologies currently developed around the Eclipse Modeling Project and the JetBrains MPS.

The proposed survey on MDE is the result of our research experience in the area throughout this last decade, during which we have designed and developed several modeling languages, tools and real-world applications following the MDE approach [69],[70], [60], [72], [58], [58] and [59]. The unified conceptual model proposed in this paper might help others to have a broad vision and a better understanding of MDE and its key concepts and terminology. First, it defines the concepts of system, model and metamodel. Second, it extensively defines the concept of modeling language, with its multiple aspects, namely abstract syntax, concrete syntax, semantics and pragmatics. Third, it defines, in a cohesive way, the remaining concepts: software product, software platform, software artefact, model-to-model and model-to-text transformations. Finally, the paper also clarifies and discusses common terminology, namely by relating MDE with MDD, MBT, MDA and other MD approaches.

As future work we consider that this survey might be extended by being applied to describe and discuss concrete modeling languages and concrete MDE approaches. Additionally, it can be used as a general and conceptual framework to better analyse MDE practices in industry such as discussed in [28].

ACKNOWLEDGMENTS

This work was partially supported by national funds through FCT – Fundação para a Ciência e a Tecnologia, under the projects POSC/EIA/57642/2004, CMUP-EPB/TIC/0053/2013, UID/CEC/50021/2013 and DataStorm Research Line of Excellency funding (EXCL/EEI-ESS/0257/2012). Thanks to my colleagues and PhD and MSc students for their strong participation and involvement in this research throughout the last decade. Finally, thanks to the anonymous reviewers for their relevant criticism and suggestions that helped to improve the paper.

REFERENCES

1. Agrawal A, Karsai G, Ledeczi A.: An end-to-end domain-driven software development framework. In: Companion of the 18th annual OOPSLA '03 ACM SIGPLAN Conference, ACM; 2003.
2. Al-Sibahi AS. On the Computational Expressiveness of Model Transformation Languages, Technical Report, IT University of Copenhagen; 2015.
3. Atkinson C, Kühne T. Model-driven development: a metamodeling foundation. IEEE Software 2003;20(5):36–41.
4. Barišić A, Amaral V, Goulao M. Usability evaluation of domain-specific languages. In: International Conference on the Quality of Information and Commuications Technology (QUATIC'2012), IEEE Computer Society; 2012.
5. Bettini L. Implementing Domain-Specific Languages with Xtext and Xtend. Packt Publishing Ltd; 2013.
6. Bézivin J, Gerbé O. Towards a Precise Definition of the OMG/MDA Framework. In: IEEE international conference on automated software engineering; 2001.
7. Booch G, Rumbaugh J, Jacobson I. The Unified Modeling Language User Guide. Addison Wesley; 1999.
8. Booch G. Object-Oriented Analysis and Design with Applications. 2nd EditionAddison Wesley; 1994.
9. Brambilla, M., Cabot, J., Wimmer, M.: Model-driven software engineering in practice. Synthesis Lectures on Software Engineering, Morgan & Claypool, 2012.
10. Bryant BR, Gray J, Mernik M, Clarke PJ, France RB, Karsai G. Challenges and directions in formalizing the semantics of modeling languages. Comput Sci Inf Syst 2011;8(2):225–53.
11. Chang CC, Keisler HJ. Model theory. Elsevier; 1990.
12. Clements P, Northrop LM. Software Product Lines: Practices and Patterns. Addison-Wesley; 2001.
13. Crane ML, Dingel J.: Towards a UML virtual machine: implementing an interpreter for UML 2 actions and activities. In: Proceedings of the 2008 conference of the center for advanced studies on collaborative research: meeting of minds. ACM; 2008.
14. Czarnecki K, Eisenecker UW. Generative programming: methods, tools, and applications. Addison-Wesley; 2000.
15. Czarnecki K, Helsen S.: Classification of model transformation approaches. In: OOPSLA workshop on generative techniques in the context of model driven architecture; 2013.
16. Deursen A, Klint P, Visser J.: Domain-specific languages: an annotated bibliography. ACM Sigplan Notices; 2000.
17. Dietz J, Proper E, Tribolet J. (Series Editors): The Enterprise Engineering Series, Springer; 2009–2014.
18. Erdweg S, van der Storm T, Völter M, Boersma M, Bosman R, Cook WR, et al. The state of the art in language workbenches. Softw Lang Eng 2013: 197–217 Springer.
19. Favre J-M, Nguyen T. Towards a megamodel to model software evolution through transformations. Electron Notes Theor Comput Sci 2005; 127:3.
20. Favre J-M. Megamodelling and Etymology. Dagstuhl Seminar (Transformation Techniques in Software Engineering); 2005.
21. Frankel D. Model Driven Architecture: Applying MDA to Enterprise Computing. Wiley; 2003.
22. Gabriel P, Goulao M, Amaral V.: Do Software Languages Engineers Evaluate their Languages? arXiv:1109.6794; 2011.
23. Gomes, C., Barroca, B., Amaral, V.: Classification of model transformation tools: pattern matching techniques. In: Model-Driven Engineering Languages and Systems, LNCS 8767, Springer; 2014. p. 619–35.
24. Greenfield J, Short K, Cook S, Kent S. Software factories: assembling applications with patterns, models, frameworks, and tools. Wiley; 2004.
25. Harel D, Rumpe B. Modeling languages: syntax, semantics and all that stuff. tech. report MCS00-16, Weizmann Institute of Science; 2000.
26. Heering J, Mernik M. Domain-specific languages in perspective. CWI; 2007 Technical Report, SEN-E0702.
27. Hermans F, Pinzger M, Van Deursen A. Domain-specific languages in practice: a user study on the success factors. In: Model driven engineering languages and systems, LNCS 5795, Springer; 2009. p.423–37.
28. Hutchinson J, Whittle J, Rouncefield M. Model-driven engineering practices in industry: social, organizational and managerial factors that lead to success or failure. Sci Comput Program 2014;89:144–61.
29. Kamandi A, Habibi J. A survey of syntax and semantics frameworks of modeling languages. In: Proceedings of Computer Science and its Applications (CSA'2009), IEEE Computer Society; 2009.

30. Kats LC, Visser E. The spoofax language workbench: rules for declarative specification of languages and IDEs. In ACM Sigplan Notices, 45(10), 2010. p. 444–63.
31. Kelly S, Tolvanen JP. Visual domain-specific modelling: benefits and experiences of using metacase tools. ECOOP Workshop on Model Engineering 2000.
32. Kelly S, Tolvanen JP. Domain-specific modeling: enabling full code generation. Wiley; 2008.
33. Kosar T, Oliveira N, Mernik M, Varanda Pereira MJ, Črepinšek M, da Cruz DC, et al. Comparing general-purpose and domain-specific languages: An empirical study. Comput Sci Inf Syst 2010;7(2):247–64.
34. Krogstie J. Model-Based Development and Evolution of Information Systems – A Quality Approach. Springer; 2012.
35. Kruchten P. The rational unified process: an introduction. Addison-Wesley Professional; 2004.
36. Kühne T, Mezei G, Syriani E, Vangheluwe H, Wimmer M. Explicit transformation modeling. Models Softw Eng 2010:240–55.
37. Kühne T. Matters of (Meta-) modeling. Softw Syst Model 2006;5(4):369–85.
38. Levendovszky T, Lengyel L, Mezei G, Charaf H. A systematic approach to metamodeling environments and model transformation systems in VMTS. Electron Notes Theor Comput Sci 2005;127(1):65–75.
39. Loniewski G, Insfran E, Abrahão S.: A systematic review of the use of requirements engineering techniques in model-driven development. In: 13th international conference on model driven engineering languages and systems (MODELS'10), Springerl; 2010.
40. Ludewig J. Models in Software Engineering – An Introduction. Softw Syst Model 2003;2(1):5–14.
41. Luoma J, Kelly S, Tolvanen JP. Defining domain-specific modeling languages: collected experiences. OOPSLA Workshop on Domain-Specific Modeling; 2004.
42. Luz MP, Silva AR. Executing UML Models. In: Proceedings of the 3rd workshop in software model engineering, IEEE Computer Society; 2004.
43. Martin J, Odell J. Object-oriented methods. Pragmatic considerations.Prentice Hall; 1996.
44. McCarthy J. History of LISP. In: History of programming languages I. ACM; 1978. p. 173–85.
45. Mellor S, Balcer M. Executable UML: a foundation for model driven architecture. Addison Wesley; 2003.
46. Mernik M, Heering J, Sloane A. When and how to develop domain-specific languages. ACM Comput Surv 2005;37(4):316–44.
47. Morais F, Silva AR.: Assessing the Quality of User-Interface Modeling Languages. In: Proceedings of ICEIS'2015 Conference, SCITEPRESS; 2015.
48. Moreira RM, Paiva AC. PBGT tool: an integrated modeling and testing environment for pattern-based GUI testing. In: Proceedings of the 29th ACM/ IEEE international conference on Automated software engineering, ACM.
49. Mussbacher G, Amyot D, Breu R, Bruel JM, Cheng BH, Collet P, et al. The relevance of model-driven engineering thirty years from now. Model-driven engineering languages and systems (MODELS'2014), Springer; 2014.
50. Nóbrega L, Nunes N, Coelho H.: The meta sketch editor. In: Proceedings of the sixth international conference on computer-aided design of user interfaces (CADUI'2006), Springer; 2008.
51. OMG: Object Management Group – MDA (Model Driven Architecture) Guide Version 1.0.1; 2001 Available at ⟨http://www.omg.org/mda/⟩.
52. OMG: Object Management Group – Common warehouse metamodel (CWM); 2003 Available at: ⟨http://www.omg.org/spec/cwm/⟩.
53. OMG. United Modeling Language Infrastructure Specification, Version 2.4.1; 2011 Available at ⟨http://www.uml.org/⟩.
54. OMG. Business Process Model and Notation (BPMN), Version 2.0.2; 2013 Available at: ⟨http://www.omg.org/spec/BPMN/⟩.
55. OMG. Object Management Group - Meta Object Facility (MOF) Core Specification, v2.4.2.; 2014 Available at: ⟨http://www.omg.org/mof/⟩.
56. OMG. Object Constraint Language (OCL), v2.4; 2014 Available at: ⟨http://www.omg.org/spec/OCL/⟩.
57. Paige RF, Kolovos DS, Polack F. A tutorial on metamodelling for grammar researchers. Sci Comput Program 2014;96:396–416.
58. Ribeiro A, Silva AR. XIS-Mobile: a DSL for Mobile Applications. In: ACM Symposium on Applied Computing (SAC), ACM; 2014a.
59. Ribeiro A, Silva AR. Evaluation of XIS-Mobile, a domain specific language for mobile application development. J\ Softw Eng Appl 2014;7(11):906–19.
60. Saraiva J, Silva AR. Evaluation of MDE tools from a metamodeling perspective. J Database Manag 2008;19(4):50–75.
61. Saraiva J, Silva AR. A reference model for the analysis and comparison of MDE approaches for web-application development. J Softw Eng Appl 2010; 3 (5):419–25.
62. Savić D, Silva AR, Siniša V, Lazarević S, Antović I, Stanojević V, et al.: Preliminary experience using JetBrains MPS to implement a requirements specification language. In: Proceedings of the Eighth international conference on the quality of information and communications technology. IEEE Computer Society; 2014.
63. Siniša V, Lazarević S, Stanojević, Antović I, Milić V, Silva M, et al. Model driven approach. In: Proceedings of the 5th international conference on information society and technology (ICIST 2015), Society for Information Systems and Computer Networks; 2015.
64. Seidewitz E. What models mean. IEEE Softw 2003;20(5):26–32.
65. Selic B. The pragmatics of model-driven development. IEEE Softw 2003;20(5):19–25.

66. Selic B. A systematic approach to domain-specific language design using UML. In: Proceedings of the international symposium on object and component-oriented real-time distributed computing (ISORC); 2007.

67. Selic B. Personal reflections on automation, programming culture, and model-based software engineering. Autom Softw Eng 2008;15(3–4):379–91.

68. Selic BV, Gaševic D, Djuric D, Bézivin J, Devedžic V.: Model driven engineering and ontology development, Springer; 2009.

69. Silva AR, Saraiva J, Ferreira D, Silva R, Videira C. Integration of RE and MDE Paradigms: the projectIT approach and tools. IET Softw J 2007;1(6):217–314.

70. Silva AR, Saraiva J, Silva R, Martins C. XIS-UML Profile for eXtreme Modeling Interactive Systems. MOMPES, IEEE Computer Society; 2007b.

71. Slonneger K, Kurtz, Barry L. Formal syntax and semantics of programming languages. Addison-Wesley; 1995.

72. Sousa L, Silva AR. Preliminary design and implementation of DSL3S – a domain specific language for spatial simulation scenarios. In: Proceedings of the International symposium on cellular automata modeling for urban and spatial systems (CAMUSS); 2012.

73. Sprinkle J, Rumpe B, Vangheluwe, H, Karsai G. 3Metamodelling – state of the art and research challenges. In: Model-based eng embedded real-time syst, Springer, 2010. p. 57–76.

74. Stahl T, Volter M. Model-driven software development. Wiley; 2005.

75. Steinberg D, Budinsky F, Paternostro M, Merks E, Eclipse EMF. Modeling framework. 2nd editionAddison-Wesley; 2009.

76. Syriani E, Gray J, Vangheluwe H. Modeling a model transformation language. Domain Eng 2013:211–37.

77. Syriani E, Vangheluwe H, Mannadiar R, Hansen C, Van Mierlo S, Ergin H. AToMPM: a web-based Modeling Environment. Demos/Posters/ StudentResearch @ MoDELS; 2013b.

78. Sztipanovits J, Karsai G. Model-integrated computing. IEEE Comput 1997; 30(4):110–1.

79. Tolvanen J-P, Rossi M.: MetaEditþ: defining and using domain-specific modeling languages and code generators. OOPSLA'2003, ACM; 2003.

80. Utting M, Legeard B. Practical Model-Based Testing: A Tools Approach. Morgan Kaufmann Publishers; 2007.

81. Vangheluwe H, De Lara J, Mosterman, PJ. An introduction to multi-paradigm modelling and simulation. In: Proceedings of the AIS'2002 conference; 2002.

82. Viyovic V, Maksimovic M, Perisic B. Sirius: a rapid development of DSM graphical editor. In: International conference on intelligent engineering systems, IEEE; 2014.

83. Voelter M, Benz S, Dietrich C, Engelmann B, Helander M, Kats LC, et al.: DSL engineering: designing, implementing and using domain-specific languages, dslbook.org; 2013.

84. Weaver P, Lambrou N, Walkley M. Practical SSADM Version 4þ. 2nd editionPrentice Hall; 1998.

85. Yourdon E. Modern structured analysis. Prentice Hall; 1999.

CHAPTER 8 CONTEXT-SENSITIVE TRACE INLINING FOR JAVA

Christian Häubl[a], Christian Wimmer[b], Hanspeter Mössenböck[a]

[a]Institute for System Software, Christian Doppler Laboratory for Automated Software Engineering, Johannes Kepler University Linz, Altenbergerstrasse 69, 4040 Linz, Austria

[b]Oracle Labs, 500 Oracle Parkway, Redwood Shores, CA 94065, USA

ABSTRACT

Method inlining is one of the most important optimizations in method-based just-in-time (JIT) compilers. It widens the compilation scope and therefore allows optimizing multiple methods as a whole, which increases the performance. However, if method inlining is used too frequently, the compilation time increases and too much machine code is generated. This has negative effects on the performance.

Trace-based JIT compilers only compile frequently executed paths, so-called traces, instead of whole methods. This may result in faster compilation, less generated machine code, and better optimized machine code. In the previous work, we implemented a trace recording infrastructure and a trace-based compiler for Java™, by modifying the Java HotSpot VM. Based on this work, we evaluate the effect of trace inlining on the performance and the amount of generated machine code.

Trace inlining has several major advantages when compared to method inlining. First, trace inlining is more selective than method inlining, because only frequently executed paths are inlined. Second, the recorded traces may capture information about virtual calls, which simplify inlining. A third advantage is that trace information is context sensitive so that different method parts can be inlined depending on the specific call site. These advantages allow more aggressive inlining while the amount of generated machine code is still reasonable.

We evaluate several inlining heuristics on the benchmark suites DaCapo 9.12 Bach, SPECjbb2005, and SPECjvm2008 and show that our trace-based compiler achieves an up to 51% higher peak performance than the method-based Java HotSpot client compiler. Furthermore, we show that the large compilation scope of our trace-based compiler has a positive effect on other compiler optimizations such as constant folding or null check elimination.

INTRODUCTION

Method-based just-in-time (JIT) compilation translates whole methods to optimized machine code, while trace-based compilation uses frequently executed paths, so-called traces, as the compilation unit [1]. This can increase the peak performance, while reducing the amount of generated machine code. Fig. 1 shows the control flow graphs (CFGs) of three methods as well as three possible traces through them. The start of a trace is called a *trace anchor*, which is block 1 for all traces in the example. It highly depends on the specific trace

Citation: Christian Häubl, Christian Wimmer, Hanspeter Mössenböck, Context-sensitive trace inlining for Java, doi:10.1016/j.cl.2013.04.002

recording implementation which blocks are chosen as trace anchors.

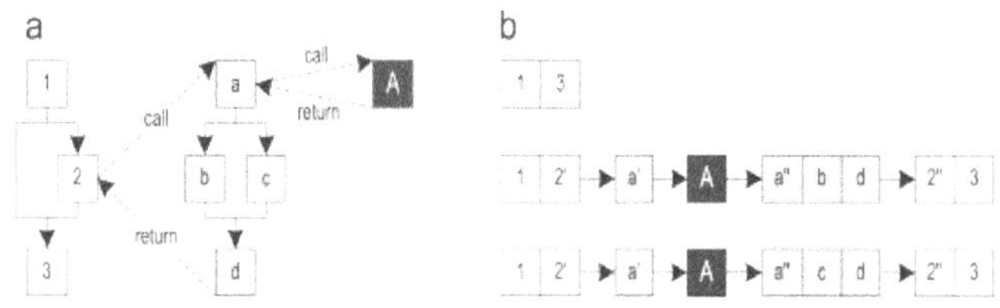

Figure. 1. Possible traces through three methods: (a) control flow graphs and (b) possible traces.

In a virtual machine (VM), traces can be recorded by instrumenting bytecode execution. Those traces are then compiled to optimized machine code. If a method part that was not compiled has to be executed, it is common to fall back to the interpreter.

Most existing trace recording implementations allow traces to cross method boundaries [1], [2], [10], [12] and [18]. This may result in large traces that must be compiled together.

In the previous work [14] and [15], we implemented a trace-based JIT compiler based on Oracle's Java™ HotSpot client compiler [19]. Our earlier conference paper [15] focused on trace inlining and contributed the following:

- We described how to perform trace inlining and discuss its advantages compared to method inlining.
- We presented multiple trace inlining heuristics implemented for our trace-based JIT compiler.
- We evaluated the impact of our trace inlining heuristics on compilation time, peak performance, and amount of generated machine code for the DaCapo 9.12 Bach [3] benchmark suite.

This paper is an extended version of our earlier conference paper [15], and contributes the following new aspects:

- We present our trace recording and our trace inlining approaches in more detail.
- We describe how compiler intrinsics for native methods can profit from the larger compilation scope that is achieved by our trace inlining.
- We additionally evaluate our inlining heuristics on the benchmark suites SPECjbb2005 [23] and SPECjvm2008 [24]. Furthermore, we also compare the peak performance of our best trace inlining heuristic to the Java HotSpot server compiler.
- We evaluate which high-level compiler optimizations do benefit from trace inlining due to the widened compilation scope.

The remaining paper is organized as follows: Section 2 gives a short overview of our trace-based Java HotSpot VM. In Section 3 we illustrate our trace recording system, and in Section 4 we explain how we perform trace inlining. Section 5 presents different trace inlining heuristics. Section 6 discusses the benchmark results. In Section 7 we discuss related work, and Section 8 concludes the paper.

OVERVIEW

In the previous work, we implemented a trace recording infrastructure and a trace-based JIT compiler for Java [14] and [15]. Fig. 2 shows the structure of our VM. Execution starts with the class loader that loads, parses, and verifies the class files. The class loader provides run-time data structures such as the constant pool and method objects to other parts of the VM. After class loading, a bytecode preprocessing step is performed that detects loops and creates tracing-specific data structures.

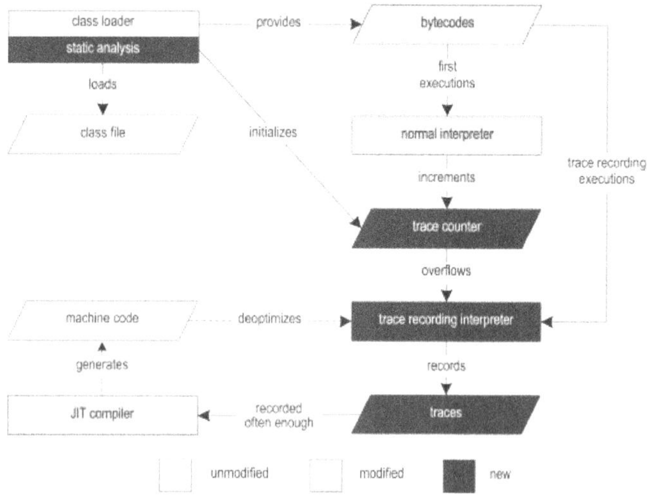

Figure. 2. Structure of the tracing VM.

For trace recording, the Java HotSpot VM template interpreter [13] is duplicated and instrumented. This results in a normal and a trace recording interpreter. The normal interpreter executes bytecodes with nearly the same speed as the interpreter of the unmodified VM and is used for the initial executions. Whenever the normal interpreter encounters a trace anchor, it increments the invocation counter of that trace anchor. When the counter overflows, the trace anchor is marked as hot and execution switches to the trace recording interpreter. The current implementation supports two different kinds of traces: loop traces anchored at loop headers, and method traces anchored at method entries.

Oracle's Java HotSpot VM ships with two different JIT compilers that share most parts of the VM infrastructure. The *client compiler* is designed for startup performance and implements basic optimizations to achieve a decent peak performance [19]. Upon compilation, the compiler generates the high-level intermediate representation (HIR), which is in static single assignment (SSA) form [7] and represents the control flow graph. During and after building the HIR, optimizations such as constant folding, null check elimination, and method inlining are applied. The optimized HIR is translated to the low-level intermediate representation (LIR), which is close to machine code but still mainly platform independent. The LIR is then used for linear scan register allocation [27] and code generation.

The *server compiler* performs significantly more optimizations than the client compiler and produces highly efficient code to reach the best possible peak performance [21]. It is designed for long-running server applications where the initial JIT compilation constitutes only a small overhead in comparison to the total execution time. The server compiler uses the following compilation phases: parsing, machine-independent optimization, instruction selection, global code motion and scheduling, graph coloring register allocation, peephole optimization, and code generation. Some additional optimizations that the server compiler performs are loop-invariant code motion, loop unrolling, and escape analysis.

Our trace-based JIT compiler is based on the HotSpot client compiler. While our techniques are general enough to be applicable to the server compiler as well, the complex structure of the server compiler is less approachable for the changes that are required for trace-based compilation, especially in the context of a research project. Therefore, we decided to use the client compiler as our base.

When traces have been recorded often enough, our compiler at first merges the recorded traces into a trace graph. This data structure is a hybrid between a control flow graph and a trace tree [10], so that merge points may exist but paths may still be duplicated if advantageous. On this level, we perform general and tracing-specific optimizations such as constant folding, aggressive trace inlining, and explicit control flow duplication. The generated machine code is then directly invoked by the interpreters or by other compiled traces.

If a precondition for an aggressive optimization is violated during execution, our system deoptimizes [17] to the trace recording interpreter. Deoptimization at first saves all values that are live in the current compiled frame and then replaces that compiled frame with one or more interpreter frames. The exact number of created interpreter frames, depends on the inlining depth of the currently executed instruction. Then, the interpreter frames are filled with the previously saved values and execution continues in the trace recording interpreter.

When the trace recording interpreter takes over, it can record a partial trace that directly starts at the point of deoptimization instead of at the trace anchor. To detect too frequent deoptimization of compiled code, a counter is incremented every time a deoptimization occurs. After reaching a threshold, the compiled machine code is invalidated and another compilation is triggered that uses the originally recorded traces and all partial traces. This allows increasing method coverage or disabling specific aggressive optimizations, which in turn reduces the deoptimization frequency.

TRACE RECORDING

Our trace recording approach restricts traces to span at most one method [14]. When a trace anchor has been executed frequently enough, execution switches from the normal to the trace recording interpreter. For trace recording, every thread holds a tracing stack that contains the traces that are currently being recorded. Information about instructions that modify the control flow is stored in the topmost trace of the tracing stack, and the tracing stack is modified as necessary.

When a method invocation is reached during trace recording, the invocation is recorded in the caller trace. For virtual method invocations, we also record the receiver class. Upon entering the callee, a new method trace is pushed on the tracing stack and recording continues there.

When the callee returns, we pop the corresponding trace from the tracing stack and store it in a trace repository. Then, we link the caller and the callee trace by storing a pointer to the callee's trace in the caller's trace and continue recording for the caller. The linking preserves context-sensitive call information over method boundaries and results in a data structure that is similar to a dynamic call graph.

When a previously stored trace is recorded again, only a counter is incremented in the already stored trace instead of storing the trace another time. We consider traces to be different if they took different paths or if they invoked different callee traces. So, trace linking allows us to record exact call information for every executed path through the whole application. To reduce the number of recorded traces to a reasonable amount, we do not link loop traces and recursive method traces to their parent trace. After trace recording was performed a certain number of times for a trace anchor, we assume that all important traces for this anchor have been recorded and compile those traces to optimized machine code.

Fig. 3 shows a trace recording example where trace recording is triggered for the methodaddData(). (1) When the trace anchor at the method entry of addData() is marked as hot, execution switches to the trace recording interpreter and a method trace is pushed on the tracing stack. The method is executed from the beginning up to the invocation of the virtual method getValue(). When doing the virtual call, the invocation and the receiver class are stored in the caller trace. (2) Upon entering the method getValue(), a new method trace is pushed on the tracing stack and trace recording continues there. (3) When getValue()returns, the corresponding trace is popped from the tracing stack and stored in the trace repository. Then, the traces are linked by storing a pointer to the trace of getValue() in the trace of addData(). Execution and trace recording continues for addData() and reaches the loop header. (4) For recording the loop, a new loop trace is pushed on the tracing stack. (5) After the first loop iteration, when execution is back at the loop header, the loop trace is popped from the tracing stack and stored. For the next loop iteration, a new loop trace is pushed on the tracing stack. The second loop iteration executes the same path as the first iteration, so the system recognizes that the same trace was already recorded and does not store it again but only increments the counter within the previously recorded trace. (6) The third loop iteration takes a different path so that the method Math.abs() is invoked for which a new method trace is pushed on the tracing stack. (7) When Math.abs()returns, the corresponding trace is stored and linked to its caller trace. (8) Then, execution reaches the loop header and the loop exits. So, the loop trace is popped from the tracing stack and stored. (9) After the loop, the virtual method setValue() is invoked. So, the invocation and the receiver class are stored in the caller trace, and a new method trace is pushed on the tracing stack upon entering setValue(). (10) When setValue() returns, the corresponding trace is popped from the tracing stack, stored, and linked to its caller trace. (11) Eventually, the method addData() returns so that also this trace is popped from the tracing stack and stored. After that, the tracing stack is empty and execution switches back to the normal interpreter.

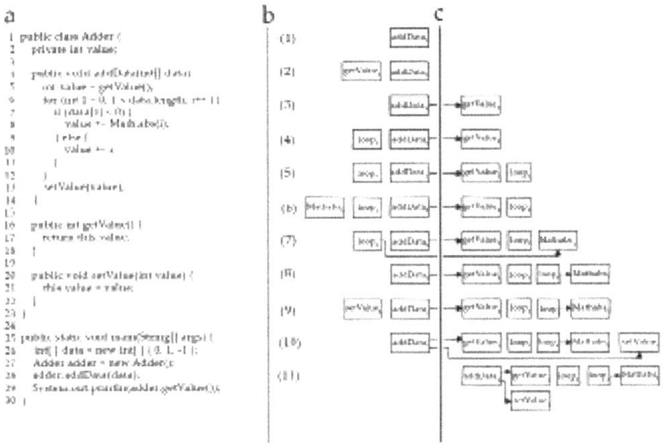

Figure. 3. Tracing stack while trace recording: (a) source code; (b) tracing stack; and (c) traces recorded in the trace repository.

In the example above, it was assumed that no traces had been compiled for the invoked methods and the loop. If traces for the method getValue() had already been compiled earlier, the invocation of getValue() would execute the compiled machine code instead of interpreting the method. So, the trace recording interpreter can neither push a new method trace on the tracing stack, nor can it record any control flow in the invoked method. In that case, our trace recording approach does not preserve exact control flow information over method boundaries. It would be possible to not invoke compiled code and instead force this code to be executed in the trace recording interpreter if a trace is currently being recorded. However, this would drastically reduce the startup performance because the application would be interpreted for a significantly longer time.

For best-possible trace recording performance, all frequently executed operations (such as recording information for specific instructions) are directly implemented in the assembler templates of the trace recording interpreter. More complex operations, such as storing the recorded traces, are implemented in the C-based runtime of the interpreter. Our trace recording infrastructure also supports efficient multi-threading so that every Java thread can switch between the normal and the trace recording interpreters independently. Each thread uses a thread-local buffer for trace recording to achieve the best-possible trace recording performance.

During trace recording, multiple threads may operate on the data structure that holds the recorded traces. We observed that for most trace anchors, only a small number of traces is recorded so that storing a new trace is required rarely, while in most cases only the execution count of an already recorded trace is incremented. Therefore, we store the recorded traces in a data structure that avoids locks and atomic instructions when data is read. When it seems that a new trace was found, we lock our data structure for other writing threads and recheck under the lock if this trace is really new before adding it to the recorded traces. So, for the most frequent case, we can avoid synchronization and atomic machine instructions, which significantly increases the trace recording performance for multi-threaded applications.

TRACE INLINING

Method inlining replaces calls with copies of the actually called code. The inlining heuristics can be categorized into static and dynamic approaches.

The Java HotSpot client compiler uses a simple, static method inlining heuristic, where the method size is compared to a fixed limit. Virtual methods are inlined using static class hierarchy analysis (CHA) [8]. This analysis determines if a method is not overridden by any loaded subclass, in which case it can be inlined optimistically. If a subclass is loaded later on that overrides an optimistically inlined method, the generated machine code is invalidated. Dynamic inlining heuristics use profiling information to decide if a call is worth inlining.

Our trace-based JIT compiler supports both static and dynamic inlining heuristics by making use of the recorded trace information. Similar to method inlining, trace inlining also replaces calls with copies of the actually called code. This increases the compilation scope and may result in a higher performance.

Advantages of Trace Inlining

Trace inlining has several advantages over method inlining:

- Trace inlining does only inline frequently executed traces instead of whole methods. Method-based compilers try to use profiling information to avoid compilation of infrequently executed method parts [9], [25] and [26]. This achieves a similar effect to trace inlining but is a complementary approach.
- The recorded traces contain context-sensitive information about which method parts are used by which caller. This information is preserved over method boundaries and can be used to avoid inlining of method parts that were executed frequently in total but are not required for the current caller.
- Traces also store information about the receivers of virtual calls and due to our trace linking, this information is also context sensitive. So, it might turn out that a certain call site invokes only methods of a specific receiver type. This information can be used for aggressive inlining of virtual methods. Method-based compilers also use profiling information for aggressive inlining of virtual calls, but in most compilers this information is not context sensitive.

Implementation

We start trace inlining by computing the maximum trace size that should be inlined at the current call site. This mainly depends on the call site's relevance (see Section 5.1) for program execution. Then, we use a heuristic to decide if it is worth to inline the invoked traces at the current call site. To a large degree, this depends on the size of the traces because inlining large traces causes code bloat.

Inlining method traces is similar to method inlining except that the traces usually do not cover all bytecodes of the callee. So, we build a trace graph from the traces that should be inlined and replace the method invocation with the contents of that trace graph. Then,return instructions that are located within the inlined bytecodes are replaced with direct jumps to the next instruction after the call and exception-throwing instructions are wired to exception handlers located in the caller trace.

Fig. 4(a) shows the control flow graphs of two methods. Two traces through those methods are shown in Fig. 4(b). After performing trace recording frequently enough, the recorded traces are getting compiled. The resulting trace graph after trace inlining (but without explicit control flow duplication) is shown in Fig. 4(c). This trace graph is then compiled to optimized machine code. If one of the removed blocks must be executed later on, the compiled code deoptimizes to the interpreter.

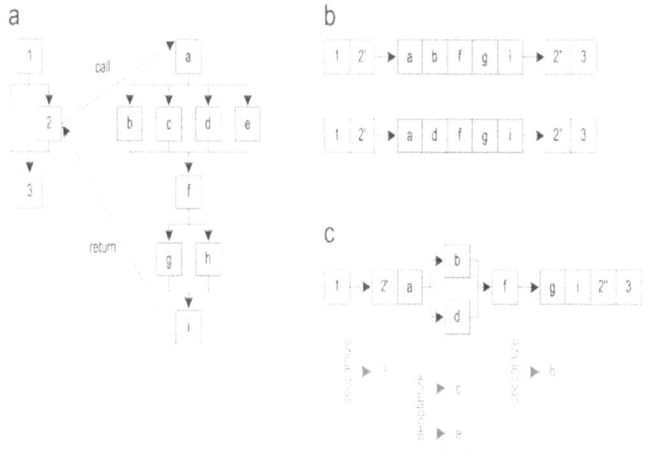

Figure. 4. Inlining method traces: (a) control flow graphs; (b) recorded traces; and (c) trace graph after trace inlining.

Another interesting aspect is that we also remove the edge from block 1 to block 3 although the trace graph does contain block 3. This is advantageous because it avoids control flow merges, which otherwise could constrain compiler optimizations. So, removing edges that are not executed results in better optimized machine code.

In most cases, we inline only those traces that were invoked by the current caller. However, if the callee traces were compiled before trace recording was started for the caller, the caller does not know which of the compiled traces it needs. In those cases, we conservatively consider all callee traces as inlining candidates, except those for which we can prove that they cannot be invoked by the current caller because of the specific parameters that the caller passes to the callee. The used technique behind that is similar to dead code elimination in a method-based compiler but allows eliminating whole traces instead of basic blocks. To further reduce the number of inlined traces, we do also filter out infrequently executed traces (see Section 4.5).

For virtual method invocations, we combine the recorded trace information with the Java HotSpot client compiler's CHA to determine the exact receiver class for the current call site. If the CHA identifies a single target method, the invoked method traces are inlined in a similar way to how the Java HotSpot client compiler inlines methods. If the CHA finds multiple possible target methods, we try to use the recorded receiver classes for inlining the method traces aggressively. For this, we add a run-time check that compares the actual receiver type with the expected type and deoptimizes to the interpreter if the types do not match. By combining CHA and context-sensitive trace information, we can inline virtual calls more frequently than most method-based compilers while emitting run-time checks only where necessary.

In addition to inlining method traces, we also support inlining loop traces. Fig. 5(a) shows a trace graph that was built for method traces that invoked loop traces. The loop traces were not inlined yet, so the loop is represented as a black box that is still unknown to the compiler. In the next step, a separate trace graph is built from the loop traces as shown inFig. 5(b). The actual inlining then replaces the black box in the caller trace graph with the loop trace graph and links all loop exits to their correct successor blocks using jump instructions. In this example, block *b* is linked to block *e* and block *c* is linked to block *d*, resulting in the trace graph shown in Fig. 5(c).

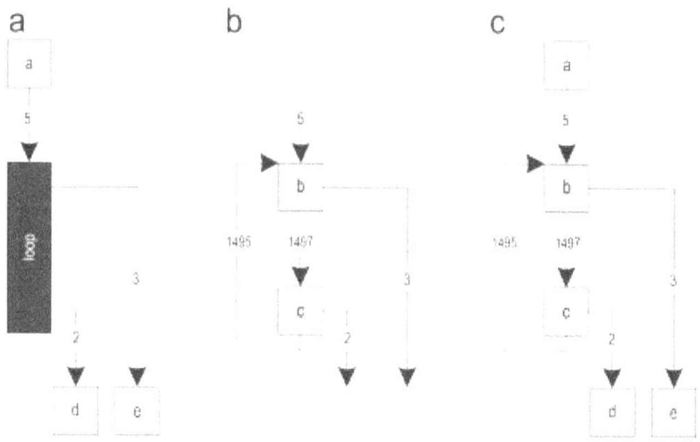

Figure. 5. Inlining loop traces: (a) method trace graph; (b) loop trace graph; and (c) after loop inlining.

When inlining loop traces, we consider all traces that were recorded for a specific loop as inlining candidates. This is necessary because loop traces are never explicitly linked to their caller trace, so no context-specific call information is available. However, we use the information about the parameters and locals that flow into the loop to eliminate those traces for which we can prove that they cannot be invoked by the current caller. Furthermore, we also eliminate traces that were not executed frequently enough.

A more difficult case is that the inlined loop can have a loop exit for which no successor exists in the caller trace graph. For example, in Fig. 5(a), block *d* could be missing because it was never recorded. However, both loop exits could still be present in the recorded loop traces as shown in Fig. 5(b). One way how this can happen is when the loop traces are compiled before trace recording is started for the method trace. Previously [15], we addressed this issue by explicitly adding deoptimization points for all loop exits that could not be linked to a successor, so that execution deoptimized to the interpreter when such a loop exit was taken. Now, we simply eliminate loop traces that end in a loop exit that is unknown to the current caller. This reduces the number of inlining candidates and results in less generated machine code.

Context Sensitivity

Our trace recording infrastructure restricts traces to span at most one method so that the trace-based compiler heavily relies on aggressive trace inlining [15]. The trace recording mechanism preserves context-sensitive information over method boundaries so that each caller knows which parts of the callee it should inline. This helps the compiler to avoid inlining of method parts that were executed frequently in total, but are irrelevant for the current caller. It reduces the generated amount of machine code, and decreases the number of merge points, which increases peak performance.

Also method-based compilers use profiling information to remove never executed code. However, their profiling information typically lacks the context-sensitivity so that they cannot decide which method parts are required for each specific caller. Context-sensitive profiling information could in principle also be recorded for a method-based compiler but we believe that trace recording and trace-based compilation simplify it.

Fig. 6 shows the method indexOf() of the JDK class ArrayList. The first part of the method handles the rare case of searching null, while the second part searches the list for non-null objects. Most callers will only require the second part of the method. However, if there is at least one caller in the application that executes the first part of the method, the profiling information in a method-based compiler would indicate that the first part has been executed. So, whenever the method-based compiler inlines the method indexOf(), it does also inline this rarely executed method part. Due to our context-sensitive trace information, our trace-based compiler can avoid that if the caller does not need that specific method part.

```
public int indexOf(Object o) {
  if (o == null) {
    for (int i = 0; i < size; i++) {
      if (elementData[i] == null) {
        return i;
      }
    }
  } else {
    for (int i = 0; i < size; i++) {
      if (o.equals(elementData[i])) {
        return i;
      }
    }
  }
  return -1;
}
```

Figure. 6. Method ArrayList.indexOf().

Because trace inlining is more selective in what it does inline, our trace-based compiler can use a more aggressive inlining policy, i.e., it can inline traces through methods that would be too large to be inlined as a whole. This increases the compilation scope without necessarily inlining a higher number of Java bytecodes than a method-based compiler. Especially, for complex applications, this results in better optimized machine code and has a significant positive effect on peak performance.

Fig. 7(a) shows the class LineBuilder that wraps an Appendable object and provides the methodappendLine(). If multiple LineBuilder objects are used to wrap instances of different classes, such as PrintStream, StringBuilder, StringBuffer, and BufferedWriter, then the invocations of append() on lines 9 and 10 will be polymorphic calls that cannot be inlined easily, as shown in Fig. 7(b).

a

```
1 public class LineBuilder {
2   private final Appendable buffer;
3
4   public LineBuilder(Appendable buffer) {
5     this.buffer = buffer;
6   }
7
8   public void appendLine(CharSequence sequence) {
9     buffer.append(sequence);
10    buffer.append("\n");
11  }
12 }
```

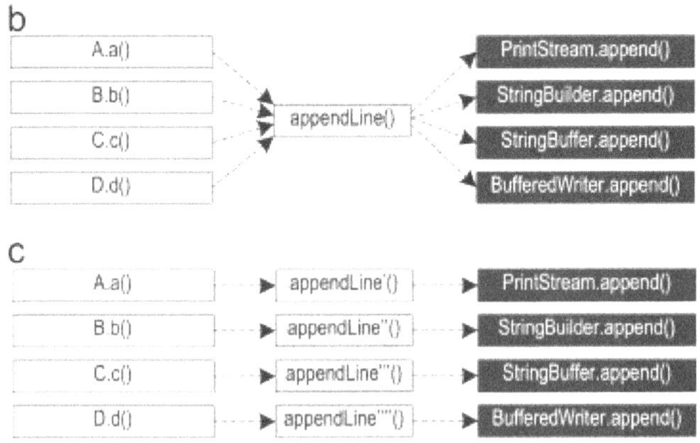

Figure. 7. Context-sensitive type information: (a) code pattern; (b) possible method invocations; (c) preferred inlining.

If the dispatch in appendLine() depends on its call site, e.g., because different LineBuilderobjects are used at different call sites, the inlining in Fig. 7(c) would be preferable. Our context-sensitive trace information also stores the receiver types of virtual calls. So, our trace-based compiler can do the preferable inlining indicated in Fig. 7(c) by using this context-sensitive information for aggressive inlining of virtual calls. If a compiler does not record the profiling information in a context-sensitive way, but just accumulates all encountered types (i.e., PrintStream, StringBuilder, StringBuffer, and BufferedWriter at buffer.append()) it will not have enough information to inline such virtual calls.

In the previous version of our trace-based compiler, we only used the type information when the recorded traces indicated that the invoked method always belonged to the same type of receiver. Such inlined traces are guarded by a *type guard* that compares the actual receiver type to the expected receiver type and deoptimizes to the interpreter if the types do not match. For this paper, we extended trace inlining in the following ways:

- If a call site always invokes the same method but does it on different receiver types, it was previously not possible to inline the method. However, this occurs frequently, for example, if an abstract base class implements a method that is not overridden by subclasses. We enabled this kind of inlining by guarding it with a so-called *method guard* that accesses the virtual method table of the actual receiver and compares the invoked method with the expected method. If the methods do not match, we deoptimize to the interpreter.
- If a call site always invokes the same method but does it via a receiver of an interface type, we extend type guards to a switch-like structure so that they can check for multiple receiver types. This is cheaper than the

interface lookup and allows us to inline invocations of interface methods in many cases. If the actual receiver type does not match any of the expected types we deoptimize to the interpreter.

- Another enhancement is the inlining of polymorphic calls. Fig. 8(a) shows a method, where a virtual call might invoke two different methods. Because these methods are small, it pays off to inline them both. This results in the control flow shown in Fig. 8(b) where block 2′ dispatches to one of the inlined methods depending on the type of the actual receiver. Here, we also use switch-like semantics so that several types can dispatch to the same inlined method. If the actual receiver type does not match any of the expected types, we deoptimize to the interpreter.

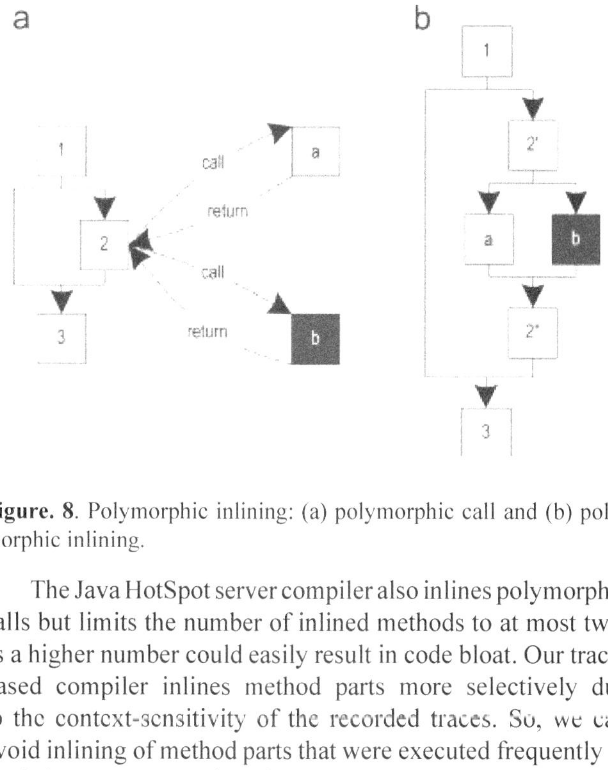

Figure. 8. Polymorphic inlining: (a) polymorphic call and (b) polymorphic inlining.

The Java HotSpot server compiler also inlines polymorphic calls but limits the number of inlined methods to at most two, as a higher number could easily result in code bloat. Our trace-based compiler inlines method parts more selectively due to the context-sensitivity of the recorded traces. So, we can avoid inlining of method parts that were executed frequently in total, but are not required for the current caller. Furthermore, the recorded type information is also context-sensitive, which reduces the number of inlining candidates. So, our trace-based compiler does not have to limit the number of inlined methods but instead only limits the total size of all inlined methods depending on the execution frequency of the specific call site. For applications with a high number of polymorphic calls, this results in significantly better inlining and therefore a higher performance, while avoiding issues with code bloat.

Native Methods

Java code can call native methods using the Java Native Interface (JNI). This mechanism is mainly used to implement platform-specific features that could not be expressed in Java otherwise. Some methods of the Java standard library, e.g.,System.arraycopy(), are implemented in a platform-specific way directly in the JVM. As no Java code is executed for such methods, trace recording is not possible for those methods.

The Java HotSpot VM uses compiler intrinsics for the most important platform-specific methods so that the JIT compiler can inline such methods. If our trace-based JIT compiler compiles a trace graph that contains the invocation of a native method that is implemented as a compiler intrinsic, we do exactly the same inlining as the method-based compiler. Still, our trace-based compiler has one advantage: traces are smaller than methods so that our trace-based compiler can inline Java traces more aggressively than a method-based compiler could inline Java methods. This results in a larger compilation scope so that the caller of a native method has specific knowledge about the parameters that are passed to the native method. The JIT compiler can use this information to optimize inlined compiler intrinsics more aggressively.

Fig. 9(a) shows pseudo-code for the implementation of the native methodSystem.arraycopy(), which is used to copy primitive type arrays. Depending on the compiler's information about the parameters that are passed to System.arraycopy(), it can optimize the intrinsic. Fig. 9(b) shows an optimized version of the method where the compiler could optimally exploit the parameter values. The necessary parameter information is for example available when the source and the destination arrays are allocated in the same compilation scope in which System.arraycopy() is inlined. So, increasing the compilation scope can help to increase the performance of inlined compiler intrinsics.

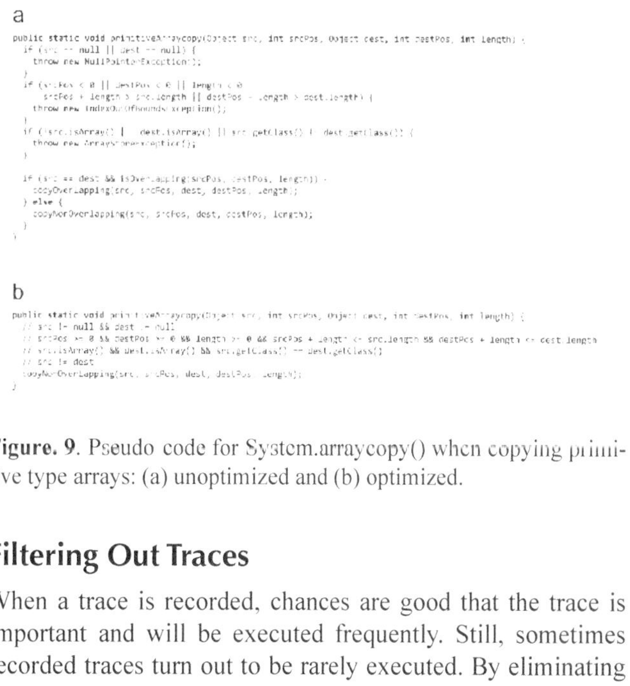

a

```
public static void primitiveArraycopy(Object src, int srcPos, Object dest, int destPos, int length) {
  if (src == null || dest == null) {
    throw new NullPointerException();
  }
  if (srcPos < 0 || destPos < 0 || length < 0 ||
      srcPos + length > src.length || destPos + length > dest.length) {
    throw new IndexOutOfBoundsException();
  }
  if (!src.isArray() || !dest.isArray() || src.getClass() != dest.getClass()) {
    throw new ArrayStoreException();
  }

  if (src == dest && isOverlapping(srcPos, destPos, length)) {
    copyOverlapping(src, srcPos, dest, destPos, length);
  } else {
    copyNonOverlapping(src, srcPos, dest, destPos, length);
  }
}
```

b

```
public static void primitiveArraycopy(Object src, int srcPos, Object dest, int destPos, int length) {
  // src != null && dest != null
  // srcPos >= 0 && destPos >= 0 && length >= 0 && srcPos + length <= src.length && destPos + length <= dest.length
  // src.isArray() && dest.isArray() && src.getClass() == dest.getClass()
  // src != dest
  copyNonOverlapping(src, srcPos, dest, destPos, length);
}
```

Figure. 9. Pseudo code for System.arraycopy() when copying primitive type arrays: (a) unoptimized and (b) optimized.

Filtering Out Traces

When a trace is recorded, chances are good that the trace is important and will be executed frequently. Still, sometimes recorded traces turn out to be rarely executed. By eliminating such traces, we can ensure that only important paths are compiled. Fig. 10(a) shows the trace graph after merging all recorded traces. The graph edges are annotated with the execution frequencies.

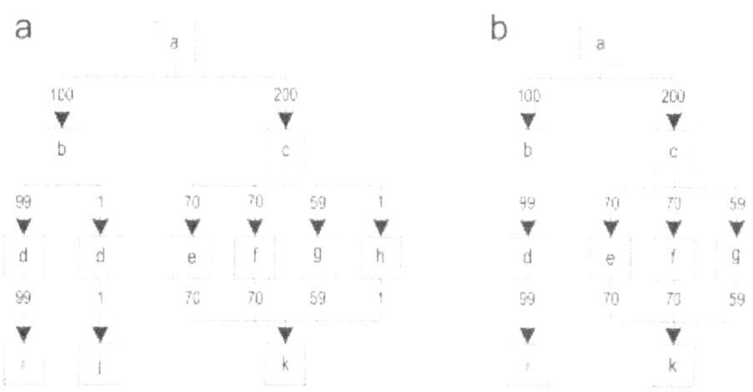

Figure. 10. Filtering out infrequently executed traces: (a) original trace graph and (b) trace graph after filtering.

For every block, we determine the most frequently executed outgoing edge and compare its frequency to those of all other outgoing edges of the same block. Then, we remove all edges with a 100× lower execution frequency. After processing all blocks, we remove no longer reachable blocks from the trace graph. Fig. 10(b) shows the resulting graph after filtering.

The recorded trace information conserves the program behavior that was observed during a specific time frame. At a later point of execution, infrequently executed (and therefore eliminated) paths might become important as the program behavior may change over time. This results in frequent deoptimization because not compiled paths get to be executed. If too frequent deoptimization is detected, the compiled machine code is invalidated and another compilation is triggered. This compilation avoids trace filtering for those cases that resulted in frequent deoptimization.

Trace filtering has the following corner cases, where extra care must be taken:

- For most loops, the loop body is executed significantly more frequently than the loop exits, see Fig. 5(c). So, the execution frequencies of the loop exits have to be compared to the frequency of the loop entry instead of to the frequency of the backward branch. Otherwise, the loop exit edges would be filtered out, so that deoptimization to the interpreter is required after executing a loop. This would increase the deoptimization frequency and it would limit the possible compilation scope.
- Aggressive trace inlining may also inline infrequently executed traces. Those inlined traces may not necessarily reflect the typical execution behavior yet so that trace filtering might eliminate important traces. This would result in frequent deoptimization so that trace filtering should be avoided for insufficiently trace-recorded methods and loops.

TRACE INLINING HEURISTICS

All inlining heuristics that are presented in the following section have in common that they first compute the relevance of a call site and then use that relevance to compute the maximum inlining size. The actual inlining decision is a simple comparison of the maximum inlining size with the actual size of the traces that should be inlined. For our evaluation, we paired several inlining heuristics with different relevance computation algorithms.

Relevance of a Call Site

The relevance of a call site is determined by the relevance of the trace graph block in which the call site is located. We evaluated three different algorithms for computing the relevance and illustrate their behavior on the two trace graph examples A and B shown inFig. 11. Example A was built from four different traces that hardly share any blocks. Example B also shows a trace graph built from four traces, but every block is shared with at least one other trace.

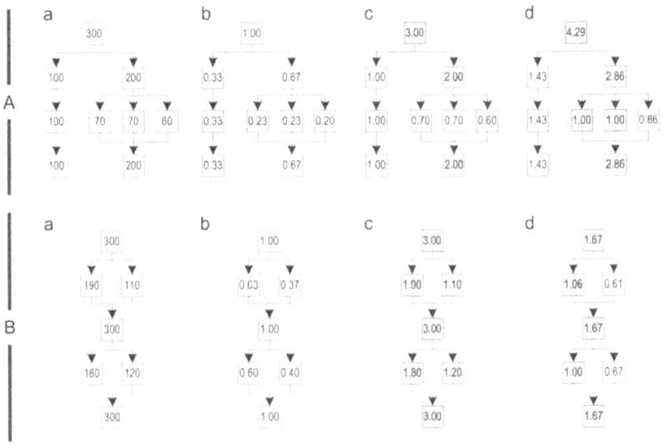

Figure. 11. Different relevance computation algorithms: (a) node execution counts; (b) simple; (c) most frequent trace; and (d) path-based.

For computing the relevance of the trace graph blocks, we first determine how often each block was executed by recorded traces. Fig. 11(a) shows the trace graphs where every block is annotated with its execution frequency. Then, we compute the relevance of each block by dividing its execution frequency with a reference value. Depending on the reference value, the relevance is scaled differently. So, we use one of the following algorithms to choose that reference value:

- *Simple*: The simplest way of computing the relevance of a trace graph block is to divide its execution frequency by the total execution frequency of all traces merged into the trace graph. The resulting value is in the range]0, 1] and assigns a high relevance to those blocks in which inlining has a positive effect during most executions, as shown in Fig. 11(b).
- *Most frequent trace*: Another way is to divide the block execution frequency by the execution frequency of the most frequently executed trace ever merged into the trace graph. Because traces are merged, trace graph blocks that are shared between multiple traces have a higher execution count than they would have without merging. So, this metric returns a high relevance for call sites that are within such shared blocks, while returning a value in the range]0, 1] for call sites that are only contained in individual traces. In Fig. 11(c), the colored blocks are shared and therefore get a higher relevance. If many different traces were recorded and many blocks are shared in the trace graph, then it can happen that every block in the trace graph has a relevance greater than 1, as shown in example B of Fig. 11(c).
- *Path-based*: Our third approach computes a variant of the most frequently executed path through the trace graph. We start at the root block of the trace graph and determine the most frequently executed successor block. Then, we mark this block as visited and continue with this block recursively until we either reach a block without successors or we are back at the loop header. All blocks that are visited due to this algorithm are colored in Fig. 11(d). Then, we use the lowest execution frequency of all visited blocks to compute the relevance of all other blocks in the trace graph. This has the advantage that important call sites, i.e., those on this path and on frequently executed split/merge points,

have a value in the range [1,∞[, while less important calls have a value in the range]0, 1[.

Configurations

We started with 15 different inlining heuristics ranging from static heuristics to dynamic ones. For each inlining heuristic, we performed a systematic search to find good parameter settings. During our evaluation, our dynamic inlining heuristics outperformed all static ones so that we omit detailed results for static inlining heuristics in this paper. Furthermore, we describe only those variants of our dynamic inlining heuristics that showed a good peak performance or a small amount of generated machine code.

- *Minimum code*: This heuristic modifies an inlining size of 35 bytecodes based on the relevance of the call site. A relevance below 1 reduces the inlining size, while a relevance greater than 1 increases the inlining size. By combining this heuristic with the *path-based* relevance computation algorithm, it shows a fairly good peak performance while generating small amounts of machine code. We also tried combining this inlining heuristic with the relevance computation algorithm *simple*. However, this has a significant negative effect on the peak performance while generating only slightly less machine code. Therefore, we omit detailed results for this second variant.
- *Balanced*: This heuristic increases an inlining size of 40 bytecodes based on the relevance of the call site. A relevance below 1 does not affect the inlining size, while a relevance greater than 1 increases the inlining size. So, decreasing the predefined size is explicitly not allowed, which makes it more likely that important calls are inlined. We use this heuristic with the *path-based* relevance computation algorithm, which results in a balance between peak performance and amount of generated machine code.
- *Performance*: This inlining heuristic uses a large inlining size of 150 bytecodes and decreases that for call sites with a relevance below 1. Increasing the inlining size beyond the predefined value is explicitly not allowed. For computing the relevance of the call sites, we again use the *path-based* relevance computation algorithm. So, this heuristic is optimized for peak performance while generating still reasonably small amounts of machine code.
- *Greedy*: Similar to the previous configuration, this heuristic uses a very large inlining size of 250 bytecodes and decreases it for call sites with a relevance below 1. To ensure that called traces are inlined greedily, we combine this heuristic with the *most frequent trace* relevance computation algorithm. However, due to the predefined maximum value, even this inlining heuristic avoids inlining of huge traces. This heuristic shows which of the benchmarks described in Section 6 profit from very aggressive trace inlining. We also experimented with even more aggressive inlining heuristics but those did not further improve the peak performance, while generating more machine code.

Similar to method-based compilers, all our heuristics make sure that tiny methods such as accessors are always inlined. This makes sense, because invoking small traces may require more machine code than the inlining. Another strategy, that is used by the Java HotSpot server compiler, is to avoid method inlining if the callee was already compiled separately and the compilation resulted in a large amount of generated machine code. This assumes that a fairly large compilation scope has already enough information for good compiler optimizations so that increasing the compilation scope beyond a certain point is not useful. We also use this technique for all our trace inlining heuristics as it reduces the generated machine code without affecting the performance measurably.

To reduce the probability of nested trace inlining, we ensure that inlined traces inherit the relevance from their parent call site. For this, we multiply the relevance of every callee block with the relevance of the caller's block. However, we limit the maximum inherited relevance to 1 as the relevance could otherwise increase with the inlining level. Relevance inheriting again reduces the amount of generated machine code without affecting the performance measurably and is also used by all our heuristics.

EVALUATION

We implemented our trace-based JIT compiler for the IA-32 architecture of Oracle's Java HotSpot VM using the early access version b12 of the upcoming JDK 8 [20]. For evaluating our inlining heuristics, we chose the benchmark suites SPECjbb2005 [23], SPECjvm2008 [24], and DaCapo 9.12 Bach [3] as those cover a large variety of benchmarks. The benchmarking system has the following configuration: an Intel Core-i5 processor with 4 cores running at 2.66 GHz, 4*256 kb L2 cache, 8 MB shared L3 cache, 8 GB main memory, and with Windows 7 Professional as the operating system.

The results are shown relative to the results for the unmodified, method-based Java HotSpot client compiler, which is denoted by 100%. For the trace-based JIT compiler, the amount of generated machine code also includes data that is specific to trace based compilation such as additional deoptimization information required for fall back to the interpreter. Each benchmark suite was executed 10 times and we report the average of those results along with the 95% confidence interval.

SPECjbb2005

The SPECjbb2005 benchmark simulates a client/server business application where all operations are performed on an in-memory database that is partitioned into so-called warehouses. The benchmark is executed with different numbers of warehouses, and each warehouse is processed by one thread. We use a system with 4 cores for benchmarking so that the official SPECjbb2005 throughput in business operations per second (bops) is defined as the geometric mean of the performance for the warehouses 4–8. A heap size of 1200 MB is used for all measurements.

Fig. 12 shows the peak performance, the generated machine code and the compilation time for the SPECjbb2005 benchmark. All our trace-based compiler variants outperform the client compiler significantly in terms of peak performance. More aggressive trace inlining results in a higher performance but does also generate more machine code and requires a longer compilation time because of the larger size of the compilation units. The peak performance of the SPECjbb2005 benchmark clearly profits up to the configuration*performance* from the increased trace inlining aggressiveness. Our configuration *greedy*increases the performance only slightly, while generating significantly more machine code. In terms of compilation time and amount of generated machine code, our configuration *minimum code* is especially efficient, while reaching a decent peak performance.

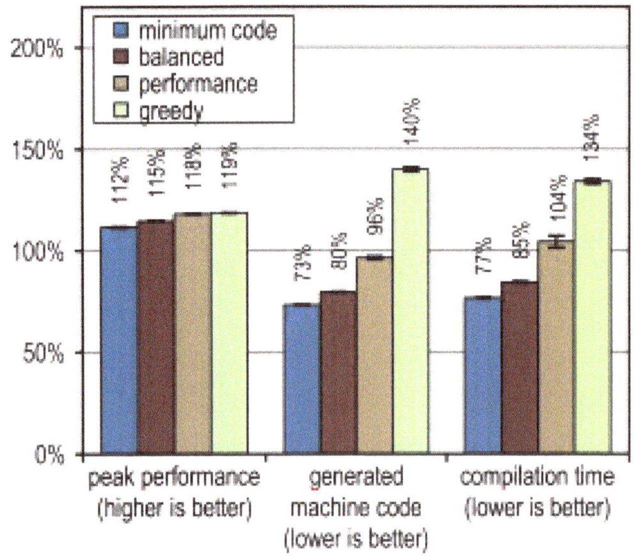

Figure. 12. SPECjbb2005 results.

Fig. 13 shows the SPECjbb2005 peak performance for different numbers of warehouses and different inlining heuristics. The maximum peak performance is reached with 4 warehouses as every warehouse is processed by one thread and our benchmarking system has 4 cores. The figure shows that our tracing configurations outperform the method-based client compiler independently of the used number of warehouses.

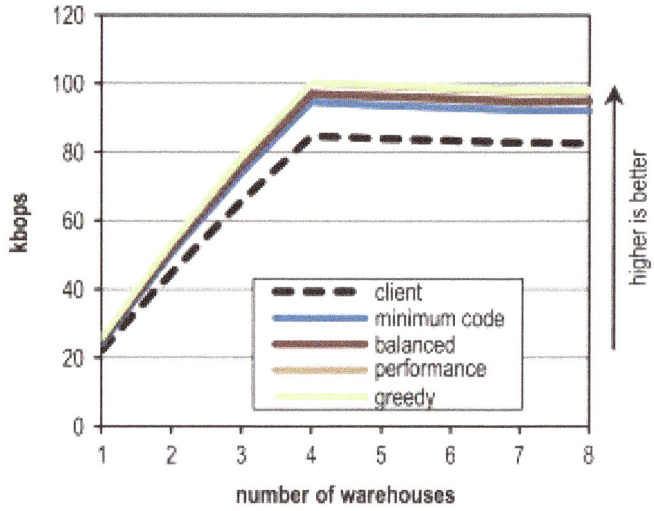

Figure. 13. SPECjbb2005 peak performance for different numbers of warehouses.

SPECjvm2008

The SPECjvm2008 benchmark consists of 9 benchmark categories that measure peak performance. Next to the individual benchmark results, we present the geometric mean of all results. A heap size of 1024 MB is used for all measurements.

Fig. 14 shows that all our tracing configurations outperform the method-based HotSpot client compiler. Our tracing configurations show the highest speedups on the benchmarks *derby* and *serial*. There, trace inlining achieves a larger compilation scope than the method inlining used by the HotSpot client compiler. A very aggressive trace inlining policy such as our configuration *greedy* does increase the peak performance especially for the benchmarks *derby* and *sunflow*. However this aggressive trace inlining also increases the amount of generated machine code and the time required for JIT compilation as shown in Fig. 15 and Fig. 16.

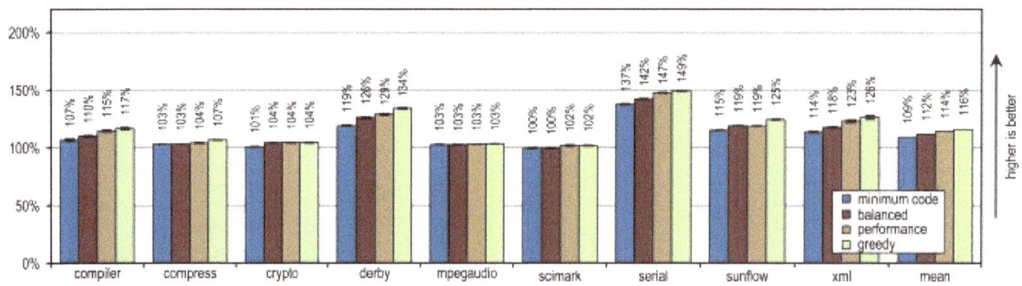

Figure. 14. SPECjvm2008 peak performance.

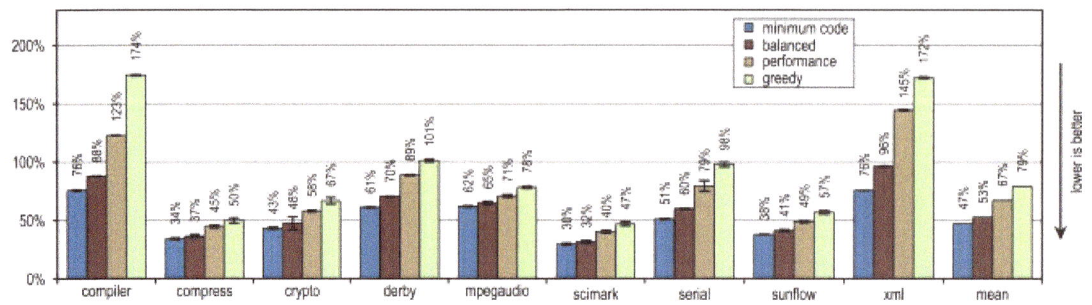

Figure. 15. SPECjvm2008 generated machine code.

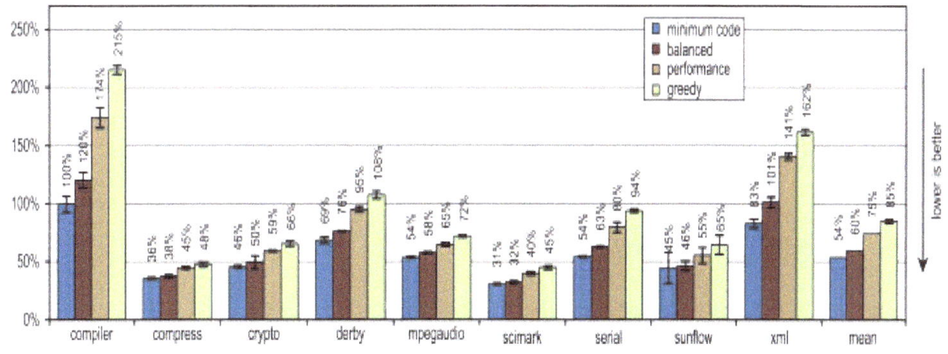

Figure. 16. SPECjvm2008 compilation time.

The small and loop-intensive benchmarks *crypto*, *mpegaudio*, and *scimark* show almost no increased peak performance because the method-based HotSpot client compiler can inline all calls in the performance critical loops as well. Due to the small size of these benchmarks, our trace-based compiler can achieve only a similar-sized compilation scope as the method-based compiler. However, our trace-based compiler inlines traces instead of whole methods so that significantly less machine code is generated and less compilation time is required, as shown in Fig. 15 and Fig. 16.

Fig. 15 shows that the amount of generated machine code is sensitive to the inlining size, so that it can easily happen that lots of machine code is generated. However, small and loop-intensive benchmarks do not show a large increase in code size, even when our most aggressive trace inlining heuristic is used. On such benchmarks, a trace inlining heuristic can only be too conservative but never too aggressive.

DaCapo

The DaCapo 9.12 Bach benchmark suite consists of 14 Java applications. Using the default data size and a heap size of 1024 MB, each benchmark is executed for 20 iterations so that the execution time converges. We present the fastest run for each benchmark and the geometric mean of all results. A heap size of 1024 MB is used for all measurements.

Fig. 17 shows the peak performance results for the DaCapo 9.12 Bach benchmarks, while Fig. 18 shows the amount of generated machine code. The inlining heuristic *greedy*shows the best peak performance, while generating more machine code than the unmodified Java HotSpot client compiler. Especially the benchmarks *luindex*, *pmd*, and*sunflow* profit from the *greedy* heuristic because of its large inlining size. However, on some of the benchmarks this heuristic is already over-aggressive so that more machine code is generated without a measurable change in peak performance.

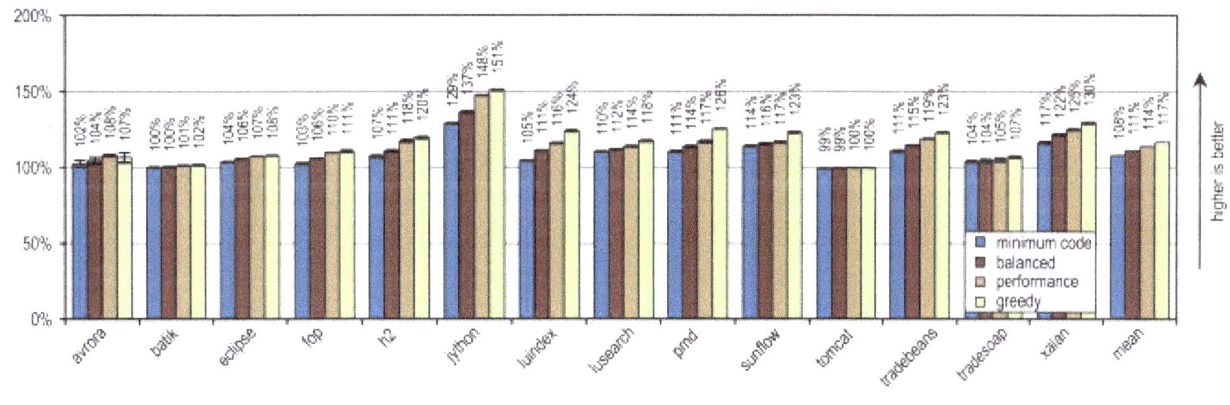

Figure. 17. DaCapo 9.12 Bach peak performance.

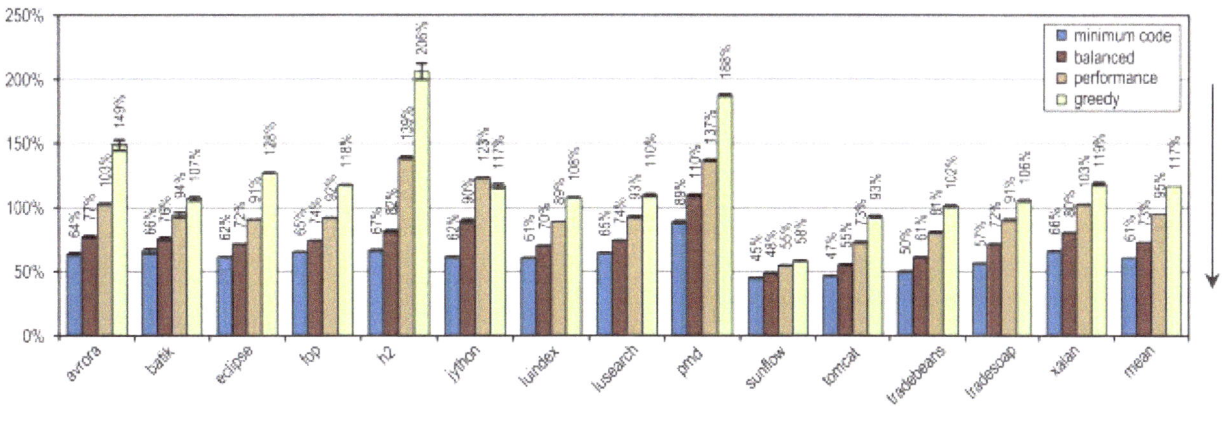

Figure. 18. DaCapo 9.12 Bach generated machine code.

The tracing configurations achieve the highest speedup for the benchmark *jython*, which executes a large number of virtual calls. Our trace-based compiler uses the recorded trace information for aggressive inlining of virtual calls. So, it achieves a large compilation scope, which results in a high peak performance.

On average, all inlining heuristics except *greedy* generate less machine code than the method-based client compiler, while still showing a higher average peak performance. One of our static inlining heuristics, which only compares the size of the traces to a fixed maximum value, reached nearly the same peak performance as *minimum code* but generated more machine code. This good result for a static inlining heuristic comes from the fact that the compiled traces contain only frequently executed paths per definition. So, for methods without much control flow, it is sufficient to compare the size of the traces to a fixed threshold. As long as the maximum inlining size was kept low, this static heuristic showed decent results but when the maximum inlining size was increased, lots of machine code was generated without a significant positive effect on peak performance.

In terms of time required for JIT compilation, Fig. 19 shows that our trace-based compiler is highly efficient so that even our most aggressive configuration *greedy* requires on average only a similar amount of time as the method-based HotSpot client compiler.

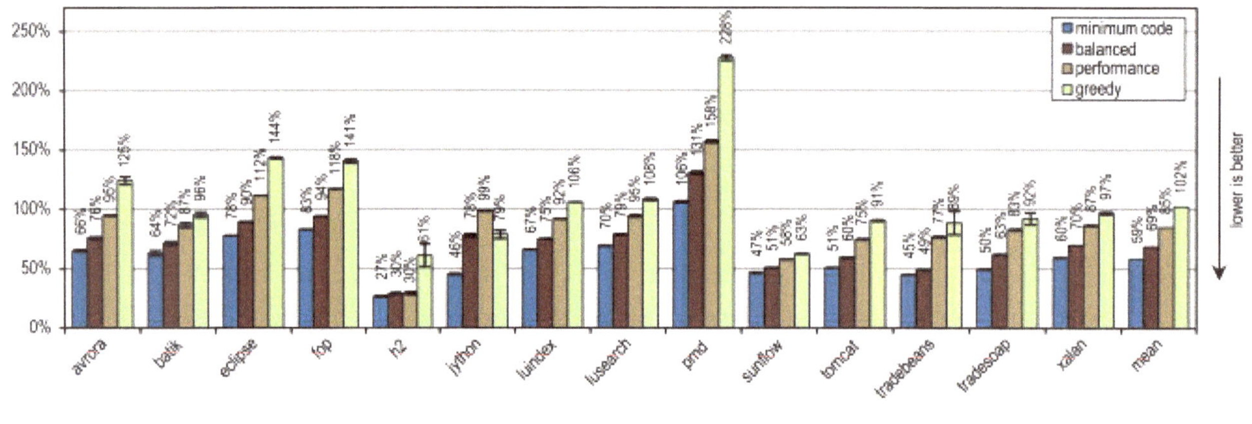

Figure. 19. DaCapo 9.12 Bach compilation time.

High-level Optimizations

Similar to method-inlining, trace inlining is an optimization that has positive effects on other compiler optimizations due to the larger compilation scope. Fig. 20 compares the impact on peak performance for different high-level optimizations that are used by both the method-based HotSpot client compiler and our trace-based compiler. Optimizations marked with [1] are local optimizations that are applied directly during bytecode parsing, while optimizations marked with [2] are global optimizations that run in a separate phase after graph building.

	client compiler speedup			tracing compiler speedup (greedy)		
	SPECjbb2005	SPECjvm2008	DaCapo 9.12	SPECjbb2005	SPECjvm2008	DaCapo 9.12
canonicalization [1]	2%	3%	1%	4%	4%	2%
conditional expression elimination [2]	1%	0%	-1%	0%	0%	0%
block merging [1,2]	0%	0%	-1%	0%	1%	1%
value numbering [1,2]	0%	2%	0%	0%	2%	1%
load/store elimination [1]	0%	1%	0%	0%	0%	0%
null-check elimination [2]	2%	2%	1%	4%	2%	1%
all optimizations [1,2]	5%	7%	4%	9%	8%	6%

Figure. 20. Impact of high-level optimizations on peak performance.

In general, aggressive trace inlining increases the compilation scope, which positively affects many optimizations. However, depending on the benchmarks the individual optimizations show different gains. For the SPECjbb2005 benchmark, our trace inlining especially increases the effectiveness of *canonicalization*, which performs simple optimizations such as constant folding and dead code elimination. The SPECjvm2008 benchmark suite contains too many small and loop-intensive benchmarks where our trace-based compiler cannot achieve a significantly larger compilation scope. Therefore, hardly any high-level optimization profits significantly here. On the DaCapo 9.12 Bach benchmark suite, the performance increase is distributed over all listed optimizations.

Server Compiler

Oracle's Java HotSpot VM has two different JIT compilers that share most parts of the VM infrastructure. Our trace-based compiler builds on the *client compiler*, which is designed for best startup performance and implements only basic optimizations to achieve a decent peak performance. The *server compiler* is designed for long-running server applications and performs significantly more optimizations to produce highly efficient code. Some additional optimizations that the server compiler performs are array bounds check elimination, loop-invariant code motion, loop unrolling, and escape analysis. Thus, the server compiler generates code with a better peak performance but requires a 6–31 times (13 times on average) longer compilation on the benchmark suites SPECjbb2005, SPECjvm2008, and DaCapo 9.12 Bach. A server executes mostly long-running applications so that the long compilation time is only a small overhead in comparison to the total execution time.

We compared our best peak performance configuration *greedy* to the HotSpot server compiler, and the results are shown in Fig. 21. The SPECjbb2005 benchmark profits heavily from some of the time-consuming optimizations of the server compiler, so that our trace-based compiler reaches only 67% of the server compiler's performance.

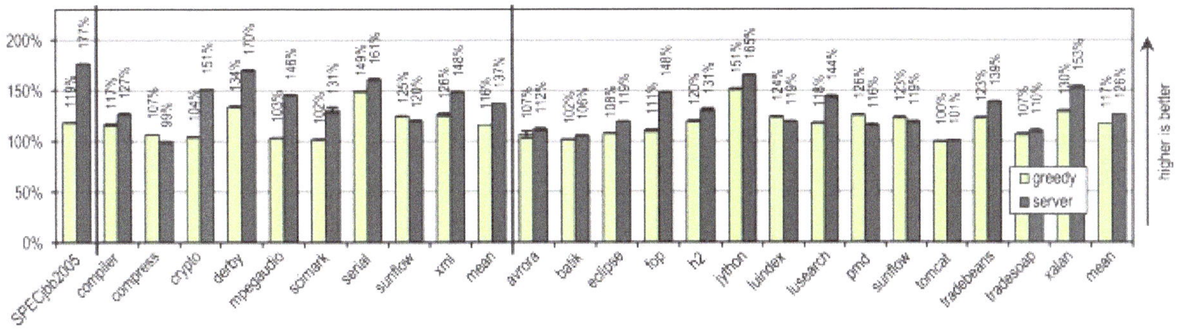

Figure. 21. SPECjbb2005, SPECjvm2008, and DaCapo 9.12 Bach peak performance.

For the SPECjvm2008 benchmark suite, our tracing configuration *greedy* reaches on average 85% of the server compiler's performance. This benchmark suite contains many loop-intensive benchmarks, such as *crypto*, *mpegaudio*, and *scimark*, where the server compiler shows a significantly higher peak performance, because it applies array bounds check elimination and sophisticated loop optimizations. However, due to our aggressive trace inlining our trace-based compiler outperforms the server compiler on the benchmarks *compress* and *sunflow*.

On the DaCapo 9.12 Bach benchmark suite, which contains significantly more complex and less loop-intensive benchmarks [14], our trace-based compiler reaches 93% of the server compiler's peak performance on average. However, although our trace-based compiler performs only basic compiler optimizations, it outperforms the server compiler's peak performance on the benchmarks *luindex*, *pmd*, and *sunflow*. This is due to our aggressive and context-sensitive trace inlining approach.

Startup Performance

The Java HotSpot client and server compilers as well as our trace-based JIT compiler are all designed for multi-threaded background compilation. So, we evaluate the startup performance in the following scenarios:

- The first scenario executes 1 *application thread*, while the VM uses up to 4 JIT compiler threads. So, on our 4 core benchmarking system, up to 3 cores can be exclusively used for JIT compilation.
- In the second scenario, 4 *application threads* are executed while the VM uses up to 4 JIT compiler threads. On our 4 core benchmarking system, the JIT compiler threads compete with the application threads. The Java HotSpot VM assigns a higher priority to JIT compiler threads as early JIT compilation has a positive effect on startup performance.

All presented results are normalized to the performance of the configuration *client* with 1 JIT compiler thread. We do not present any startup performance results for the SPECjbb2005 benchmark as this benchmark is designed to measure peak performance so that first results are obtained after 30 s where all configurations are already close to their peak-performance.

For the SPECjvm2008 benchmark suite, we measured the startup performance by executing one operation for each benchmark. Fig. 23 shows that the HotSpot client compiler and our trace-based compiler achieve good results for those scenarios where the application threads compete with compiler threads so that compilation time matters.Fig. 22 shows the different scenario when JIT compilation can be offloaded to otherwise idle cores. There, the HotSpot server compiler shows the best startup performance because the SPECjvm2008 benchmark suite contains several small benchmarks where there is little to compile and which almost reach their peak performance after compiling the innermost benchmark loop. This is the ideal case for the server compiler which does optimize loops especially well so that its peak performance advantage also affects the startup performance results if idle cores are available for compilation.

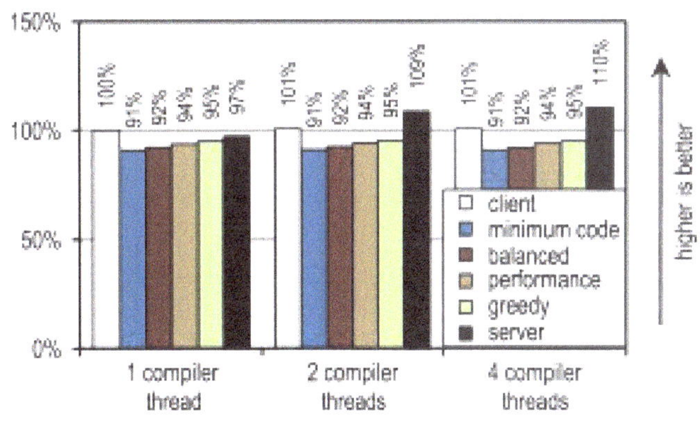

Figure. 22. SPECjvm2008 startup performance with 1 application thread.

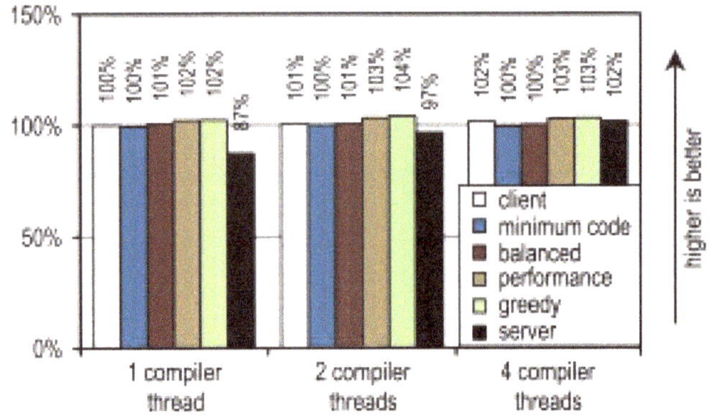

Figure. 23. SPECjvm2008 startup performance with 4 application threads.

The figures also show that the number of compiler threads does neither affect the client compiler nor our trace-based compiler because both JIT compilers require little time for compilation. The server compiler requires much time for compilation and therefore greatly profits from more than one compilation thread, especially if there are idle cores that can be used.

For the DaCapo 9.12 Bach benchmark suite, we measured the startup performance by executing one iteration for each benchmark. The benchmark results are shown in Fig. 24 and Fig. 25.

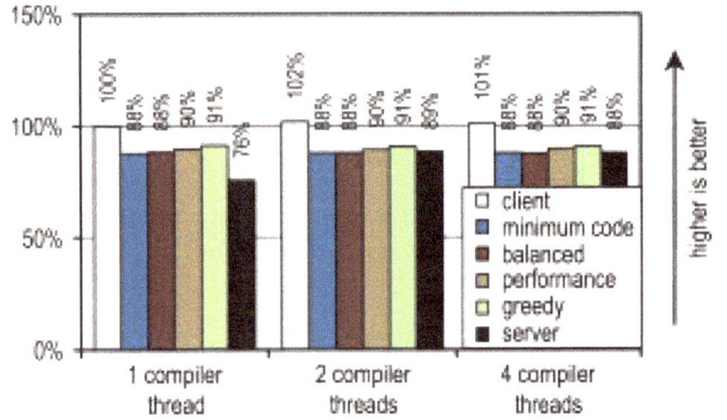

Figure. 24. DaCapo 9.12 Bach startup performance with 1 application thread.

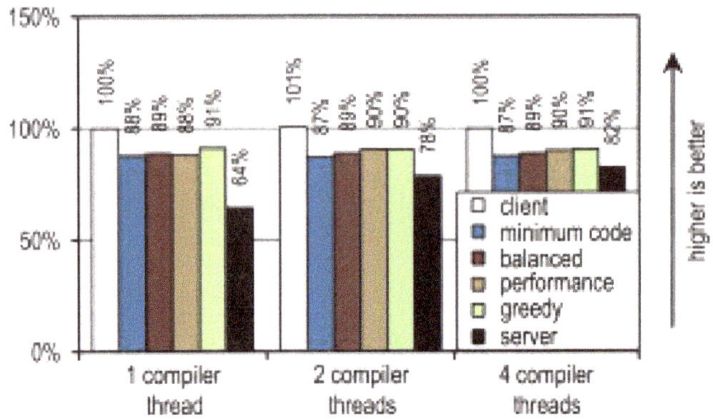

Figure. 25. DaCapo 9.12 Bach startup performance with 4 application threads.

Again, the number of compiler threads neither affects the client compiler nor our trace-based compiler because those require too little time for compilation. In contrast to that, the server compiler profits when more than one thread is used for JIT compilation. However, several of our tracing configurations always show a higher startup performance than the server compiler, even if the server compiler can use idle cores for JIT compilation. This is the case because the DaCapo 9.12 Bach benchmarks are significantly more complex than the SPECjvm2008 benchmarks [14], so that the JIT compilation performance is the dominating factor for startup performance.

So, on the DaCapo 9.12 Bach benchmarks, our trace-based configurations show a roughly 10% slower startup than the HotSpot client compiler. While our trace-based compiler often requires even less time for JIT compilation than the HotSpot client compiler, it shows a lower startup performance because of the additional overhead for trace recording and deoptimization that mainly incur during startup. However, this drawback is outweighted by the significantly improved peak performance. Unlike the HotSpot server compiler, our trace-based compiler does not need to use idle cores to achieve a good startup performance.

RELATED WORK

Bala et al. [1] implemented trace compilation for their Dynamo system to optimize native instruction streams. Hot instruction sequences are identified by executing the binary application in an interpreter. Then, those traces are compiled and the generated machine code is executed directly. The interpretation overhead decreases with the number of compiled traces, resulting in a speedup eventually. In contrast to them, we identify suitable trace anchors within Java bytecodes for which we use static analysis during class loading. We limit individual traces to at most one method and instead link the recorded traces to preserve context-sensitive trace information over method boundaries. This allows us to delay the inlining decision to the time of compilation instead of doing it already during trace recording.

Rogers [22] implemented a JIT compiler for Java where frequently executed basic blocks are detected and compiled. Related blocks, which may also span multiple methods, are grouped and optimized as an entity when executed frequently. Compared to method-based compilation, up to 18% fewer bytecodes are compiled. Our system records and compiles traces and uses context-sensitive trace inlining to increase the peak performance while at the same time generating only modest amounts of machine code.

The next approaches implemented different variants of trace-based compilation for Java[2], [11], [12] and [18]. However, all approaches have in common that traces may span more than one method, so that inlining must be performed during trace recording. In contrast to that, we assume that one method is the maximum scope of a trace and use trace linking to preserve call information between traces. This allows delaying the inlining decision to the time of compilation when more information is available. So, our inlining can be more selective while using simple inlining heuristics that result in a peak performance increase and a reduced amount of generated machine code.

Gal et al. [11] and [12] implemented trace-based compilation for Java on resource-constrained devices. Traces start at frequently executed backward branch targets and side exits of existing traces. Each trace may span multiple methods so that inlining is performed during trace recording. After recording a trace, it is compiled to machine code and linked to other compiled traces to form a tree-like structure. The simple structure of the compiled traces simplifies many optimizations but may result in excessive tail duplication and code bloat. A similar approach is also used by the Dalvik VM [4] and [6]on Android-based mobile devices. In contrast to that, we merge individual traces into a trace graph before compilation to avoid excessive tail duplication.

Bebenita et al. [2] implemented trace-based compilation for the Maxine VM. The Maxine VM uses a baseline JIT compiler instead of an interpreter for the initial executions. This baseline JIT compiler was modified to generate the trace recording instrumentation. Prior to JIT compilation, the recorded traces are merged into trace regions which have explicit control flow merge points. This avoids unnecessary tail duplication. Due to various loop optimizations, the JIT compiler achieves excellent speedups for loop-intensive benchmarks. However, it performs worse than method-based compilation on benchmarks with fewer loops. Our work is complementary as it focuses on complex applications that are not loop-intensive such as DaCapo 9.12 Bach *jython*. We achieve excellent speedups for those applications, while loop-intensive benchmarks only show small speedups as our trace-based compiler does not perform any sophisticated loop optimizations yet.

Inoue et al. [18] added a trace-based JIT compiler to the IBM J9/TR JVM by modifying the method-based JIT compiler. They record linear and cyclic traces without any inner join points and compile them to optimized machine code. In terms of peak performance, their trace-based compiler nearly reaches the performance of the similarly optimizing method-based JIT compiler. Wu et al. [28] extended that work by avoiding short-lived traces and unnecessary trace duplication. While this does not affect peak performance, it reduces both the amount of generated machine code and the compilation time. We also build on an existing production quality JVM but limit individual traces to span at most one method. So, we can delay the inlining decision to the time of compilation, which increases the peak performance.

Bradel and Abdelrahman [5] used traces for method inlining in the Jikes RVM. The traces are recorded using an offline feedback-directed system. Then, frequently executed call sites are identified within the recorded traces and this information is used to perform method inlining. Their evaluation with the benchmarks SPECjvm98 and Java Grande shows a 10% performance increase, while 47% more machine code is generated. Our system records traces during execution in the interpreter and only compiles and inlines method parts covered by traces. This increases the peak performance and can reduce the amount of generated machine code.

Hazelwood and Grove [16] implemented context-sensitive inlining for a method-based compiler. Timer-based sampling and recording of call information is used to guide inlining decisions during compilation. The amount of generated machine code and the compilation time is reduced by 10% without affecting the performance. In our system, the recorded traces contain even more detailed context-sensitive information. Depending on the inlining heuristic, this increases peak performance or reduces the amount of generated machine code.

Method inlining is a well-researched topic that is extensively covered in the literature. The remaining related work therefore concentrates on ways to inline *method parts* instead of whole methods as this is closest to our work. Still, these approaches are complementary to trace compilation as method parts are explicitly *excluded* there, while trace recording identifies method parts that should be compiled.

Partial method compilation [9] and [26] uses profiling information to detect rarely executed method parts in order to exclude them from compilation. This reduces the compilation time, increases the startup performance, and may also have a positive impact on peak performance. Our approach is even more selective as we record and compile only frequently executed traces. Furthermore, we use the saved compilation resources for more aggressive and context-sensitive inlining, which increases the peak performance.

Suganuma et al. [25] implemented region-based compilation where rarely executed method parts are excluded from compilation by using heuristics and profiling information. Then, frequently executed code is grouped into one compilation unit by heavy use of method inlining. This reduces the compilation time by more than 20% and increases the peak performance by 5% on average for the benchmark suites SPECjvm98 and SPECjbb2000. We only compile frequently executed method parts covered by recorded traces and use trace inlining to increase the performance.

CONCLUSIONS

In this paper, we presented a trace-based compiler for Java that performs trace inlining during JIT compilation instead of during trace recording. Traces have the advantage that they cover only the executed method parts. Delaying the inlining decision to the time of JIT compilation allows more selective trace inlining as more information is available at that time. Furthermore, our recorded traces are context-sensitive so that we can inline different method parts depending on the specific call site. This allows very aggressive trace inlining while generating reasonable amounts of machine code. Additionally, we propose to eliminate infrequently executed traces before compilation to ensure that only the most frequently executed traces are compiled to machine code.

The evaluation with the benchmark suites SPECjbb2005, SPECjvm2008, and DaCapo 9.12 Bach showed that good trace inlining can increase the peak performance while generating less machine code than method inlining. Furthermore, we also showed that trace inlining achieves larger compilation scopes that increase the effectiveness of common compiler optimizations and eventually result in a better peak performance.

ACKNOWLEDGMENTS

This work has been supported by the Austrian Science Fund (FWF): Project no. P22493-N18. Oracle and Java are registered trademarks of Oracle and/or its affiliates. Other names may be trademarks of their respective owners.

REFERENCES

1. Bala V, Duesterwald E, Banerjia S. Dynamo: a transparent dynamic optimization system. In: Proceedings of the

ACM SIGPLAN conference on programming language design and implementation. ACM Press; 2000. p. 1–12.

2. Bebenita M, Chang M, Wagner G, Gal A, Wimmer C, Franz M. Trace-based compilation in execution environments without interpreters. In: Proceedings of the international conference on the principles and practice of programming in Java. ACM Press; 2010. p. 59–68.

3. Blackburn SM, Garner R, Hoffman C, Khan AM, McKinley KS, Bentzur R, et al. The DaCapo benchmarks: Java benchmarking development and analysis. In: Proceedings of the ACM SIGPLAN conference on object-oriented programming systems, languages, and applications. ACM Press; 2006. p. 169–90.

4. Bornstein D. Dalvik VM Internals. Presented at the Google I/O developer conference, 2008. ⟨http://sites.google.com/site/io/dalvik-vm-internals⟩.

5. Bradel BJ, Abdelrahman TS. The use of traces for inlining in Java programs. In: Proceedings of the international workshop on languages and compilers for parallel computing, 2004. p. 179–93.

6. Cheng B, Buzbee B. A JIT compiler for Android's Dalvik VM. Presented at the Google I/O developer conference, 2010. ⟨http://www.google.com/events/ io/2010/sessions/jit-compiler-androids-dalvik-vm.html⟩.

7. Cytron R, Ferrante J, Rosen BK, Wegman MN, Zadeck FK. Efficiently computing static single assignment form and the control dependence graph. ACM Transactions on Programming Languages and Systems 1991;13(4):451–90.

8. Dean J, Grove D, Chambers C. Optimization of object-oriented programs using static class hierarchy analysis. In: Proceedings of the European conference on object-oriented programming. Springer-Verlag; 1995. p. 77–101.

9. Fink S, Qian F. Design, implementation and evaluation of adaptive recompilation with on-stack replacement. In: Proceedings of the international symposium on code generation and optimization. IEEE Computer Society; 2003. p. 241–52.

10. Gal A, Eich B, Shaver M, Anderson D, Mandelin D, Haghighat MR, et al. Trace-based just-in-time type specialization for dynamic languages. In: Proceedings of the ACM SIGPLAN conference on programming language design and implementation. ACM Press; 2009. p. 465–78.

11. Gal A, Franz M. Incremental dynamic code generation with trace trees. Technical Report. Irvine, USA: Donald Bren School of Information and Computer Science, University of California; 2006.

12. Gal A, Probst CW, Franz M. HotpathVM: an effective JIT compiler for resource-constrained devices. In: Proceedings of the international conference on virtual execution environments. ACM Press; 2006. p. 144–53.

13. R. Griesemer, Generation of virtual machine code at startup. In: OOPSLA workshop on simplicity, performance, and portability in virtual machine design. Sun Microsystems, Inc.; 1999.

14. Häubl C, Mössenböck H. Trace-based compilation for the Java HotSpot virtual machine. In: Proceedings of the international conference on the principles and practice of programming in Java. ACM Press; 2011. p. 129–38.

15. Häubl C, Wimmer C, Mössenböck H. Evaluation of trace inlining heuristics for Java. In: Proceedings of the ACM symposium on applied computing. ACM Press; 2012. p. 1871–6.

16. Hazelwood K, Grove D. Adaptive online context-sensitive inlining. In: Proceedings of the international symposium on code generation and optimization. IEEE Computer Society; 2003. p. 253–64.

17. Hölzle U, Chambers C, Ungar D. Debugging optimized code with dynamic deoptimization. In: Proceedings of the ACM SIGPLAN conference on programming language design and implementation. ACM Press; 1992. p. 32–43.

18. Inoue H, Hayashizaki H, Wu P, Nakatani T. A trace-based Java JIT compiler retrofitted from a method-based compiler. In: Proceedings of the international symposium on code generation and optimization. IEEE Computer Society; 2011. p. 246–56.

19. Kotzmann T, Wimmer C, Mössenböck H, Rodriguez T, Russell K, Cox D. Design of the Java HotSpot client compiler for Java 6. ACM Transactions on Architecture and Code Optimization 2008;5(1):7.

20. Oracle corporation. Java platform, standard edition 8 developer preview releases; 2011 ⟨http://jdk8.java.net/download.html⟩.

21. Paleczny M, Vick C, Click C. The Java HotSpot server compiler. In: Proceedings of the Java virtual machine research and technology symposium. USENIX, 2001. p. 1–12.

22. Rogers I. Optimising Java programs through basic block dynamic compilation. PhD thesis. Department of Computer Science, University of Manchester; 2002.

23. Standard Performance Evaluation Corporation. The SPECjbb2005 Benchmark; 2005 ⟨http://www.spec.org/jbb2005/⟩.

24. Standard Performance Evaluation Corporation. The SPECjvm2008 benchmarks; 2008 ⟨http://www.spec.org/jvm2008/⟩.

25. Suganuma T, Yasue T, Nakatani T. A region-based compilation technique for dynamic compilers. ACM Transactions on Programming Languages and Systems 2006;28:134–74.

26. Whaley J. Partial method compilation using dynamic profile information. SIGPLAN Notices 2001;36:166–79.

27. Wimmer C, Mössenböck H. Optimized interval splitting in a linear scan register allocator. In: Proceedings of the ACM/USENIX international conference on virtual execution environments. ACM Press; 2005. p. 132–41.

28. Wu P, Hayashizaki H, Inoue H, Nakatani T. Reducing trace selection footprint for large-scale java applications without performance loss. In: Proceedings of the ACM international conference on object oriented programming systems languages and applications. ACM Press; 2011. p. 789–804.

CHAPTER 9

IMPLEMENTING DESIGN PATTERNS AS PARAMETRIC ASPECTS USING PARAAJ: THE CASE OF THE SINGLETON, OBSERVER, AND DECORATOR DESIGN PATTERNS

Khalid Aljasser

Information and Computer Science Department, King Fahd University of Petroleum and Minerals, Dhahran, Saudi Arabia

ABSTRACT

Implementation of a design pattern can take many forms according to the programming language being used. Most of the literature presents design patterns in their conventional object-oriented implementations. Several other studies show the implementation in aspect-oriented languages such as AspectJ, EOS, and Caesar. In this work, we compare the implementation of three design patterns: singleton, observer, and decorator design patterns in these languages and also discuss the possibility of implementing them in ParaAJ: an extension to the AspectJ language that implements the idea of parametric aspects. We found that ParaAJ helps in making the implementation of the singleton and observer patterns reusable but it fails to help in the decorator case. The problem with the decorator pattern exists because of the current translation mechanism of ParaAJ's aspects to normal AspectJ's aspects. This opens the door for further work in ParaAJ to better support the idea of parametric aspects.

INTRODUCTION

Design patterns represent proven solutions to commonly recurring problems [1]. Most of the literature presents design patterns implementations in object oriented (OO) languages. Although OO languages are sufficient to implement most patterns, they lack proper constructs to make the implementation of design patterns maintainable, local, and reusable. Design patterns differ in their complexity and structure. In some cases, the pattern code gets scattered in many modules making it difficult to implement and even more difficult to maintain. As Denier and Cointe [2] state, a major problem when implementing design patterns is that they tend to disappear in the code.

Aspect oriented programming (AOP) [3] provides extra constructs to deal with crosscutting concerns. Those constructs can also be used to enhance design patterns implementation. The first study in this area is the one conducted by Hannemann and Kiczales [4] who implemented the design pattern catalog [1] in AspectJ – an aspect oriented version of the Java programming language. The implementation showed an improvement in 17 out of 23 design patterns in the original catalog [1].

Many design patterns have similar structures (and implementation) across different applications. Examples of these patterns include the observer, singleton, and decorator patterns. Other patterns depend heavily on their structure and implementation on the application they are applied in (*e.g.*, facade and adapter). For those patterns which have similar structure and implementation, it would be advantageous to

Citation: Khalid Aljasser, Implementing design patterns as parametric aspects using ParaAJ: The case of the singleton, observer, and decorator design patterns, doi:10.1016/j.cl.2015.11.002

implement them as reusable modules instead of having to go through the tedious task of creating their template code every time they are required in a new application.

For example, in the observer design pattern, there is nothing special about theaddObserver() and removeObserver() methods and they will probably be the same in all applications. Yet, we have to write them every time we use the observer pattern (considering Java as the implementation language). The AspectJ implementation of the observer pattern (as implemented in [4]) provides a better solution but it also suffers from some problems that will be discussed in Section 4.2. Other AOP languages such as EOSand Caesar have different mechanism and construct to deal with crosscutting concerns and thus can be used differently to implement the various design patterns. We will highlight the advantages and disadvantages of each approach during our discussion in the following sections. We focus mainly in this paper on aspect-oriented languages since they represent the proper tool to deal with crosscutting concerns – a problem that appears clearly in most design patterns.

ParaAJ[5] is a language extension built on top of AspectJ to facilitate the idea of*parametric* aspects. With parametric aspects, aspects can be parameterized so that they can be reused easily in different contexts. This is different from the reuse opportunities currently available in AOP languages such as AspectJ.

As we mentioned before, not every pattern can be made reusable because the *idea* of that pattern can be implemented differently according to the context in which it is applied. Hence, we are focusing on this paper on three design patterns: singleton, observer, and decorator. The reason of choosing these three patterns is the high frequency of usage among developers and therefore the need for these patterns to be made reusable.

The main contribution of this work is the implementation of some design patterns as reusable components (parametric aspects) using the ParaAJ language. Parametric aspects can be used generally but in this paper we showed how they can be effectively used to implement design patterns. The approach we are presenting is unique in the sense that the effort required to apply a design pattern in a new context is only one line of code.

The rest of this paper is outlined as follows. Section 2 provides some background about the idea of parametric aspects and ParaAJ. 3, 4 and 5 show the various ways of implementing the singleton, observer, and decorator patterns respectively in traditional object-oriented and also aspect-oriented languages. Section 6 briefly discusses why this paper focuses on these three patterns and not on other patterns. Section 7 presents some related work and finally Section 8 includes some concluding remarks.

BACKGROUND: PARAAJ

In this section, we will discuss the main constructs of the ParaAJ language and its approach toward the idea of parametric aspects [5]. This is needed for our discussion in the next few sections. A parametric aspect (para-aspect for short) is an abstract aspect that defines a self-contained piece of reusable functionality. It provides an explicit *interface* between itself and its clients and is considered abstract because it cannot be used as is; it has to be *applied* to a target component and each *application* specifies a separate concrete aspect.

Kersten and Murply [6] distinguish four types of class-aspect association: closed, open, class-directional, and aspect-directional associations. A closed association means that both the aspect and its target (usually a class) do not know about each other. In an open association, on the other hand, both know about the other by means of references in the aspect or in the class itself. Most AspectJ's aspects rely on class-directional association where aspects include information about affected class but the class is oblivious to this relation.

Parametric aspects in ParaAJ use the aspect-directional relation where the aspect is generic and oblivious to the relation and the class has all the information about the connection between the two. Thus, ParaAJ shifts the control point from the aspect to the class side. With this kind of association, the developer can see the various aspects affecting the class by looking at its source code (hence, improving visibility) and still have the crosscutting concern code encapsulated in the aspect (avoiding the tangling and scattering problems associated with most crosscutting concerns).

Another advantage in the parametric aspect approach is aspect reusability as they can be implemented without explicitly referring to their targets (*i.e.*, base code). Unlike normal aspects, a parametric aspect uses parameters as an interface between itself and its clients. This avoids any coupling resulting from hard-coding the target class in the pointcut. Mainly, parameters are used to pass target class information but they can also be used to pass any other parameters as we do in constructor and method parameters. Target class information might include pointcuts, types, field names, method names and signatures. We believe that this would be more convenient than using aspect inheritance to create a separate specialized aspect for each use of a reusable aspect.

ParaAJ[5] is an extension to the AspectJ language that allows the creation of *component*aspects, *i.e.*, modular aspects that can be applied and used in different contexts according to the supplied parameters. One of the main goals of ParaAJ is to overcome the limited reuse opportunities in AspectJ (abstract pointcuts). This can have many applications beyond implementation of design patterns but we focus in this paper in this particular topic.

ParaAJ allows either aspect-directional or closed associations. Its main distinguishing features are that aspects must be explicitly applied to the classes they affect, and that aspect applications may specify parameters that indicate how the aspect is to be applied. These features enhance maintainability, as the aspect parameters create a formal interface between aspects and classes, allowing each to be developed and maintained separately, and encouraging reuse of both aspects and classes.

It is worth noting that ParaAJ's parameters are different from the currently available parameters in AspectJ's constructs such as pointcut and advice. The parameters inAspectJ are translated simply to method parameters during the weaving process. Then, they get evaluated at run-time. In ParaAJ, on the other hand, parameters can be used to represent programming constructs (*e.g.*, fields and methods).

The parameters in parametric aspects are similar to the constructor and method parameters in normal classes except for the fact that they are evaluated at compile-time.ParaAJ's parameters come right after the aspect name in the declaration following the syntax:

```
⟨visibility⟩ aspect ⟨name⟩ (⟨formals⟩) {
    ⟨aspect body declarations⟩
}
```

where ⟨*visibility*⟩ is a visibility modifier as can be applied to a normal aspect; ⟨*name*⟩ is an aspect name; ⟨*formals*⟩ specifies the formal parameters of the aspect; and ⟨aspect body declarations⟩ are any declarations that can appear in a normalAspectJ aspect.

Similar to normal parameters in constructors and methods, each formal parameter declaration consists of a type and a name. The name can be any normal Java identifier. The type can be any primitive Java type such as int, double, char, boolean, etc. or a *meta-type*that could be one of the following: type, field, fields, method, methods, pointcut, and ident.

type is a meta-type to pass primitive or reference type names. We would be able to achieve the same thing using an identifier (ident) but using type instead helps the compiler to detect errors early if a wrong type is passed to the aspect (for example, if we pass stringinstead of String). The type 'field' and 'fields' are used to pass field names to the aspect. Such parameters can be used to construct pointcuts inside the aspect. Also, 'method' and 'methods' are used in the same way.

The ident type is a new type that we introduced to the language to allow developers to pass arbitrary identifiers to the aspects. This would be particularly useful for aspects that introduces new members to targets and we would like to parameterize the name of these members.

Using Parameters inside Aspects

Usually in methods and constructors, when a parameter is declared in the module definition, it is used inside the module as it is. For example, in the following listing, the parameters a and b appear inside the method in the same format as the method definition.

```
public int sum(int a, int b){
        return a + b;
}
```

However, inside the body of parametric aspects, parameter names should appear between '$[' and ']' symbols. The reason in using this notation is that parametric aspect parameters are evaluated during compile-time and thus we need a way to differentiate them from other symbols in the aspect body. In programming languages compiler terms, if the compiler encounters the following statement:

```
Foo x;
```

it would declare a variable of class or interface Foo. However, if the compiler encounters the following statement:

```
$[foo] x;
```

it would declare variable of type specified by aspect parameter foo. These nodes (*i.e.*, meta-nodes) are replaced during compilation with the actual values passed by the apply declaration (shown next).

As mentioned before, ParaAJ allows parameters to appear only inside the body of the aspect. However, it restricts the places where the parameter can be used according to the type of the parameter itself. For example, in Java grammar, Type is a Java rule to represent *primitive* types (such as int, char, etc.) or *reference* types (for example, String,java.util.List, user created types, etc.). This rule is used in many rules in Java and AspectJ. For example, in Java it is used in field declarations, method headers (return types), and formal parameters. Also, in AspectJ, it is used in inter-type member declarations and type patterns. ParaAJ adds a rule to the grammar to allow meta-types to appear anywhere where a type can be applied.

```
type ::=
        primitive_type  |        Java grammar
        reference_type

extend type ::= meta_type
                                 ParaAJ grammar
meta_type ::= $[ ⟨symbol⟩ ]
```

The advantage of this restriction is to ensure that ParaAJ can produce semantically correct programs. In a similar way, ParaAJ allows several other grammar rules such as meta-field declaration and meta-inter-type declaration. At this stage, ParaAJ does not support passing complete statements or a group of statements to the parametric aspect. We believe that this would add more power to the language but it is not supported yet.

Applying Parametric Aspects

Parametric aspects can be applied to a target class *internally* resulting in an aspect-directional relationship, or *externally* (from another class) resulting in a closed association between the aspect and the class. Both cases leave the parametric aspect reusable and the second case allows the target class to be reused with or without the application of that aspect. Deciding on whether we should apply an aspect internally or externally depends mainly on the aspect and on the concern it is implementing.

Internal application: In an internal application, the apply declaration resides inside the target class and only affects that particular class. It can be placed anywhere where class members can be declared and has the following syntax:

apply ⟨name⟩ (⟨**actuals**⟩);

where ⟨*name*⟩ is a parametric aspect name; ⟨*actuals*⟩ specifies the actual parameters that will be passed to the aspect.

External application: In an external application, the apply declaration resides inside one class (the *host*) but specifies that it applies to another class (the *target*). The overall effect of this kind of application is a crosscutting concern that connects the functionality of two separate classes. The syntax of the apply declaration in this case is:

⟨*target*⟩ . **apply** ⟨*name*⟩(⟨**actuals**⟩);

A Simple Example

Consider a logging requirement that logs any updates that are performed on a certain field. To implement this requirement, we create a parametric aspect that takes the field name as its interface as shown in Listing 1. This field should belong to the target that is using the aspect and can be used (*i.e.*, the field) inside the aspect to build other constructs such as pointcuts.

Listing 1.A simple parametric aspect and applying it to a class.

```
1  public aspect LogUpdates( field f ) {
2    after(): set($[f]){
3      System.out.println( $[f.toString()] +
4                          " has changed" );
5    }
6  }
```

Specifying the aspect interface (parameter)

Using the parameter inside the aspect body

```
7  public class MyClass {
8    int myField;
9    apply LogUpdates(myField);
10
11   // rest of the code
12 }
```

In AspectJ, the pointcut set(field_pattern) is used to capture any statement modifying the field matched by field_pattern. A field_pattern consists of modifier (optional), field type, host, and field name. For example, we could write:

$$\texttt{set(}\underbrace{\underbrace{int}_{type}\ \underbrace{Foo}_{host} \cdot \underbrace{bar}_{name}}_{field\ pattern}\texttt{)}$$

In ParaAJ, we need not, and must not, specify the host class, as that is determined by the class to which our aspect is applied. In this example, $[f] specifies the field whose changes should be announced. The actual name of the field will be passed in the applystatement. After defining the aspect, it can be applied to any class using the apply declaration shown in Line 9 in Listing 1.

Based on the capabilities of ParaAJ, we believe that it would be advantageous to use them in implementing design patterns. As we mentioned before, the current problem when it comes to implementing design patterns is that the implementation tends to disappear in the core logic [2]. In the aspect-oriented based implementation [4], the case is better but we still have the problem of implementation overhead *i.e.*, number of lines required to achieve a certain design pattern. Because of these reasons, we thought of using parametric aspects to implement some design patterns to achieve better maintainability, reusability, and expressiveness. In the following sections, we will discuss various implementations of three design patterns (singleton, observer, and decorator) in different object-oriented and aspect-oriented languages.

SINGLETON PATTERN

The singleton design pattern is a very well known pattern that is used to "ensure that a class has only one instance, and provides a global point of access to it" [1].

Singleton Pattern in Java

In object-oriented languages such as Java, this pattern can be implemented as shown in Listing 2. The implementation is divided into three parts: (1) an instance variable holding a reference to the created object, (2) a private constructor, and (3) a public method to get the instance. When an object of type MyClass gets created for the first time, theInstance field would be created. Later requests to create new objects would not create anothertheInstance field, but rather, would return the object that has already been created.

Listing 2. Implementing the singleton pattern in Java.

```
public class MyClass {
    private static MyClass theInstance = new MyClass();

    private MyClass(){
        //initialization
    }

    public static MyClass getInstance(){
        return theInstance;
    }
    //////////////////////////
    main class functionality
}
```

private constructor required to prevent calling the constructor externally

Although the implementation does not appear to be crosscutting, it actually mixes the singleton logic with the actual functionality of the class (not shown in the listing). The singleton pattern is widely used and the same procedure has to be followed whenever the singleton is needed.

Singleton in AspectJ

Hannemann and Kiczales [4] reimplemented the singleton design pattern using AspectJ(see Listing 3). The main component in their implementation is an abstract aspect (SingletonProtocol). In this abstract aspect, they provide an empty interface (usually called*marker interface* [7] and [8]) that is used as a parent interface (*i.e.*, the class to be made singleton should implement it). They use a pointcut that captures calls to the class constructor "call((Singleton+).new(..))" and uses an around advice to create a new instance or returns the existing one.

Listing 3. Implementing the singleton pattern in AspectJ.

```
1  public abstract aspect SingletonProtocol{
2    private Hashtable singletons = new Hashtable();
3
4    public interface Singleton {}
5
6    protected pointcut protectionExclusions();
7
8    Object around(): call((Singleton+).new(..)) &&
9                          !protectionExclusions(){
10     Class singleton =
11       thisJoinPoint.getSignature().getDeclaringType();
12     if (singletons.get(singleton) == null) {
13         singletons.put(singleton, proceed());
14     }
15     return singletons.get(singleton);
16   }
17 }
18
```

Singleton Protocol in AspectJ

```
19 public aspect SingletonPrinter extends
20                         SingletonProtocol{
21   declare parents:
22         Printer implements Singleton;
23
24   protected pointcut protectionExclusions():
25         call(( PrinterSubclass+ ).new(..));
26 }

27 public aspect SingletonScreen extends
28                         SingletonProtocol{
29   declare parents:
30         Screen implements Singleton;
31
32   protected pointcut protectionExclusions():
33         call(( ScreenSubclass+ ).new(..));
34 }
```

gray-shaded areas: difference between the two singleton instances

This implementation separates the singleton logic from the core logic of the class. TheSingletonProtocol represents the reusable building block for the singleton pattern. However, creating the actual singleton instance (Lines 19–26 and 27–34) is not as easy as we think it should be. There is a lot of code that will be the same in each singleton instance; yet, it has to be repeated every time. The gray-shaded areas in Listing 3 represent the parts that will vary in each application of the SingletonProtocol. Other un-shaded parts will remain the same and have to be duplicated in all aspects.

AspectJhas many powerful constructs and supports aspect reuse through abstract aspects. However, as we can see in Listing 3 (Lines 21 and 29), one of the main limitations of AspectJ is the inability to make inter-type declarations reusable *i.e.*, they have to be declared completely in each new concrete aspect. In other words, inter-type declarations cannot be parameterized in the current implementation of AspectJ.

Furthermore, the identifiers PrinterSubclass and ScreenSubclass that appear in the pointcuts (Lines 25 and 33) cannot be passed easily to the aspect. In other words, theprotectionExclusions pointcuts have to be repeated just to include these small parts (*i.e.*, the identifiers).

Singleton in Sally

An interesting approach is the one followed in Sally[9]. Sally is a general-purpose aspect-oriented language that has many similarities to AspectJ. However, unlike AspectJ, Sallyuses normal classes to encapsulate crosscutting code (instead of creating new constructs such as aspects). Also, it adds more power to the language by allowing variability in its static crosscutting constructs. In other words, while AspectJ pointcut language expresses only the dynamic parts of the language (for example, methods call and field access), Sally allows *introductions* to be expressed in a *parametric* way. This is useful to create generic aspects; many AspectJ aspects cannot be expressed easily in a generic way because of the inability to write *reusable introductions*. Using parametric introductions, developers can declare what to be introduced to the target class without explicitly specifying the actual target. Listing 4 shows an implementation of a generic singleton aspect in Sally.

Listing 4. Parametric singleton implementation pattern Sally.

```
pointcut singleton(?class) =
  equals(?class, ASingleton) || equals(?class, BSingleton);
introduction addSingletonMembers<?class> singleton(?class) {
    private static ?class instance = new ?class();
    public static ?class getInstance(){
        return instance;
    }
}
```

Singleton in ParaAJ

ParaAJis similar to Sally[9] in that it supports parameterization in modules. In ParaAJ, this is applied to aspects. The implementation of the singleton pattern as a parametric aspect has many similarities to the original object-oriented implementation. The only difference is the parts that refer to the actual class that need to be made as singleton. The implementation is shown in Listing 5.

Listing 5. Implementing parametric singleton aspect in ParaAJ.

```
public aspect MakeSingleton(){
  inject private static final thisTarget singleton = new thisTarget();

  inject private  thisTarget() {}

  inject public static thisTarget getInstance() {
    return singleton;
  }
}
```

thisTarget will be replaced with the actual class name during compilation

Reusable singleton aspect ParaAJ

```
class PrinterSubclass{
  apply MakeSingleton();
  //class body
}
```

applying the singleton aspect to a class

The code includes some new constructs that we did not cover in Section 2: the inject andthisTarget keywords. The inject statement is similar to inter-type declaration in AspectJexcept that it does not need to specify the target class where the member is to be introduced (*i.e.*, that contains the apply declaration). The effect of this injection is creating a member that is visible to the target class (*i.e.*, as if it was hard coded in that class). ThethisTarget is a kind of reflection mechanism that specifies the class or component which is applying the aspect. To make a class singleton, we just need to apply the MakeSingletonaspect as shown in Line 11.

The advantage of this approach is that the aspect clearly reflects the conventional object-oriented approach of implementing the singleton pattern. Any developer who is familiar with the object oriented implementation of the singleton can understand and modify the aspect (*e.g.*, to apply the double-checking mechanism required in multi-threaded applications).

The implementation in ParaAJ is different from the one in AspectJ in the sense thatAspectJ's aspect is used for all classes that need to be implemented as singleton. InParaAJ, the aspect serves as a template, whenever a class applies it, a new aspect specific to that class will be created.

Discussion

As shown in this section, the object-oriented based implementation is straightforward and simple. However, it mixes the logic of the singleton pattern with the main logic of the class. Thus, ignoring the separation-of-concerns principle [10]. The SingletonProtocol aspect shown in the AspectJ solution separates completely the singleton logic from main classes. However, as shown in Listing 3, the effort required to use the SingletonProtocol is considerable. Every time we need to make a class singleton, we have to repeat these 4 lines in the SingletonInstance aspect (Lines 19–26). In other words, it is *true* that theSingletonProtocol is reusable but it is not *easily* reusable. Another minor issue is the central management of all singleton classes. The SingletonProtocol keeps record (Line 2) of all classes that are set to use this protocol. Thus, all calls to instantiate object of *any* type is supposed to go through Line 12 to check the existence of older objects in the hashtable.

It is worth noting that some languages such as Scala[11] and [12] has built-in features implementing the singleton concept. Scala has a special keyword 'object' which creates a class and also makes it singleton in the same time without any additional coding (see the code below).

```
object ⟨Singleton⟩ {
      // class body
}
```

The singleton implementation in ParaAJ takes a different direction from the ones inAspectJ and Sally. The implementation is much closer to the object-oriented implementation. When we compare it with the AspectJsolution, we can see the *minimal*effort required to convert a class to become singleton.

OBSERVER DESIGN PATTERN

The observer design pattern is probably the most well known design pattern among the 23 patterns in the catalog of Gamma et al. [1]. It is used to allow cooperation between various classes without making a tight coupling between them. It is also known as "*publish-subscriber*" pattern [13]. Actually, the observer pattern has been used extensively in the aspect-oriented software development (AOSD) literature as an exemplar of crosscutting concerns [4], [14], [15] and [16].

As described by Gamma et al. [1], the intent of the observer pattern is to: "Define a one-to-many dependency between objects so that when one object changes state, all its dependents are notified and updated automatically". It works by specifying two types of entities: *subjects* and *observers*. A subject might change in its state and *registered*observers should be notified upon these changes. In the following sections, we will compare the implementation of this pattern in different programming languages.

Observer Pattern in Java

In an object-oriented language such as Java, this pattern can be implemented as shown in Listing 6. The Point class is the actual subject to be observed and Screen is the class representing the observer. To decrease the coupling between the actual subject and the observers, the observation logic is abstracted in two interfaces: Subject and Observer. To make the connection, the Point class has to implement the Subject interface (line 1). Similarly, the Screen class has to implement Observer interface (line 26).

Listing 6. Implementing the observer pattern in Java.

```
1  public class Point implements Subject {
2      private HashSet observers;
3      private int x, y;
4      public Point(int x, int y) {
5          this.x = x;        this.y = y;
6          this.observers = new HashSet();
7      }
8      public void setX(int x){
9          this.x = x;
10         notifyObservers();
11     }
12     public void setY(int y){
13         this.y = y;
14         notifyObservers();
15     }
16     public void addObserver(Observer o){
17         ...
18     }
19     public void removeObserver(Observer o){
20         ...
21     }
22     public void notifyObservers(){
23         ...
24     }
25 }
```

```
26 public class Screen implements Observer {
27     public void refresh(Subject s) {
28         display("update received from a "+
29             s.getClass().getName()+" object");
30     }
31 }
```

Gray-shaded areas represent the observer logic

This implementation suffers from a crosscutting presence especially in the subject part. In the Point class, whenever the *x* or *y* coordinates change, observers have to be notified by calling the notifyObservers() method. Although it is not that much (*i.e.*, only a single line in both methods), it mixes the original logic (that is, changing coordinate values) with the observation logic. Also, the Point class has to implement three methods: addObserver,removeObserver, and notifyObservers – all of which are not part of the logic of the Point class. Finally, it has to keep a record of the observers by maintaining a list as shown in line 2. The gray-shaded areas in the code represent the *observation* logic that crosscuts the point main-logic.

m:1 m:1 Another problem with the object-oriented implementation is that the observation logic cannot be used in different contexts; *i.e.*, the same code (in the gray-shaded areas) has to be repeated in all classes that need the observation logic.

Observer Pattern in AspectJ

Hannemann and Kiczales [4] reimplemented the observer pattern using AspectJ. As shown in Listing 7, the AspectJ-based implementation relies on defining an ObserverProtocolaspect that reflects the subject and observer *roles* as inner interfaces.

Listing 7. Implementing subject–observer pattern in AspectJ – ObserverProtocol.

```
1  public abstract aspect ObsProtocol"{
2   protected interface Sub { }
3   protected interface Obs { }
4   private WeakHashMap perSubObs;
5   protected List getObs(Subject s) {
6     if (perSubObs == null) {
7      perSubObs = new WeakHashMap();
8     }
9     List observers = (List)perSubObs.get(s);
10    if ( observers == null ) {
11     observers = new LinkedList();
12     perSubObs.put(s, observers);
13    }
14    return observers;
15  }
16  public void addObs(Sub s, Obs o){
17    getObs(s).add(o);
18  }
19  public void removeObs(Sub s, Obs o){
20    getObs(s).remove(o);
21  }
22  abstract pointcut subjectChange(Sub s);
23  abstract void updateObs(Sub s, Obs o);
24   after(Sub s): subjectChange(s) {
25    Iterator iter = getObs(s).iterator();
26     while ( iter.hasNext() ) {
27      updateObs(s, ((Obs)iter.next()));
28     }
29   }
30 }
```

```
31 public aspect ColorObserver extends ObsProtocol{
32
33   declare parents: Point  implements Sub;
34   declare parents: Line   implements Sub;
35   declare parents: Screen implements Obs;
36
37   protected pointcut subjectChange(Sub s):
38         ( call(void Point.setColor(Color))  ||
39           call(void  Line.setColor(Color))   )
40                                         && target(s);
41
42   protected void updateObs(Sub s, Obs o){
43         ((Screen)o).display("Color change.");
44   }
45 }
```

Creating an observer using the ObserverProtocol

Gray-shaded areas represent the duplicated code in any new aspect

The main building block in the subject-observer pattern in AspectJ

"code taken from [4] (Design Pattern Implementation in Java and AspectJ) with some modifications
Observer: Obs, Subject: Sub, perSubjectObservers: perSubObs

This ObserverProtocol represents the building block for the pattern. Users can then extend this aspect to specify the actual subject–observer behavior. The ColorObserver aspect (Lines 31–45) extends the ObserverProtocol to specify the actual observation logic. Reusing this protocol requires the following steps: (1) create a new aspect that extendsObserverProtocol, (2) assign the roles of participating classes using the 'declare parents' statement (Lines 33–35), (3) define the observation points by using the pointcut construct, and (4) define the logic that should be executed when the event happens (Line 43).

The solution in AspectJ is a generic solution for the observer pattern. It captures the relation between subjects and observer in a central ObserverProtocol. However, despite this improvement, the pattern code cannot be reused *easily* in other contexts. There is a lot of code duplication needed for each new observer required even if we are encapsulating most of the logic in the ObserverProtocol. The duplicated code is highlighted in gray in Listing7 (Lines 31–45).

Observer Pattern in EOS

Another interesting AOP language is EOS[17] – a language model designed by Rajan and Sullivan to unify classes and aspects as one modular unit called classpect [18]. The idea of classpects is to "extend classes with capabilities of aspects, and aspects with the compositionality of objects" [18].

In a study similar to the one conducted by Hannemann and Kiczales [4], Rajan [19]considered implementing some of Gamma et al.'s design patterns in the EOS language. As indicated in [19], the implementation of the observer pattern is similar to AspectJ in the sense that both depend on abstract ObserverProtocol component (aspect in AspectJ and class in EOS). The ObserverProtocol in EOS is, however, 78% smaller in size (lines of code) than its AspectJ's counterpart [19] (see Listing 8).

Listing 8. Observer pattern in EOS.

```
public abstract class ObserverProtocol {
    protected abstract pointcut subjectChange();

    protected abstract void  update ();

    after subjectChange(s): update(Subject s);
}
```

```
public class ColorObserver : ObserverProtocol{
    Point p;
    Screen s;
    public ColorObserver(Point p, Screen s){
        addObject(p); this.p=p; this.s=s;
    }
    override pointcut subjectChange():
        execution(void Point.setColor(Color));

    public override void update(){
        s.display("Color->Screen update.");
    }
}
```

A clear advantage of this approach, unlike the AspectJ implementation, is that it clearly reflects the intent of the observer pattern. One can clearly read it as: when a subject changes, update the observer (Line 6). The change to the subject is captured in Line 2 and updating the observer is defined in Line 4.

The ColorObserver can be implemented as shown in Lines 8–20. It is similar to its AspectJcounterpart. However, we find the EOS code to be more elegant and compact especially when assigning roles to the participating components. In AspectJ, we have to use thedeclare parents statement to achieve that. Also, initialization (or binding) of subjects and observers is slightly different in AspectJ and EOS. EOS makes it easier to refer to the observer unlike AspectJ which has to use the aspectOf() method.

Listing 9. Binding subjects to observers in AspectJ and EOS.

```
/* Binding subjects to observers in AspectJ */
ColorObserver.aspectOf().addObserver(p, s1);
ColorObserver.aspectOf().addObserver(p, s2);
```

```
/* Binding subjects to observers in EOS */
ColorObserver cobs1 = new ColorObserver(p, s1);
ColorObserver cobs2 = new ColorObserver(p, s2);
```

Observer Pattern in Caesar

Caesar[20] aims to build aspects as reusable components. It separates the actual definition of the aspect from its binding to the targets. Binding of aspects to their targets is done in the aspect collaboration interface (ACI). This separation of aspect implementation from aspect binding greatly improves reusability of aspects. Another feature of Caesar is that aspects can also be composed using their collaboration interfaces.

Caesarprovides a new kind of classes called *cclass* supporting family polymorphism – ability to treat inner classes the same way as methods [21]. It also has an interesting feature: *aspectual polymorphism*, which allows choosing which aspect or advice to run according to the type of the target [22].

Sousa and Monteiro [21] followed the same approach of Hannemann and Kiczales [4]and Rajan [19] in implementing some design patterns in Caesar. They chose a subset of 7 patterns (out of the 23 patterns in [1]). The ObserverProtocol in Caesar is represented as shown in Listing 10.

Listing 10. ColorProtocol in Caesar.

```
public abstract cclass ObserverProtocol^a{
  public abstract cclass Subject {
    public abstract void addObserver(Observer obs);
    public abstract void removeObserver(Observer obs);
    public abstract void removeObserver();
    public abstract void notifyObservers();

    public abstract Object getState();        | return Object with representation of internal state
  }                                             | Subject: Role of the object being watched

  public abstract cclass Observer {
    public abstract void refresh(Subject s);  | Observer role
  }
}
```

[a] code taken from author website (http://ctp.di.fct.unl.pt/~mpm/CaesarJGoF4SPLAT.rar).

Discussion

As described in Section 4.1, the pattern works by identifying one class as a subject and another class (or classes) as observers. In the subject class, the developer should add the required data structure to hold a list of observers and also add three methods namely:addObserver, removeObserver, and notifyObservers. The observer class simply implements the Observer interface and implements one method: refresh which specifies the observation logic in that specific observer.

By studying the *resulting* code, we can clearly observe the pollution that the observer code had on the original code. When we try to implement the observer pattern in a different context, we can also see that the amount of boiler-plate code in this pattern is high. The only part that need to be changed is what goes inside the refresh method in each observer.

A quick look at the solutions offered by AOP languages would show the advantage of using AOP constructs. First, the original code (*e.g.*, Point class) is not concerned or affected with the observer logic. Second, *most* of the observer logic is localized in one module (*e.g.*, the ObserverProtocol aspect in AspectJ). Third, the effort required to implement a new observer is minimized (see Listing 7). Finally, the ability to observe multiple*subjects* rather than one at a time is something unique to AOP languages. In other words, instead of creating an observer for the Line class and then creating another observer for the Point class, we can combine both in one aspect (in short: no scattering).

However, we tackle this issue from an *expressiveness* point of view. Why do we need to write this amount of code every time I need to observe a certain class? If one applies or uses the observer protocol in a different context, he would easily observe the amount of code to be repeated in each case (see gray-shaded areas in Listing 7). This is why we thought of achieving this using the parametric aspects idea in ParaAJ (next section).

Observer Pattern in ParaAJ

For the observation logic, we use a different type of aspect application. As shown in [5], parametric aspects can be applied either *internally* or *externally*. In the case of internal application, the apply declaration resides inside the target class and only affects that particular class. It can be placed directly in the class code anywhere where class members can be declared. The internal application approach is the one we used to implement the singleton pattern (Section 3).

In an external application, the apply declaration resides inside one class (the *host*) but specifies that it applies to another class (the *target*). The overall effect of this kind of application is a crosscutting concern that connects the functionality of two separate classes.

For example, if we would like to apply observer to the Point class, it is most appropriate that the code that displays the Point information should apply the observer aspect (in this case, the Screen class). This maintains a single point of control over the observation logic in the class that is responsible for that functionality. The main thing here is to determine what is required to be observed? For example, one might be interested in observing the behavior of some methods, so we can use a mechanism similar to the one used in the synchronization aspect (*i.e.*, using the 'execution' pointcut). Another one might be interested in observing some fields, so, in this case we would use a 'set' pointcut instead. Answering the previous question would determine the appropriate interface of the observer aspect.

Ignoring implementation details in Java and AspectJ, we can describe the situation as follows:

1. A subject to be observed by another component. This subject has to be oblivious to the whole monitoring requirement. It should not contain any code that belongs to the observation logic.
2. An observer that knows about the subject. It has a method that can process updates.

We can simply implement this as shown below (Listing 11). This is slightly a modified version of the original observer pattern.

Listing 11. Implementing observation logic in ParaAJ.

```
1  aspect FieldObserver(field f, method m){
2
3    private HashSet observers;
4
5    inject public void addObserver(thisHost observer) {
6      this.observers.add(o);
7    }
8
9
10   inject public void removeObserver(thisHost observer) {
11     this.observers.remove(o);
12   }
13
14
15   after (thisTarget subject): set ($[f]) &&
16                                   target(subject){
17     for (Iterator e = observers.iterator() ;
18                                    e.hasNext() ;){
19       ((thisHost)e.next()).$[m]( subject );
20     }
21   }
22 }
```

reusable observer aspect

```
23 public class Point{
24   private int x;
25   private int y;
26   private Color color;
27   // rest of the code
28 }
```

Point class is oblivious to the observation logic

Screen class applies the observation aspect

```
29 public class Screen{
30  Point.apply
31     FieldObserver(color,this.update);
32   void update(Point p){
33      // observation logic
34   }
35 }
```

Beside specifying what is to be monitored, the aspect should also specify the actual monitoring logic. Hard-coding the monitoring logic inside the aspect limits its reusability, so, it is better to *parameterize* this by passing a method name to the aspect. To apply this aspect, we have to specify the field to be monitored and also pass the method that encapsulates the observation logic as shown in Line 31 in Listing 11.

One clear advantage of this approach with parametric aspects is the simplicity of the aspect itself (in terms of development effort). Also, applying the FieldObserver aspect can be done in one line. Surely, this implementation is not equivalent to the original GoF implementation but it would serve well for many observation cases.

One would suggest using the same approach of Hannemann and Kiczales [4] in theirObserverProtocol. To link subject and observers together, we should write statements of the form:

```
Point p = new Point(5, 5, Color.blue);
Screen s1 = new Screen("s1");
ColorObserver.aspectOf().addObserver(p, s1);
```

In ParaAJ, each apply declaration results in a new aspect whose name is similar to the original parametric aspect but mangled to avoid name conflict. Thus, we will not be able to use the aspectOf() statement (as shown in the code above).

DECORATOR DESIGN PATTERN

The decorator is another interesting design pattern presented by Gamma et al. [1]. Its intent is to "attach additional responsibilities to an object dynamically" [1]. The basic implementation of the decorator design pattern in Java depends on creating a basicOutputDecorator that can include the actual concrete object implementing the type Output(Line 10 in Listing 12). When creating a concrete decorator (*e.g.*, StarDecorator orBracketDecorator), the developer has to pass the actual concrete object to the constructor (Lines 25 and 35).

The implementation is simple and straightforward. It allows the user to wrap any object with as many decorators required. For example, one can say:

```
Output o = new StarDecorator ( new BracketDecorator( new ConcreteOutput() ) );
```

However, the implementation does not help in making the various decorators reusable in other contexts. As shown in Listing 12, the two decorators are subclasses of theOutputDecorator which specifies that they can only wrap objects of type Output.

Listing 12. Implementing decorators in Java.

```
public interface Output{
    public void print(String s);
}
public class ConcreteOutput extends
                                Output{
    public void print(String s){}
}
public abstract class OutputDecorator
                    implements Output{
    protected Output outputComponent;

    public void print(String s) {
        outputComponent.print(s);
    }

    public OutputDecorator(Output output){
        this.outputComponent = output;
    }
}
```

```
public class StarDecorator extends OutputDecorator {
    public void print(String s) {
        outputComponent.print(" *** " + s + " *** ");
    }

    public StarDecorator(Output output) {
        super(output);
    }
}

public class BracketDecorator extends OutputDecorator {
    public void print(String s) {
        outputComponent.print("["+s+"]");
    }

    public BracketDecorator(Output output) {
        super(output);
    }
}
```

Decorator in AspectJ

Hannemann and Kiczales [4] reimplemented the decorator pattern using AspectJ (see Listing 13). The implementation uses a pointcut to capture any call to the print method (Lines 7 and 16). After that, it uses an around advice to *wrap* this method with a new behavior (brackets and stars) as shown in Lines 10–11. Although the implementation looks straightforward and easy to follow, it neglects a core feature of the decorator pattern: decorating *individual* objects rather than all objects of the decorated class. In other words, this implementation leaves us with a class-decorator not an object-decorator. Another problem with this implementation is that it does not allow flexible composition of different decorators [19] as it is the case in the original object-oriented implementation.

Listing 13. Implementing decorators in AspectJ.

```
1  public class ConcreteOutput {
2      public void print(String s) {
3          System.out.print(s);
4      }
5  }
```

- printCall pointcut: Identifies the execution points of interest: all calls to ConcreteOutput.print(String).

- Advice: Adds brackets or stars before and after the argument string before passing the call on to the component this decorator aspect decorates.

- Gray-shaded areas represent the duplicated code in any new aspect

```
6  public aspect BracketDecorator {
7      protected pointcut printCall(String s):
8          call(public void ConcreteOutput.print(String)) && args(s);
9
10     void around(String s): printCall(s) {
11         s = "[" + s + "]"; // Decorates the string
12         proceed(s);
13     }
14 }
15 public aspect StarDecorator {
16     protected pointcut printCall(String s):
17         call(public void ConcreteOutput.print(String)) && args(s);
18
19     void around(String s): printCall(s) {
20         s = " *** " + s + " *** ";   //Decoration
21         proceed(s);
22     }
23 }
```

Decorator in EOS

A major feature in EOS[19] is its ability to achieve instance-level advising which means that it can affect selected instances of a certain class rather than all of them (as it is the case in AspectJ). The decorator can be implemented in EOS as shown in Listing 14(Source: [19]-Figure 17).

The decorator in EOS fulfills the instance-level decoration as it is the case by the original Gang-of-Four definition of the decorator pattern. Unlike the original object-oriented implementation, the decorator should be first created as an object (Line 11) then objects can be decorated by adding them to this object (Line 12).

Listing 14. Implementing decorators pattern in EOS.

```
1  public class BracketDecorator {
2      public BracketDecorator(){}
3      protected pointcut printCall(String s):
4          execution(public void ConcreteOutput.print(String)) && args(s);
5          void around(String s): printCall(s) {
6              s = "[" + s + "]";     // Decorates the string
7          proceed(s);
8      }
9  }
10 ConcreteOutput o = new ...
11 BracketDecorator dec = new ...
12 dec.addObject(o);
13 dec.removeObject(o);
```

Pointcut and advice are similar to the AspectJ implementation

Creating object

Creating decorator

Adding decorator to object

Removing decorator from object

Decorator in Caesar

An interesting approach is the one presented by Caesar[23]. The basic idea of the decorator pattern is to *wrap* an object with an extra behavior. As shown in [21] and [24],Caesar has two ways of achieving this effect: (1) using normal pointcut and advice (as inAspectJ) and (2) using its special *language construct*: the 'wrap' keyword.

Unlike AspectJ, Caesar allows instantiating its aspects using a normal *new* keyword. With its *dynamic deployment* feature, it is easy in Caesar to add or remove decorators at runtime. However, one problem with this approach is controlling the order of different decorators. For this particular issue, AspectJ would be more flexible. The other way by which decoration can be achieved in Caesar is by using its language construct: the wrapkeyword. The wrapping mechanism works by allowing a certain object to wrap another object (or objects) so that it can extend its behavior. The wrap keyword (Lines 11 and 18 in Listing 15) reflects the decorator intent.

Listing 15. Implementing decorator pattern in Caesar.

```
1  public interface Decoratable {
2    public void print(String s);
3  }
4  public class ConcreteOutput implements Decoratable{
5    public void print(String s){
6      System.out.print(s);
7    }
8  }
9  public cclass ConcreteDecorator {
10   public cclass DollarDecorator implements
11                  Decoratable wraps Decoratable {
12     public void print(String s){
13         wrappee.print("$$"+s+"$$");
14     }
15   }
16
17   public cclass SharpDecorator implements
18                  Decoratable wraps Decoratable {
19     public void print(String s){
20         wrappee.print("##"+s+"##");
21     }
22   }
23 }
```

Interface for objects to be decorated

A family of several decorators that wrap an object identified with Decoratable interface and, of course, implements that same interface. In this way, client code does not need to be changed excluding the object creation and multiple decorators could be nested

Discussion

When considering the decorator pattern, the AspectJ solution provides class-level advising and thus all objects of the affected class will be decorated rather than selected objects. Also, as shown in Listing 13, there is a great deal of code duplication required to create new decorators. EOS, on the other hand, provides instance-level advising by providing a special method: addObject. This has a special advantage in terms of understandability of the code. In other words, we can easily associate this line of code with the idea of the decorator (since the decorator needs an object to decorate!). It is unclear to us whether EOS allows the object to be wrapped with more than one decorator or not. Caesar provides a new syntax like the keyword 'wrap' to allow a new type of composition of objects. However, the 'wrap' keyword does exactly what one wants in this case.

A modified version of the AspectJ implementation is presented by Monteiro and Fernandes [25] who achieved the effect of object-decorator by implementing a mechanism to register specific objects that need to be decorated. Thus, although the aspect is actually affecting *all* instances of the required class, the *extra behavior* will only be executed for the registered objects. It works as shown in the following code:

```
Component component1 = new Component();
Component component2 = new Component();

Decorator.aspectOf().register(component1);      | registering component1
component1.sendMessage();      | Will be executed with the aspect effect
component2.sendMessage();      | not affected by the aspect

Decorator.aspectOf().unRegister();
component1.sendMessage();      | component1 is not affected by the aspect
```

Decorator in ParaAJ

In ParaAJ, the original parametric aspect serves as a template for concrete aspects. Theapply declarations are responsible for specifying the actual values of the parameters to be filled inside the aspect. During compilation, the compiler converts each apply declaration to a new parametric aspect. The newly created aspects are exactly the same as the original parametric aspect except that their names get mangled to avoid name conflicts with the original aspect. This mechanism works fine for most cases where we want to*create-and-forget* about the aspects. In other words, in cases where we do not need to refer to the aspect at runtime. The decorator pattern is indeed different in the sense that we need to frequently refer to the decorators (aspects in this case) so that we can attach them or detach them while the program is running. For this reason, ParaAJ (at this stage) is not suitable to implement the decorator design pattern.

OTHER PATTERNS

Not every pattern has a crosscutting nature to it and thus it is not needed to apply aspect-oriented techniques to all of them. Hannemann and Kiczales [4] clearly mentioned that not all patterns would benefit from the new constructs and facilities in AspectJ. Only those patterns with crosscutting presence in their implementation *might* improve in terms of locality and reusability. Patterns such as Factory, Abstract Factory, Template Method, Builder, and Bridge cannot be made more reusable (compared to the Javaimplementation) and thus do not benefit from the AspectJ's construct. However, one feature that might be utilized is the fact that in AspectJ one would replace abstract classes with interfaces with default implementation.

This feature frees the concrete class from the *forced* inheritance relationship that is required in most object-oriented languages with single inheritance.

Also, not all patterns are applied in a similar way and hence they cannot be made reusable. In other words, many design patterns in the GoF [1] catalog represent *best practices* rather than reusable solutions (*i.e.*, components). The idea of the pattern is *recurring* and the design of the solution is reusable but the code is *not*. For example, the factory and abstract factory patterns are common in software development. However, the way they are applied differs greatly from one application to the other. In other words, we cannot design them as aspects (AspectJ, EOS, Caesar) or as parametric aspects (ParaAJ).

To summarize, if the pattern (GoF or any other pattern) has a crosscutting presence in its code, then it might benefit from the AOP constructs. If the application of the pattern is similar in different contexts, then it might benefit from the ParaAJ's constructs.

RELATED WORK

The work done by Hannemann and Kiczales [4] represents the most comprehensive study in implementing and comparing design patterns implementation in two languages:Java and AspectJ. Rajan [19] showed the need of instance-level aspects in EOS to implement patterns such as the observer and decorator. Caesar[21] is similar to EOS in the sense that both support instance-level advising. Actually, Caesar provides some language constructs that help in achieving reusable designs like the use of the wrapconstruct to implement the decorator design pattern.

In our work, we focus on aspect reusability. Hanenberg and Unland [7] noticed the insufficiency of AspectJ-like languages to provide proper reuse and proposed new idioms to overcome this issue. For example, the container-introduction idiom [7] is used to make AspectJ introductions reusable. Many other idioms such as template advice, pointcut method, and chained advice are used in other cases where other parts of the aspect need to be reused [7] and [8]. Despite their usefulness, these idioms provide an *indirect* way to achieve aspect reusability.

Meta-programming is the act of writing programs that generate other programs [26]. It is a powerful technique for developers to simplify the development process and can be used effectively to implement domain specific languages [26] and [27]. Huang and Smaragdakis [27] express the power of generating program code (meta-programming) using their language: MAJ. MAJ combines the abilities of *code generation* with the power of AspectJ[26]. As indicated by Shonle et al. [28], this could be utilized to simplify complex implementations of some patterns that are difficult to implement in AspectJ. For example, the declare-parents statements shown earlier can be easily generated with MAJ's '*quote*' ('[...]) and '*unquote*' (#[...]) operators. We share the same idea of Zook et al. [26] in the sense that there is a need for program-generating to reduce the development effort. However, their approach is general and can be applied to a range of situations. In our case, we focus on the need to generate code for some recurring patterns.

Huang and Smaragdakis [27] argue that "changing the syntax and semantics of a programming language is confusing and can lead to incomprehensible code." However, we believe that it would be useful to enrich current programming languages with constructs that can simplify development of recurring solutions such as various design patterns.

CONCLUSION

The implementation of design patterns takes many forms depending on the language being used. In this paper, we presented and evaluated implementations of three design patterns in several aspect-oriented languages including AspectJ, EOS, and Caesar. We also explored the possibility of using ParaAJ to implement these patterns. Our results show that ParaAJ can be used to provide a reusable implementation of the singleton and observer patterns (with some differences in the observer pattern). However, because of the current translation mechanism in ParaAJ, the new constructs cannot be used to successfully implement the decorator pattern as a parametric aspect. We plan to investigate the possibility of changing the translation mechanisms in ParaAJ to facilitate the support of more design patterns. By showing the different approaches to implement design patterns, this paper emphasizes the power of program generation and its advantages in reducing the development effort and also in facilitating program maintainability.

ACKNOWLEDGMENTS

The author acknowledges the support of King Fahd University of Petroleum and Minerals. This work was carried out under Grant no JF111004. The author also acknowledges the valuable comments on earlier versions of this article made by the anonymous reviewers.

REFERENCES

1. Gamma Erich, Helm Richard, Johnson Ralph, Vlissides John. Design patterns—elements of reusable object-oriented software. Addison-Wesley professional computing series. Wokingham, Reading, Menlo Park, New York-Don Mills, Amsterdam, Bonn, Sydney, Singapore, Tokyo, Madrid, San Juan, Milan, Paris, Mexico City, Seoul-Taipei: Addison-Wesley Publishing Company; 1995.
2. Denier Simon, Cointe Pierre. Understanding design patterns density with aspects: a case study in JHotDraw using AspectJ. In: Software composition. Lecture notes in computer science, vol. 4089. Berlin, Heidelberg: Springer; 2006. p. 243–58. ISBN 978-3-540-37657-6. http://dx.doi.org/10.1007/ 11821946_16.
3. Kiczales Gregor, Lamping John, Menhdhekar Anurag, Maeda Chris, Lopes Cristina, Loingtier Jean-Marc, et al. Aspect-oriented programming. In: Akşit Mehmet, Matsuoka Satoshi, editors. Proceedings European conference on object-oriented programming, vol. 1241. Berlin, Heidelberg, New York: Springer-Verlag; 1997. p. 220–42. doi: citeseer.ist.psu.edu/ kiczales97aspectoriented.html.
4. Hannemann Jan, Kiczales Gregor. Design pattern implementation in Java and AspectJ. In: OOPSLA '02: Proceedings of the 17th ACM SIGPLAN conference on Object-oriented programming, systems, languages, and applications. New York, NY, USA: ACM Press;

2002. p. 161–73. ISBN 1-58113-471-1. http://doi.acm.org/10.1145/582419.582436.

5. Aljasser Khalid, Schachte Peter. ParaAJ: toward reusable and maintainable aspect oriented programs. In: ACSC '09: Proceedings of the thirty-second australasian computer science conference, 2009. ISBN 0-7695-2778-7.

6. Kersten Mik, Murphy Gail C. Atlas: a case study in building a web-based learning environment using aspect-oriented programming. ACM SIGPLAN Not. 1999;34(10):340–52.

7. Hanenberg Stefan, Unland Rainer. AspectJ idioms for aspect-oriented software construction. In: 8th European conference on pattern languages of programs (EuroPLoP), Irsee, Germany 2003, 2003.

8. Hanenberg Stefan, Schmidmeier Arno. Idioms for building software frameworks in AspectJ. In: Coady Yvonne, Eide Eric, Lorenz David H, editors. The second AOSD workshop on aspects, components, and patterns for infrastructure software (ACP4IS), March 2003.

9. Hanenberg Stefan, Unland Rainer. Parametric introductions. In: AOSD '03: Proceedings of the 2nd international conference on aspect-oriented software development. New York, NY, USA: ACM Press; 2003. p. 80–9. ISBN 1-58113-660-9. http://doi.acm.org/10.1145/643603.643612.

10. Dijkstra Edsger W. A discipline of programming. Englewood Cliffs, New Jersey: Prentice-Hall; 1976.

11. Odersky Martin, Altherr Philippe, Cremet Vincent, Emir Burak, Maneth Sebastian, Micheloud Stéphane, et al. An overview of the Scala programming language. Technical Report 64. Lausanne, Switzerland: École Polytechnique Fédérale de Lausanne; 2004.

12. Scala. The Scala programming language. URL ⟨http://www.scala-lang.org/⟩. [accessed on 3/2014].

13. Buschmann Frank, Meunier Regine, Rohnert Hans, Sommerlad Peter, Stal Michael. Pattern-oriented software architecture: a system of patterns, vol. 1. West Sussex, England: Wiley; 1996.

14. Gybels Kris, Brichau Johan. Arranging language features for more robust pattern-based crosscuts. In: Proceedings of the 2nd international conference on aspect-oriented software development, AOSD '03, New York, NY, USA: ACM; 2003. p. 60–9. ISBN 1-58113-660-9. http://dx.doi.org/10.1145/643603. 643610. URL http://dx.doi.org/http://doi.acm.org/10.1145/643603.643610.

15. Gybels Kris, Brichau Johan. Arranging language features for more robust pattern-based crosscuts. In: Proceedings of the 2nd international conference on aspect-oriented software development, AOSD '03, New York, NY, USA: ACM; 2003. p. 60–9. ISBN 1-58113-660-9. http://dx.doi.org/10.1145/643603. 643610. URL http://dx.doi.org/http://doi.acm.org/10.1145/643603.643610.

16. Stein Dominik, Hanenberg Stefan, Unland Rainer. An UML-based aspect-oriented design notation. In: Kiczales Gregor, editor. Proceedings of the 1st international conference on aspect-oriented software development (AOSD-2002). New York, NY, USA: ACM Press. April 2002. p. 106–12.

17. Rajan Hridesh, Sullivan Kevin. Eos: instance-level aspects for integrated system design. In: Proceedings of the 9th European software engineering conference held jointly with 11th ACM SIGSOFT international symposium on foundations of software engineering. ESEC/FSE-11. New York, NY, USA: ACM; 2003. p. 297–306. ISBN 1-58113-743-5. http://dx.doi.org/10.1145/940071.940111. URL http://doi.acm.org/10.1145/940071.940111.

18. Rajan H, Sullivan KJ. Classpects in practice: a test of the unified aspect model. Technical report, Citeseer, 2005.

19. Rajan Hridesh. Design pattern implementations in eos. In: Proceedings of the 14th conference on pattern languages of programs, PLOP '07, New York, NY, USA: ACM; 2007. p. 9:1–11. ISBN 978-1-60558-411-9. http://dx.doi.org/10.1145/1772070.1772081. URL http://doi.acm.org/10.1145/1772070. 1772081.

20. Mezini Mira, Ostermann Klaus. Conquering aspects with Caesar. In: Proceedings of the 2nd international conference on aspect-oriented software development, AOSD '03. New York, NY, USA: ACM; 2003. p. 90–9. ISBN 1-58113-660-9. http://dx.doi.org/10.1145/643603.643613. URL http://doi.acm.org/10.1145/643603.643613.

21. Sousa Edgar, Monteiro Miguel P. Implementing design patterns in CaesarJ: an exploratory study. In: Proceedings of the 2008 AOSD workshop on software engineering properties of languages and aspect technologies, SPLAT'08, New York, NY, USA: ACM; 2008. p. 6:1–6:6. ISBN 978-1-60558-144-6. http://dx.doi.org/10.1145/1408647.1408653. URL http://dx.doi.org/http://doi.acm.org/10.1145/1408647.1408653.

22. Burgstaller Rainer, Fritz Thomas, Wuchner Egon. Hot-deployment of aspects. In: DAW: dynamic aspects workshop. March 2004. p. 9–22.

23. Aracic Ivica, Gasiunas Vaidas, Mezini Mira, Ostermann Klaus. An overview of CaesarJ. Trans Aspect-Oriented Softw Dev 2006;3880:135–73.

24. Sousa Edgar, Monteiro MP. An exploratory study of caesarj based on implementations of the gang-of-four patterns. Technical Report FCT-UNL-DISWE-2008-01. New University of Lisbon; 2008.

25. Monteiro Miguel Pessoa, Fernandes Joao Miguel. Pitfalls of AspectJ implementations of some of the gang-of-four design patterns. In: Fuentes Lidia, Moreira Ana, Murillo Juan Manuel, editors. Iberian workshop on aspect oriented software development (DSOA04), November 2004. URL ⟨http:// quercusseg.unex.es/juanmamu/DSOA04/papers/pessoa-fernandes.pdf⟩.

26. Zook David, Huang Shan Shan, Smaragdakis Yannis. Generating AspectJ programs with Meta-AspectJ. In: Karsai Gabor, Visser Eelco, editors. Proceedings of the generative programming and component engineering: third international conference, Springer-Verlag Lecture notes in computer science, vol. 3286. Springer, October 2004. p. 1–18. ISBN 3-540-23580-9.

27. Huang Shan Shan, Smaragdakis Yannis. Easy language extension with Meta-AspectJ. In: ICSE '06: Proceedings of the 28th international conference on

software engineering. New York, NY, USA: ACM; 2006. p. 865–8. ISBN 1-59593-375-1. http://doi.acm.org/10.1145/1134285.1134436.

28. Shonle Macneil, Lieberherr Karl, Shah Ankit. XAspects: an extensible system for domain-specific aspect languages. In: Companion of the 18th annual ACM SIGPLAN conference on object-oriented programming, systems, languages, and applications. ACM Press; 2003. p. 28–37. ISBN 1-58113-751-6. http://doi.acm.org/10.1145/949344.949349.

CHAPTER 10

MODEL-DRIVEN ENGINEERING OF INFORMATION SYSTEMS: 10 YEARS AND 1000 VERSIONS

Jim Davies, Jeremy Gibbons, James Welch, Edward Crichton

Department of Computer Science, University of Oxford, Oxford OX1 3QD, UK

ABSTRACT

This paper reports upon ten years of experience in the development and application of model-driven technology. The technology in question was inspired by work on formal methods: in particular, by the B toolkit. It was used in the development of a number of information systems, all of which were successfully deployed in real world situations. The paper reports upon three systems: one that informed the design of the technology, one that was used by an internal customer, and one that is currently in use outside the development organisation. It records a number of lessons regarding the application of model-driven techniques.

INTRODUCTION

The Object Management Group's concept of model driven architecture (MDA) [1] has been explained as the use of modelling languages 'as programming languages rather than merely as design languages [2]'. The broader concept of modeldriven engineering is a natural extension of this: using models to support automated analysis of a design, as the basis for automatic test generation, and as a source for automatically-generated documentation. It may be seen also as a natural extension of the concept of formal methods: languages and tools with a precise, mathematical foundation. If models are being used to drive processes of implementation and development, in the sense of being used to produce structures or behaviours automatically, then they must admit a precise interpretation. Furthermore, as they describe features or requirements at a higher level of abstraction than the programming notations they augment or replace, they are more amenable to mathematical characterisation.

In this paper, we will report upon our experience of a particular, original approach to model-driven engineering: one that was inspired directly by formal languages and tools. We will introduce and explain the Booster technology, the systems that we have built using it, and the lessons that we learned along the way. This explanation will focus upon three systems: one that supports our own activities, another developed for an internal customer, and a third that is presently in use outside our organisation. The lessons that we present here are informed also by the other systems we have built, and should be equally applicable to other developments using model-driven techniques.

The paper starts with an introduction to the Booster toolkit: the modelling language and the code generation process. In Section 3, we discuss the first system built using Booster: a system whose development and requirements for support had a profound influence upon the design of the toolkit. We present

Citation: Jim Davies, Jeremy Gibbons, James Welch, Edward Crichton, Model-driven engineering of information systems: 10 years and 1000 versions, doi:10.1016/j.scico.2013.02.002

some lessons in domain-specific development, data migration, and in software engineering process. In Section 4, we discuss a system built for an internal customer, supported in operation for two years, and then replaced by a supposedly-identical product built using conventional techniques on a standard platform. We present some lessons in the business and organisational context of model-driven engineering.

In Section 5, we discuss the design and operation of a system that is presently in use, for a purpose that is both important and sensitive, by a partner organisation. This system was built on the experience of the others, and we expect it to evolve and continue in use for many years. We present some lessons in dealing with legacy data, in scalability, and in migrating to other technology platforms. The paper ends with a brief summary of the experiences and lessons, an explanation of related work, and an account of prospects for further development.

BOOSTER

In 1998, following a competitive tendering and procurement process, the University of Oxford asked B-Core (UK) Limited to develop a new information system. The system would manage key aspects of the University's professional programmes in software engineering: programme finances, student registration, course attendance, on-line materials, submissions and examinations. Its development was to be managed for the University by Jim Woodcock and Jim Davies, both experienced users of formal methods: in particular, the Z notation [3]. B-Core (UK) was a company founded upon the industrial application of formal methods: in particular, the B-Toolkit [4].

Although the contract made no mention of formal methods, both sides were happy at the idea of using these techniques in the design process: indeed, given the level of expertise, and the shared, stated belief that the application of formal techniques could greatly reduce costs and increase reliability, not to do so might have seemed surprising to colleagues and customers alike. Both parties were aware that these techniques were originally developed for use in large, industrial projects, and that their application to the development of a 'simple database' could easily be counter-productive. Thus the initial plan was merely to provide a formal description of key features of the design alongside the conventional, written functional specification.

Soon after the specification, and the document, had been agreed with the developers, it became apparent that a system built exactly in accordance with it would fail to meet the users' needs and expectations. With each question from the developers, with each step of the implementation, it became apparent that the specification did not capture every aspect of the original intention, that there was scope for misinterpretation, and that some of the design decisions, so precisely expressed in the Z, were wrong. This can be explained in part by the emerging complexity of the proposed system – no longer a 'simple database' – and in part by the changing nature of the requirements: there were new regulations, new policies, and new structures to be taken into account.

It is indicative also of an inherent difficulty in the application of formal techniques: one that can be found also in the application of model-driven engineering. A precise description of intended structure and behaviour may contain a great deal of information: more than can be comfortably understood or managed by the unaided mind. Without tools for animating or otherwise validating the Z document, it served as a sketch of intentions, but nothing more; indeed, the same purpose would have been served by an object model written in a less formal language. A more concise, more abstract description might have allowed more in the way of manual exploration, and hence a more reliable, manual interpretation of the sets and symbols defined, but would have left many of the key features unspecified.

Nevertheless, the document was updated, repeatedly, to reflect changes in requirements and understanding. After several iterations, the developers observed that they might usefully treat the design document as source code for the system. This observation was based in part upon Ib Holm Sørensen's experience on the IBM CICS Project [5], where many of the Z specifications produced were deterministic at the chosen level of abstraction: that is, the value of each attribute or output included in the description would be entirely determined after each operation. This was captured as an informal principle:

Principle of Functional Specification

In a useful, formal specification, the value of each state variable should be uniquely determined after every operation.

If a variable is worth declaring, at a particular level of abstraction, then you ought to know precisely what happens to it. We leave it to the reader to suggest exceptions to this rule; we observe simply that this was proving to be the case.

At the same time, the Z notation was proving less than ideal for the description of the proposed design. We were describing the state of the system as a collection of classes, representing information held on students, courses, assignments, or invoices. As might be expected, many properties of interest concerned the relationship between attributes of different classes, causing us to adopt an idiomatic form of Z in which the model would include given sets of references to each class, and a generic dereferencing function. Furthermore, there was no mechanism for presenting each operation in the context of the 'owning' class. This led to considerable amounts of additional clutter in a model intended for manual inspection.

The Object-Z [6] notation was considered as an alternative, but a lack of tool support for presentation – drawing boxes around boxes of any significant size or number did not appear to be a scalable approach without some form of 'folding editor' – or analysis led to the decision to define a new object-based notation that could be supported by the existing B-Toolkit. Descriptions written in this notation would be translated automatically into the Abstract Machine Notation (AMN), and then refined automatically to produce an implementation of the core database functionality, based upon the toolkit's C libraries of datatypes and functions. Sørensen named this the B Object Oriented STate-based Refinement approach, or Booster.

```
SYSTEM NEWSYS              CLASS Class1[dim1]      DEFINITIONS
                              ...                    def1 == ... ;
  SETS                     END;
    set1 = ... ;                                   UTILITIES
                     IS       ...                    util1 = ... ;
  ENUMERATIONS
    CLASS Enum1            CLASS ClassN[dimN]
    ...                       ...
    END;                   END;                    END
```

Figure. 1. An outline of a Booster model.

Figure. 2. One-to-many association.

Notation

The original version of the Booster notation was presented in a conference paper in 2004 [7]. That version is the one used in the development of the three systems discussed in this paper, and is the one that we will explain here. Based upon the experiences of these and other systems, a new version of the notation has since been developed, but has yet to be used for customer applications: the changes in design are explained in Section 6.

Fig. 1 shows the outline structure of a Booster specification. The behaviour of the intended SYSTEM is described by a series of class declarations, each of which introduces a number of data attributes and operations. There are two built-in attribute types, STRING and NAT; other types are introduced directly, as sets, or indirectly, as enumeration classes or type synonyms. Direct calls to the underlying API may be declared as utility functions: to date, their use has been restricted to getting system time, managing file references, and handling user authentication. A feature of particular interest is the bound placed upon the number of instances of each class: for example, dim1 for Class1. This simplifies the allocation of memory in the implementation, and makes for more predictable behaviour: the system is guaranteed to allow the creation of a new instance of Class1 if there are fewer than dim1 instances, subject to any user-specified constraints, and guaranteed not to allow its creation when there are exactly dim1 instances.

Operations may be declared not only in the context of classes, but also in the more specific context of attributes. Each kind of attribute has a default set of operations: to set or get the value of a mandatory attribute, to set or clear the value of an optional attribute, and to add or remove a value from an attribute with multiplicity greater than one. Associations are introduced by declaring an attribute whose type is the name of a class; multiplicity and ordering information is added using the keywords SET, OSET, and SEQ, for sets, ordered sets, and sequences, respectively.

Associations in Booster are bidirectional: that is, they appear in matching pairs, allowing navigation in both directions. For example, the association shown in Fig. 2 between classes A and B would be described by a matching pair of declarations

bs : SET(O.a)[n]

in class A, and

a : A.bs

in class B. This is a one-to-many association between the classes, with a maximum cardinality of n.

Methods may be declared within the scope of a class declaration, or within the smaller, enclosed scope of an attribute declaration. A primitive method M is declared as a triple:

M(pre | change_list | post)

This should be available only if the condition pre holds for the current state and input values. If it is ever performed, then post will hold: this may refer to the values of inputs, outputs, and attributes before and after the operation, which may be expected to update the values of variables in the change_list.

This is different from the specification statement proposed by Morgan [8], in which

frame : [pre, post]

describes an operation that will achieve post if called when pre is true, changing only the values of variables mentioned in the frame list. The Booster condition pre is a partial guard, rather than a conventional precondition: the operation is guaranteed not to be available unless pre is satisfied. Furthermore, the change_list is a partial description of the frame, included as a directive to the compiler: the implementation may update other attributes, as well as leaving some or all of those listed unchanged.

The conditions pre and post are written as logical expressions in the AMN notation. In post, we may refer to values of attributes before the operation by appending _0 to the attribute name. The names of inputs and newly-created objects end with _in and _new, respectively. Where attribute names are unique within the scope of a method, any root qualification may be omitted: for example, if there is only one attribute with the name b in scope, then C.a.b may be written as b. post may include also references to other methods, and these references may be combined using method combinators. There are four in the original Booster notation: ALSO, sequential composition; ALL, universal quantification; ANY, existential quantification; and ORELSE, which produces an operation that is available whenever at least one of the components would be, and has the effect of first operation whose guard is satisfied, reading from left to right.

Expansion

The first step of the automatic refinement process is model expansion. The model is extended to include the definitions of any default operations, and operation preconditions and postconditions are strengthened where necessary to ensure that model properties – association invariants, type constraints, and user-supplied invariants – are preserved; the model transformations that calculate and provide this additional information reflect a number of domain-specific assumptions about the development of information systems. The expanded model, also in Booster, will typically be 4 or 5 times larger than the original.

Each class has two default methods: Create, to create a new object; and Destroy, to destroy an existing object. Each optional attribute has two: Set, to set the attribute; Clear, to clear it. Each set-valued attribute has four: Add, to add a reference to an existing object; Remove, to remove a reference to an existing object; New, to add a reference to a new object, creating the object; Erase, to remove a reference to an existing object, destroying it.

Each default method has a basic definition. For example, the default definition for the Add method on a set-valued attribute S of class C, containing references to objects of class D, would be defined as follows:

Add(S_in : D & S_in /: S | S | S_in : S)

The precondition insists that input S_in refers to an object of class D; and that S_in is not already an element of S. The change list indicates that the method may change the value of S. The postcondition states that, afterwards, S_in should be in S.

The cardinality constraints given in the model are added to the basic form of the default Create and New methods: for example, if class C were introduced with a dimension of N, then the Create method for that class would expand to

Create(C.card < N | C | C_new : C)

where .card is the built-in cardinality operator.

The pre- and post-conditions of Destroy and Erase are extended to take account of the association information in the model. If we are to destroy an object a1, we must ensure that there is no associated object with an attribute a whose value includes a reference to a1. If the associated object is b1, of class B, then this can be achieved in three different ways:

- if a is set-valued or optional, the postcondition is extended to require that a is changed, if necessary, to remove the reference to a1;
- if a is mandatory and B is not in the change list, the precondition is extended to require that a is not a reference to a1;
- if a is mandatory and B is in the change list, the postcondition is extended to require that b1, too, is destroyed.

The default semantics is given by 1 and 2. We may choose 3 instead by adding B to the change list when referring to either method.

Each default method has a corresponding default decoration. Within a class C, the methods Create and Destroy can use C_new and C_this to refer to the object that is to be created or, respectively, destroyed. For an optional attribute att, the methods Set and Clear can use att_in and att_this to refer to the object that is to be inserted or, respectively, removed. When referring to a default method, we may insert additional pre- or post-conditions, and add to the change list: for example, the declarations

a : Other

s : SET(Other)[5]

METHODS

Add,

Remove (s_this /= a | true)

introduce two attributes, a and s, together with a pair of methods on s. The first method is the default Add; the second extends the default Remove with an additional precondition, requiring that the object to be removed is not the same as the object currently referred to as a.

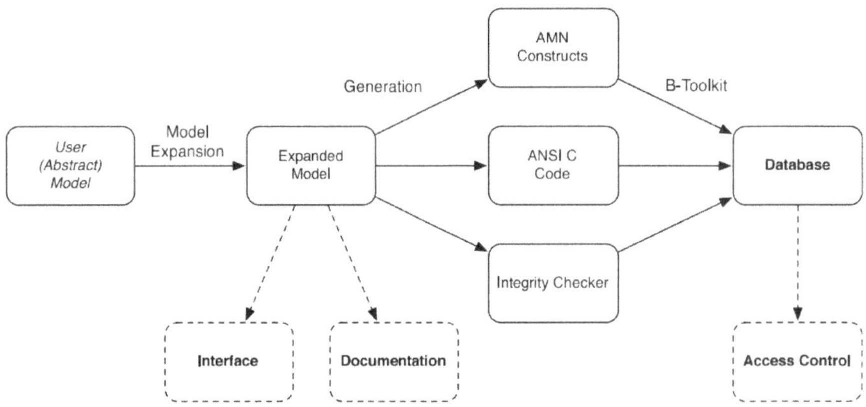

Figure. 3. The code generation process. 2.3.

Code Generation

The expanded model then serves as the source code in a subsequent compilation process: see Fig. 3. The model is translated into abstract machine notation, and then translated into C source by means of a B rulebase, before being compiled using the standard B toolkit libraries. The postcondition of each method becomes a program statement:

- the equality postcondition a = e is implemented as a simple assignment a := e;
- the membership constraints a :s and a /: s are implemented using functions that add or remove elements from sets;
- logical implication is implemented using a conditional if . . . then construction;
- logical conjunction is implemented using a sequential composition of statements: c1 ; c2

The precondition becomes a guard: a boolean expression that can be evaluated to determine whether the method in question should be available.

The resulting method implementations constitute a programming interface to the underlying data store. This interface is not accessed directly: instead, requests are queued for sequential processing by a decoder component. For a combination of pre- and post-conditions to serve as an adequate description of a method M, there must be no possibility of another method updating variables in the pre- or post-condition while M is still executing. Requests and responses are presented in a structured language, using tags that correspond to the operations of the model. The decoder logic is generated at the same time as the programming interface and the data store.

In order to generate the base object layer, the generator divides the model into single classes, removes the operation definitions, and carries out some simple syntax transformations. The B-Toolkit is used to generate a specification/implementation pair for each class, together with a set of abstract machines encapsulating state and data structures. The specifications are guaranteed to be internally consistent, and the implementations are guaranteed to meet their specification: the resulting modules are then used also in the generation of the API. Beneath this, a toolkit library layer provides support for primitive types, numbers and strings, together with basic input–output functionality.

Each method in the API may be called in one of two modes: test, which checks the precondition, and reports whether the method is currently available; and test and execute, which checks the precondition, and if it is true, executes the method. In the second mode, the implementation ensures that none of the attributes involved are updated between the precondition test and the method execution: if the test succeeds at this point, then the method is guaranteed to achieve the effect described in its original postcondition. As the system state may have changed between a test and a subsequent test and execute, any program calling the API must be ready to find that a method is no longer available.

To protect data against possible errors in the implementation of the compiler, an undo operation is generated for each primitive method. The method postcondition is checked after execution: if it is false, the operation is rolled back. A log is kept of all calls at the API, and these can be replayed to rebuild the current state from the last checkpoint, should something go awry with a complex operation or external utility function. An integrity checker for the whole data model is constructed as part of compilation process, and run whenever data is saved to disk, whenever a checkpoint is requested, and whenever there are no current requests in the decoder queue.

The decoder layer consists of a number of sub-layers. The first of these determines the nature of the request: whether it is a query or a method call. The second layer interprets the request and checkpoints the data, if necessary. The third determines which sub-decoder should be used to handle the request. The first two layers are generic, handling any query or method that can be constructed from the alphabet of attributes and methods in the expanded model. The third comprises a collection of concrete sub-decoders generated to match the class declarations and expanded method definitions. All of this functionality is implemented in ANSI C, and linked to produce a single database application.

CASE STUDY: THE SSTL SYSTEM

The first system that we will consider is the first information system that Booster was developed to implement and support. This took its name from the original contract awarded: Software Support for Teaching and Learning, or SSTL. Development of the system started in November 1998, with a functional specification and – as discussed above – a Z document outlining a proposed design. The decision to adopt a model-driven approach, treating the design document as source code, meant that a certain amount of tool building was required before the first working system could emerge.

An important lesson was learnt early in the development process. With each change to the model, the interface tier of the application would need to be redesigned. The API to the datastore, and the set of tags and codes understood by the decoder, would be updated automatically, but the Java code that generated the user interface would need to be reworked manually every time. This was time consuming, to the extent that progress on the interface had all but ground to a halt. The only solution was to generate new Java code for the interface at the same time as the rest of the system.

Lesson 1. Everything that changes with the model should change automatically.

This was enough to allow the completion of the first release of the system to administrative users, in September 1999. This release provided comprehensive support for the internal processes of course and student management, including invoicing and payments, and was well received by the administrative staff. However, there were no facilities for students to register on-line for courses, to submit assignments, or even to see what courses may be on offer. Neither were there facilities for academic staff to use the system, as lecturers, supervisors, or assessors. The development of these facilities became the next priority.

The default interface to the system is perfectly serviceable: indeed, it included many features that made it arguably superior to any product on the market at the time, at least in terms of the ease and efficiency with which experienced administrators could review and update the data in the system. It reflects the structure of the model, in terms of classes and associations, in much the same way as the object browsers defined for SmallTalk [9]. At any time, the user is looking at an 'object view', a presentation of a particular instance of one of the classes. Each primitive attribute is shown with its current value. Each reference appears as a hypertext link: clicking on this takes the user to a view of the target object. If the target class has one or more attributes identified as 'keys', then the values of these attributes appear as the labels for the links.

For example, the Course class includes an attribute attended, indicating the set of students who attended that particular course. Within the Student class, the name and student number of the individual are identified as keys. In a view of a course object, the value of attended appears as a list of name, number pairs, each a hypertext link to a view of the corresponding student. Any methods declared for a particular attribute appear as buttons against it on the screen: the method updates whatever other attributes need to be updated as a consequence of the local change, even if these are in other classes; and the button is 'greyed out' and rendered unclickable if the method's guard was not satisfied when the view was last refreshed.

Several generic features were added to minimise the number of clicks required for certain tasks, or otherwise optimise the interface to meet the needs of the administrative users. For any set-valued attribute, a 'browse' button allows the user to step through views of the target objects, moving backward or forwards at any point, and methods for that attribute can be applied to all of the targets at once. The user can create queries in an SQL-like syntax, using path expressions but without the need for joins, and associate these with classes or attributes: they then appear in the appropriate part of the view, ready to use. The user can also edit enumerations: like the queries, these are stored as data in the system. The result is a one-size fits-all interface, automatically generated, that met the needs of the 'super users'. Fig. 4 shows part of the view presented for a Subject object, that of Design Patterns.

However, it would not be appropriate to show all of this information to other classes of user; nor would it be appropriate to allow them to access to all of these methods. We needed a means of generating a view that took account of the relationship between the user and the data that they were looking at. For example, a student looking at a course object might see just the basic scheduling information and, if they had attended the course, the names of the attendees; but they should not be able to click on any of those names and move on to a view of that person's student record. Although the model included user data, the language did not present any convenient means of recording the access control information: this could be seen as quite orthogonal, or at least belonging to another layer of description.

Instead, a new language of user 'domains' or 'privileges' was introduced. Each type of user, or each user role, can be associated with a domain record that determined whether and how any particular class, attribute, or method would be presented to them. The domain language is used to express not only what specific users could do or see, but also what they would prefer to see in a given situation: for example, a lecturer is allowed to see information on every course that they have ever taught – and can obtain this from a query, or from their record – but a given object view might mention only those courses that they are currently teaching, are scheduled to teach, or for which they have yet to complete the marking.

This language was implemented using a separate compiler, which took the expanded model and the domains and generated code for the interface tier of the application. The predicates that describe the conditions under which a user may access a particular attribute or method are woven into the query. Should the query involve attributes that the current user does not have access to, the response will include empty slots or explicit 'undefined' values. Using the new language, we were quickly able to define new database views for each different kind of user.

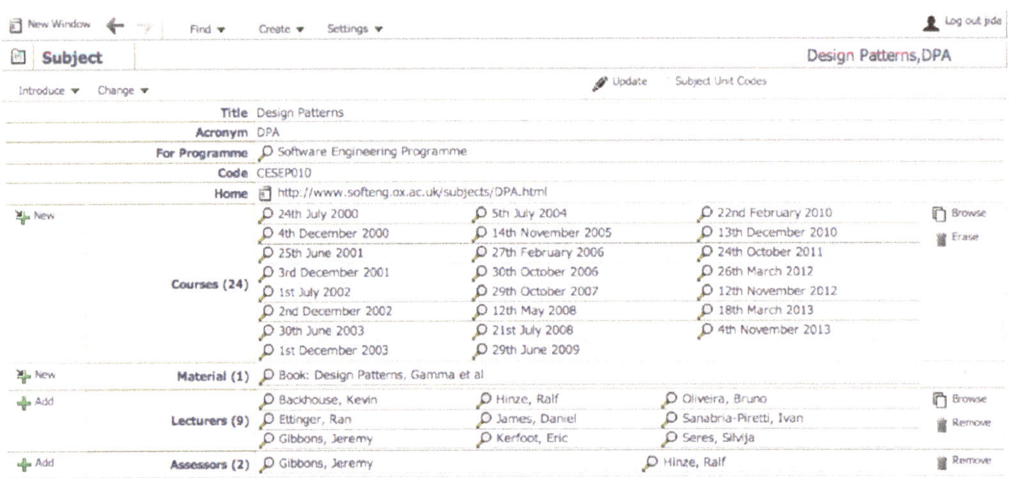

Figure. 4. A Subject object in SSTL.

***Lesson** 2*. Some aspects may be better described using a separate model in a different language.

The use of model-driven technology had an empowering effect upon the users: partly because those who could read the models had an opportunity to participate directly in the design process, something that would not be afforded them if the functionality were expressed in terms of thousands of lines of code; but mostly because of the reduction in 'cycle time'. Those who had previous experience of computerisation projects had expected the usual 'batch' mode of development, in which: meetings would be held to discuss requirements; some time later, a lengthy document would appear; much later, a system would appear, satisfying some of the requirements set out in the document; consultations with the users would be too infrequent and too abstract to result in any meaningful engagement.

In contrast, once a domain-specific framework has been established, a new version of the system takes only minutes to generate and deploy using model-driven techniques. Users can ask for a button to be moved, for a new attribute to be added to a class, or for a constraint to be modified, and the developers can make it happen there and then. What was once a 'batch' process is now interactive: users can be fully engaged in design, and can make a huge contribution to the quality of the final product. This is very much in the spirit of Agile methodology [10], with 'sprints' focused upon the development of the model rather than the implementation.

For SSTL, the extent of engagement was both beneficial and problematic: users would provide a constant stream of suggestions, based upon their own insights and priorities, and then expect them to be implemented; if these suggestions were not quickly incorporated into the working system, they would want to know the reason for the delay, or an explanation as to why someone else's suggestion has been adopted instead.

***Lesson** 3*. The easier it is to change the system, the more important change management becomes.

As changes in the implementation can now be characterised entirely in terms of changes to a concise, readable model, the emphasis here is upon change management outside the system: principally, of users and organisations. The information system is no longer acting as a brake upon organisational, structural, or process change, and some people will find it hard to keep up.

By this point, the system had several hundred users, and was handling over £1m a year in payments. It was proving particularly robust in operation, behaving precisely according to the specification, providing continuous service, and maintaining the integrity of the data. The data it held was becoming increasingly important: as the point where each transaction was enacted and recorded, the system soon became the authoritative source of information for student records, course registrations, and all of the associated invoices, payments, cancellations, and refunds.

This led to another problem, and a lesson that may be seen as a special case of Lesson 1. Whenever the model is changed, and a new version of the system is generated, we need to consider what to do with the data that has been accumulated in the existing version. The representation of data needs to change to reflect the new model, and to do this manually would be costly, error-prone, and awkward in terms of data governance—in many situations, it is recommended that developers should not have access to 'real' data from the live system. It could also act as a brake upon development, returning it to 'batch mode', and losing the engagement of the users.

Lesson 4. System evolution should be supported by automatic data migration.

The same issue would have been apparent to developers and users of Computer-Aided Software Engineering (CASE) tools during the 'maintenance' phase of the systems lifecycle [11], and a number of methods for automating aspects of data migration were proposed: see, for example [12]. The same ground is being covered again as part of the DevOps proposal for integrated development and operations in the context of enterprise computing, which is centred upon the automatic deployment of system updates [13].

In generating each new version of the system, the compiler will compare the new model with the model used to generate the previous version. If it can determine how the model has been transformed, it can apply a corresponding transformation to any data that has already been collected: the process of data migration will then be completely automatic. Code is generated to create objects, and to set attribute values, in the new version of the system; the data from the previous version is stored in a form that matches the new model; the integrity of the data is checked against the association constraints; finally, the code is then executed to create the new system and install the data.

Model transformations for which automatic migration is possible include: renaming or removing classes and attributes; adding new classes, sets, or enumerations; adding set-valued or optional attributes; adding primitive attributes. In some cases, the data from the previous version can be reloaded without modification. This will be the case when the only change to the model involves adding, removing or modifying methods or derived attributes. For more complex transformations, there are two approaches that may be employed: express the transformation as a sequence of minor transformations, each of which admits an automatic upgrade; or introduce a third, intermediate model and specify the upgrade transformation as a method in that model. In the development of SSTL, the second approach has been required once or twice a year.

As of March 2012, the current release of SSTL is V93.00. Each major release has been preceded by between 10 and 15 minor releases: Sørensen adopted the convention of incrementing the major version number whenever the new model would represent a 'significant' change in functionality, one that was clearly visible to the users. Discounting the early versions of the system, produced while the toolkit was still very much under development, there have been 1000 releases, minor and major, over the past 10 years.

In 2003, not long after the toolkit had stabilised, the system model comprised 2452 lines of sparse text, and the implementation was compiled from 232,216 lines of C, together with 691,301 lines of generated Java and Javascript. For the version of the system running in March 2012:

- the model has 9116 lines of sparse text, declaring 110 classes, with 452 primitive attributes ;
- it has 288 associations, 104 of which are mandatory, 103 are optional, and 81 are set-valued;
- there are 10 different domain models, with a total of 2948 lines of code;
- at the AMN stage, there are 1177 machines, in 1813 files, comprising 356,518 lines of code;
- the implementation is compiled from 423,607 lines of generated C code;
- there are 202,400 data objects in the live system.

This is a system that has been in continuous service since September 1999. The constant updating has allowed it to evolve to handle new degree structures, new financial procedures, and new examination regulations; it has also been steadily refined and enhanced to address new aspects of student support, including on-line applications. The cost of maintaining and developing the system in recent years has been approximately £30,000 per annum.

CASE STUDY: GSS

While the SSTL system remained in use within one department, the University as a whole moved forward with the procurement of an enterprise-level student management system, the Oracle Student System (OSS). Further development of any other information system within the University was discouraged while the Oracle system was implemented, which took a little under three years. The precise cost of that system is difficult to estimate, as more than 100 university staff were involved at some point during its implementation: however, the licencing costs alone were approximately £1m per annum.

However, as soon as the Oracle system went live, it was apparent that it would not provide support for operational aspects of student management: while its design made it possible to record and report student progress in a manner that was acceptable to the UK Higher Education Statistics Agency, there was no support for recording many of the data items needed to support processes at the department or student level. Worse still, it contained no notion of 'college', and colleges play a key role in student administration at the University of Oxford.

The schema for the underlying OSS package was, in most respects, unfit for purpose. The developers were forced to extend this in many different ways in an attempt to support at least some of the concepts and administrative processes of the University. Each extension involved a considerable amount of hand-written code in PL/SQL and Oracle Java. There was little or no modularisation, and the resulting system quickly became difficult to use and expensive to maintain. Nevertheless, a significant investment had been made, and a large development organisation – Business Services and Projects (BSP) – had been established within the University; OSS has remained the basis for 'official' student administration at Oxford, and will not be replaced until 2014.

SSTL held a wider range of data than OSS, and supported a wider range of processes; nevertheless, it was used for only four degree programmes, mostly within one department, and for only 3% of the graduate students at Oxford. Furthermore, its development was not hampered by an unsuitable core database schema. Thus a direct comparison between these two systems might be unfair. However, the expensive, inflexible nature of OSS led to the development of two other systems that provide the basis for a fairer comparison between the use of the model-driven Booster toolkit and conventional approaches to information systems development.

Every term in Oxford, a report is written upon the progress of each graduate student. Until 2006, these reports were written on paper forms, collected within departments and sent to central student administration, where three copies would be made; one copy would be returned to the supervisor, another would be sent to the director of graduate studies within the department, and a third would be sent to the student's college. Forms often went missing, and the delay between completion and review, which might be as long as three to four months, meant that the information on the form was often quite out of date. A decision was taken to computerise the process, but it was deemed too difficult to extend OSS to support it, and the cost of a new system was felt to be prohibitive.

Instead, it was proposed that the process should be implemented using email, with Word documents as attachments that would be completed and forwarded as necessary. A departmental representative objected to this, and suggested instead the Software Engineering group might be able to build a system in which the forms could be completed and processed online. Working with Sørensen, the present authors volunteered to do exactly this, on the understanding that – should the developed system be adopted – the cost of the developers' time would be paid for.

A completely new model was created for the system, as the information recorded about students, supervisors, and reports was different to that maintained in SSTL. The first version of the model was compiled on 16th August 2006, on the first day of development work. There were 10 further versions compiled that month, and a complete implementation – in the sense that it met all of the original requirements – was presented on the 1st of September. Modifications and extensions were proposed: in particular, with regard to a facility for students to provide their own report alongside that of the supervisor. There were another 9 versions compiled in September, with a further 4 before the end of the year. For the version of the system running in December 2008:

- the model had 32 classes and 180 primitive attributes;
- it had 92 associations, 17 of which were mandatory, 0 (zero) were optional, and 69 were set-valued;
- there were 8 different domain models, with a total of 3413 lines of code;
- at the AMN stage, there were 394 machines, in 597 files, comprising 104,613 lines of code;
- the implementation was compiled from 117,699 lines of generated C code;
- there were 58,888 data objects in the live system.

The system was announced to an initial cohort of 1132 students at 4.30 p.m. on the 20th February 2007. The first report was completed 60 s later. At 4.40 p.m. there were 100 students logged in to the system, each in the process of completing a report. There were 4 complaints from people unable to log in at the first attempt, due to overloading of the web server, but neither that nor the database component failed. On the 22nd of February, the team received an invitation to come to the University Offices for a celebratory drink. The system continued to perform as expected for the rest of the term, and for the following four terms, before being switched off in January 2009. Despite its initial success, the Booster-generated Graduate Supervision System (GSS) did not become a permanent part of the University's student systems provision.

It was argued that such a critical system should be supported by the BSP unit, rather than an academic department. However, the unit was staffed with business analysts, process analysts, project managers, programmers, and testers whose skills lay in the presentation or interpretation of informal documents, or in the manual production of code. The idea that one person could short-cut most of this by writing a precise model, pressing a button, and then showing a working system to the customers, was as unwelcome as it was incomprehensible. It was then argued that as the unit's development and maintenance efforts were based mainly upon Oracle technology, a non-standard, non-Oracle solution would unsupportable: at the very least, the cost of supporting it could not be reliably predicted.

***Lesson** 5*. Model-driven engineering is disruptive technology.

The arguments were won, and BSP were asked to construct a new version of GSS, using their own processes, and based on their own technology platforms, with the stipulation that it should be 'exactly like' the working Booster implementation. This development had to be treated as any other BSP project, with a preliminary requirements phase leading to a business case and project charter, prior to project initiation. Preliminary work on the new implementation began in January 2008, with a 32-page 'Requirements Definition' document issued on 26th June 2008. This included a tabular presentation of requirements, with a number of use-case diagrams and three 'swimlane' flow charts to illustrate 'as-is' processes.

The Oracle implementation went live in November 2008. The interface that it presented to supervisors lacked some of the features of the Booster version, these having been deemed too costly to implement. However, it contained enough functionality to be useable by supervisors and students alike. Behind the scenes, it was a different story: the 'super user' view of the data, the view needed by the student administration staff, was non-existent. In particular, there was no facility to search for a student report: such a facility had not been mentioned in the requirements definition, constructed over a six month period, neither had it appeared in the functional specification;

the administrative users felt that such a requirement should have been self-evident.

The Computer Science department was paid £30,000 for the initial development of GSS, and £45,000 for user support, maintenance, and data cleaning over the two years: the last of these was necessary due to erroneous or out-of-date information in the main OSS system. These payments were based upon the actual cost of developer time: principally, that of Sørensen and Edward Crichton. The total cost of developing the Oracle version was approximately £500,000: this included the time of the business and process analysts, and the project manager, as well as that of the programmers. A similar disparity appeared in the costs quoted for minor changes or enhancements; the search facility, deemed essential by the administrative staff, was costed at £8125. We estimated that the entire set of initial change requests, costed at over £100,000 and stated as requiring more than 200 person days of effort, could have been completed within two days on the Booster system, at a cost of £1200—we were charging slightly more than BSP for developer time. Even allowing a multiple of 10 for organisational costs and overheads, it seems reasonable to conclude that model-driven engineering can be more cost-effective.

Lesson 6. Model-driven engineering can reduce the cost of development by an order of magnitude.

In the case of GSS, this is a conservative estimate, given that the Booster GSS was a higher quality system, more complete in terms of intended functionality, more amenable to further development, and more reliable in operation. From February 2007 to December 2008, it required no 'downtime', whereas the Oracle version has had to be taken down repeatedly for maintenance. Furthermore, its replacement is already being actively discussed.

We are not aware of any other realistic development in which a model-driven approach can be compared directly with a conventional software process. It is unusual for an organisation to develop and deploy two versions of a business information system, over a period of two years, with precisely the same intended functionality; it is even more unusual that two such developments should proceed quite independently of one another. It should be no surprise then, that it is difficult to find reports of similar experiences, permitting a side-by-side comparison of conventional and model-driven approaches, in the literature.

It is worth observing that similar increases in productivity have been associated with the introduction of fourthgeneration languages (4GL), characterised by Martin [14] as 'non-procedural, high-level specification languages'. A comprehensive analysis of 4GL methods and tools [15] concluded that an 80% reduction in developer effort could be achieved. While the implementation of 4GLs in the 1980s and 1990s, involving direct compilation to low-level code, can be seen as quite different from the layered approach of model-driven engineering [16], we might reasonably expect that developer effort should be reduced in the same way.

CASE STUDY: TRUE COLOURS

While the SSTL and GSS systems offered several valuable lessons and insights, neither can serve as an example of realistic development for a third party: as student administration systems of one kind or another, their intended function should be entirely familiar to the academics involved. It could be argued that it was existing domain knowledge, rather than the ability to develop applications interactively, that allowed the developers to produce appropriate designs in a very short period of time. In practice, the academics did not 'own' the processes that were to be supported, these processes were subject to change, and a considerable amount of interaction with users was required; nevertheless, some doubt may remain.

To allay this, and to explore the agile, iterative approach to development that the combination of model-driven engineering and automatic data migration permits, we will consider a third system; True Colours. This is a patient- or moodmonitoring system designed to support clinical care, health research, and self-management for patients with long-term mental health conditions. The authors were asked to help develop a new version of the system, which was being used to monitor patients with bipolar disorder in Oxfordshire and Buckinghamshire. The original version had served the clinicians well, leading to two national awards, and was valued and appreciated by its users, but was in dire need of re-implementation.

To be specific, the first version of the system had been developed on an ad-hoc basis, over a number of years, without any of the supporting tools, infrastructure, or processes that one might expect. The data semantics had been destroyed: attributes had been re-purposed and invariants lost; status flags were no longer properly understood, and most of the system logic was embedded in a collection of C functions that were entirely undocumented. Further development was impossible: not only was the code base too fragile to update or refactor, but the single developer was spending all of their time updating the data in the system, providing user support, or producing weekly reports for clinicians and researchers through a combination of queries and manually-populated spreadsheets.

The new version would need to provide exactly the same service to the existing patients. For many, it had come to play a vital role in the management of their condition. It would need also to computerise many of the reporting and management activities currently performed by hand: for otherwise, the operation could not be 'scaled up' as planned. Furthermore, it would need to support a range of research projects and clinical studies: already running on the existing system, or planned for the near future. The authors met with the clinical staff responsible for the system, and with its current maintainer, and began work on an initial model. Most of the work was undertaken by Welch, with Davies contributing the design, and Crichton providing assistance with the implementation of the interface.

The first version of the model was created on 4th December 2009, with an initial collection of 7 classes, 46 attributes, and 50 methods, including all the basic functionality needed for user management. The second version was created four days later: we added 20 further classes, 122 attributes, and 100 methods, and modified three of the methods that had been defined in the first version. By this point, we had almost all of the classes that would be needed: 5 more would be added in January 2010, 1 in March, 1 in April, 2 in June, 1 in December 2010, 1 in May 2011, and 3 in June 2011. During this period, the only users of the system were the clinicians and nurses involved in the monitoring and research programmes: the system held no real patient data, and sent no messages.

The development proceeded slowly for two reasons: all of those involved were employed full-time on other tasks, and there was thus no budgeted development resource until Welch was seconded to the True Colours programme team in April 2011; also, the clinicians were keen to incorporate additional functionality in this new version, and the list of requirements was constantly being extended. Fig. 5 shows the rate of progress in terms of major versions developed, from December 2009 to June 2011. As the rate varied over the first six months, we will use the version number as the horizontal axis in a subsequent graph.

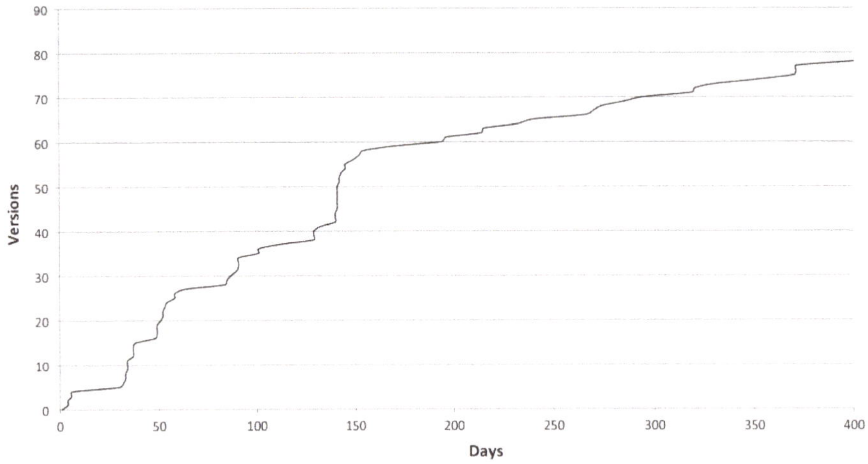

Figure. 5. True Colours versions over time.

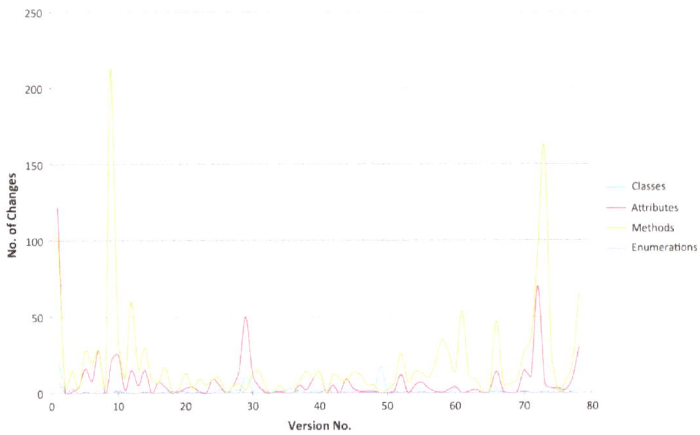

Figure. 6. True Colours changes.

As might be expected, the rate of change in the model remained fairly constant after the first ten or fifteen versions, until the point where the system was about to be exposed to a new user group: that of the patients. At this point, clinical and nursing staff became more focused upon the potential patient experience, and produced more requests for minor modifications to the design: for the most part, these would entail the addition of attributes to the model, and the modification of existing methods; the classes and enumerations would remain unchanged. Fig. 6 shows the number of changes made, for each kind of model component, against version number.

This shows a very different pattern of evolution from that experienced with SSTL and GSS. In those systems, it was quite common for attributes to be modified: a mandatory attribute might become optional, an optional attribute might become set-valued, and an association might become an association class, as the design was updated to capture some structure or process at a greater level of detail. Here, attributes are not changing: the modeller is either adding new classes, methods, and attributes, or they are modifying existing methods. We might conjecture that this is a result of the application being more tightly scoped: the data representation is relatively straightforward; the way in which the data should be accessed or updated is not.

The system was ready to go live in May 2011. At this point, however, we hit a stumbling block. In our model-driven approach, every data value must conform to the data model, and the interpretation of each attribute is easy to determine: at least, we can readily identify any constraints or relationships, and see also how the value of each attribute may be used or updated by each of the methods. To incorporate legacy data, we must first understand the model that it conforms to, and then define a mapping from this model into our own that preserves the data interpretation. If that model is encoded partly in the design of C functions and other scripts, and partly in the way that the system is used – in the surrounding data management processes – then the model may be difficult to establish.

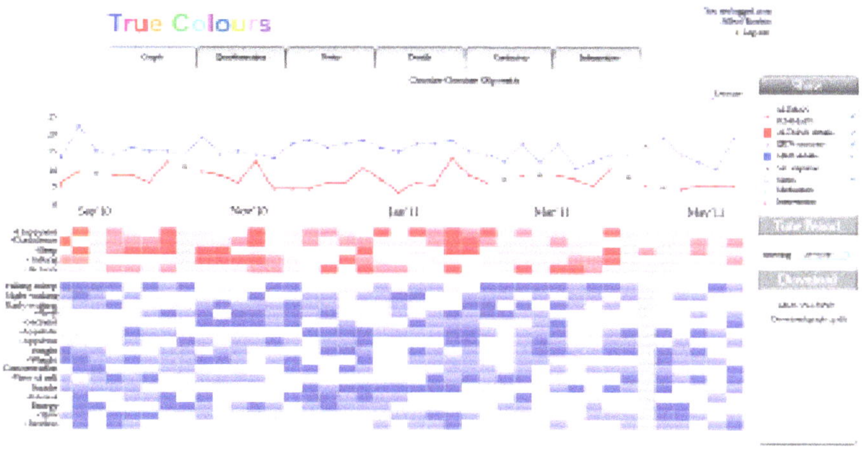

Figure. 7. Part of the participant interface in True Colours.

If the existing data is inconsistent, with attributes being used for different purposes at different times, and intended relationships not maintained, then several models may need to be established, and several mappings defined. Finally, where no values have been recorded for attributes now deemed to be mandatory, a simple mapping is not enough: appropriate values for these attributes will need to be provided. All of this was the case for the first version of True Colours, and some allowance had been made in the project schedule, but we were blissfully unaware of the full extent of the problem. The initial data migration was to be undertaken by the maintainers of the first version, who wanted to wait until the 'final' version of the new system was ready.

Although data models for the original system had been provided at the start of development, these remained untested. Had they been used as source code for the generation of tests or mappings, then the fact that much of the data in the system did not conform to them could have been detected much earlier in the process. The sensitivity of the information within the system be complicated matters – we could not be allowed access to any version containing 'real' data – but a model-driven approach to data migration would have allowed us to offer greater assistance. In the event, it took several months to define an appropriate set of mappings, and the new version of the system was not launched until September 2011.

***Lesson** 7.* A model-driven approach promotes a disciplined approach to data management, and typically leads to higher quality data.

The system has now been running for six months. Its primary function is to support patient monitoring and selfmanagement of bipolar disorder. Participants are assigned monitoring schedules in which they are prompted for a response at specified times: these could be at particular times of the day, on particular days of the week, at certain times of the month, or at random times within specified intervals. Schedules may be prescribed for days, weeks, months, or indefinite periods. Prompts are typically sent as text messages, inviting or reminding the participant to complete a questionnaire. The questionnaires are carefully designed and validated, and become familiar to the participants, who are given a credit card aide memoire of the questions. Responses may be provided by logging in to a website, by sending an email, or by texting a reply.

Each of the questionnaires has a corresponding summary calculation, yielding a single score that serves as a quick, positive or negative, indication of health. The scores are presented in a graph, providing a useful visualisation of how health has improved, or not, over time, alongside relevant clinical information: in particular, details of medication. The positive or negative responses to individual questions may be shown also: Fig. 7 shows this as a tiled visualisation, for a patient assigned the ALTMAN (Altman Self-Rating Mania Scale) and QIDS (Quick Inventory of Depressive Symptomology) questionnaires. The participant may use the system to make their own notes or diaries, allowing them to see how other factors may be affecting their condition: in the graph shown, this information appears at the top of the screen.

All of this information is automatically exported to the main patient records system used in the relevant part of the UK National Health Service (in this case, Oxford Health NHS Foundation Trust), and sent also to clinicians in encrypted PDF format. Negotiations are underway regarding wider adoption: for the monitoring of other conditions in Oxfordshire, and for the monitoring of bipolar patients across Scotland. Continuing development of the system is being funded by the National Institute for Health Research, who are supporting Welch's secondment to the project. To facilitate the proposed, wider adoption, significant additions needed to be made to the development toolkit: despite the proven reliability of the generated database, it was necessary to target an alternative implementation platform: specifically, Microsoft's SQLServer. For the servers to be running on Oxford Health Trust networks, they needed to be based upon approved technology.

Model transformations were defined to export the expanded Booster model to SQL, and to convert the method implementations into stored procedures. Further transformations were defined to generate API and interface components: it proved convenient for these to act upon the stored procedures, rather than the method descriptions, as some of the platform-dependent information required had already been incorporated. The new SQLServer-based implementation was significantly more demanding than the original platform in terms of processor time and memory, but offers significant advantages in terms of support and scalability; it is now running as the main True Colours system, and future developments of the Booster technology will include tools to target standard database platforms.

Lesson 8. In model-driven engineering, new tools are always needed.

DISCUSSION

The design of the Booster toolkit represents a particular approach to model-driven development: one that has been influenced by earlier work on formal methods. A Booster model is a partial description of intended functionality; to describe an operation, the developer writes down a predicate that explains what must be true if the operation is performed. Other properties may hold, and other changes may take place, but the compiler guarantees that this predicate – the conjunction of the pre- and post-conditions – will hold whenever the operation is made available.

The compiler may strengthen both the pre- and the post-condition in producing the implementation, using different levels of contextual information: the attribute(s) involved; the class in which the declaration appears; the content of the model as a whole; and heuristics selected by the developer or determined by the application domain. As an example, consider the way in which the compiler might treat the following method:

marry(true | partner = person_in)

Suppose that this is declared in the class Person, and that partner is an optional attribute of type Person—corresponding to a self-association with multiplicity 0..1 at each end.

Two conjuncts would be added to the postcondition:

person_in.partner = this

&

partner_0 /= person_in => partner_0.partner = {}

The first of these insists that the opposite link is established: the new partner, determined by input reference person_in, should have a partner link pointing to the current object this. The second insists that the old partner object partner_0 is updated to remove the corresponding link unless the old partner is also the new partner. The form of the antecedent ensures that the postcondition will be achieved even in the presence of aliasing: that is, even if two of the references point to the same object.

This is not enough to ensure that consistency is maintained, as the new partner object may itself have had an existing partner. The compiler adds a precondition to ensure that this is not the case:

person_in.partner = {}

As this appears in the precondition part of the declaration, the attribute name does not need to be decorated with _0. The compiler does not add any pre- or post-condition to address the possibility that person_in and this may refer to the same object, as this instance of aliasing does not prevent the postcondition from being achieved: as far as the association invariant is concerned, a person may be their own partner. If the model included also the constraint

partner /= this

as a class invariant, then the compiler would take account of this information, and extend the precondition of the operation with the constraint

person_in /= this

The completed method declarations are strong enough to guarantee that the semantic integrity of the data is maintained: in terms of the basic type and reference constraints, and also in terms of any business rules added as class or model invariants.

The resulting guard may be stronger than the weakest precondition needed for the implementation to achieve the original postcondition. The implementation will perform only those updates that the developer might reasonably anticipate. The guard is strengthened to ensure that the generated program is unavailable whenever the result might come as a surprise. The goal of the compiler is not to find some means of achieving the postcondition, but to implement the developer's intentions as far as these can be determined. The notion of what might prove surprising, and the means of determining intentions, is expressed through the design of the rules for extending the postcondition, and for translating postconditions into programs.

For example, the implementation of marry could have included a conditional assignment: to clear the partner attribute of any object originally linked to person_in. However, this object is not mentioned anywhere in the original method declaration; neither is there any path to it from the current object reference this. The developer may not have considered this object, and so the guard is strengthened to avoid the need for an assignment to one of its attributes. Subsequent developments of the Booster notation, and of the compiler, have refined this approach considerably, but the essential principle remains.

Principle. A generated method implementation should behave exactly as intended. If the intended effect is unclear, the method should be unavailable.

In a Booster implementation, there should be no surprises resulting from the effects of a method execution. Any surprise should result from a method being unavailable: because the guard is stronger than the developer had expected, or because some combination of attribute values and inputs has been presented that the developer did not anticipate. To check that no unexpected consequences will appear at run-time, we may inspect the generated method guards, present a formal proof that they will be satisfied, or construct an appropriate suite of tests to check that the system will allow the methods to be executed.

The development of an individual method can proceed as follows. We write a postcondition describing the intended effect, and the compiler generates a guard for the corresponding program. If the guard is too weak, we add an appropriate constraint to the precondition. If the guard is too strong, we modify the existing pre- or postcondition, add a conjunct explaining the intended effect upon some other attribute or object, add or remove a reference from the change list, weaken an invariant, or make a change to the structure of the model, and run the compiler again until a satisfactory solution is obtained.

The unique contribution of the Booster technology lies in the way that it facilitates the object-oriented design of information systems through declarative description of functionality, integrity constraints, and business rules. The objectoriented approach allows the description of an operation in the context of a class, where the attributes involved will be declared. In any non-trivial information system, the values of those attributes are related to the values of other attributes elsewhere in the system: there will be complex model, class, or association invariants to be maintained.

This is expected and acknowledged in many accounts of object-oriented design. For example, the opposite property for "mutually-constrained attributes" is part of the core UML language definition; the principal reference texts for OCL, including that for OCL in MDA [17], include many examples of constraints upon attributes of associated classes; and the class-responsibility-collaboration approach developed by Beck and Cunningham [18] insists that "objects do not exist in isolation" [19]. We have argued elsewhere [20] that classes are not necessarily components in the context of model-driven development: in particular, that they may not be an appropriate unit of composition for behavioural information.

The same is true of other modular approaches to imperative programming. It is a simple matter to place partial descriptions of functions that perform different actions into separate modules, files, or classes. To complete these descriptions – to know what other actions should be taken, or when that action should not be performed, in order to maintain consistency between different data items – we may need to look beyond the boundary of the current module. The Booster compiler will consider all of the constraint information in the model in determining how each method specification is translated; only by doing this is it able to ensure that the implementation will preserve every data constraint.

The current data migration technology is a simple generalisation of this approach: the changes to the model provide a specification for data transformation; a suitable method is generated, and a sufficient precondition is calculated and used as a guard. A migration method will be unavailable unless the current data, after transformation, would satisfy the constraints of the new model. Given that data migration may involve a costly interruption to service, it should be no surprise that similar methods [12] have been proposed to calculate the effect of the proposed mappings in advance, to ensure that all of the data constraints in the new system will be satisfied, before the migration process starts.

The overall impact of the Booster technology – the order of magnitude reduction in cost, the increase in software quality and maintainability – is the cumulative effect of taking a model-driven approach to every aspect of development and maintenance. There are many different contributions, including: the automatic implementation of default methods, the way in which types are inferred for variables in methods and invariants, the way in which context is inferred and qualification is unnecessary. The existence of a precise, complete model not only makes each individual contribution possible, but also ensures that they work together effectively in combination.

None of these other contributions are unique. Over the past 10 years we have seen how technologies such as Microsoft's .NET have delivered similar improvements in productivity. In January 2009, we conducted a parallel development of the Pet Store exemplar originally proposed for Java developers, comparing Booster against the current versions of .NET. The results are shown in Fig. 8, as an extension of Microsoft's original graph comparing .NET and Java developments of this application. This is a 'toy' example, with only a small number of attributes and associations, but it serves to make the point that the other, incremental contributions are also being made elsewhere, to the same effect.

Given that the development of the MDA was closely linked to the metamodelling hierarchy that underpins the Unified Modelling Language (UML), one might expect that the Booster approach could have been based upon the UML notation, making use of that notation's Object Constraint Language (OCL) instead of the formal AMN. OCL can be used to formalise preconditions, postconditions, and invariants in object models, and we have experimented extensively with its use – see, for example, [21] – in the hope of making our approach more accessible to a wider audience. However, we found two significant difficulties in using OCL:

- The notation did not support the compositional approach to method definitions afforded by the method combinators. In describing operations, we found it essential to include method references within postconditions. The ability to call methods in combination is an essential aspect of object-oriented design.
- The orientation of the notation was awkward: we wanted to describe properties of attributes in a range of different scopes; the expressions required were complex, unwieldy, and not amenable to factorisation.

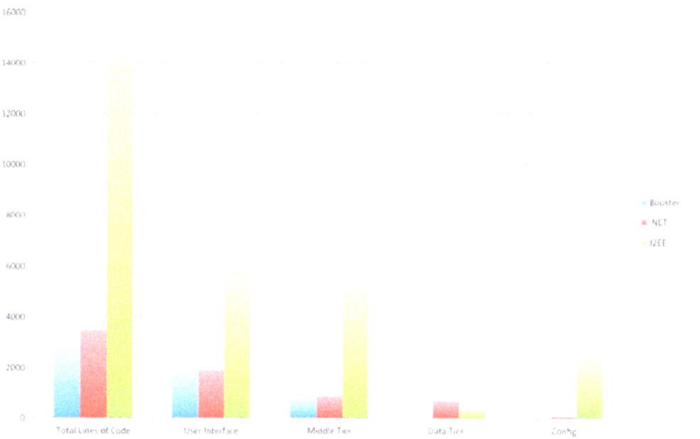

Figure. 8. The pet store in Booster.

Closer in spirit, if not in execution, is the approach advocated by [22], in which relational databases and Java web applications are generated from UML diagrams. A key difference is that functionality is described by use cases and sequence diagrams, and that there is no support for compositional design and analysis of the kind discussed here.

Some progress is being made in terms of Executable UML [23]. Based on work by Schlaer and Mellor [24], it adopts a correct-by-construction approach in which dynamic features are implemented by weaving a number of domain models. The associated development methods are based on agility and rapid delivery of working software. As with Booster, the initial model may be treated as a faithful representation of the generated system, and analysed using formal techniques: for example Turner et al. [25] shows how CSP||B models may be generated and used for analysis. We may expect further work in this area. A new OMG standard has recently been published for Foundational UML (fUML) [26]. This incorporates an action language named Alf, an Action Language for fUML, which provides Java-like functionality for modifying attributes, associations, creating and destroying objects.

George et al. [27] present a model-driven approach by which Object-Z specifications may be converted into contracts in an object-oriented implementation language: for example, as Java assertions. Tools with a sound formal basis such as JML [28] and Spec# [29] allow effective verification based upon pre- and postconditions. Dantas et al. [30] show how the B-method can be extended to support a new low-level language, at the level of abstraction of an assembly language. This helps bridge the gap between the formal language and programming constructs, giving a better guarantee of program correctness. Similarly, Edmunds and Butler [31] introduces an intermediate specification language – Object-oriented, Concurrent B (OCB) – that sits between Event-B and object-oriented implementations. This allows the specification of nonatomic operations, which may be interleaved using the; operator, and mappings are defined from OCB to Event-B, and from OCB to Java.

The experience of applying the toolkit to the development of these and other information systems, and a programme of research conducted in parallel, has informed the development of a new version of the technology, Booster 2. The most important changes are:

- The model transformations are now performed using the Stratego [32] and Spoofax technologies [33], instead of the rewrite engine of the B toolkit.
- The compilation process is targeted at standard database platforms, rather than the in-memory, bespoke database generated using the B toolkit libraries.
- The modelling language is now more expressive, and also more concise: in particular, the change list is no longer required, and the pre- and postconditions are written together as a single predicate.

At the same time, we are exploring how the model creation and editing process – the source of model changes that may later on be echoed by data migrations – can be better supported within widely-used development frameworks: see [34]. A variety of tools and platforms have been developed for identifying and acting upon model changes. Although the primary focus of this development has been model management and version control, the 'model patches' produced by tools such as EMF Compare [35] can serve as outline specifications for data transformation.

Automatic support for data migration is an essential ingredient in our emerging development methodology. Not only are we able to implement design changes reliably and efficiently, but we are also able to determine in advance whether or not the migrated data would meet the constraints of the new model. This helps us to identify and document any subtle changes in meaning or interpretation, and facilitates a deeper discussion of intentions with stakeholders or customers. In this, as in every other aspect of model development, we are critically dependent upon access to appropriate domain expertise.

In two of the three example developments reported here, there were examples of changes to the model being formulated, agreed, and deployed in the working system before it became apparent that the change was based upon some misapprehension or misunderstanding on the part of an individual customer representative. In some cases, this arose from the person having only a limited view of the processes that the system was intended to support. In others, it reflected a lack of strategic knowledge: the person had a complete understanding of existing processes, but was not aware that a decision had been taken to change the way that things were done.

To some extent, this is only to be expected, and we might comfort ourselves with the thought that a model-driven approach makes it easier to discover and reverse this kind of mistake. However, we observed also that even where sufficient domain expertise was available, the fact that changes were easily implemented meant that customers could put less effort into the consideration, articulation, and prioritisation of requirements. This underlines the importance of an appropriate methodology in making the most effective use of domain expertise and modelling effort.

The development of such a methodology, and the integration of our approach with other programming technologies, modelling tools, and development frameworks, remains the subject of future research. In the meantime, we hope that our success in applying model-driven techniques in this domain might inspire others to adopt a similar approach, and thus make a positive contribution to the quality, reliability, and sustainability of enterprise-level information systems.

ACKNOWLEDGEMENTS

We are grateful to Dave Neilson and Charles Crichton for their contributions to the work reported here. We are grateful also to our colleagues at the University of Oxford, and at Oxford Health NHS Foundation Trust, for trusting us to provide information systems that they could rely upon – that they needed to rely upon – using model-driven technology. We would like to acknowledge the support of the UK Medical Research Council (grant number G0300648) and Microsoft Research. We would like to dedicate this paper to the memory of Ib Holm Sørensen (1949–2012), without whom none of this would have happened.

REFERENCES

1. A. Kleppe, J. Warmer, W. Bast, MDA Explained, The Model Driven Architecture: Practice and Promise, Addison-Wesley, 2003.
2. D.S. Frankel, Model Driven Architecture, Wiley, 2003.
3. J. Woodcock, J. Davies, Using Z, Prentice Hall, 1996, www.usingz.com.
4. J.-R. Abrial, The B-book: Assigning Programs to Meanings, Cambridge University Press, 1996.
5. I. Hayes, Specification Case Studies, Prentice Hall, 1992.
6. G. Smith, The Object-Z Specification Language, Kluwer, 2000.
7. J. Davies, C. Crichton, E. Crichton, D. Neilson, I.H. Sørensen, Formality, evolution, and model-driven

software engineering, in: Proceedings of SBMF 2004, in: Electronic Notes in Computer Science, Elsevier, 2005.

8. C.C. Morgan, Programming from Specifications, second edition, Prentice Hall, 1998.
9. P. Coad, J. Nicola, Object-Oriented Programming, Prentice Hall, 1993.
10. R.C. Martin, Agile Software Development: Principles, Patterns, and Practices, Prentice Hall PTR, 2003.
11. E.J. Chikofsky, B.L. Rubenstein, Case: reliability engineering for information systems, IEEE Software 5 (2) (1988) 11–16.
12. J. Henrard, J.-M. Hick, P. Thiran, J.-L. Hainaut, Strategies for data reengineering, in: Working Conference on Reverse Engineering 2002, IEEE Computer Society Press, 2002, pp. 211–220.
13. M. Loukides, What is DevOps?, O'Reilly Media, 2012.
14. J. Martin, Application Development Without Programmers, Prentice-Hall, 1981.
15. R. Klepper, D. Bock, Third and fourth generation language productivity differences, Communications of the ACM 38 (9) (1995) 69–79.
16. j.O. Aagedal, J. Bezivin, P.F. Linington, Model-Driven development (WMDD 2004), in: J. Malenfant, B.M. Ostvold (Eds.), Object-Oriented Technology. ECOOP 2004 Workshop Reader, in: Lecture Notes in Computer Science, vol. 3344, Springer, 2005, pp. 148–157.
17. J. Warmer, A. Kleppe, The Object Constraint Language: Getting Your Models Ready for MDA, second edition, Addison Wesley, 2003.
18. K. Beck, W. Cunningham, A laboratory for teaching object oriented thinking, SIGPLAN Notices, 24, 10. http://dx.doi.org/10.1145/74878.74879.
19. R. Wirfs-Brock, Responsibility-driven design, The Smalltalk Report (1991).
20. J. Davies, J. Gibbons, D. Milward, J. Welch, Compositionality and refinement in model-driven engineering, in: R. Gheyi, D.A. Naumann (Eds.), SBMF, in: Lecture Notes in Computer Science, vol. 7498, Springer, 2012, pp. 99–114.
21. J. Davies, J. Welch, A. Cavarra, E. Crichton, On the generation of object databases using Booster, in: Proceedings of the 11th IEEE Conference on the Engineering of Complex Computer Systems (ICECCS 2006), IEEE Computer Society (2006). http://dx.doi.org/10.1109/ICECCS.2006.1690374.
22. A.G. Cuesta, J.C. Granja, R.V. O'Connor, A model driven architecture approach to web development, in: J. Filipe, B. Shishkov, M. Helfert, L.A. Maciaszek (Eds.), Software and Data Technologies, in: Communications in Computer and Information Science, vol. 22, Springer Berlin Heidelberg, 2009, pp. 101–113.
23. S.J. Mellor, M. Balcer, Executable UML: A Foundation for Model-Driven Architectures, Addison-Wesley Longman Publishing Co., Inc, Boston, MA, USA, 2002.
24. S.J. Mellor, Real-time development with the Shlaer-Mellor method, in: TOOLS 1997: 23rd International Conference on Technology of Object-Oriented Languages and Systems, July 28–August 1, 1997, Santa Barbara, CA, USA, IEEE Computer Society, 1997, p. 372. http://dx.doi.org/http://doi.ieeecomputersociety.org/10.1109/TOOLS.1997.10009.
25. E. Turner, H. Treharne, S. Schneider, N. Evans, Automatic generation of CSP || B skeletons from xUML models, in: J. Fitzgerald, A. Haxthausen, H. Yenigun (Eds.), Theoretical Aspects of Computing (ICTAC 2008), in: Lecture Notes in Computer Science, vol. 5160, Springer, Berlin, Heidelberg, 2008, pp. 364–379.
26. Object Management Group, Semantics of a foundational subset for executable UML models (FUML) version 1.0 – beta 1, Tech. Rep. ptc/2008-11-03 (2008).
27. N.S. George, C. Zhang, A. Radimsky, FOZCIL: a framework for converting formal specifications in Object-Z to design contracts in OO programming languages, in: Information Reuse and Integration (IRI) 2011, 2011, pp. 218 –221.
28. An overview of JML tools and applications, Eighth International Workshop on Formal Methods for Industrial Critical Systems (FMICS'03), in: ENTCS, vol. 80, Elsevier, 2003.
29. M. Barnett, K. Leino, W. Schulte, The spec# programming system: an overview, in: G. Barthe, L. Burdy, M. Huisman, J.-L. Lanet, T. Muntean (Eds.), Construction and Analysis of Safe, Secure, and Interoperable Smart Devices, in: Lecture Notes in Computer Science, vol. 3362, Springer, Berlin/Heidelberg, 2005, pp. 49–69.
30. B. Dantas, D. Déharbe, S. Galvao, A.M. Moreira, V.M. Júnior, Verified compilation and the b method: a proposal and a first appraisal, in: Proceedings of the Eleventh Brazilian Symposium on Formal Methods (SBMF 2008), Electronic Notes in Theoretical Computer Science 240 (0) (2009) 79–96. http://dx.doi.org/10.1016/j.entcs.2009.05.046.
31. A. Edmunds, M. Butler, Linking Event-B and concurrent object-oriented programs, in: Refine 2008: International Refinement Workshop, 2008.
32. M. Bravenboer, K.T. Kalleberg, R. Vermaas, E. Visser, Stratego/XT 0.17: A language and toolset for program transformation, Science of Computer Programming 72 (1-2) (2008) 52–70.
33. L.C. Kats, E. Visser, The spoofax language workbench: rules for declarative specification of languages and IDEs, in: Proceedings of the ACM international conference on Object oriented programming systems languages and applications, OOPSLA'10, ACM, New York, NY, USA, 2010, pp. 444–463. http://dx.doi.org/http://doi.acm.org/10.1145/1869459.1869497.
34. M.A. Aboulsamh, J. Davies, A formal modeling approach to information systems evolution and data migration, in: T.A. Halpin, S. Nurcan, J. Krogstie, P. Soffer, E. Proper, R. Schmidt, I. Bider (Eds.), BMMDS/EMMSAD, in: Lecture Notes in Business Information Processing, vol. 81, Springer, 2011, pp. 383–397.
35. Eclipse, EMF Compare Project, www.eclipse.org/emf/compare (accessed October 2012).

CHAPTER 11

XML FILES TYPES AND THEIR DIFFERENCES AND DENOMINATORS WITH PLAIN TXT FILE

Zahir AlHashami

Research Center, 420-Oman-Muscat

ABSTRACT

Easy and simplicity of transformation, sharing and storing files among programs, platforms and machines. From these formats are XML formats and plain and flat TXT file formats. Complex formats of the files will cause difficulty in treating with, for instance files transformation while the simple files could treat with them with insurance of no need for compatibility requirements and no virus effect. The method of this research are content size and comparison between XML file format and TXT flat file. The XML file formats are very simple to treat in structure in such as transforming and in converting among various applications. This study got that XMl files are structured programmed content and took some Kilobytes size, such as XML Spreadsheets formats which are taken for a text and a picture content just 3KB, whilst in XML PowerPoint Presentation took 97KB. TXT plain txt file is simpler than XML file which are both text based content because that, the same content after converting to TXT format took just 1KB. The plain text file format is fairly not organized and unstructured text-based content except the head section TXT file.

INTRODUCTION

XML stands for an Extensible Markup Language (XML) file format used to create, share and transform information formats and share both the format and the data on the World Wide Web (internet) by use standard ASCII text.

Usage and the aims of XML are to simplify, generalize the data across the internet. It is a textual data with strong support by coding the data for different human languages. It widely used for the representation of data such as those used in web services.

XML is similar to Hypertext Markup language (HTML). Both XML and HTML contain markup symbols to describe the contents of a page or file.

Citation: Zahir AlHashami, XML Files Types and Their Differences and Denominators with Plain TXT File, doi:10.4172/2376-130X.1000130

The identification of XML based on: Norman Walsh (1998), said: that, it is a markup language for documents containing structured information. This structured information contains the words and the pictures. In the content of XML document the section heading has a different meaning from content in a footnote, which means something different than content in a figure caption or content in a database table. Also he said the all documents have some structure [1].

XML Files Sample

```
<?xml version="1.0" encoding="UTF-8"?>
<note>
<to>Tovee</to>
<from>Jani</from>
<heading>Reminder</heading>
```

<body> Don't forget me this weekend!</body>

</note>

XML File Formats Transformation with Office Programs

In the 1990s and after advent of XML, based on Frank Rice (2006), corporation customers realize the valuable of open formats files and basic standardization in computer-regard products and applications.

As example in Microsoft Corporation the IT specialists get benefit from the files formats are possible open with XML format, because of two reasons: first the capacity and files size and second is the easily to read by many applications, and many operating system as well as internet browsers.

Historically transformation transition begun with developers to see the need to transform from binary files format to XML format. Office programs are able to do many functions but can face such challenges included transporting and easily moving data between Operating Systems and various applications.

Frank Rice also mentioned that, MS 2007 in Microsoft Corporation has the ability to transform such as: Doc, Ppt and Xls to XML files format. The new file format called Office Open XML formats. With Open office XML format can be accessed and supported with any application, Frank Rice [2].

TXT File Format

TXT file identification is a file extension for a text file, used by a variety of text editors like Note. Text is a human-readable sequence of the characters and the words they form that can be encoded into computer-readable format. There is no standard definition if a text file, though there are several common formats, including ASCCII and ANSI.

According to Varun Agarwal (2008), Flat file is generally a delimited file; with some specific delimiter such as semi-colon, comma. It shell may specify the delimiter in map properties tab in Syndicator. Whereas in case of XML file should need to specify the schema which will define the structure of XML file [3].

TXT Files Content Sample

===Plugin Name ===

Contributors: (this should be a list of wordpress.org user ID's)

Donate link: http//example.com

Tags: comments, spam

Requires at least: 3.0.1

Tested up to: 3.4

Stable tag: 4.3

License: GPL v2 or later

License URL: http://www.gnu.org/license/gpl-2.0.html

Here is a short description of the plugin. This should be no more than 150 characters. No markup here.

== Description ==

This is the long description. No limit and can use Markdown (as well as in the following sections).

For backward compatibility, if this section is missing, the full length of the short description will be used, and markdown parsed.

A few notes about the sections above:

"Contributors" is a comma separated list of wp.org/wp-plugin.org username

"Tags" is a comma separated list of tags that apply to the plugin

"Requires at least is the lowest version that the plugin will work on

"Tested up to" is the highest version that you've successfully used to test the plugin*. Not that it might work on higher version… this just the highest one you've verified.

Stable tag should indicate the subversion "tag" of the latest stable version, or "trunk," if you use /trunk/ for stable.

Application Case of XML Files Use

Analyzing data in the DrugBank aspect is included detailed drugs like chemical and pharmacological compounds by using XML documents. Each drug described with than 150 data fields. There is an application name KNIME, the XML files loaded into it. The XML processing nodes extract several information from XML file like compound name and compound description by using XPath node. The row filter is responsible to extract the information from approved drugs. In the Meta node in the XML file may extract further textual features like the organisms and manufacturer, which are including other free text fields like description and pharmacology. These are analyzed in text mining part of the XML document, Koetter, 2012 [4].

RESULTS

Content Size

The XML files of Word document, Excel book and Power Point presentation contain the same content, which is text identification of a computer and a figure of the computer as appear in the below Figure 1.

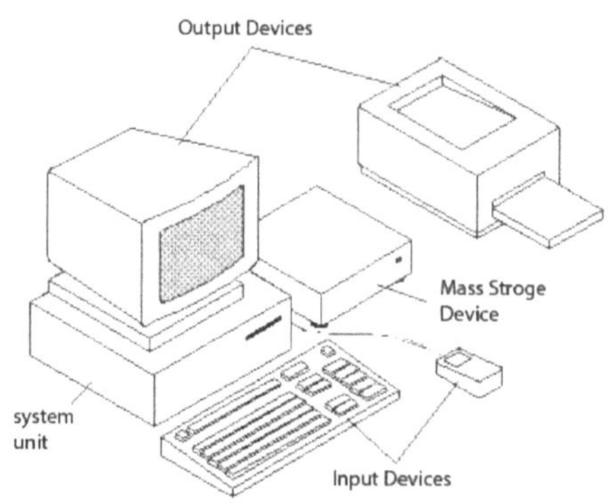

Figure 1: A computer generally means programmable machine. The two principal characteristics of a computer are: it responds to a specific set of instructions in a well-defined manner and it can execute a prerecorded list of instructions (a program).

Converting the Office programs to XML files appeared various sizes like in the Table 1.

Table 1: Converting the Office programs to XML files appeared various sizes like in this table

XML Spreadsheet	XML word document	XML Power point presentation
3KB	57KB	97KB

Size of XML Word Document and TXT Plain Text File

The same content in XML word and TXT plain text size will be like the Table 2.

Table 2: The same content in XML word and TXT plain text size will be like the table below

TXT file	XML word document
1KB	57KB

TXT and Word XML Document

TXT file:When convert and open XML word document with same content which is containing text and one picture, all the file appears just text file like the below Figure 2.

Figure 2: Conversion of open XML word document.

XML Word Document

When converting the same file that containing text and one picture as XML file, the document will appear in structured and organized XML file like the below Figure 3.

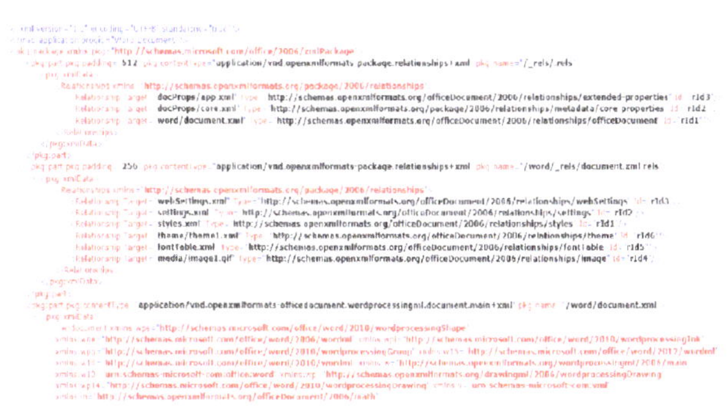

Figure 3: Structured and organized XML file.

XML document file in note:

Opening XML file document by the Note will change the structure of organized and hierarchical structure of the XML file and appear like flat TXT file Figure 4.

Figure 4: XML file and appear like flat TXT file.

DISCUSSION

XML files used for analyzing data in the DrugBank aspect which is included XML data with XML formats. These uses are like, medicine description, names of medicine and chemical and pharmacological compounds by using XML documents [4].

In the Stackoverflow.com website, Pascal Martin (2015) in his article titled: «XML file and text file» said that, XML file is structured document and standard validation consists of DTD, schema and standardized way to parsing the structure of XML. In the other hand text file is easier to write which is no need to respect and write any structured tag and that text file not necessary to have a well-defined structure [5].

Also Jacek Konieczny (2015) about the same article in Stackoverflow.com commented that the XML file is a text file, but with a well-structured framework which provides ways to respect complicated data structures.

There are attributes that XML file has like verbosity and higher processing costs. The XML file is good choice when use different applications or systems to being data exchanged, while these data is preferred to be well-structured [6].

Coombs, James and Allen (1987), said that files which contain markup or other meta-data can consider them as flat or plain text while remain text readable [6].

The flat or the plain text file is use to be recovered and to be saved for viruses trouble and loss of data. To save it in an immune disk in computer or any media and save it in case of incompatibility. According to Unicode Standard that the plain text is a pure sequence of character codes. Styled text, also known as rich text, is any text representation contains plain text with font size, color and hyperlink [7].

Vangie Beal (2015), also said about text (TXT) file that it is in each byte of the text represents one character based on ASCII Standard (American Standard Code for Information Interchange) code. He mentioned that the files that are formatted with word processor to save the formats must be as binary file to be stored.

The ASCII files are textual information or TXT data. The plain text files are supported by many applications on many machines. Because the TXT file does not include any commands in its content.

Similarity Factors between TXT File and XML

File

It can be found that there are three factors similar in XML file and TXT:

XML file is organized and neat document while txt file is fairly organized file, somewhat TXT file neat because some statement in the plain text file and its content are organized with some commands like XML an organized textual file.

XML and TXT files are easy storing and transporting among applications and platforms, both XML and TXT files are easily to transport between platform to another platform, as well as easy storing in any store device.

The XML files is organized and in neat structure and commands while the flat plain text file is not whole organized. When open XML file with Note that appears as unorganized structure like TXT file. In the meanwhile a plain text file appears not organized and not neat except the head statement.

In 2015, Paul Murrell has spoken about: "Plain Text" there is one way that is the easiest way to save data and information, which is save it as plain text file, which everything in the TXT file are stored as plain text format. He mentioned that text file format is denominator to store many file formats in many applications. He said also in his article that based on database that a data are stored as simple or plain text even the numbers saved in the flat file as plain text [8].

The file that contains computer identification text and figure of the computer, when transform it to the Word XML file, Excel XML file and Power point XML file can be found that the size differ from each one which Excel file took the lowest size 3KB, while Power point file has taken 97 KB as near multimedia file bigger than other office programs.

In contrast Word XML file compared with text (TXT) file with the same text and same figure of computer can be seen the file in the TXT taken 1 KB size. 1KB text file indicates that it is too easy and too simple file which gives advantage for the plain TXT file to storing and to transporting easily. The XML Word file taken 57KB which is also bigger much than TXT file. This size of TXT file is too small with same file text and pictures.

CONCLUSION

XML file is easy and simple file could by it store many files and transport them through applications and through platforms. From these programs are Office programs. Many application can open by XML file which is advantage for XML file meanwhile the TXT file is just unstructured plain text file.

The same file which contains text and pictures can pen through many applications like office programs (Word, Excel and Power Point). This file took 3 KB open as Excel file when opening as XML file which the lowest file among Office programs whilst the bigger application was Power point took 97KB size of the file, which explain the Power Point application as Multimedia application. The XML file is structured and organizes file and commands and in contrast flat and plaintext file is not fairly organized and not fairly structured. That appear when comparing and opening XML file by the Notepad it appeared without any neat and structured document. XML file is simple and does not take a huge amount of data but plain text file is simpler and more ease than XML.

Both files XML and TXT files text based lines and both can store and transport easily as well as XML files are in structured and commands document. The TXT is not exactly organized except header of TXT plain text file is structured and some commands appear in neat shape.

Paul Murrell has defined from plain text file attributes that, every things saved as TXT with flat text even numbers and any other values.

Like what appear in case of opening the text and figure as XML Spreadsheet, it taken just 3KB, 75 KB opened as XML Word document and taken also just 1KB text (TXT) file.

REFERENCES

1. Norman W (1998) A Technical Introduction to XML.
2. Frank R (2006) Introducing the Office (2007) Open XML File Formats.
3. Varun A (2008) Difference between XML & Flat files.
4. Koetter T (2012) DrugBank.
5. Pascal M, Jacek K (2015) XML file and text file.
6. James CH, Renear AH, DeRose SJ (1987) Plain text.
7. Vangie B (2015) ASCII file-Plain Text.
8. Paul M (2015) Plain text files-Flat Files.

CHAPTER 12

REVERSIBLE SESSION-BASED PI-CALCULUS

Francesco Tiezzi[a], Nobuko Yoshida[b]

[a]University of Camerino, Italy

[b]Imperial College London, UK

ABSTRACT

In this work, we incorporate reversibility into structured communication-based programming, to allow parties of a session to automatically undo, in a rollback fashion, the effect of previously executed interactions. This permits to take different computation paths along the same session, as well as to revert the whole session and start a new one. Our aim is to define a theoretical basis for examining the interplay in concurrent systems between reversible computation and session-based interaction. We thus propose ReSπ a session-based variant of π-calculus using memory devices to keep track of the computation history of sessions in order to reverse it. We show how a session type discipline of π-calculus is extended to ReSπ, and illustrate its practical advantages for static verification of safe composition in communication-centric distributed software performing reversible computations. We also show how a fully reversible characterisation of the calculus extends to committable sessions, where computation can go forward and backward until the session is committed by means of a specific irreversible action.

INTRODUCTION

In the field of programming languages, reversible computing aims at providing a computational model that, besides the standard forward executions, also permits backward execution steps to undo the effect of previously performed forward computations. Despite being a subject of study for many years, reversible computing is recently experiencing a rise in popularity. This is mainly due to the fact that reversibility is a key ingredient in different application domains. In particular, for what specifically concerns our interest, many researchers have put forward exploiting this paradigm in the design of reliable concurrent systems. In fact, it permits us to understand existing patterns for programming reliable systems (e.g., compensations, checkpointing, transactions) and, possibly, to develop new ones.

A promising line of research on this topic advocates reversible variants of well-established process calculi, such as CCS [2] and π-calculus [3], as formalisms for studying reversibility mechanisms in concurrent systems. By pursing this line of research, in this work we incorporate reversibility into a variant of π-calculus equipped with session primitives supporting communication-based programming. A (binary) session consists in a series of reciprocal interactions between two parties, possibly with branching and recursion. Interactions on a session are performed via a dedicated private channel, which is generated when initiating the session. Session primitives come together with a session type discipline offering a simple checking framework to statically guarantee the correctness of communication patterns. This prevents programs from interacting according to incompatible patterns.

Citation: Francesco Tiezzi, Nobuko Yoshida, Reversibility in Higher-Order Pi, doi:10.1016/j.jlamp.2015.03.004

Practically, combining reversibility and sessions paves the way for the development of session-based communication-centric distributed software intrinsically capable of performing reversible computations. In this way, without further coding effort by the application programmer, the interaction among session parties is relaxed so that, e.g., the computation can automatically go back, thus allowing to take different paths when the current one is not satisfactory. As an application example, used in this paper for illustrating our approach, we consider a simple scenario involving a client and multiple providers offering the same service (e.g., on-demand video streaming). The client connects to a provider to request a given service (specifying, e.g., title of a movie, video quality, etc.). The provider replies with a quote determined according to the requested quality of service and to the servers status (current load, available bandwidth, etc.). Then, the client can either accept, negotiate or reject the quote; in the first two cases, the interaction between the two parties shall continue. If a problem occurs during the interaction between the client and the provider for finalising the service agreement, the computation can be automatically reverted. This allows the client to partially undo the current session, in order to take a different computation path along the same session, or even start a new session with (possibly) another provider.

The proposed reversible session-based calculus, called ReSπ (Reversible Session-based π-calculus), relies on memories to store information about interactions and their effects on the system, which otherwise would be lost during forward computations. This data is used to enable backward computations that revert the effects of the corresponding forward ones. Each memory is devoted to record data concerning a single event, which can correspond to the taking place of a communication action, a choice or a thread forking. Memories are connected with one other, in order to keep track of the computation history, by using unique thread identifiers as links. Like all other formalisms for reversible computing in concurrent settings, forward computations are undone in acausal-consistent fashion [4] and [5]. This means that backtracking does not have to necessarily follow the exact order of forward computations in reverse, because independent actions can be undone in a different order. Thus, an action can be undone only after all the actions causally depending on it have already been undone.

Concerning the session type discipline, ReSπ inherits the notion of types and the typing system from π-calculus. Thus, the related results are mainly based on the ones stated for π-calculus. Besides the possibility of taking advantage of the theory already defined forπ-calculus, this also allows our investigation to focus on a standard session type setting, rather than on an ad-hoc one specifically introduced for our calculus.

The resulting formalism offers a theoretical basis for examining the interplay between reversible computations and session-based structured interactions. We notice that reversibility enables session parties not only to partially undo the interactions performed along the current session, but also to automatically undo the whole session and restart it, possibly involving different parties. The advantage of the reversible approach is that this behaviour is realised without explicitly implementing loops, but simply relying on the reversibility mechanism available in the language semantics. On the other hand, the session type discipline affects reversibility as it forces concurrent interactions to follow structured communication patterns. If we would consider only a single session, due to linearity, a causal-consistent form of reversibility would not be necessary, i.e. concurrent interactions along the same session are forbidden and, hence, the rollback would follow a single path. Instead, in the general case, concurrent interactions along different sessions may take place, thus introducing causal dependences. In this case, a session execution has to be reverted in a causal-consistent fashion. Notably, interesting issues concerning reversibility and session types are still open questions, especially for what concerns the validity in the reversible setting of standard properties (e.g., progress enforcement) and possibly new properties (e.g., reversibility of ongoing session history, safe closure of subordinate sessions).

It is worth noticing that the proposed calculus is fully reversible, i.e. backward computations are always enabled. Full reversibility provides theoretical foundations for studying reversibility in session-based π-calculus, but it is not suitable for a practical use on structured communication-based programming. In fact, reverting a completed session might not be desirable. Therefore, we also propose an extension of the calculus with anirreversible action for committing the completion of sessions. In this way, computation would go backward and forward, allowing the parties to try different interactions, until the session is successfully completed and, hence, irreversibly closed.

Summary of the rest of the paper. Section 2 reviews strictly related work. Section 3 recalls syntax and semantics definitions of the considered session-based variants of π-calculus. Section 4 introduces ReSπ, our reversible session-based calculus. Section 5 shows the results concerning the reversibility properties of ReSπ. Section 6 describes the associated typing discipline. Section 7 presents the extension of ReSπ with irreversible commit actions. Section 8 concludes the paper by touching upon directions for future work. Proofs of results are collected in Appendix A.

RELATED WORK

Our proposal combines the notion of (causal-consistent) reversibility with (typed) primitives supporting session-based interactions in concurrent systems. We review here some of the closely related works concerning either reversibility or session types.

Forms of reversible computation can be found in different formalisms in the literature. For example, backward reductions are considered in the λ-calculus to define equality on expressions [6]. Similar notions are used in the definitions of back and forth bisimulations [7] on Labelled Transition Systems, and of reversible steps in Petri nets [8]. More in practice, reversibility can be used for exploring different possibilities in a computation. For example, the Prolog language uses its backtracking capabilities to explore the state-space of a derivation to find a solution for a given goal. However, in our paper we mainly focus on the use of reversible computing as a suitable paradigm for designing and developing reliable concurrent systems, which came to prominence in recent years. Along this line of research, the works in the reversible computing field most closely related to ours are those concerning the definition of reversible process calculi. We briefly discuss the most relevant of them below, and refer the interested reader to [9] for a comprehensive survey and a larger perspective.

Reversible CCS (RCCS) [5] is the first proposal of reversible calculus, from which all subsequent works drew inspiration. The host calculus (i.e., the non-reversible calculus extended with capabilities for reversibility) is CCS without recursive definitions and relabelling. To each currently running thread is associated an individual memory stack keeping track of past actions, as well as forks and synchronisations. Information pushed on the memory stacks, upon doing a forward transition, can be then used for a rollback. The memories also serve as a naming scheme and yield unique identifiers for threads. When a process divides in two sub-threads, each sub-thread inherits the father memory together with a fork number (either $\langle 1 \rangle$ or $\langle 2 \rangle$) indicating which of the two sons the thread is. Then, in the case of a forward synchronisation, the synchronised threads exchange their names (i.e., memories) in order to allows the corresponding backward synchronisation to take place. A drawback of this approach for memorising fork actions is that the parallel operator does not satisfy usual structural congruence rules as commutativity, associativity and nil process as neutral element. It is proved that RCCS is causally consistent, i.e. the calculus allows backtrack along any causally equivalent past, where concurrent actions can be swapped and successive inverse actions can be cancelled. RCCS has been used for studying a general notion of transactions in [10].

CCS-R [11] is another reversible variant of CCS, which however mainly aims at formalising biological systems. Like the previous calculus, it relies on memory stacks for storing information needed for backtracking, which now also record events corresponding to the unfolding of process definitions. Instead, differently from RCCS, specific identifiers are used to label threads; in case of unfolding, sub-threads are labelled on-the-fly. Forking now does not exploit fork numbers, but it requires the memory stack of a given thread be empty before enabling the execution of its sons; this forces the sub-threads to share the memory that their father had before the forking. As in RCCS, in case of synchronisation, the communicating threads exchange their identifiers. The transition system of CCS-R is proved to be reversible and it is demonstrated that CCS-R is sound and complete w.r.t. CCS.

CCS with communication Keys (CCSK) [12] is a reversible process calculus obtained by applying a general procedure to produce reversible calculi. A relevant aspect of this approach is that it does not rely on memories for supporting backtracking. The idea is to maintain the structure of processes fixed throughout computations, thus avoiding to consume guards and alternative choices, which is the source of irreversibility. Past behaviour and discarded alternatives are then recorded in the syntax of terms. This is realised by transforming the dynamic rules of the SOS semantics into static-like rules. In this way, backward rules are obtained simply as symmetric versions of the forward ones. To ensure that synchronisations are properly reverted, two communicating threads have to agree on a communication key, which will uniquely identify that communication. In this way, the synchronising actions are locked together and can only be undone together. As usual, results showing that the method yields well-behaved transition relations are provided. The proposed converting procedure can be applied to other calculi without name passing, such as ACP [13] or CSP [14], but it is not suitable for calculi with name binders, as π-calculus, which we are interested in this work.

$\rho\pi$ [15] is a reversible variant of the higher-order π-calculus [16]. It borrows from RCCS the use of memories for keeping track of past actions. However, in $\rho\pi$ memories are not stacks syntactically associated to threads, but they simply are terms, each one dedicated to a single communication, in parallel with processes. The connection between memories and threads is kept by resorting to identifiers in a way similar to CCSK. Fork handling relies on specific structured tags connecting the identifier of the father thread with the identifiers of its sub-threads. Besides proving that $\rho\pi$ is causally consistent, it is also shown that it can be faithfully encoded into higher-order π-calculus. Notably, differently from the approaches mentioned before, the semantics of $\rho\pi$ is given in a reduction style. A variant of this calculus, called roll-π [17], has been defined to control backward computations by means of a rollback primitive. The approaches proposed in[15] and [17] have been applied in [18] for reversing a variant of Klaim [19].

Another reversible variant of π-calculus is Rπ [20]. Differently from $\rho\pi$, Rπ considers a standard π -calculus (without choice and replication) as host calculus, and its semantics is defined in terms of a labelled transition relation. This latter point requires to introduce some technicalities to properly deal with scope extrusion. Similarly to RCCS, this calculus relies on memory stacks, now recording events (i.e., consumed prefixes and related substitutions) and forking (by means of the fork symbol $\langle \uparrow \rangle$). Results about the notion of causality induced by the semantics of the calculus are provided.

Reversible structures [21] is a simple computational calculus, based on DSD [22], for modelling chemical systems. Since such systems are naturally reversible but have no backtracking memory, differently from most of the above proposals, reversible structures does not exploit memories. Instead, reversible structures maintain the structure of terms and use a special symbol $\wedge$ to indicate the next operations (one forward and one backward) that a term can perform. Terms of the calculus are parallel compositions of signals and gates (i.e., terms that accept input signals and emit output signals), which interact according to a CCS-style model. When a forward synchronisation takes place, the executed gate input is labelled by the identifier of the consumed signal, and the pointer symbol inside the gate is moved forward. The backwards computation is realised by executing these operations in a reverse way, thus releasing the output signal. As usual, the interplay between causal dependency and reversible structures is studied, with the novelty that in this setting signal identifiers are not necessary unique.

In our work we mainly take inspiration from the $\rho\pi$ approach. Indeed, all other approaches based on CCS and DSD cannot be directly applied to a calculus with name-passing. Moreover, the $\rho\pi$ approach is preferable to the Rπ one because the former proposes a reduction semantics, which we are interested in, while the latter proposes a labelled semantics, which would complicate our theoretical framework (in order to properly deal with scope extension of names). Specifically, we use unique (non-structured) tags for identifying threads and memories for recording taking place of actions, choices and forking. Each memory is devoted to storing the information needed to revert a single event, and memories are connected each other, in order to keep track of computation history, by using tags as links.

For what concerns the related works on session-based calculi, it is worth noticing that we consider a setting as standard and simple as possible, which is the one with synchronous binary sessions. In particular, our host calculus is the well-established variant of π-calculus introduced in [23], whose notation has been revised according to [24]. We leave for future investigation the application of our approach to formalisms relying on the other forms of sessions introduced in the literature, among which we would like to mention asynchronous binary sessions [25], multiparty asynchronous sessions [26], multiparty synchronous sessions [27], sessions with higher-order communication [24], sessions specifically devised for service-oriented computing [28], [29] and [30].

Finally, the paper with the aim closest to ours is [31], where a formalism combining the notions of reversibility and session is proposed. This calculus is simpler than ReSπ, because it is an extension of the formalism of session behaviours [32] without delegation (i.e., it is a sub-language of CCS) with a checkpoint-based backtracking mechanism. In fact, neither message nor channel passing are considered in the host calculus. Concerning reversibility, only the behaviour prefixed by the lastly traversed checkpoint is recorded by a given party that is each behaviour is simply paired with a one-size memory. Moreover, causal-consistency is not considered, because in this formalism parties just reduce in sequential way. Also committable sessions are not taken into account. On the other hand, this formalism enabled the study of an extension of the compliance notion to the reversible setting.

SESSION-BASED Π-CALCULUS

In this section we present the syntax and semantics definitions of the host language considered for our reversible calculus. This is a variant of π-calculus enriched with primitives for managing structured binary sessions.

Syntax

We use the following base sets: shared channels, used to initiate sessions; session channels, consisting on pairs of endpoints used by the two parties to exchange valueswithin an established session; variables, used to store values; labels, used to select and offer branching choices; and process variables, used for recursion. The corresponding notation and terminology are as follows:

Shared identifiers: $u, u', \ldots$ = Variables: $x, y, \ldots$; Shared channels: $a, b, \ldots$

Channels: $c, c', \ldots$ = Shared channels: $a, b, \ldots$; Session channels $s, s', \ldots$

Session identifiers: $k, k', \ldots$ = Variables: $x, y, \ldots$; Session endpoints: $s, \bar{s}, \ldots$

Labels: $l, l', \ldots$

Process variables: $X, Y, \ldots$

Values: $v, v', \ldots$ = Booleans: true, false; Integers: 0, 1, …; Shared channels: $a, b, \ldots$; Session endpoints: $s, \bar{s}, \ldots$

Notably, each session channel s has two (dual) endpoints, denoted by s and $\bar{s}$, each one assigned to one session party to exchange values with the other. We define duality to be idempotent, i.e. $\bar{\bar{s}} = s$. The use of two separated endpoints is similar to that of polarities in [33] and [23]. Notation $\tilde{\cdot}$ stands for tuples, e.g. $\tilde{c}$ means $c_1,\ldots,c_n$.

Processes, ranged over by P, Q, …, and expressions, ranged over by e , e′, … are given by the grammar in Fig. 1. We use op(·,…,·) to denote a generic expression operator; we assume that expressions are equipped with standard operators on boolean and integer values (e.g., ∧, +, …).

Processes	P	::=	$\bar{u}(x).P$	connect
		|	$u(x).P$	connect dual
		|	$k!\langle e\rangle.P$	output
		|	$k?(x).P$	input
		|	$k \triangleleft l.P$	selection
		|	$k \triangleright \{l_1 : P_1, \ldots, l_n : P_n\}$	branching
		|	if e then P else Q	conditional choice
		|	$P \mid Q$	parallel composition
		|	$(\nu c)\,P$	restriction
		|	X	process variable
		|	$\mu X.P$	recursion
		|	$\mathbf{0}$	inaction
Expressions	e	::=	v	value
		|	x	variable
		|	$\mathrm{op}(e_1, \ldots, e_n)$	composed expression

Figure. 1. Session-based π-calculus: syntax.

The initiation of a session is triggered by the synchronisation on a shared channel a of two processes of the form $\bar{a}(x).P$ and a(y).Q. This causes the generation of a fresh session channel s, whose endpoints replace variables x and y, by means of a substitution application, in order to be used by P and Q, respectively, for later communications. Primitives k! ⟨e⟩ .P and k′?(x).Q denote output and input via session endpoints identified by k and k′, respectively. These communication primitives realise the standard synchronous message passing, where messages result from the evaluation of expressions. Notably, an exchanged value can be an endpoint that is being used in a session (this channel-passing modality is called delegation), thus allowing complex nested structured communications. Constructs $k \triangleleft l.P$ and $k' \triangleright \{l_1 : P_1, \ldots, l_n : P_n\}$ denote label selection and label branching (where l_1, l_n are assumed to be pairwise distinct) via endpoints identified by k and k′, respectively. They mime method invocation in object-based programming.

The above interaction primitives are then combined by standard process calculi constructs: conditional choice, parallel composition, restriction, recursion and the empty process (denoting inaction). It is worth noticing that restriction can have both shared and session channels as argument: (νa) P states that a is a private shared channel of P ; similarly, (νs) P states that the two endpoints of the session channel, namely s and $\bar{s}$, are invisible from processes different from P (see the seventh law in Fig. 2), i.e. no external process can perform a session action on either of these endpoints (this ensures non-interference within a session). As a matter of notation, we will write $(\nu c_1,\ldots,c_n)P$in place of $(\nu c_1)\ldots(\nu c_n)P$.

$$(P \mid Q) \mid R \equiv P \mid (Q \mid R) \qquad P \mid Q \equiv Q \mid P$$

$$P \mid \mathbf{0} \equiv P \qquad (\nu c)\mathbf{0} \equiv \mathbf{0}$$

$$(\nu a)P \mid Q \equiv (\nu a)(P \mid Q) \;\text{ if } a \notin \mathrm{fc}(Q) \qquad (\nu c_1)(\nu c_2)P \equiv (\nu c_2)(\nu c_1)P$$

$$(\nu s)P \mid Q \equiv (\nu s)(P \mid Q) \;\text{ if } s, \bar{s} \notin \mathrm{fse}(Q) \qquad \mu X.P \equiv P[\mu X.P/X]$$

$$P \equiv Q \;\text{ if } P \equiv_\alpha Q$$

Figure. 2. Session-based π-calculus: structural congruence.

We adopt the following conventions about the operators precedence: prefixing, restriction, and recursion bind more tightly than parallel composition.

Bindings are defined as follows: $\bar{u}(x).P$, $u(x).P$ and $k?(x).P$ bind variable x in P; $(\nu a)\,P$; binds shared channel a in P; (νs) P binds session channel s in P ; finally, $\mu X.P$ binds process variable X in P. The derived notions of bound and free names, alpha-equivalence $\equiv_\alpha$, and substitution are standard. For P a process, fv(P) denotes the set of free variables , fc(P) denotes the set of free shared channels , and fse(P) the set of free session endpoints. For the sake of simplicity, we assume that free and bound variables are always chosen to be different, and that bound variables are pairwise distinct; the same applies to names. Of course, these conditions are not restrictive and can always be fulfilled by possibly using alpha-conversion.

Semantics

The operational semantics is given in terms of a structural congruence and of a reduction relation. Notably, the semantics is only defined for closed terms, i.e. terms without free variables. Indeed, we consider the binding of a variable as its declaration (and initialisation), therefore free occurrences of variables at the outset in a term must be prevented since they are similar to uses of variables before their declaration in programs (which are considered as programming errors).

The structural congruence, written $\equiv$, is defined as the smallest congruence relation on processes that includes the equational laws shown in Fig. 2. These are the standard laws of π-calculus. Reading the laws in Fig. 2 by row from left to right, and from top to bottom row, the first three are the monoid laws for | (i.e., it is associative and commutative, and has **0** as identity element). The second four laws deal with restriction and enable garbage-collection of channels, scope extension and scope swap, respectively. The eighth law permits a recursion to be unfolded (notation P[Q/X] denotes replacement of free occurrences of X in P by process Q). The last law equates alpha-equivalent processes, i.e. processes only differing in the identity of bound variables/channels.

To define the reduction relation, we use an auxiliary function $\downarrow$ for evaluating closed expressions: $e\downarrow v$ says that expression e evaluates to value v (where $v\downarrow v$, and $x\downarrow$ is undefined).

The reduction relation, written $\to$, is the smallest relation on closed processes generated by the rules in Fig. 3. We comment on salient points. A new session is established when two parallel processes synchronise via a shared channel a; this results in the generation of a fresh (private) session channel whose endpoints are assigned to the two session parties (rule [Con]). During a session, the two parties can exchange values (for data- and channel-passing, rule [Com]) and labels (for branching selection, rule [Lab]). The other rules are standard and state that: conditional choice evolves according to the evaluation of the expression argument (rules [If1] and [If2]); if a part of a larger process evolves, the whole process evolves accordingly (rules [Par] and [Res]); and structural congruent processes have the same reductions (rule [Str]).

$$\bar{a}(x).P_1 \mid a(y).P_2 \;\to\; (\nu s)(P_1[\bar{s}/x] \mid P_2[s/y]) \quad s,\bar{s} \notin \mathrm{fse}(P_1,P_2) \quad [\textsc{Con}]$$

$$\bar{k}!\langle e\rangle.P_1 \mid k?(x).P_2 \;\to\; P_1 \mid P_2[v/x] \quad (k=s \text{ or } k=\bar{s}),\ e\downarrow v \quad [\textsc{Com}]$$

$$\bar{k} \triangleleft l_i.P \mid k \triangleright \{l_1 : P_1,\dots,l_n : P_n\} \;\to\; P \mid P_i \quad (k=s \text{ or } k=\bar{s}),\ 1\le i\le n \quad [\textsc{Lab}]$$

$$\mathtt{if}\ e\ \mathtt{then}\ P_1\ \mathtt{else}\ P_2 \;\to\; P_1 \quad e\downarrow \mathtt{true} \quad [\textsc{If1}]$$

$$\mathtt{if}\ e\ \mathtt{then}\ P_1\ \mathtt{else}\ P_2 \;\to\; P_2 \quad e\downarrow \mathtt{false} \quad [\textsc{If2}]$$

$$\frac{P \to P'}{P \mid Q \to P' \mid Q}\,[\textsc{Par}] \qquad \frac{P \to P'}{(\nu c)P \to (\nu c)P'}\,[\textsc{Res}] \qquad \frac{P \equiv P' \to Q' \equiv Q}{P \to Q}\,[\textsc{Str}]$$

Figure. 3. Session-based π-calculus: reduction relation.

The Multiple Providers Scenario in the Session-Based Π-Calculus

The scenario involving a client and multiple providers introduced in Section 1 can be rendered in π-calculus as follows (for the sake of simplicity, here we consider just two providers):

$$P_{client} \mid P_{provider1} \mid P_{provider2}$$

where the client process P_{client} is defined as

$$\overline{a_{login}}(x).\,x!\langle \mathsf{srv\_req}\rangle.\,x?(y_{quote}).$$
$$\quad \mathtt{if}\ accept(y_{quote})\ \mathtt{then}\ x \triangleleft l_{acc}.\,P_{acc}$$
$$\quad \mathtt{else}\ (\mathtt{if}\ negotiate(y_{quote})\ \mathtt{then}\ x \triangleleft l_{neg}.\,P_{neg}\ \mathtt{else}\ x \triangleleft l_{rej}.\mathbf{0})$$

while a provider process $P_{\text{provider i}}$ is as follows

$$a_{login}(y).\,y?(z_{req}).\,y!\langle quote_i(z_{req})\rangle.\,y \triangleright \{l_{acc} : Q_{acc}\,,\ l_{neg} : Q_{neg}\,,\ l_{rej} : \mathbf{0}\}$$

We show below a possible evolution of the system, where the client contactsprovider1 and accepts the proposed quote:

$$P_{client} \mid P_{provider1} \mid P_{provider2}$$
$$\to$$
$$(\nu s)(\bar{s}!\langle \mathsf{srv\_req}\rangle.\,\bar{s}?(y_{quote}).\,\mathtt{if}\ accept(y_{quote})\ \mathtt{then}\ \bar{s} \triangleleft l_{acc}.\,P_{acc}[\bar{s}/x]\mathtt{else}\ (\dots)$$
$$\quad \mid s?(z_{req}).\,s!\langle quote_i(z_{req})\rangle.\,s \triangleright \{l_{acc} : Q_{acc}[s/y]\,,\ l_{neg} : Q_{neg}[s/y]\,,\ l_{rej} : \mathbf{0}\})$$
$$\mid P_{provider2}$$
$$\to$$
$$(\nu s)(\bar{s}?(y_{quote}).\,\mathtt{if}\ accept(y_{quote})\ \mathtt{then}\ \bar{s} \triangleleft l_{acc}.\,P_{acc}[\bar{s}/x]\mathtt{else}\ (\dots)$$
$$\quad \mid s!\langle quote_i(\mathsf{srv\_req})\rangle.\,s \triangleright \{l_{acc} : Q_{acc}[s/y][\mathsf{srv\_req}/z_{req}]\,,\ \dots\})$$
$$\mid P_{provider2}$$
$$\to$$
$$(\nu s)(\mathtt{if}\ accept(\mathsf{quote})\ \mathtt{then}\ \bar{s} \triangleleft l_{acc}.\,P_{acc}[\bar{s}/x][\mathsf{quote}/y_{quote}]\mathtt{else}\ (\dots)$$
$$\quad \mid s \triangleright \{l_{acc} : Q_{acc}[s/y][\mathsf{srv\_req}/z_{req}]\,,\ \dots\})$$
$$\mid P_{provider2}$$
$$\to$$
$$(\nu s)(\bar{s} \triangleleft l_{acc}.\,P_{acc}[\bar{s}/x][\mathsf{quote}/y_{quote}] \mid s \triangleright \{l_{acc} : Q_{acc}[s/y][\mathsf{srv\_req}/z_{req}]\,,\ \dots\})$$
$$\mid P_{provider2}$$
$$\to$$
$$(\nu s)(P_{acc}[\bar{s}/x][\mathsf{quote}/y_{quote}] \mid Q_{acc}[s/y][\mathsf{srv\_req}/z_{req}])$$
$$\mid P_{provider2}$$

REVERSIBLE SESSION-BASED Π-CALCULUS

In this section, we introduce ReSπ, a reversible extension of the calculus described in Section 3.

A reversible calculus is typically obtained from the corresponding host calculus by adding memory devices (see Section 2). They aim at storing information about interactions and their effects on the system, which otherwise would be lost during forward computations, as e.g. the discarded branch in a conditional choice. In doing this, we follow the approach of [15], which in its turn is inspired by [5] (for the use of memories) and by [12] (for the use of thread identifiers). Of course, since here we consider as host calculus a session-based variant of standard π-calculus, rather than an asynchronous higher-order variant, the technical development is different.

Roughly, our approach to keep track of computation history is as follows: we tag processes with unique identifiers and use memories to store the information needed to reverse each single forward reduction. Thus, the history of a reduction sequence is stored in a number of small memories connected each other by using tags as links. In this way, ReSπ terms can perform, besides forward reductions (denoted by $\twoheadrightarrow$), also backward reductions (denoted by $\rightsquigarrow$) that undo the effect of the former ones. As in the reversible calculi discussed in Section 2, forward computations are reverted in a causal-consistent fashion. That is, independent (more precisely, concurrent) actions can be undone in an order possibly different from the exact order of forward reductions in reverse. Specifically, an action can be undone only after all the actions causally depending on it have already been undone. We will come back on causal-consistency in Section 5.

Before introducing the technicalities of ReSπ, we informally provide a basic intuition about its main features. Let us come back to the scenario introduced in Section 1 and specified in π-calculus in Section 3.3. We can obtain a ReSπ specification of the scenario by simply annotating the π -calculus term with the (unique) tags t_1, t_2 and t_3 as follows:

$$t_1 : P_{client} \mid t_2 : P_{provider1} \mid t_3 : P_{provider2}$$

Now, the computation described in Section 3.3 corresponds to a sequence of five forward reductions leading to the ReSπ process M having the following form:

$$\begin{aligned}&(\nu s, \tilde{t})\,(t_1' : P_{acc}[\bar{s}/x][\mathsf{quote}/y_{quote}] \mid t_2' : Q_{acc}[s/y][\mathsf{srv\_req}/z_{req}]\\ &\quad \mid \langle t_1 - a_{login}(x)(y)(\nu s)P'_{client}P'_{provider1} \rightarrow t_2, t_1'', t_2'' \rangle\\ &\quad \mid \langle \ldots \rangle \mid \langle \ldots \rangle \mid \langle \ldots \rangle \mid \langle \ldots \rangle)\\ &\mid P_{provider2}\end{aligned}$$

The forward computation has created a tuple $\tilde{t}$ of fresh tags, which includes the tags t_1' and t_2' attached to the resulting processes of client and provider1, respectively. Moreover, each reduction has created a memory $\langle \ldots \rangle$, which is spawn in parallel with the two processes of the involved parties and devoted to store the information for reverting the corresponding forward reduction. Here, for the sake of presentation, we have omitted the content of such memories, except for the one generated by the first reduction: it records that the process tagged by t_1 (i.e., the client) initiates a session s along channel a login with the process tagged by t_2 (i.e., the first provider); it also records the variables replaced by the session endpoints and the continuation processes together with their tags. Notably, process M cannot immediately use this memory to revert the interaction corresponding to the session initiation. Indeed, a memory can trigger a backward reduction only if two processes properly tagged with the continuation tags are available, which is not the case of the first memory in the process M. Therefore, as expected, all the other forward reductions must be previously reverted in order to revert the session initiation one.

Syntax

The syntax of ReSπ is given in Fig. 4. In addition to the base sets used for π-calculus processes in Section 3, here we use tags, ranged over by t, t', to uniquely identify threads. Letters h, h', denote names, i.e. (shared and session) channels and tags together. Uniqueness of tags is ensured by using the restriction operator and by only considering reachable processes (see Definition 3).

ReSπ **Processes**	M	::=	$t : P$	thread
		|	$(\nu h)\,M$	channel/tag restriction
		|	$M \mid N$	parallel composition
		|	m	memory
		|	nil	empty process
Memories	m	::=	$\langle t_1 - \mathsf{A} \rightarrow t_2, t_1', t_2' \rangle$	action memory
		|	$\langle t, e?\,P{:}Q, t' \rangle$	choice memory
		|	$\langle t \rightrightarrows (t_1, t_2) \rangle$	fork memory
	A	::=	$a(x)(y)(\nu s)PQ \quad \mid \quad k\langle e \rangle(x)PQ$	action events
		|	$k \triangleleft l_i\, P\{l_1 : P_1, \ldots, l_n : P_n\}$	

Figure. 4. ReSπ syntax (π-calculus Processes P and Expressions e are in Fig. 1).

ReSπ processes are built upon standard (session-based) π-calculus processes by labelling them with tags. Thus, the syntax of π-calculus processes P, as well as of expressions e, is the same of that shown in Fig. 1 and, hence, it is omitted here. It is worth noticing that only ReSπ processes can execute (i.e., π-calculus ones cannot).

ReSπ also extends π-calculus with memory processes m. In particular, there are three kind of memories:

- Action memory $\langle t_1 - \mathsf{A} \rightarrow t_2, t_1', t_2' \rangle$, storing an action event A together with the tag t_1 of the active party of the action, the tag t_2 of the corresponding passive party, and the tags t_1' and t_2' of the two new threads activated by the corresponding reduction. An action event A, as we shall clarify later, records all information necessary to revert the corresponding interaction, which can be either a session initiation a(x)(y)(vs)PQ, a communication along an established session k $\langle$e$\rangle$ (x)PQ, or a branch selection $k \triangleleft l_i\, P\{l_1 : P_1, \ldots, l_n : P_n\}$. Notably, in the latter two events, k can only be either s or $\bar{s}$ (i.e., it cannot be a variable).
- Choice memory $\langle t, e?\,P{:}Q, t' \rangle$, storing a choice event $e?\,P{:}Q$ together with the tag t of the conditional choice and the tag t' of the new activated thread. The choice event $e?\,P{:}Q$ records the evaluated expression e, and the processes P and Q of the then-branch and else-branch, respectively.
- Fork memory $\langle t \rightrightarrows (t_1, t_2) \rangle$, storing the tag t of a splitting thread, i.e. a thread of the form t:(P|Q), together with the tags t_1 and t_2 of the two new activated threads, i.e. t_1:P and t_2:Q. The use of fork memories is analogous to that of connectors in [18].

Threads and memories are composed by parallel composition and restriction operators. The latter, as well as the notion of bound and free identifiers, extend to names. In particular, for M a ReSπ process, ft(M) denotes the set of free tags ; fv(·), fc(·) andfse(·) extend naturally to ReSπ processes. Of course, we still rely on the same assumptions on free and bound variables/channels mentioned in Section 3.1.

Not all processes allowed by the syntax in Fig. 4 are semantically meaningful. Indeed, in a general term of the calculus, the history stored in the memories may not be consistent, due to the use of non-unique tags or broken connections between continuation tags within memories and corresponding threads. For example, given the choice memory $\langle t, e?P{:}Q, t'\rangle$, we have a broken connection when no thread tagged by t′ exists in theReSπ process and no memory of the form $\langle t' \text{–A→}\, t_2, t_1', t_2'\rangle$, $\langle t_1 \text{–A→}\, t', t_1', t_2'\rangle$, $\langle t', e?P_1{:}P_2, t_1\rangle$ and $\langle t' \rightrightarrows (t_1, t_2)\rangle$ exist.

The class of meaningful ReSπ processes we are interested in consists of programs and runtime processes. The former are the terms that can be written by programmers, i.e. they are ReSπ processes with no memory. In fact, memories are not expected to occur in the source code written by programmers. We assume that the threads within a program have unique tags. The latter terms of the class are the ReSπ processes that can be obtained by means of forward reductions from programs; in this way, history consistency is ensured. Using the terminology from [20], the processes of the considered class are called reachable. We formalise their definition below.

Definition 1 Programs

The set of ReSπ programs is the set of terms generated by the following grammar

$$M ::= t : P \ \mid \ (\nu c) M \ \mid \ M \mid N \ \mid \ \mathrm{nil}$$

and whose threads have distinct tags, where P is a π-calculus process as in Fig. 1.

Definition 2 Runtime Processes

The set of ReSπ runtime processes is the set of terms obtained by the transitive closure under ↠ (see Section 4.2) of the set of ReSπ programs.

Definition 3 Reachable Processes

The set of ReSπ reachable processes is the union of the sets of programs and runtime processes.

Notice that in Definition 1 the restriction operator is defined on channels c rather than on names h. This because there is no need to restrict tags in a program. In fact, it is sufficient to use distinct tags, as required by the definition. In practice, the programmer would have to write just a π-calculus term that can be then automatically annotated with unique tags to obtain a ReSπ program. At runtime, as shown in the next subsection, it is the operational semantics in charge of generating fresh tags for the new threads by means of the restriction operator.

Semantics

The operational semantics of ReSπ is given in terms of a structural congruence and of a reduction relation.

The structural congruence ≡ extends that of π-calculus (Fig. 2) with the additional laws in Fig. 5. Most of the new laws simply deal with the parallel and restriction operators on ReSπ processes. Thus, we only focus on relevant laws (below, the laws are read by row from left to right, and from top to bottom row). The eighth law permits a restriction on a π-calculus process to be moved to the level of ReSπ processes. The ninth law lifts the congruence at π-calculus process level to the threads level. The last law is crucial for fork handling: it is used to split a single thread composed of two parallel processes into two threads with fresh tags; the tag of the original thread and the new tags are properly recorded in a fork memory.

$$
\begin{array}{ll}
(M \mid N) \mid L \equiv M \mid (N \mid L) & M \mid N \equiv N \mid M \\
M \mid \mathrm{nil} \equiv M & (\nu h)\,\mathrm{nil} \equiv \mathrm{nil} \\
(\nu t)M \mid N \equiv (\nu t)(M \mid N) \ \text{ if } t \notin \mathrm{ft}(N) & (\nu h_1)(\nu h_2)M \equiv (\nu h_2)(\nu h_1)M \\
(\nu a)M \mid N \equiv (\nu a)(M \mid N) \ \text{ if } a \notin \mathrm{fc}(N) & t : (\nu c)P \equiv (\nu c)\, t : P \\
t : P \equiv t : Q \ \text{ if } P \equiv Q & (\nu s)M \mid N \equiv (\nu s)(M \mid N) \ \text{ if } s, \bar{s} \notin \mathrm{fse}(N) \\
M \equiv N \ \text{ if } M \equiv_\alpha N & t : (P \mid Q) \equiv (\nu t_1, t_2)(t_1 : P \mid t_2 : Q \mid \langle t \rightrightarrows (t_1, t_2)\rangle)
\end{array}
$$

Figure. 5. ReSπ structural congruence (additional laws).

The reduction relation of ReSπ, written ↣, is given as the union of the forward and backward reduction relations defined by the rules in Fig. 6: $\rightarrowtail \; = \; \twoheadrightarrow \cup \rightsquigarrow$. Relations ↠ and ⇝ are the smallest relations on closed ReSπ reachable processes generated by the corresponding rules in the figure.

$$
\begin{array}{lll}
t_1 : \bar{a}(x).P_1 \mid t_2 : a(y).P_2 & s, \bar{s} \notin \mathrm{fse}(P_1, P_2) & [\text{FWCON}] \\
\quad \twoheadrightarrow (\nu s, t_1', t_2')(t_1' : P_1[\bar{s}/x] \mid t_2' : P_2[s/y] & & \\
\qquad \mid \langle t_1 \text{–}a(x)(y)(\nu s)P_1P_2 \text{→}\, t_2, t_1', t_2'\rangle) & & \\[1ex]
(\nu s, t_1', t_2')(t_1' : P \mid t_2' : Q \mid \langle t_1 \text{–}a(x)(y)(\nu s)P_1P_2 \text{→}\, t_2, t_1', t_2'\rangle) & & [\text{BWCON}] \\
\quad \rightsquigarrow t_1 : \bar{a}(x).P_1 \mid t_2 : a(y).P_2 & & \\[1ex]
t_1 : \bar{k}!\langle e\rangle.P_1 \mid t_2 : k?(x).P_2 & (k = s \text{ or } k = \bar{s}) & [\text{FWCOM}] \\
\quad \twoheadrightarrow (\nu t_1', t_2')(t_1' : P_1 \mid t_2' : P_2[v/x] & e \downarrow v & \\
\qquad \mid \langle t_1 \text{–}k\langle e\rangle(x)P_1P_2 \text{→}\, t_2, t_1', t_2'\rangle) & & \\[1ex]
(\nu t_1', t_2')(t_1' : P \mid t_2' : Q \mid \langle t_1 \text{–}k\langle e\rangle(x)P_1P_2 \text{→}\, t_2, t_1', t_2'\rangle) & & [\text{BWCOM}] \\
\quad \rightsquigarrow t_1 : \bar{k}!\langle e\rangle.P_1 \mid t_2 : k?(x).P_2 & & \\[1ex]
t_1 : \bar{k} \triangleleft l_i.P \mid t_2 : k \triangleright \{l_1 : P_1, \ldots, l_n : P_n\} & (k = s \text{ or } k = \bar{s}) & [\text{FWLAB}] \\
\quad \twoheadrightarrow (\nu t_1', t_2')(t_1' : P \mid t_2' : P_i & 1 \le i \le n & \\
\qquad \mid \langle t_1 \text{–}k \triangleleft l_i P\{l_1 : P_1, \ldots, l_n : P_n\} \text{→}\, t_2, t_1', t_2'\rangle) & & \\[1ex]
(\nu t_1', t_2')(t_1' : Q \mid t_2' : Q' & & \\
\qquad \mid \langle t_1 \text{–}k \triangleleft l_i P\{l_1 : P_1, \ldots, l_n : P_n\} \text{→}\, t_2, t_1', t_2'\rangle) & & [\text{BWLAB}] \\
\quad \rightsquigarrow t_1 : \bar{k} \triangleleft l_i.P \mid t_2 : k \triangleright \{l_1 : P_1, \ldots, l_n : P_n\} & & \\[1ex]
t : \mathtt{if}\ e\ \mathtt{then}\ P_1\ \mathtt{else}\ P_2 \ \twoheadrightarrow\ (\nu t')(t' : P_1 \mid \langle t, e?P_1{:}P_2, t'\rangle) & e \downarrow \mathtt{true} & [\text{FWIF1}] \\[1ex]
t : \mathtt{if}\ e\ \mathtt{then}\ P_1\ \mathtt{else}\ P_2 \ \twoheadrightarrow\ (\nu t')(t' : P_2 \mid \langle t, e?P_1{:}P_2, t'\rangle) & e \downarrow \mathtt{false} & [\text{FWIF2}] \\[1ex]
(\nu t')(t' : P \mid \langle t, e?P_1{:}P_2, t'\rangle) \ \rightsquigarrow\ t : \mathtt{if}\ e\ \mathtt{then}\ P_1\ \mathtt{else}\ P_2 & & [\text{BWIF}]
\end{array}
$$

$$
\frac{M \twoheadrightarrow M'}{M \mid N \twoheadrightarrow M' \mid N}\ [\text{FWPAR}]
\qquad
\frac{M \rightsquigarrow M'}{M \mid N \rightsquigarrow M' \mid N}\ [\text{BWPAR}]
$$

$$
\frac{M \twoheadrightarrow M'}{(\nu h)M \twoheadrightarrow (\nu h)M'}\ [\text{FWRES}]
\qquad
\frac{M \rightsquigarrow M'}{(\nu h)M \rightsquigarrow (\nu h)M'}\ [\text{BWRES}]
$$

$$
\frac{M \equiv M' \twoheadrightarrow N' \equiv N}{M \twoheadrightarrow N}\ [\text{FWSTR}]
\qquad
\frac{M \equiv M' \rightsquigarrow N' \equiv N}{M \rightsquigarrow N}\ [\text{BWSTR}]
$$

Figure. 6. ReSπ reduction relation.

We comment on salient points. When two parallel threads synchronise to establish a new session (rule [fwCon]), two fresh tags are created to uniquely identify the two continuations of the synchronising threads. Moreover, all relevant information is stored in the action memory $\langle t_1 \text{–}a(x)(y)(\nu s)P_1P_2 \text{→}\, t_2, t_1', t_2'\rangle$: the tag t_1 of the initiator (i.e., the thread executing a prefix of the form $\bar{a}(\cdot)$), the tag t_2 of the thread executing the dual action, the tags t_1' and t_2' of their continuations, the shared channel a used for the synchronisation, the replaced variables x and y, the generated session channel s , and the processes P_1 and

P_2 to which substitutions are applied. All such information is exploited to revert this reduction (rule [bwCon]). In particular, the corresponding backward reduction is triggered by the coexistence of the memory described above with two threads tagged t_1' and t_2', all of them within the scope of the session channel s and tags t_1' and t_2' generated by the forward reduction (which, in fact, are removed by the backward one). Notice that, when considering reachable processes, due to tag uniqueness, the two processes P and Q must coincide with $P_1[\bar{s}/x]$ and $P_2[s/y]$; indeed, as registered in the memory, these latter processes have been tagged with t_1' and t_2' by the forward reduction. The fact that two threads tagged with t_1' and t_2' are available in parallel to the memory ensures that all actions possibly executed by the two continuations activated by the forward computation have been undone and, hence, we can safely proceed to undone the forward computation itself.

Rules [fwCom], [bwCom], [fwLab], [bwLab], [fwIf1], [fwIf2] and [bwIf] are similar. Notably, in the first two rules mentioned above, besides tags and continuation processes, the action memory stores the session endpoint k of the receiving party (the other endpoint $\bar{k}$ is obtained by duality), the expression e generating the sent value, and the replaced variable x. It is also worth noticing that, since all information about a choice event is stored in the corresponding memory, we need just one backward rule ([bwIf]) to revert the effect of the forward rules [fwIf1] and [fwIf2]. The meaning of the remaining rules, dealing with parallel composition, restriction and structural congruent terms, is straightforward.

The Multiple Providers Scenario in *ReSπ*

Let us consider again the multiple providers scenario. We have shown at the beginning of this section that a ReSπ specification can be obtained by simply annotating the π-calculus term with unique tags as follows:

$$t_1 : P_{client} \mid t_2 : P_{provider1} \mid t_3 : P_{provider2}$$

Now, the computation described in Section 3.3 corresponds to the following sequence of forward reductions:

$$t_1 : P_{client} \mid t_2 : P_{provider1} \mid t_3 : P_{provider2}$$

$$\twoheadrightarrow \twoheadrightarrow \twoheadrightarrow \twoheadrightarrow \twoheadrightarrow$$

$$\begin{aligned} M = (\nu s, t_1^1, t_2^1, t_1^2, t_2^2, t_1^3, t_2^3, t_1^4, t_1^5, t_2^4) \\ (t_1^5 : P_{acc}[\bar{s}/x][\mathsf{quote}/y_{quote}] \mid t_2^4 : Q_{acc}[s/y][\mathsf{srv\_req}/z_{req}] \\ \mid \langle t_1 - a_{login}(x)(y)(\nu s)P'_{client} P'_{provider1} \rightarrow t_2, t_1^1, t_2^1 \rangle \\ \mid \langle t_1^1 - s\langle \mathsf{srv\_req}\rangle (z_{req}) P''_{client} P''_{provider1} \rightarrow t_2^1, t_1^2, t_2^2 \rangle \\ \mid \langle t_2^2 - \bar{s}\langle \mathsf{quote}\rangle (y_{quote}) P'''_{provider1} P'''_{client} \rightarrow t_1^2, t_2^3, t_1^3 \rangle \\ \mid \langle t_1^3, accept(\mathsf{quote})?\, P_{client\_t} : P_{client\_e}, t_1^4 \rangle \\ \mid \langle t_1^4 - s \triangleleft l_{acc}\, P_{acc}[\bar{s}/x][\mathsf{quote}/y_{quote}] \\ \{l_{acc} : Q_{acc}[s/y][\mathsf{srv\_req}/z_{req}], \ldots\} \rightarrow t_2^3, t_1^5, t_2^4 \rangle\,) \\ \mid P_{provider2} \end{aligned}$$

Basically, five memories have been generated, each one dedicated to revert the effects of the corresponding forward reduction.

If a problem occurs during the subsequent interactions between the client and the provider for finalising the service agreement, the computation can be reverted to the initial state. In particular, the backward rules [bwCon], [bwCom], [bwLab] and [bwIf] can be applied only if the ReSπ term contains a memory in parallel with thread(s) appropriately tagged by the continuation tag(s) stored in the memory. For example, to apply the rule [bwCon] in the process M, two threads tagged by t_1^1 and t_2^1 must be in parallel with the first memory, which actually is not the case. In fact, in M, only the last memory can trigger a backward step, by means of the application of rule [bwLab]:

In this way, the threads labelled by t_1^5 and t_2^4 are removed, while the threads performing the selection and offering the branching choice, labelled by t_1^4 and t_2^3 respectively, are restored.

Then, in the process M′, only the last memory can trigger a backward reduction, which undoes the conditional choice performed by the client thread. Similarly, other backward reductions can be subsequently triggered by the other memories, consuming them from the bottom to the top of the term. In this way, the forward computation can be completely reverted:

$$M' \rightsquigarrow \rightsquigarrow \rightsquigarrow \rightsquigarrow t_1 : P_{client} \mid t_2 : P_{provider1} \mid t_3 : P_{provider2}$$

Now, the client can start a new session, possibly with provider2.

Notice that in ReSπ there is no need of explicitly implementing loops for enabling the client to undo and restart sessions. Notice also that here we do not consider specific primitives and techniques that avoid interacting again with the same provider. This would break the Loop Lemma (see Lemma 5) and complicate our theoretical framework; we refer to [34] for a definition of some of such controlled forms of reversibility.

PROPERTIES OF THE REVERSIBLE CALCULUS

We present in this section some properties of ReSπ, which are typically enjoyed by reversible calculi. We exploit terminology, arguments and proof techniques of previous works on reversible calculi (in particular, [15], [5] and [20]). As a matter of notation, we will use P and R to denote the set of π-calculus processes and of ReSπ processes, respectively.

Correspondence with π-calculus

We first show that ReSπ is a conservative extension of the (session-based) π-calculus. In fact, as most reversible calculi, ReSπ is only a decoration of its host calculus. Such decoration can be erased by means of the forgetful map φ, which maps ReSπ terms intoπ-calculus ones by simply removing memories, tag annotations and tag restrictions.

Definition 4 Forgetful map

The forgetful map $\phi : \mathcal{R} \rightarrow \mathcal{P}$, mapping a ReSπ process M into a π-calculus process P, is inductively defined on the structure of M as follows:

$$\phi(t : P) = P \qquad \phi((\nu c)N) = (\nu c)\phi(N)$$

$$\phi((\nu t)N) = \phi(N) \qquad \phi(N_1 \mid N_2) = \phi(N_1) \mid \phi(N_2)$$

$$\phi(m) = \mathbf{0} \qquad \phi(\mathrm{nil}) = \mathbf{0}$$

To prove the correspondence between ReSπ and π-calculus, we need the following auxiliary lemma relating structural congruence of ReSπ to that of π-calculus.

Lemma 1

Let M and N be two ReSπ processes. If M≡N then φ(M)≡φ(N).

Proof

We proceed by induction on the derivation of M≡N (see Appendix A.1.1).

Now, we can show that each forward reduction of a ReSπ process corresponds to a reduction of the corresponding π-calculus process.

Lemma 2

Let M and N be two ReSπ processes. If M↠N then φ(M)→φ(N).

Proof

We proceed by induction on the derivation of M↠N (see Appendix A.1.1).

The correspondence between ReSπ and π-calculus reductions is completed by the following lemmas, which intuitively are the inverse of Lemma 1 and Lemma 2.

Lemma 3

Let P and Q be two π-calculus processes. If P≡Q then for any ReSπ process M such that φ(M)=P there exists a ReSπ process N such that φ(N)=Q and M≡N.

Proof

The proof is straightforward (see Appendix A.1.1). □

Lemma 4

Let P and Q be two π-calculus processes. If P→Q then for any ReSπ process M such that φ(M)=P there exists a ReSπ process N such that φ(N)=Q and M↠N.

Proof

We proceed by induction on the derivation of P→Q (see Appendix A.1.1).

Loop Lemma

The following lemma shows that, in ReSπ, backward reductions are the inverse of the forward ones and vice versa.

Lemma 5 Loop lemma

Let M and N be two reachable ReSπ processes. M↠Nif and only if N⇝M.

Proof

The proof for the if part is by induction on the derivation of M↠N, while the proof for the only if part is by induction on the derivation of N⇝M (see Appendix A.1.2).

Causal Consistency

We show here that reversibility in ReSπ is causally consistent. Informally, this means that an action can be reverted only after all the actions causally depending on it have already been reverted. In this way, in the presence of independent actions, backward computations are not required to necessarily follow the exact execution order of forward computations in reverse. We formalise below the notions of independent (i.e., concurrent) actions and of causal consistency.

As in [15] and [5], we rely on the notion of transition. In ReSπ, a transition is a triplet of the form $M \xrightarrow{m,\mathcal{M},\twoheadrightarrow} N$ (resp. $M \xrightarrow{m,\mathcal{M},\rightsquigarrow} N$), where M and N are closed reachable ReSπ processes such that M↠N (resp. M⇝N), m is the action or choice memory involved in the reduction, and M is the set of fork memories possibly involved in the reduction. A memory is involved in a reduction if it is created or removed by the reduction. We use η to denote transition labels (m,M,↠) and (m,M,⇝). If η is (m,M,↠), then its inverse is $\eta_{\bullet}$=(m, M,⇝) and vice versa. In a transition $M \xrightarrow{\eta} N$, we call M the source of the transition and N its target. We use τ to range over transitions; $\tau_{\bullet}$ denotes the inverse of transition τ.

Two transitions are coinitial if they have the same source, cofinal if they have the same target, composable if the target of one is the source of the other. A sequence of transitions, where each pair of sequential transitions is composable, is called a trace; we use σ to range over traces. Notions of target, source and composability extend naturally to traces. We use ε_M to denote the empty trace with source M and $\sigma_1;\sigma_2$ the composition of two composable traces σ_1 and σ_2.

We consider only transitions $M \xrightarrow{\eta} N$ where M and N do not contain threads of the form t:(P|Q). This condition can be always satisfied by splitting all threads of this kind into sub-threads, until their disappearance in the considered terms, using the structural law t:(P|Q)≡($\nu t_1,t_2$)(t_1:P|t_2:Q| ⟨t⇉(t_1,t_2)⟩). Moreover, since conflicts between transitions are identified by means of tag identifiers (see Definition 5 below), we only consider transitions that do not use α -conversion on tags, and that generates fork memories in a deterministic way, e.g. given a memory ⟨t⇉(t_1,t_2)⟩ tags t_1 and $t_2$are generated by applying an injective function to t.

The stamp $\lambda(\eta)$ of a transition label η identifies the threads involved in the corresponding transition, and is defined as follows (we use T to denote a set of tags$\{t_i\}_{i\in I}$):

$$\lambda(m,\mathcal{M},\twoheadrightarrow) = \lambda(m,\mathcal{M},\rightsquigarrow) = \lambda(m) \cup \lambda_{\lambda(m)}(\mathcal{M})$$

$$\lambda(\langle t_1 \text{—A}\!\rightarrow t_2, t'_1, t'_2\rangle) = \{t_1, t_2, t'_1, t'_2\}$$

$$\lambda(\langle t, e?\,P{:}Q, t'\rangle) = \{t, t'\}$$

$$\lambda_T(\{m_i\}_{i\in I}) = \bigcup_{i\in I} \lambda_T(m_i)$$

$$\lambda_T(\langle t \rightrightarrows (t_1, t_2)\rangle) = \begin{cases} \{t_1, t_2\} & \text{if } t \in T \\ \emptyset & \text{otherwise} \end{cases}$$

The stamp of fork memories permits us to take into account the relationships between a thread and its sub-threads. This is similar to the closure over tags used in [18]. Notably, as in [15], the tags of continuation processes are inserted into a stamp, in order to take into account possible conflicts between a forward transition and a backward one. Notice also that it is instead not necessary to include in the stamp the fresh session channel created or used by a reduction. In fact, this would allow to detect conflicts between the transitions involving the memory corresponding to the creation of the channel and the transitions where such channel is used. Such conflicts, however, are already implicitly considered, since after its creation the channel is only known by the threads corresponding to the continuation processes, which are already considered in the stamp as discussed above.

We can now define when two transitions are concurrent.

Definition 5 Concurrent Transitions

Two coinitial transitions $M \xrightarrow{\eta_1} M_1$ and $M \xrightarrow{\eta_2} M_2$ are in conflict if $\lambda(\eta_1) \cap \lambda(\eta_2) \neq \emptyset$. Two coinitial transitions are concurrent if they are not in conflict.

Intuitively, two transitions are concurrent when they do not involve a common thread.

The following lemma characterises the causally independence among concurrent transitions.

Lemma 6 Square Lemma

If $\tau_1 = M \xrightarrow{\eta_1} M_1$ and $\tau_2 = M \xrightarrow{\eta_2} M_2$ are two coinitial concurrent transitions, then there exist two cofinal transitions $\tau_2/\tau_1 = M_1 \xrightarrow{\eta_2} N$ and $\tau_1/\tau_2 = M_2 \xrightarrow{\eta_1} N$.

Proof

By case analysis on the form of transitions τ_1 and τ_2 (see Appendix A.1.3).

In order to study the causality of ReSπ reversibility, we introduce the notion of causal equivalence [4] and [5] between traces, denoted $\asymp$. This is defined as the least equivalence relation between traces closed under composition that obeys the following rules:

$$\tau_1 ; \tau_2/\tau_1 \asymp \tau_2 ; \tau_1/\tau_2 \qquad \tau ; \tau_\bullet \asymp \epsilon_{\mathtt{source}(\tau)} \qquad \tau_\bullet ; \tau \asymp \epsilon_{\mathtt{target}(\tau)}$$

Intuitively, the first rule states that the execution order of two concurrent transitions can be swapped, while the other rules state that the composition of a trace with its inverse is equivalent to the empty transition.

Now, we conclude with the result stating that two coinitial causally equivalent traces lead to the same final state. Thus, in such case, we can rollback to the initial state by reversing any of the two traces.

Theorem 1 Causal Consistency

Let σ_1 and σ_2 be coinitial traces. Then, $\sigma_1 \asymp \sigma_2$ if and only if σ_1 and σ_2 are cofinal.

Proof

By construction of $\asymp$ and by applying Lemma 6 and other two auxiliary lemmas (see Appendix A.1.3).

TYPE DISCIPLINE

In this section, first we recall the session type discipline of session-based π-calculus then we discuss how we could exploit it to type ReSπ processes.

Typing Session-based ϖ-calculus

The type discipline presented here is basically the one proposed in [23], except for the notation of the calculus that has been revised according to [24].

Types

The syntax of sorts, ranged over by S , S′, ..., and types, ranged over by α, β, ..., is defined in Fig. 7. The type ![S].α represents the behaviour of first outputting a value of sort S, then performing the actions prescribed by type α . Type ![β].α represents a similar behaviour, which starts with session output (throw) instead. Types ?[S].α and ?[β].α are the dual ones, receiving values instead of sending. Type $\&[l_1 : \alpha_1, \ldots, l_n : \alpha_n]$ describes a branching behaviour: it waits with n options, and behave as type α_i if the i -th action is selected (external choice). Type $\oplus[l_1 : \alpha_1, \ldots, l_n : \alpha_n]$ represents the behaviour which would select one of l_i and then behaves as α_i, according to the selected l_i (internal choice). Type end represents inaction, acting as the unit of sequential composition. Type μt.α denotes a recursive behaviour, representing the behaviour that starts by doing α and, when variable t is encountered, recurs to α again. As in [23], we take anequi-recursive view of types, not distinguishing between a type μt.α and its unfoldingα[μt.α/t], and we are interested on contractive types only, i.e. for each of sub-expressions $\mu t.\mu t_1 \ldots \mu t_n.\alpha$ the body α is not t . The result is that, in a typing derivation, types μt.α and α[μt.α/t] can be used interchangeably.

Sorts	S	::=	bool	boolean
		|	int	integer
		|	$\langle\alpha\rangle$	shared channel
Types	α, β	::=	$![S].\alpha$	output
		|	$?[S].\alpha$	input
		|	$![\beta].\alpha$	throw
		|	$?[\beta].\alpha$	catch
		|	$\oplus[l_1 : \alpha_1, \ldots, l_n : \alpha_n]$	selection
		|	$\&[l_1 : \alpha_1, \ldots, l_n : \alpha_n]$	branching
		|	end	end
		|	t	type variable
		|	$\mu t.\alpha$	recursion

Figure. 7. Syntax of sorts and types.

For each type α , we define $\bar{\alpha}$, the dual type of α, by exchanging ! and ?, and & and ⊕. The inductive definition is in Fig. 8.

$$\overline{![S].\alpha} = ?[S].\bar{\alpha} \qquad \overline{![\beta].\alpha} = ?[\beta].\bar{\alpha} \qquad \overline{\oplus[l_i : \alpha_i]_{i\in I}} = \&[l_i : \overline{\alpha_i}]_{i\in I}$$

$$\overline{?[S].\alpha} = ![S].\bar{\alpha} \qquad \overline{?[\beta].\alpha} = ![\beta].\bar{\alpha} \qquad \overline{\&[l_i : \alpha_i]_{i\in I}} = \oplus[l_i : \overline{\alpha_i}]_{i\in I}$$

$$\overline{\mathsf{end}} = \mathsf{end} \qquad \overline{\mu t.\alpha} = \mu t.\bar{\alpha} \qquad \bar{t} = t$$

Figure. 8. Dual types.

Typing System

A sorting (resp. a typing, resp. a basis) is a finite partial map from shared identifiers to sorts (resp. from session identifiers to types, resp. from process variables to typings). We let Γ, Γ′, ...(resp. Δ, Δ′, ..., resp. Θ, Θ′, ...) range over sortings (resp. typings, resp. bases). We write Δ·k:α when k∉dom(Δ); this notation is then extended to Δ·Δ′.

Typing judgements are of the form $\Theta; \Gamma \vdash P \triangleright \Delta$ which stands for "under the environment Θ; Γ, process P has typing Δ". The typing system is defined by the axioms and rules in Fig. 9. We call a typing completed when it contains only end types. A typing Δ is called balanced if whenever

$s:\alpha, \bar{s}:\beta \in \Delta,$, then $\alpha = \bar{\beta}$. We refer the interested reader to [23] for detailed comments on the rules.

$$\Gamma \vdash \mathtt{true} \triangleright \mathsf{bool}\ [\mathrm{BOOL}_{tt}] \qquad \Gamma \vdash \mathtt{false} \triangleright \mathsf{bool}\ [\mathrm{BOOL}_{ff}] \qquad \Gamma \vdash 1 \triangleright \mathsf{int}\ [\mathrm{INT}] \ \ldots$$

$$\frac{\Gamma \vdash e_1 \triangleright \mathsf{int} \quad \Gamma \vdash e_2 \triangleright \mathsf{int}}{\Gamma \vdash +(e_1, e_2) \triangleright \mathsf{int}}\ [\mathrm{SUM}] \qquad \frac{\Gamma \vdash e_1 \triangleright \mathsf{bool} \quad \Gamma \vdash e_2 \triangleright \mathsf{bool}}{\Gamma \vdash \wedge(e_1, e_2) \triangleright \mathsf{bool}}\ [\mathrm{AND}] \ \ldots$$

$$\Gamma \cdot u:S \vdash u \triangleright S\ [\mathrm{ID}] \qquad \frac{\Delta \text{ completed}}{\Theta;\Gamma \vdash \mathbf{0} \triangleright \Delta}\ [\mathrm{INACT}]$$

$$\frac{\Gamma \vdash u \triangleright \langle\alpha\rangle \quad \Theta;\Gamma \vdash P \triangleright \Delta \cdot x:\bar{\alpha}}{\Theta;\Gamma \vdash \bar{u}(x).P \triangleright \Delta}\ [\mathrm{REQ}] \qquad \frac{\Gamma \vdash u \triangleright \langle\alpha\rangle \quad \Theta;\Gamma \vdash P \triangleright \Delta \cdot x:\alpha}{\Theta;\Gamma \vdash u(x).P \triangleright \Delta}\ [\mathrm{ACC}]$$

$$\frac{\Gamma \vdash e \triangleright S \quad \Theta;\Gamma \vdash P \triangleright \Delta \cdot k:\alpha}{\Theta;\Gamma \vdash k!\langle e\rangle.P \triangleright \Delta \cdot k:![S].\alpha}\ [\mathrm{SEND}] \qquad \frac{\Theta;\Gamma \vdash P \triangleright \Delta \cdot k:\beta}{\Theta;\Gamma \vdash k!\langle k'\rangle.P \triangleright \Delta \cdot k:![\alpha].\beta \cdot k':\alpha}\ [\mathrm{THR}]$$

$$\frac{\Theta;\Gamma \cdot x:S \vdash P \triangleright \Delta \cdot k:\alpha}{\Theta;\Gamma \vdash k?(x).P \triangleright \Delta \cdot k:?[S].\alpha}\ [\mathrm{RCV}] \qquad \frac{\Theta;\Gamma \vdash P \triangleright \Delta \cdot k:\beta \cdot x:\alpha}{\Theta;\Gamma \vdash k?(x).P \triangleright \Delta \cdot k:?[\alpha].\beta}\ [\mathrm{CAT}]$$

$$\frac{\Theta;\Gamma \vdash P \triangleright \Delta \cdot k:\alpha_j}{\Theta;\Gamma \vdash k \lhd l_j.P \triangleright \Delta \cdot k:\oplus[l_1:\alpha_1,\ldots,l_n:\alpha_n]}\ (1 \le j \le n)\ [\mathrm{SEL}]$$

$$\frac{\Theta;\Gamma \vdash P_1 \triangleright \Delta \cdot k:\alpha_1 \quad \ldots \quad \Theta;\Gamma \vdash P_n \triangleright \Delta \cdot k:\alpha_n}{\Theta;\Gamma \vdash k \rhd \{l_1:P_1,\ldots,l_n:P_n\} \triangleright \Delta \cdot k:\&[l_1:\alpha_1,\ldots,l_n:\alpha_n]}\ [\mathrm{BR}]$$

$$\frac{\Gamma \vdash e \triangleright \mathsf{bool} \quad \Theta;\Gamma \vdash P \triangleright \Delta \quad \Theta;\Gamma \vdash Q \triangleright \Delta}{\Theta;\Gamma \vdash \mathtt{if}\ e\ \mathtt{then}\ P\ \mathtt{else}\ Q \triangleright \Delta}\ [\mathrm{IF}]$$

$$\frac{\Theta;\Gamma \vdash P \triangleright \Delta \quad \Theta;\Gamma \vdash Q \triangleright \Delta'}{\Theta;\Gamma \vdash P \mid Q \triangleright \Delta \cdot \Delta'}\ [\mathrm{CONC}] \qquad \frac{\Theta;\Gamma \cdot a:S \vdash P \triangleright \Delta}{\Theta;\Gamma \vdash (\nu a)P \triangleright \Delta}\ [\mathrm{RES1}]$$

$$\frac{\Theta;\Gamma \vdash P \triangleright \Delta \cdot s:\alpha \cdot \bar{s}:\bar{\alpha}}{\Theta;\Gamma \vdash (\nu s)P \triangleright \Delta}\ [\mathrm{RES2}] \qquad \frac{\Theta;\Gamma \vdash P \triangleright \Delta \quad s \text{ not in } \Delta}{\Theta;\Gamma \vdash (\nu s)P \triangleright \Delta}\ [\mathrm{RES3}]$$

$$\Theta \cdot X:\Delta;\Gamma \vdash X \triangleright \Delta\ [\mathrm{VAR}] \qquad \frac{\Theta \cdot X:\Delta;\Gamma \vdash P \triangleright \Delta}{\Theta;\Gamma \vdash \mu X.P \triangleright \Delta}\ [\mathrm{REC}]$$

Figure. 9. Typing system for π-calculus.

Results

We report here the main results concerning the type discipline, namely Subject Reduction and Type Safety, borrowed from [23]. The former result states that well-typedness is preserved along computations, while the latter states that no interaction errors occur on well-typed processes.

Theorem 2 Subject Reduction

If $\Theta;\Gamma \vdash P \triangleright \Delta$ with Δ balanced and $P \rightarrow^* Q$,, then $\Theta;\Gamma \vdash Q \triangleright \Delta'$ and Δ′ balanced.

Proof

See proof of Theorem 3.3 in [23].

The notion of error, necessary to formalise Type Safety, is also taken from [23]. A k-process is a process prefixed by subject k, while a k-redex is the parallel composition of two k-processes either of the form $(k!\langle e\rangle.P_1 \mid k?(x).P_2)$, or $(k \lhd l_i.P \mid k \rhd \{l_1 : P_1,\ldots,l_n : P_n\})$. Then, P is an error if P≡(νc)(Q|R) where Q is, for some k, the parallel composition of either two k-processes that do not form a k-redex, or of three or more k-processes.

Theorem 3 Type Safety

A program typable under a balanced channel environment never reduces to an error.

Proof

See proof of Theorem 3.4 in [23].

Typing *ReSϖ*

We show here how the notion of types, the typing system and the related results given for the π-calculus (Section 6.1) can be reused for typing ReSπ. The key point is that we only consider reachable ReSπ processes originated from ReSπ programs that are well-typed (according to the typing discipline of π-calculus). In fact, by statically type checking ReSπprograms, we already check all possible interactions that they will perform. More specifically, Subject Reduction and Type Safety ensure that all runtime processes obtained from a program by means of (forward) reductions are interaction safe. Thus, since backward computations cannot lead to new runtime processes, but just go back to terms reachable from the program via forward reductions, there is no need of type checking the content of the memories in runtime processes.

Now, before formally showing how the typing discipline of π-calculus extends to ReSπ, we introduce a few auxiliary definitions and results.

Definition 6 Reachable Processes for typed ReSϖ

The set of reachable processes for the typed ReSπ only contains: (i) programs M such that $\Theta;\Gamma \vdash \phi(M) \triangleright \Delta$ with Δ balanced, and (ii) runtime processes M obtained by forward reductions from the above programs.

Property 1

Let M be a reachable process. If M↣M′then M′is a reachable process.

Proof

The proof follows from Definition 6 and Lemma 5 (see Appendix A.2).

The notion of well-typedness for ReSπ, expressed by the judgement $\Theta;\Gamma \vdash_r M \triangleright \Delta$,, is defined in terms of the well-typedness notion introduced for the π-calculus.

Definition 7 Well-typedness

$\Theta;\Gamma \vdash_r M \triangleright \Delta$ if and only if $\Theta,\Gamma \vdash \psi(M) \triangleright \Delta$,, with Δ balanced.

Thus, Subject Reduction extends to ReSπ terms as follows.

Theorem 4 Subject Reduction

Let M be a reachable process. If $\Theta;\Gamma \vdash_r M \triangleright \Delta$ with Δ balanced and M↣M′, then $\Theta;\Gamma \vdash_r M' \triangleright \Delta'$and Δ′ balanced.

Proof

The proof relies on Theorem 2 (see Appendix A.2).

We conclude by showing how the notion of error and Type Safety of π-calculus extends to ReSπ. A ReSπ process M is an error if and only if φ(M) is an error.

Theorem 5 Type Safety

A ReSπ program typable under a balanced channel environment never reduces to an error.

Proof

By the notion of ReSπ error and by Theorem 3, we have that typable programs are not errors. Then, by Theorem 4 we have the thesis.

Typing the Multiple Providers Scenario

Coming back to the scenario introduced in Section 3.3 and specified in ReSπ in Section4.3, we can easily verify that the process

$$t_1 : P_{client} \mid t_2 : P_{provider1} \mid t_3 : P_{provider2}$$

is well-typed (assuming that the unspecified processes P_{acc}, P_{neg}, Q_{acc} and Q_{neg} are properly typable). In particular, the channel a login can be typed by the shared channel type

$$\langle\, ?[\text{Request}].\,![\text{Quote}].\,\&[l_{acc} : \alpha_{acc},\, l_{neg} : \alpha_{neg},\, l_{rej} : \text{end}]\,\rangle$$

where we use sorts Request and Quote to type requests and quotes, respectively.

Let us consider now a scenario where the client wishes to concurrently submit two different requests to the same provider, which would be able to concurrently serve them. Consider in particular the following specification of the client (the provider one is dual):

$$\overline{a_{login}}(x).\,(\,x!\langle \text{srv\_req\_1}\rangle.\,P_1 \mid x!\langle \text{srv\_req\_2}\rangle.\,P_2\,)$$

The new specification of the scenario is clearly not well-typed, due to the use of parallel threads within the same session. This forbids us from mixing up messages related to different requests and wrongly delivering them. In order to properly concurrently submit separate requests, the client must instantiate separate sessions with the provider, one for each request.

The session type discipline, indeed, forces concurrent interactions to follow structured patterns that guarantee the correctness of communication. For what concerns reversibility, linear use of session channels limits the effect of causal consistency, since concurrent interactions along the same session are prevented and, hence, the backtracking of a given session follows a single path. Of course, interactions along different sessions are still concurrent and, therefore, it is important to use a causal-consistent rollback to revert them.

COMMITTABLE SESSIONS

The calculus ReSπ discussed so far is fully reversible, i.e. backward computations are always enabled. Full reversibility provides theoretical foundations for studying reversibility in session-based π-calculus, but it is not suitable for a practical use on structured communication-based programming. Therefore, in this section, we enrich the framework to allow computation to go backward and forward along a session, allowing the involved parties to try different interactions, until the session is successfully completed. This is achieved by adding a specific action to the calculus for irreversibly committing the closure of sessions.

It is worth noticing that the fully reversible characterisation of the calculus permits us to prove that its machinery for reversibility (i.e., memories and their usage) soundly works with respect to the expected properties of a reversible calculus. This remains valid also for the extension proposed here. In fact, as clarified below, the extended calculus basically prunes some computations allowed in ReSπ, which corresponds to backward and forward actions that are undesired after a session closure.

ReSϖ with Commit

The syntax of ReSπC (Reversible Session-based π-calculus with Commit) is obtained from that of ReSπ (given in Fig. 4) by extending the syntactic category of processes P with process commit(k).P, and by extending the syntactic category of memories mwith the commit memory $\langle t_1 - \surd(s) \rightarrow t_2 \rangle$. This new memory simply registers the closing event of the session identified by s due to an agreement of threads tagged by $t_1$and t_2.

The irreversible closure of a session is achieved by the synchronisation on its session channel s of two threads of the form $t_1 : \mathtt{commit}(\bar{s}).P_1$ and t_2:commit(s).P_2. This synchronisation acts similarly to the 'cut' operator in Prolog, as both mechanisms are used to prevent unwanted backtracking. After the synchronisation, since the session s is closed, the continuations P_1 and P_2 can no longer use the session channel s ; this check is statically enforced by the type system for ReSπC (presented later on).

Formally, the semantics of ReSπC is obtained by adding the following rule to those defining the reduction relation of ReSπ (Fig. 6):

$$\begin{array}{ll} t_1 : \mathtt{commit}(\bar{k}).P_1 \mid t_2 : \mathtt{commit}(k).P_2 & (k = s \text{ or } k = \bar{s})\ [\text{COMMIT}] \\ \twoheadrightarrow\ (\nu t_1', t_2')(t_1' : P_1 \mid t_2' : P_2 \mid \langle t_1 - \surd(s) \rightarrow t_2 \rangle) & \end{array}$$

Since commit is an irreversible action that will never be backtracked, there is no need to remember information about the continuation processes in the generated memory. For the same reason, there is no backward rule inverse to [commit].

For what concerns the type discipline, types α (defined in Fig. 7) are extended with type $\surd$, while the typing system is extended with the following rule:

$$\frac{\Theta; \Gamma \vdash P \rhd \Delta \cdot k : \text{end}}{\Theta; \Gamma \vdash \mathtt{commit}(k).P \rhd \Delta \cdot k : \surd}\ [\text{COMMIT}]$$

which ensures that after the commit the session is closed.

Irreversibility Propagation

When a commit action is executed, all actions that caused it became unbacktrackable, although they were themselves reversible. In other words, a commit action creates adomino effect that disables the possibility of reversing the session actions previously performed.

To formalise the domino effect caused by the commit irreversible action, we have to introduce the following notions of head and tail of memories:

$$\begin{array}{ll} \text{head}(\langle t_1 \text{ –A}\rightarrow t_2, t_1', t_2' \rangle) = \{t_1, t_2\} & \text{tail}(\langle t_1 \text{ –A}\rightarrow t_2, t_1', t_2' \rangle) = \{t_1', t_2'\} \\ \text{head}(\langle t, e?\, P{:}Q, t' \rangle) = \{t\} & \text{tail}(\langle t, e?\, P{:}Q, t' \rangle) = \{t'\} \\ \text{head}(\langle t \rightrightarrows (t_1, t_2) \rangle) = \{t\} & \text{tail}(\langle t \rightrightarrows (t_1, t_2) \rangle) = \{t_1, t_2\} \\ \text{head}(\langle t_1 - \surd(s) \rightarrow t_2 \rangle) = \{t_1, t_2\} & \text{tail}(\langle t_1 - \surd(s) \rightarrow t_2 \rangle) = \emptyset \end{array}$$

Using the terminology of [5], we say that a memory is locked when the event stored inside can never be reverted, because the conditions triggering the corresponding backward reduction will never be satisfied. Specifically, to perform a backward reduction is required the coexistence of a memory with threads properly tagged, and the latter will never be available due to an irreversible action. Let us now formalise, given a process M , its setL_M of locked memories.

Definition 8 Locked Memories

Let M be a ReSπC process and M_M stand for the set of memories occurring in M. The set L_M of locked memories of M is defined as follows:

- $\langle t_1 - \surd(s) \rightarrow t_2 \rangle \in \mathcal{M}_M \quad \Rightarrow \quad \langle t_1 - \surd(s) \rightarrow t_2 \rangle \in \mathcal{L}_M$
- $m \in \mathcal{L}_M,\ m' \in \mathcal{M}_M,\ t \in \mathrm{head}(m),\ t \in \mathrm{tail}(m') \quad \Rightarrow \quad m' \in \mathcal{L}_M$

The first point says that a commit memory is locked, while the second point describes the propagation of the locking effect, i.e. the event within m depends on the event within m'(because the latter generates a thread involved in the former) and hence also m' is locked. Of course, $L_M \subseteq M_M$.

Now, we can demonstrate the main result about ReSπC, stating that committed sessions cannot be reverted (Theorem 6). This result is based on the notion of reversible memory (Definition 9) and on Lemma 7, ensuring that locked memories cannot be reverted. We use $\rightsquigarrow^+$ to denote the transitive closure of $\rightsquigarrow$.

Definition 9

Let M be a ReSπC process. A memory $m \in M_M$ is reversible if there exists a processM' such that $M \rightsquigarrow^+ M'$ and $m \notin M_{M'}$.

Intuitively, a memory can be reverted if there exists a backward computation that consumes it to restore the threads it memorises.

Lemma 7

Let M be a ReSπCprocess. If $m \in L_M$ then m is not reversible.

Proof

The proof proceeds by contradiction (see Appendix A.3).

Theorem 6

Let M be a ReSπCprocess and s a session committed in M. Then, all interactions performed along s cannot be reverted.

Proof

The proof relies on Lemma 7 (see Appendix A.3).

The Multiple Providers Scenario in *ReSϖC*

Let us consider again the multiple providers scenario specified in ReSπ in Section 4.3.

Suppose now that, for the sake of simplicity, the client and the first provider commit the session immediately after the acceptance of the quote. That is, Pacc and Qacc stand forcommit(x) and commit(y), respectively. Thus, the computation described in Section 3.3 in ReSπC corresponds to:

$$t_1 : P_{client} \mid t_2 : P_{provider1} \mid t_3 : P_{provider2}$$

$$\twoheadrightarrow \twoheadrightarrow \twoheadrightarrow \twoheadrightarrow \twoheadrightarrow$$

$$\begin{aligned} M = {} & (\nu s, t_1^1, t_2^1, \ldots, t_1^5, t_2^4) \\ & (t_1^5 : \mathtt{commit}(\bar{s}) \mid t_2^4 : \mathtt{commit}(s) \\ & \mid \langle t_1 - a_{login} \ldots \rightarrow t_2, t_1^1, t_2^1 \rangle \mid \ldots \mid \langle t_1^4 - s \triangleleft l_{acc} \ldots \rightarrow t_2^3, t_1^5, t_2^4 \rangle) \\ & \mid P_{provider2} \end{aligned}$$

M can now evolve as follows:

$$\begin{aligned} M \twoheadrightarrow M' = {} & (\nu s, t_1^1, t_2^1, \ldots, t_1^5, t_2^4, t_1^6, t_2^5) \\ & (t_1^6 : \mathbf{0} \mid t_2^5 : \mathbf{0} \mid \langle t_1^5 - \surd(s) \rightarrow t_2^4 \rangle \\ & \mid \langle t_1 - a_{login} \ldots \rightarrow t_2, t_1^1, t_2^1 \rangle \mid \ldots \mid \langle t_1^4 - s \triangleleft l_{acc} \ldots \rightarrow t_2^3, t_1^5, t_2^4 \rangle) \\ & \mid P_{provider2} \end{aligned}$$

The memory $\langle t_1^5 - \surd(s) \rightarrow t_2^4 \rangle$ generated by this last forward reduction is locked (first point of Definition 8). Thus, also memory $\langle t_1^4 - s \triangleleft l_{acc} \ldots \rightarrow t_2^3, t_1^5, t_2^4 \rangle$ is locked, since its tail contains tags belonging to the head of the commit memory (second point of Definition 8). Repeatedly applying the second point of Definition 8, we obtain that $L_{M'} = M_{M'}$, i.e. all memory of M' are locked. This means that $M' \not\rightsquigarrow$ and hence, as desired, the computation along session s cannot be reverted.

CONCLUDING REMARKS

To bring the benefits of reversible computing to structured communication-based programming, we have defined a theoretical framework based on π-calculus that can be used as formal basis for studying the interplay between (causal-consistent) reversibility and session-based structured interaction. We conclude the paper by discussing the main directions of ongoing and future work.

Concerning the reversible calculus, we plan to investigate the definition of a syntactic characterisation of consistent terms, which statically enforces history consistency in memories (as in [15]), rather than using the current definition of reachable process (as in [20] and [18]). In line with [17], we also plan to enrich the language with primitives and mechanisms to control reversibility.

For what concerns the typing discipline of ReSπ, we intend to investigate the definition of a typing system capable of type checking contents of memories, in order to identify interaction errors that could be caused by terms restored from memories. This permits us to extend the class of ReSπ programs to include also processes with memories, thus allowing programmers to write also this kind of reversible code. We think that the required checks would resemble the semantics of the roll primitive in [17], which can be then used as a source of inspiration.

Coming to the extension with committable sessions, it is worth noticing that action commitmust be carefully used in case of subordinate sessions. For example, let us consider the typical three-party scenario where a Customer sends an order to a Seller that, in his own turn, contacts a Shipper for the delivery. We have that the session between the Seller and the Shipper is subordinated to the session between the Customer and the Seller. Now, when the main session is committed, also the subordinate session is involved in the commit. This is usually desirable, because the commit acts on the whole transaction and, hence, after the commit the interaction with the Shipper cannot be reverted. However, if the subordinate session is previously committed, the main session is affected, because interaction performed before the commit cannot be reverted. This latter situation is typically undesirable; therefore, as a best practice, commit should be not used by subordinate sessions. We plan to devise a static analysis technique supporting this disciplined use of commit in presence of subordinate sessions.

As longer-term goal, we intend to apply the proposed approach to other session-based formalisms, which consider, e.g., asynchronous sessions and multiparty sessions. We also plan to investigate implementation issues that may arise when incorporating the approach into standard programming languages, in particular in case of a distributed setting. The rollback mechanism incorporated in the semantics of the language would require low-level synchronisations between the involved parties.

Appendix A. Proofs

A.1. Proofs of Section 5

A.1.1. Correspondence with π-calculus

Lemma 1

Let M and N be two ReSπ processes. If M≡N then φ(M)≡φ(N).

Proof

We proceed by induction on the derivation of M≡N. For most of the laws in Fig. 5 the conclusion is trivial because φ(M)≡φ(N) directly corresponds to a law for π-calculus in Fig. 2. Instead, for the eighth and twelve laws, we easily conclude because by applying φwe obtain the identity.

Lemma 2

Let M and N be two ReSπ processes. If M↠Nthen φ(M)→φ(N).

Proof

We proceed by induction on the derivation of M↠N. Base cases:

- [fwCon]:: We have that $M = t_1 : \bar{a}(x).P_1 \mid t_2 : a(y).P_2$ and $N = (\nu s, t'_1, t'_2)(t'_1 : P_1[\bar{s}/x] \mid t'_2 : P_2[s/y] \mid \langle t_1 - a(x)(y)(\nu s)P_1 P_2 \rightarrow t_2, t'_1, t'_2\rangle)$ with $s, \bar{s} \notin \mathrm{fse}(P_1, P_2)$. By definition of φ, we obtain $\phi(M) = \bar{a}(x).P_1 \mid a(y).P_2$. Now, by applying rules [Con] and [Str], we have $\phi(M) \rightarrow (\nu s)(P_1[\bar{s}/x] \mid P_2[s/y] \mid \mathbf{0}) = P$. By definition of φ , we have φ(N)=P that permits us to conclude.
- [fwCom], [fwLab], [fwIf1], [fwIf2]: These cases are similar to the previous one.

Inductive cases:

- [fwPar]: We have that $M = M_1 \mid M_2$ and $N = M'_1 \mid M_2$. By the premise of rule [fwPar], we also have $M_1 \twoheadrightarrow M'_1$ from which, by induction, we obtain $\phi(M_1) \rightarrow \phi(M'_1)$. By definition of φ, we get $\phi(M) = \phi(M_1) \mid \phi(M_2)$. By applying rule [Par], we have $\phi(M) \rightarrow \phi(M'_1) \mid \phi(M_2) = P$. Thus, by definition of φ, we have $\phi(N) = P$ that directly permits us to conclude.
- [fwRes]: This case is similar to the previous one. In particular, when the restricted name is a tag, it is not even necessary to apply rule [Res], because the forgetful map erases the restriction.
- [fwStr]: By the premise of rule [fwStr], we have M≡M′, M′↠N′ and N′≡N. By induction, we obtain φ(M′)→φ(N′). By applying Lemma 1, we have φ(M)≡φ(M′)and φ(N′)≡φ(N) that allow us to conclude.

Lemma 3

Let P and Q be two π-calculus processes. If P≡Q then for any ReSπ process M such that φ(M)=P there exists a ReSπ process N such that φ(N)=Q and M≡N.

Proof

The proof is straightforward. Indeed, given a ReSπ process M such that φ(M)=P, it must have the form $(\nu\tilde{t})(t : P \mid \prod_{i\in I} m_i)$ up to ≡. Thus, the process N, such that φ(N)=Q, can be defined accordingly: $N \equiv (\nu\tilde{t})(t : Q \mid \prod_{i\in I} m_i)$. Now, we can conclude by exploiting the ninth law in Fig. 5, i.e. t:P≡t:Q if P≡Q, and the fact that relation ≡ on ReSπ processes is a congruence.

Lemma 4

Let P and Q be two π-calculus processes. If P→Q then for any ReSπ process M such that φ(M)=P there exists a ReSπ process N such that φ(N)=Q and M↠N.

Proof

We proceed by induction on the derivation of P→Q. Base cases:

- [Con]: We have that $P = \bar{a}(x).P_1 \mid a(y).P_2$ and $Q = (\nu s)(P_1[\bar{s}/x] \mid P_2[s/y])$ with $s, \bar{s} \notin \mathrm{fse}(P_1, P_2)$. Let M be a ReSπ process such that φ(M)=P, it must have the form $(\nu\tilde{t})(t_1 : \bar{a}(x).P_1 \mid t_2 : a(y).P_2 \mid \prod_{i\in I} m_i)$ up to ≡ up to ≡. Thus, by applying rules [fwCon], [fwPar], [fwRes] and [fwStr], we get $M \twoheadrightarrow (\nu\tilde{t}, s, t'_1, t'_2)(t'_1 : P_1[\bar{s}/x] \mid t'_2 : P_2[s/y] \mid \langle t_1 - a(x)(y)(\nu s)P_1 P_2 \rightarrow t_2, t'_1, t'_2\rangle \mid \prod_{i\in I} m_i) = N$. We conclude by applying φ to N, since we obtain φ(N)=Q.
- [Com], [Lab], [If1], [If2]: These cases are similar to the previous one.

Inductive cases:

- [Par]: We have that P = P1 | P2 and $Q = P'_1 \mid P_2$. Let M be a ReSπ process such thatφ(M)=P_1|P_2. We have $M \equiv (\nu\tilde{t})(t_1 : P_1 \mid t_2 : P_2 \mid \prod_{i\in I} m_i) \equiv (\nu\tilde{t'})(M_1 \mid t_2 : P_2 \mid \prod_{j\in J} m_j)$ with $M_1 \equiv (\nu\tilde{t''})(t_1 : P_1 \mid \prod_{k\in K} m_k)$, $\tilde{t} = \tilde{t'}, \tilde{t''}$, and J∪K=I. By the premise of rule [Par], we also have $P_1 \rightarrow P'_1$ from which, by induction, since φ(M_1)=P_1, there exists M'_1 such that $\phi(M'_1) = P'_1$ and $M_1 \twoheadrightarrow M'_1$. Thus, by applying rules [fwPar], [fwRes] and [fwStr], we get $M \twoheadrightarrow (\nu\tilde{t'})(M'_1 \mid t_2 : P_2 \mid \prod_{j\in J} m_j) = N$. We conclude by applying φ to N, because $\phi(N) = \phi(M'_1) \mid P_2 = P'_1 \mid P_2 = Q$.
- [Res]: This case is similar to the previous one.
- [Str]: We have that P≡P′, Q≡Q′ and P′→Q′. Let M be a process such that φ(M)=P. By applying Lemma 3, there exists M′ such that φ(M′)=P′ and M≡M′. By induction, there is N′ such that φ(N′)=Q′ and M′↠N′. By applying Lemma 3again, there exists N such that φ(N)=Q and N≡N′. By applying rule [fwStr], we conclude M↠N.

A.1.2. Loop lemma

Lemma 5

Let M and N be two reachable ReSπ processes. $M \twoheadrightarrow N$ if and only if $N \rightsquigarrow M$.

Proof

The proof for the if part is by induction on the derivation of $M \twoheadrightarrow N$. Base cases:

- [fwCon]: We have that and $N = (\nu s, t_1', t_2')(t_1' : P_1[\bar{s}/x] \mid t_2' : P_2[s/y] \mid \langle t_1 - a(x)(y)(\nu s)P_1 P_2 \rightarrow t_2, t_1', t_2' \rangle)$ with $s, \bar{s} \notin fse(P_1, P_2)$. By applying rule [bwCon], we can directly conclude $N \rightsquigarrow M$.
- [fwCom], [fwLab], [fwIf1], [fwIf2]: These cases are similar to the previous one.
- Inductive cases:
- [fwPar]: We have that $M = N_1 | N_2$, $N = N_1' \mid N_2$ and $N_1 \twoheadrightarrow N_1'$. By induction $N_1' \rightsquigarrow N_1$. Thus, we conclude by applying rule [bwPar], since we get $N = N_1' \mid N_2 \rightsquigarrow N_1 \mid N_2 = M$.
- [fwRes]: We have that $M = (\nu h)M_1$, $N = (\nu h)M_1'$ and $M_1 \twoheadrightarrow M_1'$. By induction $M_1' \rightsquigarrow M_1$. Thus, we conclude by applying rule [bwRes], since we get $N = (\nu h)M_1' \rightsquigarrow (\nu h)M_1 = M$.
- [fwStr]: We have that $M \equiv M'$, $N \equiv N'$ and $M' \twoheadrightarrow N'$. By induction $N' \rightsquigarrow M'$. Thus, we conclude by applying rule [bwStr], since we directly get $N \rightsquigarrow M$.
- The proof for the only if part is by induction on the derivation of $N \rightsquigarrow M$. Base cases:
- [bwCon]: We have that $N = (\nu s, t_1', t_2')(t_1' : P \mid t_2' : Q \mid \langle t_1 - a(x)(y)(\nu s)P_1 P_2 \rightarrow t_2, t_1', t_2' \rangle)$ and $M = t_1 : \bar{a}(x).P_1 \mid t_2 : a(y).P_2$. Since N is a reachable process, memory $\langle t_1 - a(x)(y)(\nu s)P_1 P_2 \rightarrow t_2, t_1', t_2' \rangle$ has been generated by a synchronisation between threads $t_1 : \bar{a}(x).P_1$ and $t_2 : a(y).P_2$, producing a session channel s and two continuation processes $P_1[\bar{s}/x]$ and $P_2[s/y]$ tagged by t_1' and t_2', respectively. Now, by tag uniqueness implied by reachability and use of restriction in tag generation, Pand Q must coincide with $P_1[\bar{s}/x]$ and $P_2[s/y]$, respectively. Therefore, by applying rule [fwCon], we can directly conclude $M \twoheadrightarrow N$.

[bw • Com], [bwLab], [bwIf]: These cases are similar to the previous one.

Inductive cases:

- [bwPar]: We have that $N = N_1 | N_2$, $M = N_1' \mid N_2$ and $N_1 \rightsquigarrow N_1'$. By induction $N_1' \twoheadrightarrow N_1$. Thus, we conclude by applying rule [fwPar], since we get $M = N_1' \mid N_2 \twoheadrightarrow N_1 \mid N_2 = N$.
- [bwRes]: We have that $N = (\nu h)N_1$, $M = (\nu h)N_1'$ and $N_1 \rightsquigarrow N_1'$. By induction $N_1' \twoheadrightarrow N_1$. Thus, we conclude by applying rule [fwRes], since we get $M = (\nu h)N_1' \twoheadrightarrow (\nu h)N_1 = N$.
- [bwStr]: We have that $N \equiv N'$, $M \equiv M'$ and $N' \rightsquigarrow M'$. By induction $M' \twoheadrightarrow N'$. Thus, we conclude by applying rule [fwStr], since we directly get $M \twoheadrightarrow N$.

A.1.3. Causal consistency

Lemma 6

If $\tau_1 = M \xrightarrow{\eta_1} M_1$ and $\tau_2 = M \xrightarrow{\eta_2} M_2$ are two coinitial concurrent transitions, then there exist two cofinal transitions $\tau_2/\tau_1 = M_1 \xrightarrow{\eta_2} N$ and $\tau_1/\tau_2 = M_2 \xrightarrow{\eta_1} N$.

Proof

By case analysis on the form of transitions τ_1 and τ_2.

$M \xrightarrow{m_1, \mathcal{M}_1, \rightarrow} M_1$ and $M \xrightarrow{m_2, \mathcal{M}_2, \rightarrow} M_2$. The two transitions can be any combination of forward reductions. Let us consider the case of two communication (the other cases are similar). Since the two transitions are concurrent, the involved threads are four distinct threads (two sending threads and two receiving ones). In particular, we consider below two communications along different sessions; in fact, the type discipline in Section 6 forbids concurrent communications along the same session (although, in this proof, this kind of concurrent communications would not cause any problem). Thus, in the considered case, the source of the two transitions is as follows:

$$M \equiv (\nu s_1, s_2, \tilde{t})(t_1 : \bar{s}_1!\langle e_1 \rangle.P_1 \mid t_2 : s_1?(x_1).P_2 \\ \mid t_3 : \bar{s}_2!\langle e_2 \rangle.P_3 \mid t_4 : s_2?(x_2).P_4 \mid M')$$

where t_1, t_2, t_3, t_4 are in $\tilde{t}$. Then, $M \twoheadrightarrow M_1$ with

$$M_1 \equiv (\nu s_1, s_2, \tilde{t}, t_1', t_2')(t_1' : P_1 \mid t_2' : P_2[v_1/x_1] \mid m_1 \\ \mid t_3 : \bar{s}_2!\langle e_2 \rangle.P_3 \mid t_4 : s_2?(x_2).P_4 \mid M')$$

where $e_1 \downarrow v_1$ and $m_1 = \langle t_1 - \bar{s}_1\langle e_1 \rangle(x_1)P_1 P_2 \rightarrow t_2, t_1', t_2' \rangle$. Similarly, $M \twoheadrightarrow M_2$ with

$$M_2 \equiv (\nu s_1, s_2, \tilde{t}, t_3', t_4')(t_1 : \bar{s}_1!\langle e_1 \rangle.P_1 \mid t_2 : s_1?(x_1).P_2 \\ \mid t_3' : P_3 \mid t_4' : P_4[v_2/x_2] \mid m_2 \mid M')$$

where $e_2 \downarrow v_2$ and $m_2 = \langle t_3 - \bar{s}_2\langle e_2 \rangle(x_2)P_3 P_4 \rightarrow t_4, t_3', t_4' \rangle$. Now, we have that $M_1 \twoheadrightarrow N$with

$$N \equiv (\nu s_1, s_2, \tilde{t}, t_1', t_2', t_3', t_4')(t_1' : P_1 \mid t_2' : P_2[v_1/x_1] \mid m_1 \\ \mid t_3' : P_3 \mid t_4' : P_4[v_2/x_2] \mid m_2 \mid M')$$

As desired, we also have that $M_2 \twoheadrightarrow N$.

$M \xrightarrow{m_1, \mathcal{M}_1, \rightarrow} M_1$ and $M \xrightarrow{m_2, \mathcal{M}_2, \rightsquigarrow} M_2$. The two transitions can be any combination of a forward rule and a backward one, respectively. Let us consider the case of a forward communication and the undo of a choice (again, the other cases are similar). Thus, in the considered case, the source of the two transitions is as follows:

$$M \equiv (\nu s, \tilde{t}, t_3')(t_1 : \bar{s}!\langle e_1 \rangle.P_1 \mid t_2 : s?(x_1).P_2 \\ \mid t_3' : P_3 \mid m_2 \mid M')$$

where $m_2 = \langle t_3, e_2 ? P_3 : P_4, t_3' \rangle$, $e \downarrow true$, and t_1, t_2, t_3 are in $\tilde{t}$. Notably, since the two transitions are concurrent, the continuation tag in m_2 can be neither t_1 nor t_2(indeed, in the above process M this tag is t_3'). Then, $M \twoheadrightarrow M_1$ with

$$M_1 \equiv (\nu s, \tilde{t}, t_3', t_1', t_2')(t_1' : P_1 \mid t_2' : P_2[v_1/x_1] \mid m_1 \\ \mid t_3' : P_3 \mid m_2 \mid M')$$

where $e_1 \downarrow v_1$ and $m_1 = \langle t_1 - \bar{s}\langle e_1 \rangle(x_1)P_1 P_2 \rightarrow t_2, t_1', t_2' \rangle$. Now, we also have that$M \rightsquigarrow M_2$ with

$$M_2 \equiv (\nu s, \tilde{t})(t_1 : \bar{s}!\langle e_1 \rangle.P_1 \mid t_2 : s?(x_1).P_2 \\ \mid t_3 : \mathtt{if}\ e_2\ \mathtt{then}\ P_3\ \mathtt{else}\ P_4 \mid M')$$

As desired, both M_1 and M_2 can then evolve with a backward and forward reduction, respectively, to N:

$$N \equiv (\nu s, \tilde{t}, t'_1, t'_2)(t'_1 : P_1 \mid t'_2 : P_2[v_1/x_1] \mid m_1 \mid t_3 : \texttt{if}\ e_2\ \texttt{then}\ P_3\ \texttt{else}\ P_4 \mid M')$$

$M \xrightarrow{m_1, \mathcal{M}_1, \rightsquigarrow} M_1$ and $M \xrightarrow{m_2, \mathcal{M}_2, \rightsquigarrow} M_2$. Similar to the first case.

$M \xrightarrow{m_1, \mathcal{M}_1, \rightsquigarrow} M_1$ and $M \xrightarrow{m_2, \mathcal{M}_2, \twoheadrightarrow} M_2$. Similar to the second case.

The proof of the Causal Consistency theorem follows the (standard) pattern used in [15] and [5]. In particular, the proof relies on two auxiliary lemmas. The first lemma permits us to rearrange a trace as a composition of a backward trace and a forward one. The second lemma permits a forward trace to be shortened.

Lemma 8

Let σ be a trace. There exist σ′and σ″both forward traces such that $\sigma \asymp \sigma'_\bullet; \sigma''$.

Proof

We prove this by lexicographic induction on the length of σ, and the distance to the beginning of σ of the earliest pair of transitions in σ contradicting the property. If there is no such contradicting pair, then we are done. If there is one, say a pair of the form $\tau; \tau'_\bullet$ with τ and τ′ forward transitions, we have two possibilities: either τ and τ′ are concurrent, or they are in conflict. In the first case, τ and $\tau'_\bullet$ can be swapped by using Lemma 6, resulting in a later earliest contradicting pair. Then, the result follows by induction, since swapping transitions keeps the total length constant. In the second case, there is a conflict on a tag, because it belongs to the stamps of both transitions. Again, we have two sub-cases: either the memory involved in the two transitions is the same or not. In the first sub-case we have τ=τ′, and then we can apply Lemma 5 to remove $\tau;\tau_\bullet$. Hence, the total length of σ decreases and, again, by induction we obtain the thesis. Instead, the second sub-case never happens. Indeed, let τ generate a memory $m_1 = \langle t, e?P:Q, t' \rangle$ (the case with the action memory is similar). A conflict with τ′ would be caused by the presence of t or t′ in the memory m_2 removed by $\tau'_\bullet$ (and, by hypothesis, different from m_1). However, t cannot occur in m_2, because the transition τ consumed the thread uniquely tagged by t, which then cannot be involved in the other transition. Also t′ cannot occur in m_2, because the thread uniquely tagged by t′ has been generated by τ; thus, another forward transition must take place before $\tau'_\bullet$ to involve this thread so that t′ could occur in m_2.

Lemma 9

Let σ_1 and σ_2 be coinitial and cofinal traces, with σ_2 forward. Then, there exists a forward trace σ'_1 of length at most that of σ_1 such that $\sigma'_1 \asymp \sigma_1$.

Proof

The proof is by induction on the length of σ_1. If σ_1 is a forward trace we are already done. Otherwise, by Lemma 8 we can write σ_1 as $\sigma_\bullet;\sigma'$ (with σ and σ′ forward). Due to its form, σ_1 contains only one sequence of transitions with opposite direction, say $\tau_\bullet;\tau'$. Let m_1 be the memory removed by $\tau_\bullet$. Then, in σ′ there is a forward transition generating m_1; otherwise there would be a difference with respect to σ_2, since the latter is a forward trace. Let τ_1 be the earliest such transition in σ_1. Since τ_1 is able to put backm_1, it has to be the opposite of $\tau_\bullet$, i.e. τ_1=τ. Now, we can swap τ_1 with all the transitions between τ_1 and $\tau_\bullet$, in order to obtain a trace in which τ_1 and $\tau_\bullet$ are adjacent. To do so, we use Lemma 6, since all the transitions in between are concurrent. Assume in fact that there is a transition involving memory m_2 which is not concurrent to τ_1. A possible conflict could be caused by the presence of a continuation tag, say t, of m_1 in m_2. But this case can never happen, since t is freshly generated by the forward rule used to produce τ_1 and thus, thanks to tag uniqueness, t cannot coincide with any tag of a previously executed transition. The other possible conflict could be caused by the presence of a continuation tag of m_2 in m_1. Since $\tau_\bullet$ removes m_1, this memory cannot contain a fresh tag generated by a subsequent transition when m_2 is created. Thus, also this case can never happen. Now, when $\tau_\bullet$ and τ are adjacent, we can remove both of them using ≍. The resulting trace is shorter, thus the thesis follows by inductive hypothesis.

Theorem 1

Let σ_1 and σ_2 be coinitial traces. Then, $\sigma_1 \asymp \sigma_2$ if and only if $\sigma_1$and σ_2 are cofinal.

Proof

By construction of ≍, if $\sigma_1 \asymp \sigma_2$ then σ_1 and σ_2 must be coinitial and cofinal, so this direction of the theorem is verified. Thus, it just remains to prove that σ_1 and σ_2 being coinitial and cofinal implies that $\sigma_1 \asymp \sigma_2$. By Lemma 8, we know that the two traces can be written as composition of a backward trace and a forward one. The proof is by lexicographic induction on the sum of the lengths of σ_1 and σ_2 and on the distance between the end of σ_1 and the earliest pair of transitions τ_1 in σ_1 and τ_2 in σ_2 which are not equal. If all the transitions are equal then we are done. Otherwise, we have to consider four cases, depending on whether the two transitions are forward or backward.

- τ_1 forward and τ_2 backward. One has $\sigma_1 = \sigma_\bullet;\tau_1;\sigma'$ and $\sigma_2 = \sigma_\bullet;\tau_2;\sigma''$ for some σ , σ′, and σ″. Lemma 9 applies to $\tau_1;\sigma'$, since it is a forward trace, and to $\tau_2;\sigma''$; indeed, σ_1 and σ_2 are coinitial and cofinal by hypothesis, thus also $\tau_1;\sigma'$ and $\tau_2;\sigma''$are coinitial and cofinal. We then have that $\tau_2;\sigma''$ has a shorter equivalent forward trace, and so σ_2 has a shorter equivalent forward trace. We can conclude by induction.
- τ_1 backward and τ_2 forward. This case is similar to the previous one.
- τ_1 and τ_2 forward. We have two possibilities: they are concurrent or are not. In the latter case, they should conflict on a thread, say t: P, that they both consume and store in different memories. Since the two traces are cofinal, there should be a transition τ'_2 in σ_2 creating the same memory as τ_1. However no other thread t:P is ever created in σ_2; hence, this is not possible. Therefore, we can assume that $\tau_1$and τ_2 are concurrent. Let τ'_2 be the transition in σ_2 creating the same memory of τ_1. We have to prove that τ'_2 is concurrent to all the previous transitions. This holds since no previous transition can remove one of the processes needed for triggering τ'_2

and since forward transitions can never conflict on t. Thus we can repetitively apply Lemma 6 to derive a trace equivalent to σ_2 where τ_2 and τ_2' are consecutive. We can apply a similar transformation to σ_1. Now, we can apply Lemma 6 to τ_1 and τ_2 to have two traces of the same length as before but where the first pair of different transitions is closer to the end. We then conclude by inductive hypothesis.

- τ_1 and τ_2 backward. Let m_1 be the memory removed by τ_1, which is surely different from the memory removed by τ_2 (indeed, the two backward transitions cannot remove the same memory). Since the two traces are cofinal, either there is another transition in σ_1 putting back the memory or there is a transition τ_1' in σ_2 removing the same memory. In the first case, τ_1 is concurrent to all the backward transitions following it, but the ones that consume processes generated by it. Thus, all such transitions have to be undone by corresponding forward transitions (since they are not possible in σ_2). Consider the last such transition: we can use Lemma 6to make it the last backward transition. The forward transition undoing it should be concurrent to all the previous forward transitions (the reason is the same as in the previous case). We can then use Lemma 6 to make it the first forward transition. Finally, we can apply $\tau_\bullet ; \tau \asymp \epsilon_{\mathtt{target}(\tau)}$ to remove the two transitions, thus shortening the trace. In this way, we obtain the thesis by inductive hypothesis.

A.2. Proofs of Section 6

Property 1

Let M be a reachable process. If $M \rightarrowtail M'$ then M' is a reachable process.

Proof

The proof follows from Definition 6. Indeed, since M is a reachable process, there exists a typed program N such that $N \twoheadrightarrow^* M$, where $\twoheadrightarrow^*$ denotes the reflexive and transitive closure of $\twoheadrightarrow$. Now, we distinguish two cases:

- $M \twoheadrightarrow M'$. In this case, we have $N \twoheadrightarrow^* M \twoheadrightarrow M'$, that is $N \twoheadrightarrow^* M'$.
- $M \rightsquigarrow M'$. Here we have to sub-cases:

  M' is a process encountered in the computation $N \twoheadrightarrow^* M$. Thus, $N \twoheadrightarrow^* M' \twoheadrightarrow^* M$. In particular, since from $M \rightsquigarrow M'$ by Lemma 5 we have $M' \twoheadrightarrow M$, we obtain $N \twoheadrightarrow^* M' \twoheadrightarrow M$.

  M' is not encountered in $N \twoheadrightarrow^* M$. Since M' is obtained from M by a backward reduction, the memories of M' are the same of M except for the one consumed by the backward reduction (which, of course, is missing in M'). Being M a reachable process, the content of such memories is consistent. Thus, consuming all memories in M' inevitably leads to the program N, i.e. $M' \rightsquigarrow^* N$. By applying Lemma 5 to all reductions in this backward computation, we obtain $N \twoheadrightarrow^* M'$.

In all cases, M' is originated from the same program of M, hence it is a reachable process too.

Theorem 4

Let M be a reachable process. If $\Theta; \Gamma \vdash_r M \triangleright \Delta$ with Δ balanced and $M \rightarrowtail M'$, then $\Theta; \Gamma \vdash_r M' \triangleright \Delta'$ and Δ' balanced.

Proof

We distinguish two cases:

- $(\rightarrowtail = \twoheadrightarrow)$. By Definition 7, from $\Theta; \Gamma \vdash_r M \triangleright \Delta$ we obtain $\Theta; \Gamma \vdash \phi(M) \triangleright \Delta$. By applying Lemma 2 to the hypothesis $M \twoheadrightarrow M'$, we have $\varphi(M) \rightarrow \varphi(M')$. Thus, byTheorem 2, we get $\Theta; \Gamma \vdash \phi(M') \triangleright \Delta'$ with Δ' balanced. Finally, by Definition 7, we have the thesis $\Theta; \Gamma \vdash_r M' \triangleright \Delta'$.
- $(\rightarrowtail = \rightsquigarrow)$. By Property 1, we get that process M' is reachable. Thus, by Definition 6, there exists a program N such that $\Theta; \Gamma \vdash \phi(N) \triangleright \Delta''$ with Δ'' balanced, and $N \twoheadrightarrow^* M'$. Now, we can proceed as in case 1, by applying Lemma 2 and Theorem 2 to obtain $\Theta; \Gamma \vdash \phi(M') \triangleright \Delta'$ with Δ' balanced. Again, by Definition 7, we get the thesis.

A.3. Proofs of Section 7

Lemma 7

Let M be a ReSπCprocess. If $m \in L_M$ then m is not reversible.

Proof

The proof proceeds by contradiction. Suppose that there exists a memory m such that $m \in L_M$ and m is reversible. By Definition 9, there exists M' such that $M \rightsquigarrow^+ M'$ and $m \notin M_M'$. We have two cases:

- 1.m= $\langle t_1 - \surd(s) \rightarrow t_2 \rangle$: this case is trivial because no rule is able to revert this kind of memory (in fact, the forward rule [Commit] is not paired with a corresponding backward rule). Thus, no process M' such that $m \notin M_M'$ can be derived from M, which contradicts the hypothesis.
- 2.m$\neq$ $\langle t_1 - \surd(s) \rightarrow t_2 \rangle$: since $m \in L_M$, by Definition 8, there exists a memory $m' \in L_M$ and tag t such that $t \in tail(m)$ and $t \in head(m')$. To revert m, according to rules [bwcon], [bwcom], [bwlab], and [bwif], for each tag $t' \in tail(m)$ a thread tagged by t' must be in parallel with the memory. However, the tag t in tail(m) also belongs to head(m'), meaning that the thread tagged by t (which, we recall, is unique) has been already executed (in fact, data concerning such execution is stored in m'). Thus, no backward rule can be applied to revert m in one step. The only possibility is to revert m' before. Now, if m' is a commit memory, then we proceed as in case 1, i.e. m' cannot be reverted and, hence, m is not reversible, which is a contradiction. Otherwise, we repeat the same reasoning of case 2 for $m'$and proceed in this way until a commit memory is found. Indeed, this commit memory must exist by construction of L_M (Definition 8, first point). As in case 1, this memory cannot be reverted and, hence, all involved memories, included m, are not reversible, which is a contradiction.

Theorem 6

Let M be a ReSπCprocess and s a session committed in M. Then, all interactions performed along s cannot be reverted.

Proof

Since s is committed in M, then there exists a memory m of the form $\langle t_1 - \surd(s) \rightarrow t_2 \rangle$ such that $m \in M_M$. By Definition 8, $m \in L_M$. Now, we have to prove that all other interactions performed along s corresponds to memories in L_M. By linearity of sessions (ensured by the type discipline in Section 6), each interaction in s causally depends on one of the threads produced by the previous interaction along s. Since m corresponds to the last interaction along s (as ensured by rule [Commit] of the type system), m causally depends on all memories corresponding to the interactions along s. Since $m \in L_M$, by Definition 8 (second point), all such memories are included in L_M. Thus, by applying Lemma 7, we obtain the thesis.

REFERENCES

1. F. Tiezzi, N. Yoshida, Towards reversible sessions, in: PLACES, in: Electron. Proc. Theoret. Comput. Sci., vol. 155, 2014, pp. 17–24.
2. R. Milner, Communication and Concurrency, Prentice-Hall, 1989.
3. R. Milner, J. Parrow, D. Walker, A calculus of mobile processes. I, Inf. Comput. 100 (1992) 1–40; R. Milner, J. Parrow, D. Walker, A calculus of mobile processes. II, Inf. Comput. 100 (1992) 41–77.
4. G. Berry, J. Lévy, Minimal and optimal computations of recursive programs, J. ACM 26 (1979) 148–175.
5. V. Danos, J. Krivine, Reversible communicating systems, in: CONCUR, in: Lect. Notes Comput. Sci., vol. 3170, Springer, 2004, pp. 292–307.
6. H. Barendregt, The Lambda Calculus: Its Syntax and Semantics, Stud. Logic Found. Math., Elsevier Science, 1985.
7. R. De Nicola, U. Montanari, F.W. Vaandrager, Back and forth bisimulations, in: CONCUR, in: Lect. Notes Comput. Sci., vol. 458, Springer, 1990, pp. 152–165.
8. W. Reisig, Understanding Petri Nets – Modeling Techniques, Analysis Methods, Case Studies, Springer, 2013.
9. I. Lanese, C.A. Mezzina, F. Tiezzi, Causal-consistent reversibility, Bull. Eur. Assoc. Theor. Comput. Sci. 114 (2014).
10. V. Danos, J. Krivine, Transactions in RCCS, in: CONCUR, in: Lect. Notes Comput. Sci., vol. 3653, Springer, 2005, pp. 398–412.
11. V. Danos, J. Krivine, Formal molecular biology done in CCS-R, Electron. Notes Theor. Comput. Sci. 180 (2007) 31–49.
12. I.C.C. Phillips, I. Ulidowski, Reversing algebraic process calculi, J. Log. Algebr. Program. 73 (2007) 70–96.
13. J.A. Bergstra, J.W. Klop, Process algebra for synchronous communication, Inf. Control 60 (1984) 109–137.
14. S.D. Brookes, C.A.R. Hoare, A.W. Roscoe, A theory of communicating sequential processes, J. ACM 31 (1984) 560–599.
15. I. Lanese, C.A. Mezzina, J.-B. Stefani, Reversing higher-order pi, in: CONCUR, in: Lect. Notes Comput. Sci., vol. 6269, Springer, 2010, pp. 478–493.
16. D. Sangiorgi, Bisimulation for higher-order process calculi, Inf. Comput. 131 (1996) 141–178.
17. I. Lanese, C.A. Mezzina, A. Schmitt, J.-B. Stefani, Controlling reversibility in higher-order pi, in: CONCUR, in: Lect. Notes Comput. Sci., vol. 6901, Springer, 2011, pp. 297–311.
18. E. Giachino, I. Lanese, C.A. Mezzina, F. Tiezzi, Causal-consistent reversibility in a tuple-based language, in: PDP, IEEE, 2015, in press.
19. R. De Nicola, G.L. Ferrari, R. Pugliese, Klaim: a kernel language for agents interaction and mobility, IEEE Trans. Softw. Eng. 24 (1998) 315–330.
20. I. Cristescu, J. Krivine, D. Varacca, A compositional semantics for the reversible p-calculus, in: LICS, IEEE, 2013, pp. 388–397.
21. L. Cardelli, C. Laneve, Reversible structures, in: CMSB, ACM, 2011, pp. 131–140.
22. A. Phillips, L. Cardelli, A programming language for composable DNA circuits, J. R. Soc. Interface 6 (2009).
23. N. Yoshida, V.T. Vasconcelos, Language primitives and type discipline for structured communication-based programming revisited: two systems for higher-order session communication, Electron. Notes Theor. Comput. Sci. 171 (2007) 73–93.
24. D. Mostrous, N. Yoshida, Session-based communication optimisation for higher-order mobile processes, in: TLCA, in: Lect. Notes Comput. Sci., vol. 5608, Springer, 2009, pp. 203–218.
25. M. Coppo, M. Dezani-Ciancaglini, N. Yoshida, Asynchronous session types and progress for object oriented languages, in: FMOODS, in: Lect. Notes Comput. Sci., vol. 4468, Springer, 2007, pp. 1–31.
26. K. Honda, N. Yoshida, M. Carbone, Multiparty asynchronous session types, in: POPL, ACM, 2008, pp. 273–284.
27. A. Bejleri, N. Yoshida, Synchronous multiparty session types, Electron. Notes Theor. Comput. Sci. 241 (2009) 3–33.
28. M. Boreale, R. Bruni, R. De Nicola, M. Loreti, Sessions and pipelines for structured service programming, in: FMOODS, in: Lect. Notes Comput. Sci., vol. 5051, Springer, 2008, pp. 19–38.
29. R. Bruni, I. Lanese, H.C. Melgratti, E. Tuosto, Multiparty sessions in SOC, in: COORDINATION, in: Lect. Notes Comput. Sci., vol. 5052, Springer, 2008, pp. 67–82.
30. L. Caires, H.T. Vieira, Conversation types, Theor. Comput. Sci. 411 (2010) 4399–4440.
31. F. Barbanera, M. Dezani-Ciancaglini, U. de'Liguoro, Compliance for reversible client/server interactions, in: BEAT, in: Electron. Proc. Theoret. Comput. Sci., vol. 162, 2014, pp. 35–42.

32. F. Barbanera, U. de'Liguoro, Sub-behaviour relations for session-based client/server systems, Math. Struct. Comput. Sci. (2014), in press, http://dx.doi.org/ 10.1017/ S096012951400005X.

33. S.J. Gay, M. Hole, Subtyping for session types in the pi calculus, Acta Inform. 42 (2005) 191–225.

34. I. Lanese, C.A. Mezzina, J.-B. Stefani, Controlled reversibility and compensations, in: RC, in: Lect. Notes Comput. Sci., vol. 7581, Springer, 2013, pp. 233–240.

CHAPTER 13

KERNELS, IN A NUTSHELL

Jeremy Gibbons

Department of Computer Science, University of Oxford, United Kingdom

ABSTRACT

A classical result in algebraic specification states that a total function defined on an initial algebra is a homomorphism if and only if the kernel of that function is a congruence. We expand on the discussion of that result from an earlier paper: extending it from total to partial functions, simplifying the proofs using relational calculus, and generalising the setting to regular categories.

INTRODUCTION

When is a function a fold? In one sense, the definition of *fold* says it all:

$$\begin{aligned}&\mathit{fold} : \mathit{Functor}\,\mathsf{F} \Rightarrow (\mathsf{F}A \to A) \to \mu\mathsf{F} \to A\\&\mathit{fold}_{\mathsf{F}}\,f\,(\mathrm{in}_{\mathsf{F}}\,x) = f\,(\mathsf{F}\,(\mathit{fold}_{\mathsf{F}}\,f)\,x)\end{aligned}$$

A function $h{:}\mu\mathrm{F}{\to}a$ can be written in the form of a fold precisely when there exists an $f{:}\mathrm{F}A{\to}A$ such that $h{=}\mathit{fold}_{\mathrm{F}}f$. For example, with $\mathrm{L}A{=}1{+}\mathit{Nat}{\times}A$ as the shape functor for lists of naturals, $\mathit{sum}{:}\mu\mathrm{L}{\to}\mathit{Nat}$ is a fold: indeed, $\mathit{sum}{=}\mathit{fold}_{\mathrm{L}}\,\mathit{add}$ where

$$\begin{aligned}&\mathit{add}\,(\mathit{Inl}\,()) &&= 0\\&\mathit{add}\,(\mathit{Inr}\,(m, n)) &&= m + n\end{aligned}$$

But $\mathit{allEqual}{:}\mu\mathrm{L}{\to}\mathit{Bool}$, the predicate testing that all elements of a list have the same value, is not a fold: with a little effort (for example, considering lists of length 0, 1, and 2), one can convince oneself that there exists no f with $\mathit{allEqual}{=}\mathit{fold}_{\mathrm{L}}f$

However, this criterion is a little unsatisfying. One can use the existence of f as a criterion to prove that h is a fold, by exhibiting the f; but it is harder to use it to disprove that h is a fold, since it is harder to provide evidence for the non-existence of any such f. The criterion is *intensional*, referring to some property f of the implementation of h, which we may not yet have to hand. We might hope for an *extensional* criterion instead, expressed purely in terms of the behaviour of h rather than of any possible implementation.

An extensional but incomplete answer is given by the observation that if h is injective, so that there exists a post-inverse h' with $h'{\circ}h{=}\mathit{id}$, then

$$h = \mathit{fold}_{\mathsf{F}}\,(h \circ \mathrm{in}_{\mathsf{F}} \circ \mathsf{F}\,h')$$

and so h is a fold. But injectivity is only a sufficient condition, not a necessary one—indeed, *sum* is a fold, despite not being injective. So again this observation is no help in showing that a function is not a fold.

Citation: Jeremy Gibbons, Kernels, in a nutshell, doi:10.1016/j.jlamp.2015.10.006

In this paper, we discuss a necessary and sufficient condition for h to be a fold. The result was presented in an earlier paper [6]. It turns out to be a standard result in algebraic specification; see for example [4, §3.10]. We elaborate on that earlier work here. Our original presentation was purely in set-theoretic terms, treating functions as sets of pairs, and limited to total functions. Here, we point out a straightforward extension to *partial functions*, and we consider an *allegorical* (that is, axiomatic relational) presentation, which turns out to be rather simpler, and one in terms of *regular categories*, which is a bit more flexible.

In the interests of brevity, we talk only about folds and postfactors. There's a dual story about prefactors, but the most useful connection with unfolds isn't quite one of duality (because dualising 'partial function' isn't very helpful). We leave the details for the curious reader to explore for themselves.

TOTALLY

In this section, we work in the category *Set*, in which the objects are sets and the arrows are total functions between sets. In particular, a function $f{:}A{\to}B$ is a triple consisting of the source A, the target B, and the graph, the set of pairs $\{(a,b) | a{\in}A{\wedge}b{=}fa{\in}B\}$. We write $\mathsf{ran}\,f \subseteq B$ for the range of f.

A crucial ingredient in the construction is the notion of the *kernel* of a function, that is, the set of pairs of arguments identified by the function.

Definition 1

The kernel $\mathsf{ker}\,f$ of a total function $f{:}A{\to}B$ is the set of pairs

$$\mathsf{ker}\,f = \{(a,a') \mid a,a' \in A \wedge f\,a = f\,a'\}$$

It is easy to see that this definition yields an equivalence relation on A.

Given $h{:}A{\to}C$ and $f{:}A{\to}B$, when can h be factorised into $g{\circ}f$ for some $g{:}B{\to}C$? It is clearly necessary for the function space $B{\to}C$ to be non-empty, that is, either $C{\neq}\emptyset$or $B{=}\emptyset$; otherwise, there can be no such g. Given that proviso, a necessary and sufficient condition for the existence of such a postfactor g is for the kernel of h to include the kernel of f:

Theorem 2

Given $h{:}A{\to}C$and $f{:}A{\to}B$such that $B{\to}C{\neq}\emptyset$,

$$(\exists g : B \to C \,.\, h = g \circ f) \quad \Leftrightarrow \quad \mathsf{ker}\,h \supseteq \mathsf{ker}\,f$$

Proof

From left to right, suppose that $h{=}g{\circ}f$. Then

$$\begin{array}{l} (a,a') \in \mathsf{ker}\,h \\ \Leftrightarrow \quad [\![\text{ definition of kernel }]\!] \\ h\,a = h\,a' \\ \Leftrightarrow \quad [\![h = g \circ f]\!] \\ g\,(f\,a) = g\,(f\,a') \\ \Leftarrow \quad [\![\text{ Leibniz }]\!] \\ f\,a = f\,a' \\ \Leftrightarrow \quad [\![\text{ definition of kernel }]\!] \\ (a,a') \in \mathsf{ker}\,f \end{array}$$

which establishes the inclusion. From right to left, suppose that $\mathsf{ker}\,h \supseteq \mathsf{ker}\,f$; we construct g as follows. For $b \in \mathsf{ran}\,f$, pick any a such that $fa{=}b$, and define $gb{=}ha$; by the hypothesis, the choice of a does not affect the value of gb. For $b \notin \mathsf{ran}\,f$, definegb arbitrarily; by the assumption that $B{\to}C{\neq}\emptyset$, this is possible (classically).

Remark 4

One can show that $\mathsf{ker}\,(\mathsf{F}h) = \mathsf{Rel}_\mathsf{F}(\mathsf{ker}\,h)$, where $\mathrm{Rel}_\mathrm{F}R$ denotes the *relational lifting* of the relation R on A to a relation acting pointwise on FA. Moreover, since in_F is a bijection, $\mathsf{ker}\,(h \circ \mathsf{in}_\mathsf{F})$ is equivalent to just $\mathsf{ker}\,h$. Finally, given an F-algebra $f{:}\mathrm{F}A{\to}A$, we say that a relation R is an F-*congruence for* f if pointwise-related arguments are taken by f to related results:

$$(x,x') \in \mathsf{Rel}_\mathsf{F}R \quad \Rightarrow \quad (f\,x, f\,x') \in R$$

Then the condition $\mathsf{ker}\,(h \circ \mathsf{in}_\mathsf{F}) \supseteq \mathsf{ker}\,(\mathsf{F}h)$ in Corollary 3 is equivalent to saying that $\mathsf{ker}\,h$ is an F-congruence for in_F, which is the more traditional but less manipulable formulation.

PARTIALLY

The simple characterisation above of the kernel of a total function needs adaptation, if it is to continue to serve as an equivalence relation on the source of a *partial* function:

Definition 5

The kernel $\mathsf{ker}\,f \subseteq A \times A$ of a partial function $f{:}A{\nrightarrow}B$ is the set of pairs

$$\begin{array}{l} \mathsf{ker}\,f = \{(a,a') \mid a,a' \in \mathsf{dom}\,f \wedge f\,a = f\,a'\} \\ \qquad \cup \{(a,a') \mid a,a' \in A - \mathsf{dom}\,f\} \end{array}$$

(writing $\mathsf{dom}\,f \subseteq A$ for the domain of definition of f). This denotes an equivalence relation again: two elements are equivalent iff they are treated equivalently by f. When f is in fact total, $\mathsf{dom}\,f = A$ and Definition 5 reduces to Definition 1.

A postfactor theorem similar to Theorem 2 can be proved for partial functions. The conditions need to be strengthened in one sense: clearly now it is necessary for $\mathsf{dom}\,f$ to include $\mathsf{dom}\,h$. But they may be weakened in another sense: we no longer need to assume a non-empty space of results, because partial functions exist even to empty sets.

Theorem 6

Given partial functions $h{:}A{\nrightarrow}C$and $f{:}A{\nrightarrow}B$,

$$(\exists g : B \nrightarrow C \,.\, h = g \circ f) \quad \Leftrightarrow \quad \mathsf{ker}\,h \supseteq \mathsf{ker}\,f \wedge \mathsf{dom}\,h \subseteq \mathsf{dom}\,f$$

However, the proof is rather more awkward. It depends on the fact that dom $(g \circ f) = \{a \in \mathrm{dom}\ f \mid f\,a \in \mathrm{dom}\ g\}$..

Proof

From left to right, suppose that $h{=}g{\circ}f$. Then

$$\begin{array}{l} a \in \mathsf{dom}\,h \\ \Leftrightarrow \quad [\![h = g \circ f]\!] \\ a \in \mathsf{dom}\,(g \circ f) \\ \Leftrightarrow \quad [\![\text{ domain }]\!] \\ a \in \mathsf{dom}\,f \wedge f\,a \in \mathsf{dom}\,g \\ \Rightarrow \quad [\![\text{ weakening }]\!] \\ a \in \mathsf{dom}\,f \end{array}$$

As for the kernel inclusion, suppose $(a,a') \in \mathsf{ker}\,f$,

, so either (i) $a, a' \in \mathsf{dom} f$ and *fa=fa'*, or (ii) $a, a' \notin \mathsf{dom} f$. In case (i), either $fa, fa' \in \mathsf{dom} g$, when $a, a' \in \mathsf{dom}\, h$ and *ha=g(fa)=g(fa')=ha'*, so $(a, a') \in \ker h$; or $fa, fa' \notin \mathsf{dom} g$, when $a, a' \notin \mathsf{dom}\, h$, so $(a, a') \in \ker h$. Finally, in case (ii), again $a, a' \notin \mathsf{dom}\, h$ and so $(a, a') \in \ker h$.

From right to left, suppose that $\ker h \supseteq \ker f$ and $\mathsf{dom}\, h \subseteq \mathsf{dom} f$; we construct *g* with $\mathsf{dom}\, g = \{f\, a \mid a \in \mathsf{dom}\, h\}$ as follows. For b ∈ dom g, pick any a ∈ dom h such that *fa=b*, and define *gb=ha*; by the hypothesis, the choice of *a* does not affect the result (for if $a, a' \in \mathsf{dom}\, h \subseteq \mathsf{dom} f$ with *fa=fa'*, then $(a, a') \in \ker f \subseteq \ker h$ and so *ha=ha'*). Of course, we do not have to consider b ∈/ dom g, so we need no longer resort to classical reasoning.

ALLEGORICALLY

The construction in the proof of Theorem 2 essentially involves inverting *f*; this suggests that it might be worth exploring a presentation in terms of the relational calculus [2]. Rather than work concretely with relations as sets of pairs, as we did in Section 2 and in[6], we use the axiomatic presentation of a *division allegory* [5], falling back on sets of pairs only for the purposes of illustration. Formally, we consider typed relations *R*:*A*~*B*'from *A* to *B* '; intersection *R*∩*S* forming a semi-lattice, and inducing inclusion *R*⊆*S* as a preorder on relations of a common type; identity *id* and composition *R*∘*S*, forming a monoid, with composition monotonic with respect to ⊆; converse R° forming an involution, contravariant with respect to composition and monotonic with respect to inclusion; and division operators *R*/*S*, *R**S* discussed in more detail below. One additional and non-obvious axiom is required, the so-called *modular law* $(R \circ S) \cap T \subseteq (R \cap (T \circ S^\circ)) \circ S$.

Four special classes of relations are identified as follows:

R injective:	$R^\circ \circ R \subseteq id$	*R* simple:	$R \circ R^\circ \subseteq id$
R entire:	$R^\circ \circ R \supseteq id$	*R* surjective:	$R \circ R^\circ \supseteq id$

We say that *R* is *coreflexive* if *R*⊆*id*. The *domain* of a relation is defined by

$$\mathsf{dom}\, R = (R^\circ \circ R) \cap id$$

with the universal property that dom R is the smallest coreflexive *S* that may be extracted as a prefactor:

$$\mathsf{dom}\, R \subseteq S \quad \Leftrightarrow \quad R \subseteq R \circ S \qquad \text{– for coreflexive } S$$

Lemma 7 R ∘ dom R = R

Proof.

We have:

$$\begin{array}{l} R \circ \mathsf{dom}\, R \\ \subseteq \quad [\![\ \mathsf{dom}\, R \text{ is coreflexive }]\!] \\ R \\ \subseteq \quad [\![\text{ instantiate } S = \mathsf{dom}\, R \text{ in universal property of domain }]\!] \\ R \circ \mathsf{dom}\, R \end{array}$$

Right and left division are characterised by their universal properties

$$\begin{array}{lllll} T \subseteq R/S & \Leftrightarrow & T \circ S \subseteq R & & \\ T \subseteq S \backslash R & \Leftrightarrow & S \circ T \subseteq R & \Leftrightarrow & S \subseteq R/T \end{array}$$

These are the least familiar of the operators of the relational calculus, but they are truly central: (/*S*) forms a Galois connection with (∘*S*), and (*S*\) with (*S*∘), and Galois connections—more generally, adjunctions—underlie most of the structural equivalences we use in program calculation [9].

The appropriate notion of kernel for relations in general is as follows [1]:

Definition 8

The kernel ker R of a relation *R* is given by

$$\begin{aligned} \ker R &= (R \backslash R) \cap (R \backslash R)^\circ \\ &= (R \backslash R) \cap (R^\circ / R^\circ) \end{aligned}$$

In terms of concrete sets of pairs, the quotients reduce to the following constructions:

$$\begin{array}{lll} (a, b) \in R/S & \Leftrightarrow & (\forall c \,.\, (a, c) \in R \Leftarrow (b, c) \in S) \\ (a, c) \in S \backslash R & \Leftrightarrow & (\forall b \,.\, (b, c) \in R \Leftarrow (b, a) \in S) \end{array}$$

and therefore

$$\ker R = \{(a, a') \mid \forall b \,.\, (a, b) \in R \Leftrightarrow (a', b) \in R\}$$

In particular, when *R* is simple, so equivalent to a partial function, this agrees with the definition of kernels in Section 3.

We identify three useful lemmas about kernels, which we will need for the proof of Theorem 12 on postfactors for simple relations, analogous to Theorem 2 and Theorem 6.

Lemma 9

Kernels enjoy the universal property that

$$\ker R \supseteq S \quad \Leftrightarrow \quad R \supseteq R \circ S \wedge R \supseteq R \circ S^\circ$$

Proof

This follows from the universal properties of the components:

$$\begin{array}{l} \ker R \supseteq S \\ \Leftrightarrow \quad [\![\text{ definition of kernel }]\!] \\ ((R \backslash R) \cap (R \backslash R)^\circ) \supseteq S \\ \Leftrightarrow \quad [\![\text{ universal property of intersection }]\!] \\ (R \backslash R \supseteq S) \wedge ((R \backslash R)^\circ \supseteq S) \\ \Leftrightarrow \quad [\![\text{ converse preserves inclusion }]\!] \\ (R \backslash R \supseteq S) \wedge (R \backslash R \supseteq S^\circ) \\ \Leftrightarrow \quad [\![\text{ universal property of division }]\!] \\ R \supseteq R \circ S \wedge R \supseteq R \circ S^\circ \end{array}$$

Lemma 10

$R^\circ \circ R \subseteq \ker R$ for simple R.

Proof

We have

$$\begin{array}{l} \ker R \supseteq R^\circ \circ R \\ \Leftrightarrow \quad [\![\text{ universal property of kernel }]\!] \\ R \supseteq R \circ R^\circ \circ R \wedge R \supseteq R \circ (R^\circ \circ R)^\circ \\ \Leftrightarrow \quad [\![\text{ the conjuncts are equivalent, by contravariance of converse }]\!] \\ R \supseteq R \circ R^\circ \circ R \\ \Leftarrow \quad [\![\text{ monotonicity }]\!] \\ id \supseteq R \circ R^\circ \end{array}$$

Lemma 11

$R \circ \ker R \subseteq R$

Proof

We have:

$R \circ \ker R \subseteq R$
$\Leftrightarrow$ [[universal property of division]]
$\ker R \subseteq R \backslash R$
$\Leftrightarrow$ [[definition of kernel]]
true

Theorem 12

For simple T:A~Cand R:A~B, there exists simple S:B~Cwith T=S∘Riff $T = S \circ R$ *iff* $\ker R \subseteq \ker T$ and $\mathrm{dom}\, R \supseteq \mathrm{dom}\, T$.

Proof

From left to right, suppose $T=S \circ R$. Then

$\ker R \subseteq \ker T$
$\Leftrightarrow$ [[assumption]]
$\ker R \subseteq \ker (S \circ R)$
$\Leftrightarrow$ [[universal property of kernel]]
$S \circ R \supseteq S \circ R \circ \ker R \wedge S \circ R \supseteq S \circ R \circ (\ker R)^{\circ}$
$\Leftrightarrow$ [[$\ker R$ is symmetric, so the two conjuncts are equivalent]]
$S \circ R \supseteq S \circ R \circ \ker R$
$\Leftarrow$ [[monotonicity]]
$R \supseteq R \circ \ker R$
$\Leftrightarrow$ [[Lemma 11]]
true

and

$\mathrm{dom}\, R \supseteq \mathrm{dom}\, T$
$\Leftrightarrow$ [[assumption]]
$\mathrm{dom}\, R \supseteq \mathrm{dom}\, (S \circ R)$
$\Leftrightarrow$ [[universal property of domain ($\mathrm{dom}\, R$ is coreflexive)]]
$S \circ R \circ \mathrm{dom}\, R \supseteq S \circ R$
$\Leftrightarrow$ [[Lemma 7]]
true

(We don't actually need the assumption that R, S, and hence T are simple.) Conversely, suppose the kernel and domain inclusions on R,T, and define $S=T \circ R^{\circ}$. Then $T=S \circ R$:

T
$=$ [[Lemma 7]]
$T \circ \mathrm{dom}\, T$
$\subseteq$ [[assumption]]
$T \circ \mathrm{dom}\, R$
$\subseteq$ [[definition of domain]]
$T \circ R^{\circ} \circ R$ — which is $S \circ R$
$\subseteq$ [[Lemma 10—by assumption, R is simple]]
$T \circ \ker R$
$\subseteq$ [[assumption]]
$T \circ \ker T$
$\subseteq$ [[Lemma 11]]
T

Moreover, S is simple:

$S \circ S^{\circ}$
$=$ [[definition of S]]
$S \circ R \circ T^{\circ}$
$=$ [[by the above, $S \circ R = T$]]
$T \circ T^{\circ}$
$\subseteq$ [[by assumption, T is simple]]
id

Note that this proof establishes the result in the more general setting of simple relations, that is, partial rather than total functions, with no extra fuss. In contrast, the proof ofTheorem 6 is rather more complicated than the proof of Theorem 2, with an awkward case analysis.

CATEGORICALLY

One might wonder whether the full structure of a division allegory is necessary for the postfactors result to hold: the proof in Section 4 uses division heavily, but the more concrete one in Section 2 does not. What abstract structure is actually required?

Definition 13 Kernel Pair

The categorical analogue of the kernel of a function is the *kernel pair* of an arrow, the pullback of the arrow along itself:

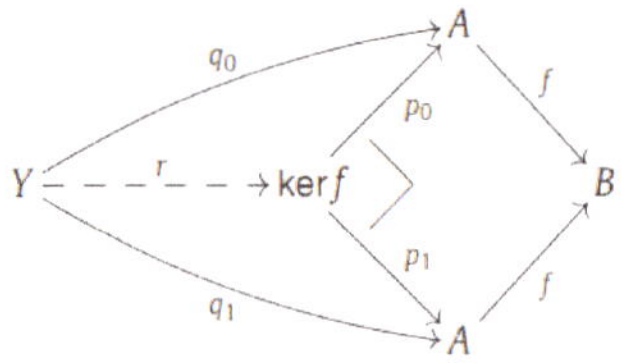

That is, the kernel pair of $f{:}A \rightarrow B$ is an object X and arrows $p_0,p_1{:}X \rightarrow A$ satisfying $f \circ p_0 = f \circ p_1$, with the universal property that, for any other object Y with arrows $q_0,q_1{:}Y \rightarrow A$ satisfying $f \circ q_0 = f \circ q_1$, there is a unique mediating arrow $r{:}Y \rightarrow X$ such that $q_0 = p_0 \circ r$ and $q_1 = p_1 \circ r$.

Such pullbacks do not always exist. They always do in S*et*, when the object X is just the set of pairs kerf from Definition 1, and p_0, p_1 are the left and right projections; that justifies the use of "ker f" for X in the commuting diagram above. More generally, a *finitely complete* category possesses all finite limits, and in particular pullbacks and hence kernel pairs. But for these kernel pairs to be in some sense well behaved, we need a couple of extra conditions as well.

Definition 14 Epimorphism, Monomorphism

An arrow $g{:}B \rightarrow C$ is an *epimorphism* if it is right-cancellable, in the sense that for any $h_0,h_1{:}C \rightarrow D$, if $h_0 \circ g = h_1 \circ g$ then $h_0 = h_1$.

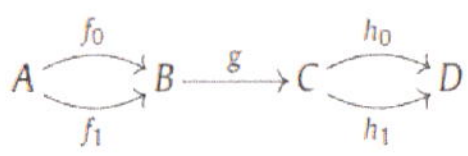

Dually, g is a *monomorphism* if it is left-cancellable: for any $f_0,f_1{:}A \rightarrow B$, if $g \circ f_0 = g \circ f_1$ then $f_0 = f_1$. ⋄

In S*et*, the epimorphisms are the surjections, and the monomorphisms the injections. By convention, we draw epimorphisms in commuting diagrams with double headed arrows $\twoheadrightarrow$ and monomorphisms with hook-tailed arrows $\hookrightarrow$.

Definition 15 Coequaliser

We say that arrow $g{:}B \rightarrow C$ *coequalises* a parallel pair of arrows $f_0,f_1{:}A \rightarrow B$ if $g \circ f_0 = g \circ f_1$. The *coequaliser* of f_0,f_1 is a universal such C and g—that is, for any other object D and arrow $h{:}B \rightarrow D$ that coequalises f_0,f_1, there is a unique mediating arrow r: $C \rightarrow D$ such that $h = r \circ g$.

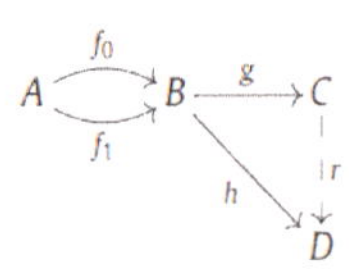

In S*et*, the coequaliser object C is the quotient of B by the smallest equivalence relation $\equiv$ such that $\forall a \in A \circ f_0 a \equiv f_1 a$; that is, the reflexive, symmetric, transitive closure of the relation induced by f_0, f_1. It is an instructive exercise to verify that the coequaliser is necessarily an epimorphism (whatever the category). Not all epimorphisms arise as coequalisers; those that do are called the *regular epimorphisms*.

Definition 16 Regular Category

A *regular category* is one: that is finitely complete (so in particular has all kernel pairs); in which every kernel pair has a coequaliser; and in which regular epimorphisms are stable under pullbacks—that is, if g in the commuting diagram below is a regular epimorphism, then so is p_1.

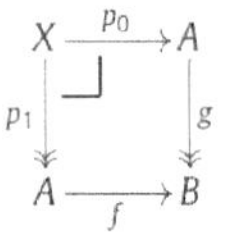

The category *Set* is regular.

Definition 17 Relation

One can define a notion of 'relation' $R{:}A{\sim}B$ via a span $A{\leftarrow}R{\rightarrow}B$: in a Cartesian category (that is, one with products), R is modelled as a monomorphism $R \hookrightarrow A \times B$ into the product:

(To be more precise, one should consider equivalence classes of such spans under isomorphisms between their apices R. One can also remove the dependence on products by requiring that the two legs of the span are *jointly monic*, suitably defined.)

In *Set*, this directly corresponds to thinking of R as a subset of $A{\times}B$. But constructing the composition of relations involves taking a pullback of spans:

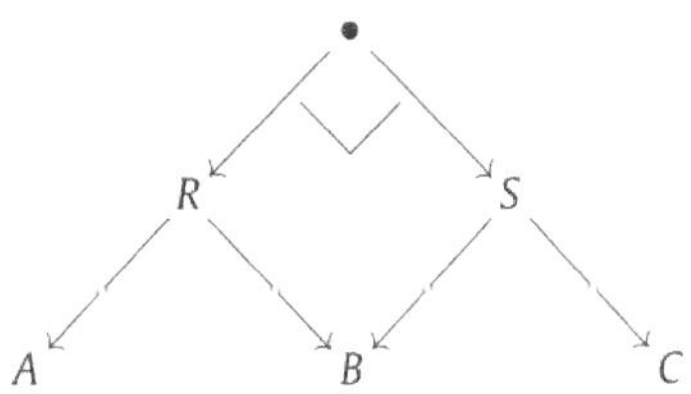

(and then taking the 'image', as discussed above: the arrow from the apex to $A{\times}C$ is typically not a monomorphism); in order for this composition to be associative, one needs the additional well-behavedness properties of a regular category [5, §1.569]. So regular categories are a somewhat necessary phenomenon in thinking about relational programming; for a recent crisp summary, see [7, Section 2].

Definition 18 Partial Map

Similarly, one can define a *partial map* $f : A \rightharpoonup B$ in a category as a span with a monomorphic left leg:

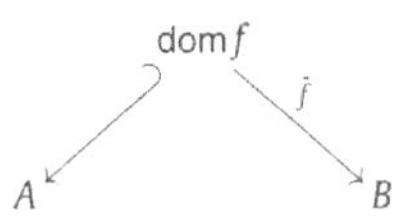

writing $\bar{f} : \mathrm{dom} f \rightarrow B$ for the restriction of f to its domain (again, up to equivalences arising from isomorphisms on the apices). Composition is again constructed by pullbacks of spans.

Lemma 19 Image Factorisation

An important result about regular categories is that every arrow f:A→Bfactorises into a regular epimorphism followed by a monomorphism.

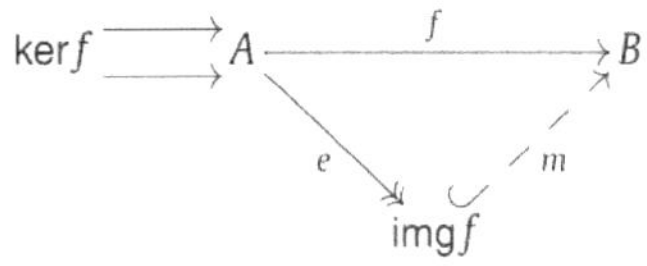

Indeed, an alternative chacterisation of regular categories is that they have finite limits and image factorisations, stable under pullbacks.

In *Set*, img f is $A_{/f}$, the quotient of A into equivalence classes according to f; that is, two elements $a,a' \in A$ are equivalent iff $fa{=}fa'$ (in other words, $(a, a') \in \mathrm{ker} f$). So one can think of e as taking an element of A to its equivalence class, and m mapping this class into B. Equivalently, one can think of e as being f but with the target restricted precisely to the range of f, and m as the embedding of the range back into the target: $A_{/f}$ is isomorphic to ran f. For more about image factorisation, see Taylor [13].

Theorem 20

Given arrows f:A→Band h:A→Cin a regular category, there exists a partial map g:B Csuch that h=g∘fif and only if there exists an arrow $i : \mathrm{ker} f \rightarrow \mathrm{ker} h$ satisfying $p_0{=}q_0$ iand $p_1{=}q_1{\circ}i$, where $p_0,p_1$and $q_0,q_1$are the kernel pairs of f and h respectively.

Proof

The situation is illustrated in the diagram below:

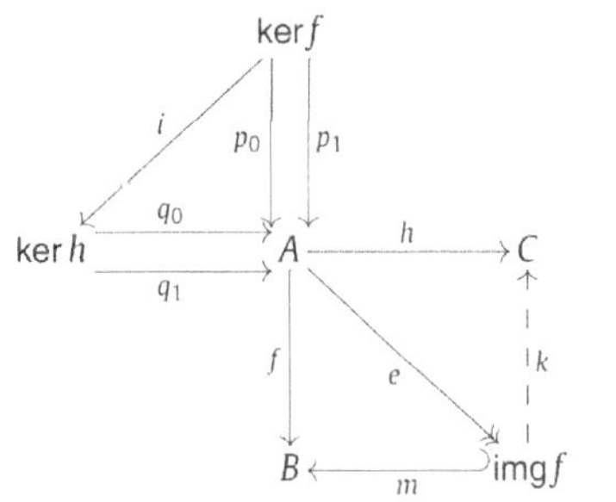

From right to left, suppose we are given i making the two upper left triangles commute; we construct g as follows. Let $m{\circ}e$ be the image factorisation of f (making the lower left triangle commute), so that e is the coequaliser of p_0,p_1. Now h also coequalises p_0, p_1:

$$h \circ p_0 = h \circ q_0 \circ i = h \circ q_1 \circ i = h \circ p_1$$

so by the universal property of the coequaliser there exists a unique mediating arrow $k : \mathrm{img} f \rightarrow C$ making the upper right triangle commute. We define partial map $g : B \rightharpoonup C$ to be the span $B \xleftarrow{m} \mathrm{img} f \xrightarrow{k} C$.

We have to show that $h{=}g{\circ}f$ as partial maps. Since f and h are in fact total, their domain coincides with their source, and the monomorphic left legs of the spans are the identity. So for the composition $g{\circ}f$, we have the following situation:

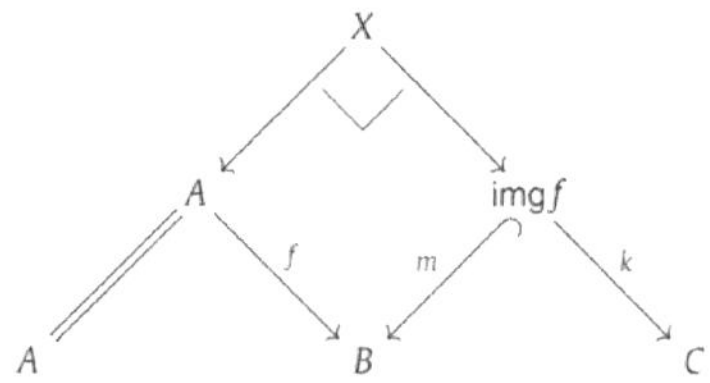

and we have to show that the outer span equals h. Let us factor f into $m\circ e$, and see what effect this has on the pullback diamond:

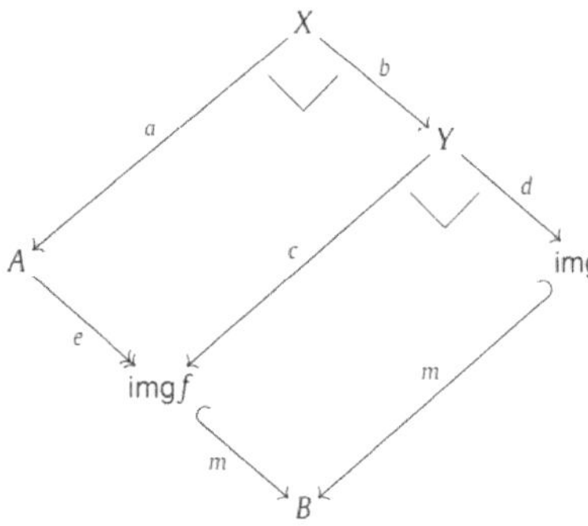

We use two simple standard facts about pullbacks, both of which are straightforward to prove. Firstly, the pullback of a monomorphism along itself is the identity; so Y = img f, and $c=d=id$. Secondly, a pullback of the identity (c) is again the identity; so $a=id$, and hence $X=A$ and $b=e$. Therefore, the outer span is indeed $A = A \xrightarrow{k\circ e=h} C$ as required.

Conversely, given $h=g\circ f$, and kernel pairs p_0,p_1 for f and q_0,q_1 for h, we construct the mapping as follows:

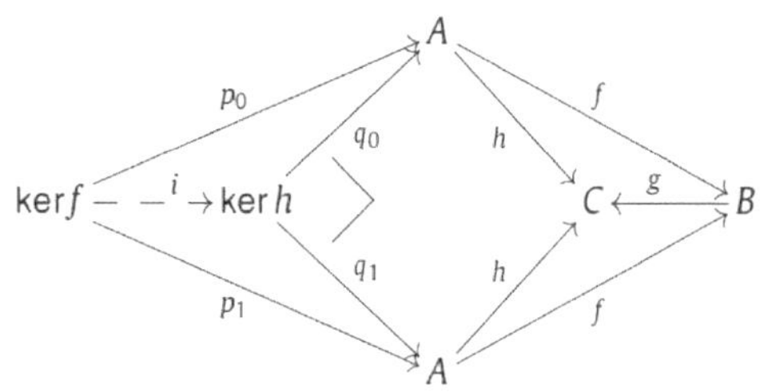

We have that p_0,p_1 form a cone over $A \xrightarrow{h} C \xleftarrow{h} A$:

$$h \circ p_0 = g \circ f \circ p_0 = g \circ f \circ p_1 = h \circ p_1$$

so by the universal property of the pullback, there exists a (unique) mediating arrow i : kerf → ker h making the triangles $p_0=q_0\circ i$ and $p_1=q_1\circ i$ commute.

CONCLUSIONS

I presented a preliminary version of Section 2 at Meeting #55 of IFIP WG2.1 in Cochabamba in January 2001; Lambert Meertens simplified my proofs there. The work was subsequently published at CMCS 2001 [6], jointly written with Graham Hutton and Thorsten Altenkirch, whose contributions were invaluable. Bart Jacobs also made some helpful observations about congruences and images, pointing me towards his paper [8].

Thanks to comments received at CMCS, I saw how to generalise from total functions to partial functions; I presented the more general results at Meeting #56 of WG2.1, in Ameland in September 2001—precisely while the tragedy of the twin towers was unfolding. Roland Backhouse encouraged me there to use the relational definition $\ker R = (R\backslash R) \cap (R\backslash R)^\circ$ of kernels from Section 4, but we didn't manage to complete the proof in the relational style at the meeting. (This notion of kernel turns out to date back at least to 1948 [12]; it is a special case ker R = syq(R, R) of the 'symmetric quotient' used by Schmidt and by Winter in this volume.) In October 2005, José Oliveira invited me to take part in a PURe Workshop in Braga; that was the spur I needed to complete the relational proofs (helped by Shin-Cheng Mu), which I presented there. José liked the results, because it turned out to be related to work he was doing on pointfree functional dependency theory [10]; he encouraged me to write those results up, but I've never had the excuse to make time for it-until now! (Note that the relational definition of kernels used here is in general incomparable to the definition $\ker R = R^\circ \circ R$ used by José himself [10] and [11] as a stepping stone towards his 'injectivity preorder' on relations.)

For help with the categorical construction, I am indebted to Maciej Piróg for pointing me towards regular categories; to James McKinna, Ohad Kammar, and Bob Harper, for enlightening discussions; and especially to Sam Staton, who sketched out the proof of Theorem 20 for me.

ACKNOWLEDGEMENTS

This work was partially supported by EPSRC grants *Datatype-Generic Programming* (GR/S27078/01) and *A Theory of Least Change for Bidirectional Transformations*(EP/K020919/1).

REFERENCES

1. Roland C. Backhouse, Jaap van der Woude, Domain operators and domain kinds, in: STOP Workshop on Galois Connections, Utrecht, 1993. Available from http://www.cs.nott.ac.uk/~rcb/MPC/perorder.ps.gz.
2. Richard Bird, Oege de Moor, Algebra of Programming, Prentice-Hall, 1997.
3. Francis Borceux, Handbook of Categorical Algebra, vol. 2, Cambridge University Press, 1994.
4. Hartmut Ehrig, Bernd Mahr, Fundamental of Algebraic Specification, EATCS Monographs on Theoretical Computer Science, vol. 1, Springer-Verlag, 1985.
5. Peter J. Freyd, Andre Scedrov, Categories, Allegories, in: Mathematical Library, vol. 39, North-Holland, 1990.
6. Jeremy Gibbons, Graham Hutton, Thorsten Altenkirch, When is a function a fold or an unfold? Electron. Proc. Theor. Comput. Sci. 44 (1) (April 2001), Coalgebraic Methods in Computer Science.
7. Chris Heunen, Sean Tull, Categories of relations as models of quantum theory, in: Chris Heunen, Peter Selinger, Jamie Vicary (Eds.), Proceedings of the 12th International Workshop on Quantum Physics and Logic (QPL 2015), Oxford, U.K., July 15–17, 2015, Electron. Proc. Theor. Comput. Sci. 195 (2015) 247–261, http://dx.doi.org/10.4204/EPTCS.195.18, arXiv:1506.05028.
8. Bart Jacobs, Mongruences and cofree coalgebras, in: V.S. Alagar, M. Nivat (Eds.), Algebraic Methodology and Software Technology, in: LNCS, vol. 936, Springer, 1995, pp. 245–260.
9. Shin-Cheng Mu, José Nuno Oliveira, Programming from Galois connections, J. Log. Algebr. Program. 81 (6) (2012) 680–704.

10. José Nuno Oliveira, Functional dependency theory made 'simpler', Technical report DI-PURe-05.01.01, Departamento de Informática da Universidade do Minho, January 2005.

11. José Nuno Oliveira, Transforming data by calculation, in: Ralf Lämmel, Joost Visser, João Saraiva (Eds.), Generative and Transformational Techniques in Software Engineering II, in: LNCS, vol. 5235, Springer, 2008, pp. 134–195.

12. Jacques Riguet, Relations binaires, fermetures, correspondances de Galois, Bull. Soc. Math. Fr. 76 (1948) 114–155.

13. Paul Taylor, Practical Foundations of Mathematics, Studies in Advanced Mathematics, Cambridge University Press, 1999.

CHAPTER 14 POSSIBLE VALUES: EXPLORING A CONCEPT FOR CONCURRENCY

Cliff B. Jones[a], Ian J. Hayes[b]

[a]School of Computing Science, Newcastle University, UK

[b]School of Information Technology and Electrical Engineering, The University of Queensland, Australia

ABSTRACT

An important issue in concurrency is interference. This issue manifests itself in both shared-variable and communication-based concurrency — this paper focuses on the former case where interference is caused by the environment of a process changing the values of shared variables. Rely/guarantee approaches have been shown to be useful in specifying and reasoning compositionally about concurrent programs. This paper explores the use of a "possible values" notation for reasoning about variables whose values can be changed multiple times by interference. Apart from the value of this concept in providing clear specifications, it offers a principled way of avoiding the need for some auxiliary (or ghost) variables whose unwise use can destroy compositionality.

INTRODUCTION

High on the list of issues that make the design of concurrent programs difficult to get right is 'interference'. Reproducing a situation that exhibited a 'bug' can be frustrating; attempting to reason informally about all possible interleavings of interference can be exasperating; and designing formal approaches to the verification of concurrent programs is challenging.

Recording post conditions for sequential programs applies the only real tool that we have: abstraction is achieved by winnowing out what is inessential in the relationship between the initial and final states of a computation. Post conditions record the required relationship without fixing an algorithm to bring about the transformation; furthermore, they record required properties only of those variables which the environment will use. The rely/guarantee approach (see Section 1.1) uses abstraction in the same way to provide specifications of concurrent software components that are more abstract than their implementations: for any component, rely conditions are relations that record interference that the component must tolerate and guarantee conditions document the interference that the environment of the component must accept.

This paper explores a concept that fits well with rely/guarantee reasoning but probably has wider applicability. In relational post conditions, it is necessary to be able to refer to the initial value x and final value x' of a variable x (e.g. $x \le x' \le x+9$). If however it is necessary to record something as simple as the fact that a local variable x captures one of the values of a shared variable y , it is inadequate to write $x'=y \vee x'=y'$ in the case where y might be changed many times by the environment. Enter 'possible values': the suggested notation is that $\bar{y}$ denotes the set of values which variable y contains during the execution of the operation in whose

Citation: Cliff B. Jones, Ian J. Hayes, Possible values: Exploring a concept for concurrency, doi:10.1016/j.jlamp.2016.01.002

specification $\hat{y}$ is written. So, (assuming the access to read the value of y is atomic):

$$post\text{-}Op : x' \in \widehat{y}$$

is satisfied by a simple assignment of y to x.

```
                                   f ← wr;
while true do                        ||  while true do
   ··· produce v ···                 ||     while f = wr do skip od;
   while f = rd do skip od;          ||     r ← b;
   b ← v;                            ||     f ← wr
   f ← rd                            ||     ··· consume r ···
od                                   ||  od

guar (f = rd ⇒ b′ = b) ∧                 rely (f = rd ⇒ b′ = b) ∧
     (f = rd ⇒ f′ = rd)                       (f = rd ⇒ f′ = rd)
rely f = wr ⇒ f′ = wr                     guar f = wr ⇒ f′ = wr
```

Figure. 1. A one-place buffer.

Rely/Guarantee Thinking

Before going into more detail on the possible values notation (see Section 2), a brief overview of background work is offered. The specifications given in Section 3 are written in the notation of VDM [12] and [15]. It is unlikely that they will present difficulties even to readers unfamiliar with that specific notation because similar ideas for sequential programs are present in Z [6], B [1], Event-B [2], and TLA [23]. The basic idea is of state-based specifications with operations (or events) transforming the state and being specified by something like pre and post conditions. Pre conditions are predicates over states that indicate what can be assumed about states in which an operation can be initiated. Post conditions are relations over initial and final states that specify the required relations between the initial and final values of state components. Good sequential specifications eschew any details of implementation algorithms: they do not specify anything about intermediate states; in fact an implementation might use a state with more components. At first sight, it might appear surprising that there is not a precise functional requirement on the final state but using non-determinism in specifications turns out to be an extremely useful way of postponing design decisions.

The use of abstract objects in specifications is a crucial tool for larger applications. Moreover, datatype invariants can make specifications clearer: restricting types by predicates simplifies pre/post conditions and also offers a way for the specifier to record the intention of a specification. Another useful aspect of VDM is the ability to define more tightly the 'frame' of an operation by recording whether access to state components is for (only) reading or for both reading and writing.[1]

[1]Most of the literature on rely/guarantee conditions is limited to normal (or 'scoped') variables; [21] shows how 'heap' variables can be viewed as representations of more abstract states.

The basic rely/guarantee [13] and [14] idea[2] is simple: interference is documented and proof rules are given which support reasoning about interference in concurrent threads. Just as in sequential specifications, the role of a state is central to recording rely/guarantee specifications. For concurrency, it is accepted that the environment of a process can change values in the state during execution of an operation.[3] Such changes are however assumed to be constrained by a rely condition. In order to reason about the combined effect of operations, the interference that a process can inflict on its environment is also recorded; this is done in a guarantee condition. Both rely and guarantee conditions are, for obvious reasons, relations over states. In the original form – and after many experiments – both conditions are reflexive and transitive covering the possibility of zero or many steps. Such relations often indicate monotonic evolution of variables.

[2]The literature on rely/guarantee approaches continues to expand; see [9, 11] for further references. For a reader who is completely unfamiliar with rely/guarantee concepts, a useful brief presentation can be found in [16].

[3]Notice that there is an essential difference here from 'actions' [5] or 'events' [2] which view execution of a guarded action as atomic.

It is useful to compare the roles of rely and guarantee conditions with the better known pre/post conditions. Pre conditions are essentially an invitation to the designer of a specified component to ignore some starting states; in the same way, the developer can ignore the possibility that interference will make state changes that do not satisfy the rely condition. In neither case should a developer include code to test these assumptions; there is an implicit requirement to prove that the component is only used in an appropriate context. In contrast, post conditions and guarantee conditions are obligations on the running code that the developer has to create; these conditions record properties on which the deployer can depend.

The simplest form of relation that could be used in rely or guarantee conditions is to state that the value of a variable remains unchanged (e.g. $b'=b$). Such unconditional constraints are normally better handled by marking an operation (or part thereof) as having only read access. There is however an important way to combine 'monotonic' changes to flags with assertions about variables remaining unchanged. Consider a simple one-place buffer in which a producer process places a value in a buffer variable b from which a consumer process extracts values. Testing and setting flag f in Fig. 1ensures that the producer and consumer alternate their access to b. During its read phase, the consumer needs to rely on the fact that the value of b cannot change but this is too strong as a rely condition for the whole of the consumer process — the producer process could never insert anything into the buffer if it were required to achieve a guarantee condition of $b'=b$. But the consumer process can instead rely on $f=rd \Rightarrow b'=b$, which in turn is easy for the producer to guarantee. The 'monotonic' behaviour of the flags means that the producer has also to guarantee that $f=rd \Rightarrow f=rd$ and the consumer must guarantee $f=wr \Rightarrow f=wr$. This example shows one way in which rely/guarantee conditions can be used to reason about race-free programs. It also illustrates a technique that is used in Section 3 to locate what is going on in the environment without adding auxiliary variables. The example tackled in Section 3 is however much more challenging than this simple one-place buffer.

Law for Mutual Strengthening of Guarantee and Rely

As part of the example in Section 3, a new facet of rely/guarantee refinement is needed: it allows mutual strengthening of both rely and guarantee conditions for a portion of one process. The approach is a contribution to rely/guarantee refinement and it makes it possible to avoid introducing additional auxiliary variables (see Section 4.3) in order to handle the example in Section 3.

In the standard approach to rely/guarantee refinement, when two parallel processes are introduced each has an associated rely/guarantee pair and there is an obligation to show that the guarantee of each implies the rely of the other. Normally the one rely/guarantee pair suffices to handle the refinement of a process but for the example in Section 3 that is not sufficient.

In the standard theory, rely/guarantee pairs are often mutually dependent: for the two-process case, a process P maintaining its guarantee may be dependent on its environment (process Q) maintaining the rely of P (by Q maintaining its guarantee) and vice versa. For example, P may guarantee to maintain $x \geq 0$ provided it can rely on its environment maintaining $x \geq 0$. The guarantee, g, of a process has to hold for every atomic program step it makes and hence g has to be weak enough to be maintained by every step. However, for a subpart S of P, all the atomic steps of S may imply a stronger guarantee gs. As P forms the environment of process Q, while P is executing subpart S, Q may assume a stronger rely condition of gs and as a consequence of this its own guarantee may be strengthened from r to rs, which in turn allows process P to assume a stronger rely condition rs, but only while it is executing subpart S. Note that while only a subpart S of P is of concern, the whole of Q has to be considered for the strengthening of its rely and guarantee.

In order to establish the strengthened rely/guarantee pair for the duration of S, the state when P enters S may need to satisfy an initial condition j. For the example in Section 3 a special case of the above reasoning applies in which the guarantee of P is strengthened to state that P does not modify any shared variables. In this case one needs to show that process Q maintains the stronger rely rs from any initial state satisfying j provided Q suffers no inference from P.

Connection to Data Abstraction/Reification

It is important to appreciate how rely relations abstract from the detail of the actual environmental interference of an operation. Obviously, the most detailed information about an environment is the actual state changes it makes. But designing to such concrete detail would create a component that is not robust to change. Just as post conditions deliberately omit implementation details of a specified operation, it is useful to strive for an abstract documentation of interference. It is clear that relations cannot record certain sorts of information but, if they are adequate for a given task, their use will yield a more compositional development than the detail of the environment.

The extended example in Section 3 shows the importance of linking rely/guarantee ideas with data abstraction and reification. Specification using abstract mathematical objects and the process of stepwise introduction of more concrete (i.e. closer to hardware) objects is well established for sequential programs and for significant applications is often more telling than the abstraction that comes from post conditions — see, for example, [15]. In addition to layering design decisions, careful use of abstract objects in the development of concurrent programs offers other advantages. In particular, developments can appear to allow data races at an abstract level that are removed by careful choice of a concrete representation — this is discussed in [17]. One reason that this is interesting is Peter O'Hearn's suggested dichotomy in [24] that separation logic is appropriate for reasoning about race avoidance whilst rely/guarantee methods fit 'racy' programs. The distinction between abstract and concrete data races is perfectly illustrated in Section 3 but the example is not easy to summarise. A simpler example is searching an array to find the lowest index of an element that satisfies a predicate P by means of two parallel processes that search the elements with, respectively, even and odd indices (for a full development of this example, see [9]). If a single variable t were used to record the least index of an element that satisfies P, it would be necessary to have locks in the two processes to avoid a data race on t. A neat way to avoid the 'write/write' race is to represent t by the minimum of two variables, et and ot that record the least value of, respectively, even and odd indices where the array element satisfies P. The 'write/write' race, which is useful in an abstract description of the design, is reduced to a 'read/write' race because the actual code for each process updates only one of the variables although it reads the other variable in its loop test (and on the completion of both processes t can be retrieved as $min(et,ot)$).

The citations above relate to the original form of rely/guarantee reasoning in which the (potentially) four conditions are combined. More recent work has shown how separate rely and/or guarantee constraints can be wrapped around any command including conventional refinement calculus style specifications. The presentation in [9] and [11] of rely/guarantee thinking makes algebraic properties clearer.

Plan of This Paper

This paper provides evidence of the usefulness of the possible values concept. Section 2presents a notation for the concept while Section 3 is an extended example using the concept and notation. Section 2.2 outlines how a semantic model can be provided and looks at the form of laws that would fit the newer presentation of rely/guarantee reasoning [9] and [11]. The current authors recognise that this paper represents the start of an exploration — some avenues to be investigated are mentioned in Section 4.

POSSIBLE VALUES

It is argued above that the confessed expressive weakness of rely/guarantee specifications serves the purpose of preserving some form of compositionality in the design of concurrent programs. However, if notations can be found that increase expressive power, they should be evaluated both for expressiveness and tractability. The simple case mentioned above of using one or more possible values terms in a post condition is considered first and issues about extension are deferred to Section 4.

Possible Values of Variables

If an operation only has read access to a shared variable y and x is a local variable of the process, then:

$$post\text{-}Op : x' \in \widehat{y} \tag{1}$$

requires that the final value of the variable x should contain one of the values that the environment places in the variable y — this includes the (initial) value of y at the time *Op* began execution. So $\widehat{y}$ denotes a set of values whose elements have the type of y.

Notice that the post condition above is 'stable' in the sense that the environment might change the value of y after *Op* accesses the variable and the post condition is still true. In contrast, it would be unwise to write a post condition that contained $x' \notin \widehat{y}$ because this would not be stable and it would appear to require that every possible change that the environment makes to the value of y is observed. (In some cases, it would be possible to establish such a result under a suitable rely condition; but some form of (local) datatype invariant should also be considered in such cases.)

So, for the straightforward case, the post condition (1) can be established by the atomic assignment x←y. As is reported in Section 3.2, an instance of this simple case was the inspiration for the possible values notation. There are however several vectors of extension. If the process in which the $\widehat{y}$ term is written also has write access to the variable y, it is necessary to take a position on whether both environment assignments to y and those of the component itself are reflected in $\widehat{y}$; the view of the current authors is that $\widehat{y}$ contains all values of y that could be observed by the process.

Semantics and Laws

It is not difficult to see how a formal meaning can be given to the simple form of the possible values notation in a semantics such as that in [9]: basically, that portion of the sequence of states that corresponds to the execution of an operation is distinguished so as to identify the first and last states in order to give a semantics to post conditions. It is only necessary to consider all of the states in that portion and to extract the set of values of the relevant variable.

Another interesting semantic issue concerns locking. In fact, the possible values notation forces consideration of a number of facets of 'atomicity'. Locking may be used to ensure mutually exclusive access to a set of variables. A process may lock a resource protecting a set of variables. While it owns the lock, it may make multiple changes to the variables protected by the lock, however, any other processes accessing the protected variables cannot observe any of the intermediate states of the protected variables. Hence a process in the scope of a resource with a set of protected variables can only observe the initial and final states of a protected block within another process. Throughout the body of a protected block a process can rely on the protected variables being stable. Furthermore, any guarantee involving just the protected variables has to hold only between the initial and final states of the protected block.

Just as the semantics for the straightforward use of possible values terms in a post condition poses no difficulties in terms of the underlying traces, a rather simple law suffices to reason about the notation. Here, it is convenient to switch to the refinement calculus style of [9] and [11] in which the specification statement x:[q] establishes the postcondition q and modifies only x, and the command c in a rely context of r is written $\mathbf{rely}\ r \cdot c$. Assuming a read of y is atomic, the following law holds.

$$\mathbf{rely}\ (x' = x) \cdot x : [x' \in \widehat{y}] \sqsubseteq x \leftarrow y \qquad (2)$$

The rely condition x′=x is required to ensure that the environment doesn't change x after the assignment is made. For example, x may be a local variable or, as below in Section 3.3, annotated owns wr$x$.

Possible Values of Expressions

For the set of possible values of an expression, $\widehat{e}$, one needs to consider the corresponding set of states of the execution and form the set of values of e, each evaluated in one of those states. Importantly, all values of program variables used in e are sampled in a single state for each evaluation. For example, for the specification

$$x : [x' \in \widehat{y + y}] \qquad (3)$$

both occurrences of y are sampled in the same state and hence the resultant value is always even (assuming the variables are integer valued). Note that there is a subtle difference between (3), which samples y once, and

$$x : [\exists v, w \cdot v \in \widehat{y} \wedge w \in \widehat{y} \wedge x' = v + w]$$

which samples y twice so that the values of v and w may differ.

Replacing y in the law (2) with an expression e introduces the complication that each variable reference in the evaluation of e in the assignment could be accessed in a different state. Note that if e has multiple references to a single variable y, each reference could be accessed in a different state. However, if e has only a single reference to a variable y and all other variables in e are stable, any evaluation of e is equivalent to evaluating it in the state in which y is accessed and the law is valid. Let S be a set of variables such that the free variables of e are contained in S∪{y} and e has only a single reference to y and accesses to y are atomic, then

$$\mathbf{rely}\ (x' = x \wedge (\textstyle\bigwedge z \in S \cdot z' = z)) \cdot x : [x' \in \widehat{e}] \sqsubseteq x \leftarrow e\,. \qquad (4)$$

If e is of the form d(f) for a mapping d and expression f, stability is required on the program variables in f but stability is not required for the whole of d, just d(f), because the other elements of d have no effect on the expressions value.

If the expression e contains multiple references to a variable x, saving x in a local variable t and then evaluating e in terms of t ensures that the value used for x is from a single state. The following refinement law ensures x is sampled once. It is assumed that r and t are local variables (and hence the environment cannot change them) and that r and t do not occur free in e.

$$t, r : [r' \in \widehat{e[x/v]}] \sqsubseteq \langle t \leftarrow x \rangle\,;\ r : [r' \in \widehat{e[t/v]}] \qquad (5)$$

For this to be valid one needs to rely on the environment maintaining $\widehat{e[t/v]} \subseteq \widehat{e[x/v]}$, for the duration of the command. This holds provided the rely condition

$$x' \neq t \wedge t' = t \Rightarrow e[t/v]' = e[t/v]$$

is maintained by the environment, where e[t/v]′ stands for e[t/v] evaluated in the after state, i.e. e′ is e with every program variable y in e replaced by y′.

Law (5) can be justified as follows. The atomic statement ⟨t←x⟩ establishes e[t/v]=e[x/v]. An environment step that has a final state in which $x'=t$ establishes$e[t/v]'=e[x/v]'$ otherwise the environment establishes $e[t/v]'=e[t/v]=e[x/v]$.

As an example consider the case in which the expression *e* is d(v). Applying (5) gives

$$t, r : [r' \in \widehat{d(x)}] \sqsubseteq \langle t \leftarrow x \rangle ; r : [r' \in \widehat{d(t)}] \quad (6)$$

provided its environment ensures the condition: $x' \neq t \Rightarrow d'(t)=d(t)$. Immediately after the atomic assignment to *t*,

$$d(t) = d(x) \in \widehat{d(x)} . \quad (7)$$

If the environment makes a step that does not change *x*, (7) is maintained because $d'(t')=d'(x')$ but if the environment changes *x* so that it no longer equals *t* one can no longer rely on $d'(t')$ being the same as $d'(x')$. However, if one can rely on d(t) being stable and because d(t)=d(x) and $d'(t')=d(t)$, one can still deduce $d'(t')=d(x)$.

ASYNCHRONOUS COMMUNICATION MECHANISMS

An Asynchronous Communication Mechanism (ACM) logically provides a one-place buffer between a single writer and a single reader (see Fig. 2). This sounds trivial but the snag is in the adjective: ACMs are asynchronous in the sense that neither the reader nor the writer should ever be held up by locks.[4] Unless the value being communicated via the buffer is small enough to be read and written atomically, it should be obvious that one slot is not enough to realise the buffer; a little thought shows that a buffer representation with two slots is also inadequate; the topic of how many slots are required is returned to in Section 3.4. In [28], Hugo Simpson proposed a 'four-slot' algorithm to implement an ACM for which, while the code is short, extremely subtle reasoning is required for its justification.

[4]This contrasts with the simple one-place buffer in Section 1 where the code would 'busy wait' on the value of a flag to control alternation between the producer and consumer.

while true **do** ···produce *v*··· *Write*(*v*) **od**	**while** true **do** $r \leftarrow Read()$ ···consume *r*··· **od**

Figure. 2. Code to clarify reader/writer structure.

ACM Requirements

The requirement is to communicate the "most recent" value from a single producer to a single consumer via a shared buffer. More precisely, it must satisfy the following.

- It is assumed that there is only a single reader and a single writer but the reader and writer processes operate completely asynchronously
- A write puts a new value in the buffer
- A read gets a completely written value from the buffer
- The value read is at least as fresh as the last completely written value when the read started – this implies that, for two consecutive reads, the value read by the second read will be at least as fresh as that read by the first
- Reads and writes must not block (no locks)
- Reads and writes of values can't be assumed to be atomic (i.e. a single value may be larger than the atomic changes made by the hardware)
- The only thing Simpson assumes to be atomic is the setting of single bits (and they are actually realised by wires)
- The buffer is initialised with a data value (so there is always something to read)
- The buffer is shared by the reading and writing processes alone (i.e. no third process can modify the buffer)

In the terminology of Lamport [22] this can be summarised as implementing a single-reader wait-free atomic register in terms of atomic Boolean control registers.

Approaches to Specifying ACM

There is an interesting range of approaches as to how the requirements that are listed above can be expressed in a formal specification. Without surveying all of them, it fits the theme of this paper to review two strands of publications[5]: one motivated by (Concurrent) Separation Logic [24] and [25] and the other by rely/guarantee methods. Surveying the latter also pinpoints the origin of the possible value notation.

[5]Other approaches include [2, 8].

Richard Bornat is an expert on separation logic so it is interesting to look at how he has formalised the specification and development of Simpson's 'four slot' algorithm. In [3], separation logic is certainly used but it is interesting to see that the paper also uses rely/guarantee concepts. In contrast, [4] makes no real use of separation logic and the specification uses the concept of linearisability [10]. The reason that this history is enlightening is that the essence of Simpson's algorithm is the exchange of 'ownership' of the four slots between the reader and writer processes. This is done precisely to ensure (data) race freedom so one would anticipate that separation logic would be in its element. There is, in fact, one paper that uses separation logic for precisely this form of argument; unfortunately [31] does not include an argument that the reader always gets the 'freshest' value and a recent private correspondence with one of the authors indicates that they have not extended their work to cover this essential property.

It is only fair to make an equally critical assessment of two papers [19] and [20] that use rely/guarantee ideas. In the development recorded in [19],[6] it is necessary to assert that the value of one variable (*lw*) is assigned to another variable (*cr*); this assertion was recorded as:

$$cr' = lw \vee cr' = lw' .$$

[6]The variable names in the Jones/Pierce papers are hold-r/fresh-w; for the reader's convenience, these have been changed in the extracts in the current paper to match the names used here (cr/lw).

This plausible attempt says that the final value of *cr* is either the initial or final value of *lw*. Unfortunately, during the operation being specified, the value of *lw* could potentially be changed more than once. This observation was precisely the stimulus that led to the invention of the notation for possible values. In addition to various improvements and clarifications in the development, the journal version [20] resolves the problem by using

$cr' \in \widehat{lw}$.

Rushby [27] noted a similar issue in model checking Simpson's algorithm: a version checking for just the before or after values fails in the case of multiple writes overlapping a single read. To handle this in the model checking context, Rushby restricts the sequence of data values written so that they are strictly increasing in value, and then checks that the sequence of values read is nondecreasing, which he concludes is necessary but may not be sufficient. He concedes that this is a limitation of the expressiveness of the model checking specification language (which does not have the (unbounded) expressive power of the possible values notation).

There is however a deeper objection to both of the Jones/Pierce specifications of ACMs. In both cases, the most abstract specification uses a variable (*data*-w) that contains the entire history of values written by the write process. This is in spite of the fact that a read operation cannot access values in the sequence earlier than the last value added before the read began. This sort of redundancy is deprecated in [15, Sect. 9.3] as using a 'biased' representation: the state contains values that have no influence on subsequent operations. Where there is no bias in the representation underlying a specification, a homomorphism (retrieve function) relates a representation back to the abstraction; in the case of a biased representation, a relation between the abstraction and the representation is used to argue that the operations on the latter fit those on the former. In situations where it is necessary to express non-determinism in a specification that can be removed in the design process, biased specifications are sometimes unavoidable — but, where there is an alternative, unbiased specifications should normally be preferred because they make it easier to see the range of possible implementations. One further surprising fact about the specifications in [19] and [20] is that, even at the most abstract level, the specifications of both *Read* and *Write* are each split into two sub-operations which are joined by sequential composition. Although the semantics of such a specification are clear, it means that the task of convincing users that their requirements have been adequately captured involves a rather algorithmic discussion.

Having been self-critical of these specifications, there is one important positive point that needs preserving in the approach below: the issue of data-race freedom is handled in[20] at the level of an abstract intermediate representation. This is an important general point: rely/guarantee conditions can be used to record interference on an abstraction where the final code is certainly not 'racy'.

Specification Using Possible Values

In contrast to the above attempts, a top-level specification using 'possible values' notation appears to be much more natural and perspicuous. The abstract specification uses a state with just a single value buffer *b* of type *Value*. The use of this intuitively simple state is only made possible by employing the possible value notation in the post condition of *Read*, where $\tilde{b}$ stands for the set of possible values of *b* during the execution of *Read*. The *Read* operation is described as returning a value (*r*) so the post condition is simply $r' \in \tilde{b}$. This means that a single read operation can return the value of the write most recently completed at the time the read begins or of any write that executes an assignment to *b* during the execution of the read operation. Notice that there is no danger of a subsequent read operation obtaining an older value than the current read because the reference point for the possible values of the newer read is the start of its execution.

As in [20], the specification can be made clearer by annotating whether the external state variables accessed by an operation can be only read (rd) or both read and written (wr).

Thus, the specification of *Read* can be given simply as:

Read() *r* : *Value*

ext rd *b* : *Value*

post $r' \in \widehat{b}$

When generating proof obligations, the ext rd is equivalent to a guarantee condition $b'=b$.

The specification of the *Write* operation is interesting. If the parameter to *Write* is *v*, one would expect the post condition to be $b'=v$ — and this is certainly required. In addition, it is necessary to rule out the possibility that *Write*(v) puts some spurious value(s) into *b* that might be accessed by *Read* before the *Write*(v) corrects its wayward behaviour and achieves its post condition. This can be expressed in a guarantee condition $b' \neq b \Rightarrow b' = v$. Extending (again, as in [20]) the ext annotation to mark write ownership yields a specification:

Write(*v* : *Value*)

ext owns wr *b* : *Value*

guar $b' \neq b \Rightarrow b' = v$

post $b' = v$

Here, the proof obligation expansion of ext owns wr is a rely condition $b'=b$, which matches the implicit guarantee of *Read* courtesy of its ext rd annotation.

The role of the guarantee of *Write* here is to provide an intuitive specification; the more standard use is to show that processes can co-exist and this usage occurs in the development below. The guarantee of *Write* ensures that only valid values are observable in the buffer (by *Read*). It is an important part of the specification of *Write* but note that there is no corresponding rely condition in *Read*. Firstly, there is the technical issue that *v* is local to *Write* and hence cannot be referred to in (the rely of) *Read*. Secondly, several *Write* operations might take place during a single *Read* and hence there may be multiple changes to the buffer during a *Read*, even though each *Write* only changes the buffer (at most) once. In fact, the possible multiple changes of the buffer during a *Read* motivates the use of $\tilde{b}$ in its post condition. It is worth observing that $\tilde{b}$ is applied to an abstract variable *b* — the development that follows employs a representation of *b* that is by no means obvious.

The guarantee of *Write* requires that the observable effect of the operation takes place in a single atomic step and the use of the possible values notation in the post condition of *Read* ensures that the observable effect of *Read* also takes place in a single atomic step.

The initial value of *b* is assumed to contain a valid *Value* so that it is possible for a *Read*operation to precede the first *Write*.

Thus far, the possible values concept – that was devised in order to document an intermediate design – has here been shown to offer a short and clear overall specification of ACM behaviour. Freshness comes from the possible values notation and the effect of it being relative to the start of each *Read* operation. The implementation has to find a way of achieving the atomic change behaviour of *b* in the abstraction without such an atomicity assumption.

Understanding Simpson's Representation

The challenge of presenting a specification that makes sense to potential users is addressed in Section 3.3. A development using a single data reification step to a version of Simpson's code is presented in Section 3.5 — that development makes interesting further use of the possible values concept and is thus presented in some detail. The current section attempts to provide an intuition of the 'four-slot' data structure. The operations corresponding to *Write* and *Read* of Section 3.3 are here named $Write_i$ and $Read_i$.

The importance of data abstraction and reification are commented in Section 1.3. Rather than jump immediately to Simpson's decision to use exactly four slots to represent the abstract variable *b*, a useful intermediate refinement step uses a data structure that contains an abstract map of an indexed set of 'slots' $X \xrightarrow{m} Value$. Here, this part of the state is named *dw*. There is also a data type invariant that requires that the (potentially partial) map has a value in every slot: $\mathbf{dom}\, dw = X$.[7]

[7] Note that, in the concurrent context, the data type invariant must hold for every step, not just initially and at the end of each operation.

As in [20], the index set *X* is deliberately left unspecified at this stage. $Write_i$ is decomposed into a three parts:

- $Write\text{-}ch_i$ chooses an index ($\in X$) that is safe to use
- $Write\text{-}upd_i(v)$ updates the map *dw* at the chosen index to *v*
- $Write\text{-}com_i$ commits the index by exposing it to $Read_i$
- $Read_i$ is split into two parts:
- $Read\text{-}sel_i$ selects the most recently written index and stores that index in a local variable
- $r \leftarrow Read\text{-}acc_i$ accesses the indexed slot

$Write_i$ must inform $Read_i$ of the index of the slot which has been (most recently) written. In addition, $Read_i$ must have a way of alerting $Write_i$ to the index of the slot that is claimed for reading. Remember that the reader and writer processes are in no way synchronised and the implementation is designed to allow (multiple) reads to occur during a write or multiple writes to overlap with a single read.

It should be clear that the potential number of slots (the cardinality of the set *X*) must be at least three because the writer has to select a member of *X* that is neither the most recently written nor one which the reader might access (these could be the same but are not necessarily so). It is possible to build a 'three slot' implementation *providing* there is an atomic way of communicating index values between *Read* and *Write*.

It is tempting to make $Read_i$ reserve a single element of *X* to $Write_i$ but this does not actually provide an abstraction of Simpson's code. What that code effectively does is to reserve more than one slot. This is shown here as *pr* being a set of indexes.

The intermediate state is thus:

$\Sigma_i ::$	$dw : X \xrightarrow{m} Value$	– space for values
	$lw : X$	– index of the last committed write
	$cw : X$	– index claimed by the writer
	$cr : X$	– index claimed by the reader
	$pr : X\text{-}\mathbf{set}$	– potential elements of *X* that the reader might use

It is an interesting observation that none of the variables can be modified by both operations. The final letter of each variable name records which process, reader or writer, can write to that variable (e.g. *lw* can only be modified by $Write_i$).

It is not difficult to see the lines of the data reification required here: the retrieve function isb=*dw*(*lw*). The initial state must, of course, satisfy the invariant; the initial value in the buffer must be *dw*(*lw*) and there must be some arbitrary value in every slot to ensure that dom dw = X.

It is interesting to note that the issue of (data) race freedom on the slots is worked out at this level of abstraction with rely/guarantee conditions. This can be contrasted with Peter O'Hearn's view in [24] that separation logic is the tool of choice for reasoning about race freedom and rely/guarantee reasoning is for 'racy' programs. The decisive point appears to be that, here, race freedom is established on a data structure that is more abstract than the final representation.

Although the observation is made above that three slots would be adequate to avoid clashing,[8] the genius of the representation proposed by Hugo Simpson is that – if four slots are used – communication can be reduced to using single bits; furthermore, in a physical implementation, these bits can be realised as wires connecting the $Read_f$ and $Write_f$ processes running on separate processors. Simpson describes the algorithm in terms of choosing 'pairs' and 'slots'. As in [20], this intuition is followed by using two sets *P* and *S* each of which has two possible values. However, here, toggling between the two values is achieved by a "¬" operator. Although both sets *P* and *S* can be implemented as Booleans, the temptation to use Booleans is resisted at this stage because separating the types *P* and *S* provides useful information as to whether each index variable refers to a pair or a slot (and has the potential to flag incorrect use as a type error).

[8] In fact, [4] also considers a three slot implementation

The final representation (Σ_f) is given in Fig. 3. This is related to Σ_i by a retrieve function where:

- dw is directly modelled by dsw with the set X reified to a (P, S) pair
- cw is represented by (cpw,¬sw(cpw))
- cr is represented by (cpr,csr)
- lw is represented by (lpw,sw(lpw))
- pr is represented by {(cpr,sl)|sl∈S}

$\Sigma_f ::$	$dsw : P \times S \xrightarrow{m} Value$	– two pairs of two data slots each
	$sw : P \xrightarrow{m} S$	– $sw(p)$ is the last written slot for pair p
	$lpw : P$	– last written pair
	$cpw : P$	– current write pair
	$cpr : P$	– current read pair
	$csr : S$	– current read slot

Figure. 3. The final state Σf.

One Step Argument

This section presents a single-step data refinement from the top level specification using possible values to Simpson's algorithm. Although the approach to refining the code from the specification is new, the end code comes from Simpson's insights and motivates the approach. The final state representation is as in Fig. 3 and the relationship between the abstract buffer *b* and this representation state is

$$b = dsw(lpw, sw(lpw)) .$$

The code for Simpson's algorithm is given in Fig. 4. First note that the $Write_f$ operation has the following guarantee[9]:

$$\forall i, j \cdot (i, j) \neq (cpw, \neg sw(cpw)) \Rightarrow dsw'(i, j) = dsw(i, j) \qquad (8)$$

and that when the write operation is not active, the writing process does not modify any of the variables in the representation.

[9] Although ACMs are much more complicated than the one-place buffer, the idea mentioned in Section 1.1 of locating where a key value is unchanged without adding auxiliary variables is evident here.

```
Read_f()r : Value                Write_f(v : Value)
  var t ∈ P;                       ⟨cpw ← ¬cpr⟩;
  ⟨t ← lpw⟩;                       dsw(cpw, ¬sw(cpw)) ← v;
  ⟨cpr ← t⟩;                       ⟨sw(cpw) ← ¬sw(cpw)⟩;
  ⟨csr ← sw(cpr)⟩;                 ⟨lpw ← cpw⟩
  r ← dsw(cpr, csr)
```

Figure. 4. Code for Simpson's algorithm.

The specification of the $Read_f$ operation after mapping through the representation relation and extending the frame with an appropriate subset of the representation variables is

$$t, cpr, csr, r : [r' \in \widehat{dsw(lpw, sw(lpw))}] \qquad (9)$$

The first refinement step uses law (5) from Section 2.2 with *lpw* corresponding to *x* and *dsw*(v,*sw*(v)) corresponding to *e*. In fact the law needs to be extended to accommodate extra variables in the frame but that is straightforward.

$$(9) \sqsubseteq \langle t \leftarrow lpw \rangle; \qquad (10)$$

$$cpr, csr, r : [r' \in \widehat{dsw(t, sw(t))}] \qquad (11)$$

For this one needs to rely on

$$lpw' \neq t \Rightarrow dsw'(t, sw'(t)) = dsw(t, sw(t)) . \qquad (12)$$

Note that *sw*(t) is only changed by $Write_f$ if t=*cwp* but the code also guarantees that t=*cpw*⇒t=*lpw* and hence *sw*(t) can be changed only if *lpw'*=t and hence(12) holds. If *sw*(t) does not change, (12) is guaranteed by $Write_f$ by (8) because(t,*sw*(t))≠(*cpw*,¬*sw*(*cpw*)) because either t≠*cpw* or if t=*cpw* then*sw*(t)=*sw*(*cpw*)≠¬*sw*(*cpw*). This use of the slots vector *sw* in Simpson's algorithm is one of the smart parts of how it works.

The second refinement step uses law (5) once more to refine (11).

$$(11) \sqsubseteq \langle cpr \leftarrow t \rangle; \qquad (13)$$

$$csr, r : [r' \in \widehat{dsw(cpr, sw(cpr))}] \qquad (14)$$

provided one can rely on t'≠*cpr*⇒*dsw'*(*cpr*,*sw'*(*cpr*))=*dsw*(*cpr* ,*sw*(*cpr*))which holds trivially as t=*cpr* is invariant over (14).

The third refinement step again uses law (5) to refine (14).

$$(14) \sqsubseteq \langle csr \leftarrow sw(cpr) \rangle; \qquad (15)$$

$$r : [r' \in \widehat{dsw(cpr, csr)}] \qquad (16)$$

provided one can rely on

$$sw'(cpr) \neq csr \Rightarrow dsw'(cpr, csr) = dsw(cpr, csr) \qquad (17)$$

being maintained by $Write_f$ for the duration of (16). Here (17) can be strengthened to

$$dsw'(cpr, csr) = dsw(cpr, csr) \qquad (18)$$

and this can be shown to be maintained by $Write_f$ using the approach outlined in Section 1.2. For the duration of (16), $Read_f$ strengthens its guarantee to state that it does not modify any shared variables (*r* is local to $Read_f$). Because (15) establishes

$$(cpr, csr) \neq (cpw, \neg sw(cpw)) \qquad (19)$$

it is sufficient to show that $Write_f$ maintains (18) from initial states satisfying (19)provided there is no interference on its shared variables. If $Write_f$ is executing its write phase from any state satisfying (19), it guarantees (18) because the slot being written is not (*cpr*,*csr*). Once $Write_f$ finishes its write phase (or if it is not initially in its write phase) it does not modify *dsw* at all (and hence maintains (18)) until after it executes *cpw*←¬*cpr* which re-establishes (19) for the next write phase.

The final refinement step uses law (4) to refine (16).

$$(16) \sqsubseteq r \leftarrow dsw(cpr, csr)$$

This is valid provided *dsw*(*cpr*,*csr*) is stable, which follows from the argument given above for the previous refinement step.

A pleasing aspect of the above refinement is that, having started from a specification (9)using the possible values concept (which allows for non-determinism in the value read), the refinement steps have maintained the use of possible values (and hence the non-determinism) until the last step, when it is clear which slot is being read (and that the slot is stable).

Using the approach of locally strengthening a guarantee – and hence indirectly strengthening a rely – (see Section 1.2) obviates the need to introduce and reason about auxiliary variables. However, a development using auxiliary Boolean variables *reading*and *writing* is also possible, where *reading* is true if and only if the *Read* process is actually reading from *dsw* and *writing* is true if and only if the *Write* process is actually writing *dsw*. With these auxiliary variables the important invariant is,

$$reading \wedge writing \Rightarrow (cpr, csr) \neq (cpw, \neg sw(cpw))$$

which ensures that the *Read* and *Write* processes are not simultaneously using the same slot. This represents the weakest invariant to ensure correct operation of the algorithm.

Because the specification of $Write_f$ does not make use of possible values notation its refinement is not presented in detail here. An important property of $Write_f$ is that during its writing phase the slot being written differs from any slot that could be read concurrently, which has been covered in the refinement of $Read_f$. The other aspect of $Write_f$ worth noting is that its guarantee in the abstract specification requires the buffer b to be updated to v atomically. Recalling that b is represented by $dsw(lpw,sw(lpw))$, that guarantee is achieved by (non-atomically) assigning to slot$(cpw,\neg sw(cpw))$, which can never correspond to b. The switch of $(lpw,sw(lpw))$ to $(cpw,\neg sw(cpw))$ is then achieved either by the assignment $sw(cpw)\leftarrow\neg sw(cpw)$ if lpw already equals cpw, or by the following assignment $lpw\leftarrow cpw$ if they differed initially.

Finally note that all of the atomic assignments in Fig. 4 are now in a form in which they can be implemented by the corresponding non-atomic assignment, assuming each read and write of a shared variable other than dsw is atomic. This assumption is in line with the requirements because the shared flags can be implemented as single bits (or, indeed, realised as wires).

CONCLUSIONS AND FURTHER WORK

The concept of possible values arose in an attempt to provide a clear design rationale of code which is delicate in the sense that slight changes destroy its correctness. A seemingly simple and intuitive notational idea contributed to the description of a layered development. The proposal was clearly motivated by a need in a practical application. The next bonus came in the link to the non-deterministic state ideas: this connection is set out in [7]. The current paper contains the first publication of the specification given in Section 3.3 and the simplicity of the overall specification comes as strong encouragement for the concept and notation of possible values. This is further reinforced by the development of Simpson's algorithm in Section 3.5 which retains the use of the possible values notation and utilises laws taking advantage of the possible values notation.

This closing section points to further avenues that appear to have potential but certainly require more work. As with the steps to date, the motivation for the decisions should come from practical examples.

Further Applications

It can perhaps be mentioned that the possible values notation appears to have some potential for recording arguments about brain-teaser puzzles. At the March 2015 meeting of IFIP WG 2.3 in Istanbul, Michael Jackson posed a hide-and-seek puzzle which is apparently described in several contexts. Here, a mole is what must be located. There are five holes in a line; the mole moves each night to an adjacent hole; the seeker can only check one hole per night and must devise a strategy that eventually locates the mole whose non-deterministic nocturnal movements are only constrained at either end of the line of holes. This paper doesn't spoil the reader's fun by providing an answer; it only mentions that one of the authors recorded the argument for termination using the possible values notation.

Sadly, most of the examples (see [26], [29] and [30]) using 'weak memory' (a.k.a. 'relaxed memory') also give the feeling that they are gratuitous puzzles. At a recent Schloss Dagstuhl meeting (15 191), one of the authors tried to use the possible values notation to record the non-determinism that results from not knowing when the various caches are flushed. It must be conceded that, on the pure puzzle examples, possible values are doing little more than providing an alternative notation for disjunctions. A challenge is to find a genuinely useful piece of code that, despite non-determinism, satisfies a coherent overall specification under, say, total store order (TSO) or partial store order (PSO) memory models. Only on such an application should the judgement about the usefulness of possible values be based.

There are also alternative views of the possible values notation itself. For example, $\widehat{b}$ could yield a sequence of values rather than a set. There is however an argument for preserving a (direct) way of denoting the set of possible values.

Possible Evaluations of Expressions

As well as possible values of an expression $\widehat{e}$ that is the set of values of e evaluated in each state of the execution, one can define $\widehat{\widehat{e}}$ as the set of all possible evaluations of e over the execution interval: each instance of a variable x in e takes on one of the values of x in the interval so that different occurrences of x within e may take on different values, and the values of separate variables x and y may be taken from different states. The set of evaluations includes those in which the values of all the variables are taken in a single state and hence $\widehat{e} \subseteq \widehat{\widehat{e}}$. In [7] the possible values concept was linked to different forms of nondeterministic expression evaluation corresponding to $\widehat{e}$ and $\widehat{\widehat{e}}$.

The following simple rule requires no restriction on e other than it does not contain references to x because x is in the frame of the specification.

$$\textbf{rely}\ x' = x \cdot x : [x' \in \widehat{\widehat{e}}] \ \sqsubseteq \ x \leftarrow e\,.$$

If e satisfies the single reference property over the execution interval (as defined earlier) then $\widehat{\widehat{e}} = \widehat{e}$ and hence

$$\begin{aligned} & \textbf{rely}\ x' = x \wedge (\textstyle\bigwedge z \in S \cdot z' = z) \cdot x : [x' \in \widehat{e}] \\ = \ & \textbf{rely}\ x' = x \wedge (\textstyle\bigwedge z \in S \cdot z' = z) \cdot x : [x' \in \widehat{\widehat{e}}] \\ \sqsubseteq \ & x \leftarrow e\,. \end{aligned}$$

Auxiliary Variables

The statement is made in [18] that using auxiliary (a.k.a. ghost) variables in the specification of a software component *can* destroy compositionality by encoding too much information about the environment. Studying possible values has helped put the position more clearly:

- having the code of the environment gives maximum information — but minimal compositionality
- the same distinction is actually there with sequential programs where post conditions provide an abstract description of functionality without committing to an algorithm (they can also leave unconstrained the values left in temporary variables etc.)
- for concurrency, things are much more sensitive: one ideal is that the visible variables (read and write) of parallel processes are 'separate' — this might be true on a concrete representation even when an abstract description appears to admit interference — see [21]

- rely/guarantee conditions are an attempt to state only what matters
- the expressive 'weakness' of rely/guarantee conditions (is conceded and) can be a positive attribute
- auxiliary variables can be used to encode extra information about the environment — in the extreme, with use of statement counters, they can encode as much as the program being executed by the environment

The advice is to minimise the use of auxiliary variables — even when writing assertions, abstraction from the environment can be lost if gratuitous information is recorded in auxiliary variables. The 'possible values' notation appears to offer an intuitive specification tool and a principled way of avoiding the need for some auxiliary variables.

One indication of the compositional nature of rely conditions is that, if a component with a rely condition r is refined to a sequential composition, each subcomponent inherits the rely condition r. Conversely, a sequential composition guarantees a relation g if each component of the sequential composition guarantees g.

ACKNOWLEDGEMENTS

An earlier version of this paper was prepared for a conference that celebrated José Nuno Oliveira's sixtieth birthday. The authors of the current paper thank the organisers of that memorable event in Guimarães and take the opportunity to renew their warmest good wishes to José.

Outlines of material on possible values were presented at the 2015 meeting of IFIP WG 2.3 and at the Schloss Dagstuhl meeting 15191 — on both occasions comments were made that have helped clarify the ideas and their explanation. In Dagstuhl, useful discussions with Viktor Vafeiadis helped one author understand the issues around weak memory. Useful comments on a draft from Diego Machado Dias are gratefully acknowledged as are those of the anonymous journal referees.

The research reported here is funded by the EPSRC responsive mode grant on "Taming Concurrency" EP/K011707/1, the EPSRC Platform Grant "TrAmS-2" EP/J008133/1 and the ARC grant DP130102901; the authors express their thanks for this support.

REFERENCES

1. J.-R. Abrial, The B-Book: Assigning Programs to Meanings, Cambridge University Press, 1996.
2. J.-R. Abrial, Modeling in Event-B, Cambridge University Press, 2010.
3. Richard Bornat, Hasan Amjad, Inter-process buffers in separation logic with rely-guarantee, Form. Asp. Comput. 22 (6) (2010) 735–772.
4. Richard Bornat, Hasan Amjad, Explanation of two non-blocking shared-variable communication algorithms, Form. Asp. Comput. 25 (6) (2013) 893–931.
5. R.J.R. Back, A method for refining atomicity in parallel algorithms, in: Eddy Odijk, Martin Rem, Jean-Claude Syre (Eds.), PARLE '89 Parallel Architectures and Languages Europe, in: LNCS, vol. 366, 1989, pp. 199–216.
6. Ian Hayes (Ed.), Specification Case Studies, second edition, Prentice Hall International, 1993.
7. Ian J. Hayes, Alan Burns, Brijesh Dongol, Cliff B. Jones, Comparing degrees of non-determinism in expression evaluation, Comput. J. 56 (6) (2013) 741–755.
8. Neil Henderson, Formal modelling and analysis of an asynchronous communication mechanism, PhD thesis, University of Newcastle upon Tyne, 2004.
9. Ian J. Hayes, Cliff B. Jones, Robert J. Colvin, Laws and semantics for rely-guarantee refinement, Technical report CS-TR-1425, Newcastle University, July 2014.
10. Maurice Herlihy, Jeannette M. Wing, Linearizability: a correctness condition for concurrent objects, ACM Trans. Program. Lang. Syst. 12 (3) (1990) 463–492.
11. Cliff B. Jones, Ian J. Hayes, Robert J. Colvin, Balancing expressiveness in formal approaches to concurrency, Form. Asp. Comput. 27 (2015) 475–497.
12. C.B. Jones, Software Development: A Rigorous Approach, Prentice Hall International, 1980.
13. C.B. Jones, Development methods for computer programs including a notion of interference, PhD thesis, Oxford University, June 1981, Printed as: Programming Research Group, Technical Monograph 25.
14. C.B. Jones, Specification and design of (parallel) programs, in: Proceedings of IFIP'83, North-Holland, 1983, pp. 321–332.
15. C.B. Jones, Systematic Software Development Using VDM, second edition, Prentice Hall International, 1990.
16. C.B. Jones, Accommodating interference in the formal design of concurrent object-based programs, Form. Methods Syst. Des. 8 (2) (March 1996) 105–122.
17. C.B. Jones, Splitting atoms safely, Theor. Comput. Sci. 375 (1–3) (2007) 109–119.
18. C.B. Jones, The role of auxiliary variables in the formal development of concurrent programs, in: Cliff B. Jones, A.W. Roscoe, Kenneth Wood (Eds.), Reflections on the Work of C.A.R. Hoare, Springer, 2010, pp. 167–188, Chapter 8.
19. Cliff B. Jones, Ken G. Pierce, Splitting atoms with rely/guarantee conditions coupled with data reification, in: ABZ2008, in: LNCS, vol. 5238, Springer, 2008, pp. 360–377.
20. Cliff B. Jones, Ken G. Pierce, Elucidating concurrent algorithms via layers of abstraction and reification, Form. Asp. Comput. 23 (3) (2011) 289–306.
21. Cliff B. Jones, Nisansala Yatapanage, Reasoning about separation using abstraction and reification, in: Radu Calinescu, Bernhard Rumpe (Eds.), Software Engineering and Formal Methods, in: LNCS, vol. 9276, Springer, 2015, pp. 3–19.
22. Leslie Lamport, On interprocess communication, part II: algorithms, Distrib. Comput. 1 (2) (1986) 86–101.
23. Leslie Lamport, Specifying Systems: The TLA+ Language and Tools for Hardware and Software Engineers, Addison Wesley, 2003.

24. P.W. O'Hearn, Resources, concurrency and local reasoning, Theor. Comput. Sci. 375 (1–3) (May 2007) 271–307.

25. John C. Reynolds, Separation logic: a logic for shared mutable data structures, in: Proceedings of 17th LICS, IEEE, 2002, pp. 55–74.

26. Tom Ridge, A rely-guarantee proof system for x86-TSO, in: Verified Software: Theories, Tools, Experiments, Springer, 2010, pp. 55–70.

27. John Rushby, Model checking Simpson's four-slot fully asynchronous communication mechanism, Technical report, Computer Science Laboratory, SRI International, Menlo Park CA 94025, USA, July 2002.

28. H.R. Simpson, Four-slot fully asynchronous communication mechanism, IEE Proc., Comput. Digit. Tech. 137 (1) (1990) 17–30.

29. Jaroslav Sev ˆ cik, ˇ Viktor Vafeiadis, Francesco Zappa Nardelli, Suresh Jagannathan, Peter Sewell, Relaxed-Memory Concurrency and Verified Compilation, ACM SIGPLAN Not., vol. 46, ACM, 2011, pp. 43–54.

30. Viktor Vafeiadis, Francesco Zappa Nardelli, Verifying fence elimination optimisations, in: Eran Yahav (Ed.), Static Analysis, in: LNCS, vol. 6887, Springer, 2011, pp. 146–162.

31. Shuling Wang, Xu Wang, Proving Simpson's four-slot algorithm using ownership transfer, in: Markus Aderhold, Serge Autexier, Heiko Mantel (Eds.), VERIFY-2010, in: EPiC Series, vol. 3, EasyChair, 2012, pp. 126–140.

CHAPTER 15

DESIGN OF A FLOW VISUALISATION FRAMEWORK

Matthew Edmunds, Chao Tong and Robert S. Laramee

Department of Computer Science, Swansea University, Swansea, SA2 8PP, Wales, UK

ABSTRACT

Research software often consists of individual, isolated prototype applications. Small proof of concept applications are usually enough for demonstrating new algorithms. However, the unification of new research algorithms into a cohesive software framework has advantages. Adding new features to an existing pipeline reduces implementation overhead. The researcher is more able to compare and contrast existing or previous work with new research. Utilizing previously implemented techniques, researchers are able to combine visualization options in new ways that typical research prototypes cannot. The software application can be made available to the domain expert for evaluation and future use. These goals are in part realized by utilizing recent advancements in game design technology and by leveraging features available with recent graphics hardware. Described is the design of a feature-rich flow visualization software framework in more detail than a typical research paper. In contrast to most research prototypes, the system we present handles real-world simulation datasets by interfacing directly with the commercial package called tecplot. We present a description of our system in detail, whereas previously published work focuses on the research contribution. The effectiveness and scalability of the approach is also discussed.

INTRODUCTION

Computational fluid dynamics (CFD) is a rapidly developing tool for fluid analysis [1]. With wide reaching industrial applications, such as automotive, aerospace, weather and medical, it is an increasingly important software application used to speed up the design process while reducing costs. With increasing data complexity and size, the ability of the user to interpret the CFD results becomes increasingly difficult. Post processing software aims to alleviate this challenge by providing visualization methods for the evaluation and correlation of simulation results. Our visualizations include the latest state-of-the-art flow visualization techniques. Bridging the gap between current visualization software techniques and the latest research techniques is an important goal of our work.

Illustrated in Figure 1 is the CFD simulation pipeline which highlights the inputs, outputs and processing steps. This process is described in three stages:

1. *Preprocessing*: A surface and the volumetric mesh is generated to model a physical object. This mesh is generated from computer-aided design (CAD) geometry utilizing mesh generation and manipulation tools. Boundary conditions and fluid properties are defined and specified.

Citation: Matthew Edmunds, Chao Tong and Robert S. Laramee, Design of a Flow Visualisation Framework, doi:10.3390/computers4010024

2. *Simulation*: A computational simulation of the fluid is performed using numerical methods applied to the mesh, with respect to the boundary conditions and fluid properties.
3. *Post Processing*: The simulation result is explored, analyzed and visualized using a range of techniques dependent on the requirements of the CFD engineer.

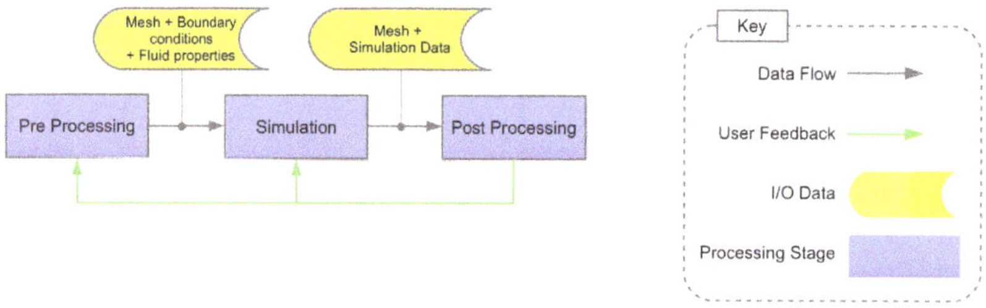

Figure 1. The computational fluid dynamics (CFD) simulation pipeline is comprised of a preprocessing stage, the simulation stage and the post-processing stage. This illustration shows the inputs and outputs of each stage and highlights where the different tasks reside.

In order to present a visualization toolkit that is capable of dealing with large simulation data and complex algorithms, a comprehensive and versatile visualization framework is needed. It is the focus of this chapter to describe the design and implementation of a state-of-the-art flow visualization framework that provides scientists and engineers with effective solutions for the visualization of CFD simulation data. By drawing on recent developments in the game and graphics card hardware industry and by combining several scientific visualization techniques, our visualization framework yields the following benefits:

- A platform independent flexible framework, which implements state of the art research algorithms in flow visualization. In particular, stream surface seeding algorithms are incorporated, which were not available in previous systems, such as the VTK or Visit [2].
- A framework specifically designed to enable quick integration of new algorithms for study, testing and evaluation.
- A smooth and efficient threaded user interface, even when processing large data and complex algorithms.
- Simultaneous comparisons of different techniques.

What we have developed is a novel research prototype for flow visualization. However, unlike most prototypes, it interfaces directly with commercial software. Thus, it combines the best of both worlds: state-of-the-art flow visualization with commercial-grade datasets. The visualizations are novel for flow and also offer fast performance. The flow visualization techniques are more current then previous systems such as the VTK or Para-view [2]. What we present here are the design and implementation considerations for our software. The information necessary to implement these features is missing from our previous papers [3, 4] because of the strict focus on visualization and space limitations. Furthermore, to see performance details, for example how our software performs compared to previous systems, we refer the reader to Edmunds *et al.* [3, 4].

The remainder of this paper is organized as follows: Section 2 outlines the software application framework. Section 3details the design of the GUI. Section 4 describes the services subsystem. Section 5 details the logic subsystem. Section 6highlights our conclusions and proposed future work.

SYSTEM OVERVIEW

In this section we start by discussing some design and implementation related work. We then provide an overview of our application framework and related subsystems. Laramee *et al.* [5] describe the design and implementation of a flow visualization subsystem which utilizes the geometric and texture-based flow visualization techniques.

In order to guarantee the quick responsiveness for user interaction, even when dealing with large data, Piringer *et al.* [6] present a generic multi-threading architecture, which enables early cancellation of the visualization thread due to user interaction without the common pitfalls of multi-threading. They also present an interactive visualization toolkit, HyperMoVal [7], as an implementation of this architecture in practice.

McLoughlin and Laramee [8] describe a flow visualization software framework that offers a rich set of features. Their application also serves as a basis for the implementation and evaluation of new algorithms. The application is easily extendable and provides a clean interface for the addition of new modules. Peng *et al.* [9] present a multi-linked framework that provides customized visualization techniques for engineers to gain a fast overview and intuitive insight into the flow past the marine turbine.

Our software application system is divided into three main subsystems; the GUI, the Logic and the Services. See Figure 2. We divide the system into smaller, easier to maintain subsystems using logical groupings of similar functionality. The GUI subsystem is responsible for capturing the user input for computing a visualization, displaying the resultant visualization and supporting user interaction with the visualization. The Logic subsystem encapsulates the algorithms used to compute the visualizations. This subsystem processes the input data as specified by the user and computes the visualization based on the given user input parameters and selected algorithm. Providing a central point of storage for input and derived data is the service subsystem.

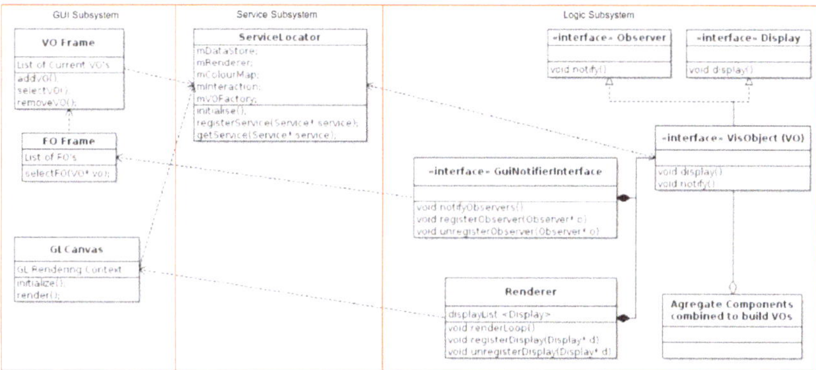

Figure 2. This top level overview of the system shows three main subsections of the software application framework. The GUI subsystem provides the user interface and all associated user interaction and feedback. The logic subsystem encapsulates the processing aspects of the framework. The services subsystem provides system-wide services for use by the other subsystems.

Another feature of our framework is the Visualization Object (VO). The VO is an encapsulating aggregate of all the elements of an individual feature or individual algorithm. Some examples of features are: interaction VOs, which encapsulate the interaction with the visualization, e.g., panning, zooming and rotating; color map VOs, encapsulating color map functionality; stream surface VOs, which encapsulate the stream surface generation algorithms [10].

For each VO within our framework, there is an associated frame object (FO); an interface for encapsulating the I/O with the VO. This design approach creates a simple interface for adding new functionality quickly and easily. We further discuss VOs and FOs within our application, along with the detailed description of the structure of our framework in Section 3, Section 4 and Section 5.

GUI SUBSYSTEM DESIGN

The GUI, shown in Figure 3, is divided into three main frames. The centre frame for rendering the current list of VOs, the left frame for listing the current VOs and the right frame area, which displays the FO for the currently selected VO and lists the VO's currently available options; refer to Figure 3.

VOs are added by right mouse clicking the parent VO category and selecting the required VO from the drop-down menu. The VO categories (data, view, scene, visualization) can be seen in the left frame of Figure 3. Right mouse clicking a VO in the list enables the user to delete it. Left mouse click the listed VO and its associated FO is displayed in the right frame area. The FO lists the attributes of the VO that can be manipulated. In Figure 3, the selected VO is a seeding object. The right frame displays the the options available to the seeding object. At the top of this FO, a track pad is available for seeding curve manipulation; under this, we can specify type and size. We can save and load previously specified seeding curves. At the bottom of this FO, we have options for the generation of stream surfaces.

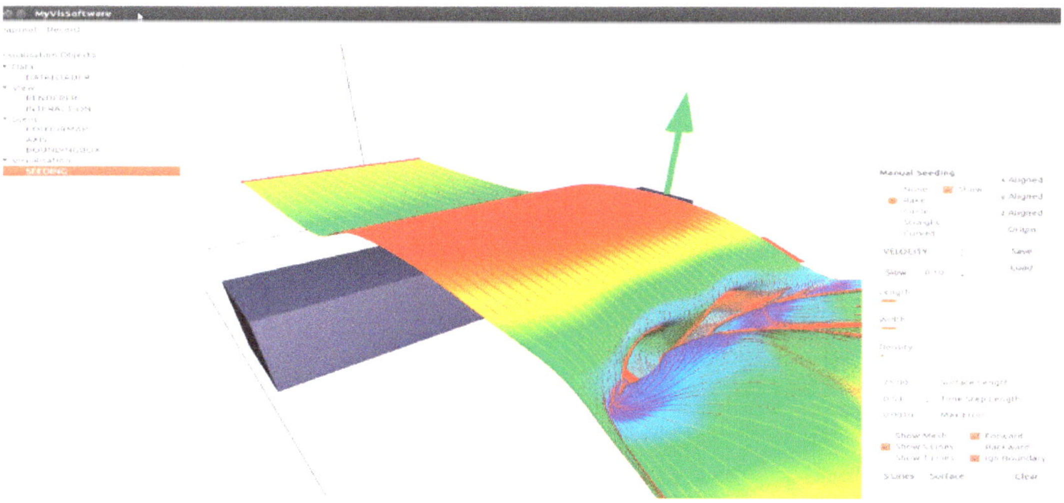

Figure 3. This illustration shows the layout of the user interface.

Once we add the required VOs and set FO options, we can see the results rendered in the centre frame. Interaction with the visualization is achieved using the mouse. For example: to pan, press, hold and drag the right mouse button; to zoom, press, hold and drag the left mouse button; to rotate the view, press, hold and drag the left and right mouse buttons together.

Each of the three frames within the interface run their actions in separate threads. This allows continued interaction with the interface (such as panning and rotation of the visualization), while waiting for lengthy processes and computations (such as loading large datasets) to finish. As a result of our design approach, the application of thread locks to specific VOs is trivial [11].

SERVICES SUBSYSTEM DESIGN

Some objects in an application can end up communicating with almost all other objects within the code base. It is difficult to find a component of our application that does not need access to objects which encapsulate either input or derived data at some point. Other examples are objects which encapsulate color maps or OpenGL rendering. A method of accessing these objects via interfaces is also desirable. The interface can allow swapping of a given object for an alternative or allow intermediate objects to be installed, which can perform additional tasks, such as logging. Systems like these can be thought of as services that need to be available to the entire application.

The service locator design pattern [12, 13, 14] is used to meet these requirements in our application. The service locator pattern decouples code that needs a service from both who it is (the concrete implementation type) and where it is (how we get to the instance of it). The service subsystem utilizes the service locator design pattern to provide a robust, type safe, central location for accessing system services.

In our services subsystem, we focus on data storage and accessibility. The services we implement include raw data storage, derived data storage, model data storage, render object storage, colour map storage, interaction matrix storage and a VO factory.

In Listing 1, we see the basic layout of the service locator class. The listing shows an initialization function, a register function and a get function. The service locator is reliant on a service being registered with it before any other objects try to use the service. One challenge here is that a null pointer may be returned if not initialized or a service is registered. It is also important to note that the service is not aware of the concrete service class, just the service interface. The only object in the code that knows about the concrete class is the function that registers the service.

```
#ifndef SERVICELOCATOR_H_
#define SERVICELOCATOR_H_

class ServiceLocator {
public:
        static void InitializeDataStore() {
                mDataStore = &mNullData;
        }

        static void Register(DataStoreInterface* service){
                if (service == nullptr) {
                        mDataStore = &mNullData;
                } else {
                        mDataStore = service;
                }
        }

        static DataStoreInterface& GetDataStore() {
                return *mDataStore;
        }

private:
        static DataStoreInterface* mDataStore;
        static NullDataStore mNullData;
}

#endif /* SERVICELOCATOR_H_ */
```

Listing 1: Service Locator Pattern.

If we try to use the service before a provider has been registered, it returns a null pointer. If the calling code does not check this, we will crash the application. To address the null pointer, we implement the null object design pattern [15] or, in our case, a null service. A null service inherits the same service interface, but its implementation does nothing. This allows code that receives the object to safely continue on. The calling code will never know that the service is not available, and we do not have to handle a null pointer. We are guaranteed a valid object.

Our service locator is initialized within the main function prior to any other calls. The initialization function registers the null objects. We can then register any additional services as required. Registering a replacement service is a simple case of just registering the service. We do not delete any services within the service locator class, which provides us the flexibility of swapping services back and forth if required. An example of this is two interaction services storing different view matrices; whichever service is currently registered dictates from which viewpoint the visualization is viewed in the centre frame.

Another important feature of this design pattern is the logging or debugging capabilities. Using a decorator design pattern [16] we can easily add an intermediate object which can output either logging or debugging information. Accessing the services is a simple matter of calling the accessor function. This returns a reference to the currently registered service object. Unregistering a service can be achieved by registering a null pointer. The service locator will then register the default null service.

LOGIC SUBSYSTEM DESIGN

The Logic subsystem encapsulates the algorithms used to compute the visualizations. This subsystem processes the input parameters selected by the user and computes the visualization based on the selected algorithm. Figure 4 shows the communication route from user interaction with the GUI to the selected VO generating the visualization data. There are three main subsets of the logic subsystem responsible for manipulation of the VO. These are the factory class, the observer class and the renderer class. In this section, a discussion of the factory and observer design patterns takes place. This is followed by a discussion of the render loop and finishes with an examination of the aggregate VO and its life cycle.

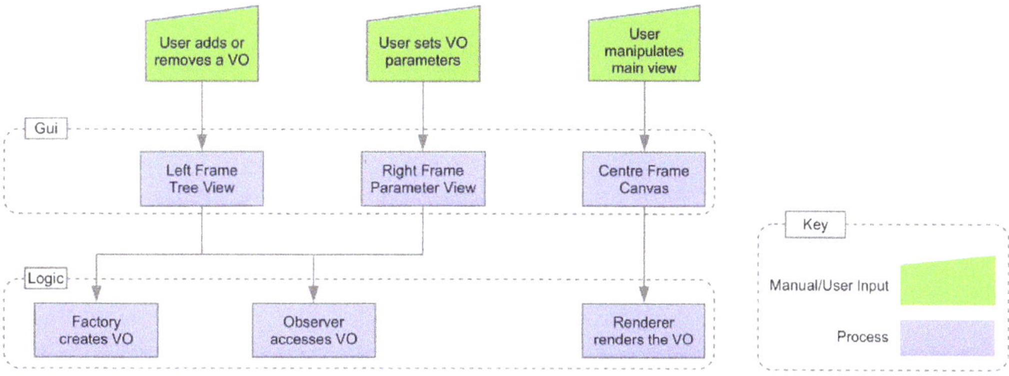

Figure 4. Communication routes from the user to the logic subsystem. User interaction with the GUI is communicated to the visualization object (VO) responsible for the selected visualization algorithm via dedicated subsets of the logic subsystem.

The Factory

There are many cases when a class needs to create several types of object. This class can have this responsibility, but it has to know about each and every object type. The possibility that the class cannot anticipate all the required objects in advance is clear. The idea of the factory pattern is to encapsulate the creation of a multitude of different classes utilizing a common interface. A factory is the location of a class in the code where multiple types of object are constructed. The purpose of utilizing this pattern is to isolate the creation of objects from their usage and to create groups of similar objects without the need to depend on their concrete classes. This has the advantage of introducing new derived types with no change to the code that leverage the base class type. Using this pattern also introduces the possibility of interchanging the concrete implementations without code modification. An example of the factory pattern can be seen in Listing 2. If the user chooses to add a new VO in the treeview (on the left of GUOI), the GUI instructs the factory to create a new VO of a type indicated by a type ID. A reference to the factory is stored in and accessed from the service locator.

```
#ifndef COMPONENTFACTORY_H_
#define COMPONENTFACTORY_H_

class ComponentFactory {
public:
        ComponentFactory();
        ~ComponentFactory();

        VisObjectInterface* genObject(const VisTypeEnum& ID) {

                switch(ID) {
                        case VisTypeEnum::surfacevisobject:
                                return new SurfaceVisObject();
                                break;
                        case VisTypeEnum::axisvisobject:
                                return new AxisVisObject();
                                break;
                        default:
                                return new DefaultVisObject();
                }

        }
};

#endif /* COMPONENTFACTORY_H_ */
```

Listing 2: Factory Pattern.

The Observer

The observer design pattern is used to communicate an object change of state to all dependent objects. These dependent objects are then automatically updated. This pattern controls the communication between classes. An object known as the subject is able to publish a change of state. A set of observer objects that depend on the subject are registered with the subject, such that they can then be automatically notified when the state of the subject changes. This design pattern provides a loose coupling between the subject and its observers. The subject has access to a set of observers that are registered at runtime. The observers must inherit an observer interface; thus, the base class and its functionality is not known to or required by the subject.

Figure 5 shows the the use case in our software framework. The VOs inherit the observer interface, which includes the notify function, which must be appropriately overridden in the base class. The VO is registered with the subject, which, in our case, is the GuiNotifier class. When a frame object (FO) state changes, it calls the notifyObservers function, which notifies all registered VOs that the state has changed. The base class implementation overriding the notify function then checks for changes and updates itself accordingly where applicable.

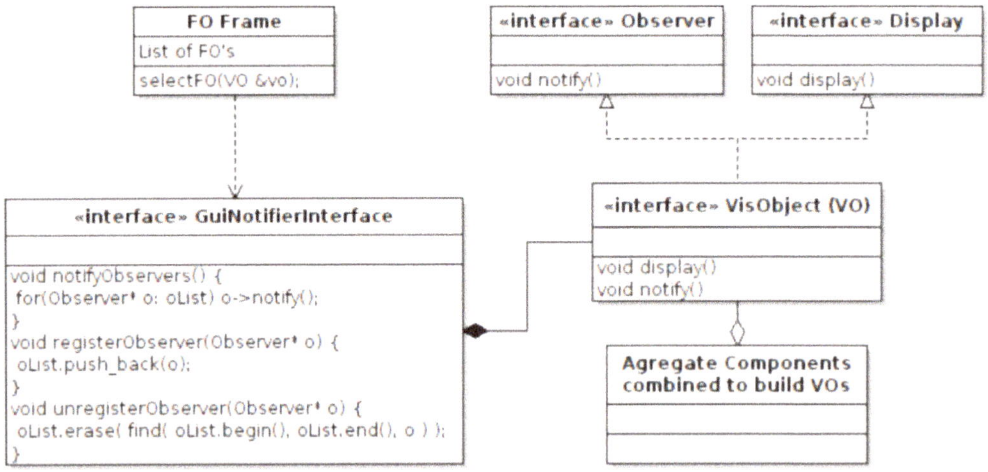

Figure 5. This UML (Unified Modeling Language) diagram shows the layout of the observer design pattern utilized for communication between the GUI frame objects (FOs) and the visualization objects (VOs).

The Rendering Loop

The GUI centre frame renders the current OpenGL rendering context to its canvas for viewing by the user; Section 3. An example of this can be seen in the following illustration; Figure 3. In Figure 6, the centre frame encapsulates the GLCanvas class. When the GLCanvas class render event is triggered, it calls the renderLoop function from the Renderer class.

The Renderer class is designed to encapsulate the collection of OpenGL calls required to set the state of the OpenGL state machine. This class also has functionality based on the observer design pattern. VO objects are registered with the renderer, and when the renderLoop function is called by the GLCanvas class, the overridden display function called on the list of registered VOs. The detail of this is shown in the UML (Unified Modeling Language) diagram of Figure 6.

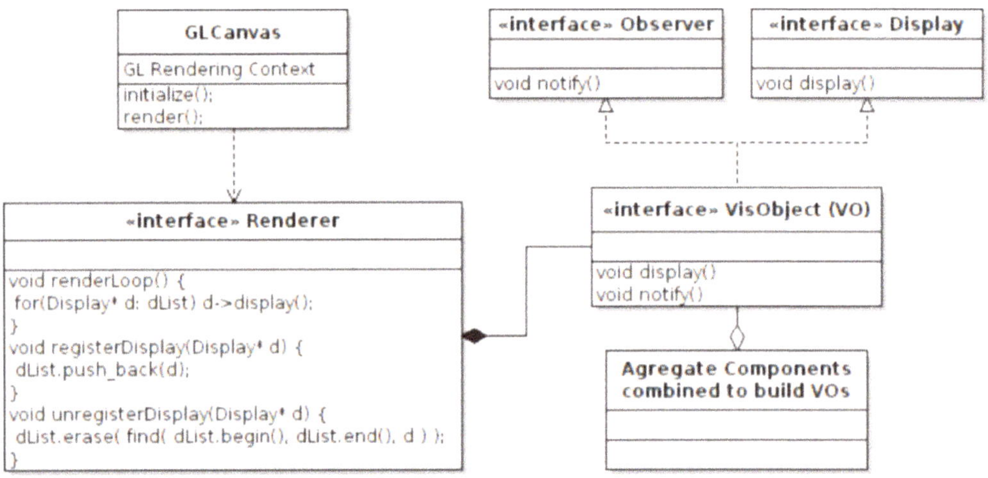

Figure 6. This UML diagram shows the relationship between the renderer and the visualization objects (VOs). Note the similarity with the observer design pattern shown in Figure 5.

The general state of the scene is set from the renderer's associated frame object (FO). This includes features, such as perspective parameters, light source locations and lighting intensitys, e.g., ambient, diffuse and specular. The type of OpenGL Shader is also selected from this frame object. The renderer class defines how to render the scene data, whereas the VO defines what data are to be rendered.

The Renderer interface is used to provide a general interface for the specific OpenGL implementation. There are differing versions of OpenGL available, supported by different specifications of hardware. The advantage of our system is the ability to interchange the Renderer class depending on the hardware support for a particular version of OpenGL. The required version of the Renderer class is registered with the service locator. This is also useful for testing revised OpenGL or Graphics Library Shading Language (GLSL) [17] implementations.

- ***What is GLSL:*** GLSL or Graphics Library Shading Language is a high level shading language, which uses a syntax close to that of the C programming language. It was created for the purpose of providing developers with more precise control over the built-in graphics pipeline. Previously, developers would be required to use OpenGL assembly or graphics card-specific programming languages to implement modifications to the fixed functionality pipeline.

In our implementation, we use a combination of per pixel Phong lighting, edge highlighting using a Gaussian filter to detect sudden changes in depth, and depth peeling for order-independent transparency. These algorithms are discussed in more detail in [3, 4, 10] and in the work by Born *et al.* [18] and Hummel *et al.* [19].

The Visualization Object (VO)

The visualization object (VO) is a key element in the functionality of this software framework. The entire framework is built around the idea of a single object interface type used for all implemented features within the application. In this subsection we describe the lifecycle of a typical VO. We then describe the aggregate style implementation of the VOs and discuss some advantages of this approach over more traditional methods in the context of a robust visualization framework for prototyping, testing and comparing new techniques.

The life cycle of a VO is illustrated in Figure 7. The life cycle of the VO starts with its creation as the result of user input. The factory is responsible for the generation of VOs, which are then passed to the GuiNotifierInterface detailed in Figure 5. Communication with the VO can then take place. The next step is setting the parameters of the VO required as input to the particular algorithm the VO encapsulates. Once these parameters are set, the visualization data are then generated.

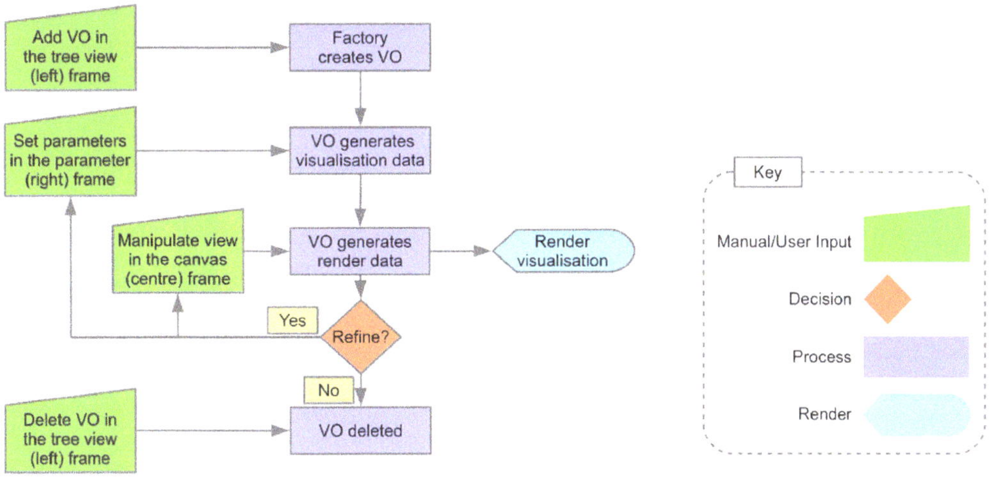

Figure 7. The Visualization Object (VO) lifecycle.

During the visualization generation process, data external to the VO may be required. An example of this is the vector and scalar data made available by another VO (the data storage VO) registered with the service locator. This data can be accessed via the service locator interface, along with other data such as colour maps *etc.*

Once the visualization data is generated, in the form of a triangulated mesh, the next step is to generate the render data. The mesh data is usually generated in dual arrays, one representing the vertex, normal, colour data and one representing the node indices. This data is sent directly to the VBO (Vertex Buffer Object) class encapsulating the OpenGL Vertex Buffer Object. This class registers the pointers to the data, then specifies the required rendering parameters needed by the OpenGL state machine to correctly render the mesh.

Once the visualization algorithm is rendered to the centre frame, the user is able to interact with the visualization. The user can directly pan, zoom and rotate the rendered scene by dragging the mouse over the scene in combination with the mouse buttons. The right mouse button is pressed to pan the scene; the left mouse button is pressed to zoom the scene; and both mouse buttons are used to rotate the scene. While interacting with the visualization, the user can also set new parameters for the visualization and generate a modified visualization, which is then rendered to screen; see Figure 7.

The final part of the process is deletion of the VO. If the user removes the VO from the left frame 3 by selecting delete from the VO context menu, the VO is then passed back to the factory for deletion ending this VO's lifecycle. All VO objects are created and deleted by the factory. This centralized approach makes for easy debugging of erroneous VO's during the VO lifecycle.

The VOs are constructed by aggregating the set of sub classes needed to compute the required algorithm. The more traditional method of class hierarchies implement features available in a set of classes by extending them and therefore maximizing code reuse. The design of the class hierarchy is made in advance with anticipation of possible additions to the code at a later date. This approach is tried and tested and generally works well.

However, a more recent approach is being more commonly utilized, particularly within the games industries: the aggregate design pattern [20,21]. With the more traditional hierarchical inheritance approach, problems can arise in a number of ways. If the insight into the type of additions to the inheritance hierarchy were not well predicted, the code base can easily end up struggling to cope with the required changes leading to major refactoring of the code base. Furthermore, with more and more features being added, the interwoven complexity of the inheritance hierarchical tree can quickly become unwieldy and difficult to maintain. These scenarios do not lend themselves to quick and simple implementations of new features.

The aggregate design pattern provides an alternative approach which is more applicable to the type of framework discussed in this paper. We need to be able to add new algorithms quickly and easily, but without the issues and complexity associated with large inheritance hierarchies. Another advantage of this approach is the ability to minimize the inherited overhead of unrequired features when extending a class of which only some of the functionality is required.

The parent class is constructed from an aggregation (collection) of a set of components classes. The component classes separate all the functionality required by the system into individual components, which are independent of each other. The parent class becomes a wrapper for communication between each of the individual components *i.e.*, the parent class performs no computation or stores any data with the exception of the aggregated component classes; see Figure 8 and Figure 9. Distinct new functionality is implemented in the system by creating a new component. New combinations of component classes are aggregated together to form new base classes providing the required system functionality.

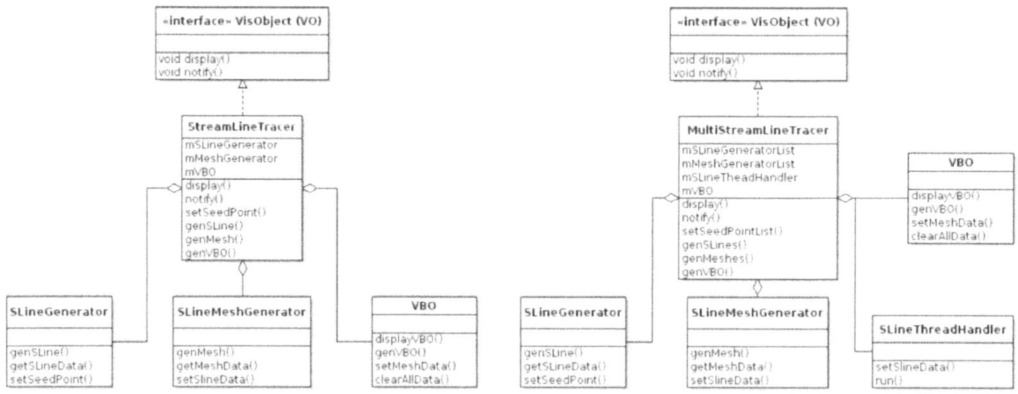

Figure 8. This UML diagram illustrates a simplified version of a streamline tracer class and a multi threaded streamline tracer class. Rather than inherit the original streamline class and adding the multi threading implementation into the new class, we instead assemble a new class from the original components plus a new thread-handling component. If threading was an original intention, then the hierarchical inheritance could be designed more efficiently, but now, we must refactor the code. With the component-based approach, foresight into how the software will involve in the future is not required. This is particularly useful in a system which is subject to adding a lot of new functionality.

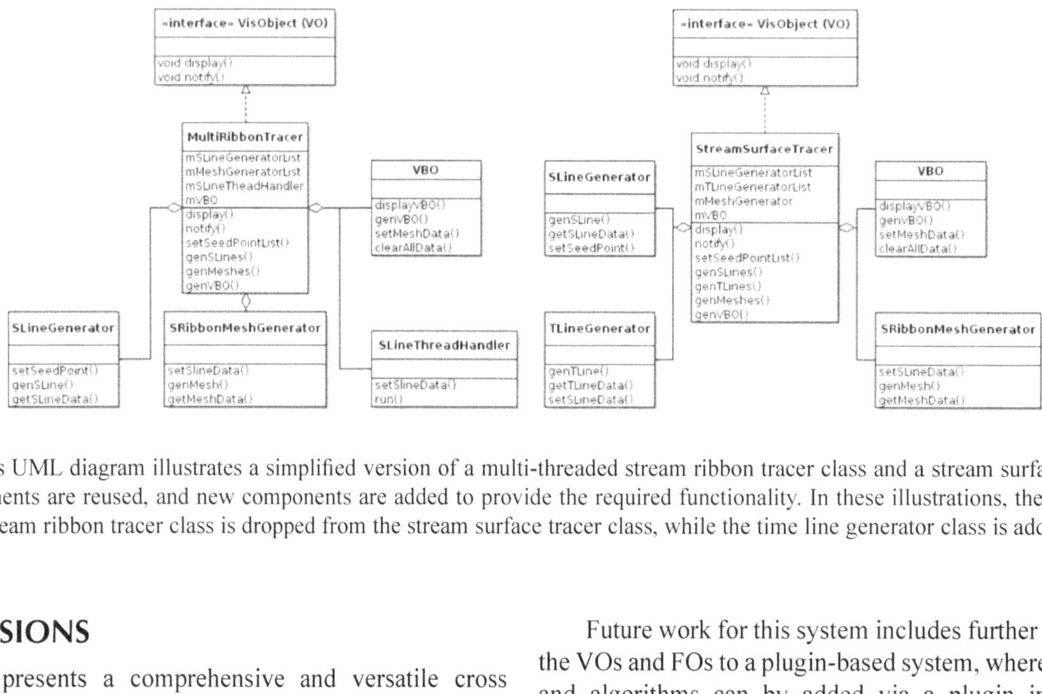

Figure 9. This UML diagram illustrates a simplified version of a multi-threaded stream ribbon tracer class and a stream surface tracer class. Some components are reused, and new components are added to provide the required functionality. In these illustrations, the thread handler used in the stream ribbon tracer class is dropped from the stream surface tracer class, while the time line generator class is added for timeline refinement.

CONCLUSIONS

This paper presents a comprehensive and versatile cross platform state-of-the-art flow visualization toolkit. This framework has the flexibility to add new algorithms fast and efficiently for testing, evaluation, comparing results and for study by the domain experts. We focus on describing the design and implementation of a generic visualization framework, which provides scientists and engineers with effective solutions for the visualization of CFD simulation data.

The simple and intuitive layout of the GUI is effective for reducing the software-related learning curve by the domain experts. The subdivision of the GUI, service locater and logic into logical subsystems not only greatly simplifies the system, but also simplifies the communication between the different subsystems and provides greater flexibility when accessing the raw data. The use of aggregation with the VOs proved very successful and flexible when adding new algorithms and features to the software stack.

Future work for this system includes further abstraction of the VOs and FOs to a plugin-based system, where new features and algorithms can by added via a plugin interface. This would further simplify implementation and remove the need to modify the main code base. Another area of further work is extending the aggregate pattern of composite components to an XML based approach for constructing the VOs. This combined with a plugin interface for the components would produce a very flexible way to add new features and algorithms to the software.

ACKNOWLEDGMENTS

The Authors would like to thank the Department of Computer Science at Swansea University, UK.

AUTHOR CONTRIBUTIONS

Matthew Edmunds wrote the software framework and contributed to the writing of this paper. Chao Tong contributed to the writing of this paper. Robert S. Laramee contributed to the design and implementation of the software as well as authorship of the paper. All authors have read and approved the final manuscript.

REFERENCES

1. ANSYS UK. Fluent Engineering Simulation. Available online: http://www.fluent.co.uk/ (accessed on 11 March 2015).
2. Laramee, R.S. Comparing and evaluating computer graphics and visualization software. *Softw. Pract. Exp. (SP&E)*2008, *38*, 735–760. [Google Scholar]
3. Edmunds, M.; Laramee, R.; Chen, G.; Zhang, E.; Max, N. Advanced, Automatic Stream Surface Seeding and Filtering. In Proceedings of Theory and Practice of Computer Graphics 2012, Didcot, UK, 13–14 September 2012; pp. 53–60.
4. Edmunds, M.; Laramee, R.S.; Evans, B.; Chen, G. *Stream Surface Placement for a Land Speed Record Vehicle*; Technical Report; The Visual and Interactive Computing Group, Computer Science Department, Swansea University: Wales, UK, 2013. [Google Scholar]
5. Laramee, R.S.; Hadwiger, M.; Hauser, H. Design and Implementation of Geometric and Texture-Based Flow Visualization Techniques. In Proceedings of the 21st Spring Conference on Computer Graphics, Budmerice, Slovakia, 12–14 May 2005; pp. 67–74.
6. Piringer, H.; Tominski, C.; Muigg, P.; Berger, W. A Multi-threading Architecture to Support Interactive Visual Exploration. *IEEE Trans. Vis. Comput. Graph.* 2009, *15*, 1113–1120. [Google Scholar] [CrossRef]
7. Piringer, H.; Berger, W.; Krasser, J. HyperMoVal: Interactive Visual Validation of Regression Models for Real-Time Simulation. In *Computer Graphics Forum*; Blackwell Publishing Ltd.: Hoboken, NJ, USA, 2010; Volume 29, pp. 983–992. [Google Scholar]
8. McLoughlin, T.; Laramee, R.S. *Design and Implementation of Interactive Flow Visualization Techniques*; INTECH Open Access Publisher: Rijkka, Croatia, 2012; Chapter 6; pp. 87–110. [Google Scholar]
9. Peng, Z.; Geng, Z.; Laramee, R.S. Design and Implementation of a System for Interactive, High-Dimensional Vector Field Visualization. In *Horizons in Computer Science Research*; Nova Science Publishers: Hauppauge, NY, USA, 2013; Volume 8, pp. 175–200. [Google Scholar]
10. Edmunds, M.; Laramee, R.; Malki, R.; Masters, I.; Croft, T.; Chen, G.; Zhang, E. Automatic Stream Surface Seeding: A Feature Centered Approach. *Comput. Graph. Forum* 2012, *31*, 1095–1104. [Google Scholar] [CrossRef]
11. Cppreference.com. Std::lock. Available online: http://en.cppreference.com/w/cpp/thread/lock (accessed on 11 March 2015).
12. BlackWasp. Service Locator Design Pattern. Available online: http://www.blackwasp.co.uk/ServiceLocator.aspx(accessed on 11 March 2015).
13. Code Project. A Basic Introduction On Service Locator Pattern. Available online: http://www.codeproject.com/Articles/18464/A-Basic-Introduction-On-Service-Locator-Pattern (accessed on 11 March 2015).
14. Martin Fowler. Inversion of Control Containers and the Dependency Injection pattern. Available online: http://martinfowler.com/articles/injection.html (accessed on 11 March 2015).
15. BlackWasp. Null Object Design Pattern. Available online: http://www.blackwasp.co.uk/NullObject.aspx (accessed on 11 March 2015).
16. BlackWasp. Decorator Design Pattern. Available online: http://www.blackwasp.co.uk/Decorator.aspx (accessed on 11 March 2015).
17. OpenGL.org. OpenGL GLSL. Available online: http://www.opengl.org/wiki/OpenGL_Shading_Language (accessed on 11 March 2015).
18. Born, S.; Wiebel, A.; Friedrich, J.; Scheuermann, G.; Bartz, D. Illustrative Stream Surfaces. *IEEE Trans. Vis. Comput. Graph.* 2010, *16*, 1329–1338. [Google Scholar] [CrossRef]
19. Hummel, M.; Garth, C.; Hamann, B.; Hagen, H.; Joy, K. IRIS: Illustrative Rendering for Integral Surfaces. *IEEE Trans. Vis. Comput. Graph.* 2010, *16*, 1319–1328. [Google Scholar] [CrossRef] [PubMed]
20. Nystrom, R. Game Programming Patterns. Available online: http://gameprogrammingpatterns.com/component.html(accessed on 11 March 2015).
21. West, M. Refactoring Game Entities with Components. Available online: http://cowboyprogramming.com/2007/01/05/evolve-your-heirachy (accessed on 11 March 2015).

INDEX